The BIG Book of Bugs!

Consulting Editor Matthew Robertson

Welcome

New York

Published in 1999 by Welcome Enterprises, Inc.
588 Broadway, New York, NY 10012
(212) 343-9430 Fax (212) 343-9434

Photo credit for title page: Lee Gibbons/WLAA

Library of Congress Cataloging-in-Publication Data
The big book of bugs!
p. cm.
Summary: A collection of unusual facts, games, puzzles, activities, and artwork centering around the world of insects.
ISBN 0-941807-33-9 (hardcover)
1. Insects Miscellanea Juvenile literature. [1. Insects Miscellanea.] I. Welcome Enterprises.
QL467.2.B524 1999
595.7--dc21 99-29014
CIP

Printed in Singapore
10 9 8 7 6 5 4 3

CREATURE FILE

Tarantula

As big as a dinner plate and with eight eyes and eight bristly legs, the tarantula looks fearsome. But how scary is it?

There are many different kinds of tarantula, from different parts of the world. For most people, though, 'tarantula' means one of the large, hairy spiders that come from North, Central and South America. Some of these live in dry, semi-desert areas, such as Arizona, USA, or in Mexico. Others are found in the jungles of South America. The best-known of these spiders is the Mexican red-kneed tarantula.

BIG AND HAIRY

Tarantulas are big. The bodies of North American tarantulas can be longer than an adult's middle finger, and their leg span is as wide as an adult's hand. Their South American cousins are even bigger – legs included, they can be as big as this page.

LONG-LIVED

Some tarantulas live for only a few months, others for up to 18 months, but tarantulas can live for as long as 25 years or more. In Mexico, one female tarantula was found that had lived for nearly 30 years.

FINAL WARNING

Although usually peaceful, a threatened Mexican red-kneed tarantula, right, rears up and displays the red bristles on its body.

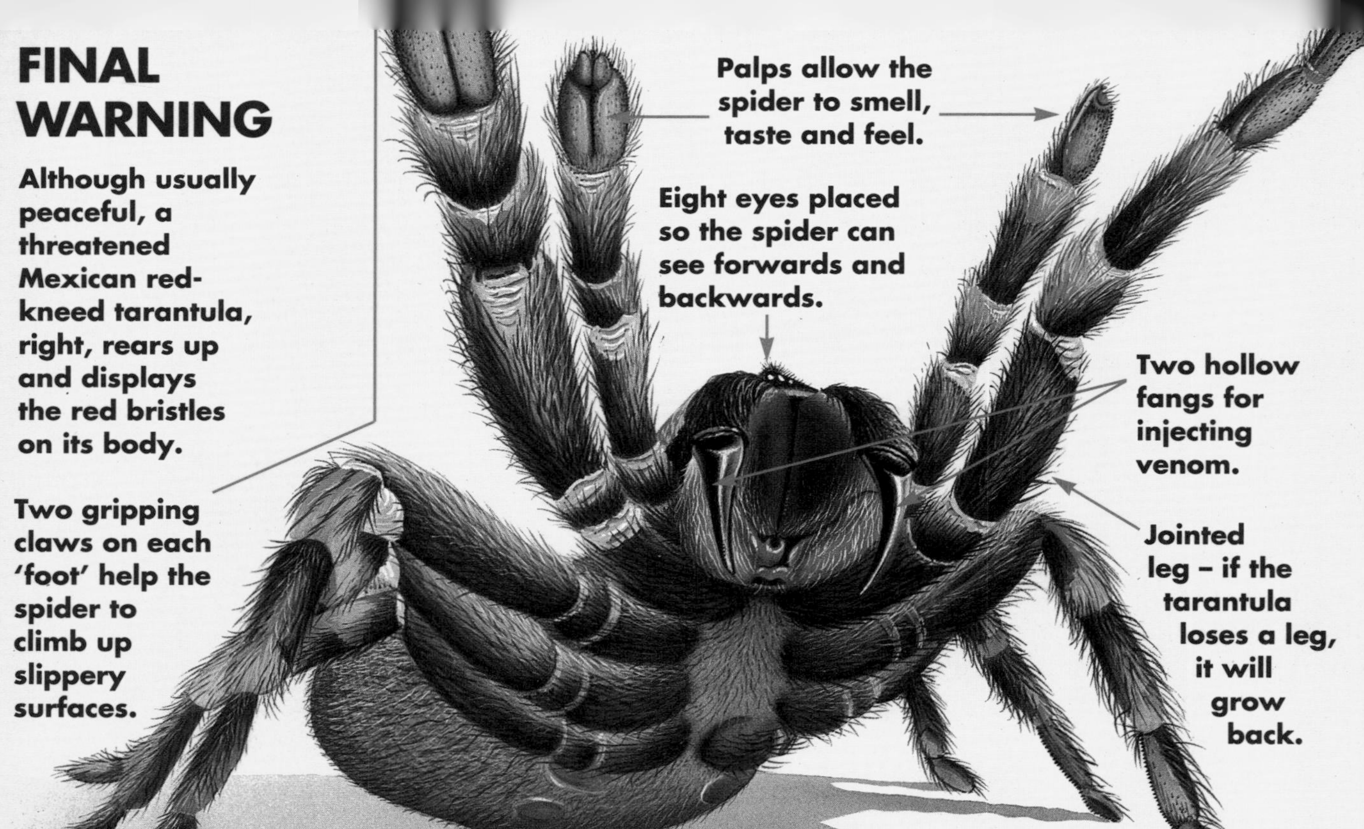
Palps allow the spider to smell, taste and feel.
Eight eyes placed so the spider can see forwards and backwards.
Two hollow fangs for injecting venom.
Jointed leg – if the tarantula loses a leg, it will grow back.
Two gripping claws on each 'foot' help the spider to climb up slippery surfaces.

LYING IN WAIT

Tarantulas live in burrows underground, which they dig with their fangs. They line the insides with ribbons of a special substance called spider's silk. Unlike common garden spiders, they don't make webs to catch prey. Instead, they wait to pounce when a likely-looking snack comes along. In the heat of the day tarantulas rest, and do their hunting at night, when they catch insects such as beetles. They also enjoy a special treat of small frogs, toads, mice, or small birds.

SHY SPIDERS

Although they look fierce, tarantulas are in fact shy creatures, which stay in their burrows most of the time, rarely coming outside. During the mating season, however, swarms of long-legged male tarantulas roam about, looking for females

Small Talk

TARANTULA BABIES

Tarantulas are excellent mothers. Mexican red-kneed tarantulas have up to 700 babies a year. They wrap their eggs in a silk parcel, which they carry between their fangs, turning the parcel occasionally to make sure that the eggs on the bottom are not crushed. Once the eggs have hatched, the tarantulas rip the silk open with their fangs to let the babies out. They guard the young spiders (spiderlings) for several weeks until they are able to look after themselves.

The red-kneed tarantula gets its name from its colourful, hairy 'knee pads'. The bald patch on the back of its body shows where this spider (right) has flicked irritating hairs out on the enemy.

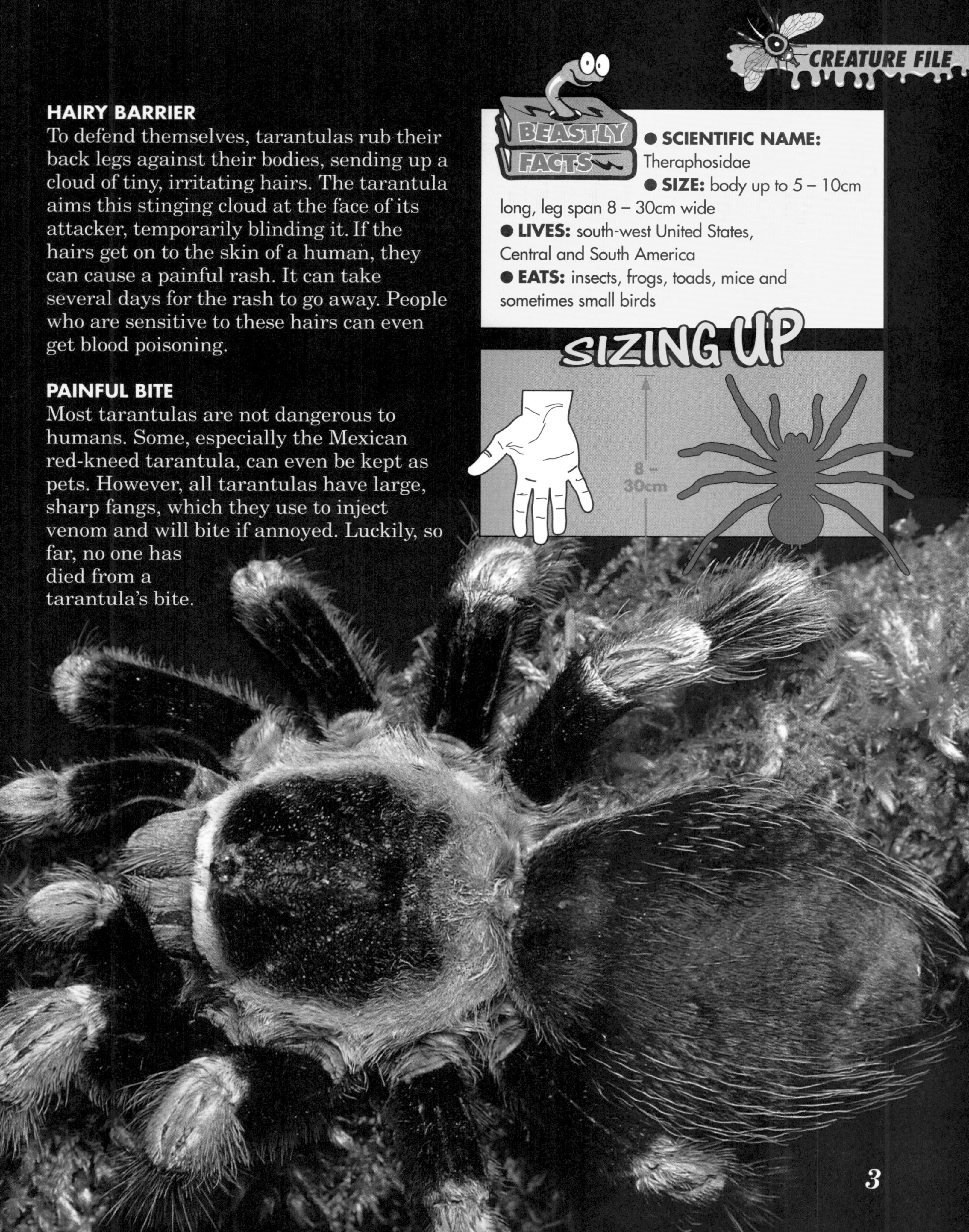

HAIRY BARRIER
To defend themselves, tarantulas rub their back legs against their bodies, sending up a cloud of tiny, irritating hairs. The tarantula aims this stinging cloud at the face of its attacker, temporarily blinding it. If the hairs get on to the skin of a human, they can cause a painful rash. It can take several days for the rash to go away. People who are sensitive to these hairs can even get blood poisoning.

PAINFUL BITE
Most tarantulas are not dangerous to humans. Some, especially the Mexican red-kneed tarantula, can even be kept as pets. However, all tarantulas have large, sharp fangs, which they use to inject venom and will bite if annoyed. Luckily, so far, no one has died from a tarantula's bite.

- **SCIENTIFIC NAME:** Theraphosidae
- **SIZE:** body up to 5 – 10cm long, leg span 8 – 30cm wide
- **LIVES:** south-west United States, Central and South America
- **EATS:** insects, frogs, toads, mice and sometimes small birds

Velvet Worm

The velvet worm changes the shape of its bendy body to make itself longer or shorter, fatter or thinner.

The velvet worm, or 'walking worm', can have anything between 14 and 40 pairs of legs, depending on which worm species it belongs to and how old it is. Hundreds of bristles all over its body give it its velvety appearance.

STRETCHY BODY

The velvet worm's body has lots of folds, like a concertina, so that it can stretch itself out to twice its length. Because it has no hard skeleton, it can squeeze itself into, and get through, very narrow spaces.

SLIME ATTACK

On the inside of its mouth, the velvet worm has two glands that produce a sticky liquid. It uses the liquid to catch small bugs which it eats. If threatened, it squirts its attacker with this liquid to scare it away.

LIVE BABIES

In most species of velvet worm, the young grow inside the mother's body, and are born live, like human babies. They can find their own food as soon as they are born.

SIZING UP

1 – 7cm

- **SCIENTIFIC NAME:** *Peripatus capensis*
- **SIZE:** 1 – 7cm long
- **LIVES:** forests of South and Central America
- **EATS:** worms and insects, especially termites

Hornet

Hornets are able to attack even large insects, such as wasps and bees. A hornet's sting can also be dangerous to humans.

The hornet is one of the largest members of the wasp family. It is also known as the yellow jacket because of its bright colouring. Its vivid orange-yellow and black stripes warn us and other animals to keep away.

NEST BUILDING

Hornets build large papery nests made from wood that they chew to a paste. They make their nests in hollow trees, in the ground or in an empty building. The nest hangs upside-down, and is made up of layers of cells (small chambers).

- **SCIENTIFIC NAME:** *Vespa crabro*
- **SIZE:** 19 – 35mm long
- **LIVES:** all over Europe, Asia, north Africa and North America
- **EATS:** insects and sweet foods

HORNET HOUSEWORK

The queen hornet starts the nest in spring. She lays her eggs inside a few of the cells. Young workers grow from the eggs. When they are a little older, they add new layers of cells, clean the nest and feed the larvae (young hornets). In the autumn, the old queen and the other hornets all die. Only new queens survive the winter, after which they each start making a new nest.

Life in a leaf-cutter

Imagine waking up one morning to find that an enormous tree outside your home had been stripped bare overnight. This is what could happen if you lived in South America near a colony of leaf-cutter ants.

Like many other insects, ants live together in large groups called colonies. They all have different jobs and duties within their society. Like our own villages, towns and cities, ant colonies may have from one hundred to several million inhabitants. In most colonies, there are three main types of ant – males, workers and queens.

LEAF-CUTTERS

The tropical forests of South America are home to leaf-cutter ants. The leaf-cutters are gardeners. They cut pieces of leaves from plants and trees and carry them back to their nest. They then chew the leaves to a pulp, which they use to grow a special fungus. This fungus provides the whole colony with food, and is all the ants eat.

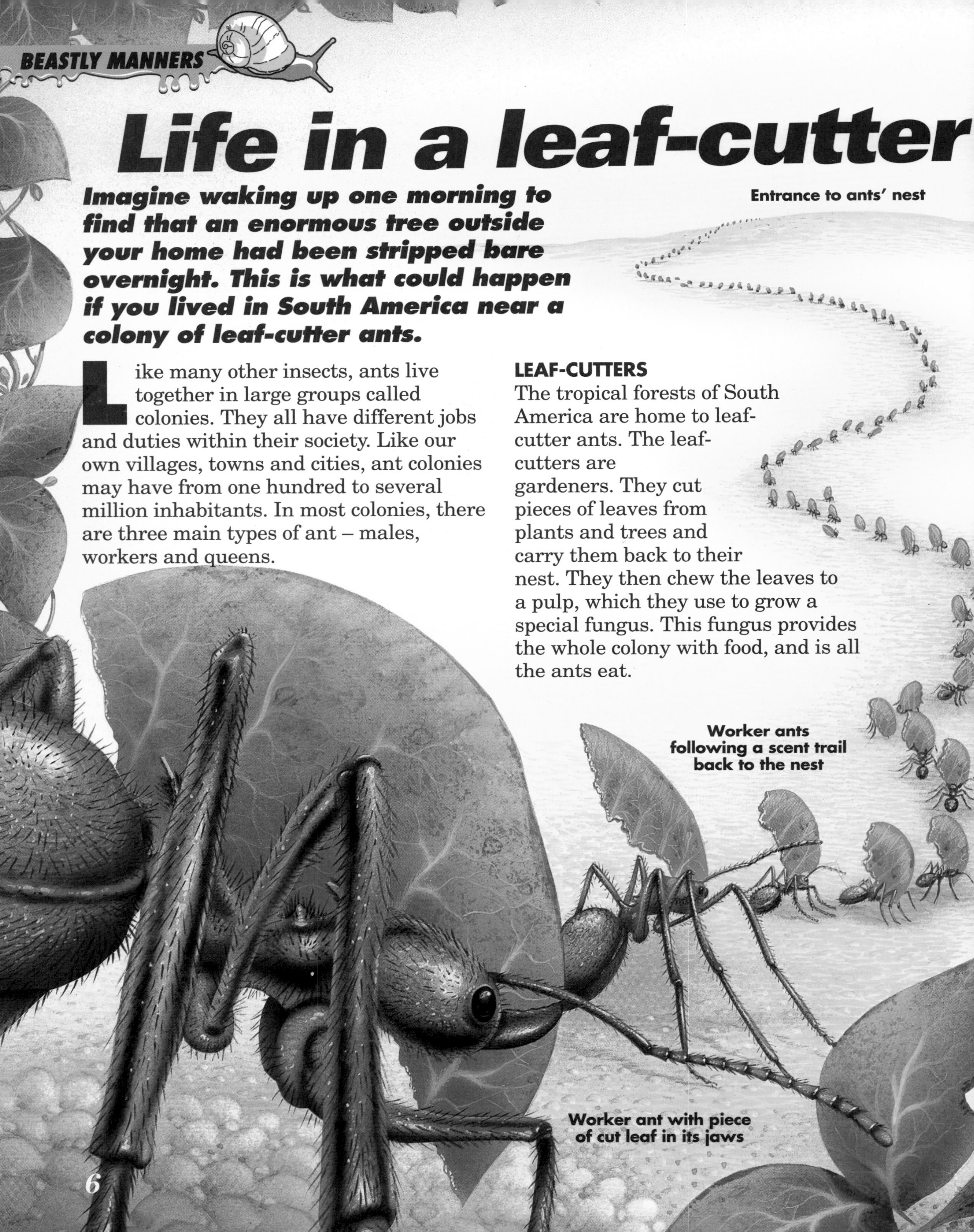

Entrance to ants' nest

Worker ants following a scent trail back to the nest

Worker ant with piece of cut leaf in its jaws

ant colony

AMAZON WEIGHT-LIFTERS
A fully-grown leaf-cutter can be up to 2cm long, and can carry a gigantic weight in its jaws. Holding a large piece of leaf above its head is like a man carrying a small car in his teeth!

LEFT: The leaf-cutter ant is capable of carrying a very large weight, about three times its size and ten times its weight.

MIDNIGHT RAIDS
Leaf-gathering often takes place at night. Large numbers of ants march along well-worn trails to a tree, which they climb and strip of its leaves. Then columns of leaf pieces move through the forest! These are in fact the ants carrying their load back to the nest.

Is it true... that the queen is the mother of the whole colony?
Yes, the queen is the only ant that lays eggs. On a summer's day, the queen flies off, followed by winged males. After mating, she finds a spot for a new nest, bites off her wings, digs a hole and plants some fungus. She lays eggs on the fungus and guards them until they hatch into larvae. In time, the larvae turn into pupae and finally emerge as young workers.

FINDING THEIR WAY
Leaf-cutter workers lay scent trails from the nest to the tree or plants they are stripping for others to follow. They touch the ground with the tip of their abdomen to leave an invisible path.

Defending the nest

The soldiers that guard both the nest and the other ants have very big heads, strong muscles and a vicious bite. If an ant is attacked, it squirts out an alarm scent. This tells the soldiers where help is needed so they can rush to the scene.

Soldier ant

Inside the nest

Under the ground the leaf-cutter ants' nest is 6m deep and covers about the same area as a tennis court. It is home to a highly organised society.

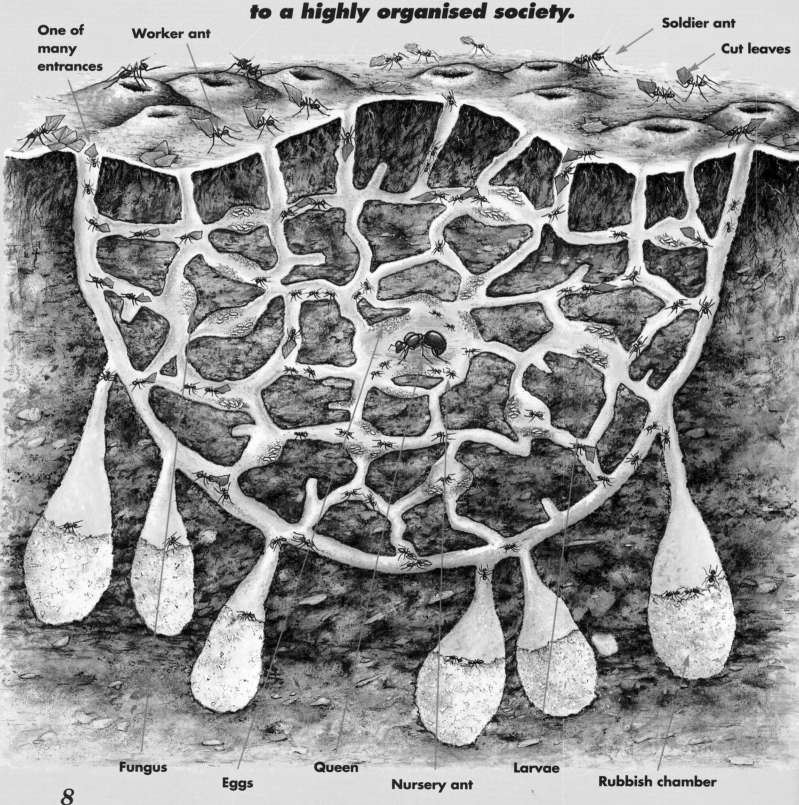

Small Talk

- A queen ant can grow to the size of a small fieldmouse.
- South American Indians used leaf-cutter soldier ants to stitch wounds! They got them to bite the two edges of the wound together and then twisted off the ants' bodies.

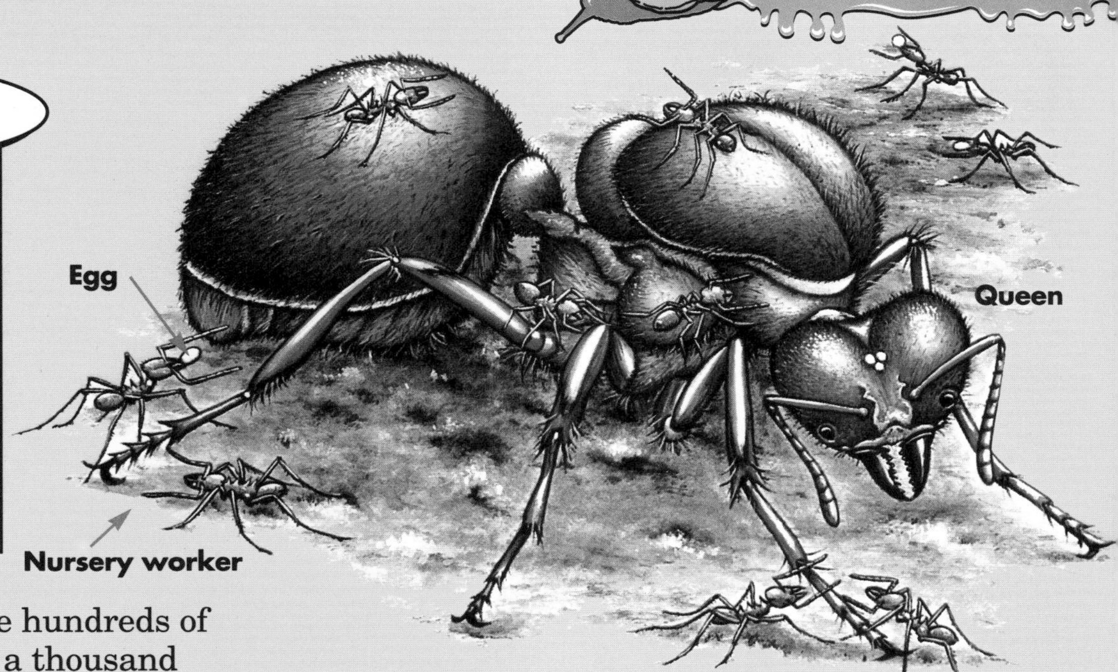

The queen can lay up to one egg every ten seconds. Nursery workers collect them from her chamber and take them to the nursery.

A large nest may have hundreds of entrances and over a thousand chambers where the leaf-cutters grow fungus. Underground chambers provide perfect conditions for the fungus to thrive. The chambers are linked by tunnels. The nest also has its own air-conditioning system made up of air inlets.

IN THE NURSERY

The queen is waited on by her own servants in her special chamber. These tiny nursery workers feed her with fungus and look after the eggs until they hatch. They feed the very young ants, or larvae, and in time these change into pupae. The pupae then develop into adult ants.

A WORKING LIFE

Work is divided up between individual ants, according to their size and experience. While larger workers are out leaf-cutting and strong soldiers ferociously guard the nest entrances, the smaller workers dig new tunnels and look after the fungus gardens.

KISS AND TELL

Leaf-cutters pass on messages by gently touching antennae. Another way of giving instructions is by kissing. Leaf-cutters do this by passing tiny pieces of food from one mouth to another. The queen makes a chemical which she passes on to her nursery ants. In turn, they pass the chemical on to the workers. The chemical allows the ants to recognise other members of their colony.

What is... fungus?

Fungus is very similar to a plant. However, unlike a plant, it has no stem, leaves or flowers. It grows on plants or decaying substances. The mushroom is the best-known fungus. The leaf-cutter ants' fungus only grows inside the nest. They grow it by chewing leaves into a pulp and mixing this with their droppings. The fungus grows as a grey spongy mass of fine threads.

Jumping Spider

Between the leaves on the forest floor, a male jumping spider stalks its prey. With its six small eyes watching out for danger, its two larger front eyes scan the ground ahead for food. Suddenly, it spots a small beetle nearly 30cm away. The spider tenses and then springs through the air, landing on top of its victim. Its fangs sink into the writhing beetle's back and inject it with fast-acting poison.

Making a

A wormery is both easy to make and easy to keep

A wormery is an indoor place for worms to live. It is made from soil and dead leaves placed inside a container with clear sides, so you can watch the worms.

Worms munch their way through the soil in search of dead plants to eat. They also drag leaves from the surface and eat these. As they chew, they also swallow bits of earth, which mix with the dead plants. Once the worm has digested, it goes to the toilet. Worm droppings are full of food for plants. This makes the worm one of the most important animals on Earth.

You will need:

- 2 clean, clear plastic fizzy drink bottles, one thinner than the other
- scissors
- water
- dead leaves
- grass cuttings
- gravel
- peat
- sand
- a large sheet of thick, light-proof plastic (a black bin liner is perfect for this)
- a black bin liner under which to catch your worms

WHAT TO DO

1 Wash and rinse out both fizzy drink bottles. Cut the top off the fatter bottle.

2 Half-fill the thinner bottle with water and stand it inside the fatter bottle. This both helps to keep the wormery cool and stops it falling over.

5 Put a few worms on the top layer of dead leaves. Now wait for them to burrow down into the peat. Always wash your hands after touching worms and soil.

6 Make a cover for your wormery, by wrapping it with a sheet of thick dark plastic or cloth, through which you can't see the light (remember that worms are used to living underground). This should be big enough to form a tube round the outer bottle. Put the wormery in a cool, sheltered place. The soil should be kept damp, but should not become soaked with rain, as the worms could drown. Leave the wormery outside in a sheltered place for two weeks.

wormery

3 Put a layer of gravel into the space between the two bottles. Add alternating layers of peat and sand, starting with peat. (Gravel, peat and sand are all available at garden centres.) Make each layer about 2cm deep. Continue until the wormery is almost full. Lastly, add a thick layer of dead leaves and grass cuttings.

4 Make a drawing of the wormery, and label each layer. You will then be able to see how it has changed at the end of the experiment.

7 After two weeks, bring the wormery indoors and take off the cover. Compare what you can see now with the picture you made before you put in the worms. The different layers of leaves, sand and peat will show you how the worms have moved the soil. Don't keep the wormery indoors for longer than one or two days. Finally, return the worms to the place where you found them.

Now catch your worms

Worms usually only come to the surface of the soil at night, when there are very few birds about and so they are not in danger of being eaten. They are particularly likely to come to the surface when it's been raining. This is because the rain loosens the soil and makes it easier for worms to travel through it. You can make them think it's been raining by watering the ground. Put a black bin liner over the damp earth. Weigh it down with a few stones. Check under the plastic every ten minutes or so. You should eventually find several worms underneath.

What is an

There are more insects on Earth than any other type of animal. Scientists know about one million kinds of insect and they are still counting. So what makes all these different creatures part of the same group – the insects?

Mouth parts

Antenna

Compound eye

Head

Thorax

Head
Look closely and you will find the mouth, eyes and antennae on an insect's head.

Thorax
The muscles that work the insect's wings are found in the thorax.

Legs
Every insect has six jointed legs. These are arranged in three pairs either side of its body. Depending what kind it is, the insect uses its legs to walk, run or jump.

Insects are invertebrates, which means that they have no backbone. Mammals (like you), fish, birds and reptiles all have a skeleton inside their bodies which gives them their basic shape. An insect gets its shape from its hard outer skin, called an exoskeleton. This tough skin also helps to protect the animal, like medieval knights wore metal suits of armour to protect themselves.

insect?

Wings
Most – but not all – insects also have wings, which allow them to escape from danger. Wings enable them to travel in search of food as well. Some insects have two wings; others have four.

Abdomen

Abdomen
The surface of the abdomen is covered with a thin layer of wax. Like wearing a raincoat, this waterproofs the insect. It also stops it losing water from its body.

BODY TALK
All adult insects have a body that is divided into three parts. These are the head, the thorax and the abdomen.

THREE PARTS
The head has the insect's eyes, jaws and antennae. The thorax has the legs and wings. The abdomen is where the insect breaks down its food and where eggs are made.

IS THIS AN INSECT?

Can you tell which of these animals is an insect?

Remember the 3 + 3 rule: an insect has three parts to its body and three pairs of legs.

A
Spider
Clue: count the legs

B
Scorpion
Clue: count its body parts

C
Housefly
Clue: count its legs and its body parts.

D
Garden worm
Clue: look at its body

Turn the page to find the answers.

Welcome or unwelcome?

People often think of insects as being harmful. We tend to notice them only when they are a nuisance and this gives them a bad reputation. But, in fact, most of the millions of insects around us are totally harmless and many insects have an important role to play in the world.

DID YOU SPOT THE INSECT?

A No, spiders are not insects. Spiders have eight legs and they do not have a separate head and thorax. All insects have six legs and a separate head and thorax.

B No, scorpions are not insects. The head and the thorax on a scorpion are not separate. They are separate on an insect.

C Yes, flies are insects. Like all insects, flies have three pairs of legs and three body parts.

D No, worms are not insects. Worms have soft bodies. Insects have hard outer bodies.

Below are some of the ways in which insects are welcome and unwelcome. Some insects are both.

WELCOME INSECTS

Bees, flies and butterflies carry pollen on their bodies from plant to plant. In this way they help to pollinate flowers and crops and so make sure that new plants grow the following year.

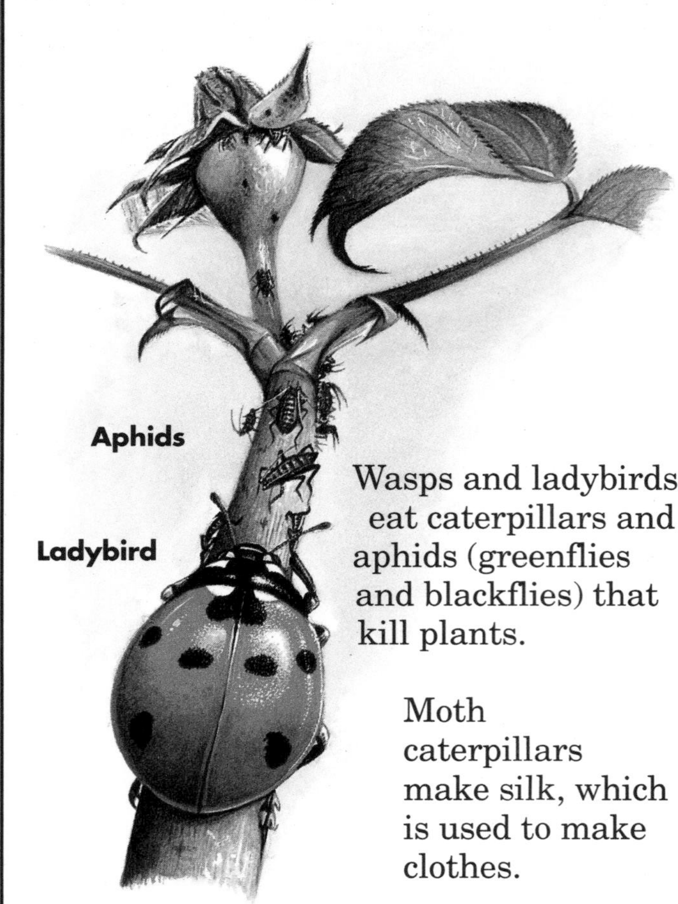

Wasps and ladybirds eat caterpillars and aphids (greenflies and blackflies) that kill plants.

Moth caterpillars make silk, which is used to make clothes.

Small Talk

- There are thought to be more than 10,000,000,000,000,000,000 insects alive at any one time. That's about 1,500 million insects for every person alive.
- The first animals ever to fly were insects – millions of years before birds took to the air. Monster-sized dragonflies with wings 70cm across flew 300 million years ago, before the Age of the Dinosaurs.

Beetles and flies clean up animal droppings and the rotting bodies of dead plants and animals.

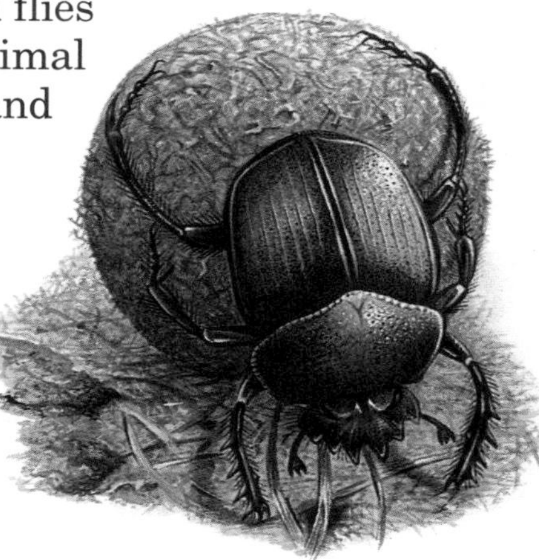

Dung beetle

Honey bee

Bees provide us with honey to eat and beeswax, which is used to polish furniture.

UNWELCOME INSECTS

Mosquitoes spread diseases, such as malaria and yellow fever.

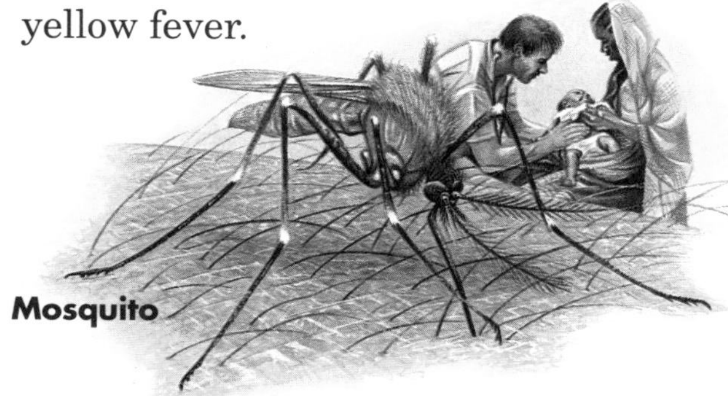

Mosquito

Bees, wasps and hornets have a painful sting, which can be dangerous to some people.

Termites and woodworms damage furniture and buildings.

Colorado beetles eat and ruin potato crops.

Death-watch beetle

Death watch beetles munch through timber in buildings.

Locusts gather in huge groups called swarms and can eat all the plants in an area, leaving the people living there without food.

Cockroaches infest food stores and spread germs.

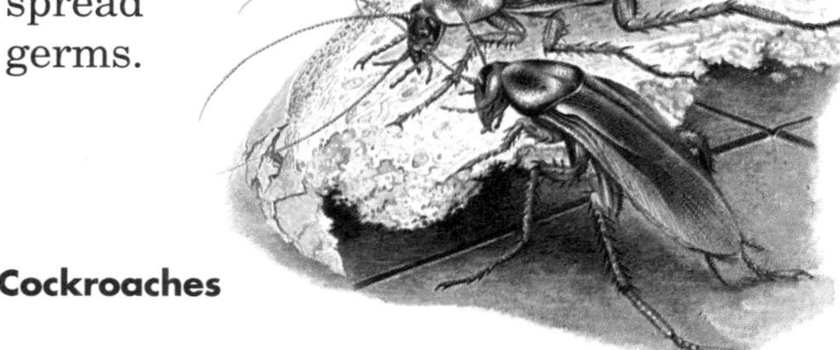

Cockroaches

GRUB'S UP!

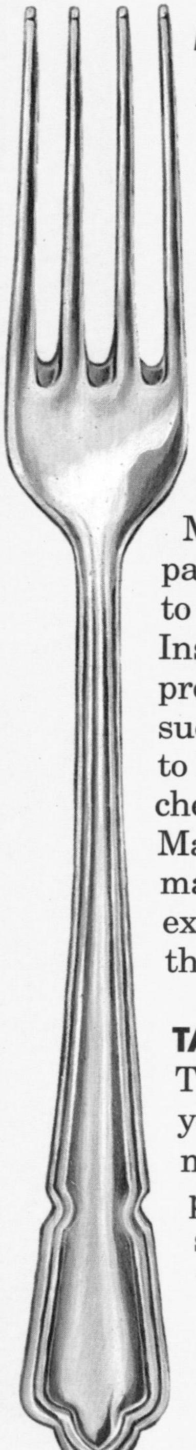

Bugs can be as good for you as beef, lamb or pork. In some countries they are an important food.

Many people in the western world turn up their nose at the idea of eating bugs but there is no reason why they should. Munching bugs can be good for you!

FULL OF GOODNESS

Most bugs are clean and unlikely to pass on germs. Their flesh is similar to that of other animals that we eat. Insect larvae (young) are full of protein, which is found in foods such as cheese. People need protein to help keep them strong. Unlike cheese, however, bugs are low in fat. Many animals eat bugs – birds make a meal out of mealworms for example, though we do not suggest that you do!

TASTY PLANT-EATERS

The food an animal lives on helps tell you whether it is fit to eat. In general, meat-eaters should be avoided. Many plant-eaters, though, make healthy snacks. Most bugs are plant-eaters, which makes them good to eat.

IN THE POT

Some people use bugs in their cooking. There are many types of edible bug and each country has its own favourites. Here is what you might find on an international bug menu.

Queen termite

Edible tarantula

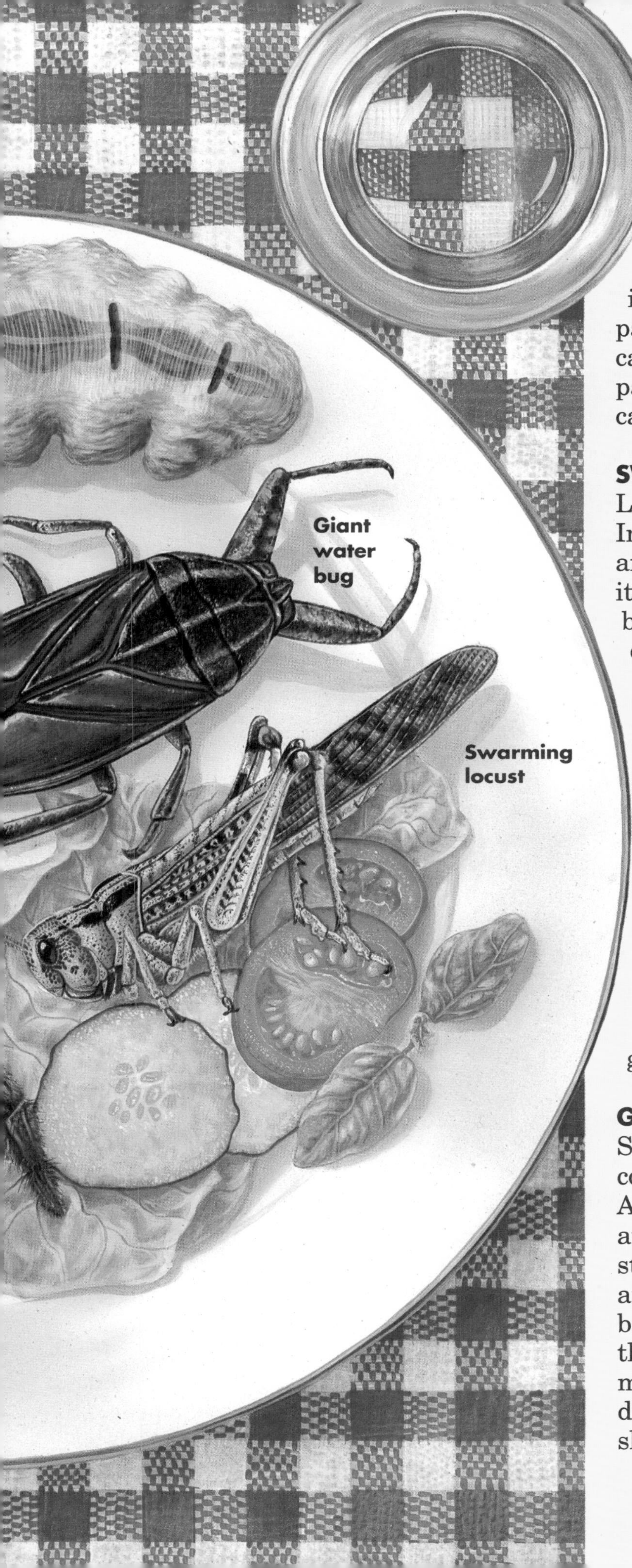

QUEEN TERMITE

It's hard work digging up a queen termite – not to mention painful if you find yourself under attack from the soldiers guarding her – but it's worth it. She contains thousands of eggs, packed with protein and vitamins. She can be eaten straight away or, if she's particularly large and luscious, she can be cooked over an open fire.

SWARMING LOCUST

Locusts are major destroyers of crops. In the past, people collected, cooked and ate them. These days, however, it is not a good idea to do this because they are often sprayed with chemicals which can make them poisonous to humans.

EDIBLE TARANTULA

Large, hairy spiders up to 20cm across live in the forests of south-east Asia. They are not dangerous and can easily be lured out of their burrows. They are killed and threaded on to skewers then roasted over an open fire so that the stinging hairs that cover their body are singed off. These spider kebabs are full of goodness and absolutely delicious!

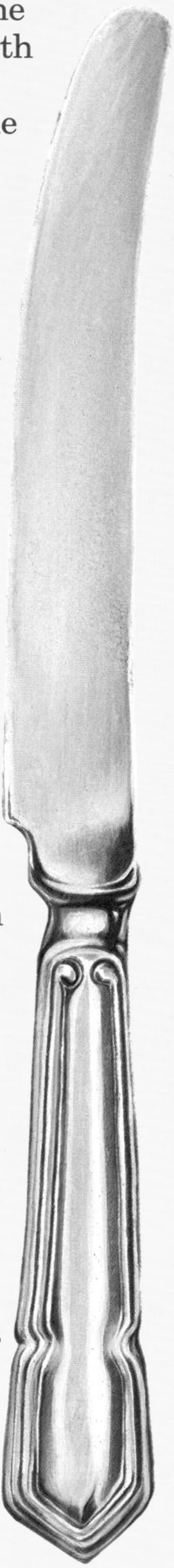

GIANT WATER BUG

Some south-east Asian markets contain small stalls selling snacks. Among the usual pancakes and rice, are giant water bugs roasted on sticks. Sometimes large grasshoppers are also on sale. The giant water bugs should be eaten with caution as they are sometimes very old, or they might have come from a local sewage ditch. The wise water bug eater shops carefully!

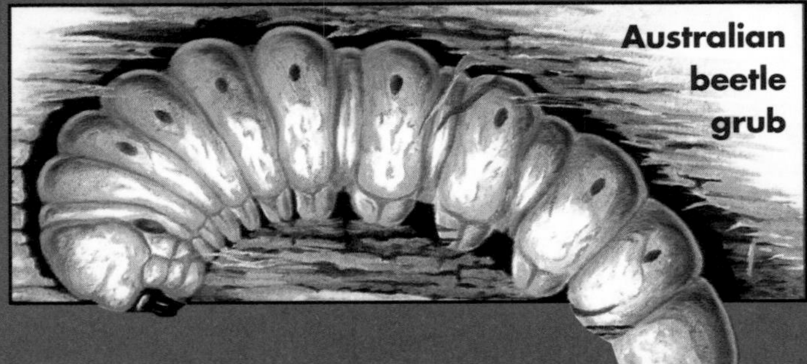

Australian beetle grub

AUSTRALIAN BEETLE GRUB

In dry countries, it can be difficult to grow food in fields, so people have to eat what they can find. One of the favourite snacks of Aborigines in Australia is the larvae of large beetles that live in rotting wood or soil. The large white grubs, known as witchetty grubs, can be over 13cm long. They can be eaten raw or cooked, and are said to taste rather like peanuts.

Is it true... that water contains bugs?

Yes, even a simple glass of water can contain a miniature world of bugs. Almost all of them are harmless to humans and when you drink tap water most of them have been removed. Some of these creatures are important to humans. They live in us and help clean our insides. However, water that doesn't come from the tap can contain bugs which will make you ill.

Floating in this water are jelly-like amoeba, which are so small a crowd of them could sit on a full stop. These slide around looking for bits of food. Other amoeba are hunters. They hunt their minute prey as they whizz through the water, pushed along by hundreds of oar-like hairs that cover their bodies.

BOGONG MOTH

Bogong moths sometimes form huge swarms made up of millions of individuals. These swarms travel across parts of Australia, flying by night and resting in caves by day. Aborigines collect the large moths in huge numbers, then make them into bogong balls and gently bake them.

Bogong moth

GOLDEN ORB SPIDER

The golden orb weaver spider lives in tropical forests. It is easy both to spot and to catch because it builds a huge 2m web. Although it can bite, its venom is very mild and does not put off the Papua New Guinea tribespeople. They roast and eat them with great relish. Only the abdomen is eaten. The legs and the thorax are thrown away.

Golden orb spider

HONEY-POT ANT

In Australia and USA the workers of some kinds of ant store sap (juice) from plants inside their abdomens. Although their nests are deep underground, the taste of these sugar-filled bugs is enough to get people digging. The ants are usually eaten straight from the ground. But some people in the Western world dip them in chocolate!

CHEESE-SKIPPER FLY
Some bugs are eaten by accident. The maggots of the cheese-skipper fly spend their short lives burrowing through soft, ripe cheese. They are difficult to spot because they are the same colour as the cheese. If they are disturbed, the maggots can curl up their bodies and 'skip' up to 20cm. They are quite harmless.

Chocolate-covered honey-pot ants are about 1.5cm long. Only their abdomens are eaten

WATCH IT!

Although people do eat bugs, there are some creepy-crawlies that will make you very ill. So, don't eat any bugs unless your parents tell you you can.

Improve and test your knowledge with...

CREEPY~CRAWLY FACTS

Meet some aphids that are out of this world and try your hand at our BUGS! quiz.

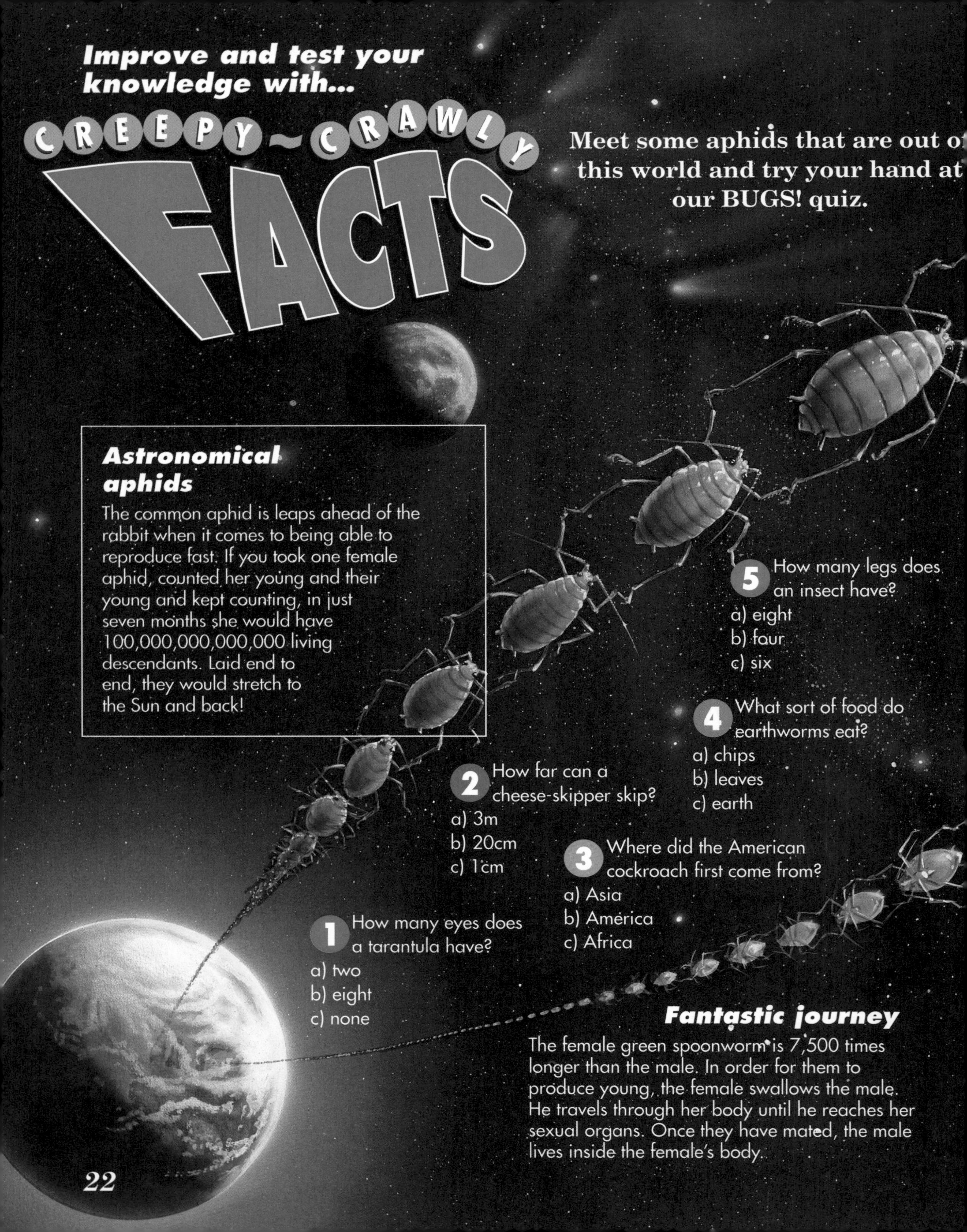

Astronomical aphids

The common aphid is leaps ahead of the rabbit when it comes to being able to reproduce fast. If you took one female aphid, counted her young and their young and kept counting, in just seven months she would have 100,000,000,000,000 living descendants. Laid end to end, they would stretch to the Sun and back!

1 How many eyes does a tarantula have?

a) two
b) eight
c) none

2 How far can a cheese-skipper skip?

a) 3m
b) 20cm
c) 1cm

3 Where did the American cockroach first come from?

a) Asia
b) America
c) Africa

4 What sort of food do earthworms eat?

a) chips
b) leaves
c) earth

5 How many legs does an insect have?

a) eight
b) four
c) six

Fantastic journey

The female green spoonworm is 7,500 times longer than the male. In order for them to produce young, the female swallows the male. He travels through her body until he reaches her sexual organs. Once they have mated, the male lives inside the female's body.

10 Which of these creatures is an insect?
a) a scorpion
b) a housefly
c) a blackwidow spider

7 How many kinds of ants are there?
a) 100
b) 8,800
c) 5,000

9 Which bug can run the fastest?
a) windscorpion
b) tarantula
c) worm

6 Why are hornets orange and black striped?
a) so they cannot be seen
b) to warn enemies of their sting
c) to look cool

8 What did the Australians use to clear up their cow dung?
a) shovels
b) beetles
c) flies

Holy mothnappers

One of the first cases of industrial spying involved two monks, a couple of walking sticks and a moth. Silk is made by silkworms, which grow into moths. In the 5th century A.D. silk was rare and expensive outside China. The Roman Emperor Justinian wanted silk, so two monks stole a batch of moth eggs, hid them inside the sticks and brought them to him in Rome. They took a big risk as the punishment for moth rustling in China was death.

What's in a name?

When something goes wrong with a computer it is often blamed on a 'bug'. The first computer bug lived up to its name. It turned out to be a grey moth, which had made its home in one of the early computers. By electrocuting itself, the moth had caused the machine to stop working.

Dung roamin'

Settlers who took the first cattle to Australia were faced with a very smelly problem. The local bugs had never seen cowpats before and so they didn't remove them from the fields. To solve the growing problem, experts brought over dung beetles from Africa. As the toilet attendants of the animal world, they cleared away the cowpats.

Answers to the questions on the inside back cover

Q and A

Matthew Robertson, who spent 12 years working with bugs at London Zoo, here answers all your creepy-crawly questions.

Which is the fastest bug?

The fastest bug on land is the windscorpion. This relative of the true scorpion can sprint along the ground at up to 12 km/h (kilometres per hour). However, some flying bugs, such as the hawk moth, can reach speeds of 30 km/h. In water, none can swim faster than the flying squid, which manages swift bursts of over 42 km/h.

Do insects have ears?

Nearly all insect have ears but they look very different from our own. For a start, very few insects have them anywhere near their head. Katydid grasshoppers, for instance, hear through their knees, whilst praying mantids have a single ear in the middle of their chest.

What is a bug?

Bugs are all those creatures that do not have a backbone or skull. They include a huge range of creatures. The smallest bug is so small that you could fit more than half a million of them on a pinhead. The biggest is longer than two buses. Bugs are sometimes also known as minibeasts, which is a general term that is used to describe any very small animal.

Which is the most venomous bug?

The most venomous bug is the Brazilian wandering spider. Although its bite is extremely dangerous, few people die from it as humans rarely come into contact with it. More people are injured by the blackwidow spider because it often makes its home in people's houses.

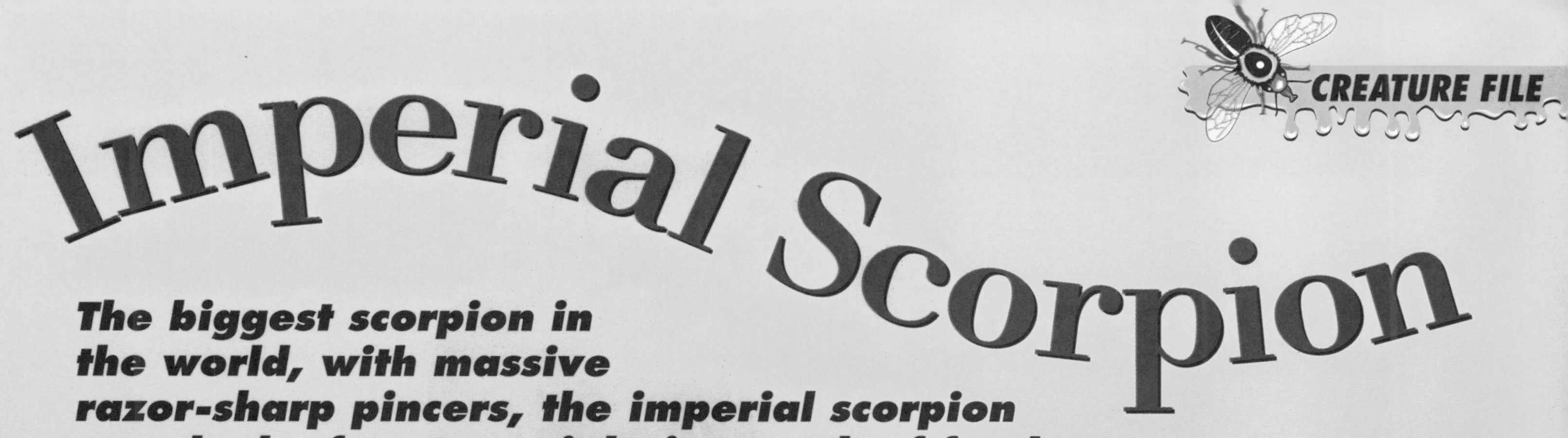

Imperial Scorpion

The biggest scorpion in the world, with massive razor-sharp pincers, the imperial scorpion prowls the forest at night in search of food.

From the tip of its head to the end of its tail, the imperial scorpion is over 15cm long. This huge scorpion eats anything from bugs to small lizards and mammals. Yet, despite its fearsome appearance, large sting and massive pincers, the imperial scorpion is not dangerous to humans.

OUT AT NIGHT

The imperial scorpion lives in the hot and humid forests of central Africa. It is found among the fallen leaves that collect at the base of trees. Like most scorpions, it is nocturnal, coming out only at night. The imperial scorpion can live for a surprisingly long time – over eight years.

BIG AND STRONG

Because of its size, this scorpion does not need a powerful venom to kill. It holds its prey with its scissor-like pincers and stings it several times until it stops struggling. The scorpion takes the food back to its burrow where it pulls its prey apart. The prey is shredded further by a smaller set of pincers, which the scorpion uses to place the food in its mouth.

The long flexible tail can whip forward like lightning to deliver its sting.

The sting is only used against animals that fight back.

Bristle-like hairs on the feelers help the scorpion detect prey.

Powerful pincers with razor-sharp edges can rip even large prey to bits.

The mouth parts have tiny pincers that cut food into chunks small enough to swallow.

GREEN AND GLOWING

Because imperial scorpions are black and only come out at night, they are very difficult to spot. When experts study them in the wild, they take torches that give off a special kind of light called ultraviolet. The outer shell of this scorpion glows bright green when it is lit up with this light.

DANGER SIGNS

Scorpions with big pincers – like the imperial scorpion – do not usually need a strong venom because they are strong enough to hold their prey still. A scorpion is more likely to be dangerous if its pincers are small. This means it needs to rely on venom to overpower its prey.

CAUTIOUS MOVER

When he wants to mate, the male imperial scorpion approaches the female slowly and very carefully. Once he is quite sure she knows he is there and that she no longer thinks he might be a tasty snack, he moves forward.

MATING DANCE

The two of them then lock their pincers together. It looks rather as though they are doing some sort of strange, complicated dance together as they pull each other around. In fact, the male is trying to position the female over a drop of his sperm, which he has placed on the ground. This mating 'dance' can last for several hours, or up to two days. A few months after the scorpions have mated, the female gives birth. She usually has between 20 and 50 babies.

HITCHING A LIFT

Baby scorpions are small white creatures that look a bit like woodlice. As each baby is born, the mother helps it crawl on to her back. While the babies are there, they rely on her completely for transport, food, and safety. After a few weeks, the babies shed their skins. They then look like miniature versions of the mother. They stay with her for several weeks. When the young scorpions are able to feed themselves, they wander off.

A CHANGE OF CLOTHES

Like all bugs that have a hard skeleton on the outside, the imperial scorpion has to shed its skin in order to grow. It usually does this once a year throughout its life.

- **SCIENTIFIC NAME:** *Pandinus imperator*
- **SIZE:** 15cm long
- **LIVES:** rainforests of central Africa
- **EATS:** bugs, lizards, small mammals

SIZING UP

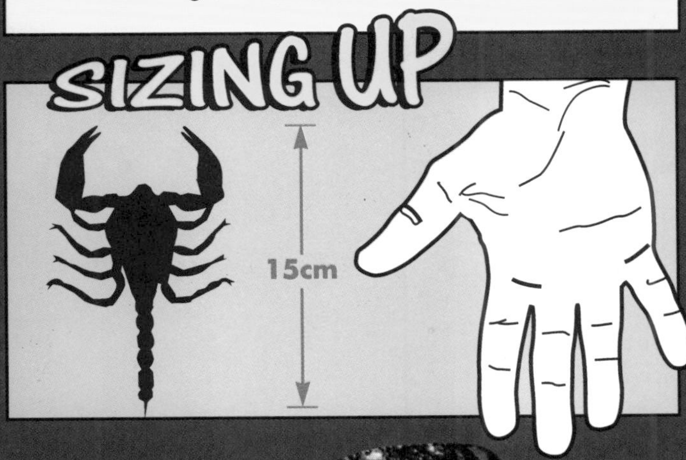

Is it true... that when scorpions fight they can sting each other to death?

No. Scorpions cannot be hurt by their own venom so they cannot sting each other – or themselves. Their powerful pincers, however, are quite capable of ripping their opponent to pieces.

The babies on the mother's back are soft and helpless.

The red admiral can fly so fast that in a race it would beat most birds.

Red Admiral

The red admiral is one of the biggest butterflies in North America and Europe. It has beautiful scarlet markings on its wings.

BEASTLY FACTS

- **SCIENTIFIC NAME:** *Vanessa atalanta*
- **SIZE:** wingspan 5.5 – 6.5cm
- **LIVES:** Central and North America, Europe, north Africa, western Asia
- **EATS:** leaves of nettles, sometimes hops (as a caterpillar), nectar of flowers, juice of rotting fruit, tree sap (as a butterfly)

LEAF COVER

The female red admiral can lay 100 eggs a day. She lays them one by one, usually on nettle leaves. When the young caterpillars hatch, they wrap the leaves around themselves with threads of their silk.

KEEPING ENEMIES AWAY

The fully-grown caterpillars have bold markings and spiny bodies that keep most birds away, but they may be attacked by wasps or flies. The butterflies are such fast fliers that few birds could catch them.

SENSE OF TASTE

Red admirals taste things with their feet! Using the special organs in this part of their body, they can pick out the tiniest differences in taste between foods.

In one night, this starfish can eat an area of coral half as wide as itself.

Crown-of-thorns

The spiky, crown-of-thorns starfish lives in the warm, south Pacific Ocean. It comes out at night, in search of coral – its favourite midnight snack.

SLOW EATER

The crown-of-thorns clamps itself on to the coral with the suckers on its feet. Then it turns its stomach 'inside out' by pushing it out through its mouth. It covers the coral with its stomach and sucks it out of the rock.

LEGS AND FEET

The crown-of-thorns starfish has 15 – 20 legs. If one of them is lost, it just grows a new one! Along the bottom of its legs are rows of hollow feet that it moves in and out by pumping sea water through them.

KEEPING CLEAN

On top of its body, it has tiny 'jaws'. These pick up any anything that falls on to it, and help to keep it clean.

BEASTLY FACTS

- **SCIENTIFIC NAME:** *Acanthaster planci*
- **SIZE:** 40 – 70cm across
- **LIVES:** south Pacific Ocean, South America
- **EATS:** coral

SIZING UP

Imagine walking through a desert under the blazing sun, when suddenly the sky goes black. A cloud has blocked out the sunlight – a cloud of desert locusts.

Swarm!

In a matter of hours a locust swarm can munch its way through tonnes of vegetation. No wonder some farmers (above left) take to the air to protect their crops from the locusts.

Desert locusts collect in huge numbers and eat all the crops in their path. They can travel for hundreds of kilometres and they are particularly common in Africa and Asia.

WEATHER CHECK

For desert locusts to go on the rampage, the weather has to be just right. Usually, only a few of the eggs that are laid by the females survive. But if weather conditions are good, more eggs hatch. As they become overcrowded and food runs out, the young locusts swarm. Here are the six stages that result in a swarm.

1 SHOWER POWER

The best time for the females to lay their eggs is after rain. This is because the rain makes the crops grow so there is plenty for the young to eat. Also, it is easier for the babies to get out of the ground when the soil is wet.

- As much as £5 million worth of food is lost to locusts each year.
- Locusts are a good source of protein. In some parts of Africa, people eat them.

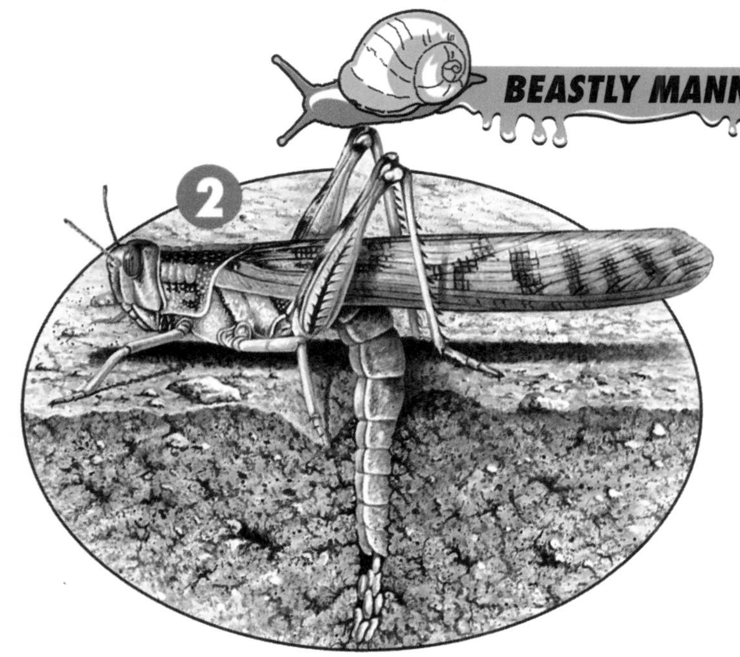

2 EGG LAYING

After mating, the female lays a pod (group) of sausage-shaped eggs in a warm sandy area. There can be up to 100 eggs in one egg pod. She digs a hole by extending her abdomen and puts her eggs in it. She then blocks the hole with some froth, which she makes in her abdomen. The froth hardens to protect the eggs and also helps prevent them drying out.

3 HATCHING HOPPERS

The baby locusts hatch after nine to 11 days. The young locusts are known as hoppers or nymphs. They are exact miniatures of the adults, only without wings. The young hoppers start to feed as soon as they hatch. They have very strong jaws – perfect for biting into plants.

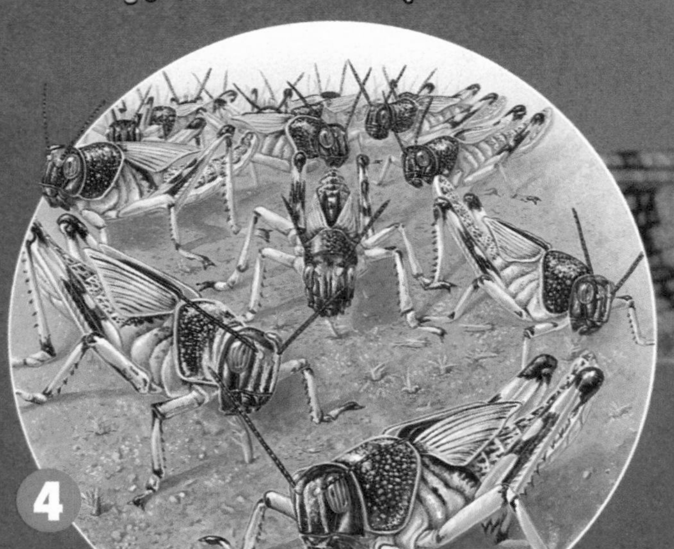

This locust (right) is an adult. It has shed its skin and grown wings. Now it's ready to swarm! Locusts have two phases in their lives – a solitary one, when they live alone, and a sociable one, when they swarm.

4 EATING ON THE MOVE

The hoppers go on a march that lasts for 4 – 5 weeks. This is when they cause most damage. There can be 15,000 per square metre. During the day the young locusts hop in groups called bands. At dusk they feed. Their favourite foods are maize, millet, citrus fruits and wild grasses.

5

The skin splits down the hopper's back and the adult begins to emerge.

The new adult turns around and holds on to the skin.

Blood begins to pump around the wings. The adult eats its old skin.

5 TAKING TO THE SKIES

The locust adult (left) grows to full size by moulting (shedding its skin). It does this six times in its life. When its four wings are fully grown it is an adult. It is then able to fly off and find new areas to feed. It flies at 10 – 25 km per hour, depending on the direction and speed of the wind. During this adult stage it eats its own weight in food each day.

Small Talk

POOL POISON

Chemicals called insecticides are sprayed on to pests to kill them. It would take nearly 4 million litres of insecticide to get rid of a large locust swarm. That's enough to fill four Olympic-size swimming pools.

6

6 SWARMING
Once the locusts have eaten all they can in an area they fly off. A typical swarm (above) can contain 10 billion locusts and cover an area of 1,875 square kilometres. It would consume over 20,000 tonnes of food each day. Swarms can cause complete devastation to farmers' fields.

SNAIL WATCH

How snails eat

Snails are mainly herbivores, which means that they only eat plants. They do not have teeth like we do. Instead, they have a tongue with rough edges called a radula. The uneven edges help the snail pick up food.

ACTION

You will need:
- ground oatmeal • water
- sheet of clear plastic
- magnifying glass • a snail

1 Mix some ground oatmeal in water, using two parts oatmeal to one part water.

2 When you've made a thick paste, smear this on to a sheet of clear plastic.

3 Place a snail on the oatmeal paste.

4 You can watch it gliding along and see its mouth opening and closing.

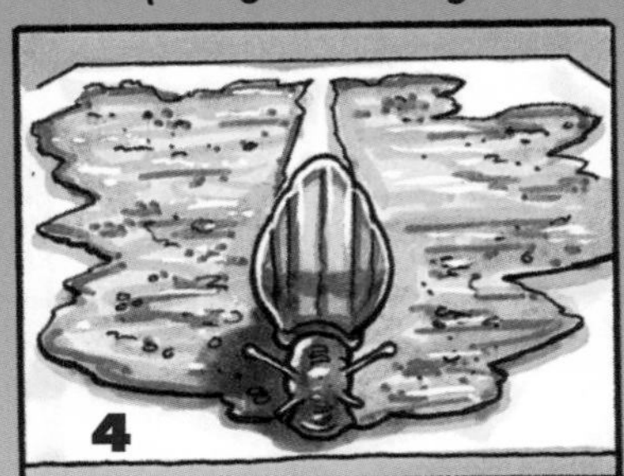

5 If you look at it through a magnifying glass, you might be able to see the radula moving backwards and forwards. As the snail moves, you will see a clear path through the oatmeal.

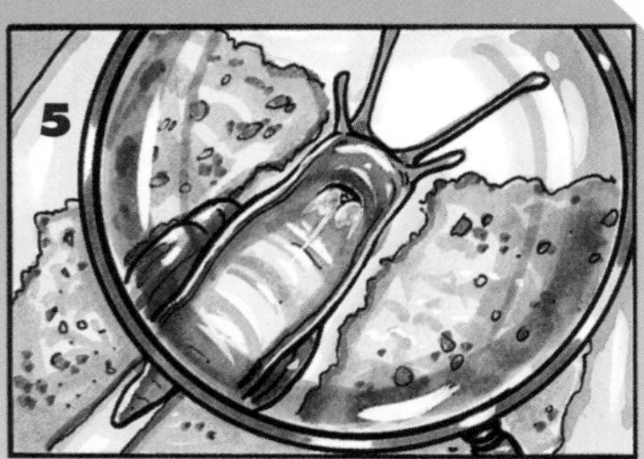

Moving about

A major problem faced by snails on land is how to get about without any legs. In the water they can swim or glide. To get around on land, snails produce a layer of thick slime. This lets them slide along on almost any surface. Because of this slippery slime and their bendy bodies, they can crawl over pointed objects – even a sharp knife.

You will need: • a snail • clear plastic

ACTION

1 Put one on a sheet of clear plastic.

2 You will see ripples moving from its tail to its head. These are caused by muscles that lift the snail slightly off the ground and push it forward.

3 You will also be able to see its trail of slime.

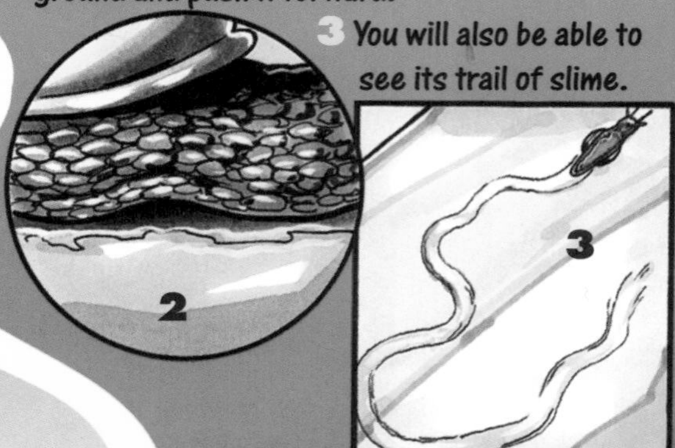

Snails are fascinating bugs to watch. Here are some tests for you to do, which will show you how they live.

Wet or dry?

Water is very important to snails. If a snail finds itself in a dry place, it will either crawl into its shell or go in search of better conditions. You can see how it does this.

You will need:
- small tank with clear sides at least 60cm x 30cm x 30cm
- netting for lid, with elastic bands to hold it in place
- water • a snail
- soil

ACTION

1 Put a layer of dry soil into the tank. 2 Leave one end of the tank dry and make the other end damp. 3 Place the snail in the middle of the tank. 4 Cover the top with netting kept in place with rubber bands.

5 Leave the tank in a dark place overnight. In the morning you can see whether the snail went towards the dry or damp soil. You should find that the snail moves towards the damp end. This is because snails can't store water easily so they need to stay as close to water as possible.

You can also discover whether snails prefer night or day.

Dark or light?

You will need:
- small tank with clear sides at least 60cm x 30cm x 30cm
- netting for lid, with elastic bands to hold it in place
- soil
- thick cloth or a large piece of paper
- at least one snail
- a lamp (optional)

ACTION

1 Use the same tank as you used to test if snails prefer wet or dry soil, but this time make sure that the soil is damp all over. 2 Place at least one snail in the tank and cover the top with netting. 3 Put a thick cloth or large piece of paper over half of the tank and leave the other end uncovered, apart from the netting. Leave the tank in a bright place or under a lamp and watch which end the snails travel to.

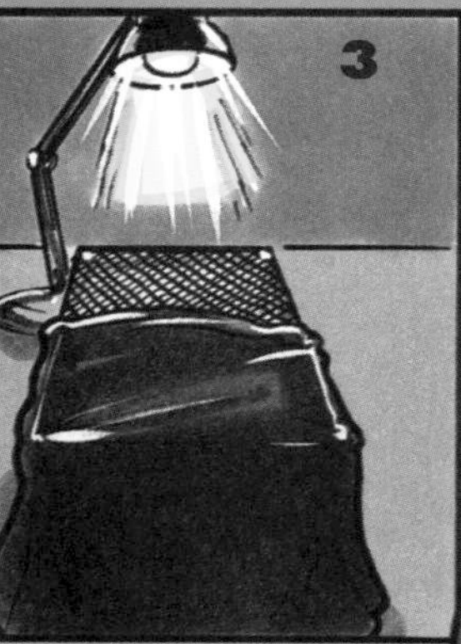

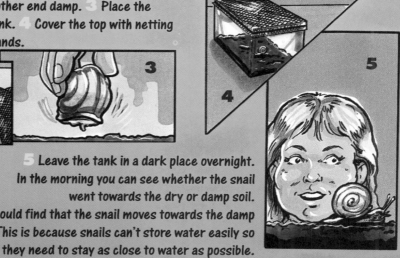

4 The snails should prefer the dark end. This is because they like to come out at night when it is cooler. The dark also helps prevent some enemies spotting them.

REMEMBER - ALWAYS WASH YOUR HANDS AFTER TOUCHING BUGS AND SOIL.

Millipede

A determined scavenger, the millipede slowly trundles its worm-like body through dead leaves that lie on the ground. This bug is in search of its favourite food – decaying plant matter. When the millipede comes face to face with danger, its antennae stand upright and the bugs rolls its body up into a tiny ball. Its long body is made up of many segments which enables the millipede to curl up small. Two rows of stink glands along the sides of its body secrete a nasty substance capable of killing – or at least repelling – any attacking insects.

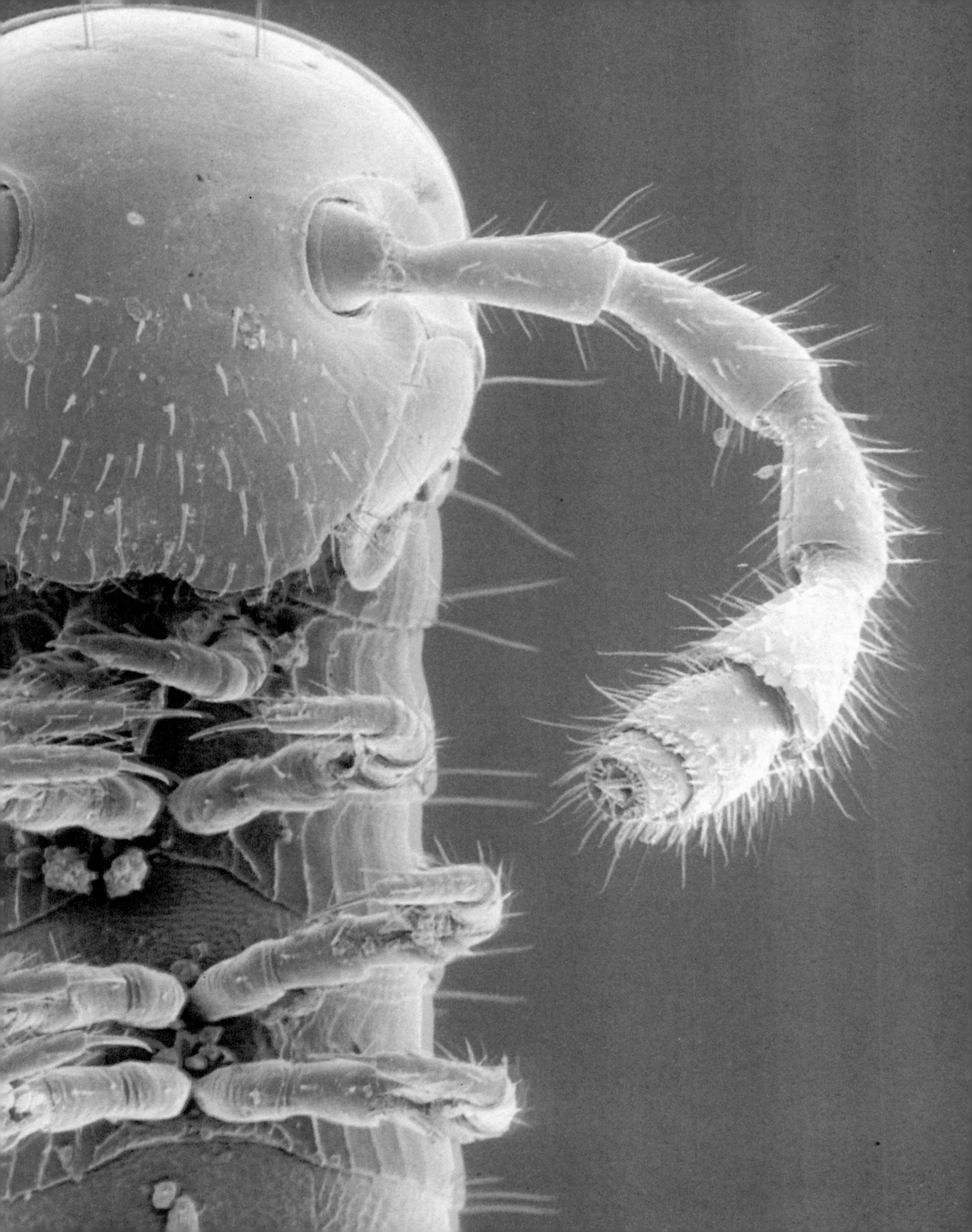

Small Talk

MULTI-TALENTED

Animals are not the only things that bugs mimic. They also mimic a whole range of other things, including plants and rocks. There are even spiders and beetles that do very convincing impressions of bird droppings!

Look-alike

Many bugs mimic other bugs and animals, either to protect themselves or to fool other bugs into coming close enough to be eaten.

Spectacled owl

Mimicry is when an animal or plant pretends to be something it is not. One of the most common forms is when one bug pretends to be another type of bug that is poisonous or has a painful bite or sting. Others pretend to be birds or leaves. Meet the masters of disguise.

THE OWL BUTTERFLY

The owl butterfly normally relies on its resemblance to a leaf to keep it out of harm's way. However, if it is disturbed it has a trick up its sleeve. Suddenly, it opens its wings to reveal two huge 'eyes'. At the same time it sticks out its body. To any predator the dead leaf has turned into an owl – one of the most feared enemies of small animals.

THE LANTERN BUG

Like the owl butterfly, the peanut or lantern bug uses its wings to do a good impersonation of an owl. However, if you come at it from the front you are in for a surprise. For there staring back at you is an alligator! It is true that it is only a few centimetres long, but with staring eye, flaring nostrils and two rows of gleaming teeth, it would take a brave animal to start a fight with this cunning bug.

This bird (left) has had the shock of its life. A harmless butterfly, the owl butterfly, has opened its wings and turned into a clawed hunter – an owl. The real bird doesn't wait to take a second look, it flies off to safety.

The harmless viceroy butterfly (below) has the same warning colours as the poisonous monarch butterfly (right).

Monarch butterfly

Viceroy butterfly

Wasps

The hover fly (below) looks and flies just like a wasp (above). Unlike its look-alike, the hover fly only eats nectar and doesn't sting.

Hover fly

THE ANT-MIMICKING FLY

The slit-legged fly is unable to defend itself. Like a lot of flies, it does not have a bite or sting. To try to scare off attackers it imitates a bug that can bite – an ant.

FIREFLIES

Fireflies use light to attract a mate. Each species has a special code of light flashes. The North American firefly uses its light for another purpose. By imitating the light flashes of another species of firefly, the female can lure an unsuspecting male to her. While the male is busy impressing the female, she lunges at him and eats him!

STINK BUGS

When baby stink bugs are born they group together, face inwards and waggle their legs and antennae in the air. Together, they do an impressive impersonation of a caterpillar with irritating hairs on its body. Even a hungry bird won't be tempted.

The harmless stilt-legged fly (below) wants to look dangerous. It has very small wings, which it folds flat against its body so that it will be mistaken for a fierce ant (right).

These two animals look similar, but they are not even distant relatives. This cunning caterpillar (above left), which lives in Costa Rica, South America, does a brilliant impression of a snake (above right).

Is it true... that some bugs imitate different things as they get older?

Yes. There is one bug, for example, called Macleay's spectre stick insect, which mimics four different things at different stages of its life. A master of mimicry, it can look like a seed when it's in the egg, a vicious ant when it hatches, a scorpion when it's young, and finally a dead leaf when it reaches adulthood.

Macleay's spectre stick insect (above) is constantly changing its image. Here, the young stick insect is doing its scorpion imitation.

BUG

There are more than 2,300 types of endangered bugs. That's over 10 times the number of threatened mammals. For bugs to survive, they must be protected.

There are over 30 million species of bug but they need protection. Without bugs, many plants and animals would die. Some bugs are food for larger animals, others carry pollen from one flower to another (pollinate) helping plants to grow.

WHY WORRY?
The natural world depends on a balance of plants and animals. If a lot of bugs disappear, this balance will be lost and many animals could also become extinct.

WHAT THREATENS BUGS?
There are three main threats to bugs:

● **Pollution**
Bugs that live in water are easily killed by chemicals dumped into lakes and rivers by factories. Fertilisers and insecticides are washed from fields into streams and oil spillages are a big threat to sea bugs.

● **Other animals**
The introduction of animals from one area to another has also caused many bugs to become rare and to die out. For instance, humans have taken rats, mice, cats and pigs all over the world. These animals eat the bugs and can easily alter the balance of nature.

● **Habitat destruction**
Since humans first appeared on Earth, over half of all forests where many bugs live have been cut down for the wood or to make way for farm land.

Is it true... that hundreds of bug species have died out in the last 50 years?

Yes, although the exact number will never be known. All over the world, animals are slowly dying out. These bugs have disappeared forever: 16 species of pearly mussel from (USA), the Lord Howe stick insect (Australasia), and the green sphinx of Kauai (Hawaii). In Britain, the large blue butterfly and the mole cricket are both extinct.

Going, going...

Every time a tree in a tropical forest is cut down, a species of bug dies. All the bugs on this page are in danger because of the action of humans. The future of many bugs depends on you.

THE ROBBER CRAB

The largest land bug, the robber crab, has already been practically wiped out. These huge crabs, which can measure up to 1m wide, are hunted by humans for food.

TOO MANY PEOPLE

In the past there were fewer humans on Earth. Over the years, the number of humans has increased, while the number of robber crabs has fallen. Animals that prey on robber crabs, such as rats, monkeys, cats and lizards, have also helped reduce the number of crabs.

TOURIST TRAP

Many robber crabs are killed, stuffed with foam, and sold as ornaments to tourists. The Pacific islands where they live, have been used as test sites for nuclear bombs, which means that the crab's chances of survival are even smaller.

Robber crab

BUG HIT LIST

These bugs are so rare that any one of them could disappear tomorrow.

1 Moorean tree snail
2 No-eyed big-eyed wolf spider
3 New Zealand's giant weta cricket
4 St Helena giant earwig
5 Fine-rayed pearly mussel
6 UK's wart-biter cricket
7 Coral reefs
8 Yorba Linda weevil
9 Malaysia's ghost walker beetle
10 Xerxes blue butterfly

SNAIL-EAT-SNAIL

In the 1970s, a giant African land snail farm was set up on islands in the Pacific. The snails escaped and in 10 years there was a plague of them eating the crops! Another snail was introduced to eat the giant snail. But the snail-eating snails ate the local tree snails and soon made them extinct! Fortunately, a few of the local snails had been taken from the islands for research so it was possible to collect some snails together and to set up a breeding programme for 15 species.

BYE BYE BUGS

Most bugs live in rainforests – around 20 million species. It has been calculated that somewhere in the region of 60,000 species of bug will disappear every year, simply because of the destruction of the rainforests. That works out at seven species of bug an hour, every hour of the day. If the same rate were applied to mammals, all 4,000 different kinds of mammal would be extinct in less than a month – just 24 days, to be exact. Frightening, isn't it?

Giant American land snail

European medicinal leech

LIFE-SAVING LEECHES

The European medicinal leech has now become very rare. For hundreds of years, these animals were used to suck the blood out of sick people. It was thought that leeches would remove the poison from their bodies and make them well. However, as more and more leeches were prescribed by doctors, their numbers dropped dramatically. In addition, the places where they lived were being cleared for farm land and housing. Soon the leech was on the verge of extinction.

NEW POWERS

It is quite possible that the leech would eventually have vanished completely. But in the nick of time, scientists discovered that a chemical produced by the leech helps stop blood clotting during delicate operations. The leech is now in great demand and is bred on special leech farms.

mprove and test your
nowledge with...

EEPY~CRAWLY FACTS

Watch out for the bug with the strong left hook and test your friends with these brainteasers.

1 The pyramids at Giza are made of
) concrete
) fossilized wood
dead bugs

2 How many army ants are here in an army?
ı) 7,000
ɔ) 700,000
:) 7,000,000

3 What does millipede mean?
ı) ten legs
ɔ) one hundred legs
:) one thousand legs

4 What does the crown-of-thorns starfish use to move its feet?
ı) sea water
ɔ) flippers
:) electricity

5 When is the best time for female locusts to lay eggs?
ı) at night
ɔ) after rain
:) on holiday

6 What animal does the hover fly mimic?
a) snake
b) wasp
c) giraffe

7 How many things does Macleay's spectre stick insect mimic?
a) four
b) twenty
c) two

8 What do red admirals use their feet for?
a) digging holes
b) attacking birds
c) tasting food

9 How much forest has been cut down since humans first appeared?
a) over half
b) a third
c) none

10 Which bug glows bright green in ultraviolet light?
a) cabbage greenfly
b) imperial scorpion
c) locust

Munching millions

Early in the 1870s, a vast swarm of locusts appeared in the heart of North America. A passing bug expert tried to count them as they flew by. He lost count, but estimated 10 million million. A swarm this size would have covered an area the size of the United Kingdom. Each day it would have eaten over 1 million tonnes of food.

Strong swimmers

If you were to shrink to the size of one of the smallest bugs, you would only be visible under a microscope. If you tried to go swimming you would be in for a shock. At this size the water seems thicker – about 1 million times thicker. It would be like jumping into a pool of treacle!

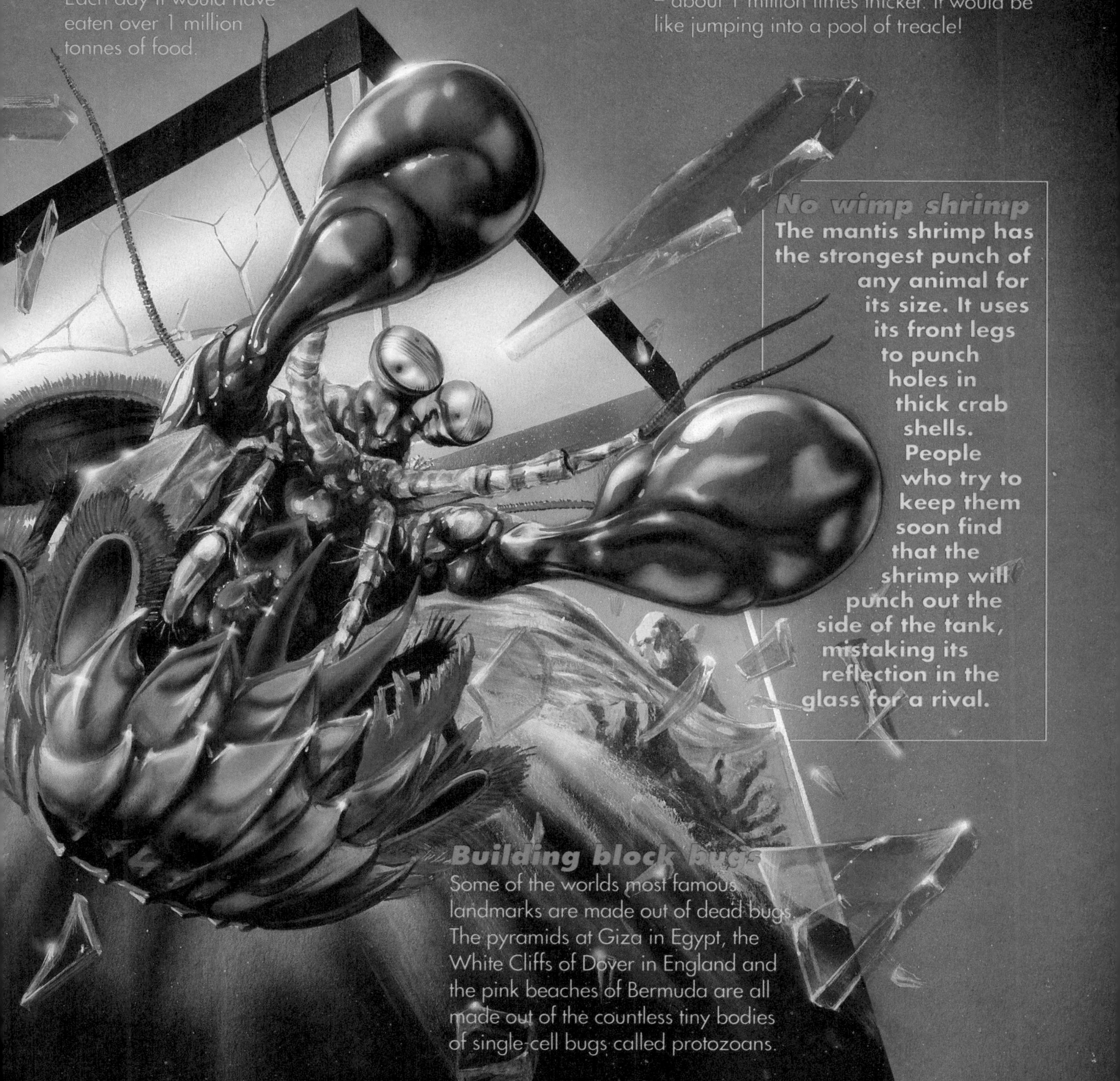

No wimp shrimp

The mantis shrimp has the strongest punch of any animal for its size. It uses its front legs to punch holes in thick crab shells. People who try to keep them soon find that the shrimp will punch out the side of the tank, mistaking its reflection in the glass for a rival.

Building block bugs

Some of the worlds most famous landmarks are made out of dead bugs. The pyramids at Giza in Egypt, the White Cliffs of Dover in England and the pink beaches of Bermuda are all made out of the countless tiny bodies of single-cell bugs called protozoans.

Q and A

Matthew Robertson, who spent 12 years working with bugs at London Zoo, here answers all your creepy-crawly questions.

Which is the most intelligent bug?

The octopus is probably the cleverest bug of all. It has a large brain (for a bug), good eyesight, and its tentacles are agile and sensitive. Experts have found that they can do quite complex puzzles. They can even take the top off a screw-top jar.

What is the most dangerous bug in the world?

The mosquito and the single-cell parasite that causes malaria are among the most dangerous creatures on Earth. Between the two of them they have caused more deaths than any other living thing (including humans). Every year, over 1,200,000 people die from malaria and a further 150,000,000 people become infected.

Which bug has the most legs?

The millipede (it literally means *a thousand legs*) has more legs than any other living creature although none has been recorded with this number. The giant Seychelles millipede, which grows to nearly 30cm long, has over 600 legs. However, the leggiest of them all is an American millipede which boasts an impressive 752 legs.

Stag Beetle

Male stag beetles use their huge jaws to wrestle with each other. They are strong enough to pick up an opponent and fling him aside.

Stag beetles have huge, claw-like jaws which look like the antlers of a stag. This is how they got their name. Only the male beetles have jaws this size, which can be as big as their bodies, and are edged with teeth. The male beetles don't use their jaws for killing prey, but they do use them for fighting each other.

LOOKING FOR A FIGHT

In the forests where they live, each male stag beetle has his own 'territory', or part of the forest. He can mate with all the females there. If another male enters his territory, he attacks, using his sharp jaws to try to push the intruder off the log or branch where he is standing. If this doesn't work, he may even lift up his enemy in his jaws, and try to drop him to the ground.

IN DANGER

Such battles don't usually end in death – the loser often just gives up and goes away. But if one beetle's shell is pierced by the jaws of the other, it can die. A beetle that falls on to its back, and cannot get to its feet, may also become the victim of ants.

LIFE STORY
Stag beetles live under old logs or pieces of bark. Like other insects, they begin their life as eggs. The females lay the eggs in old, rotting wood, or in the roots of trees. The European stag beetle can dig down 75cm into the earth to place her eggs in the roots of oak trees. Out of the eggs come the larvae (say 'lar-vee'), which look a bit like plump, c-shaped worms.

GETTING TOUGH
Some larvae can be up to 10cm long, which is almost as long as an adult's forefinger. They feed on wood, which they chew with their powerful jaws. When the time is right, the larvae grow a hard shell around themselves. Inside the shell they slowly turn into beetles. Changing from an egg to a beetle can take from three to five years.

EVENING MEAL
Most stag beetles come out in the early evening, when they fly about noisily, or scurry up and down tree branches. Many feed on the sweet sap, or juice, of oak trees. Others, which come out during the day, like to eat flowers or young leaves.

BIG, SMALL, AND SHINY
The male stag beetles are almost always bigger than the females, and vary tremendously in length. They may be as short as 5cm, or as long as 10cm. The common stag beetle, from Europe, is brownish-black in colour, which makes it very hard to see when it's flying through the night sky. Other kinds may be a deep blue-green or reddish-brown, with a pearly shine.

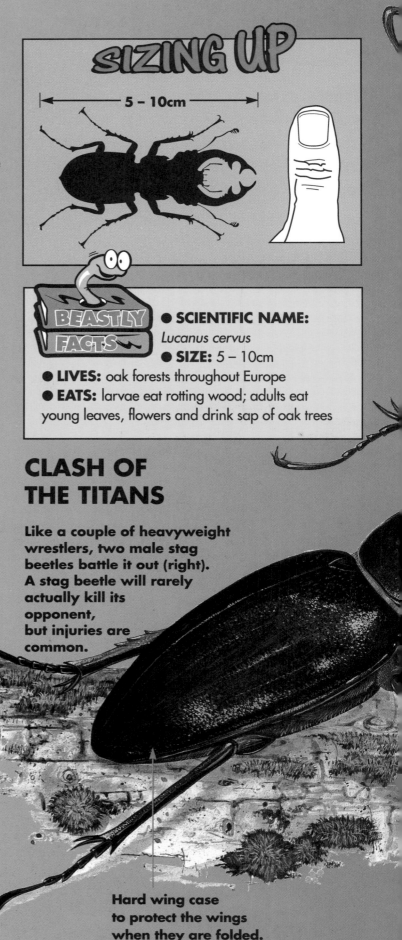

SIZING UP

5 – 10cm

BEASTLY FACTS

- **SCIENTIFIC NAME:** *Lucanus cervus*
- **SIZE:** 5 – 10cm
- **LIVES:** oak forests throughout Europe
- **EATS:** larvae eat rotting wood; adults eat young leaves, flowers and drink sap of oak trees

CLASH OF THE TITANS

Like a couple of heavyweight wrestlers, two male stag beetles battle it out (right). A stag beetle will rarely actually kill its opponent, but injuries are common.

Hard wing case to protect the wings when they are folded.

By flapping its wings the beetle can flip itself the right way up if it has toppled over. This wing has been damaged in the fight.
Powerful claws on its legs help the beetle to pull itself along branches.
Large antennae help pick up the female's scent so the male can find her.
The male's jaws, like the antlers of a stag, are very strong. They are used to fight, not to kill.
Two palps for sensing food.
The male's sponge-like mouth sucks up sweet liquids like sap.

Small Talk

BEETLE MAGIC

About five hundred years ago stag beetles were thought to have healing powers – they were widely used in folk medicine. The beetles were boiled in oil and what was left in the bottom of the pan was either drunk or rubbed on parts of the body to cure fevers and treat earache. Stag beetles were also used to prevent children wetting the bed!

CREATURE FILE

Moon Moth

Moon moths are one of the largest moths in the world. They have huge, pale green wings with long 'tails', rather like the shape of an old-fashioned kite.

With a wingspan of up to 15cm, which is as wide as the length of a pencil, moon moths are huge. They get their name from the moon-like markings on their wings.

FINDING A MATE

Male moon moths have an impressive sense of smell. During the mating season, the females give off a scent to attract the males. Using their antennae, the males can pick up the tiniest traces of this scent from over 6km away.

FAT CATERPILLARS

After mating, the females lay clusters of eggs, from which hatch caterpillars with huge heads. The caterpillars grow up to 7cm long, and change colour as they get older. They live on leaves and they must eat as much as they can at this stage. Once they become moths, they can't eat as the moth has no mouth!

SHARP SPINES

The caterpillars spin tough cases, or cocoons, of silk around themselves. Inside, they slowly change into moths. The moths pierce their way out of the cocoons with the sharp spines on their wings.

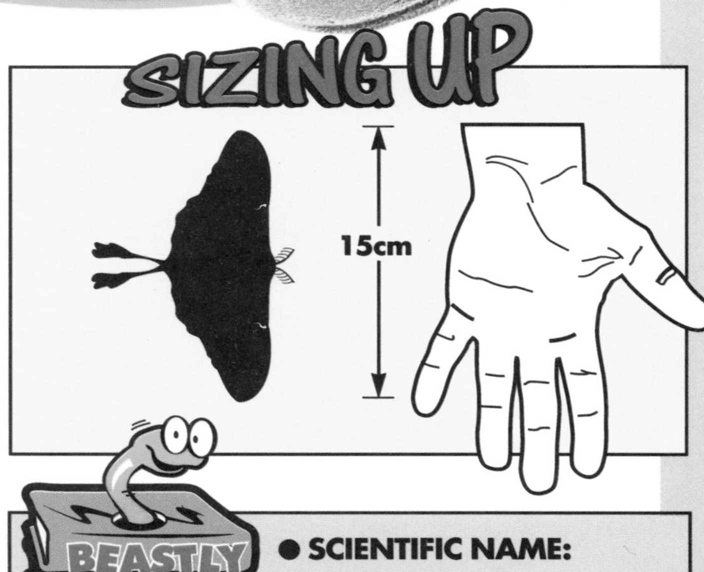

BEASTLY FACTS

- **SCIENTIFIC NAME:** *Actias luna*
- **SIZE:** length 12cm including tail, wingspan 12.5 – 15cm
- **LIVES:** forests of North America
- **EATS:** the caterpillar eats leaves; the moth doesn't eat anything

Giant Centipede

Fast on its feet and armed with poison, the giant centipede is a fierce and armoured hunter.

The giant centipede is the biggest centipede in the world. It lives in warm, damp, dark places – like moist soil or in tree bark or under rotting leaves.

FIERCE HUNTERS

With poisoned claws at the end of every leg and antennae for picking up any movement, giant centipedes go hunting at night. Instead of looking for their prey, they feel around for it. When something tasty comes along, they grab it with their claws, inject it with paralyzing poison – and then eat it!

LOTS OF LEGS

'Centipede' means '100 legs' – but in fact giant centipedes have between 40 and 44 legs, arranged in pairs along their bodies. (That's enough legs for about seven insects.) Even if a giant centipede loses a leg or two, this doesn't mean it has to limp because the other legs make up for the missing ones. Later, new legs grow to replace the lost ones.

THREE-LEGGED RACE

When it is running at top speed, a giant centipede may have only three of its legs on the ground at the same time.

- **SCIENTIFIC NAME:** *Scolopendra gigantea*
- **SIZE:** 23 – 30cm long, 2cm wide
- **LIVES:** in the forests of Central and South America
- **EATS:** insects, sometimes frogs and lizards

SIZING UP

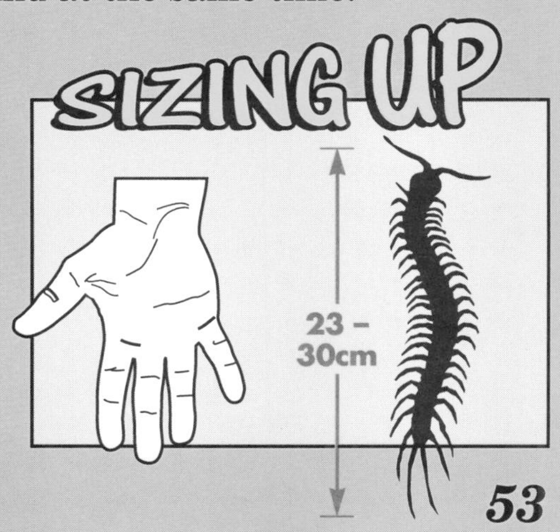

Trapdoor

The crafty trapdoor spider uses its burrow to capture bugs. But when an enemy drops by, the spider vanishes, as if by magic.

Trapdoor spiders are underground architects, building cleverly-designed burrows. They use these as nests, hide in them when hunting insects, and are protected from their enemies in them. Trapdoor spiders live all over the world and there are hundreds of different types.

BUILDING A HOME

Trapdoor spiders make deep burrows. Using their very sharp fangs like rakes, they dig the soil. They sweep it into little lumps, and then brush it outside. Once the burrow is finished, they close the top with a hinged lid, or trapdoor, which is level with the ground.

HOUSE PROUD

Some burrow lids are thin flaps, but most are thick slabs built up from layers of silk and soil. The spider spends ages carefully making sure the lid is a perfect fit.

The waiting game

1 The spider sits under the trapdoor with its front legs sticking out from under the lid, waiting...

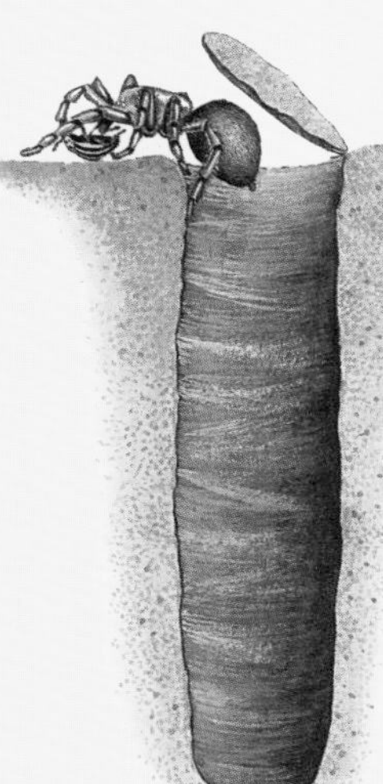

2 The hairs on the spider's legs pick up vibrations on the ground. It knows an insect is approaching and pounces.

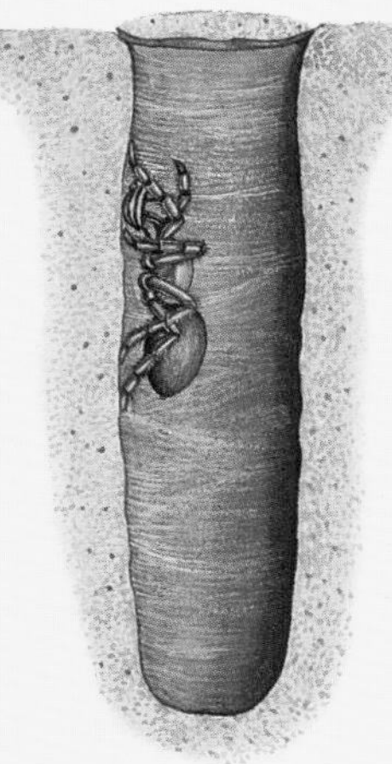

3 It takes some kinds just 0.03 seconds to grab their victim. That's faster than the time it takes to blink! They then inject their victim with poison and pull it down the burrow to be eaten.

OPEN AND SHUT CASE

The lid has a silk hinge so that it can be opened and closed, like a trapdoor. This is how the spider got its name. When it is finally satisfied, the spider pulls bits of moss and plants over the lid so that it is hidden. Now the spider sets its trap.

HUNTING FOR FOOD

Trapdoor spiders hunt from home. Most live in damp places, where there are plenty of insects. This means they don't have to wait long before an unsuspecting victim comes along.

WATCHING AND WAITING

The spider sits at the top of the burrow, with the lid slightly open. Its front legs stick out under the lid. Then it waits to pounce, like the spider in the pictures above.

TRIP WIRES

Some spiders lay complicated traps using twigs or silken wires. The spider arranges these as lines coming out from the burrow entrance, like the spokes of a wheel. If a wire or twig moves, the spider knows that a small animal has stumbled across it and rushes out on the attack.

WATCH OUT

The trapdoor spider stays in the same spot for most of its life, so its enemies often go hunting for it. Its worst enemy is the spider-hunting wasp, which forces its way into the spider's burrow, paralyses it with its sting and lays an egg. When the wasp grub hatches, it eats the spider alive.

CLINGING ON FOR LIFE

Spiders have different ways of outwitting their enemies. When an enemy attempts to force open the lid, some spiders cling to the bottom of the lid, trying to resist the intruder. The Californian trapdoor spider can hold down a force 38 times heavier than itself. That's like one adult man having a tug-of-war contest with three and a half football teams on the other side – and winning!

BOTTOMS UP

The back of the flat-bottomed trapdoor spider looks as if it has been chopped off. Its end is covered in a special kind of armour plating. The bottom of the burrow fits the spider's body exactly. A threatened spider can scoot down the burrow and plug it with its body, like a cork in a bottle (right). All the predator finds is the spider's hard, flat body, which it can't grip properly. The spider is safe.

This trapdoor spider heads for home. Its best defence is its craftily designed burrow.

Bottoms up! The spider blocks the burrow. The predator can't grip the spider's bottom, which is covered in a kind of armour plating, keeping it safe.

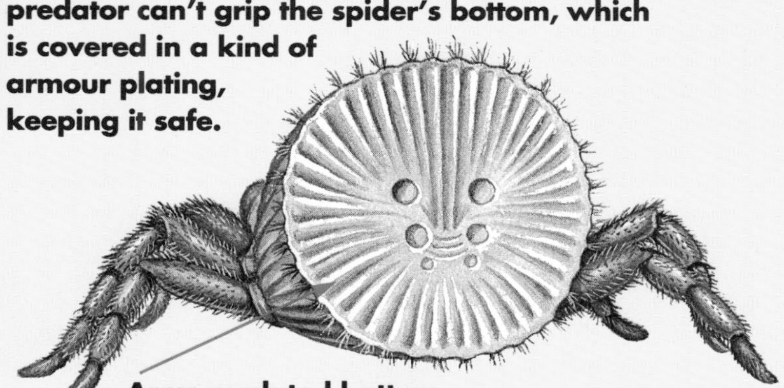

FRONT DOOR, BACK DOOR

Some spiders build burrows with side chambers and more than one entrance. These act as escape routes. When a predator appears at one opening, the spider darts up the other and escapes (below).

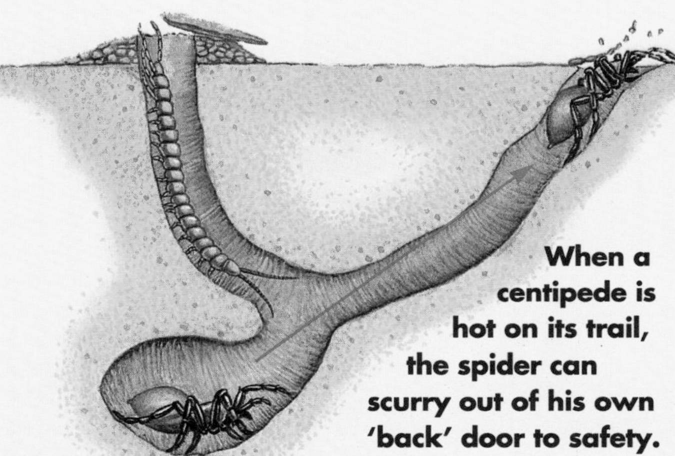

When a centipede is hot on its trail, the spider can scurry out of his own 'back' door to safety.

IN HIDING

Other trapdoor spiders line the lower part of their burrows with silk. They leave an open collar half way up, like the top of a bag. The spider makes a pear-shaped pellet from silk, saliva and mud. This sits in a hollowed-out chamber at the side of the collar (right). If a hungry centipede, or other predator, peers down the burrow, the spider tugs at the collar. The pellet topples over, making a barrier to hide behind, and the spider has vanished!

FLOOD WARNING

It's not just hungry predators that trapdoor spiders have to cope with. Sometimes water floods their burrows. To avoid drowning, some spiders build a side chamber half way up the burrow. They can sit here safe and dry as the water at the bottom rises (right).

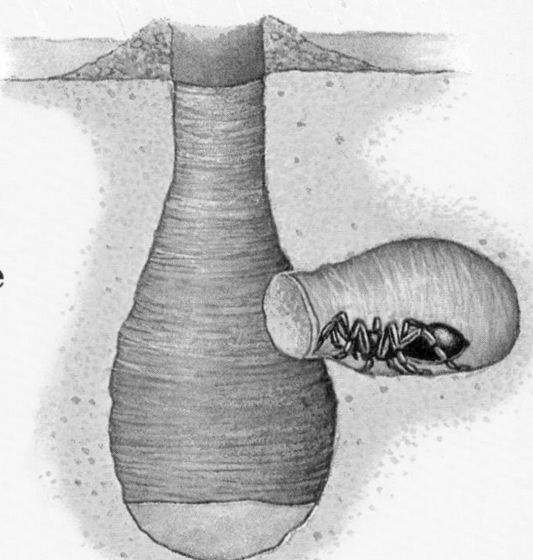

The spider hides in its own little Noah's Ark, safe from flooding in the burrow.

Small Talk

- Trapdoor spiders will pounce on anything that moves near their burrows. Sometimes they accidentally catch something that doesn't taste good. If this happens, the spider flings the offending animal out from its burrow.
- A female trapdoor spider may spend her whole life inside her burrow. As she gets bigger, she makes her burrow bigger too.

Chased by a bull ant, the spider climbs into its home and hides behind its pellet of silk and mud.

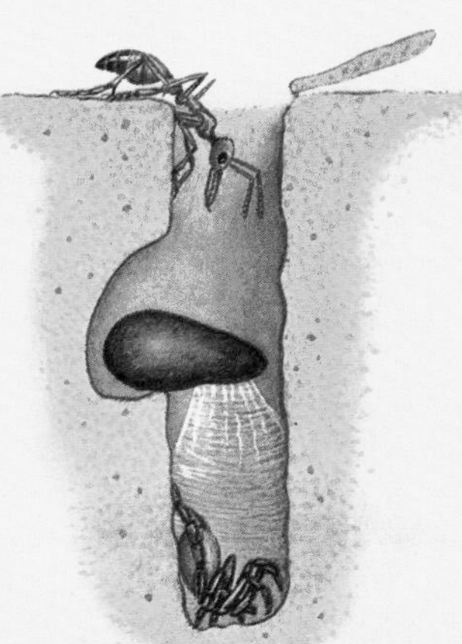

Keeping

WHAT TO DO

Stick insects are easy and fun to keep indoors. They cost nothing to feed, and live quite happily at room temperature.

The best stick insects to keep – and the ones you're most likely to find – are the privet or Indian stick insects. These are easily available from pet shops. As their name suggests, they feed on privet though they will also eat ivy or bramble.

Several stick insects can live together in a tank at the same time. You can also set up a special nursery in which to breed them.

You will need:

- small fish tank
- narrow-necked jam jar
- privet
- cotton wool
- net curtain fabric
- string

1 Stand the tank on one end, with the open part (where the lid would be) facing you.

2 Fill the jam jar with water and put pieces of privet about the height of the tank into it. It's important to use a narrow-necked jar, otherwise the insects might get into it and drown. Pack cotton wool into any gap left around the neck of the jar. Stand the jar inside the tank.

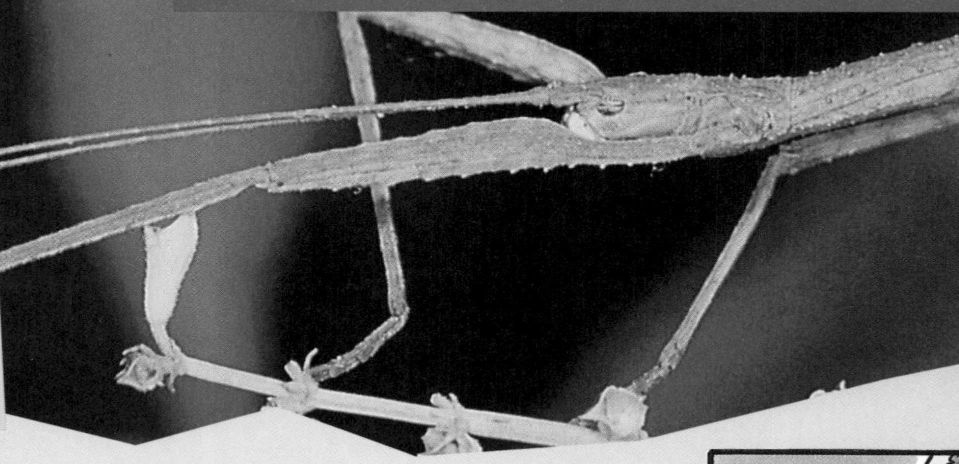

Breeding stick insects

Unlike most other animals, these stick insects do not need to mate in order to produce babies. The eggs of the stick insect are only 3mm in diameter and look like small brown seeds. They have a little hatch at one end through which the baby stick insect emerges. You will find the eggs on the bottom of the tank, among the stick insect droppings (called frass).

You will need:

- plastic container with a lid
- peat or sheets of kitchen towel
- water

WHAT TO DO

1 First put a 1cm layer of peat or half a dozen sheets of kitchen towel in a plastic container.

stick insects

4 Arrange a few privet twigs running from the base of the tank up into the foliage. This helps the stick insects if they fall off the foliage because it gives them something they can crawl back up on.

5 Cover the open part of the tank (where the lid would be) with curtain netting. Fix it in place by tying string all round the tank. The holes in the netting allow the stick insects to breathe.

3 Put the stick insects inside the tank. Handle them carefully because they are fragile and lose their legs easily.

Small Talk

Virtually all privet stick insects are female. Males are almost unheard of – perhaps as few as one in 400,000 insects.

3 Sprinkle the eggs on the surface.

2 Damp this down slightly.

5 The babies hatch into miniature replicas of the adult. You can transfer them straight to the adults' tank. Alternatively, you can rear them in another tank, reserved specially for babies. They should reach the adult stage in three to six months.

4 Replace the lid and make a few air holes in it. This is not for the eggs to 'breathe' but to prevent the tub going mouldy. If the eggs are kept at a temperature of between 19° and 23°C, they should hatch in three or four months. Check once a week that the eggs are not getting too dry. At the same time, make sure that they are not becoming mouldy. If they are, replace the peat or the paper towels.

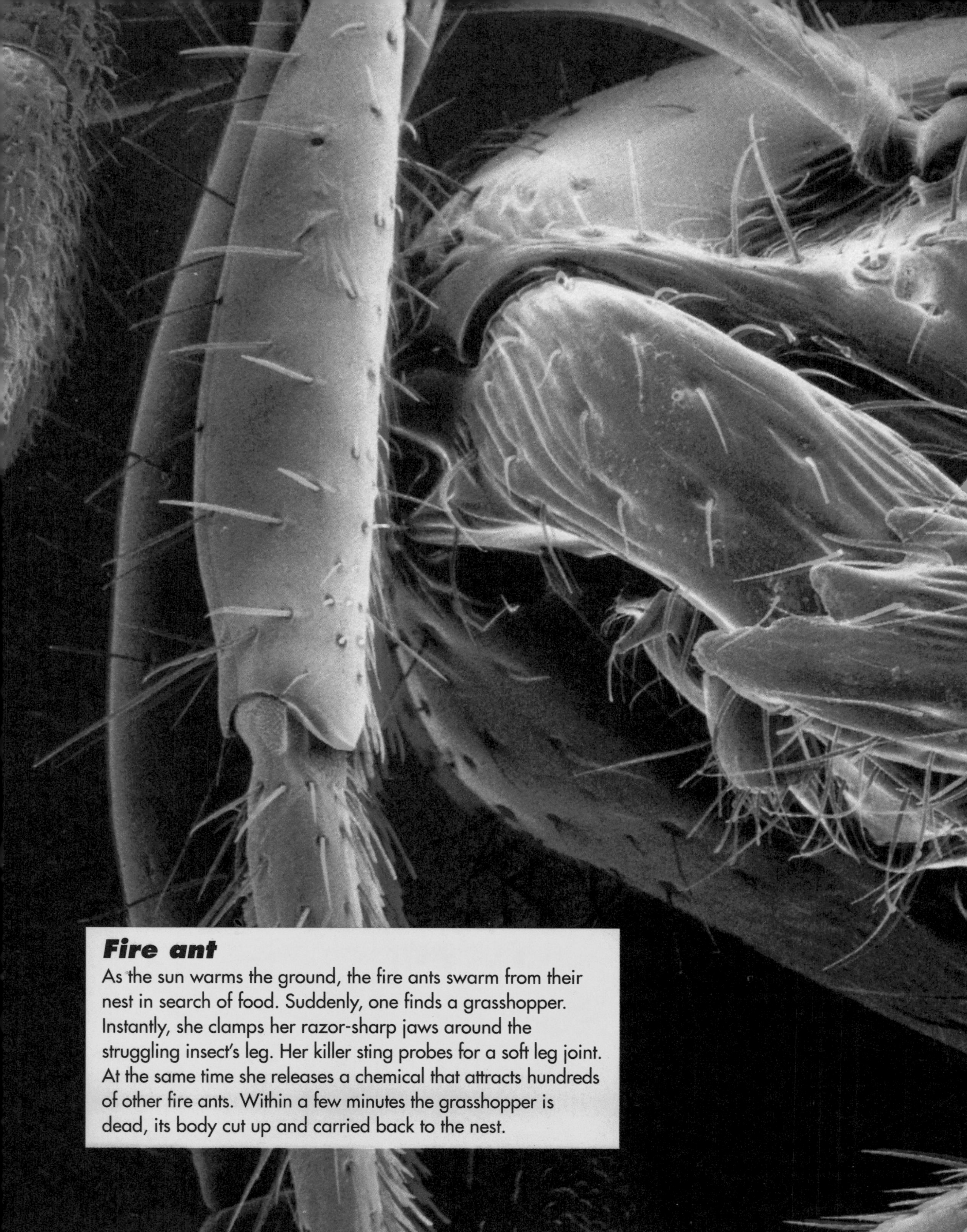

Fire ant

As the sun warms the ground, the fire ants swarm from their nest in search of food. Suddenly, one finds a grasshopper. Instantly, she clamps her razor-sharp jaws around the struggling insect's leg. Her killer sting probes for a soft leg joint. At the same time she releases a chemical that attracts hundreds of other fire ants. Within a few minutes the grasshopper is dead, its body cut up and carried back to the nest.

3-D
MINIBEASTS

How bugs see

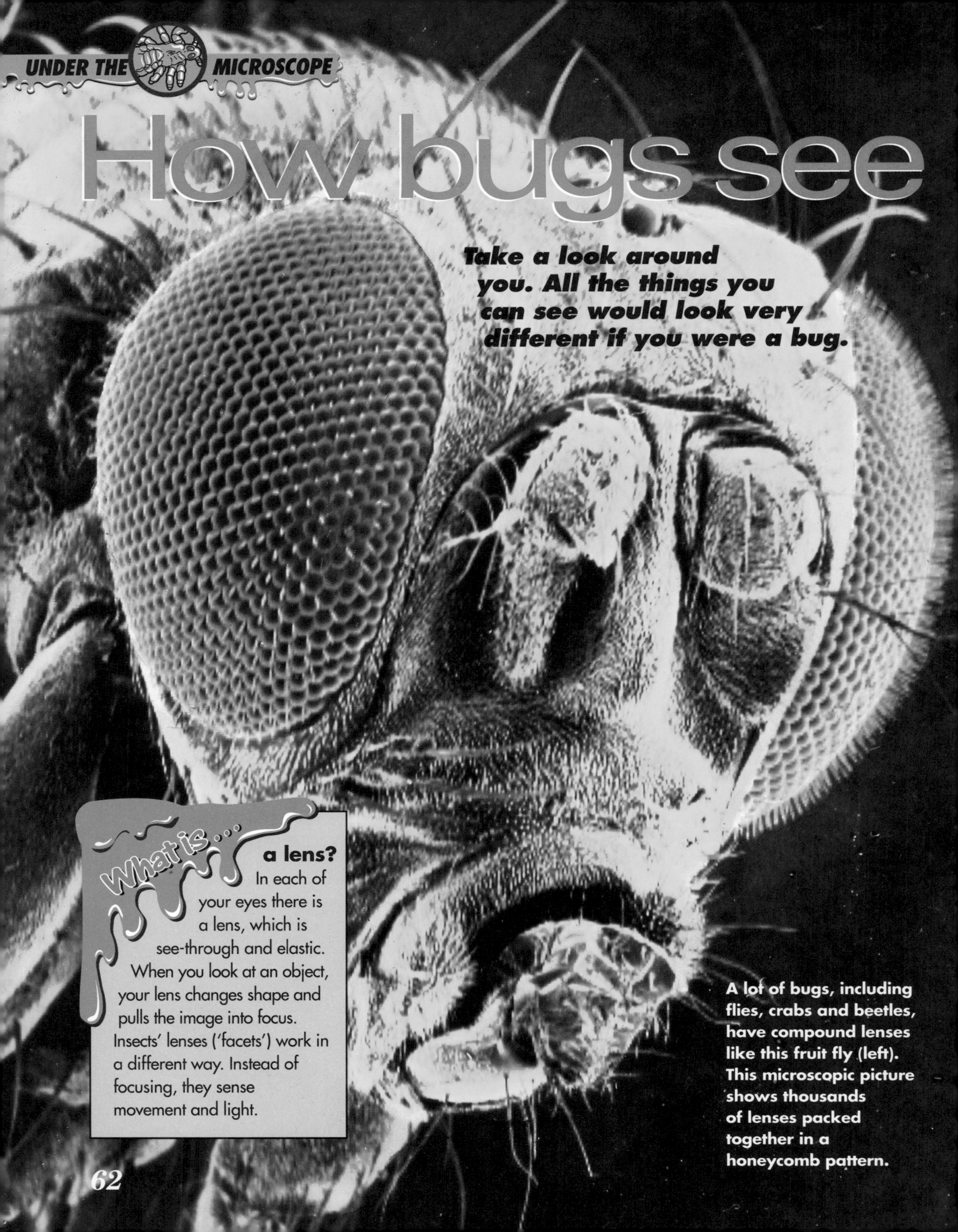

Take a look around you. All the things you can see would look very different if you were a bug.

What is... a lens?

In each of your eyes there is a lens, which is see-through and elastic. When you look at an object, your lens changes shape and pulls the image into focus. Insects' lenses ('facets') work in a different way. Instead of focusing, they sense movement and light.

A lot of bugs, including flies, crabs and beetles, have compound lenses like this fruit fly (left). This microscopic picture shows thousands of lenses packed together in a honeycomb pattern.

Bugs see things differently from humans. Their eyes don't look like ours and they work differently too. A lot of bugs have very sharp eyesight, while others can barely see the light of day.

ON THE LOOK OUT

There is a huge variety of bug eye. Each one is designed to help the animal spot food, avoid danger and find a mate. Each of our eyes has one lens, which puts everything into focus. Bugs that dart about hunting for their next meal have large eyes and lots of lenses. Bugs that are slow-moving or spend a lot of time underground usually have only a few lenses.

EYE PATCH

Our bodies are made up of millions of tiny cells, which are invisible unless you look at them under a microscope. A simple bug, like *Euglena*, is made up of just one cell. Because its body is so small, it only needs one eye. This is inside its body and is made up of a patch of light-sensitive chemicals. This means that though *Euglena* can't see the world around it, it can tell the difference between light and dark.

***Euglena* – the one-eyed bug**

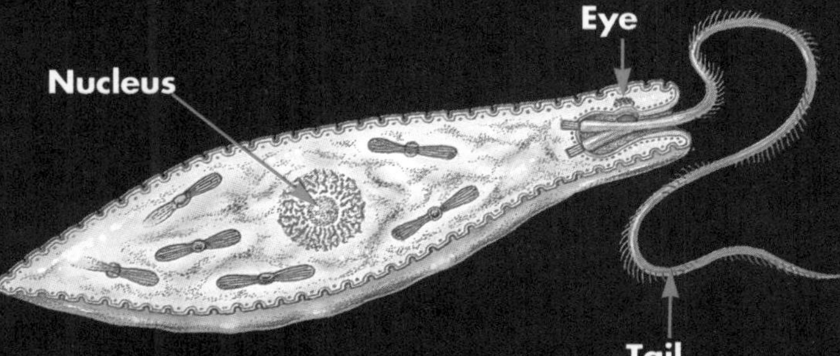

BUG-EYED

If you've ever tried to catch a fly, you'll know that it is almost impossible. Many bugs are hard to creep up on because their special compound eyes can detect the tiniest movement. Beetles, flies, crabs and many other bugs have big, compound eyes.

BLEARY EYED

They are called 'compound' because they are made up of lots of separate lenses – less than 12 or more than 56,000. You look very blurred to a bug with compound eyes, but it will certainly see your movements. Compound eyes are also excellent for seeing in the dark.

COLOUR VISION

Bugs see colours differently from us. They can pick out blue easily, but they can't see red very well. They can also see a kind of light called ultraviolet – which the human eye can't detect. Experts have invented machines that allow them to see ultraviolet light. Using this equipment, scientists can see patterns on flower petals that are usually invisible to humans. These 'secret' patterns guide insects to the nectar and pollen (their food).

Honey guides

Above: This is how the flower on the left would look through a compound eye. The dark lines act as 'honey guides', leading the insect to the nectar.

BEHIND YOU!

Flies, like many other bugs with compound eyes, can see in all directions at once. Without moving your head, see how far you can see behind you. Now imagine being a fly on a wall. Using your compound eyes, you would be able to see the ceiling, the floor, the other walls and the other side of the room without even moving your head – which is handy if you're being chased by someone waving a fly-swatter!

Each of the bug eyes on this page is designed to help the animal survive. Take a close look and try to work out how.

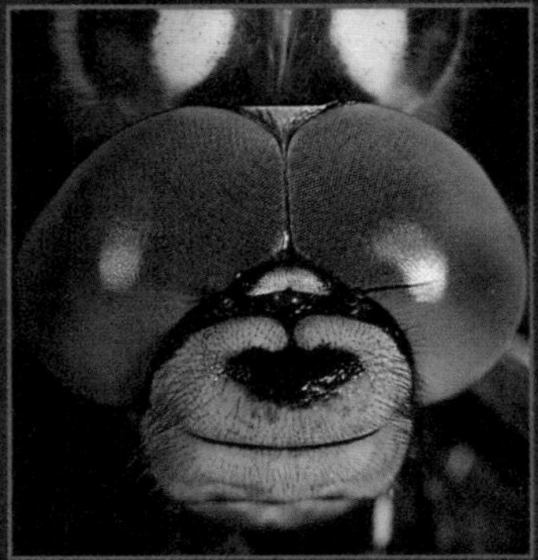

SNAIL
This snail's eyes are on stalks. If it retreats quickly into its protective shell, it can pull its eyes in towards its head.

FIDDLER CRAB
Up periscope! If this fiddler crab needs to hide in the sand, it won't miss out on the action. Its eyes are on stalks and, if it needs to look about, it sticks them up through the ground.

DRAGONFLY
Dragonflies hunt while they are flying. They have good timing and excellent eyesight. Their large compound eyes can see tiny insects coming from any angle – even in poor light.

SCALLOP

Imagine having a security camera outside your front door – a scallop does. A circle of tiny eyes around the edge of the shell allows this mollusc to see all around without opening its protective shell too far.

JUMPING SPIDER

Looking before it leaps is vital to this jumping spider if it is to catch its supper. Its huge front eyes are excellent for spotting passing insects. The jumping spider can focus on objects up to 36cm away.

OCTOPUS

Octopuses 'talk' to each other by changing the colour of their bodies. So they need eyes that can see these colours. When an octopus is angry, its whole body turns red, warning others to keep their distance.

SPOT THE KITCHEN

Five bugs have wandered into this kitchen – they're easy to spot. But there are tell-tale clues to six more uninvited visitors. Can you spot them?

Bugs find the kitchen irresistible. More than any other room, it is likely to have food in it. This is an open invitation to any hungry creature.

KITCHEN FEAST

Peckish bugs are on the look out for food that is about to be prepared. However, they don't just visit the kitchen for a fresh snack. Leftover food on dirty plates waiting to be washed up or bits of food in the rubbish bin are just as tempting. The thought of stale or second-hand food may not be very tempting to you, but it's enough to make a bug's mouth water!

THIRSTY BUGS

Some bugs, such as slugs and scorpions, are also attracted by the humid (warm and damp) air in most kitchens. Thirsty bugs head for the kitchen so they can drink.

SAFE AS HOUSES

Bugs also like to come indoors so that they can hide from birds and other enemies that eat them. But they're not necessarily safe. Some cunning hunters, such as blackwidow spiders and house centipedes, actually go into kitchens because they know there are other bugs living there which they can eat.

SPICK AND SPAN

It's not a good idea to encourage bugs to live in your kitchen. They're unlikely to do you any direct harm, but they can infest food and spread germs. The best way of limiting the bug population is to keep your kitchen as clean as possible and to throw away rubbish regularly.

TELL-TALE SIGNS

This picture contains clues to eleven bugs you might find in kitchens around the world. See if you can spot them and guess which creatures might have been visiting. Turn the page to find the answers.

Small Talk

OTHER CLUES

Some of the signs that show a bug is about are not things you can see but rather sounds or smells. A chirping noise from behind your fridge, for instance, means you have house crickets. Even an army of tiny termites can make a noise as they eat through the woodwork. A strange plastic-like smell means you have cockroaches. This smell is difficult to describe, but once smelled, never forgotten!

BUGS...

A deserted kitchen – or is it?
Take a closer look.

...they're everywhere!

CLUE: trail of tiny black ants
GUEST: pharaoh's ant *(Monomorium)*
FOUND: worldwide

The pharaoh's ant is tiny, about 2mm long. Unlike most ants, it is a keen meat-eater. It comes into the kitchen in search of food – cat and dog bowls being a favourite haunt. Pharoah's ants build their nest in any quiet, sheltered place, such as in a food cupboard.

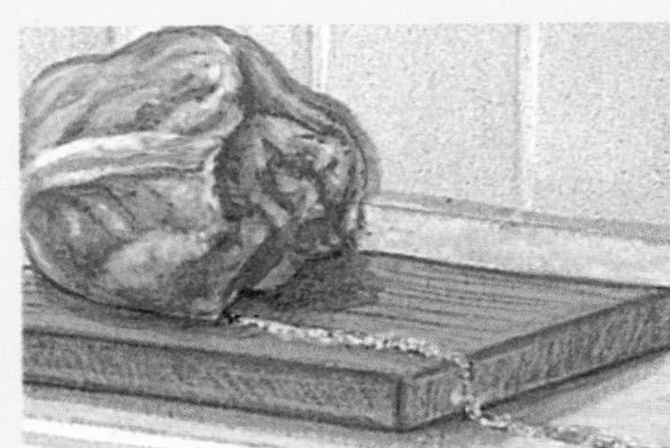

CLUE: a trail of slime
GUEST: giant slug *(Ariolimax)*
FOUND: worldwide

The giant slug can grow as long as 20cm. It likes humid air and the smell of food in a kitchen. It produces a slime trail, which helps to make movement easier.

CLUE: a tail sticking out of a glove
GUEST: scorpion *(Centruroides)*
FOUND: worldwide

Scorpions are easy to recognise because of their large pincers and the stinger at the tip of their tail. They are about 7-8cm long. They come into the kitchen in search of water. A kitchen glove left on a window or an equally dark and cosy place, such as a wellington boot, is an ideal home for a scorpion. Dangerous scorpions are only found in hot countries, like Africa, Central America and the Middle East.

CLUE: a web inside a cupboard
GUEST: Blackwidow spider *(Latrodectus)*
FOUND: throughout most of the world

The blackwidow spider comes into the kitchen in search of shelter and food, in the form of other small bugs. It is about 1cm long, with a leg span of about 3cm. Its bite is extremely painful and causes stiffness.

CLUE: a greasy brownish-yellow stain and a centipede hunting cockroaches
GUESTS: house centipede *(Scutigera)* and oriental cockroach *(Blatta)*
FOUND: centipede: worldwide, especially in warm countries; cockroach: worldwide

The house centipede likes humid places, such as kitchens. It eats silverfishes, cockroaches, flies and other small bugs, and is therefore a welcome visitor. It leaves no clues to show where it's been.

The oriental cockroach hides in cracks by day and feeds on any food it can find by night. It contaminates food and may carry germs. It leaves an easily recognisable musty smell, as well as a greasy brownish yellow stain on the wall around the crack. There may also be a little pile of droppings underneath it.

CLUE: black specks in flour
GUEST: confused flour beetle *(Tribolium)*
FOUND: worldwide

This is a tiny beetle which lives on stored granary products such as flour. It leaves small black specks behind it – these are beetles, larvae, eggs and droppings. Wherever you find stored grain or flour you will find these beetles, but eating them won't harm you.

CLUE: a black line
GUEST: termite *(Reticulitermes)*
FOUND: warm countries

Termites live in colonies, feeding on wood. They build a covered walkway, made out of droppings and small bits of rubbish, running, perhaps, from a cupboard to behind a shelf. A pile of sawdust under a shelf is also a clue.

CLUE: eggs on a piece of meat
GUEST: flesh fly *(Sarcophaga)*
FOUND: North America and cooler countries in Europe

About 13-15mm long, the speckled flesh fly is often found near humans. The females search for meat in which they lay their eggs. The eggs are visible as small white specks. In this way, they are often responsible for the spread of disease.

CLUE: a web near a window with a flesh fly caught in it
GUEST: garden spider *(Araneus)*
FOUND: worldwide

Garden spiders often come indoors in search of food and warmth. They build their webs near windows. This is because flies inside the house try to get out through the window. All the spider has to do to find its next meal is sit and wait!

Improve and test your knowledge with...

CREEPY~CRAWLY FACTS

Dive down to the murky depths of the sea and test yourself with our BUGS! quiz.

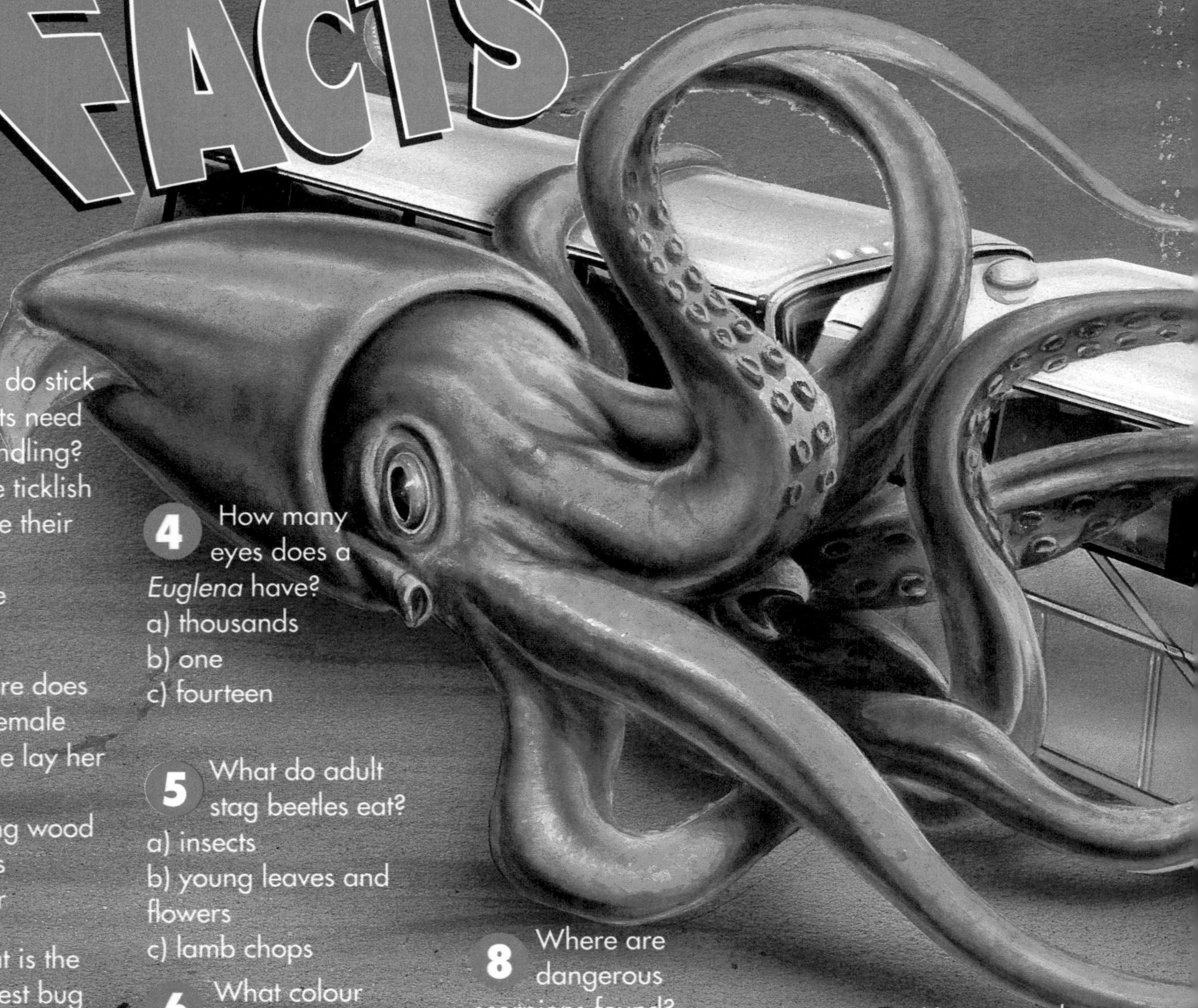

1 Why do stick insects need careful handling?
a) they are ticklish
b) they lose their legs easily
c) they bite

2 Where does the female atlas beetle lay her eggs?
a) in rotting wood
b) in grass
c) in water

3 What is the biggest bug in the world?
a) blue whale
b) giant cockroach
c) giant squid

4 How many eyes does a *Euglena* have?
a) thousands
b) one
c) fourteen

5 What do adult stag beetles eat?
a) insects
b) young leaves and flowers
c) lamb chops

6 What colour does an octopus turn when it's angry?
a) blue
b) green
c) red

7 Which bug makes the loudest noise?
a) cicada
b) grasshopper
c) cricket

8 Where are dangerous scorpions found?
a) in hot countries
b) in cold countries
c) at the North Pole

9 Why do blister beetles bleed?
a) to lose weight
b) to get rid of poisons
c) to stop predators eating them

10 How many legs does a giant centipede have?
a) 100
b) 40-44
c) 60-64

Super squid!

The biggest bug of all lives in the dark depths of the Atlantic ocean. Longer than two coaches, heavier than a hippo and with eyes the size of footballs, the giant squid is an awesome beast. Only the huge sperm whale can defend itself against it.

The blob

The South American bolas spider uses a blob of sticky liquid to catch its prey. The blob has a smell that attracts male moths. The spider attaches the smelly blob to the end of a piece of silk, which it twirls around. Eventually a male moth will fly into the blob and become stuck. All the spider has to do now is haul in its lunch.

It's a girl, girl, girl...

Humans usually produce one baby at a time after nine months. The next 16 or so years are spent taking care of it. The pork, or human, tapeworm can produce up to 105 million babies at once and they are always female. It does not look after its young at all.

Beetle juice

The large African blister beetle spends its day wandering around untroubled by predators. Most animals have learned not to try to swallow these beetles as they can force acidic blood out of the tops of their legs. Not only does this blood burn, but it also contains a powerful chemical that can kill.

Fingerprint food

Some bugs will eat almost anything, but experts were baffled when they found pharaoh's ants in Trinidad, the West Indies, munching their way through the plastic coating of electrical cables in a radio factory. The cable had no goodness in it, so why were they eating it? Eventually, the experts realised the ants were feeding on the sections that had been touched by the 'greasy' fingers of people working in the factory.

Answers to the questions on the inside back cover

Q and A?

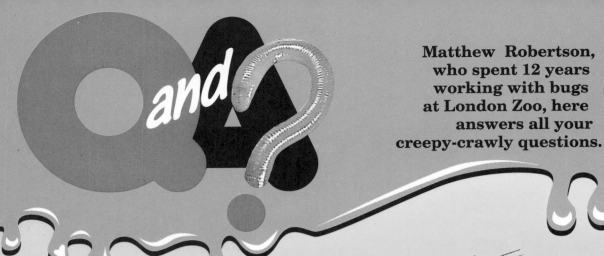

Matthew Robertson, who spent 12 years working with bugs at London Zoo, here answers all your creepy-crawly questions.

Which bug makes the loudest noise?

Although grasshoppers and crickets can both make loud calls, they are no match for the cicada. There are over 3,000 different species (kinds) of cicada, and each one makes a different call. Some of the large cicadas can be heard half a kilometre away.

Why do bugs hate the cold?

Small animals, like bugs, lose heat quicker than large ones so they are affected by cold temperatures sooner. Many bugs try to avoid cold weather by hiding in sheltered places. Some flies and jellyfish, however, have special chemicals in their blood that stop them freezing. This means that they can carry on as normal even in very low temperatures.

What is the rarest bug in the world?

There are many species of bug which we know about because individuals have been spotted once or twice, but then never seen again. Every time a patch of rainforest is pulled down, many types of bugs that scientists have never seen or studied become extinct (die out). However, the rarest known bug would have to be a small snail from an island in the Pacific ocean. This snail is extinct in the wild and now only one lone snail remains in captivity.

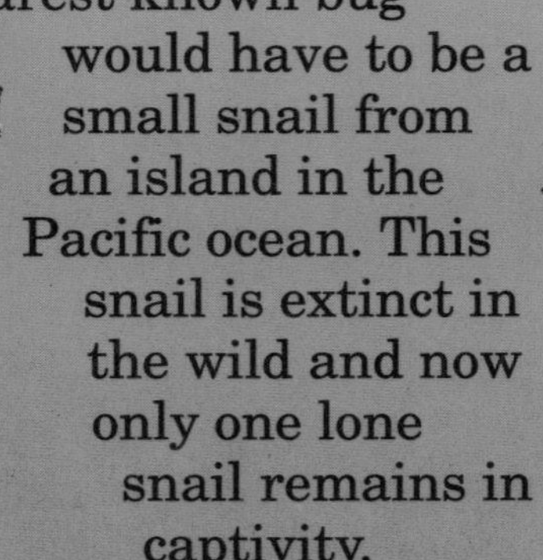

Praying Mantis

The praying mantis disguises itself so it can launch a vicious surprise attack on its victims.

There are about 1,800 species of praying mantis. They live in trees and grassland in warm places, where there is a regular supply of food.

DELICATE WINGS

The praying mantis has a long, slender body and three pairs of legs. It also has two pairs of very fine wings, but in general only the smaller male uses these for flying.

PERFECT DISGUISE

With its green or brown colouring and its stick-like body, the praying mantis looks like a leaf or twig. Some of the more unusual species of praying mantis are more colourful, and look like flowers. These clever disguises help the insect blend into its background so that predators – and prey – cannot easily spot it.

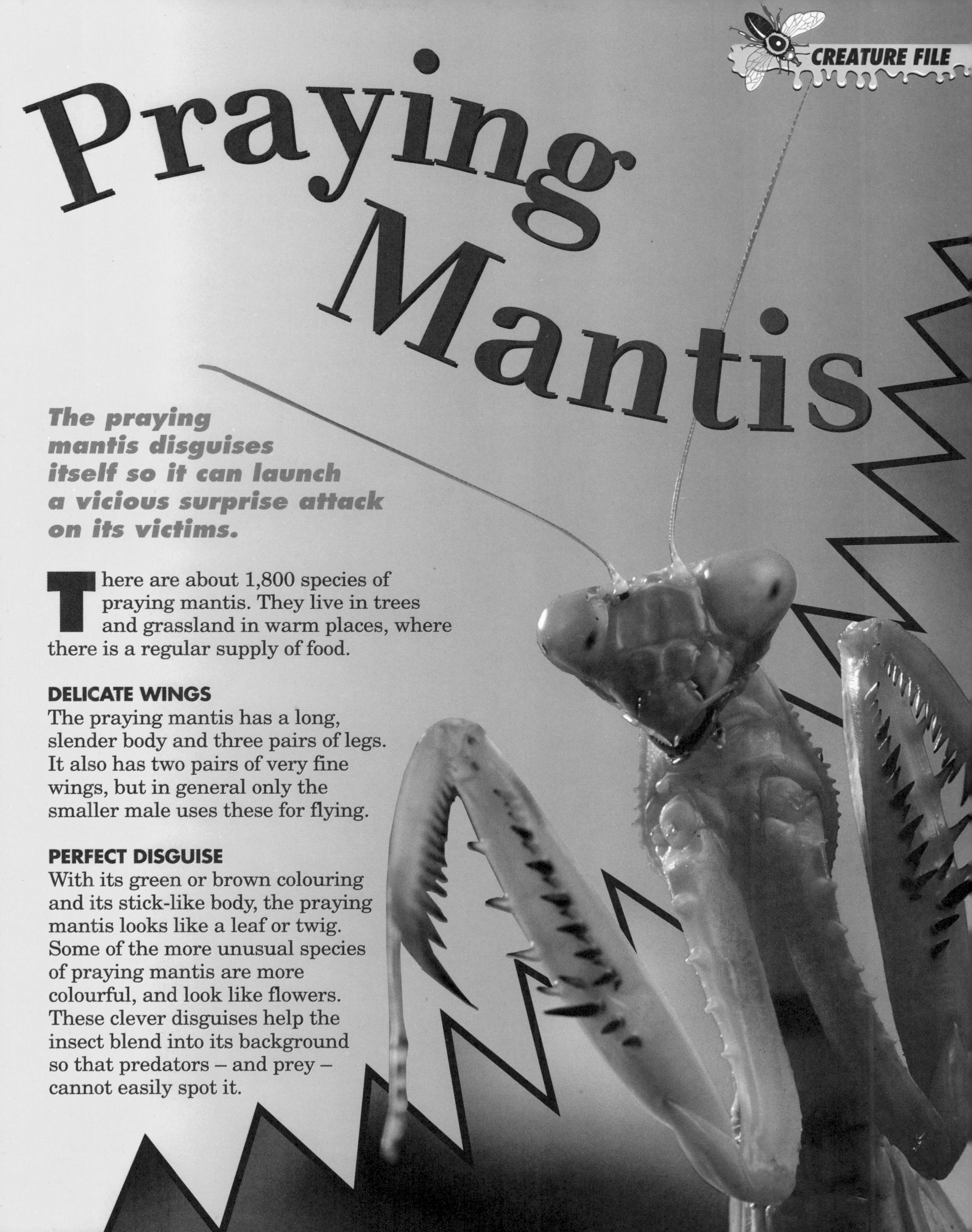

Small Talk

FRIEND OR FOOD?

For the male praying mantis, mating is a dangerous time. The male is slightly smaller and more delicate than the female and, when they are mating, she might mistake him for food and try to eat him! Even if the female praying mantis bites off his head though, he can still go on mating because his body takes a while to die.

PRAYING FOR FOOD

The praying mantis has another trick that makes it even harder to see. It can stay very still, without moving at all, for hours on end. Sitting up on its hind legs with its forelegs folded neatly together in front, it looks like a person praying – which is how it got its name. Perched in this position, it waits to pounce on any unsuspecting insect that comes along.

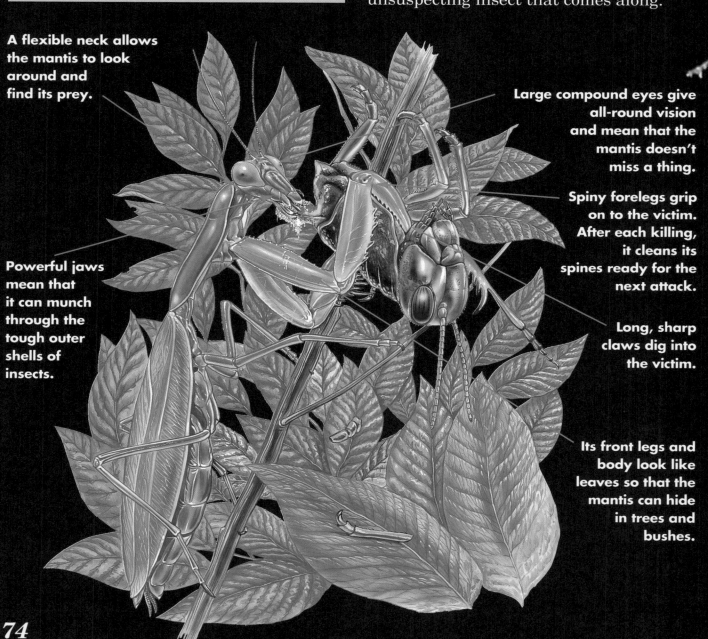

A flexible neck allows the mantis to look around and find its prey.

Powerful jaws mean that it can munch through the tough outer shells of insects.

Large compound eyes give all-round vision and mean that the mantis doesn't miss a thing.

Spiny forelegs grip on to the victim. After each killing, it cleans its spines ready for the next attack.

Long, sharp claws dig into the victim.

Its front legs and body look like leaves so that the mantis can hide in trees and bushes.

This male praying mantis is in mid-flight. The fore legs, usually folded in front of its body, are stretched out in front to balance itself.

WATCHING

The huge, saucer-shaped eyes on the sides of its head give the praying mantis all-round vision – it can even see behind itself. It can watch its prey approaching from any direction, without turning its head. When its victim is close enough, the mantis leaps on it, gripping it firmly with its strong, spiny forelegs so that it cannot escape. Its jaws are strong enough to chew through even the toughest insect. The praying mantis is a fussy eater, though, so it may not finish its meal.

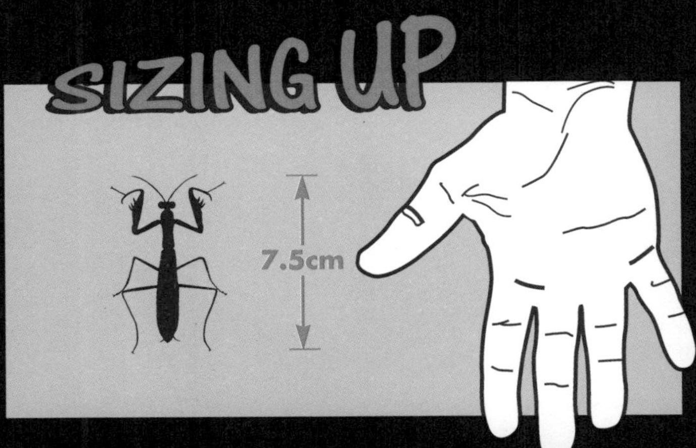

HUNGRY BABIES

Even the tiny praying mantis babies are hungry hunters. They hatch from eggs that the female lays inside a large cocoon, or hard shell. She lays about 200 – 400 eggs at a time. The tiny insects that come out of the eggs are pale green and only 6mm long, but they begin hunting almost at once – and may even eat each other!

- **SCIENTIFIC NAME:** *Mantis religiosa*
- **SIZE:** 4–7.5cm long
- **LIVES:** trees and grassland in tropical and warm countries
- **EATS:** insects and spiders

NO DEFENCE

Although the praying mantis is a fierce hunter, it is not very good at defending itself. Its main hope is that predators – such as certain kinds of bird – won't notice that it is there. If an enemy does threaten it, it rises up to its full height, spreads out its wings, and tries to look big and scary. This doesn't always work, though, and the praying mantis just gets eaten.

Tsetse Fly

Although it belongs to the same family as the housefly, a bite from the tsetse fly could kill you!

The tsetse (say 'tet-sea') fly lives in tropical parts of Africa, where it feeds on the blood of cattle and people.

DEADLY DISEASE
When a tsetse fly bites, it injects some of its saliva into its victim's skin. This saliva may contain the germs of diseases that can kill cattle and horses, and sleeping sickness that can kill people. A person with sleeping sickness feels exhausted and extremely sleepy, and may eventually die.

A GOOD MEAL
The tsetse fly likes to have a good, long meal, and may take up to 10 minutes to suck up all the blood it wants. When it is full, its abdomen swells and turns red (below). It won't need to feed again for about another three days.

SMALL FAMILIES
Unlike other insects that lay eggs, the female tsetse fly gives birth to live young. In her short lifetime of about six months, she may produce only two offspring a month.

SIZING UP

2cm

- **SCIENTIFIC NAME:** *Glossina palpalis*
- **SIZE:** 2cm long
- **LIVES:** tropical Africa
- **EATS:** animal blood, including humans'

Beware, the Spanish dancer's bright colours are a warning that it stings!

Spanish Dancer

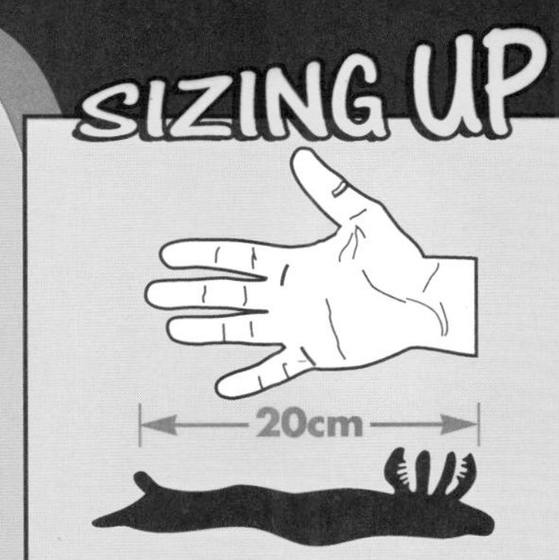

Spanish dancers are a type of sea slug. They have bright red bodies with pink tuft-like gills on their backs, through which they breath. Bold colours are often a warning that an animal is dangerous. Spanish dancers use their colour to warn predators to keep away.

SNAKY MOVEMENT

Most sea slugs stay on the bottom of the ocean, but some can swim by wriggling their bodies up and down, or by moving them sideways, like a snake. The Spanish dancer gets its name because of the way it moves through the water.

BEASTLY FACTS

- **SCIENTIFIC NAME:** *Hexabranchus sanguineus*
- **SIZE:** up to 20cm long
- **LIVES:** warm waters such as the Mediterranean Sea and Red Sea
- **EATS:** sponges and sea anemones

STINGING SLUGS

Some sea slugs feed on algae (say 'al-gee'), plants that grow in the sea, while others eat sea creatures such as sponges or barnacles. The clever Spanish dancer is able to eat whole stinging sea anemones without getting stung. It just swallows the stings, stores them in the waxy tips of its bright pink gills and uses them as weapons against any fierce predators that try to eat it!

Armed and dangerous

Collected in this glass case are four of the world's most dangerous land bugs. All of them could kill you or cause great pain. Take a step closer and find out what would happen to you if you were bitten or stung. Also, discover your chances of survival!

Fat-tailed scorpion

RECLUSE SPIDER
Loxosceles
From United States, South America, Europe, Asia

Sometimes causes death in humans.

Bite causes burning pain, blisters on the skin, bleeding inside the body, vomiting, fits and fever. The blisters are difficult to heal.

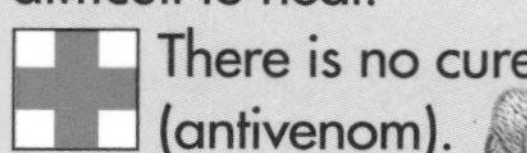

There is no cure (antivenom).

FAT-TAILED SCORPION
Androctonus
From north Africa, Middle East

Humans can die in 6 –7 hours. (Most venomous scorpion.)

Very painful sting. The muscles that help us to breathe may stop working, so may the heart.

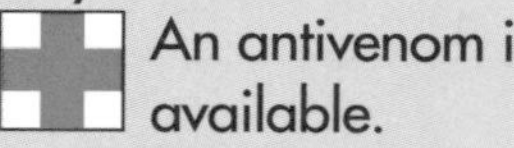

An antivenom is available.

Recluse spider

Giant centipede

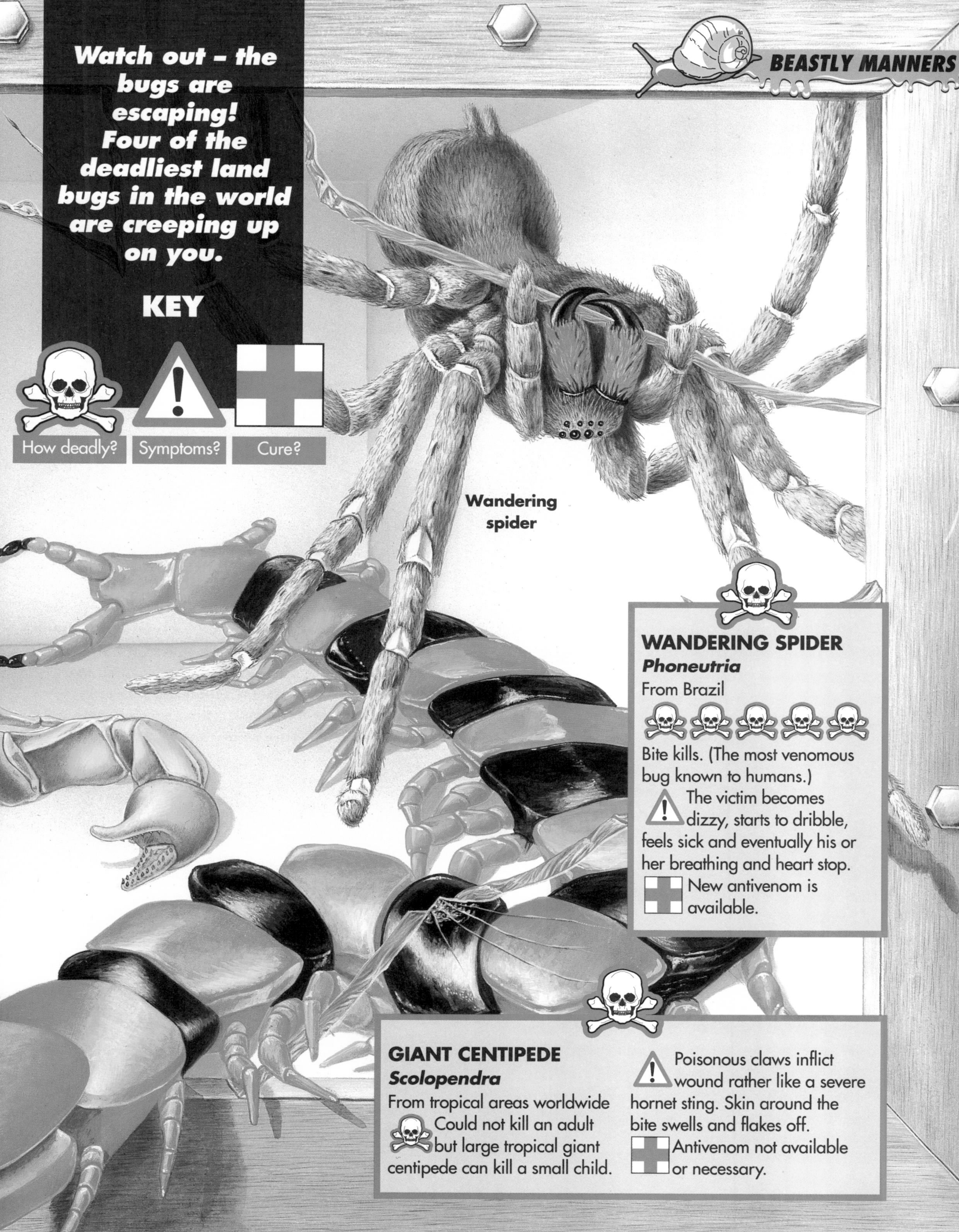

Watch out – the bugs are escaping! Four of the deadliest land bugs in the world are creeping up on you.

KEY

How deadly? | Symptoms? | Cure?

WANDERING SPIDER

Phoneutria

From Brazil

Bite kills. (The most venomous bug known to humans.)

The victim becomes dizzy, starts to dribble, feels sick and eventually his or her breathing and heart stop.

New antivenom is available.

GIANT CENTIPEDE

Scolopendra

From tropical areas worldwide

Could not kill an adult but large tropical giant centipede can kill a small child.

Poisonous claws inflict wound rather like a severe hornet sting. Skin around the bite swells and flakes off.

Antivenom not available or necessary.

Why do bugs inject venom? Are they hungry, nervous or just very vicious?

Venomous bugs inject humans and other animals for two reasons. They either want to cripple and kill their victims or they want to defend themselves against attack.

A PAINFUL DEATH

The most vicious land bugs known to humans are certain scorpions, bees, spiders and centipedes. All these creatures use sharp parts of their bodies to puncture their victim's outer shell or skin and inject their prey with powerful chemicals. This weakens or kills the victim and makes it much easier to catch and eat.

CONFUSING THE ENEMY

As soon as the bug's venom enters the victim's bloodstream, it begins to suffer. If its victim is in intense pain it cannot concentrate on defending itself and the venomous bug moves in for the kill.

What is... the difference between venom and poison?

A poison is something that is harmful to eat. If an animal eats a poisonous bug, it will get sick and may even die. All the creatures on this page have a special type of chemical in their bodies called venom. Animals are said to be venomous if they inject their enemies with venom.

Venomous bugs have fangs, stings or poisonous claws, which they use to pierce the flesh of their victim before they inject it with a deadly chemical. Scientists have developed cures for some venoms – these are called antivenoms.

If you were to inject someone with venom, you would need a sharp needle to puncture the skin. Bugs inject their victims in different ways. Often they have a sting (like bees) or a bite, others have venomous claws.

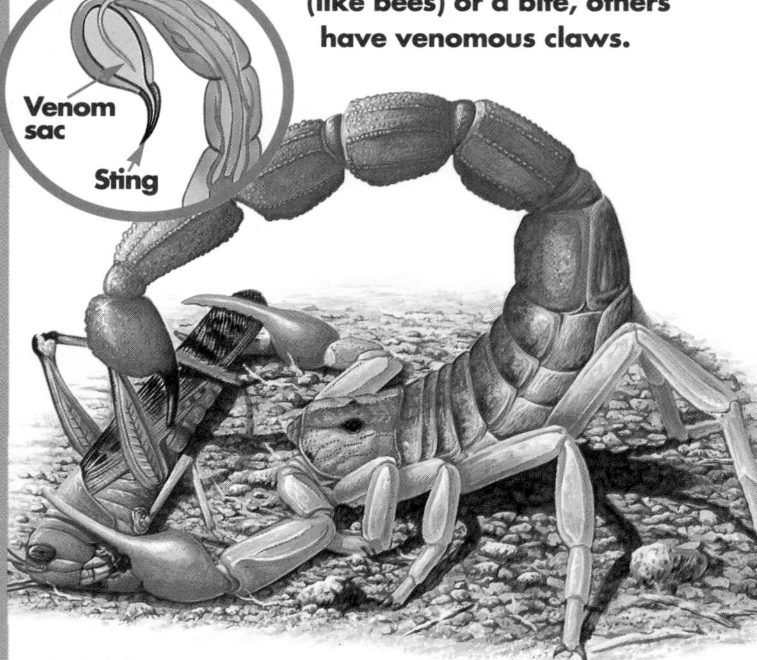

STINGS

At the end of a scorpion's tail (above) is a fat bulb-shaped segment and a sharp point that injects the venom. In the tail is a pair of sacs, which are surrounded by muscles. When the scorpion wants to inject the venom, the muscles in its tail tighten and squeeze out the venom.

BITES
The wandering spider (below) injects its venom through a pair of sharp fangs. Above each fang and just behind its eyes is a large venom gland filled with a deadly chemical.

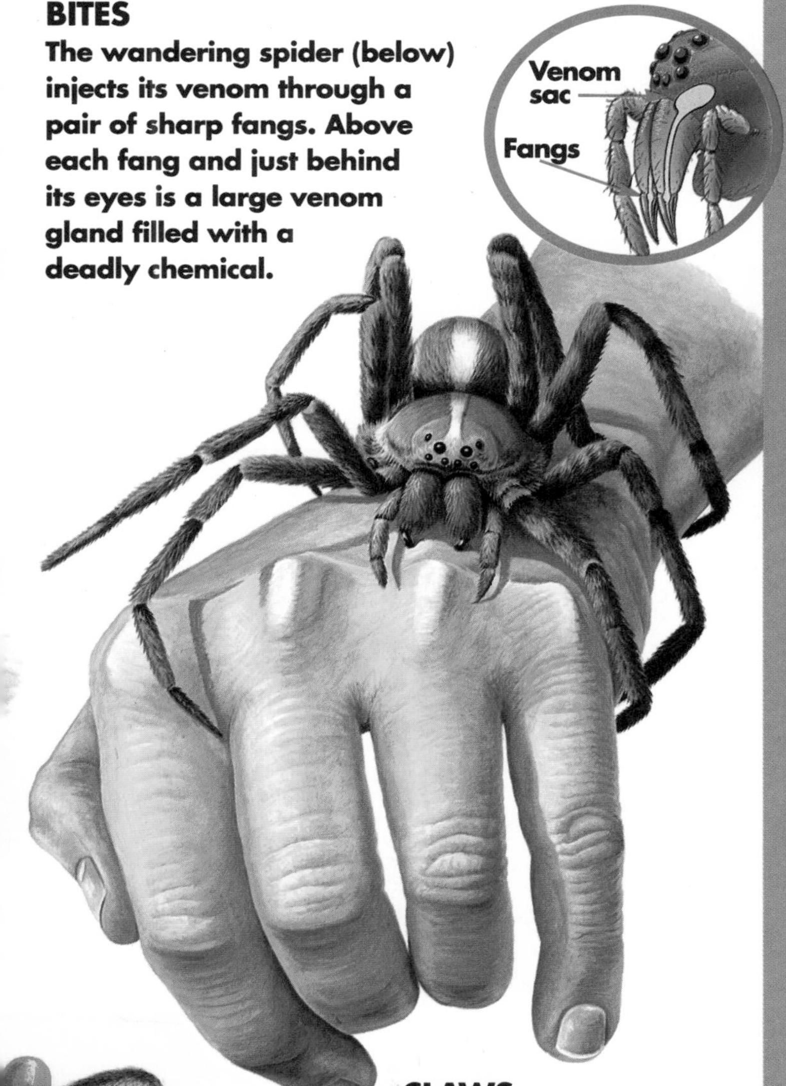

Venom sac
Fangs

CLAWS
The giant centipede (left) bites and injects venom with its two front feet! Over millions of years this creature has adapted its two front feet into biting claws, which contain a nasty venom.

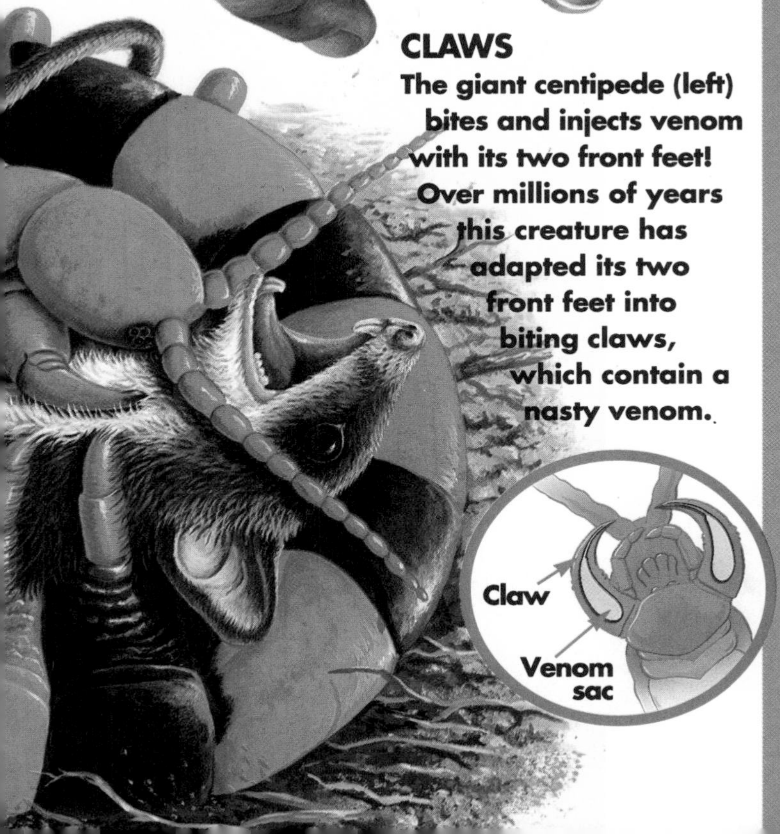

Claw
Venom sac

VENOM POUCHES

The deadly venom is stored in pouches or sacs in the bug's body. Often they are found near the animal's mouth. This is because venom also helps bugs to eat. Just like the saliva in your mouth, the venom contains chemicals that help the bugs to break down their food before it reaches their stomachs.

NO FEELINGS

Some venoms contain chemicals that numb the victim or make it less aggressive. This makes it much easier to handle and kill. For instance, some ticks feed off the blood of another animal. To make sure that the animal it is feeding on does not know that it is there, the blood-sucking tick injects its victim with a special numbing venom. The tick can then feed in peace.

VEGGIES FIGHT BACK

Not all venomous bugs are meat-eating killers. Some vegetarian (plant-eating) bugs also use a nasty dose of venom to keep their attackers at bay. Flick-knife caterpillars have spines that they shoot out to inject their attackers with venom. The venom can cause intense pain and blisters.

Small Talk

SURPRISE KILLER

The group of bugs that kills the most humans each year is not scorpions or spiders, but the common wasp and bee group – Hymenoptera. For most people a wasp sting is harmless, though painful, but for the few people who are allergic to them they can be very dangerous. These bugs probably kill more people in the USA each year than all the other venomous creatures put together.

POND DIPPING

Become an underwater explorer without getting your feet wet! Go pond dipping.

To go pond dipping, you will need a net, which you can use to trawl a pond for bugs. You can buy one or make your own using the instructions given here. Once you've got your equipment, you're ready to go.

TO MAKE YOUR NET

You will need:

- a wire coathanger
- a piece of fine netting
- a broom handle
- a clip with a key for tightening, like you find on a hosepipe. This is called a jubilee clip or plastic cable clip
- pins
- a needle and strong thread
- you may also need an adult to help you

1 Start by measuring the length of each of the sides of the triangular shape of the coathanger. Add these together. This will give you the width of netting you need. It should be approximately 90cm.

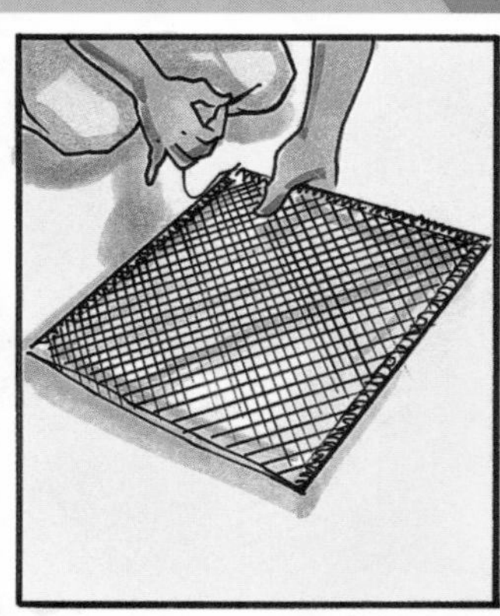

2 Cut the netting to the width you measured by about 40cm deep. Fold it in half and sew up the two short sides, to make a bag. Pull out the coathanger so it makes a circle. Straighten the hook.

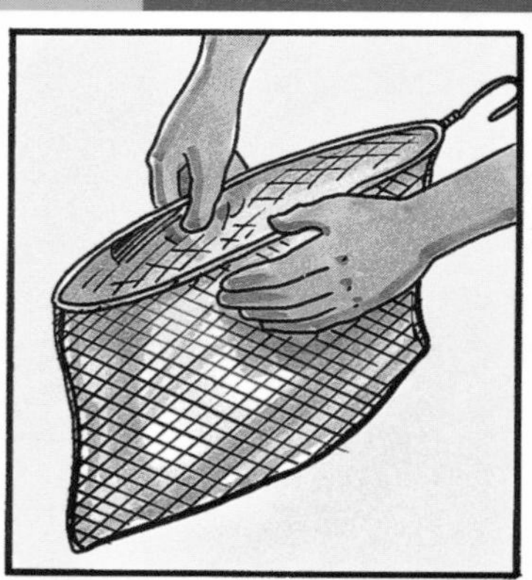

3 Fold the netting bag over once to make a small hem. Fold it over again, this time including the wire. Pin the netting in place. Sew around the top of the net, making sure it is very secure.

4 Put the end of the broom handle against the straightened-out hook of the coathanger. Secure it in place with the jubilee clip or a plastic cable clip. You have now made your net.

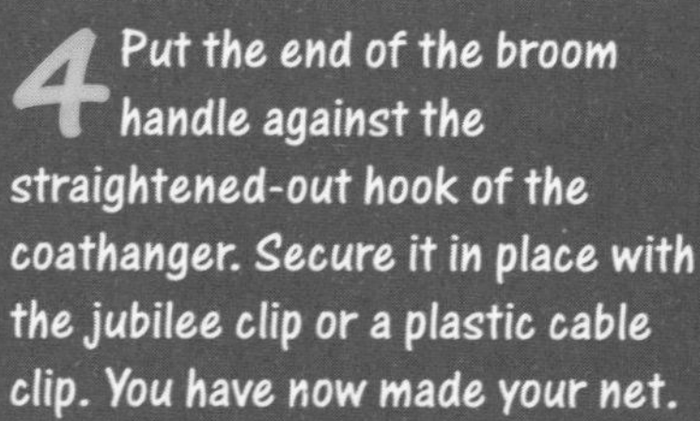

Small Talk

- Always make sure someone is with you when you go pond dipping. This makes the expedition fun and also means you have someone on hand to help you. Adults are ideal assistants.
- Wear waterproof clothing and footware.
- Spring and summer are the best times to go pond dipping, and wild ponds with lots of greenery and plant life are better than well-kept ponds.

THE EXPEDITION

You are now ready to lead your expedition to a suitable spot. This must be on firm ground, preferably close to water plants. Avoid going over boggy ground or near deep water. You must also make sure your expedition does not actually enter the water. This is for your own safety but it also stops the animals being frightened away. Walk up to your site slowly and quietly.

WHAT TO DO

You will need:
- large white or clear plastic container
- notebook
- pencil

1 When you reach your site, start by filling your tub with water. This will become the place where you put the things you catch, where they will be able to breathe.

2 Sweep the net through the water near any underwater plants. Take the net out of the water and empty it into your tub. Wait for the water to settle.

3 You can list all your finds in your notebook and put them into separate groups based on the number of legs they have. Look for things with no legs too – like fish, flatworms, leeches and water snails.

4 Make a note of the date. Some creatures, such as tadpoles, may have no legs, two legs, or four legs, depending on the stage in their development.

5 Now look at animals with six legs, such as water scorpions with their long, snorkel-like tails, pond skaters on the surface of the water, or whirligig beetles. Below the surface, look for water boatmen. You might also find hungry dragonfly larvae.

6 Look out, too, for animals with eight legs, such as spiders. If you find something you don't recognise, draw a sketch and look it up when you get home. When you have finished, carefully pour the water and the animals back into the pond.

3-D
MINIBEASTS

Dust Mite

A dust mite trundles across a vast plain of kitchen lino searching for bits of tasty dead skin. Stopping to munch on a particularly crunchy flake, it is suddenly swept into the air by a huge yellow duster. As the spring-cleaning person comes closer, the mite is sucked into a huge dark damp cavern and finds itself in a human nose! Surprised, the mite settles itself and begins to walk towards the light. With no warning it is shot from the cavern by a tremendous blast of air and a deafening noise: 'atishoo'!

What is a

There are so many of them that they have been called 'the insects of the sea'. They can be smaller than a full stop or as big as a sofa. Some live only a couple of weeks; others live as long as a human. They are part of the same group: they are all crustaceans.

THINK OF A NUMBER

When scientists divide bugs into groups in order to study them, they put more than 35,000 into a single group – the crustaceans. The best-known crustaceans are lobsters and crabs, but this group also includes water fleas and barnacles. So what makes experts group these animals together?

Two pairs of long antennae (feelers) help the lobster sense its surroundings in the dingy depths of the ocean.

The lobster's large pincers are very powerful. It uses them to crack the tough shells of its food.

crustacean?

WHAT'S IN A NAME?

The name crustacean comes from the word 'crustacea'. This term is used to describe any animal with a hard crust that is jointed like a suit of armour. These shells contain calcium, a substance that is found in your teeth. But one other thing makes crustaceans special. They have two pairs of antennae (feelers). Insects only have one pair of antennae.

OCEAN GOING

While many crustaceans are found in fresh water, and some even live on the ground, most of them inhabit the oceans. Sea-living lobsters and crabs are the giants of the crustacean world. The body of the male lobster may be 60cm long. However, most crustaceans are tiny animals, usually less than just a few centimetres long.

The shell is jointed like a suit of armour.

Gills let the lobster breathe underwater.

The swimmeret not only helps the lobster swim but also, in the female, holds the eggs.

With a flick of its tail the lobster can swim backwards very quickly.

THE LOBSTER

The lobster is a crustacean. Although not all crustaceans are the same, it has many of the features that are found in this group. The North Atlantic lobster in the picture is found along the east coast of North America. If you turn the page, you'll discover some of the other incredible creatures that make up this group.

The weird and wacky

KEEP AN EYE OUT

The one-eyed cyclops (right) is a type of crustacean known as a copepod. There are more copepods found on Earth than any other animal.

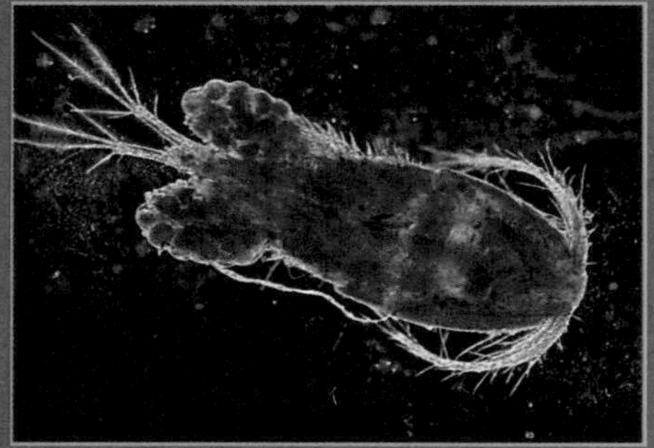

SMASH AND GRAB

If a mantis shrimp (below) hit you, it would be like being punched by a boxer. The shrimp needs this strength in order to crack open the hard shells of other crustaceans, such as crabs, upon which it feeds.

HARD AS NAILS

Crustaceans are the tough guys of the bug world and the brine shrimp (below) is no exception. It can live in water that is hotter than a bath and many times saltier than the sea.

WET, WET, WET

Tadpole shrimps (below) need to live in water. But over millions of years, they have changed to be able to survive when there is not much water about. For instance, hundreds of adults can live in a shallow puddle and, unlike most other creatures, their eggs do not hatch after a certain length of time. Instead, they only hatch after it has rained.

world of crustaceans

Small Talk

FLIGHTS OF FANCY

Years ago, experts believed that some crustaceans were baby birds! Every year, when flocks of geese flew in from the sea, people wondered where they came from. One day a scientist cut open a barnacle and thought he could see a baby goose inside. Today, we know he was wrong and that barnacles are crustaceans, but these ones (below) are still called goose barnacles.

TEENY WEENY

The water flea (main picture) is not a real flea, but is the same size and shape. Some water fleas are only 0.25mm long, smaller than a full stop.

CRUSHING DEFEAT

Any animal that wants to feast off a crustacean has to resort to strong arm tactics. The edible crab (right) has the largest claw of any animal and uses it to shatter the shells of other, smaller, crustaceans.

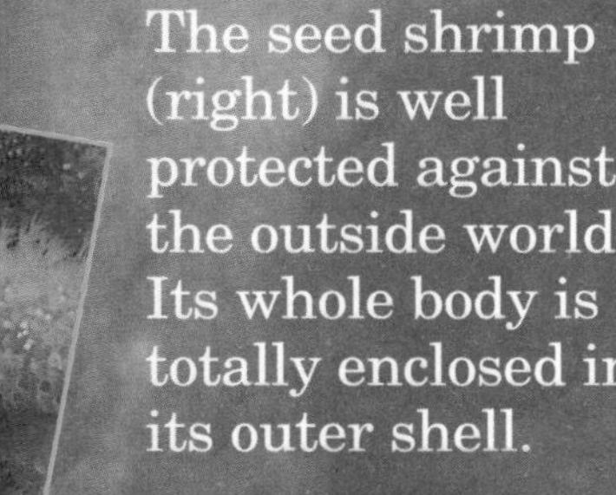

INTO ITS SHELL

The seed shrimp (right) is well protected against the outside world. Its whole body is totally enclosed in its outer shell.

LAND LUBBERS

Of all the crustaceans only the woodlouse, or sowbug (right), is able to live all its life on land. However, it still needs to live in damp places, such as under rocks or logs.

Creepy caves

Most people are afraid of the dark, but bugs aren't. There are some creatures that spend their whole lives in caves and rarely see the light of day.

A dark, dripping cave may not be your idea of a good home, but to some bugs it is ideal. Cave bugs are protected by the darkness and prey on other animals that creep into their home or already live there. Peer into the gloom to find out how these bugs cope in the dark.

NEED FOR CHANGE

Bugs that live in the dark have evolved (changed very slowly over millions of years) so that they can move about and feed without needing to see. If you found yourself in a dark room you would hold your arms out in front of you and feel your way around. You would also walk slowly; if you ran you would probably bump into the furniture. Cave bugs behave in the same way. They often have extra long feelers and are sometimes quite slow-moving.

The peacock butterfly (above) hibernates in caves during the winter. After hibernation it opens its wings and basks in the sun. Lives: Asia and Europe.

What is... guano?

Guano is bird or bat droppings. Bats fly about at night looking for insects and a colony of 50 million bats may eat 6,000 tonnes of bugs each year. Every morning they return to the cave with full bellies. During the day guano drops down on to the cave floor. It is made up of parts of dead insects and minerals. It is grey or black and cave bugs, such as cockroaches, love to eat it.

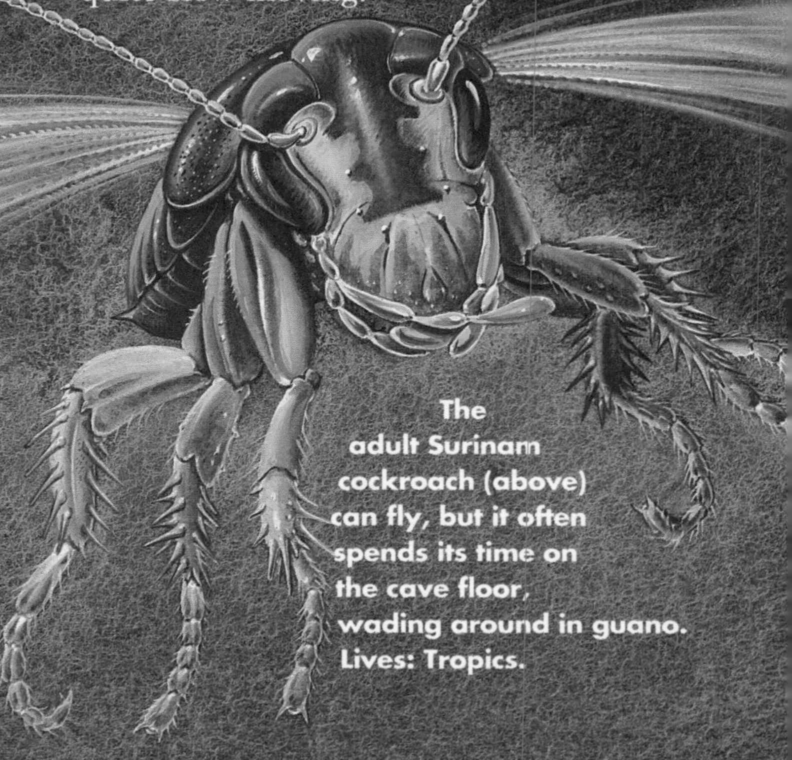

The adult Surinam cockroach (above) can fly, but it often spends its time on the cave floor, wading around in guano. Lives: Tropics.

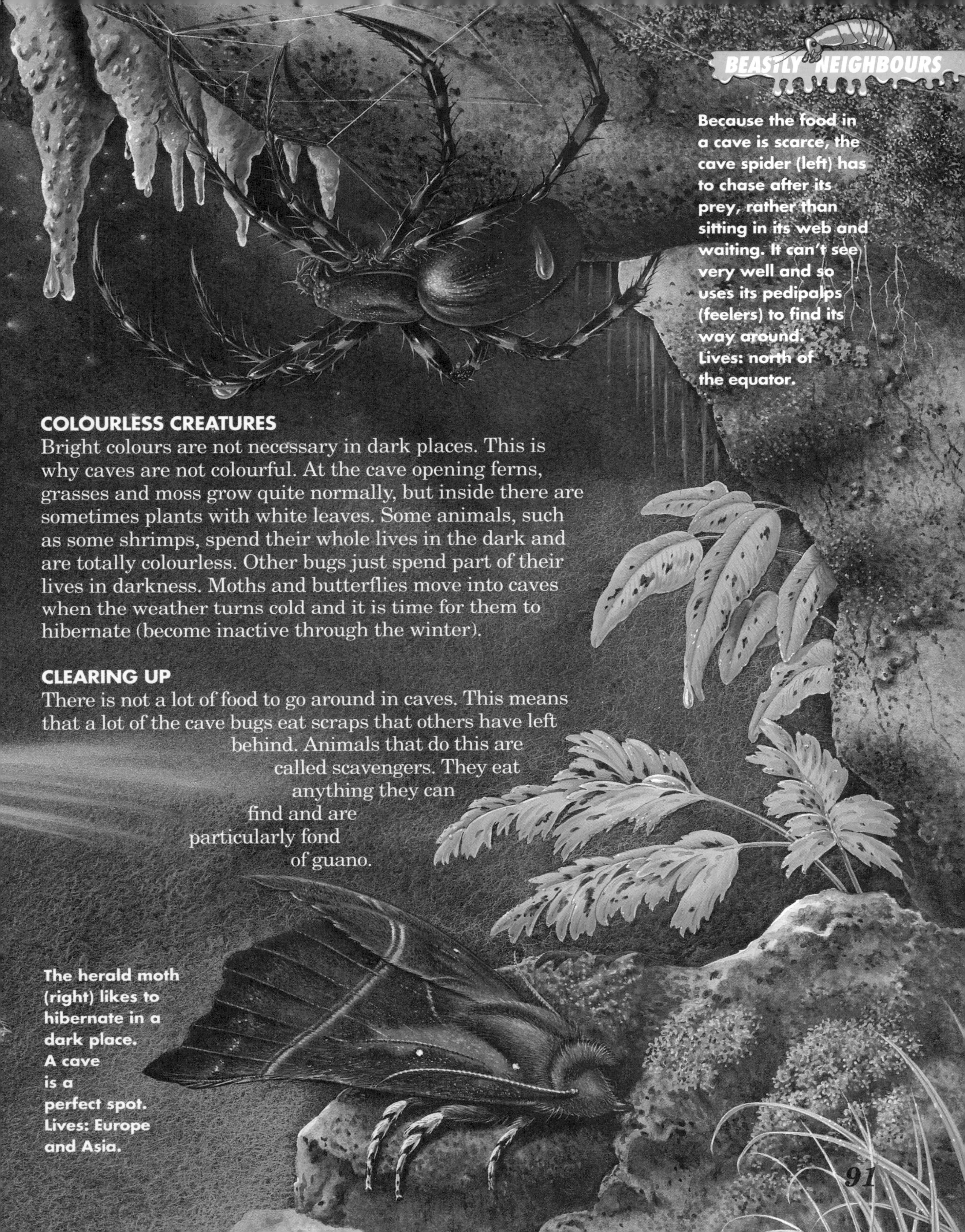

Because the food in a cave is scarce, the cave spider (left) has to chase after its prey, rather than sitting in its web and waiting. It can't see very well and so uses its pedipalps (feelers) to find its way around. Lives: north of the equator.

COLOURLESS CREATURES

Bright colours are not necessary in dark places. This is why caves are not colourful. At the cave opening ferns, grasses and moss grow quite normally, but inside there are sometimes plants with white leaves. Some animals, such as some shrimps, spend their whole lives in the dark and are totally colourless. Other bugs just spend part of their lives in darkness. Moths and butterflies move into caves when the weather turns cold and it is time for them to hibernate (become inactive through the winter).

CLEARING UP

There is not a lot of food to go around in caves. This means that a lot of the cave bugs eat scraps that others have left behind. Animals that do this are called scavengers. They eat anything they can find and are particularly fond of guano.

The herald moth (right) likes to hibernate in a dark place. A cave is a perfect spot. Lives: Europe and Asia.

Going underground

Take a step inside, let your eyes get used to the darkness and look at the bugs that lurk deep inside the cave.

Bugs that live in pitch dark caves get used to life in the dark, some even make their own light.

MAKING LIGHT

Caves in Waitomo, New Zealand glimmer with the light of millions of glow-worms. These glow-worms are not worms at all, but the larvae of gnats. They don't glow to light up the cave, but to attract their prey. As well as their bodies glowing in the dark, they also spin luminous webs, which are like sticky strings of glow-in-the-dark candyfloss. Flying insects become trapped in the web and are eaten by the glow-worms.

PALE, BUT INTERESTING

In caves in Jamaica, there are crabs which are the size of a hand. They are totally white. Like cave shrimps and crayfish, which live in the USA, they have spent so long in the dark that they have not developed colour.

FEELING WELL

As well as being colourless, the cave crayfish is also totally blind. Like crayfish that live in the sea, it has eye stalks, but it doesn't use them to see. The stalks are used as feelers instead. Like many cave dwellers, cave crayfish find their way around by touch

Glow-worms (above) catch flying bugs in their sticky traps. Live: New Zealand.

White crabs (below left) get their food from underground rivers. Live: Jamaica.

You will only see a crayfish (below) if a light shines on it and forms a shadow. Its bod is colourless and it is blind. Live: North America.

Tailless whip

THE SILENT HUNCHBACK

The cave or camel cricket is born to live underground. It has very long, bendy feelers, which it uses to grope around in the darkness, and spikes on its feet, which allow it to cling upside-down on smooth cave ceilings. On its bottom are three sharp spikes, which it uses to tell if a bug is creeping up behind it in the dark. Crickets are usually noisy bugs, but the cave cricket seldom chirps – it prefers to lurk silently in the dark and surprise its victims.

SENSING DANGER

The tailless whip scorpion and the centipede are both well adapted to life in a cave. They have long legs, which help them to hold on to the cave walls, and extra-long antennae, which the whip scorpion uses to find out what is going on in the dark cave.

Cave crickets (above) rest by day and forage for food during the night. Their long antennae can be three times the length of their bodies. Live: North Africa, southern Europe and North America.

The cave flatworm (below left) reaches 18mm in length and clamps on to its prey with suckers before it eats them. Lives: North America and Asia.

Cockroaches (below) feed on guano. Live: worldwide.

In the dark, the cave centipede's legs (below) act as feelers. Lives: warm countries worldwide.

Small Talk

TROPICAL TERRORS

Caves in the tropics are warm and wet. They generally contain more life than caves in cooler climates. In such warm conditions, whip scorpions grow very large. They can become as big as an adult's hand, while their legs may span 50cm, which is wider than these two pages. Tropical caves are sometimes so full of guano that the cave floor becomes a moving mass of munching cockroaches.

Improve and test your knowledge with...

CREEPY~CRAWLY FACTS

Steal a glance at the light-fingered robber crab and test your friends with this mind-boggling quiz.

1 What is a Spanish dancer?
a) a barnacle
b) a sponge
c) a sea slug

2 How many species of praying mantis are there?
a) about 18
b) about 1,800
c) about 8

3 What disease does the tsetse fly carry?
a) malaria
b) sleeping sickness
c) flu

4 What is a bee-louse?
a) a fly
b) a bee
c) a louse

5 Which of these bugs could kill a human with its bite?
a) black widow spider
b) bee-louse
c) praying mantis

6 How big is a blood-splashing cricket?
a) about the size of a mouse
b) about the size of a football
c) about the size of a ladybird

7 The cave cricket has another name. What is it?
a) bat dropping cricket
b) field cricket
c) camel cricket

8 Which animal has the largest claw?
a) lobster
b) lion
c) edible crab

9 How many pairs of legs does a praying mantis have?
a) six
b) three
c) two

10 Which bug gives off a steady light?
a) shrimp
b) fire ant
c) glow-worm

Night stalker

Watch out, there's a thief about! The robber crab gets its name from its habit of sneaking into beach camps at night and scuttling off with anything from milk bottles to cookers. At more than 1m across, and with claws that can cut through metal sheeting, it is the largest land bug in the world. Sadly, the crab is dying out because its island homes are being destroyed.

Bugs library

It is thought that there are about 30 million kinds of bug. If this magazine series were to include all of them, it would need over 150 million pages of creature file alone. To keep the whole set, you would need 550km of book shelf able to support 20,000 tonnes.

Bath time

As the places they live are destroyed by humans, many kinds of bugs have to find new homes. The Socorro sowbug, a kind of freshwater bug that looks like a woodlouse, made a clean break when it was forced out of its mountain home in New Mexico. The last few remaining bugs moved into an abandoned wash house!

Glowing in the wind

Global warming, or the greenhouse effect, is a serious threat to many species of animal, including humans. The gases that cause it can come from strange places. As much as one fifth of the gas methane that adds to global warming is produced by insects when they pass wind!

Answers to the questions on the inside back cover

Matthew Robertson, who spent 12 years working with bugs at London Zoo, here answers all your creepy-crawly questions.

When did the first bug appear?

Bugs were the first animal rulers of the world, until fish appeared about 100 million years later. The first bugs to leave fossils (remains of animals or plants preserved in rocks) were jellyfish and worms, which appeared over 650 million years ago. Bugs were almost certainly around before this time, but their soft bodies rotted quickly and so they did not leave fossils.

Do bugs shiver?

Yes, like humans, some bugs do shiver. Flying insects shiver to warm up before they take off. They do this by working their muscles very quickly. This builds up their body heat and makes the muscles work more efficiently. Many flying insects need to do this otherwise they cannot move their wings quickly enough to take off.

What is the most common bug?

This is a very difficult question, but it would have to be one of those bugs that occurs all around the world. Bugs such as the honey bee, housefly or oriental cockroach must be close to the top. Perhaps the most common bugs are krill (tiny sea shrimps), which whales eat in huge numbers.

Which is the smelliest bug?

The Florida stick insect squirts a chemical that is so smelly it can knock a human out! Bugs use smells for many reasons. Some bugs use them to attract mates – silk moths can pick up a smell 11km away. Smells are also used by some bugs to put other animals off eating them.

Bombardier Beetle

Like a soldier in a shoot-out, the bombardier beetle blasts away at its attackers.

The bombardier beetle is a member of the huge ground beetle family, that lives on the surface of the ground. Most of the time, the bombardier keeps itself safely out of sight, hiding among the roots of trees or under stones. You might find several of these beetles together under a single stone.

- **SCIENTIFIC NAME:** *Brachynus crepitans*
- **SIZE:** 1cm
- **LIVES:** central and southern Europe, north Africa, Siberia
- **EATS:** caterpillars, snails and other bugs

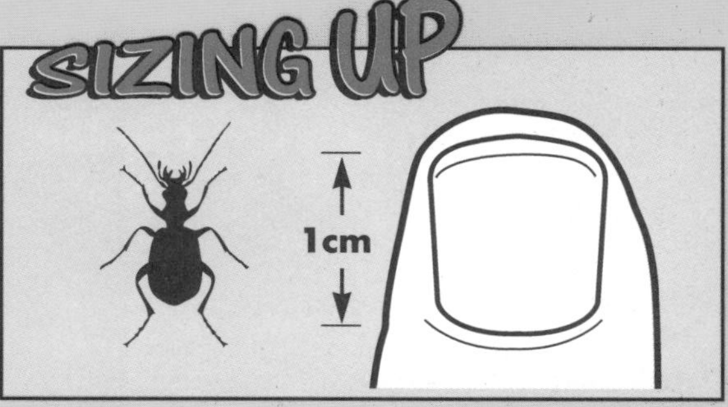

Is it true... that a bombardier beetle can spray its opponent more than once before it gives up?

Yes. When the bombardier beetle is defending itself against an attacker, it sprays in small, short bursts. It can go on doing this for some time before all the spray is used up, producing up to 80 small, but powerful, 'explosions' in four minutes.

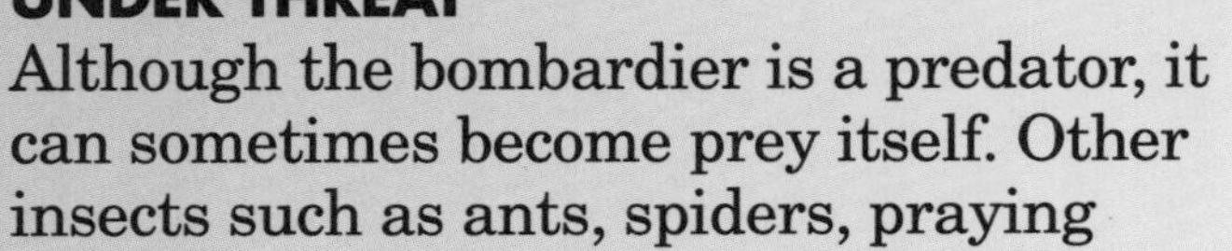

UNDER THREAT

Although the bombardier is a predator, it can sometimes become prey itself. Other insects such as ants, spiders, praying mantids – or sometimes even frogs or small mammals – may try to attack it.

TWO-COLOUR BODY

The top two parts of the bombardier's body – its head and thorax – are small and brown. The third part, its abdomen, is much bigger, and may be a shiny black, blue-black or greenish black in colour.

FAST FOOTWORK

The bombardier is a carnivore, and likes to eat the flesh of soft-bodied insects. Like other meat-eating beetles, it is fast on its feet – which means that it can run after its prey and overtake it.

A NASTY SHOCK

Ready, aim, fire! The bombardier beetle rears up and points its bendy abdomen towards the snout of a nosy puppy.

Small, brown thorax.

Wing covers fold flat when the beetle isn't flying.

Flexible abdomen points upwards to aim at the attacker.

Chemical spray.

STINK BOMBS
When a bombardier feels threatened, it has an unusual way of defending itself – it blasts its attacker with an explosion of gas from the back of its body. The gas looks like a puff of blue smoke, and comes out with a loud pop! This startles the attacker, and gives the beetle time to scurry away. These gas 'bombs' give the beetle its name.

GASWORKS
Whenever the beetle is in danger, its body produces a burning, chemical liquid, in a sac near the back of its abdomen. It also produces the gas oxygen. The oxygen presses on the sides of the sac and forces the liquid out – rather like squirting paint out of a spray can. When the liquid comes into contact with the air, some of it turns into an explosive gas.

HOT AND SMELLY
The temperature inside the beetle's abdomen rises to 100°C – that's hot enough to make water boil. So, when the liquid comes out, it is boiling hot, and smelly, too! It can cause blisters on other insects, but on human skin it only causes a mild burning feeling.

PERFECT AIM
The tip of the beetle's abdomen can move in any direction, which means that it can aim very accurately. By rotating the tip, it can spray an attacker wherever it is – in front, to the side, or behind.

Small Talk

POWERBOAT BUGS

The bombardier beetle isn't the only beetle to use chemicals to defend itself. One of the rove beetles, a distant relative of the bombardier beetle, lives in ponds and escapes from predators using a chemical to propel itself across the surface of the water. Like the bombardier beetle, this water beetle makes the chemical in its abdomen. It drops a tiny amount of the chemical from the tip of its abdomen on to the water's surface. This expands very rapidly and pushes the bug along at great speed.

Although it is related to the ordinary earthworm, the medicinal leech has a diet of blood!

- **SCIENTIFIC NAME:** *Hirudo medicinalis*
- **SIZE:** up to 15cm long
- **LIVES:** Europe, Middle East, western Asia
- **EATS:** blood

Medicinal Leech

The medicinal leech lives in still ponds and slow-moving rivers. It feeds on the blood of the animals that come to drink at the water's edge, particularly horses and cattle.

BLOOD-SUCKER

The leech has a sucker at either end of its body that helps it hold on to things. Clamping itself on to its victim, it bites the animal with its three jagged jaws. The jaws inject a fluid into the animal's skin that stops the blood clotting (thickening and drying up), and another that numbs the area around the bite. This gives the leech time to suck up plenty of blood and get a decent meal. Unlike ordinary bug bites, a leech bite can go on bleeding for 24 hours.

QUIET EATER

Quietly feeding, the leech may drink five times its own weight in blood before it lets go. Its meal may take months to digest.

CRUEL CURE

In the past, doctors used leeches on their patients. Letting a leech drain off some blood was thought to cure illnesses. In the middle of the 19th century, this idea fell out of fashion. Today, some doctors think that blood-sucking leeches might have medicinal powers after all.

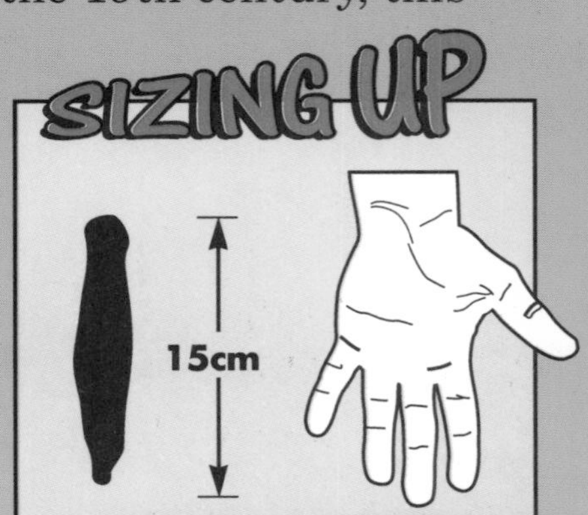

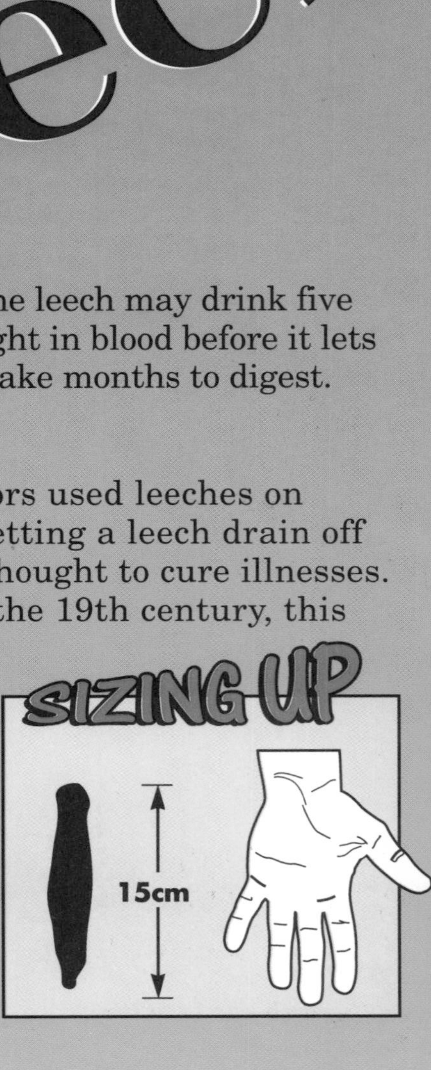

Like an enormous fishing net, the tentacles of the lion's mane jellyfish spread out into the depths of the ocean.

Lion's Mane Jellyfish

The lion's mane jellyfish is huge! Its body, or 'bell', can grow to 2m wide – that's the same as the height of a door. Its tentacles, around the edge of the bell, can reach an incredible 40m long – about the same size as a 10-storey building!

CATCHING FOOD

Floating in the cold, ocean waters, this monster jellyfish waits for prey to come along. Its tentacles work like a giant sieve or fishing net, stinging and paralysing any tiny sea creatures that swim through and touch them. Then the tentacles carry their catch to the jellyfish's mouth, underneath its body. The four flaps, or 'lobes', around its mouth also help to catch food.

PAINFUL STING

This jellyfish can sting people too. Its body can be 35m away, but this creature can still reach you with its tentacles. Even a sting from a small one causes painful, red swellings on your skin. A jellyfish washed up on a beach is still dangerous because it can go on stinging long after it is dead.

BEASTLY FACTS

- **SCIENTIFIC NAME:** *Cyanea capillata*
- **SIZE:** bell up to 2m wide, tentacles up to 40m long
- **LIVES:** north Atlantic Ocean
- **EATS:** tiny sea creatures (plankton)

BEASTLY MANNERS
The body-snatchers
The wasp dives in – its jaws are designed for chewing meat.
The scorpion fly tucks into a meal of blood and guts.
Flies lay their eggs inside the body of the mouse. They hatch into squirming maggots.
Earwigs usually eat flowers, but they will occasionally tuck into dead flesh.
A garden snail finds a piece of bone to munch.
The bluebottle, attracted by the smell of the mouse, arrives too late to lay its eggs.

A dead mouse can disappear from a garden in 24 hours. With the body-snatchers about it's a case of now you see it, now you don't!

Young greenbottles emerge from the ground around the mouse and fly off.

Wood ants are the vacuum cleaners of the forest, they'll eat almost anything.

Devil's coach horse beetles often live in cemeteries. They feed on the bugs that feed on dead flesh.

When a small mammal, such as a field mouse, dies, its body can vanish in a day. This is not magic, but busy bugs at work. Some bugs snatch and eat the rotting flesh of animals (known as carrion). Rotting bodies often carry germs so the bugs' quick and easy clean-up service removes the source of diseases. Meet some of the body-snatchers.

BABY GROW
The greenbottle lays its eggs in moist, shaded parts of a dead body, such as the mouth or the ears. Twenty four hours later, the eggs hatch. The young maggots squirt a special substance that turns the mouse's flesh into a soup-like liquid. Feeding on their revolting soup, they grow quickly.

ROVING EYE
The devil's coach horse is a type of rove beetle. These beetles hang around dead bodies, not to eat the flesh itself, but to feed on the larvae of insects that gather to eat the decaying animal.

BLOOD SUCKERS
Scorpion flies use their long, sucking mouth parts to suck up the runny remains of dead animals. They also drink the blood of freshly killed or badly injured animals.

FLESH STRIPPERS
During the early part of the year, wasps eat meat – both fresh and rotting. They take it back to their nests to feed the larvae.

TEAM WORK
Ants scurry around in huge groups, stripping meat from the body and taking it back to their nest. A snail arrives late for its meal at the carcass. It likes to eat the dead animal's bones because they are a good source of calcium, which the snail needs to keep its shell strong.

The grave-diggers

Burying beetles don't snatch bits of the flesh from a corpse, they bury the whole body so they can enjoy their dinner later in peace and quiet.

Burying, or sexton, beetles can smell the dead body of their prey more than 1km away. When they have found the meat, they work in pairs and start burying it underground.

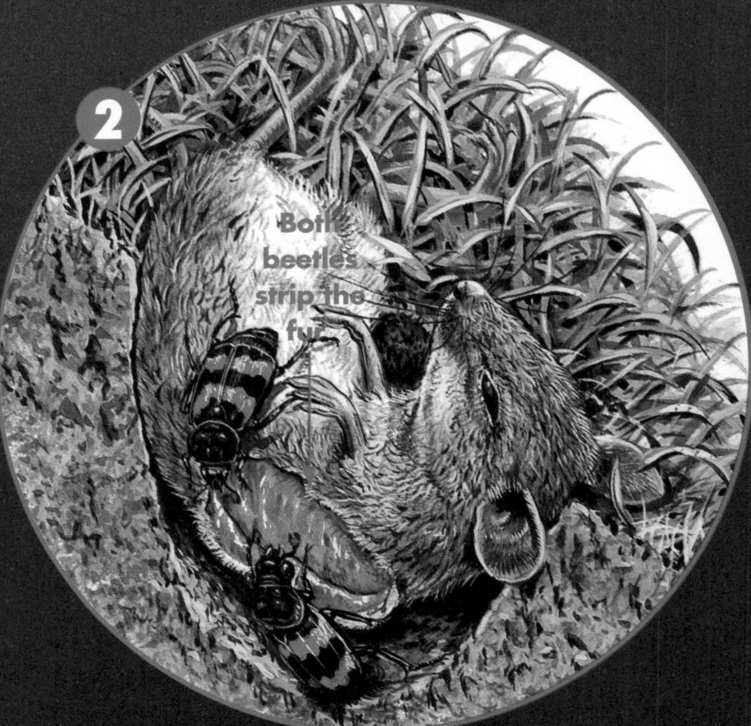

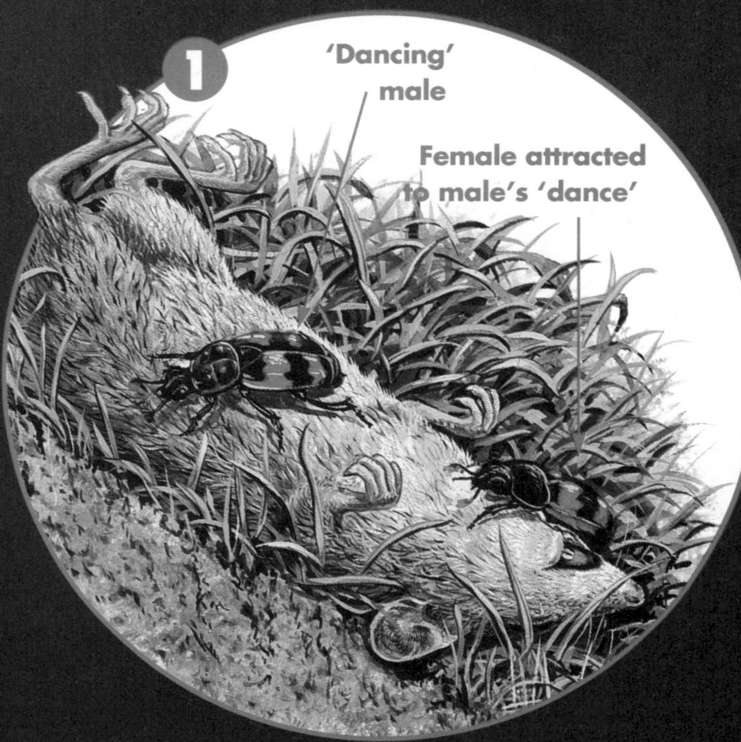

2 DIGGING DEEP

The beetles begin to dig a pit for the dead animal. Their legs are specially designed for digging. Once the beetles have pushed the mouse to the bottom of the grave, they strip it of all its fur, and chop its body into small pieces.

1 DIRTY DANCING

When the male finds a suitable dead body he climbs up on top of it. If there is no female around to join him, he stretches his body diagonally upwards and starts swaying backwards and forwards. This 'dancing' catches the attention of a passing female and she climbs up on top of the corpse with her new partner.

SOUNDS GOOD

Unlike most bugs, burying beetles 'talk' to their young using sounds. The female chirps softly as she looks after her brood. As soon as they hatch, the young larvae follow the noises she makes to find their way along the underground tunnel to the chamber where all the food is stored.

3 HAVING BABIES

In some species the female drives the male away once they have mated. She then digs a tunnel and lays up to 24 eggs in its walls. Clambering back into her chamber, she eats away at the top of the dead prey's flesh and bones, leaving a shallow pit in the ball of rotting meat. She stays in the chamber and picks at the food while she waits patiently for her eggs to hatch.

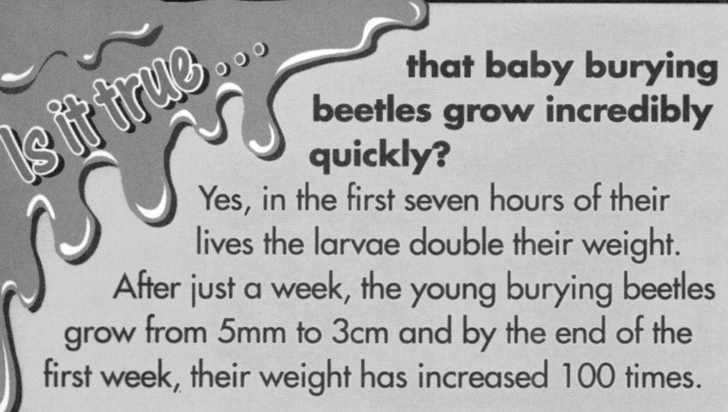

that baby burying beetles grow incredibly quickly?

Yes, in the first seven hours of their lives the larvae double their weight. After just a week, the young burying beetles grow from 5mm to 3cm and by the end of the first week, their weight has increased 100 times.

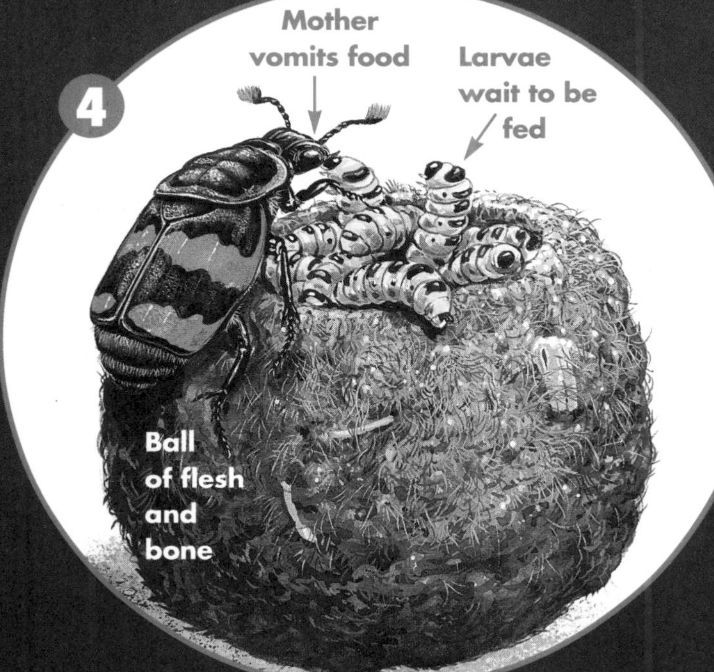

4 WAITRESS SERVICE

Five days later the young appear. The mother's 'singing' leads them to the chamber where they fall on to the ball of animal flesh and bones. For the first six hours of their lives, the young are unable to feed themselves and rely on their mother for food – she vomits partly digested food for them to eat. For the next five days they feed themselves on the ball of remains. Just before the larvae are fully grown, they need their mother to give them one last meal. With all this good food inside them, the young wriggle away and finally turn into beetles.

Keeping millipedes

Millipedes are easy to keep and fun to watch.

In the wild, millipedes live in damp dark places, such as under stones or among fallen rotting leaves. They are not easy to find as they are shy creatures that hide away from light. Most types of millipede are also very small so it is difficult to study them. Keeping your own giant millipedes as pets allows you to keep a closer watch on them.

You will need:

- compost
- water
- leaves
- fruit and vegetables

From a good pet shop:

- a tank, about 60 x 30 x 30cm, with a lid
- heat pad about one-third the size of the bottom of the tank
- plug
- plastic strip thermometer
- cuttlefish
- millipedes

WHAT TO DO

1 Get an adult to put a plug on the heat pad. Place the tank on top of the heat pad so that it warms one end of the tank. This will vary the temperature in the tank so that the millipedes can choose just how warm or cool they want to be.

5 If the compost is dry, sprinkle some water on it until it is all slightly damp. Don't add too much water or the millipedes will not like it and will eventually die.

6 Allow the tank to warm up overnight. Place four or six millipedes in the tank. They are fragile animals and should be handled with care as they can split open if dropped.

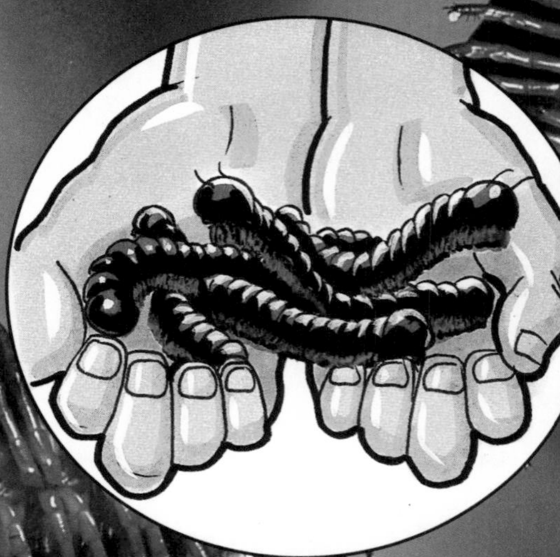

2 The best soil temperature is 70 – 80°C. Use the strip thermometer to check that the temperature in the middle of the tank is somewhere between these two figures.

3 Put at least 10cm of compost in the bottom of the tank. Lay the cuttlefish on top of the compost. The millipedes need this in order to get calcium for their hard external skeletons.

Small Talk

HEALTHY BUGS

When you buy your millipedes, check that they are healthy. A limp one might be unwell. The best type of giant millipede to buy is the East African species known as the Mombasan train, *Epibolus pulchripes*. Unlike some giant millipedes, which spray defence chemicals, the Mombasan train millipede is not aggressive.

4 Next wash a selection of leaves under a running tap and scatter them over the soil. Watch which leaves the millipedes like to eat best of all. Collect a bag full of leaves in the autumn so that you can feed your millipedes during the winter.

7 Millipedes eat a variety of foods, including fruit, leaves, dead animals, even droppings. Give them lettuce, fruit and vegetables. Wash all food beforehand, as it may have chemicals on it. Try a wide variety of foods, so you can find out which are their favourites. Change any food after two or three days, before it becomes mouldy.

8 After a few months baby millipedes might appear. These are pale and only about 1 – 2cm long. They hatch from eggs buried in the soil. Be careful not to throw them away with the old food. Millipedes live for about 18 months.

Blowfly

The blowfly homes in on its next tasty meal. On the menu today are a rotting dead bird, bits of leftover food and a pile of dung. The blowfly can't chew or swallow solid food. Instead, it vomits some of its previous meal on to the food, which turns it to liquid. Yum! This mixture of rotting food and vomit is hoovered up using a special straw-like feeding tube (proboscis). Perhaps you'll think twice before you invite a blowfly for tea.

the munch bunch

Take a look at the different types of bugs on the opposite page. Can you match the creepy-crawly to the way it eats?

Some humans may prefer bacon to cabbage, or chocolate to fruit but, on the whole, we eat the same *types* of food. We also all eat in the same way; we have hands to pick up our food (or a knife and fork), and jaws to chew the food. But bugs eat all sorts of different food in lots of different ways and their bodies are tailor-made to suit their eating habits.

MIX AND MATCH

All the bugs on this page eat in different ways. These are described in the green box (right). Take a look at the pictures (far right) and see if you can match the bug to the way it eats. Then turn the page to discover the answers and more details.

WAYS OF EATING

PARASITE: lives and feeds in or on another 'host' animal. Parasites that absorb food through their skin need to have bodies with large surface areas so they can get as much food as possible.

CARNIVORE: is a meat-eater. It needs large, strong claws to grab and hold its victims, and sharp jaws to rip them to pieces.

HERBIVORE: eats only plants. It needs to be difficult to spot so it won't be attacked by carnivores when eating.

FILTER FEEDER: takes food from the water in which it lives. Its eating parts act like a sieve. As water trickles over them, they collect tiny bits of food and let the rest of the water run away.

LIQUID FEEDER: doesn't eat solid food. It 'drinks' liquids, such as nectar from flowers, with a long straw-like mouth part. When it is not drinking, it curls up its mouth part.

TAPEWORM

GIANT WHIP SCORPION

BUTTERFLY

STICK INSECT

BARNACLES

THE TAPEWORM IS A PARASITE

The tapeworm lives in the gut of other animals, such as pigs and humans, and absorbs food directly from this 'host' animal. To do this, its body needs to have the largest surface area possible. This is why its body is so long and wrinkled. The tapeworm attaches itself to the other animal with suckers and hooks on its head. The largest tapeworm, found in sperm whales, is over 30m long, which is as long as four double-decker buses!

Wrinkled, large surface area

THE GIANT WHIP SCORPION IS A CARNIVORE

The scorpion has very large and powerful claws to catch and grip on tightly to its victims. It comes out at night when it uses its long pair of whip-like legs to explore the ground. The giant whip scorpion is also known as the 'vinegaroon' because it defends itself by spraying a stream of strong-smelling acid, just like vinegar, from its bottom.

Mouth

Jaws

Claws

THE STICK INSECT IS A HERBIVORE

The stick insect cannot be seen very easily. The colour and shape of its legs makes it look like a plant and difficult for a predator to spot. The stick insect has jaws that can cut through and grind tough leaves. It sometimes lives in large groups which can strip large areas of woodland.

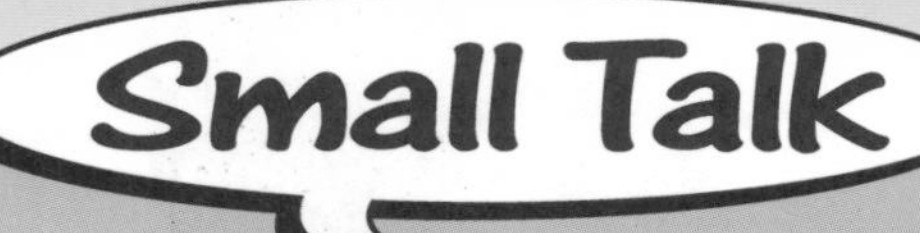

PSYCHIC SCIENTIST

The famous scientist Charles Darwin guessed that the Madagascan hawkmoth existed even before it had been discovered! He found a type of flower (an orchid) that could only be pollinated by a liquid-feeding insect with straw-like mouth parts over 30cm long. Until then, nobody had ever seen an insect like that, but Darwin was right and the hawkmoth was discovered many years later.

THE BARNACLE IS A FILTER FEEDER

Filtering tentacles

Mouth

The barnacle feeds on tiny pieces of food that float in water. Food is carried towards the barnacle by currents in the water. It is sieved by the barnacle's tentacles, pulled down into the shell and carried to the mouth. Barnacles are not hunters – they just sit around and wait for food to turn up.

Flaps guide the food into the mouth

Jaw

THE BUTTERFLY IS A LIQUID FEEDER

The butterfly feeds on the nectar in flowers. Its long, straw-like mouth parts (proboscis) are perfect for sucking up liquid. They look like one, long curly straw, but in fact there are two parts joined together, forming a tube. Not all liquid feeders drink nectar. Some suck animals' blood while others drink sap (the juices found in plants). Unlike the butterfly, liquid feeders that feed on blood, such as female mosquitoes, have short, sharp mouth parts to pierce the skin.

Straw-like mouth parts

CRAB SPREAD

The sack crab parasite is not content to stay and feed in the gut of its host animal. It really makes itself at home. It spreads its whole body throughout every centimetre of the crab until it takes on the shape of the crab's insides.

Death traps

Bugs are at risk from attack by hungry predators, but they are also in danger from plants – killer plants.

Most plants make their food from a mixture of sunlight, air, water and minerals, but there are a few that can't do this so they catch and kill bugs instead. These meat-eating plants are called carnivorous.

GOOD LOOKING PLANTS

A trap needs a bait. Just as humans use cheese to lure a mouse into a trap, so killer plants have their own ways of making their traps tempting. Insects spend most of their days buzzing from flower to flower in search of nectar and pollen. They usually aim for bright petals and the sweet smell of nectar. Bug-eating plants tempt their prey with a strong odour and attractive colouring.

WHO'S THERE?

Carnivorous plants often have a way of sensing if a gullible bug has landed in the trap. Some have sensitive hairs, which act as triggers when the insect brushes past them. Once a plant has caught its victim it will not let it scurry off. Some, like the venus flytrap, hold their victims in a 'cage', while others have a pool of sticky liquid, which bogs the animal down until, eventually, it drowns.

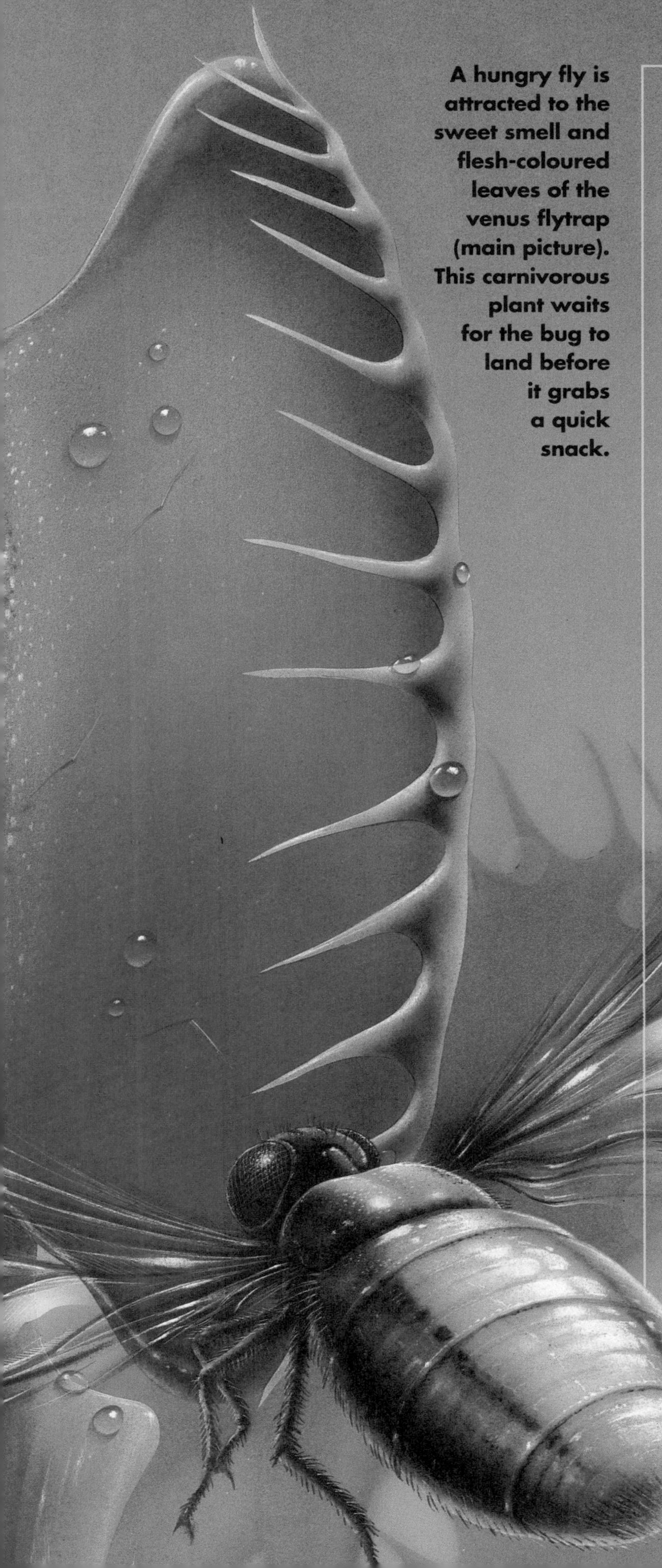

A hungry fly is attracted to the sweet smell and flesh-coloured leaves of the venus flytrap (main picture). This carnivorous plant waits for the bug to land before it grabs a quick snack.

All these plants may look innocent, but they're killers. Turn over to see the evidence.

SUNDEW

Sundews grow all over the world either in tiny clumps just 2cm across or in large bushes. Flying insects love the look of their colourful, shiny leaves.

TRUMPET PITCHER PLANT

A bug flying across a piece of marshy ground in North America may well be attracted to the smell of nectar and the bright colours of the trumpet pitcher plant. If it lands, though, the bug is in for trouble.

BLADDERWORT

Water bugs are not safe from meat-eating plants. The bladderwort, which lives in ponds all over the world, vacuums up its victims as they swim past.

BUTTERWORT

Warm, wet places around the world are home to the butterwort. Some bugs like the fungus-type odour that it gives off, and fly straight towards its deadly leaves.

TUCKING IN

Plants don't have teeth or stomachs, so how do they eat? In your stomach there are juices, which break down the food that you eat. Carnivorous plants have similar juices (enzymes) that turn the soft parts of the insect into a nourishing liquid, which is absorbed into the plant. The bug's tough outer shells are left behind. Often the empty shells of past victims can be seen on or near bug-eating plants.

EVIL SERPENT

The cobra lily, from North America, looks like a deadly snake ready to pounce. To an insect, it's just as dangerous. Bugs crawl up the tongue-shaped leaf, eager to get at the nectar that they can smell. Once they have climbed inside, they get confused by clear patches on the 'roof' of the plant. The bug thinks they are escape routes and tries to fly out of them, but finds it cannot escape and falls down into the pool of water at the bottom of the flower and drowns.

KILLING FOR A CAUSE

Tropical water-lilies kill insects so that they can pollinate their flowers. Pollination happens when a bug accidentally brings pollen from the male parts of one flower to the female parts of another. The insect, which is carrying pollen from another plant, lands at the centre of the water-lily where it is dragged down into a pool of liquid. The bug dies, but the pollen that was stuck to its body is put to good use – it is used by the water-lily to produce more plants.

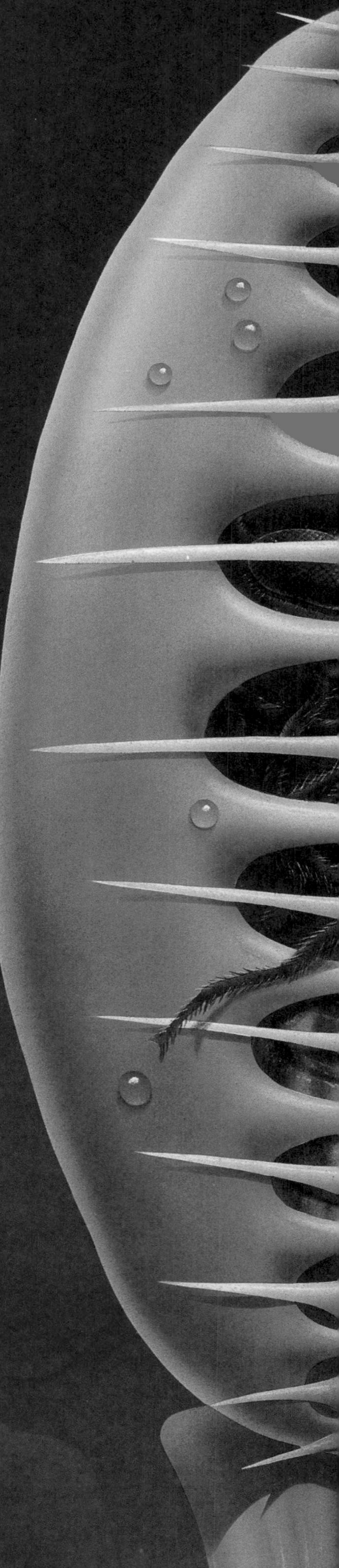

In a flash, the venus flytrap slams shut (main picture), trapping its prey inside. All the goodness from the insect's body is soaked into the plant. Once the meal is finished the trap reopens for business – and its next victim.

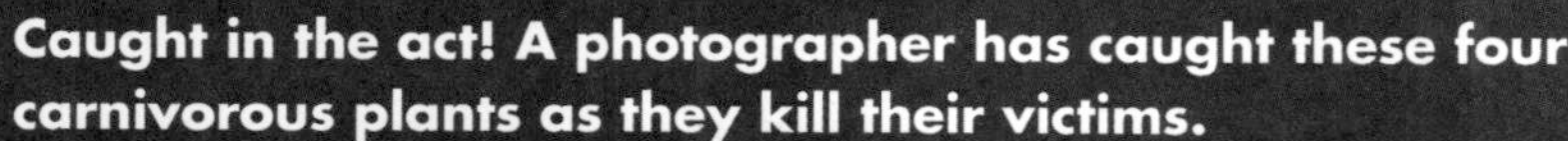

Caught in the act! A photographer has caught these four carnivorous plants as they kill their victims.

STICKY DROPLETS (SUNDEW)

As the insect lands on the sundew, it finds its feet are stuck to sticky droplets on the leaves. The leaves curl around the insect and eat the struggling victim.

A JUG OF DEADLY WATER (TRUMPET PITCHER PLANT)

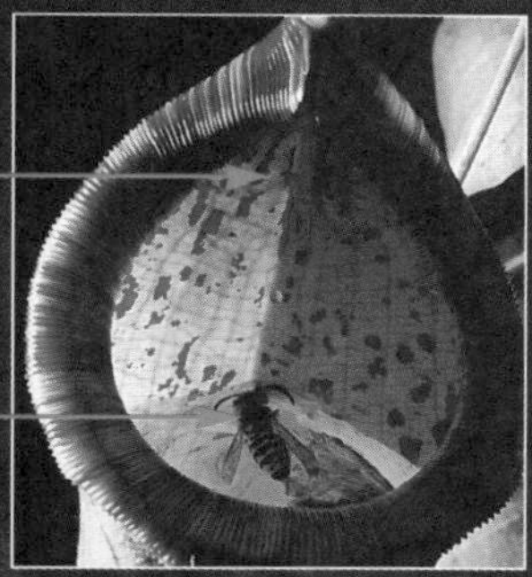

These plants are shaped like jugs or pitchers and can grow up to almost 1m long. Their walls are waxy, which means that the bug cannot get a foothold and falls to its death in a pool of water inside the plant.

DEATH BY VACUUM CLEANER (BLADDERWORT)

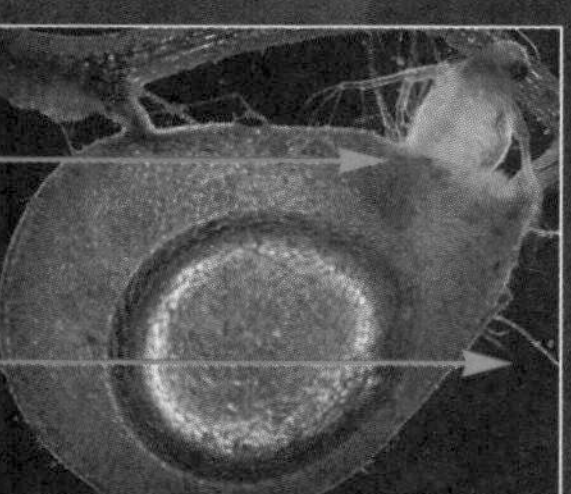

As the bug swims by, it brushes past sensitive hairs on the plant. A trapdoor opens and in a fraction of a second, the bug is vacuumed up and eaten inside.

A SMELLY TRAP (BUTTERWORT)

This plant's leaves have a buttery coating that smells of fungus. Some bugs love this smell. Insects land on the sticky leaves and suffocate in the smelly slime before they are eaten.

Improve and test your knowledge with...

CREEPY~CRAWLY FACTS

Jump to it and test your friends with our BUGS! teaser...

1 Which of these plants does not eat bugs?
a) butterwort
b) buttercup
c) bladderwort

2 Where is the lion's mane jellyfish's mouth?
a) at the end of one of its tentacles
b) on the top of its head
c) underneath its body

3 How does the blue-ringed octopus warn its enemies that it is dangerous?
a) with its colours
b) it sprays them with ink
c) it curls up in a ball

4 How long does the adult booklouse live for?
a) just over 2 weeks
b) just over 2 months
c) just long enough to finish the book

5 How far can a zebra jumping spider jump?
a) 3 times its own length
b) 365 times its own length
c) 36 times its own length

6 How long does the medicinal leech grow?
a) up to 15cm long
b) up to 5cm long
c) up to 5m long

7 Which spider traps its prey with a sticky ball of silk?
a) monkey spider
b) tarantula
c) bolas spider

8 What does the bombardier beetle eat?
a) other bugs
b) dead plants
c) fresh leaves

9 A burying, or sexton, beetle can smell a dead body
a) 1km away
b) 100m away
c) 150km away

10 What is a filter feeder?
a) a bug that only eats filters
b) a meat-eating animal
c) an animal that sieves water for food

Banned bugs

Before the age of powerful insecticides people had to use whatever means they could to get rid of pests. In Europe during the 15th century all manner of crop-destroying bugs, from caterpillars to weevils, were put on trial by the Church. As not one bug offered any defence they were all banned by the Church.

Jump start

Many bugs are capable of jumping long distances, but few jump as far or as accurately as the jumping spider. Some species, like the zebra jumping spider, can leap 36 times their own length. That's the same as a person jumping from one side of a football pitch to the other. Even at this distance, the spider can land right on top of its prey. As it leaps, it attaches a silk safety thread in case it needs to pull itself back to safety quickly.

Sonic pop!

For many years scientists thought the bot fly was the fastest animal on Earth. They claimed it could fly at over 1,367 km/h. However, experts eventually realised this was impossible. This speed is quicker than the time it takes for the sound of your voice to travel. To move so fast, the fly would need so much energy that it would have to eat the equivalent of one sugar cube per second. Its wings would also have to beat incredibly fast, at over 14,000 times a second!

One for all

In the deserts of Ethiopia there are many night predators. To ensure that its colony is safe, one species of ant fills in the entrance of its nest each night. One ant stays outisde to disguise the opening. Sadly, this ant will be eaten by a night-time prowler. This sacrifice means the others ants are safe.

Answers to the questions on the inside back cover

Q and A

Matthew Robertson, who spent 12 years working with bugs at London Zoo, here answers all your creepy-crawly questions.

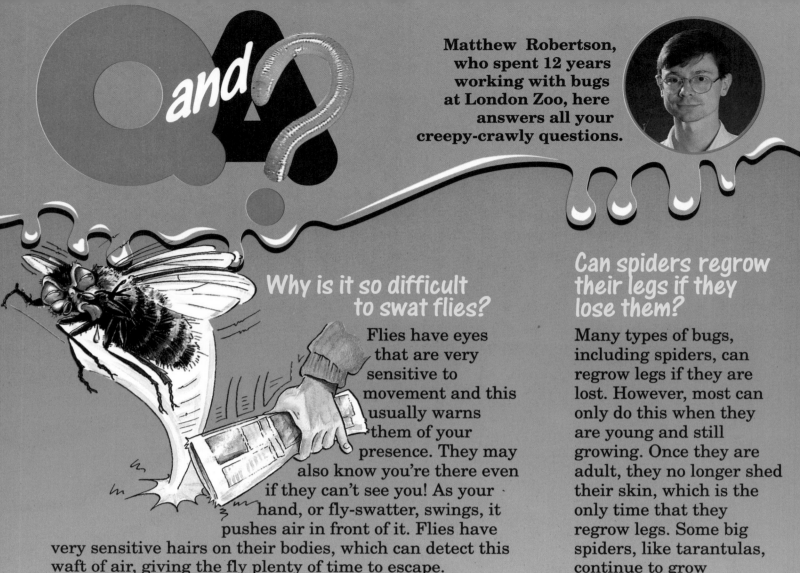

Why is it so difficult to swat flies?

Flies have eyes that are very sensitive to movement and this usually warns them of your presence. They may also know you're there even if they can't see you! As your hand, or fly-swatter, swings, it pushes air in front of it. Flies have very sensitive hairs on their bodies, which can detect this waft of air, giving the fly plenty of time to escape.

Which is the biggest ant nest in the world?

The biggest ant colony with one queen belongs to the African driver ant. There can be over 20 million ants in total. However, they do not build nests. The biggest nests are built by Japanese wood ants. One super-colony built a nest on the coast of Hokkaido (an island in the north of Japan) that has more than 306 million workers, 900,000 queens and covers an area of 3 square kilometres.

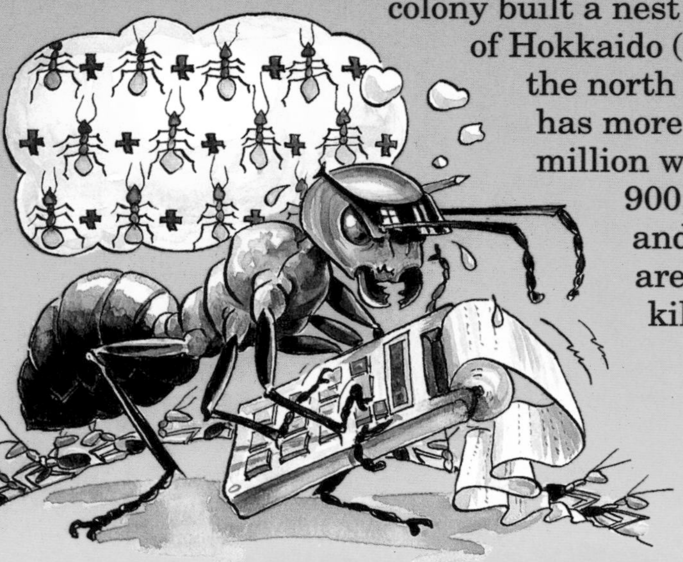

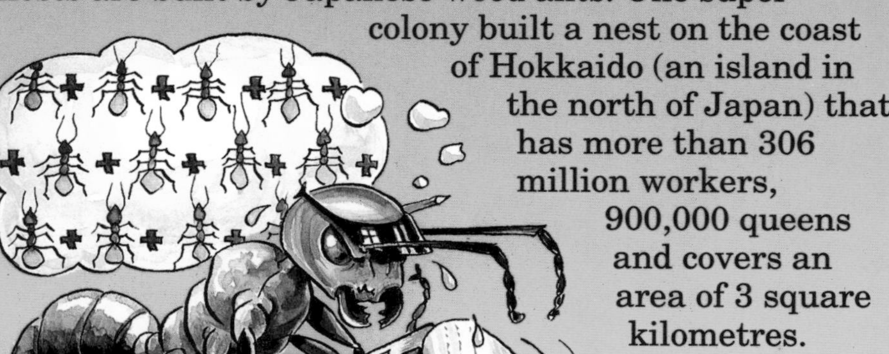

Can spiders regrow their legs if they lose them?

Many types of bugs, including spiders, can regrow legs if they are lost. However, most can only do this when they are young and still growing. Once they are adult, they no longer shed their skin, which is the only time that they regrow legs. Some big spiders, like tarantulas, continue to grow throughout their lives so they are always able to grow new legs.

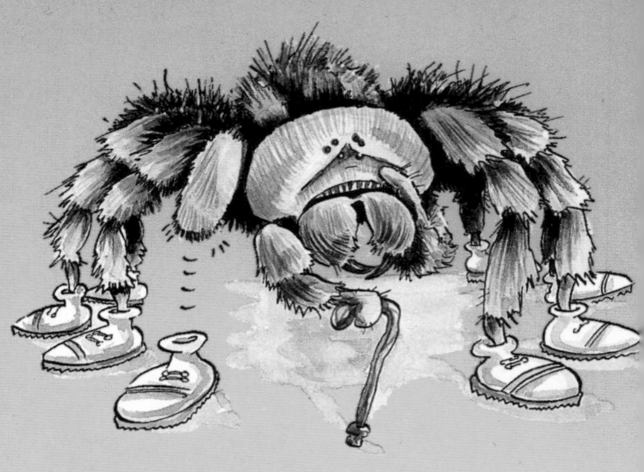

Army Ant

When army ants swarm over the forest floor, there is little escape for the creatures in their path.

The army ant lives in an enormous colony of up to several hundred thousand other army ants. At the heart of the colony is the queen ant, who lays all the eggs. The other ants are either workers or soldiers.

TEAM WORK

The workers and soldiers work together to feed and protect the queen and her young. The workers' job is to catch and bring back prey and look after the young. The soldiers' job is to defend the colony.

TRAVELLERS

Army ants have no permanent home. They stay in one place for only about three weeks at a time. Then they go on the march again, looking for another place to set up home. Scientists believe that they keep moving on in this way in order to find new food supplies.

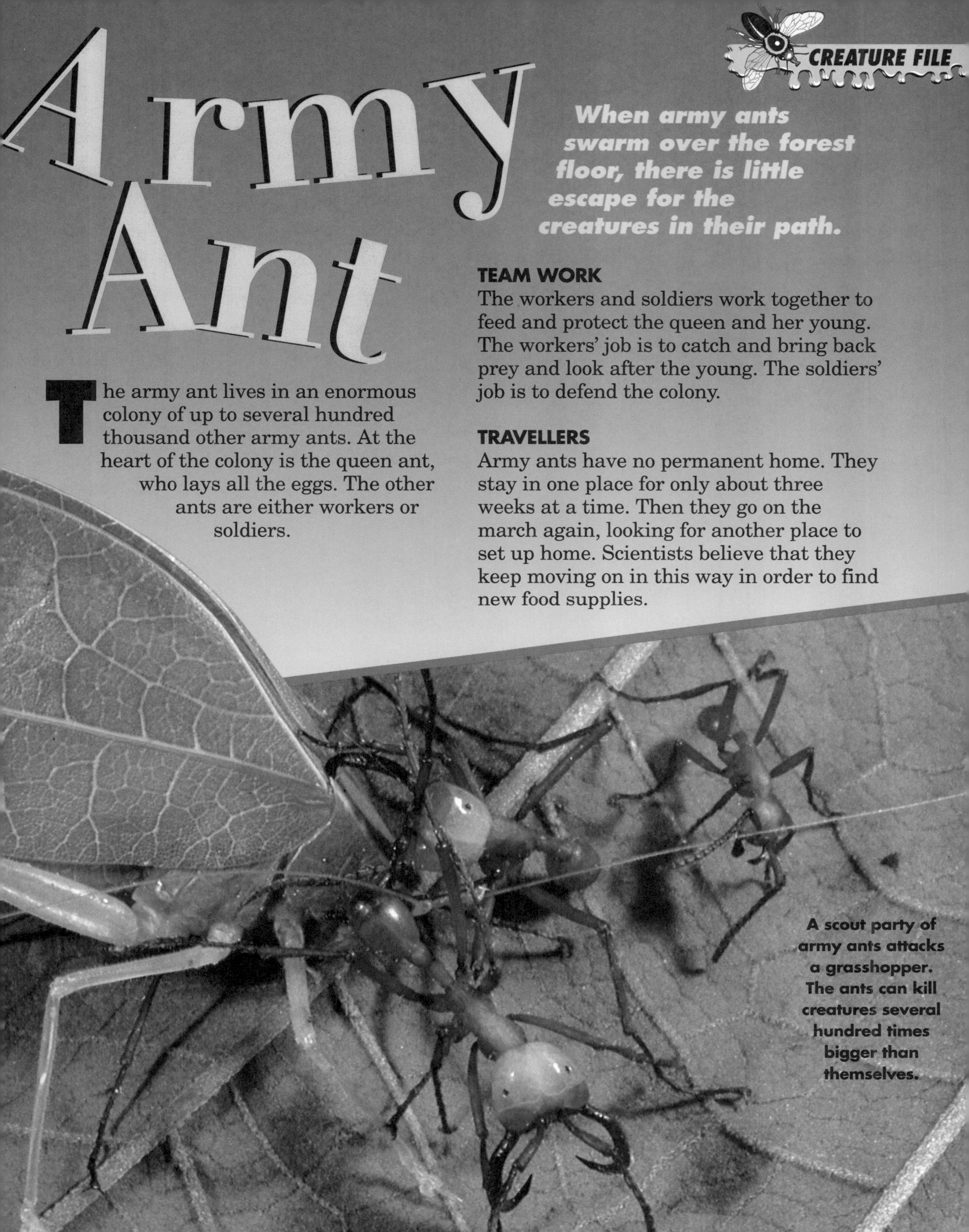

A scout party of army ants attacks a grasshopper. The ants can kill creatures several hundred times bigger than themselves.

When on the move, the ants carry everything with them, including their young. Here they are transporting pupae.

SETTING UP CAMP

Every night, the ants stop to rest. When it is dark they begin building a nest. But this nest isn't made of twigs – it's made of the ants' own bodies! First, some of the workers choose a sheltered spot, perhaps under a log. They hang on to the log with their claws, then more and more workers join on, gradually building up long chains with their bodies – rather like making chains out of paper clips. The chains all link together, and form a huge ball, about 1m wide, made up of 150,000 – 700,000 ants! By midnight, the nest is finished, and the queen and her young are safely inside.

ON THE MARCH

The ants march in a column, with some of the workers acting as scouts. The scouts find the best direction to take, and lay down a trail of scent for the others to follow. The soldiers move along the outside of the column. Twice as big as the workers, they have large jaws and a deadly sting. They attack any creature that gets too close, stinging it and pulling it to pieces.

DAWN RAIDS

After about two or three weeks on the march, the ants stop and set up a new base, called a bivouac (say 'biv-oo-wack'). They build the same kind of nest as before. In the morning, as the sun warms the nest, the workers wake. Thousands of them stream out into the forest to go hunting.

ON THE ATTACK!

Spreading out into a fan shape, the swarm can be 15m wide in front. The ants attack any creatures that do not get out of their way, killing them with thousands of stings, or ripping them to pieces with their powerful jaws. The ants go 100m away from the nest to find and bring back food.

NEW COLONIES

About eight times a year, the queen lays about 100,000-300,000 eggs. Out of the young that hatch, only one will become a new queen with her own colony.

Is it true . . . that all the members of an army ant colony are female?

Yes, the workers, soldiers and the queen are all female, but only the queen is fertile (can produce eggs). When her eggs hatch, there will be about six new, fertile females, and about 1500 – 3000 males. The males mate with the fertile females, and then die. Usually only one of the fertile females survives to start up her own colony.

BEASTLY FACTS

- **SCIENTIFIC NAME:** *Eciton burchelli*
- **SIZE:** up to 2cm
- **LIVES:** forests of South and Central America
- **EATS:** insects and other small animals, sometimes snakes, birds or mammals

SIZING UP

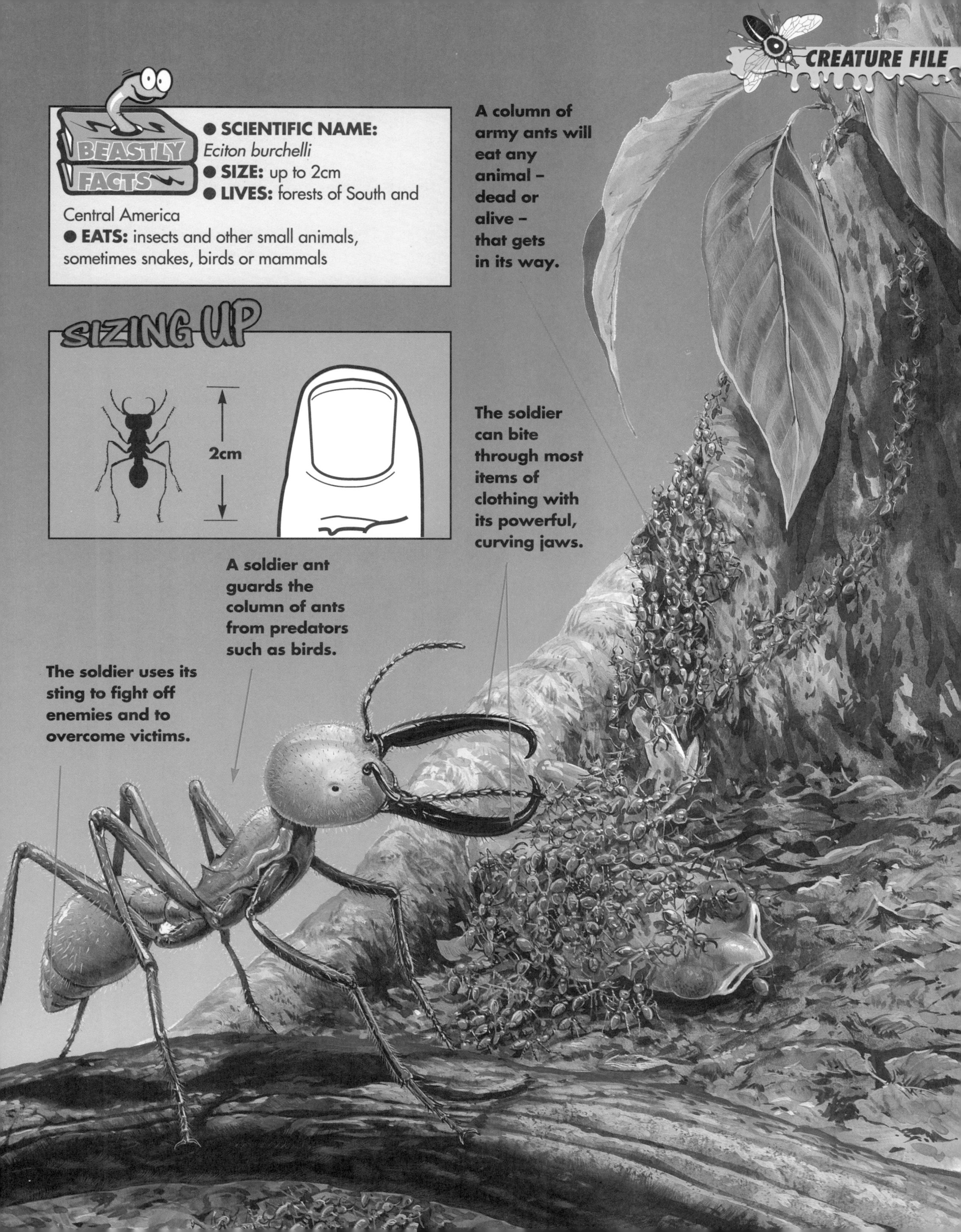

2cm
A column of army ants will eat any animal – dead or alive – that gets in its way.
The soldier can bite through most items of clothing with its powerful, curving jaws.
A soldier ant guards the column of ants from predators such as birds.
The soldier uses its sting to fight off enemies and to overcome victims.

Violin Beetle

By night this giant beetle glides noiselessly along the ground, sneaking up on its prey like a ghost.

The violin beetle is the largest ground beetle in the world. Adults can grow up to 10cm long – that's as long as 10 bombardier beetles!

SIZING UP

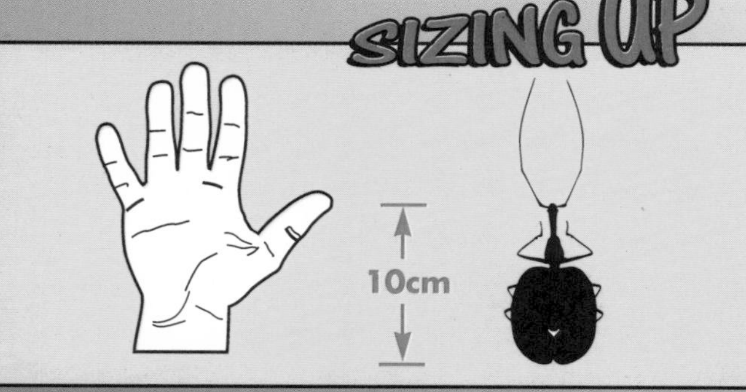

- **SCIENTIFIC NAME:** *Mormolyce phyllodes*
- **SIZE:** up to 10cm long
- **LIVES:** South-East Asia
- **EATS:** caterpillars, snails and other bugs, including small beetles

HOMES IN THE TREES

As larvae, violin beetles crawl slowly along the ground. But when they grow to their full size they climb up trees and make their homes in the gaps in the bark. Even though they are so large, violin beetles have a very flat shape so they can easily wriggle under bark.

MIDNIGHT FEAST

The violin beetle crawls out of its hiding place as soon as it's dark and scuttles off in search of prey. It eats caterpillars, snails and, sometimes, other beetles. By night it's hard to see this animal. This is because it's almost see-through and scuttles about very quickly.

IN DANGER

Sadly, the violin beetle is now extremely rare because the dense rainforests of South-East Asia where it lives are being destroyed. Amazingly, in this part of the world, most trees are cut down to make chopsticks!

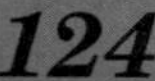

Needle-spined Sea Urchin

With its long, prickly spines, this sea urchin helps to save the lives of other sea creatures.

The needle-spined sea urchin lives close to the seashore. It is covered with long spines, which are usually dark purple, but can be white. Between these long spines, there are shorter ones.

SIZING UP

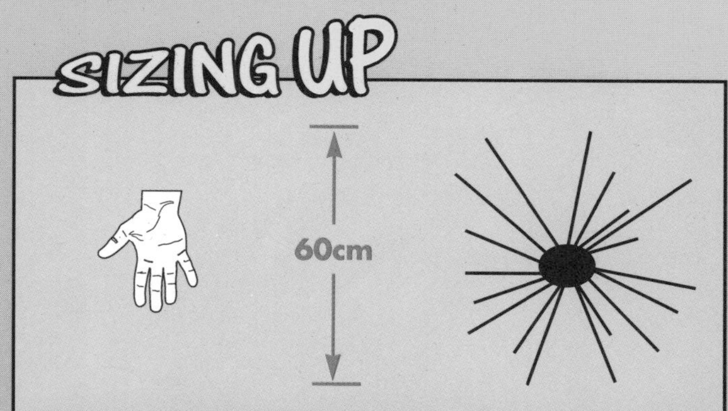

- **SCIENTIFIC NAME:** *Diadema setosum*
- **SIZE:** body 10cm wide, spines span 60cm
- **LIVES:** in coastal areas in the Indian and Pacific Oceans
- **EATS:** algae

WALKING ABOUT

The urchin can move its spines – and even point them in different directions. Balancing on these moving spines, it slowly 'walks' about.

GIVING SHELTER

The urchin's spines provide shelter for other sea creatures, such as tiny fish and shrimps. These little animals dive in among the spines, where predators cannot reach them.

PAINFUL WOUND

Although they are probably not poisonous, the urchin's spines are very sharp and break easily. If you got one in your hand, it would be very difficult to get it out, and it would cause a painful wound.

SCRAPING UP FOOD

The urchin's mouth is under its body. It eats algae – a kind of seaweed – which it scrapes off coral with its sharp jaws.

Spinning

Spiders' webs are beautiful works of art, but they are also deadly traps.

The orb-web is probably the most dangerous of all types of web. Flying insects can't see the silky trip wires until it's too late. They are called orb-webs because of their round shape.

ROUTINE WORK

Female spiders are the homemakers – only they, and spiderlings (young spiders), know how to spin webs. The female spiny-bellied orb weaver spider (or kite spider) is an expert at spinning the deadly orb-web. She doesn't hang about – she normally finishes her housework in just one hour.

HOUSE BOUND

Once the exhausted spider has built its web, it can relax. It sits right in the centre and waits patiently, day and night, for prey to get trapped in its web. Then it pounces.

WHAT SPIDER'S WEB?

The orb-web is hard to see unless it is covered in frost, or the spider is in it. The silk used to make an orb-web is almost invisible but it is very strong and elastic. Spiders are not very welcoming. Visitors to their beautiful homes are likely to be eaten!

WASTE NOT, WANT NOT

Spiders that spin orb-webs build a new one every night. Some old lines are used again. The spider usually winds up damaged threads and eats them.

Is it true... that a spider never gets trapped in its own web?

Yes, a spider uses several tricks to avoid getting stuck in its own web. As it builds its web, the spider makes sure that some parts of the web are not sticky. The spider knows where these 'dry' areas are and it uses them as it dashes across its web to grab its prey. Web-builders have special feet with an extra claw and little hairs, to help them cling on to the silk threads. They also have an oily coating on their legs, which stops them getting tangled up.

The more this greenbottle struggles, the more entangled it becomes in the spiny-bellied orb weaver spider's web. Its legs are stuck

a trap

GOOD VIBRATIONS

The spider knows it has finally managed to trap some food in its web when the web's silky threads start to vibrate as its victim lands on them. The spider relies on these tiny vibrations to tell it the size and the position of its prey. The spider cannot rely on its eyesight as it is very short-sighted.

The spider makes the silk for its web inside its body. It forces the liquid silk out through nozzles on its underbelly, called spinnerets. These are surrounded by smooth, hard skin, which stops the silk sticking to the spider.

How spiders make orb-webs

It takes the spiny-bellied orb weaver spider just one hour to build her web. Once she has finished, the orb-web works twenty-four hours a day to ensnare both daytime and nighttime flying bugs. Follow the steps to see how she makes her death trap.

A web-weaver doesn't hang around in the web to eat her meal. She wraps the insect like a parcel in a wide ribbon of silk and carries it to a quiet spot. After making sure that her supper is safe, she scuttles back to her web to repair it. Now she can enjoy her meal in peace.

Victim wrapped in silk.

Wide ribbon of silk.

Small Talk

- Adult male spiders are usually much smaller than the females. They do not build webs to catch food. Instead, they are always out looking for females to mate with.
- Both male and female spiderlings, or baby spiders, can produce perfect webs shortly after hatching from the egg sac.

The most important part of a web is the first line. From point **a** the spider drops a silk thread into the air. This is carried by air currents until it catches on a leaf or branch, **b**. The spider pulls it tight, anchors it at **a** and crawls along to point **b**, spinning behind her a second, stronger line.

The spider crawls back along the first line, dropping a loose loop of silk as she goes. She secures the loop at **a**. Moving to the centre of the loop, **c**, she drops a line below it. Clinging to the end of this line, the spider drops down onto a hard surface, **d**. Then she pulls the silk and anchors it. She has now made a 'Y'-shaped fork. The middle of the 'Y' forms the web centre.

The spider continues spinning threads, laying them like spokes of a bicycle wheel across the first 'Y'. As she works, she feels for gaps that need filling. There are usually about 50 spokes.

The spider moves to the middle of the web and spins circles around its centre, **e**. Leaving a small gap, she works away from the middle, spinning larger spirals, **f**, until she reaches the edge of her web. Then she goes back the way she came, making the web stronger and sticky. She keeps the centre of the web 'unsticky' so she can sit in it without getting stuck.

Make a nature

Given a little encouragement, your garden can be home to many creatures.

Every garden attracts hundreds of different minibeasts, even if you don't want it to. But there are many things that you can do that will actually encourage them to come and make their home with you. All you have to do is to create the right habitats, or places for them to live. If you don't have a garden, you can plant flowers to encourage bugs in a window box. Here's how to invite bugs to stay.

Compost

Compost is made up of decaying dead plants. It contains tiny bugs, which break down the plants and attract larger bugs that eat them.

You will need:

- bag or bin
- vegetable peelings
- house bricks
- sticks, such as privet hedge clippings

WHAT TO DO

1 The first place to start when making compost is in the kitchen. Get a bag or bin and collect vegetable peelings, old apple cores or any bits of plant material that would normally be thrown away. Take all this waste outside to a corner of the garden.

2 Choose a corner of the garden that is unlikely to be disturbed. Arrange the bricks in lines, close together. Do this until you have covered an area about 1m square.

3 Then lay sticks on top of the bricks. Privet hedge clippings are really good for this. This makes a platform that allows air to move up through the compost so that the bugs can breathe.

4 Now pile your kitchen waste on top of the base. You have now made a compost heap – a brilliant home for a community of bugs. You can try adding garden waste, but avoid too many grass clippings, which can turn your compost heap from a minibeast city full of worms, beetles and springtails into a slimy mess.

Log pile

Log piles made from thick branches and bits of wood give shelter to many bugs, such as spiders and beetles, which live in rotting wood. Some, such as woodlice, even eat it.

You will need: • thick branches and bits of wood

WHAT TO DO

1 Simply leave bits of dead trees in a small heap on the ground. Choose a good spot, such as in the corner of a garden, where they won't be kicked over. Avoid wood that has been treated with paint or preservative.

2 If you are lucky, you will quickly see different colours of fungus growing. Then wood-eating bugs will move in, and bug-eating bugs, such as wasps and spiders, will soon follow.

Rocky home

WHAT TO DO

Many minibeasts – like worms, beetles, spiders, centipedes, and many types of larvae – like dark, moist places. Most of all, they love to lurk under stones.

You will need:

- stones
- plants to attract bugs (optional)

1 Collect some stones and spread them around on the ground in a corner of the garden. Any stones will do.

2 You can use plants to attract minibeasts. If you have a big garden, plant a buddleia. These large bushes attract butterflies. Michaelmas daisies and iceplants are also good for butterflies and provide them with food late in the year before they start to hibernate. Nettles are excellent plants for caterpillars to grow up on.
Insects love colourful, smelly plants. Honesty and sorrel are both jolly plants and honeysuckle smells gorgeous – especially to a moth. Sunflowers, which are bright yellow in colour, attract hoverflies and bees.

Why encourage bugs?

Bugs should be encouraged because they perform many useful jobs.

Bees carry pollen from one flower to another, which – in turn – encourages the plant to develop seeds, from which new plants grow. This is called pollination.
Beetles hunt down caterpillars which eat and destroy plants in the garden.

Butterflies help pollinate flowers.
Centipedes eat other bugs, so keeping their numbers down.

Hoverflies are good because their larvae eat bugs like greenfly, which destroy plants.
Moths attract bigger animals that want to eat them, such as birds and bats, into your nature reserve.

Spiders eat flies and stop them getting out of control.
Springtails help break down dead plants and animals.
Wasps keep down numbers of caterpillars and other bugs.

Woodlice break down old pieces of wood.
Worms help air get into the soil and help break down leaves when they fall in autumn.

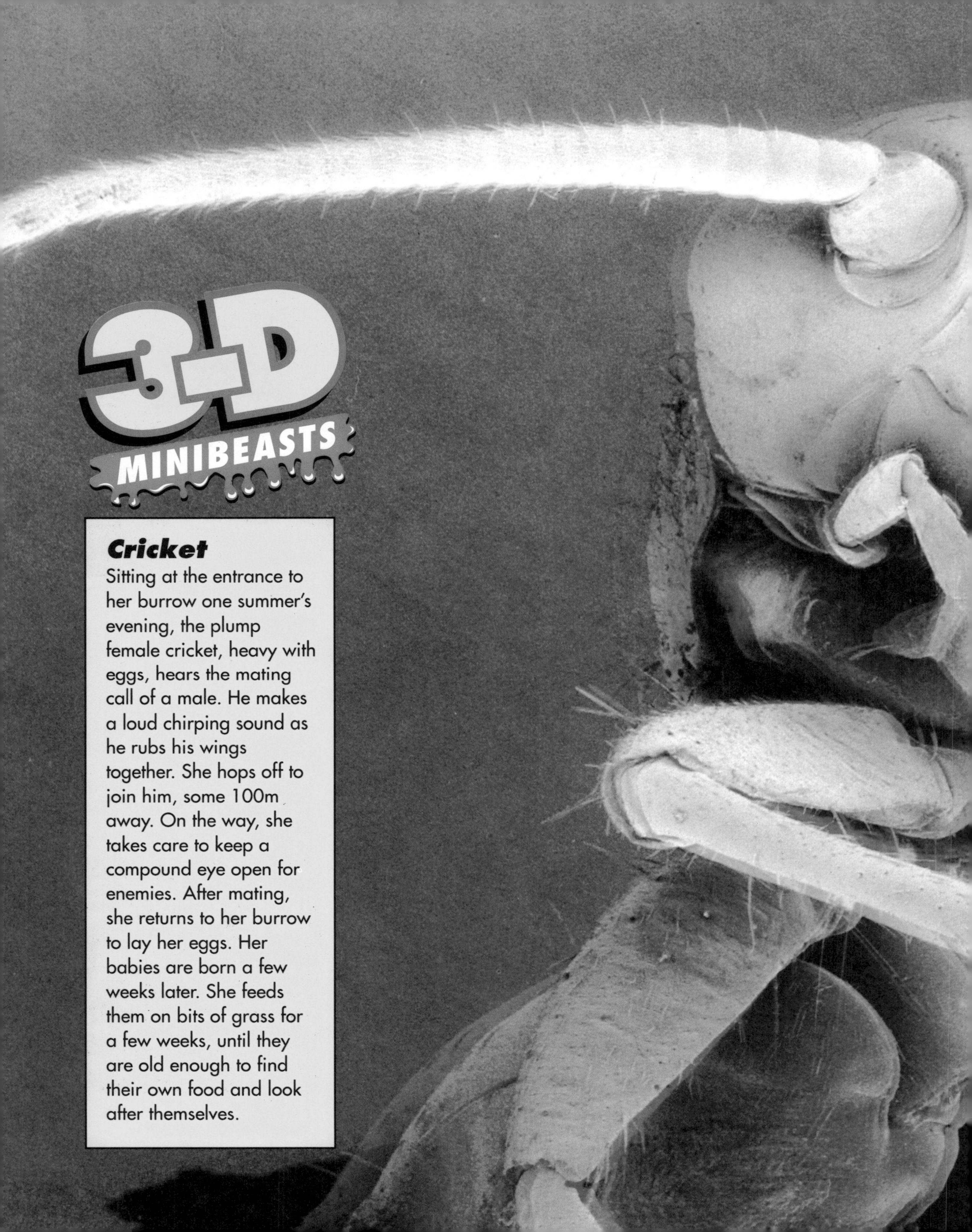

3-D MINIBEASTS

Cricket

Sitting at the entrance to her burrow one summer's evening, the plump female cricket, heavy with eggs, hears the mating call of a male. He makes a loud chirping sound as he rubs his wings together. She hops off to join him, some 100m away. On the way, she takes care to keep a compound eye open for enemies. After mating, she returns to her burrow to lay her eggs. Her babies are born a few weeks later. She feeds them on bits of grass for a few weeks, until they are old enough to find their own food and look after themselves.

Take off!

Long before birds or bats existed, insects developed wings and took to the air.

Like most adult insects, the harlequin beetle (left) can fly. Even this huge bug, with its 4.5cm long body, can take to the air.

Flying bugs first grew wings to escape from danger and to fly off to look for food. Later on in the history of bug development, insects began to use their wings to attract mates.

GLIDING ON A WING

The earliest winged insects probably did not flap their wings. They glided through the air, rather like modern flying squirrels, which glide from tree to tree using the flaps of skin on either side of their bodies.

LEARNING TO FLAP

Early gliding creatures may simply have had wings that stuck out from the sides of their bodies, but did not move. Later on, they became able to use these 'wings' for greater control and then to flap them.

What is... an insect's wing made of?

Insects' wings are made of a tough substance called chitin. It is so strong that long after insects have died and rotted, their wings often remain behind. Wings are stiffened by a network of veins. Air tubes, nerves and blood are carried through these veins. Experts use these patterns of veins to identify insects. Each species has a slightly different pattern.

Tiny pin-like halteres, or balancers, help very small flying insects, like this robber fly, to balance in gusty winds.

WINGS IN ROCK

Insects flew through the air 300 million years ago. Fossils of these early bugs prove that some of the early insects were monsters – *Meganeura* was a massive dragonfly with a wingspan of about 75cm.

ONE PAIR, OR TWO?

Dragonflies have two pairs of wings, which are almost exactly the same size. Most flying insects also have two pairs of wings, but they are different sizes. Some bugs, such as flies, only have one pair of wings. Some experts think that these insects are the best fliers.

Damselflies' wings are not joined together. This allows them to fly forwards, backwards and sideways.

AIR TRAFFIC CONTROL

Flies only have one pair of wings, but they also have special rods where their second pair of wings would be. These thin rods have a knob on the end and are called halteres. They help the insect to balance while it's flying and to sense objects around it. Without these rods, flies would be unable to stay upright in the air and would crash.

ZIP UP YOUR WINGS

Some insects have improved their flying by 'zipping' their front wings to their back wings. They have a row of hooks along the front of their back wings. After millions of years, these have locked on to the front wings and the two pairs of wings beat as one pair. Butterflies and many moths have two pairs of wings that overlap so that they also beat as one pair.

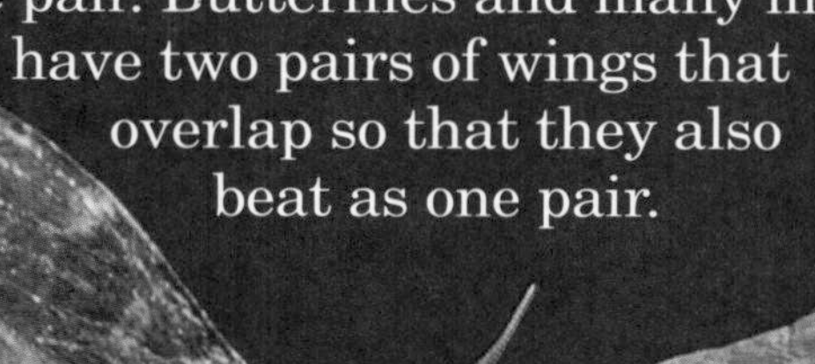

Compared with other insects, most moths beat their wings very slowly (only 4 – 12 times per second). Their two pairs of wings overlap to improve the moths' flight.

With such light and delicate looking wings, how do insects manage to take off and stay in the air?

Modern humans have been around for about 30,000 years, but it is only in the 20th century that we have learned to build aeroplanes and fly. Insects have been flying for about 345 million years. No wonder they're so good at it.

WARM-UP

Just as an Olympic swimmer stretches and warms up before he or she dives in, many flying bugs give the muscles in their wings a good flap before they actually take off. These pre-flight warm-ups are necessary because an insect's wings need to be several degrees warmer than its body before they are ready for take off.

TESTING THE AIR

Some insects check the weather conditions before taking off. The green-bottle fly tests the speed of the wind with its antennae before moving. If the wind speed is more than 9km/h, it stays put.

Beetles, like this ladybird (left), have two pairs of wings. The front pair are curved and tough. They protect the soft hind wings, which do all the hard work when the beetle flies.

HOW WINGS WORK

One set of muscles runs from the top of the thorax to the bottom and is attached to the wings. The other set runs lengthways along the insect's thorax.

1

Muscles inside the insect's body, close to the wings, pull down the top wall of the thorax. This makes the wings go up.

2

Another set of muscles, which runs from the front of the insect's body to the back, becomes thicker. The top of the insect's body springs back into shape and the wings go down.

1

2

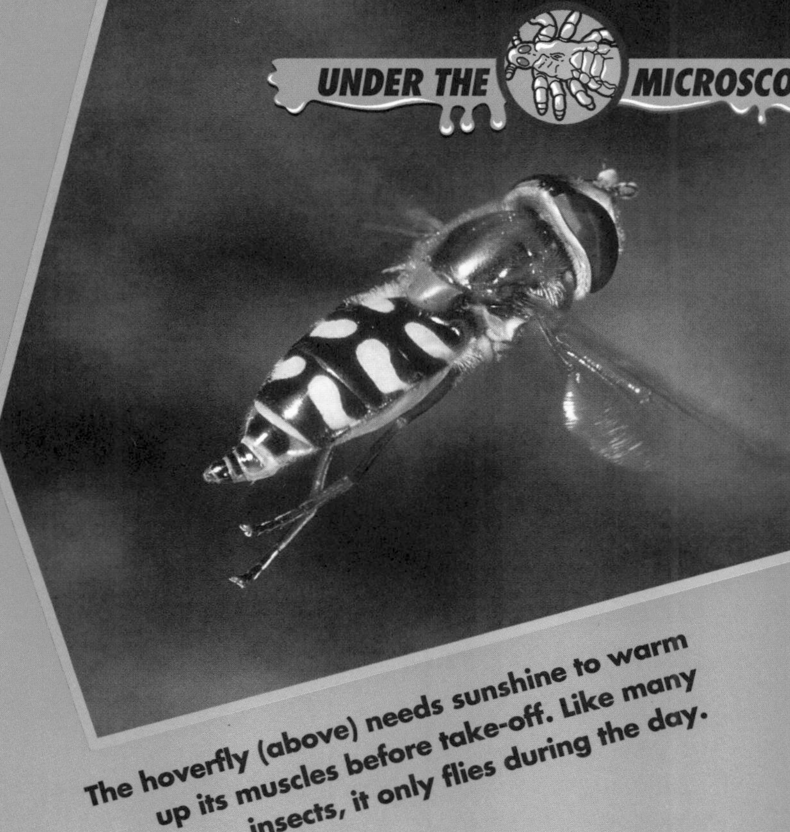

The hoverfly (above) needs sunshine to warm up its muscles before take-off. Like many insects, it only flies during the day.

WIMPS ON THE WING

Unlike the wings of bats and birds, insects' wings do not contain muscles. Instead, they are usually powered by muscles inside the creature's thorax. Insects' thoraxes are made of a very elastic substance, called resilin. If you could make a ball out of this substance, it would carry on bouncing for much longer than a rubber ball. There are two sets of muscles inside the bug's thorax, which do all the work.

FLAP-O-METER

Insect	Number of beats in 1 second
Midge	up to 1,750
Mosquito	up to 600
Fruit-fly	250
Housefly	200
Bees	190 – 200
Large moths	50 – 70
Dragonfly	20 – 30
Locust	18 – 20
Butterfly	4 –12

ALL IN A FLAP

Midges can flap their wings over 1,000 times in one second. Most butterflies, however, only manage 4 – 12 beats per second. As a rule, a very small insect beats its wings faster than a larger bug, such as a moth.

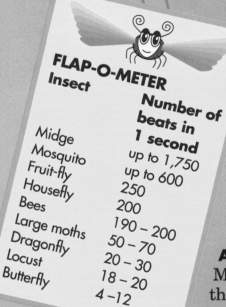

NO WING SITUATION

Although most insects have wings, many don't. Some, such as springtails, which are very simple bugs that leap through the air, never developed them. Others don't need wings because they spend all their lives on the ground. Over millions of years, these land-bound bugs have lost the power of flight. Fleas and lice, which live off other animals' blood, stay in one place once they have found a good spot to feed. Some bugs, such as the red-legged weevil, live under the ground, so they don't need to be able to fly.

Is it true... that some insects have to 'row' through the air?

Some insects, such as fairy wasps (0.2mm long), are so small that the air around them seems very thick. If you wade across the shallow end of a swimming pool you have to push your body through the water. To the fairy fly wasp, the air is as thick as water is to us. This tiny member of the wasp family has wings shaped like oars to pull itself through the air.

IN THE DESERT

If you suddenly found yourself in the middle of a desert, you probably wouldn't see many signs of life. But lift up a rock, kick up some sand, and you might be in for some nasty surprises!

The desert can get as hot as an oven during the day and freezing cold at night. Most bugs would be dead within minutes at these temperatures. Sometimes it doesn't rain for years and there aren't many juicy plants to eat. Only the toughest and meanest bugs can survive in the desert.

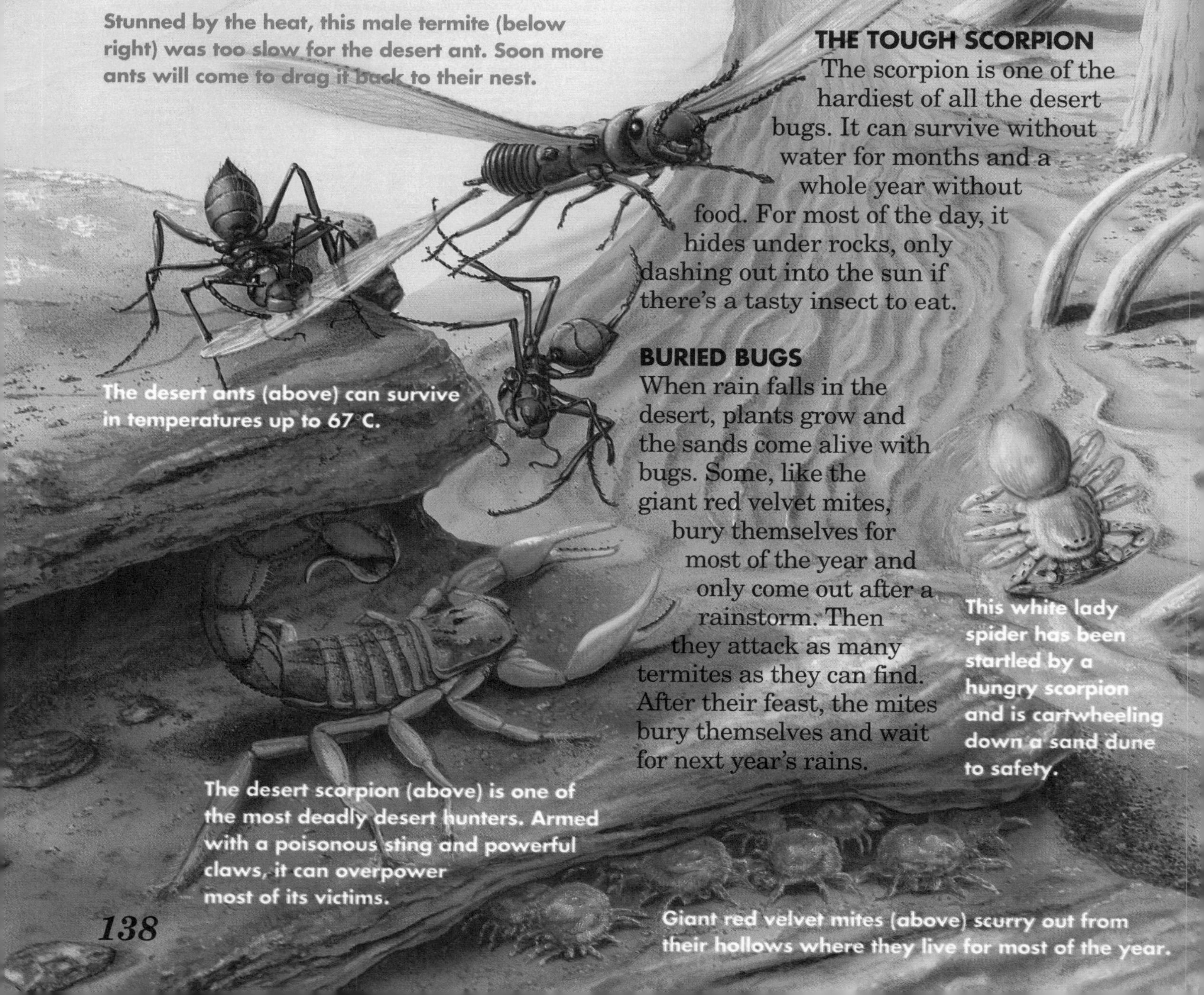

Stunned by the heat, this male termite (below right) was too slow for the desert ant. Soon more ants will come to drag it back to their nest.

THE TOUGH SCORPION

The scorpion is one of the hardiest of all the desert bugs. It can survive without water for months and a whole year without food. For most of the day, it hides under rocks, only dashing out into the sun if there's a tasty insect to eat.

The desert ants (above) can survive in temperatures up to 67°C.

BURIED BUGS

When rain falls in the desert, plants grow and the sands come alive with bugs. Some, like the giant red velvet mites, bury themselves for most of the year and only come out after a rainstorm. Then they attack as many termites as they can find. After their feast, the mites bury themselves and wait for next year's rains.

This white lady spider has been startled by a hungry scorpion and is cartwheeling down a sand dune to safety.

The desert scorpion (above) is one of the most deadly desert hunters. Armed with a poisonous sting and powerful claws, it can overpower most of its victims.

Giant red velvet mites (above) scurry out from their hollows where they live for most of the year.

COPING WITH THE SUN

Bugs that build nests in the desert need to make sure that their eggs and young do not get too hot. Compass termites build thin, wedge-shaped nests. When the sun is at its hottest, it is exactly overhead and only shines on the thin ridge that runs along the top of the nest. The main part of the nest stays at a bearable temperature. Desert ants, on the other hand, avoid the sun by building their nests 20 – 40cm under the ground. The temperature inside the nest stays exactly the same day and night.

Termites avoid the blazing midday sun by building clever nests (left), which can be 3.5m high.

The giant centipede (below) can be found in most deserts. They survive by hunting around for creatures, such as lizards, in the sand and can grow to 28cm in length.

ITCHING A RIDE

The camel bot fly survives by hitching a ride on a camel. The adult bot flies lay eggs on the camel's skin. These hatch into maggots, which burrow into its flesh and begin eating their way towards the camel's nostrils, where the larvae grow. When they are ready to turn into adult flies, they irritate the camel's nostrils, making it sneeze them out.

THE EIGHT-LEGGED CARTWHEEL

Many desert bugs have clever ways of moving across the dunes. Some crickets have large feet with widely spaced toes. These stop them sinking into the sand. Others have long legs that keep the burning sand away from their bodies. If threatened, the white lady spider cartwheels away at top speed.

FOOD FOR BABY

It's always a problem finding food in the desert. The tarantula-hawk wasp lays its egg on the body of a paralysed spider and buries it in a burrow. When the egg hatches, the young have a meal waiting for them.

The desert snail (above) survives the scorching heat by sealing itself inside its tough shell for long periods. Some will even stay like this in their shells for over four years.

This tarantula-hawk wasp (above) drags a paralysed tarantula into a hole and lays its egg on the spider's body.

Nightfall is the time when most desert bugs crawl out from their lairs and go looking for food. Scorpions and spiders creep over the desert sands and flying insects fill the skies.

Desert bugs love the night. It is a time for hunting and scavenging. Some desert bugs have even developed special night-hunting skills.

LAST ONE HOME GETS EATEN!

As night falls, desert ants rush back to their underground nest to escape being eaten by bigger bugs. But the last ant home has a raw deal. Its job is to hide the front door of the nest with sand so that it won't be found by nest raiders. Once the nest is hidden, the ant must fend for itself alone in the dark desert.

INTO THE LION'S PIT

Some insects in the desert build traps for others to fall into. The ant lion larva buries itself at the bottom of a pit and waits with its jaws open for an insect to fall in. When it grows up it takes to the air and goes hunting for small flying bugs at night.

An ant lion (below right) has dug its pit and is ready for business. A desert ant (below left), is about to stumble into the trap. Lives: Africa.

WHERE DEW GET A DRINK?

Sometimes it doesn't rain in the desert for years. So some desert insects have developed very clever ways of getting a drink. The Namib desert beetle waits until morning and then raises its back into the air. As the morning dew forms, little drops of water collect on the beetle's back and trickle down to its open mouth.

An adult ant lion (left) sets off to find a mate. Lives: Africa.

These Namib desert beetles (below left) are having a drink of water. The morning dew settles on their raised backs and trickles into their mouths. Lives: Namib desert, Africa.

HAIRY LEGS

At night the scorpion crawls out from its hiding place and goes hunting. It has four pairs of eyes but doesn't see well. Instead it uses special hairs on its legs to feel in the dark. These hairs can sense the tiny movements of other bugs. They can even tell the scorpion where its victim is, and in which direction it is moving.

FASTEST BUG ON EIGHT LEGS

The windscorpion is a relative of the spider and can grow to 10cm in length. It is a terrifying hunter and the fastest-moving land bug. Its jaws are huge; it has the largest jaws compared with its body size of any animal. This fast-moving bug has a huge appetite. It eats until it is so big that it can hardly move.

A speedy windscorpion (below left) opens its jaws and pounces on a desert cricket (below). Lives: Africa and Asia.

Improve and test your knowledge with...

CREEPY~CRAWLY FACTS

Don't get gunged by the exploding ant or bogged down by the minibeast quiz.

Bugged bugs

Much of what we know about the habits of big mammals has been learned by tracking the animals in the wild. This is often done with radio transmitters that are attached to the animal with a collar. Today, transmitters can be made so small that they are being used to track the incredibly rare giant weta cricket from New Zealand. The tiny transmitters are attached to the back of the cricket with a blob of sticky putty.

Up, up and away

A worm called a fluke spends the first part of its life in an ant and the second half in a bird. It has a clever way of getting from one animal to the other. While the worm is living in the ant, it takes over the ant's brain and forces the ant to climb up to the top of a blade of grass. Here it can easily be seen by a passing bird, which will swoop down for an ant snack and will itself become infected with the worm.

Vacancies

Some bugs have very close relationships with plants. The thorn ant lives inside the hollow thorns of the acacia tree. Not only does it have a ready-made home, but also a constant supply of nectar from the tree. The acacia also produces buds at the tips of new leaves, for the young ants to eat. In return, the thorn ant keeps the tree free of plant-eating bugs and makes sure that no other plants grow too near the tree.

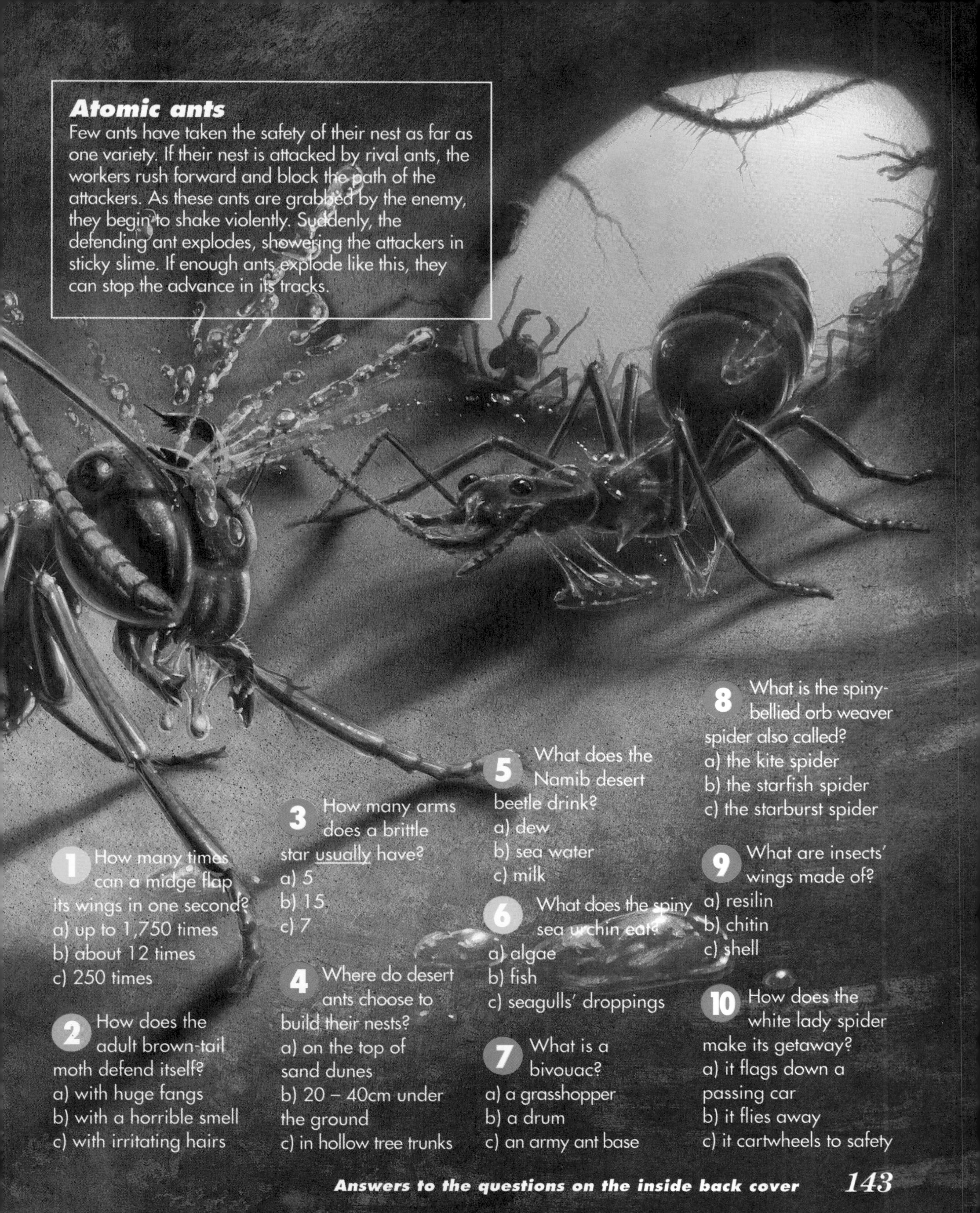

Atomic ants

Few ants have taken the safety of their nest as far as one variety. If their nest is attacked by rival ants, the workers rush forward and block the path of the attackers. As these ants are grabbed by the enemy, they begin to shake violently. Suddenly, the defending ant explodes, showering the attackers in sticky slime. If enough ants explode like this, they can stop the advance in its tracks.

1 How many times can a midge flap its wings in one second?
a) up to 1,750 times
b) about 12 times
c) 250 times

2 How does the adult brown-tail moth defend itself?
a) with huge fangs
b) with a horrible smell
c) with irritating hairs

3 How many arms does a brittle star usually have?
a) 5
b) 15
c) 7

4 Where do desert ants choose to build their nests?
a) on the top of sand dunes
b) 20 – 40cm under the ground
c) in hollow tree trunks

5 What does the Namib desert beetle drink?
a) dew
b) sea water
c) milk

6 What does the spiny sea urchin eat?
a) algae
b) fish
c) seagulls' droppings

7 What is a bivouac?
a) a grasshopper
b) a drum
c) an army ant base

8 What is the spiny-bellied orb weaver spider also called?
a) the kite spider
b) the starfish spider
c) the starburst spider

9 What are insects' wings made of?
a) resilin
b) chitin
c) shell

10 How does the white lady spider make its getaway?
a) it flags down a passing car
b) it flies away
c) it cartwheels to safety

Answers to the questions on the inside back cover

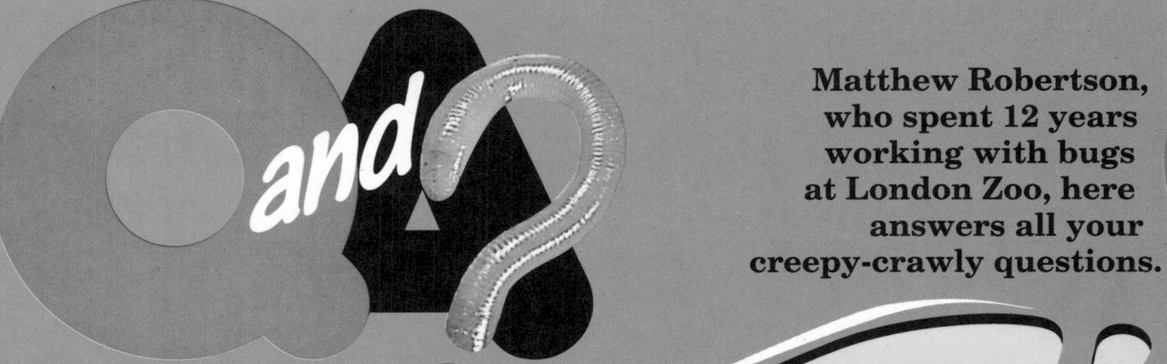

Matthew Robertson, who spent 12 years working with bugs at London Zoo, here answers all your creepy-crawly questions.

Why are people scared of spiders?

No one really knows. Some people think that our fear is handed down from our ancestors. They believe that when early humans lived in caves in hot countries, they learned to hate spiders because they knew that a few of them were dangerous. Their hatred has been passed down from parents to children over hundreds of thousands of years. Although most spiders are completely harmless to humans, many people still hate them.

Do bugs get ill?

Like most other animals, bugs can become ill. Scientists have worked out how to make some bugs unwell. They are particularly interested in the pests that eat crops. Once scientists have discovered germs that will make pest bugs ill, they breed them in huge numbers. Then they spray the crops and bugs with germs. Soon all the bugs die. This method is very effective because the illness usually only attacks the destructive bugs and leaves helpful animals alone.

Are slugs really snails that have lost their shells?

In a way they are. Over millions of years, some snails turned into slugs. They did this because of where they lived. Snails need to live in areas with chalky soil. The chalk keeps their shells in good condition. If they live in an area with acid soil, their shells eventually dissolve. Millions of years ago, snails that lived in acid areas began to lose their shells because they could not look after them. Today you will tend to find snails in chalky areas, while slugs can live in areas with acid soil.

Ladybird

During its lifetime, a single ladybird can gobble up as many as 8,000 greenflies.

The ladybird is a kind of beetle. It is usually red, yellow or black, with spots or stripes in one of these colours. The number of spots varies a lot. One ladybird may have only a single spot, while another may have over 10. Some ladybirds are all one colour – they have neither spots nor stripes.

KEEP-OFF SIGNS

The ladybird's bright colours and bold markings are Nature's ways of warning predators to stay away. The ladybird is definitely not good to eat – not only does it smell nasty, but it tastes horrible, too! If a predator attacks, the ladybird may ooze a sticky liquid, which gums up the mouth and antennae of the predator. When they are in danger, some ladybirds tuck their legs and antennae under their shells.

BIG APPETITE

The ladybird is always hungry! Its favourite food is aphids, especially greenflies. These tiny, green insects gather in great colonies to feed on plants, sucking out their sap and slowly killing them. When the ladybird strikes, there is no escape for the defenceless greenflies, and huge numbers of them are gobbled up.

The female ladybird does not stay to look after her young. After laying her eggs she flies off.

BABY FOOD

The female ladybird lays her tiny, yellowy-orange eggs in batches of about 100 – 200. She lays them on the undersides of leaves or in slits in the stems of plants, near places where there are plenty of greenflies. As she lays the eggs, the ladybird produces a glue, which sticks the eggs to the plant. When the eggs hatch, five to eight days later, the hungry young are surrounded by food. The newly hatched ladybirds tuck straight into their ready-made meals.

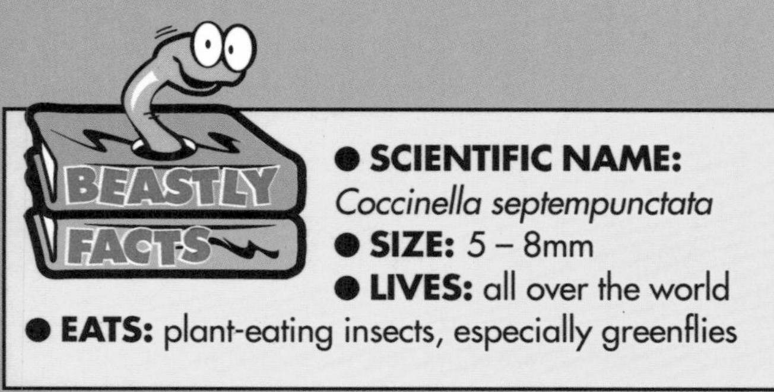

- **SCIENTIFIC NAME:** *Coccinella septempunctata*
- **SIZE:** 5 – 8mm
- **LIVES:** all over the world
- **EATS:** plant-eating insects, especially greenflies

LUCKY LADIES

Some people believe that ladybirds have special powers. In southern France, for example, if a ladybird settles on a young man, it is supposed to be a sign that he will get married. Another belief says that if a girl wants to know when she will marry, she must place a ladybird on her index finger and count. The number she has reached when the ladybird flies away will be how many years need to pass until she marries.

GARDENER'S MATE

Because it eats so many greenflies and other plant pests, the ladybird can be a big help to people who grow plants, such as gardeners, farmers and foresters. Greenflies can destroy huge numbers of plants and trees. Using ladybirds to eat greenflies is much safer for the Earth than using poisonous chemicals to kill them.

FLYING AWAY

Like most other beetles, the ladybird can fly. Its wings are tucked away under the hard 'wing cases' that cover its back. The wing cases lift up when it wants to fly. If the food supply is low in one area, or the weather gets bad, the ladybird will fly long distances to find a better place.

GATHERING TOGETHER

In the summer, the ladybird lives and hunts alone. But as winter approaches, it gathers together with other ladybirds to take shelter from the cold. Hundreds of them, from different species, may collect under bark or in people's homes – in the cracks in walls, or even in hidden places on balconies! They stay there all winter, until spring arrives.

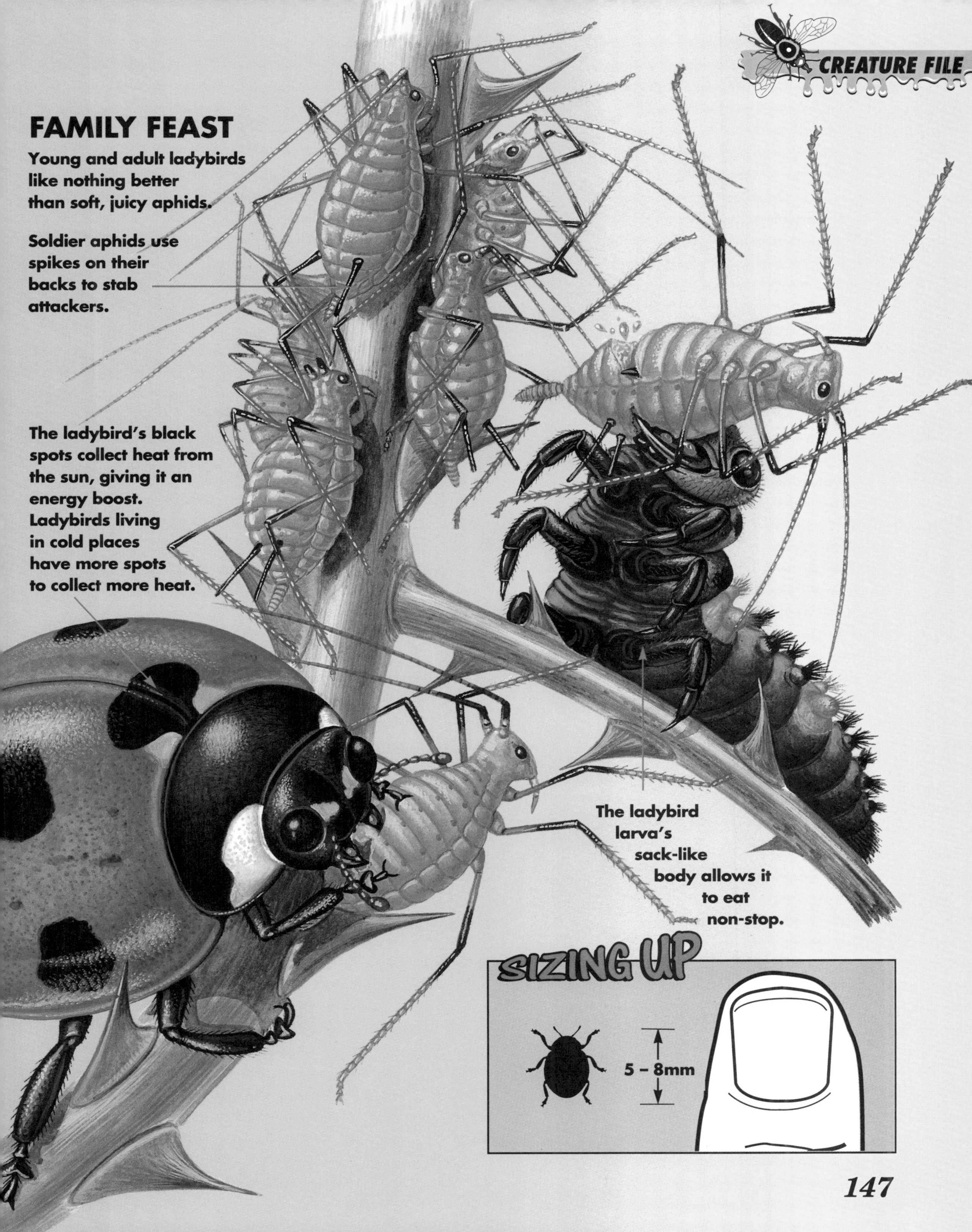

FAMILY FEAST
Young and adult ladybirds like nothing better than soft, juicy aphids.
Soldier aphids use spikes on their backs to stab attackers.
The ladybird's black spots collect heat from the sun, giving it an energy boost. Ladybirds living in cold places have more spots to collect more heat.
The ladybird larva's sack-like body allows it to eat non-stop.
SIZING UP
5 – 8mm

Bed Bug

Bed bugs were once found in nearly every home. Luckily for us, few modern homes have them.

The bed bug likes to live in human houses, where there is plenty of shelter – and food! It lives on human blood, and that of other animals, such as mice or poultry.

NIGHT FEEDS

During the day, the bed bug rests in warm, dark hiding places, such as cracks and holes in walls, or in old carpets or furniture. At night, it creeps out into the open to feed on people while they sleep. The bed bug pierces the skin of its victim with the sharp, needle-like tube that is part of its mouth, and sucks up the blood.

HUNGRY FEMALES

To be able to lay her eggs, the female needs more blood than the male. In 10 minutes, she can suck up five times her own body weight in blood!

SURVIVOR

If food is scarce, or if the weather is really cold, the bed bug becomes 'dormant', which means it rests and stops growing. It can survive in freezing temperatures, without food, for several months.

- **SCIENTIFIC NAME:** *Cimex lectularius*
- **SIZE:** 5 – 7mm
- **LIVES:** in homes of humans and animals all over the world
- **EATS:** blood of humans and other animals

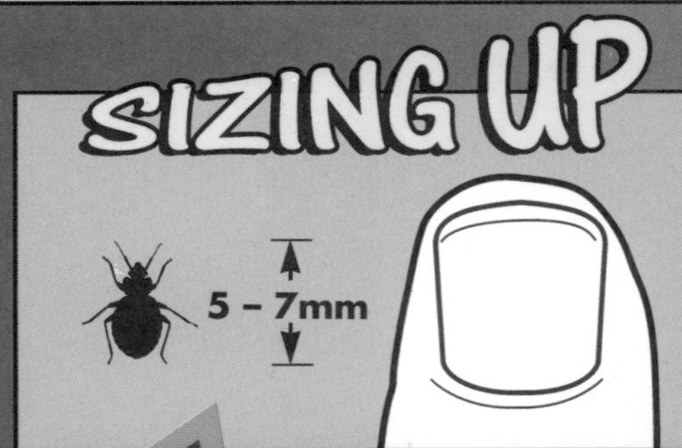

Elephant Hawk-moth

In its caterpillar stage, the elephant hawk-moth makes itself look more dangerous than it really is.

● **SCIENTIFIC NAME:** *Deilephila elpenor*
● **SIZE:** 58 – 65mm
● **LIVES:** most parts of Europe, north Africa and Asia
● **EATS:** nectar from different flowers

As soon as the sun sets, the elephant hawk-moth begins to fly about, darting from flower to flower and sucking up the nectar from inside them. It goes on eating late into the night.

SIZING UP

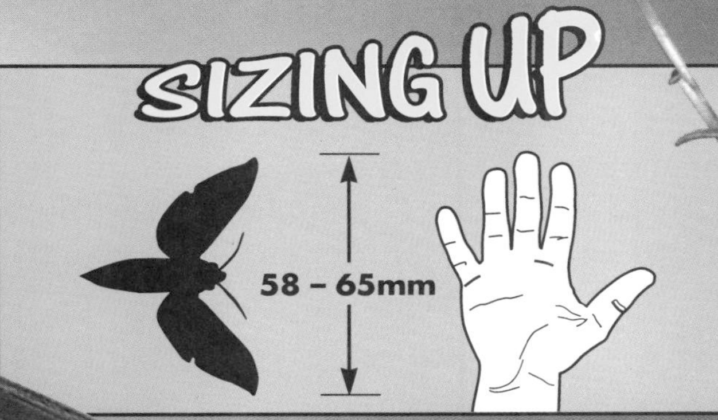

UNDER THE LEAVES

The moth lays her eggs on a plant called willowherb. She places the eggs, one at a time, on the undersides of the leaves. Caterpillars hatch from the eggs and, later, turn into moths themselves.

WARNING SIGNS

Each caterpillar has a wonderful way of keeping predators away – it fools them into thinking it is a snake! On either side of its head are two pairs of large, dark spots. When the caterpillar is threatened, it rears up and squeezes its head and body together so that they change shape and look like a snake's head. Predators get a nasty shock when the dark spots on the sides of the caterpillar's head stand out and look like black eyes.

The master builders

Some people live in flats, some live in houses, others live in igloos, or on boats. Termites live in nests, but their homes also come in different shapes and sizes.

How many people live in your home? In a termite mound there's room for about one million bugs. They work together like a team of builders, to make a nest that will keep the termites safe.

AIR-CONDITIONING

Instead of bricks, the termites use spit, earth and droppings to build the walls of their homes. Spaces inside the nest allow the air to circulate. This stops the termites getting too hot during the day, or freezing at night.

A MAZE OF ROOMS

Most nests stick up above the ground, but a lot of the action takes place underground, where there is a maze of tunnels. The queen lies in a room at the centre of the maze, where the temperature is always 30°C.

COMING OF AGE

Some mature queens can be 14cm long and live to be 21 years old. Most termites are around 4 – 5mm long, but some measure up to 2cm.

HOUSE GUESTS

Termites have to put up with a lot of lodgers. They don't mind when cockroaches come to stay because they eat the termites' rubbish. Others are unwelcome – some ants and beetles, for instance, live inside the nest and eat the termites' babies.

Winged male and female termites escape from the damaged nest.

The soldier termites try to protect the queen with their powerful jaws.

The aardvark is one of the termites' fiercest enemies. Its strong claws and long, sticky tongue make short work of the termites.

A CHANGE OF SCENE
Termites live mainly in the hot tropical zones of Africa, South-East Asia, Australia and North and South America. They can be found in cold regions, too. Some termites live in the Rocky Mountains, in Canada, at 2,000m above sea-level.

DAMAGE
Because they feed on wood, termites can cause a lot of damage. Houses, fences, sheds, roofs, foundations, telegraph poles and furniture are all termite targets. These bugs will also eat leather, cloth, rubber and will even munch on electrical cables if there is nothing better around!

Funny Houses

Here's a selection of strange termite homes.

STAYING OUT OF THE SUN
The 3.5m-tall nests of the compass termite of northern Australia look like thin tents. In the morning and evening, the sun shines on the sides. At midday, when the sun is overhead and at its fiercest, it only shines on the thin edge at the top, so the nest doesn't get too hot.

ROOFING EXPERTS
Some termites build their mounds in the shape of 1m-tall mushrooms. The broad tops are umbrellas, which protect the mounds from the sun and rain.

PROPPED UP
Termites build their mounds against the sides of trees for two reasons. First, the wood provides them with a good meal on their doorstop. Second, the tree casts some welcome shade in the hot weather. These termite nests can be more than 9m tall.

HIGH RISE
Some termites build mounds, 50 – 70cm tall, in trees. They like to eat wood and the height also keeps them safe from predators on the ground, such as an aardvark.

Small Talk

- To avoid being eaten by birds, some termites pretend to be dead! This trick might fool the birds, but not the ants which eat them instead!

Enemies on the doorstep

Termites have a lot of enemies, but none as threatening as the ant.

Hard-working termites have to put up with attacks from spiders, lizards, birds and aardvarks. But the ant is probably the termites' greatest enemy. When a gang of ants meets a colony of termites – it's war!

FOLLOW THAT SMELL

Some ants send a single worker out to look for termites. Once it has found them, it releases a scent which the other ants follow. When the rest of the ants arrive at the termite nest, they split up and invade the nest from all directions. Each ant grabs a termite and drags it to the surface, then goes back down into the nest for more. When they have each dragged about six termites to the surface, the whole ant army regroups outside. Each ant picks up as many of the struggling termites as it can carry, usually three or four, and the invading ant army marches home.

STUNNING ATTACK

Some ants send out spies to look for termites. When they return to their own nest, the spies recruit a small team of 10 – 30 helpers. They set off for the termite nest and sting the termites. Leaving their prisoners stunned, the ants return to their own nest to get an even larger group to take home the paralysed termites.

A heavily armoured driver ant.

A fierce battle rages outside a termite nest. Shiny, black driver ants have knocked a hole in the side of a termite mound.

STOP THIEF!

Thief ants build their nests close to termite mounds. They sometimes actually move in with the termites and build their nests in the walls of the termite mounds. Sneaking into the termite chambers, the ants steal the termites' eggs.

ON FULL ALERT

The soldier termites defend their nest with their large, powerful muscles and sharp jaws. Some soldier termites have big heads, which block the holes in the nest like plugs. An invader finds it very difficult to get around them. If the nest is attacked, soldiers line up outside of the nest and try to keep the invaders at bay by forming 'walls' with their bodies.

What is... the difference between a termite and an ant?

Ants and termites both live in colonies and both have a queen (which produces eggs), soldiers and workers. But ants and termites are not closely related. Ants have three clearly defined body parts, whereas termites appear to have only two. Also termites don't have compound eyes like ants – in fact they are usually blind. Queen ants only mate once, but queen termites have a mate (king) for life.

A termite worker carries on with its work and tries to rebuild the damaged nest.

The soldier termite's pincer-like jaws are designed for slicing off ants' heads.

A headless driver ant.

CHOPPED IN HALF

Some soldier termites have lethal jaws as sharp as razors. They snap shut around the ants' bodies, chopping them in half. Other soldiers are so keen to defend their nests that they kill themselves in an attack. As they attack, their mouths produce a sticky, yellow liquid, which entangles the victim. Sometimes the termites explode, like walking bombs, spraying the yellow gunge in all directions.

GLUE GUNS

Another type of soldier termite has developed its own weapon – a glue gun. It squirts out a thick, sticky liquid from a nozzle in its head. At the same time, it sprays another liquid that signals to other termites that the nest is under attack.

THE WEB GAME

KEY

You feel a tug on the web. It feels like a small fly. You quickly follow the vibrations until you reach the fly. Yummy!
GO FORWARD ONE PLACE

A cat has killed a mouse. The mouse's body attracts flying insects, which you can catch and eat.
GO FORWARD THREE PLACES

Is it a bird? Yes! Too late. You've just become lunch for one of the spider's biggest enemies.
GO BACK TO THE START

Heavy rain has damaged your web and you will have to stop to repair it.
MISS A GO

Food, glorious food. This dustbin is covered in flies, which might fly into your web.
GO FORWARD TWO PLACES

A strong wind has picked up. Bugs aren't flying and it is too dangerous for you to move.
MISS A GO

That was clumsy! You've broken your web. Stop to fix it.
MISS A GO

Your web is covered in frost and is totally useless.
MISS A GO

Oh no! You've caught an angry wasp. Watch out for its sting. Throw the dice to see how lucky you are. If you get a 1 or 2 – you manage to wrap the wasp in silk without getting stung.
STAY WHERE YOU ARE
If, on the other hand, you throw a 3, 4, 5 or 6 – the wasp stabs you with its sting and you both die slowly in the web.
GO BACK TO THE START

Phew! It's a lovely hot day and the insects are warm and are flying around. You'll eat well today!
GO FORWARD TWO PLACES

You've been shut in a matchbox by a bug fan. Throw the dice again. If you throw a 4, 5 or 6 – the person only wants a quick look at you.
TAKE YOUR NEXT GO AS USUAL
If you throw a 1, 2 or 3 – the person keeps you for a while.
MISS A GO

What's that tugging at your web? You are slightly short-sighted and can't tell what it is. Throw the dice to find out and to discover your fate! If you get a 1 or 2 – you strike out at your victim without looking. Oops! You've just eaten a male spider. You can't mate now and there will be no baby spiders next year.
GO BACK TO THE START
If you throw a 3, 4 or 5 – well done! **YOU HAVE REACHED THE CENTRE** and found yourself a mate. Next year there will be hundreds of baby spiders. Watch out flies!

Life's not easy for a spider. Play the web game and find out why.

Move around the web and try to avoid the dangers in your way. Can you get to the middle of the web, or will you come to a sticky end?

You will need:

- one or more friends to play with
- a dice
- one counter for each player

Place the counters on **START**. Take it in turns to throw the dice and see where you land. There are pictures in the centres of some circles. Look at the picture on the circle where you land and check the key (far left) to see what happens to you. Good luck!

Small Talk

MAKING COUNTERS

If you want to make your own spider counters, either draw a picture of a spider on a circular piece of card, or trace the counter (below) through a thin piece of paper. Colour in your traced picture and stick it on to a piece of circular card. If you like, you could use a coin or a small toy instead.

Cat flea

This hungry cat flea is waiting for the family cat to come in from the cold. The flea wants to suck its blood. It doesn't matter that it is only 1mm long, because it can jump about 200 times its own height. Once it has leapt into the cat's soft fur, its piercing mouth parts puncture the cat's skin and it starts to suck. The cat won't be able to shake the flea off because it is holding on tightly with its feet. When the cat goes out at night, the flea goes too. Perhaps this jumping bug will leap into the fur of another cat. By morning, this flea could be in another cat's home.

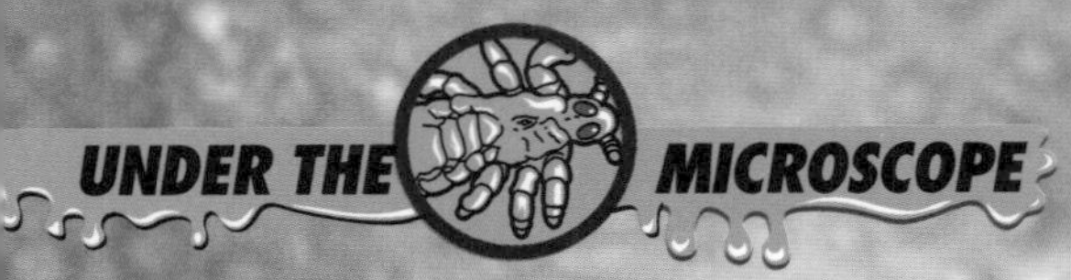

Introducing th

Armed with vicious spikes and some with deadly poisons, the spiny skins lurk in the murky depths of the sea. Their different colours and shapes turn the ocean into a vivid kaleidoscope. This group of creatures is called the echinoderms.

The word echinoderm (say 'ek-i-no-derm') means spiny skinned and that's exactly what this family of bugs is. Each family member has a skin covered in hard spines or spikes, which protects it. Any attacking predator gets a nasty mouthful of spikes. All echinoderms live in the sea.

THE STARFISH

The starfish is the most famous echinoderm. As well as having a protective spiny skin, starfish also produce poisons that can kill fish if they attack. Starfish eat animals and dead plants. In particular, they prey on snails and clams, using their suckered feet to force open their closed shells and pull out the soft-bodied animals.

If a spiny skin loses an arm, it just grows another one! This starfish has grown a very long replacement arm.

e spiny skins

STUCK ON
Unlike fish, echinoderms can't swim. They would be lost at sea if they didn't have a way of grabbing on to rocks and other solid objects. Most echinoderms have special 'feet' that anchor them in one place. These feet are really suckers that make a sticky goo, which sticks to anything it touches. Using these suckers, echinoderms can cling so tightly to a rock that only the most powerful waves can budge them.

WATER POWER
An echinoderm's suckers don't only help it stay still – they help it move around, too! When you move about you use muscles in your body. An echinoderm uses sea water, which it stores in its body. When it wants to move, it forces sea water into its suckers to make them rigid. This is how an echinoderm becomes unstuck from its rock. Then the bug uses small muscles to move it in the direction it wants to go.

MIRROR IMAGE
If you were to draw an imaginary line through the centre of an echinoderm's body, each half would look exactly the same. This is called symmetry. All echinoderms can be divided in five different ways like this.

What is... symmetry?
An object has symmetry (say 'sim-met-ree') if it can be divided up by an imaginary line so there are two identical shapes on either side of the line. Some objects and animals can be divided by more than one imaginary line to make several identical shapes. The shape on the right shows a starfish, which can be divided by five lines to make identical shapes. Each dotted line is called a line of symmetry.

1 2 3 4 5

Every colour o

Starfish are just one type of echinoderm, but the spiny skins come in a wide range of shapes and shades.

▲ FEATHER STAR

The feather star has between five and 200 thin arms, which look like feathers, round the edge of its body. These arms help it to flap food towards its mouth. The feather star doesn't move very much, but if it does want to get about it pulls itself along with its arms.

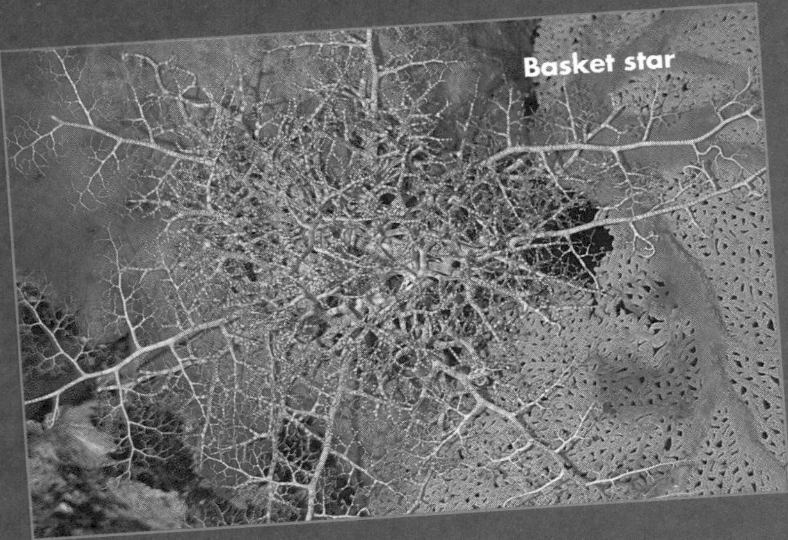

▼ SEA CUCUMBER

The sea cucumber gets its name because of its long, tube-like shape. It can make itself soft enough to squeeze through small spaces or hard enough so it can't be knocked off a rock. Many sea cucumbers can make themselves burst open at one end and spit out their insides towards an attacker, leaving the enemy to die tangled up in the sticky mess. The sea cucumber heals itself quickly after doing this.

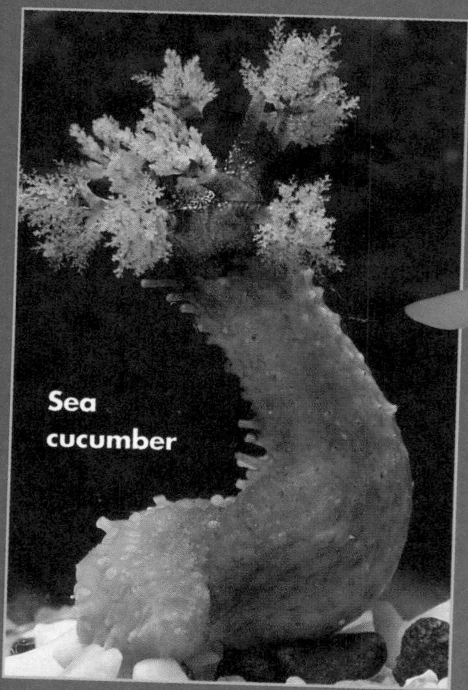

◄ BASKET STAR

Basket stars come out of their hiding places at night to eat. They feed on the tiny sea creatures that happen to float past them in the water. Basket stars can grow to over 1m across.

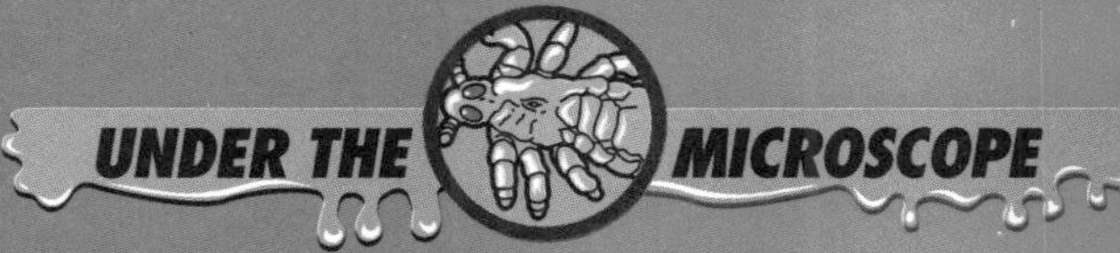

f the rainbow

Sea urchin

◀ SEA URCHIN
The sea urchin is sometimes called the sea hedgehog because of its sharp spines, which can cause a lot of pain. Each one is attached to a ball and socket joint, like the one in your shoulder, and can move round in all directions. The spines can be as thick as a pencil. Most sea urchins are about the size of a tennis ball (6 – 12cm in diameter).

Brittle star

Small Talk

• From time to time the sea cucumber cleans its feathery tentacles by putting them into its mouth one by one.
• Sea urchins might not look very tasty but a lot of people all round the world like to eat them. They eat the raw insides of the creature. So many have been eaten in Japan that they have become very rare. The Japanese now ship them in from Chile, the USA and Australia.

▲ BRITTLE STAR
The brittle star can't defend itself as well as other echinoderms. But it can move faster so can always run away! It moves by rowing itself along the sea bed with its strong arms. Sometimes it casts off a still-wriggling leg to confuse any enemy chasing after it.

PICNIC PATROL

Eight different types of bug have gate-crashed this picnic. They are all mentioned on these two pages. Can you identify them?

When you go for a picnic, you will probably attract a lot of bugs. Which bugs you meet depends on where you go. But remember, wherever you decide to have your picnic, you're invading their home.

DIFFERENT HOMES

Some bugs like to live near water, others like drier ground. Some like the shelter of trees, while others love wide, open spaces, such as fields.

CATTLE CRAZY

If you choose a field for your picnic, or lay your rug out near a farm, you will probably come across bugs that hang around livestock. The cattle horsefly eats animal blood, which it sucks up with its dagger-like, sucking mouth parts. It can be 2 – 2.5cm in length and has a nasty bite. It is probably the largest flying bug you are likely to see on your picnic. Other bugs that live near cattle have different reasons for being there.

6

STRANGE TASTES
Another bug that you might come across in a cow field is the yellow dung fly. It does not feed on the blood of cattle though. This bug feeds on smaller insects that hang around cow pats.

SHADY HOMES
If you start sipping a refreshing drink in a forest and find yourself covered in wood ants, try not to be annoyed. Wood ants build their nests in forests to protect them from the wind and rain. On a hot day, you might shelter in the shade of an oak, but you may not be alone. The caterpillar of the brown-tail moth hatches from eggs, which are covered in irritating hairs. If your skin brushes against these hairs, you may get a nasty rash. The caterpillars are often found in large numbers.

WATER LOVERS
A peaceful spot by a stream may seem like the perfect picnic site, but watch out for the black-flies! They like to stay near water and there can be thousands in one swarm. The mosquito is also a water lover. It flies away from water to feed, but always returns to lay its eggs.

HUNGRY SUCKERS
If you decide to have a nap in long grass, beware of the hard tick. Ticks drink blood, and can survive a year without eating. They are just waiting for a warm-blooded animal like you to come along.

NO ESCAPE
Some bugs, such as hornets, will always be around. In a good year, there can be up to 10,000 in a single nest. But you won't see them all at once!

Your picnic will attract bugs for several different reasons.

If you're unlucky enough to be invaded on a picnic, here's an instant guide to some of your likely attackers and why they want to join you.

HORNET ▼
Hornets, the largest European member of the wasp family, make their nests in the hollow trunks of trees. The hornet population varies quite a lot from year to year, so you might not see one, or you might be plagued with them, especially if you have sweet food with you. If one comes close, sit still and try not to scare it.

Hornets have a strong craving for sugar in late summer so watch out when eating anything sweet.

Small Talk

SWEET-TOOTHED WASPS

In early summer you are unlikely to be bothered by wasps. At this time, they are happy to feed on other insects and are busy looking after their young. In late summer, however, the young have grown up and go in search of sugar to eat. This is when they are likely to invade your picnic.

TIPS FOR A BUG-FREE PICNIC

- Choose a good site. Check the ground where you decide to sit and look our for piles of loose soil – they may be ants' nests.
- Cover up your food. Some insects, such as wasps, are attracted by the smell of food, especially sugary drinks or sweets.
- It could be a perfume that ruins your picnic. Some perfumes in shampoos attract bugs, while insects mistake other scents for alarm signals, causing the creatures to buzz about your head.

HARD TICK ▼
A hard tick's body is only about 3mm across, but once it's filled with blood, it could swell to about seven times its normal size. Hard ticks normally suck the blood of sheep or deer, but they will also latch on to humans. If one attaches itself to your skin, don't try to pull it off. Go to your doctor.

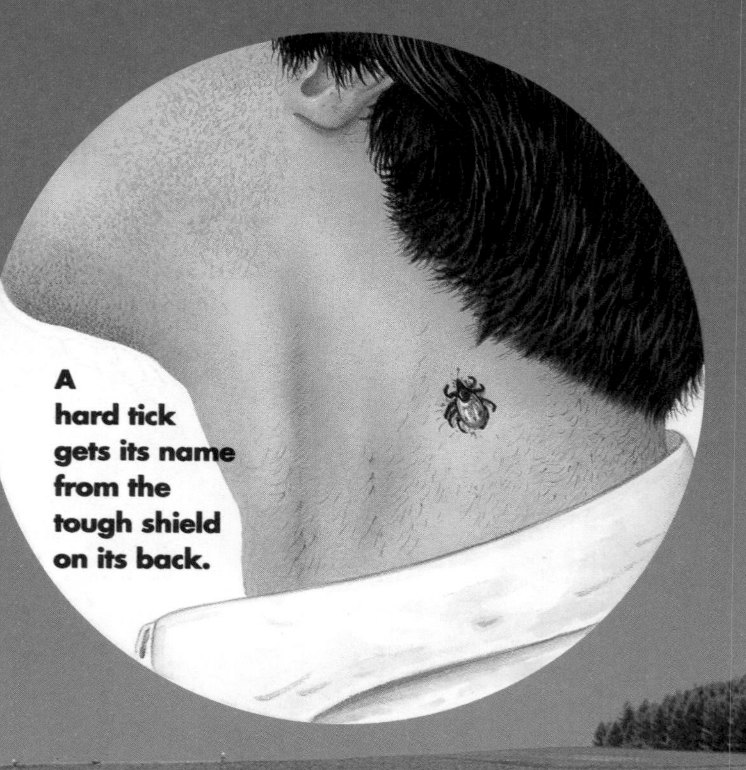

A hard tick gets its name from the tough shield on its back.

HORSEFLY ▼

Although male horseflies like to snack peacefully on nectar, the females enjoy nothing better than the blood of animals. If one starts to dive-bomb you, it is probably looking for a quick snack. They particularly like to attack arms and shoulders. You may have to move picnic spots because they are not easily put off.

Dung flies are attracted to the sugar on these biscuits and bring traces of dung with them on their feet.

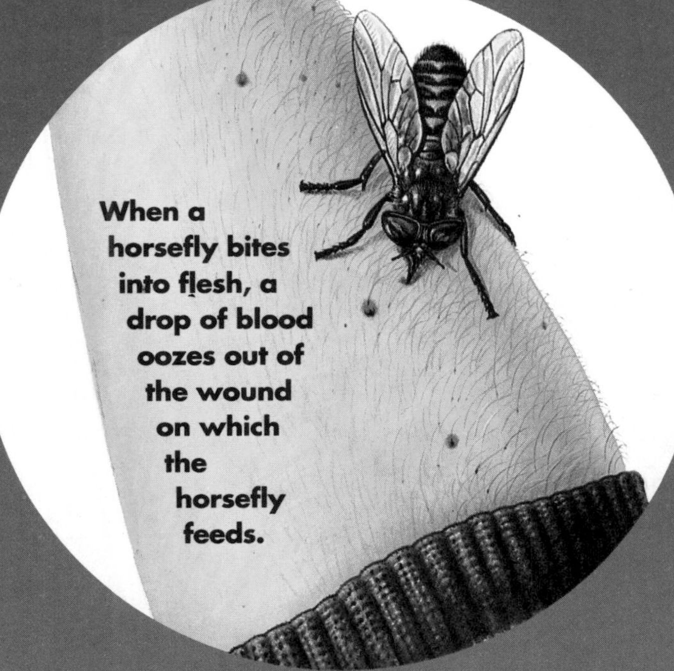

When a horsefly bites into flesh, a drop of blood oozes out of the wound on which the horsefly feeds.

YELLOW DUNG FLY ▲

Yellow dung flies are easy to spot. Their bodies are covered in yellow hairs and they fly with their legs dangling beneath their bodies. They feed on cow dung. If you want to avoid sharing your food with them, go on a picnic on a very blustery day as, like all flies, they tend to lie low when the wind's blowing.

WOOD ANTS ▶

In the wild, wood ants really like to eat other bugs, but they are not fussy. They will certainly be attracted to anything sweet, such as a fizzy drink. If they are disturbed as they go about their hunt for food, they may spray you with a stinging liquid, called formic acid.

Wood ants can spray formic acid up to 45cm.

Improve and test your knowledge with...

CREEPY~CRAWLY FACTS

Dive down to the murky depths of the sea and test yourself with our BUGS! quiz.

1 Where do compass termites build their nests?
a) northern Europe
b) northern Australia
c) southern France

2 How many greenfly can a ladybird eat in a lifetime?
a) 1,000
b) 8,000
c) 50,000

3 What does a bed bug do during the day?
a) it looks for food
b) it travels long distances
c) it rests

4 What does the elephant hawk moth caterpillar imitate?
a) a snake
b) a hawk
c) an elephant

5 How long can a tick last without a meal?
a) one year
b) over 3 years
c) over 10 years

6 What is an echinoderm?
a) a sea bug with a spiky skin
b) a type of termite
c) a relative of the army ant

7 How many years can a queen termite live?
a) 21
b) 102
c) no more than one

8 How big can a bull ant grow?
a) 20cm long
b) 2 – 3cm long
c) 2mm long

9 Which bug is the burrowing sea cucumber related to?
a) a caterpillar
b) a starfish
c) a burying beetle

10 Which bugs spray formic acid?
a) butterflies
b) slugs
c) wood ants

Worm warmer

Many bugs are attacked by microscopic worms, which live inside their bodies. Some of these tiny creatures actually make the bug ill. Locusts have worked out how to get rid of the worms. The infected locust basks in the hot rays of the sun until its body is as hot as it can stand. Inside, the minute worms begin to overheat until they eventually 'cook' and die.

Lazy bones

Animals that chase after their food have to rest a lot when they are not hunting. The common European wolf spider is an expert in energy conservation. Although its name makes it sound like an active hunter, in reality it spends less than three minutes a day hunting. The rest of the time it just sits still and waits.

War bugs

In 1964, in a bay off the coast of Vietnam, American sailors saw lights moving quickly through the water. They thought that they were being attacked by Vietnamese torpedoes. Soon after this sighting, the Vietnam War began. It is now thought that what the US sailors saw was a colony of pyrosomes – bugs that live together in huge 15m-long tubes. The flashing lights are caused when the bugs communicate with each other.

Gold diggers

Many types of ant decorate the entrance to their nests with objects that they have dug out of the ground. Gold diggers used to look out for these ant nests, which were sometimes decorated with pieces of gold. This told the diggers to search for gold in this area. Other ants have been known to decorate their nests with fossilised teeth and bits of ancient bone.

Answers to the questions on the inside back cover

Matthew Robertson, who spent 12 years working with bugs at London Zoo, here answers all your creepy-crawly questions.

Do butterflies and moths only drink nectar from flowers?

No. Although most drink nectar, some suck the juices from ripe fruits, while others drink other animals' urine. Some butterflies have a taste for alligators' tears. Possibly the strangest diet of all is the vampire moth's. It sucks its victim's blood, but is less dangerous than a mosquito.

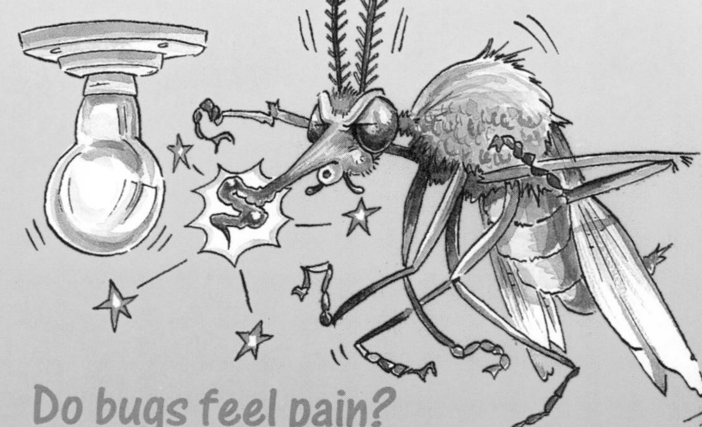

Do bugs feel pain?

This is a difficult question because bugs can't tell us how they feel! Bugs probably feel pain, though not in quite the same way as we do. They do not appear to suffer pain as much as we do. Like most animals, bugs try to avoid getting hurt. If they did not do this, they wouldn't survive for long.

How do bugs walk on glass?

There are two reasons why some bugs are able to climb up glass. Many bugs have pads at the ends of their legs. These are covered in tiny hairs and a thin layer of oil, which oozes out of holes at the base of each hair. When the fly walks up a pane of glass, the oil acts like glue. Bugs that can walk on glass are also very light. If they were heavy, they would not be able to cling on to slippery surfaces.

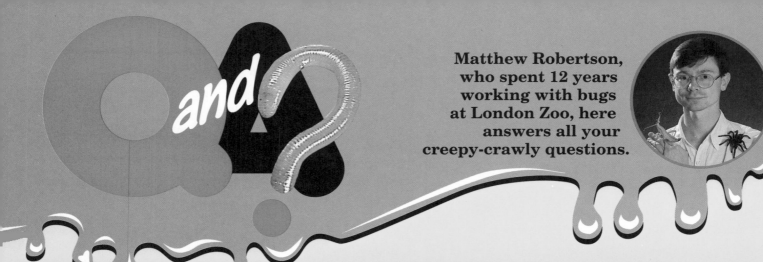

Earwig

The earwig got its name from the old belief that it crawled into people's ears and bit holes in their eardrums.

With its short legs and long, flat body, the earwig can squeeze itself into the narrowest spaces. During the day, it keeps out of sight, resting in dark hideaways.

CROWDED HOUSE

The earwig makes its home under logs, stones or piles of leaves. Large groups of earwigs gather together in places like these – you might find as many as 100 under one log!

FINDING FOOD

At night, earwigs come out to look for food, feeling around for it with their antennae. They eat all kinds of things – rotting fruit, vegetables and plants or decaying dead animals. They also like the occasional meal of fresh fruit or flowers, and may sometimes catch and eat small, live insects. Such a wide diet means that the earwig is never short of food, and has a good chance of survival.

USEFUL PINCERS

The earwig catches insects with the pincers at the back of its body. Arching them right up over its body, it brings its catch to its mouth. When it is under attack, it arches its pincers in the same way to scare off its attacker. You can easily tell an earwig's sex by looking at its pincers: the male's are long and curved, but the female's are shorter and much straighter.

HIDDEN WINGS

Like many other flying insects, the earwig keeps its wings tucked away under its tough, leathery wing cases. When it wants to fly, it lifts up the wing cases. The wings are large and delicate, so unfolding them is tricky. To get them back under the wing cases, they have to be folded up into more than 40 layers.

BABY CARE

Female earwigs make excellent mothers. After mating, in late summer or autumn, the female earwig finds a safe place in which to spend the winter. She and her mate then stay here together, as part of a larger earwig group. In the early spring, she lays her eggs – between 20 and 50 of them. They are creamy white in colour.

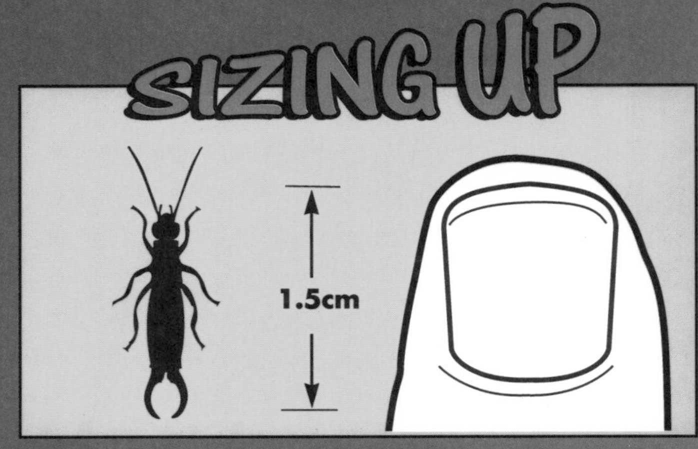

MOTHER LOVE

Unlike many other insect mothers, the earwig does not leave her eggs. Instead, she stays with them all the time and protects them, covering them with her head and forelegs. And she will attack any intruder that dares to come inside her home and threaten them.

HEALTHY EGGS

Earwig eggs have very thin shells, which can easily dry out. They can also become infected by germs and mould. So that the eggs stay clean, free of germs and healthy, the mother keeps turning them round and licking them.

Small Talk

EAR PIERCING

Earwigs get their name because of an old belief that says that earwigs crawl into people's ears, and bite holes in their eardrums. Earwigs may like dark, secret places, but they have never been known to bite through someone's ear – although their pincers could give your finger a sharp nip!

- **SCIENTIFIC NAME:** *Forficula auricularia*
- **SIZE:** up to 1.5cm long
- **LIVES:** all over the world
- **EATS:** dead plants and animals, fruit, flowers and small insects

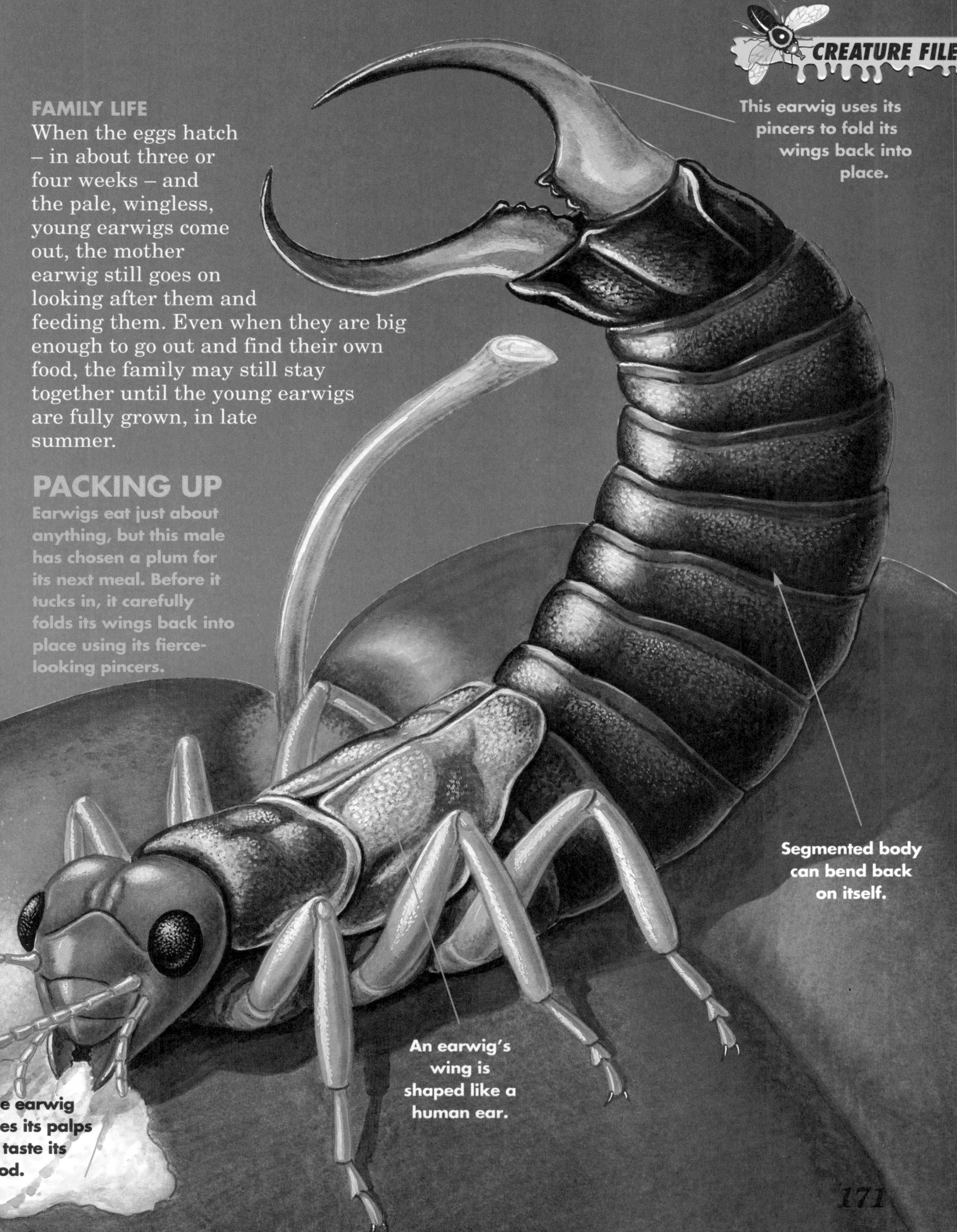

This earwig uses its pincers to fold its wings back into place.
Segmented body can bend back on itself.
An earwig's wing is shaped like a human ear.
he earwig uses its palps o taste its ood.

FAMILY LIFE

When the eggs hatch – in about three or four weeks – and the pale, wingless, young earwigs come out, the mother earwig still goes on looking after them and feeding them. Even when they are big enough to go out and find their own food, the family may still stay together until the young earwigs are fully grown, in late summer.

PACKING UP

Earwigs eat just about anything, but this male has chosen a plum for its next meal. Before it tucks in, it carefully folds its wings back into place using its fierce-looking pincers.

The human flea has survived for thousands of years by feeding on the blood of human beings.

The human flea lives on or near its victims – in people's clothes, or perhaps in their bedding or in cracks and crevices in the floor or carpets.

DOING A HEADSTAND
On its mouth, the flea has a tube with three needle-like points that it uses to pierce the skin of its victim and to suck up their blood. As it jabs through the skin, its head is pulled down and its body tilts up in a kind of headstand.

ITCHY BITE
When it bites, the flea injects some of its saliva (spit) into the skin to stop the blood clotting. It is this saliva that makes a flea bite feel so itchy.

HIGH JUMP
The flea is a champion jumper. If you could jump as well as a flea, you could reach the top of a skyscraper, shooting upwards at around 300km/h. Fleas jump about in their quest for new victims. A hungry flea can do 600 jumps an hour in its search for food.

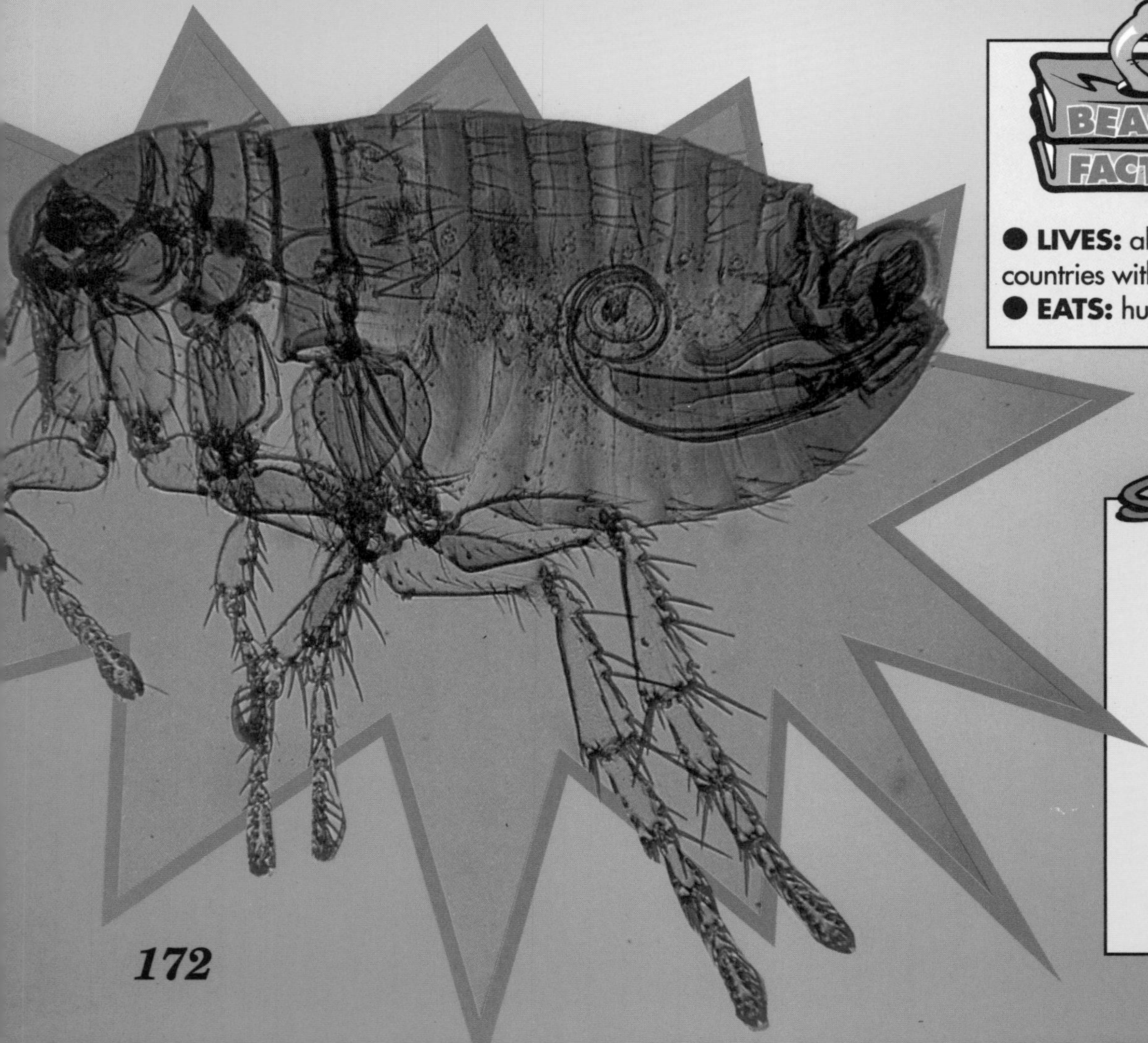

BEASTLY FACTS

- **SCIENTIFIC NAME:** *Pulex irritans*
- **SIZE:** 2 – 3mm
- **LIVES:** all over the world, in countries with mild, damp climates
- **EATS:** human blood

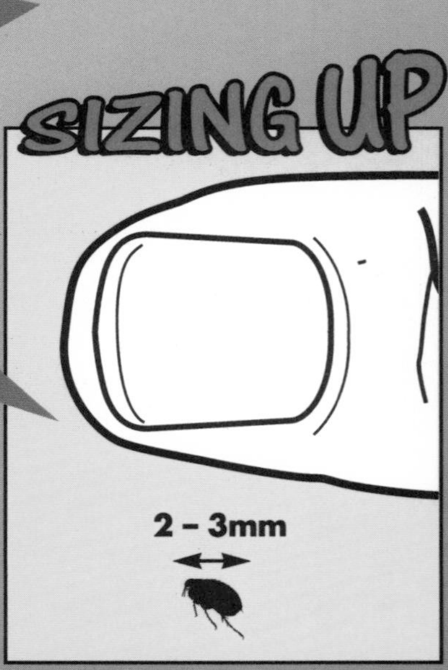

SIZING UP

2 - 3mm

Tailless whip scorpion

Despite its ferocious looks, the tailless whip scorpion is a shy creature, and quite harmless to humans.

The tailless whip scorpion quietly creeps out at night from its dark, damp hiding places under stones, logs, bark or leaves.

NIGHT-TIME EXPLORER

Although it has eight eyes, the scorpion uses its legs to feel its way in the dark. Stretching out its two long, delicate front legs, it gently taps everything in a wide circle around it to find out whether it is predator or prey. It uses its six back legs for walking, and can move forwards, sideways and backwards very quickly.

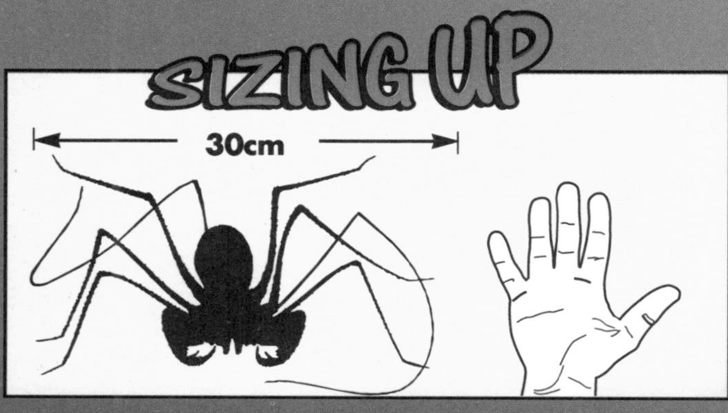

- **SCIENTIFIC NAME:** *Charinus sp. milloti*
- **SIZE:** body length 3cm – 4.5cm, legspan 20cm – 30cm
- **LIVES:** tropical and subtropical parts of Africa
- **EATS:** small bugs

SPINY CLAWS

When it finds some prey, the tailless whip scorpion pins it down with the two large, spiny claws on the front of its head. The claws can also give a sharp pinch to any predator that gets too close. Luckily for other creatures, the scorpion is not a fierce hunter and has a small appetite.

BABY CARE

After mating, the female lays 20 – 40 eggs, which she carries in a pouch under her body. When the eggs hatch, she carries the young on her back.

Ambush!

Eating dinner can be dangerous for some bugs – especially when the 'dinner' turns round and eats them!

A bug must always watch out when it is tucking into its favourite snack. It may not be the only bug nearby that is thinking about food! Some bugs lie in wait for other bugs to start eating – then they pounce. Other bugs disguise themselves to look like their prey's favourite food.

LAST SUPPER

The jumping spider (above) hides behind leaves until it sees a bug feeding nearby. Before you can say 'ambush!', the jumping spider dives into the air and leaps on top of the unsuspecting animal. Some jumping spiders can grab insects in mid flight!

HOME DELIVERY

The other bugs shown here don't need to hide because they are so difficult to see. They lay traps or give off confusing signals until prey comes close, then they pounce.

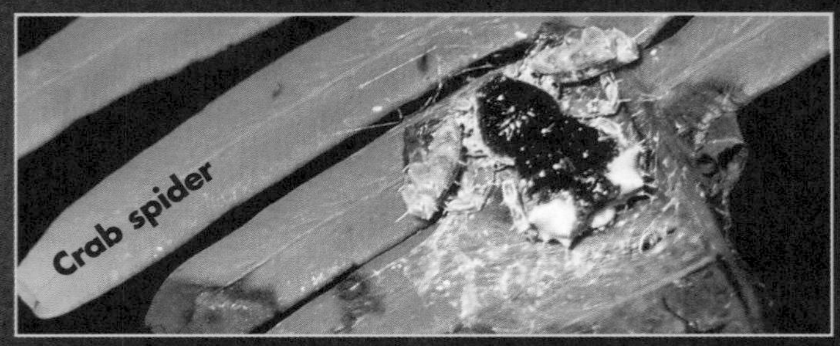

Crab spider

SMELLS PECULIAR

The splodge (above) may look like a bird dropping, but it is a type of crab spider. The spider has left some of its web as a smear that looks and smells just like real bird dung. The spider sits in clear view on top of a leaf. When a passing fly comes near to feed, the spider pounces.

PINK PERIL

This pretty pink orchid flower (right) is hiding a deadly orchid crab spider, which has been waiting for a bee to fall into its trap. Insects that eat pollen and nectar, such as bees, are attracted to the flower and fly towards their death.

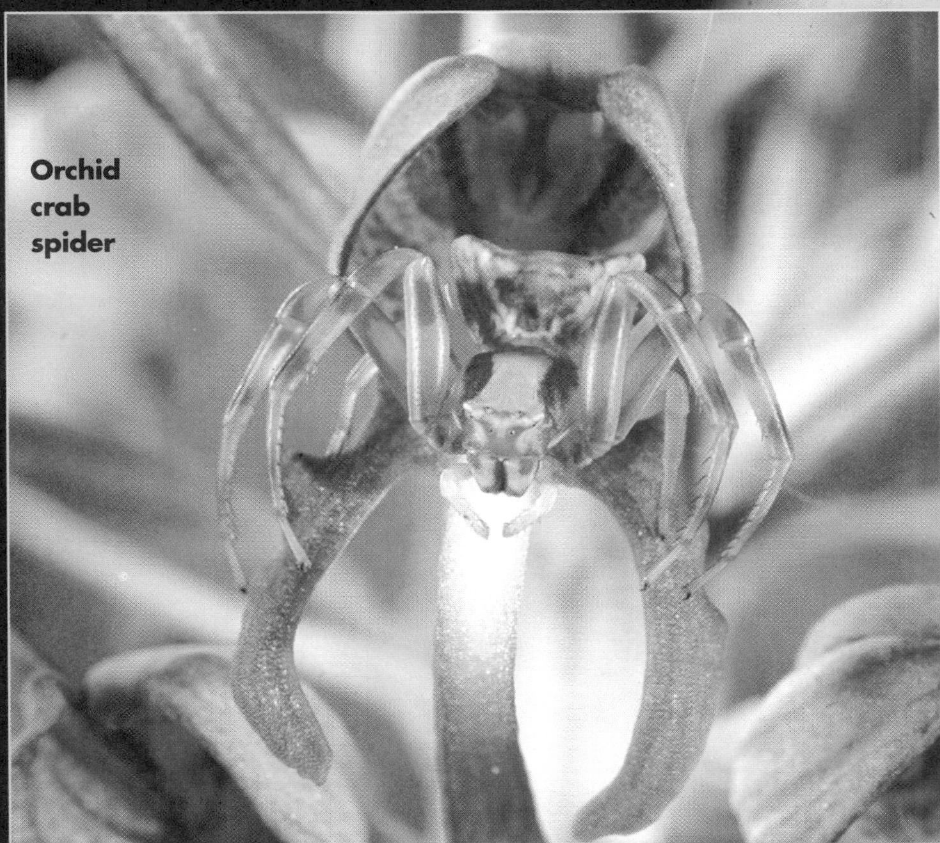

Surprise! Surprise! Don't look now, but a jumping spider is about to land on top of this unsuspecting bee, which is feeding on a flower. The bee's dinner will soon be over and the jumping spider will soon be tucking into its freshly caught snack.

FISHING FOR TROUBLE

The termite in this picture (left) is in danger. An assassin bug, which lives on the side of the termite's nest, has disguised itself using termite droppings and is waiting to pounce. Assassin bugs sometimes dangle a dead termite from their mouths and wriggle it about. The assassin bugs use the carcasses as bait – rather like a fisherman does – to attract other termites. Members of the colony think the termite is in trouble and rush to help. The assassin bug is ready for lunch.

FLOWER POWER

As a butterfly dips into the bright yellow flower head to feed on the nectar, it suddenly realises that a type of crab spider is lurking in the centre of the flower (main picture). But it is too late: the spider catches the butterfly before it has chance to escape. Crab spiders are small but they are powerful, with very strong venom. The spider knows the butterfly is there, and when exactly to attack, because it senses the insect's movements, and because it has fairly good eyesight.

A BITE LIKE DRACULA

The spider's legs fold round the butterfly and its fangs bite into the back of its neck, just like Dracula. The butterfly's main nerve is in the back of its neck so it is paralysed by the bite. Now the spider can enjoy its meal. Crab spiders are not always bright yellow, they can be pink, purple or white. They choose a flower to match their own colour, so they are always difficult to see.

The nectar of this brilliant yellow flower draws butterflies near to investigate. But hiding in the centre of the flower is a vicious crab spider, which is poised ready to attack.

TIDY EATER

Once the crab spider has grabbed its prey, it tries to eat it as quickly, cleanly and tidily as possible. It is making sure it doesn't blow its cover! The crab spider has another trick up its sleeve to fool passing bugs. It holds its legs out at strange angles. This changes the shape of its body and so tricks other bugs into thinking it is not a spider at all.

ARMED AND DANGEROUS

Lurking in the coral beds, heavily disguised, is an octopus (below). It grabs a fish that comes too near with its long arms, and eats it. The unfortunate fish doesn't even see the octopus before it is eaten because the octopus can change its colour and blend so well with its surroundings.

Octopus

The bug-

There are several things that are useful to have if you want to be a bug watcher.

Many bugs are very difficult to find, either because they're hidden or they're very small. Even if you can find them, many are so tiny that you cannot see them in any detail and they don't seem to be very interesting. But with some equipment and a little patience, you will soon be able both to easily find and watch these tiny bugs. Here is the instant guide for the well-equipped bug watcher.

There are several places you can look for bugs. These include in garden soil, on plants and underneath rocks and pieces of wood.

Magnifying glass

A magnifying glass allows you to see bugs in close-up. You can buy one from most hardware stores. Attach a length of string to it and wear it around your neck. In this way, you're unlikely to lose it and it will be handy at all times.

Notebook

Choose a notebook with a stiff back, so you can write in it without having to lean on anything. If you have a spiral-bound notebook, you will be able to tear off pages as you use them and keep together all the notes you have made on any particular bug. Use a pencil to write notes, then they won't smudge if it rains.

Always write down the date and time when you saw the bug. Make a note of the place where you found it, and what the weather was like. If you find something you would particularly like to look at again, draw yourself a map showing exactly where you found it.

Make rough notes while you are watching the bug – you can always write them up in more detail later on. Make quick sketches of the bugs you find. Show the size, colour and anything unusual about its markings, wings or legs.

Clear container

A clear plastic container with a tight-fitting lid makes a good 'hotel' for keeping bugs so you can watch them for a short while. Puncture some air holes in the lid to let them breathe and always be gentle with bugs you catch.

- Make sure you put bugs back where you found them as soon as possible.

Small paintbrush

You can use a paintbrush to help move small bugs without damaging them.

watcher's kit

Pooter

A pooter is useful for collecting small bugs without damaging them. You can buy a pooter from specialist pet shops or you can make one yourself. It is easy to make and costs very little.

Making a pooter

You will need:

- a clear jar with a lid
- a pair of scissors
- 40cm length of 8mm-diameter plastic tubing
- modelling clay
- a small elastic band
- a small piece of muslin

1 Take the lid off the jar and ask an adult to make two crosses in it with the scissor blades.

2 Cut the plastic tubing in half so that you have two 20cm lengths. Push each piece through the holes in the lid so that about 3cm is sticking into the jar. Hold them in place and seal any gaps with modelling clay.

3 On the inside of the lid, cover the end of one of the lengths of plastic tubing with a piece of muslin. Hold this in place with a small elastic band. The muslin is important as it stops bugs going into your mouth when you suck on the straw.

4 Put the lid on the jar. You have now made a pooter. To use it, hold the end of the plastic tubing without the muslin near a bug and suck on the end of the other tube. This draws air into the pooter, carrying any small bugs with it. Only use your pooter for catching very small bugs – larger ones might get stuck.

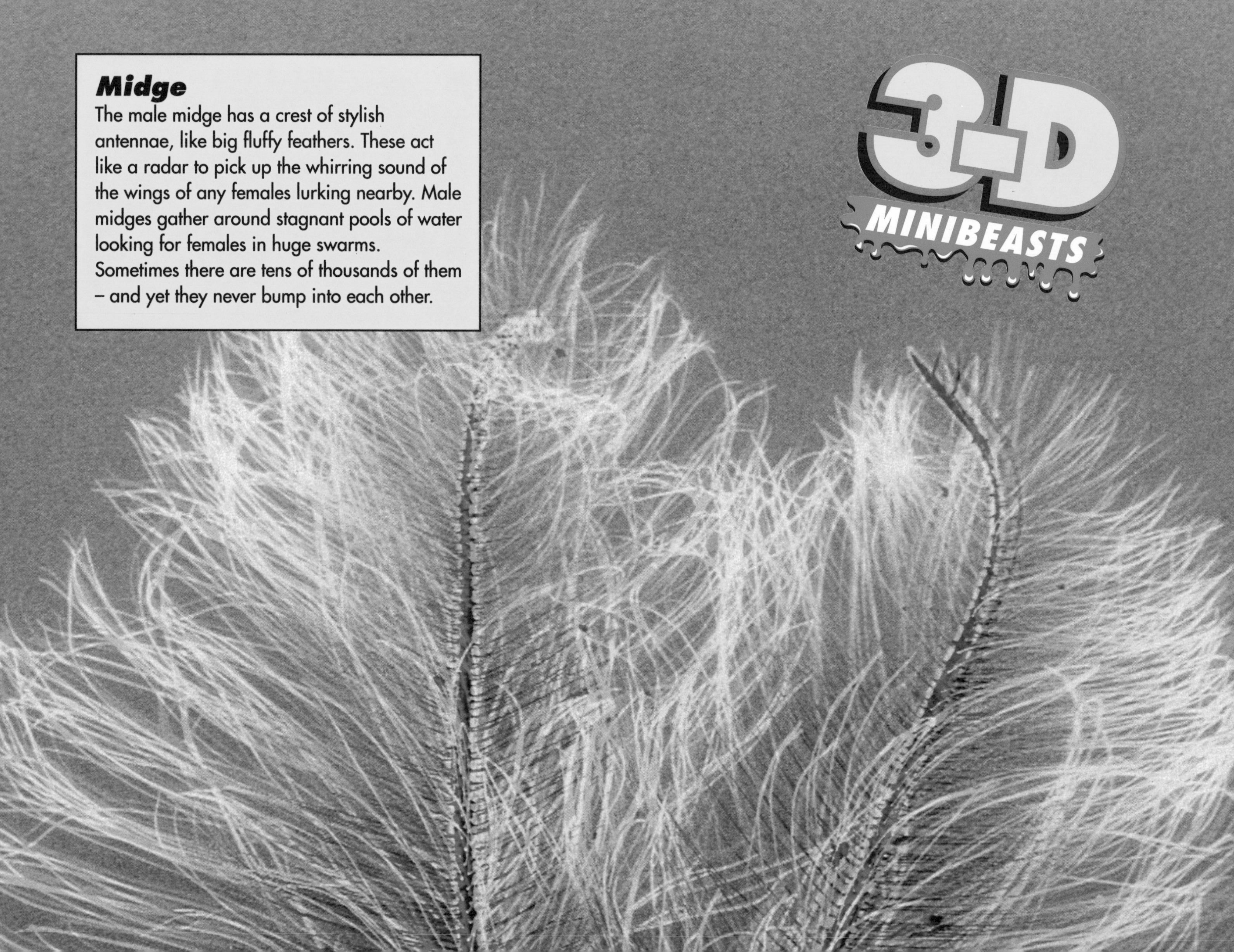

Midge

The male midge has a crest of stylish antennae, like big fluffy feathers. These act like a radar to pick up the whirring sound of the wings of any females lurking nearby. Male midges gather around stagnant pools of water looking for females in huge swarms. Sometimes there are tens of thousands of them – and yet they never bump into each other.

Prehistoric water bugs

Millions of years before humans existed, and before dinosaurs walked across the Earth, the oceans were full of bugs. Some of them were as big as cars.

Ammonite

We know that these huge water bugs existed because their bodies formed fossils. Fossils are the remains (or prints) of animals or plants that have been preserved in rocks for a very long time. Often it is the hard parts of animals, such as their shells or wings, that form fossils.

CLUES TO THE PAST

Fossils of prehistoric water bugs give us excellent clues to life in the seas millions of years ago. From just one fossil, experts can tell when a bug lived, how big it was and sometimes even how it died. Experts who study fossils are called palaeontologists (say 'pay-lee-on-toll-o-jists').

HOW A BUG BECAME A FOSSIL

A dead bug or animal had to be very lucky to become a fossil. The first thing a dead bug (above) had to avoid was being eaten by other animals as it sank to the sea floor.

The bug was buried quickly in fine-grained mud or sand before any scavengers found it. Over the years, layers of mud covered the bug and its flesh gradually rotted away.

This ammonite is about 170 million years old. Sea creatures like this disappeared about 65 million years ago. Dinosaurs died out at the same time – no one knows why.

FLOATING CONES

Early ancestors of today's squid and octopus swam through the prehistoric waves. Members of this family are called cephalopods (say 'kef-a-lo-pods'), which means 'tentacled head'. Their tentacles formed a circle around their mouths. The very first cephalopods had shells that were shaped like long, thin ice-cream cones. One of the oldest cephalopods was *Orthoceras* (say 'orth-o-kir-us'). Inside its cone were a number of air-filled spaces, which the creature used to help it float.

CURLY-WURLY CREATURES

Another type of cephalopod was the ammonite. This animal was basically the same as *Orthoceras*, but its shell was quite different. Instead of a straight cone, it carried around a spiral shell.

LARGER THAN LIFE

The fossils on this page may not look very scary, but just imagine if massive versions of these bugs were brought back to life. Turn the page to see these bugs in action.

This shell (below) belonged to an *Orthoceras* that lived about 450 million years ago. Spaces inside the shell allowed this water bug to float or sink. If it wanted to sink to the sea bed, it filled the spaces with water to make itself heavier. If it wanted to float to the surface, it let the water out, filling its body with air, which made it float.

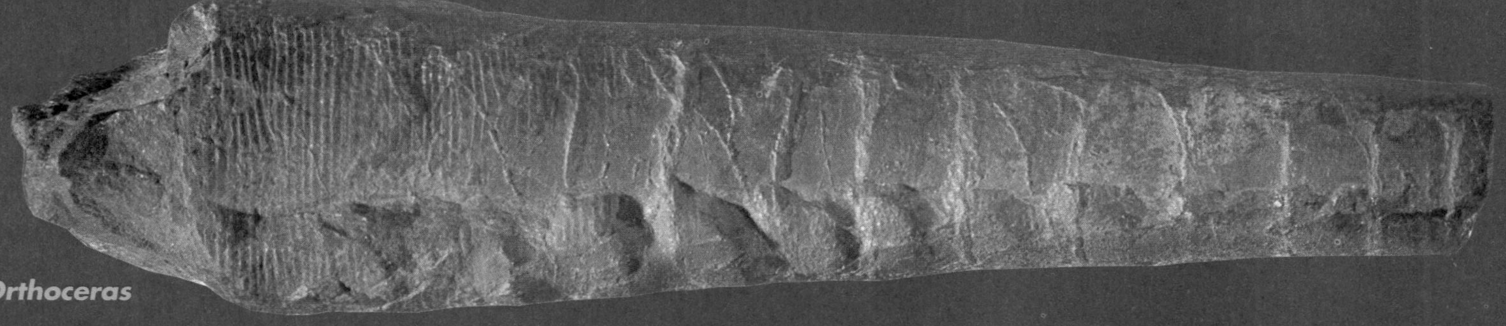

Orthoceras

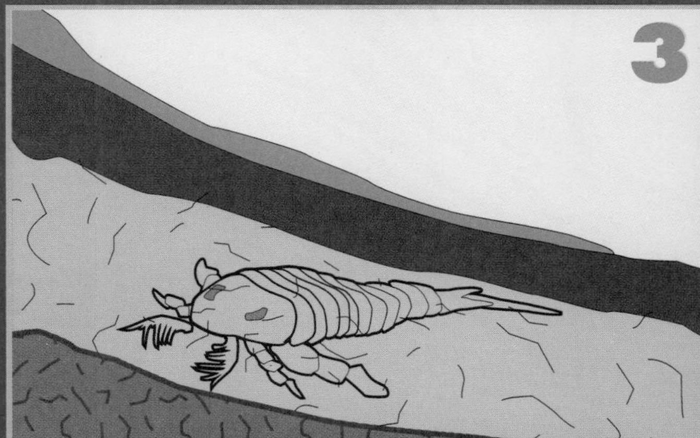

The hard parts of the bug's body, such as the tough outer skeleton, left an imprint in the mud. Over millions of years, the mud turned to stone and preserved the shape of the bug's body.

Millions of years later, the level of the sea dropped. The wind and rain wore away the rock to reveal the fossil – evidence that bugs lived millions of years ago.

Imagine swimming through the ocean and coming across a group of massive prehistoric water bugs.

TIME TRAVELLER

Of course, you could never meet these bugs. But if you travelled back in time millions of years, this is what you would see.

- **AMMONITE (say 'a-mon-ite')**
- **2.5m diameter**
- **Lived 390 – 65 million years ago**
- **Ate fish and other sea bugs**

Ammonite fossils are quite common. If you found one on a beach you could probably hold it in the palm of your hand, but some are larger. One of the largest ammonite fossils that has been found was 2.5m wide. This monster was a bottom feeder, which meant that it shuffled along the sea bed looking for crabs and fish.

***ORTHOCERAS* (say 'orth-o-kir-us')**

- **4m long**
- **Lived 500 – 440 million years ago**
- **Ate fish and other sea bugs**

Orthoceras was an early member of the octopus and squid family but, instead of a soft skin, it had a tough shell. Most *Orthoceras* were small, but over millions of years they developed into monsters. This one (right) is 4m long – that's twice as long as your bed.

- ***PTERYGOTUS* (say 'terry-goat-us')**
- **2.3m long**
- **Lived 439 – 409 million years ago**
- **Ate fish and other sea bugs**

Pterygotus was a giant sea scorpion. The proper name for sea scorpions is eurypterids (say 'u-rip-ter-ids'). This particular monster was almost as long as a small car (2.3m long)! Two broad paddles at the end of its tail helped it move easily through the water, grabbing prey with two huge pincers.

Ammonite

FROZEN WITH FEAR

Trilobites (say 'try-lo-bites') lived long before dinosaurs. They looked a bit like woodlice – they had armoured backs and jointed legs. If a trilobite was threatened, it curled itself up into a ball, just like a woodlouse or pillbug millipede. Some trilobites fossilised in this curled-up position.

A trilobite viewed from above.

A trilobite with its body curled up tightly.

The pillbug millipede (right) defends itself by curling up like the ancient trilobite.

This huge fossil shows two water scorpions side by side. Their bodies are well preserved because their tough outer shells did not have a chance to rot before they were fossilised in mud.

THE BUG WAR

Bugs are not always popular with humans. In large numbers they can be pests. Humans try to fight back – with very mixed results.

Humans have waged war on bugs on many occasions. Farmers, gardeners and foresters will try anything to defend their crops, flowers or trees. Sometimes their tactics work well, but often their weapons are totally useless and the bugs win the battle.

FIERY FIEND

The fire ant, for example, is a really tough opponent. Millions of US dollars have been spent trying to wipe out this tiny bug. But it always bounces back – in its millions.

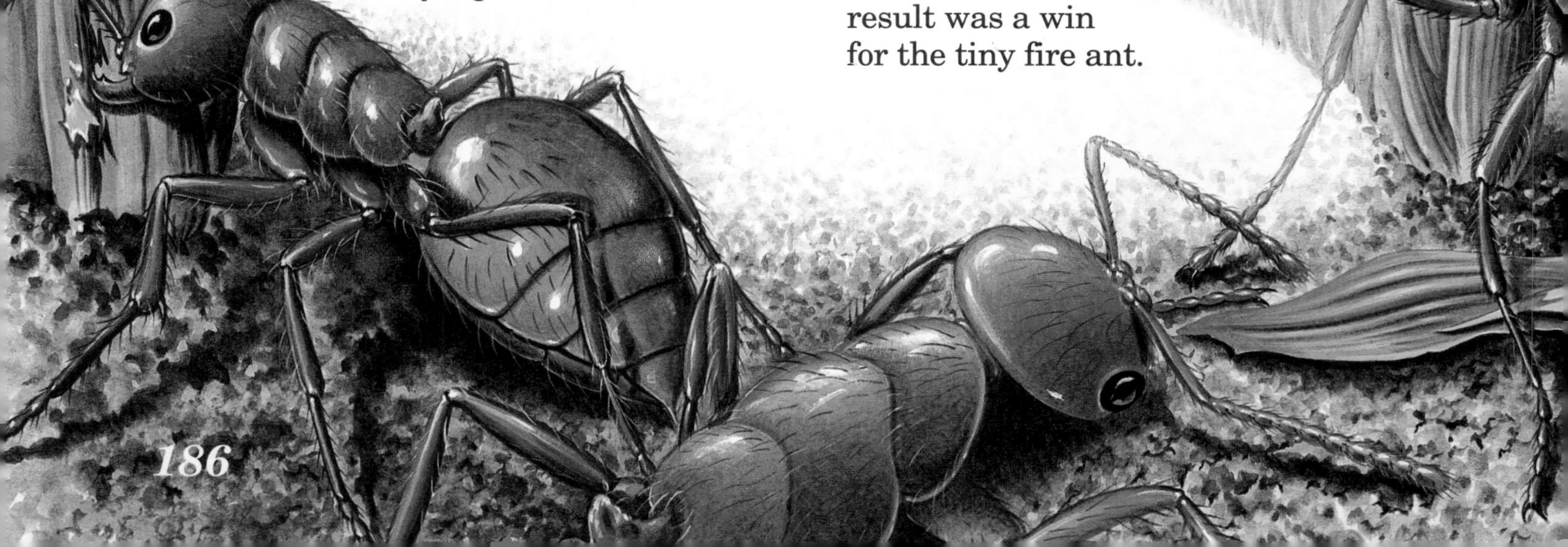

Fire ants (below) normally enjoy the taste of other bugs, but a field full of newly sprouted seeds is a tempting alternative.

FIRE ANT SUCCESS

A fire ant colony expands rapidly. In just three years, its members can grow from 1,000 to 250,000. All these ants need to eat constantly. Fire ants usually eat other bugs, but when meat is scarce, the fire ant gladly munches on newly sprouted seeds instead. Fire ants also build hard mounds, which can damage farm machinery, and they sometimes gnaw through electric cables. It's not surprising they are so unpopular with farmers.

EXPENSIVE MISTAKE

In the 1950s, the fire ant infested a large area of the southern states of the USA. Farmers asked scientists to help them get rid of the dreaded fire ant. The scientists made a new pesticide (a chemical for killing pests). Large war planes called B17s sprayed the pesticide over the fields. But the result was a win for the tiny fire ant.

BAD RESULT

The battle plan had misfired – the new pesticide killed livestock, such as cattle, wildlife, fish and even some pets. For a while almost all of the fire ants were wiped out, but in a very short time they were back to full strength. When scientists gave this pest its scientific name they decided to call it the Latin for 'unbeatable' ant.

AROUND THE WORLD

Pests can spread quickly. In the 1870s, the Colorado beetle spread from the west to the east coast of the USA, across the Atlantic Ocean and into Europe. By the 1960s, it was eating potatoes – its favourite food – in Poland. That's a journey of 15,000km! When the scientists took on the Colorado beetle, they had more success. Again they used pesticides, but this time they were the winners. Today, pesticides still control the march of the Colorado beetle.

The Colorado beetle (left) was once considered to be a pest, but today humans have controlled the spread of this stripy bug with the use of pesticides.

INSECTS' TACTICS

Bugs do a lot of good work, but if their numbers get out of control they can become a problem. Different bugs attack crops in different ways. Some insects use their mouths to suck the sap from leaves and buds. Chewers, such as weevils and worms, gnaw away at leaves and eat bark. Tiny leaf borers tunnel in between the layers in a leaf. Some insects, such as the gall wasp, actually cause plants to grow cancers, while tunnelling insects destroy delicate roots.

Scientists are always looking for different ways to fight the war against pests. Some of their ideas work well, others are total disasters.

PESTICIDES

A pesticide is a substance for destroying pests, particularly insects. Each pesticide is designed to combat a certain type of bug without killing everything else around it. In the case of the fire ants, this idea didn't work! They disappeared for a while, then came back stronger than ever, while other animals around them died out.

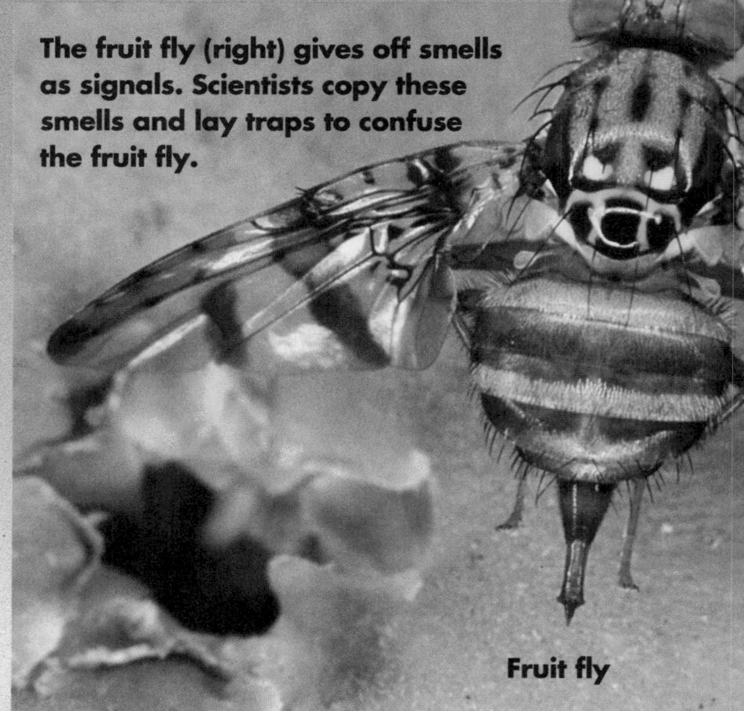

The fruit fly (right) gives off smells as signals. Scientists copy these smells and lay traps to confuse the fruit fly.

Fruit fly

PREDATORS

Sometimes a farmer introduces an animal that will prey on the pest. This seems sensible, but it doesn't always work. In Australia, cane beetles became such a pain that the cane toad was brought in from South America to eat them all. Sadly, the cane toad did not eat the beetles and its numbers also increased. Before long, the toad had also become a pest.

PARASITES

Experts have discovered that they can encourage tiny bugs to live inside larger bugs, and to eat away at their insides. Bugs that do this are called parasites. Gardeners combat slugs by putting tiny worms, called nematodes, on their flower beds. The slugs eat these worms, which live happily inside their bodies and slowly eat away at the slugs' insides.

Cane toad

The cane toad refused to eat the swarms of cane beetles in Australia. Instead it ate reptiles, other bugs and small mammals. Today the cane toad is itself a major pest!

War planes full of pesticide (right) were not enough to get rid of the the 'unbeatable' fire ant. About 90 per cent of the bugs died out, but they later came back stronger than ever. Instead, the pesticide damaged wildlife, fish and even cattle.

CHEMICAL COPYING

Some bugs 'talk' to other members of their group by giving off smells. These smells are called pheromones (say 'fe-ro-moans'). Scientists can imitate these smells using chemicals. Farmers who grow fruit in greenhouses use these man-made pheromones to attract and kill male Mediterranean fruit flies. They cover sticky boards with the smell of female fruit flies. These attract the males, which stick to the boards and die. By killing the males, the farmers keep the fruit flies in check.

BACTERIA

Tiny bugs, called bacteria, are made of only one cell. They can cause disease and are sometimes sprayed over crops to kill the insects that eat them. Farmers use this method to fight a moth caterpillar called the army worm, which eats everything in sight. These bugs are covered with bacteria, which kill the worms.

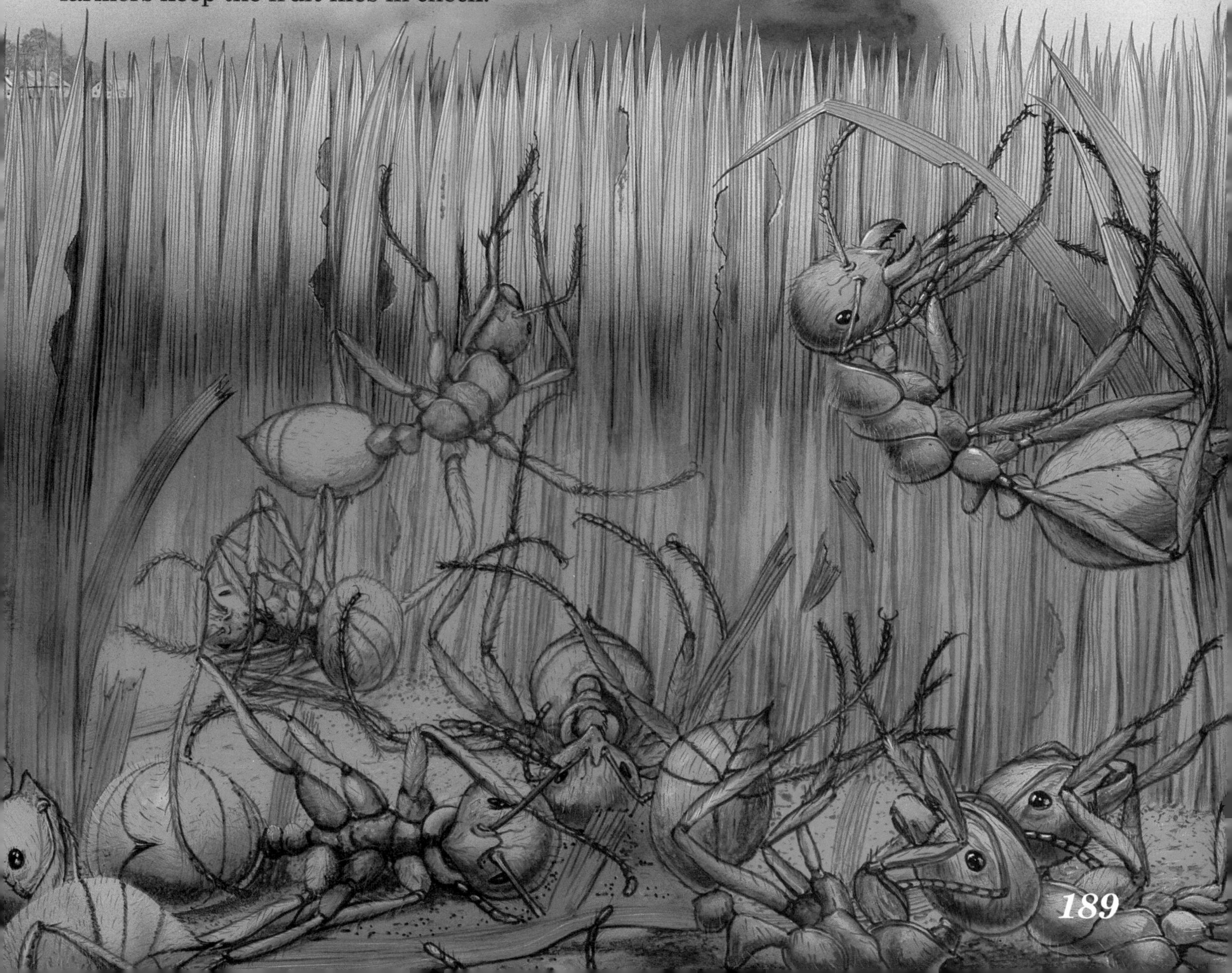

Improve and test your knowledge with...

CREEPY~CRAWLY FACTS

Wade through the blizzard of bugs and try to get the drift of the BUGS! quiz.

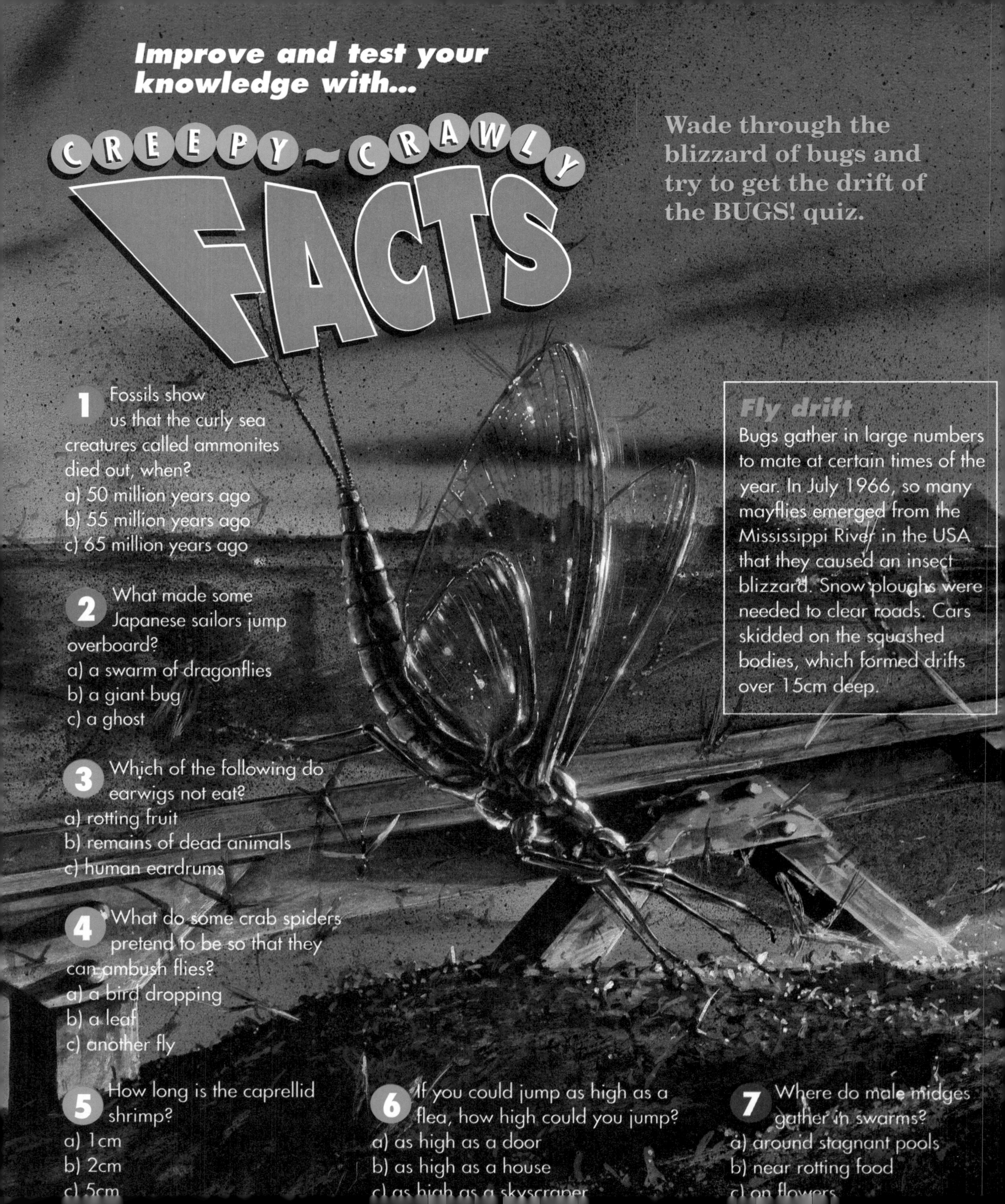

1 Fossils show us that the curly sea creatures called ammonites died out, when?
a) 50 million years ago
b) 55 million years ago
c) 65 million years ago

2 What made some Japanese sailors jump overboard?
a) a swarm of dragonflies
b) a giant bug
c) a ghost

3 Which of the following do earwigs not eat?
a) rotting fruit
b) remains of dead animals
c) human eardrums

4 What do some crab spiders pretend to be so that they can ambush flies?
a) a bird dropping
b) a leaf
c) another fly

Fly drift

Bugs gather in large numbers to mate at certain times of the year. In July 1966, so many mayflies emerged from the Mississippi River in the USA that they caused an insect blizzard. Snow ploughs were needed to clear roads. Cars skidded on the squashed bodies, which formed drifts over 15cm deep.

5 How long is the caprellid shrimp?
a) 1cm
b) 2cm
c) 5cm

6 If you could jump as high as a flea, how high could you jump?
a) as high as a door
b) as high as a house
c) as high as a skyscraper

7 Where do male midges gather in swarms?
a) around stagnant pools
b) near rotting food
c) on flowers

Bugs ahoy!

Oil tankers have to be careful not to hit other boats or large objects, so they use radars to help them 'see'. The crew of a Japanese tanker off the coast of Japan was confused when a massive blip appeared on their radar. It was heading straight for them! The ship's look-out spotted a shimmering shape, over 700m wide, closing in fast. In their panic, some crew members jumped overboard. The massive shape turned out to be a huge – but harmless – swarm of dragonflies.

Mum munching

Making sure babies grow up strong is important for all animals. However, there are few that take it as far as the Asian eresid spider. The mother feeds her babies with food she has already digested. Eventually, the young spiders demand more food than she can supply, so she digests her own body and turns it into a nourishing soup. By killing herself, she makes sure her babies have one last meal before they have to look after themselves.

Antibiotic ant aerosol

Ants have to keep their eggs and larvae clean. South American fire ants have a neat way of doing this. First, they carefully lick the eggs. Then the ant lifts up its abdomen and squeezes a drop of venom on to the unhatched larvae. The venom acts as an antibiotic, killing any germs near the eggs. This venom is also used to sting other bugs!

8 Where does the female tailless whip scorpion carry her young?
a) on her back
b) in a pouch under her body
c) between her delicate front legs

9 In July 1966, thousands of mayflies emerged from the Mississippi River. What did they cause?
a) a drought
b) an insect blizzard
c) a riot

10 What does the scientific name for the fire ant mean?
a) bossy ant
b) unbeatable ant
c) blue ant

Answers to the questions on the inside back cover

Matthew Robertson, who spent 12 years working with bugs at London Zoo, here answers all your creepy-crawly questions.

Which bugs fly the fastest?

Several groups of insect (and one flying squid!) all come close to the title of fastest flier. At present, the record holder is an Australian dragonfly that has been clocked at nearly 35km/h. However, it is unlikely that any bugs are able to fly any faster than 40km/h. If they did so their wings would probably break because of the air pressure on them.

How long is an inch worm?

Inch worms can be any length from 3mm to 6cm. They are the caterpillars of the geometer moths. Unlike most other caterpillars, which just crawl along, inch worms move by looping their backs high into the air and moving their back legs up to their front legs. As they march along, it looks like they are measuring how far they have gone. In a metric world, inch worms should really be called 2.5399cm worms!

Can bugs be friendly?

Most bugs see humans either as an enemy or as a source of food. Intelligent bugs, however, like squids and octopuses, seem to recognise the people who look after them in zoos and aquariums, and will swim towards them. But it may just be cupboard love as they think they're about to be fed!

Cuttlefish

The cuttlefish is designed to be a nice little mover.

The cuttlefish lives in seas and oceans all over the world. It spends most of its time swimming along through the water, using the flexible fins on either side of its rigid body.

LONG ARMS

On the sides of its head, the cuttlefish has two big eyes. Sticking out from the front of its head are 10 tentacles, or arms, with suckers on them for holding on to things. Two of its tentacles are extra long. These are used for grabbing prey.

GOING UP, GOING DOWN

Although the cuttlefish looks soft on the outside, it has a large, hard, rounded shell inside its body. Its shell is filled with lots of little holes – rather like a sponge. Inside the holes is a mixture of gas and liquid. To make itself lighter so that it can float upwards, the cuttlefish forces more gas into the holes. To make itself heavier so that it can sink, it forces in more liquid.

GOING BACKWARDS

The cuttlefish can also dart backwards. It draws in water through slits behind its eyes, and then forces out the water through a funnel-like tube underneath its mouth. As the jet of water shoots forward, it pushes the cuttlefish back – a bit like letting air out of a balloon to make it shoot backwards.

The cuttlefish moves through the water on the look out for prey. If it comes across a predator, this bug can slip into reverse and make a speedy getaway.

SIZING UP

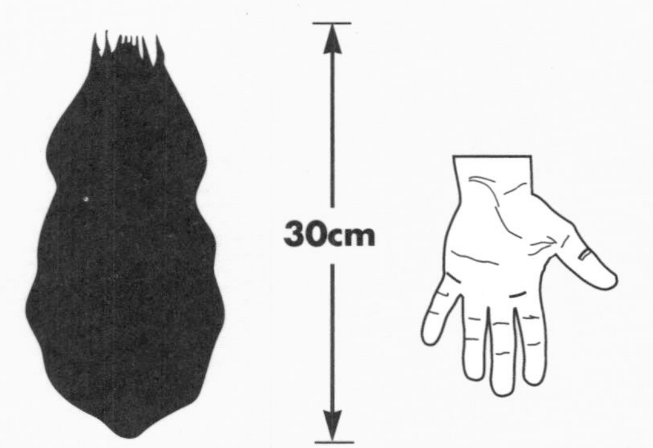

- **SCIENTIFIC NAME:** *Sepia officinalis*
- **SIZE:** 30cm long
- **LIVES:** seas and oceans all over the world
- **EATS:** small fish and sea bugs

COLOUR CLASH!

These two male cuttlefish are about to start fighting. The dominant one changes its colours and thrusts out its tentacles, hitting its weaker rival.

Changing colour tells the other cuttlefish that it is preparing for attack.

Thousands of suckers firmly hold even the most slippery prey.

The tentacles shoot out to grasp prey or chase off a rival.

The rippling fin on the side of its body lets it move smoothly in any direction.

INK ATTACK

Inside the cuttlefish's body is a sac, or bag, containing a dark, inky liquid. When a cuttlefish comes under attack, it squirts out this 'ink' to distract its predator. While the predator looks at the ink, the cuttlefish makes its escape. If this doesn't work, the cuttlefish whips up a 'sandstorm' on the sea-bed with jets of water from its funnel-like tube and buries itself.

Razor-sharp beak slices easily through the tough bodies of prawns, crabs and fish.
Tentacles also help position food in front of mouth.
Excellent eyesight helps spot prey and rivals.
A squirt of thick, dark ink screens the prey from its attacker, and gives it time to escape.

COLOUR CHANGE

When it senses danger, the cuttlefish can also disguise itself by quickly changing colour to blend in with the sea-bed. Deep in its skin, it has tiny cells that contain colouring. These cells can change size, becoming bigger or smaller, and so make the cuttlefish lighter or darker. It can also change its patterns. In just one second, it can go from being striped, like a zebra, to spotted, like a leopard. These sudden changes help scare off unwanted predators.

ATTRACTIVE MATE

When a male cuttlefish chooses a female for a mate, he has to put on quite a show to interest her. To persuade the female to mate with him, the male makes himself attractive by changing colour hundreds of times. After mating, the female lays her eggs on seaweed or coral.

BLACK EGGS

At first, the eggs are soft and transparent, but they soon harden. Ink oozing out of the tiny ink sacs inside each egg turns the eggs black, so that they look like bunches of black grapes! When the eggs are about 1cm long, the young cuttlefish break out.

Small Talk

COLOURING IN

The common cuttlefish is called *Sepia officinalis* and, for hundreds of years, the 'ink' of the cuttlefish was used to make a brown colour called 'sepia'. Artists used it in their ink and watercolour paints.

The millipede's legs are like lines of soldiers on parade, marching together in step.

Millipede

The name 'millipede' means '1,000 legs'. Although the millipede doesn't really have this many legs, it does have quite a few. Each one has 40 – 400 legs, depending on the species.

GIANT STEPS

Because the millipede has so many legs, it uses more than one leg at a time to take each step. When it is walking slowly, a big millipede, like the giant millipede from Kenya (above), may use 50 of its legs for each step. If it wants to go faster, it lengthens its stride and uses as few as 10 legs at a time.

COAT OF ARMOUR

The millipede's body is split into lots of segments, or 'folds', which make it very bendy. Each segment is covered by a hard shell. When danger threatens, the millipede curls up into a tight ball, and the shells overlap each other to form a solid coat of armour. If you want to know how many legs a millipede has, all you have to do is to count its segments, and then multiply this number by four.

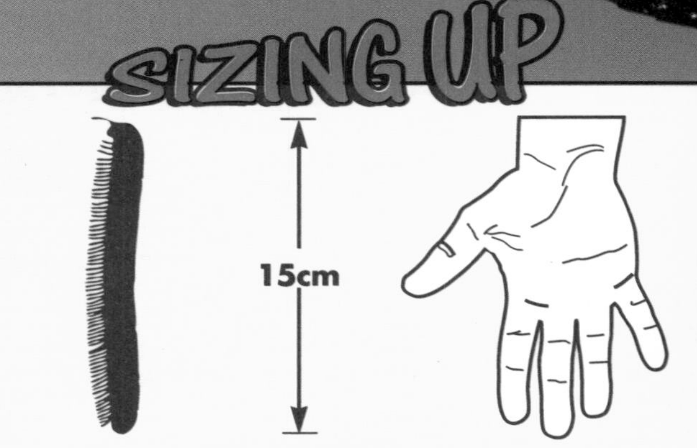

- **SCIENTIFIC NAME:** *Epibolus pulchripes*
- **SIZE:** 15cm long
- **LIVES:** in the soil, or under leaves in East Africa
- **EATS:** rotting plants, dead insects and other small animals

Leaf Insect

From the time it begins life as an egg, the leaf insect is a master of disguise.

Warm, wet jungles are home to the leaf insect. It comes out at night to feed on the leaves of the guava tree, and other tree leaves.

HIDDEN EGGS

Up in the trees, the female leaf insect lays about 100 eggs altogether, flicking them from her so that they fall to the forest floor below. The floor is covered with the droppings of the silk moth caterpillar. Because the eggs look just like these droppings, it's hard to tell them apart. This is the eggs' clever disguise to fool predators, such as birds and monkeys.

IMITATION ANTS

The eggs lie on the ground for about six months, and then hatch. The skinny, 1cm-long babies are bright red, just like the ants in the jungle – another trick against predators.

LEAF SHAPES

As the young grow, they turn green or brown, and develop flaps of skin on either side of their bodies that look just like the leaves of the trees around them.

SHORT LIVES

Leaf insects mate when the male is about 15 weeks old, and the female about 18 weeks. The male dies a week or so later, but the female lives on for another six weeks after laying her eggs.

SIZING UP

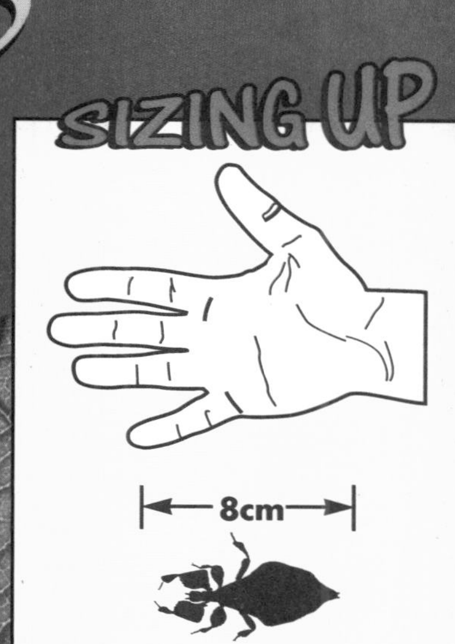

BEASTLY FACTS

- **SCIENTIFIC NAME:** *Phyllium gigantium*
- **SIZE:** female up to 15cm long, male up to 8cm long
- **LIVES:** Malaysia
- **EATS:** leaves

Bugs on Bugs

Just like you, every bug needs food and shelter. Some bugs fend for themselves, build their own homes and look for their own food. Others rely on other bugs for all their creature comforts.

An animal that lives on or in another animal, and gets its food directly from it, is called a parasite. The animal that provides the home is called a host. Many bugs are parasites. Fleas can live on cats and dogs. Tapeworms live inside pigs and humans. Some bugs live in other bugs!

FRIEND OR FOE?

Some parasites are harmless and eventually move on without causing too much harm. Other parasites suck out all the blood and goodness from their host's body until it loses strength and dies.

HANG ON!

Many bugs only stay on their host for part of their lives, taking what they need and then moving on. Some live on several bugs during the course of their lives. Others just hitch a lift from one place to another. Many bugs live inside their host's body. Others live on the outside and have to hang on for dear life. They have clever ways of attaching themselves to another bug. Fleas have special spikes, ticks have spiky mouth-parts, and lice have gripping arms.

HOME HELP

The Madagascan hissing cockroach (main picture) is host to a tidy mite. This mite, which eats scraps, lays its eggs and sticks them on to the cockroach. When the young start to move about, they act like miniature vacuum cleaners, sucking up dirt from around the cockroach's mouth and generally tidying up.

Parasite: mite

Host: Madagascan hissing cockroach

OUT THE BACK DOOR

About half of all the aphids that are ever born become infested by a wasp. This parasite lays its eggs inside aphids. Once they are born, the wasp larvae munch away at the host's body until just before they are ready to turn into adults. When they are fully grown, they bite out a tiny skylight in the top of the aphid's body, swing it open and get out.

EATING OUT

The female braconid wasp chooses a host for her babies. She lays her eggs underneath a caterpillar's skin. The eggs hatch into larvae, which munch away at the caterpillar's insides. The caterpillar carries on living because the hungry babies only eat the parts of its body that aren't needed for it to stay alive. Once the larvae have had their fill, they burrow out and make white silken cocoons. Young adult wasps emerge from these and fly away.

DIGGING DINERS

The tarantula-hawk wasp is big enough (about 5cm long) to tackle large spiders, such as tarantulas. Hunting at night, the female attacks a tarantula and paralyses it with venom. She then drops the stunned, but still living, spider into a burrow along with her other victims. The wasp lays a single egg on each spider, then fills in the burrow. When her young hatch, they feed on the spider until they are old enough to go in search of nectar.

The story of a parasite

Some parasites use more than one host. This is the story of a worm-like bug that starts life in a snail and ends in a bird.

The trematode, a parasitic worm-like bug, spends some of its life in a snail and some of it in a bird. These larger animals provide the worm with food, shelter and even transport. Start at number one and follow the arrows to find out how the trematode makes its incredible journey.

1 STRANGE MEAL
A snail eats bird droppings as they fall to the ground. Inside the droppings are tiny eggs, which have been laid by the trematode.

3 SUN WORSHIP

The snail usually likes dark places. But because of the bug inside its eye-stalks, it feels a sudden urge to move towards the light. It climbs to the top of a blade of grass to get as much sunlight as possible.

4 LOOKS TASTY

A passing bird mistakes the snail's swollen eye-stalks for caterpillars, which it loves to eat. The hungry bird swoops down and eats the whole snail along with the trematode larvae inside its antennae.

5 DROPPING OFF

The bird eats the trematode and carries the bug in its stomach to a new site. The life cycle begins again when another snail eats the bird's droppings.

2 MOVING UP

The eggs hatch inside the snail and trematode larvae travel around its body. Two of these worm-like larvae make their way up into the snail's eye-stalks. The stalks, which are striped green and brown, swell up, start throbbing and look remarkably like fat, juicy caterpillars.

Small Talk

SUN-SEEKING SNAIL

Land snails, like the one below, don't usually venture out into bright sunlight. This means that birds, which go looking for food in the daytime, can't spot them easily because the snails are lurking in dark places. Once the trematode has burrowed its way into the snail's eye-stalks, the snail is forced to change its habit of a lifetime. It suddenly craves sunlight, crawls up into the open and gets eaten by a hungry bird.

A passing bird could easily mistake these antennae for fat, juicy caterpillars.

In the wild, land hermit crabs live on islands in tropical seas. They feed on plants and the remains of dead animals. They live in the discarded shells of dead molluscs and move to bigger shells as they grow. Keeping your own land hermit crabs allows you to watch them closely. They can live for as many as seven years or even longer. They are almost impossible to breed in captivity.

Keep some pet land hermit crabs – they are fascinating bugs and you'll have a lot of fun watching them.

You will need:

- a 25-60 watt lightbulb
- electric plug
- half a clay flowerpot or a piece of slate
- a few rocks and a branch
- a dish of clean water at least 15 x 15 x 2cm
- fruit and vegetables
- dried cat or dog food

From a good pet shop:

- an aquarium, with a light fitting in the lid, at least 60 x 30 x 30cm
- heat pad about one-third the length of the aquarium
- coral or silver sand
- plastic strip thermometer
- a piece of cuttlebone
- a variety of different-sized shells
- 4 or 5 land hermit crabs

WHAT TO DO

1 Get an adult to put a plug on the heat pad. Place the aquarium on top of the heat pad so that it gets warm at one end. This is so that the crabs can choose just how warm or cool they want to be.

2 The best sand to use is coral or silver sand, which is cleaner and has a better texture than ordinary sand. Wash the sand to get rid of any chemicals that could harm the crabs. Then put a layer of sand at least 8cm deep in the aquarium.

3 Land hermit crabs can't survive underwater for more than a few minutes. But without water they will suffocate. So you need to put a large, flat dish of fresh water in the aquarium. The dish should measure at least 15 x 15 x 2cm. Remember to change the water every day.

LAND HERMIT CRABS...

6 Land hermit crabs are not fussy eaters. They like fruits, vegetables and fresh meat. Try different foods to see which they like best. A small amount of dried cat or dog food with cuttlebone grated over it is usually a favourite. Make sure there is always a piece of cuttlebone in the aquarium so the crabs can eat it to get calcium. To stop the food contaminating the sand, it should be put on a small dish. You must change the food every day, because in this heat it goes off very quickly.

4 Although they carry their homes around with them, land hermit crabs also need somewhere to hide. You can make a home from half a clay flowerpot or a piece of slate on top of a few rocks. You might need to put another rock on top of the slate to hold it in place. Now you can put in the shells. The crabs will move into these as they moult (shed their skin) and get bigger. Without a new, larger shell to move into, the crabs would eventually die. Land hermit crabs like to climb, so you should also put a branch in the aquarium. Wedge it firmly into one of the bottom corners, so that it is diagonal to an opposite top corner.

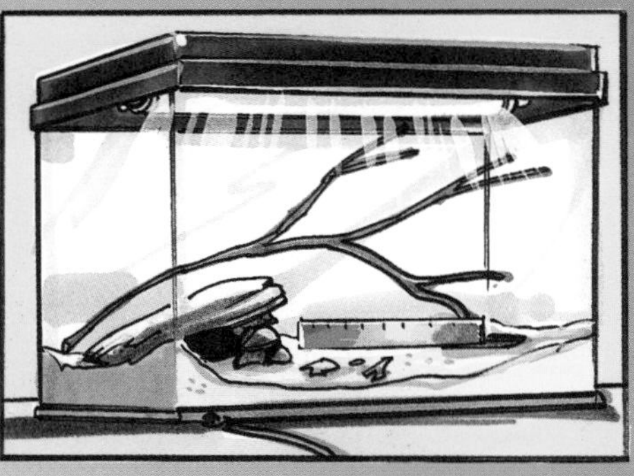

5 Leave the aquarium to warm up inside the house overnight. Fix the lightbulb or strip light into the fitting on the inside of the lid. In the morning, put four or five crabs in it. You should keep the light on all day and only turn it off at night. This gives them light which they would normally get from the sun. On the whole, land hermit crabs like a daytime temperature of between 27 and 29°C and between 23 and 26°C at night-time. You can check the temperature inside the aquarium by using your strip thermometer. Attach it just above the layer of sand on the outside of the aquarium. Put the crabs into the aquarium, then quickly put the lid on, making sure it fits tightly. Land hermit crabs are surprisingly strong and they could easily escape if the lid isn't on properly.

Small Talk

NEW SKIN

About once a year, you may see your crabs shed their skin. Before they do this, they first crawl out of their shell. THEY MUST NOT BE TOUCHED AT THIS TIME. After shedding, they will either return to their old shell or – more likely – they will search out a new, larger one. They must be allowed to eat their old skin if they want to as it gives them extra calcium.

Woodlouse

As night falls, the woodlouse crawls out from under a smelly piece of bark and stretches its jointed legs. It has been asleep all day and now it's woken up – and it's hungry. It sets off on a night-time scavenging trip in the hope of finding some tasty food. Perhaps it will discover its favourite food – rotting leaves. The woodlouse is a tough bug. It is covered in a coat of armour, but it doesn't have any weapons to defend itself. If it gets into trouble, this minibeast curls up into a ball and waits for danger to pass.

Fancy Feelers

Bugs would be lost without their antennae. They wouldn't be able to tell where they were or what was going on around them.

Joints in the antennae allow them to bend.

The ends of the antennae are particularly sensitive.

Antennae are sometimes called feelers, but they don't just feel. They are complicated sense organs that help bugs to work out what is going on around them. Antennae also tell bugs where there is food and even how to stay out of trouble.

THE LONG AND THE SHORT OF IT

Some bugs, such as flies, have tiny antennae that are difficult to see without a microscope. Others, like crickets, have huge feelers that are several times the length of their bodies. Antennae come in all different shapes, too, including some that are made up of as many as 100 parts. Female and male insects of the same kind often have totally different antennae.

MULTI-PURPOSE ANTENNAE

Antennae are mostly used to feel and smell. Sight is very important to humans, and we rely on it more than our sense of smell or taste. But although some bugs have very sharp vision, others can't see at all, so they have to rely on their antennae to feel, taste and 'sniff' their way around! Feelers also tell a bug in which direction the wind is blowing and can detect any food.

WHAT A CON!

The paussid beetle (right) uses its antennae as bait. It lives in ants' nests and has two antennae that are shaped like the oars of a rowing boat. They ooze a sweet gunge, which ants find irresistible. The ants flock towards the beetle, which promptly eats them. The paussid beetle has been known to suck out the soft bodies of 10 ant larvae in five minutes.

The paussid beetle (1.5cm long) lives in tropical countries. It makes its home in ants' nests, where there is always a meal close by.

The longhorn beetle (main picture) lives up to its name. Its antennae are so long that it finds flying difficult. The beetle's antennae are jointed like its legs. If the beetle wants to squeeze into a tight spot, it bends its antenna back out of the way.

This is a male longhorn beetle. Male insects often have larger or fancier antennae than females.

Is it true... that some bugs don't need long antennae?

Yes. Some bugs have quite good eyesight and so they don't need long antennae to feel their way about. The golden-ringed dragonfly (right) can see very well and can even catch and eat fast-flying prey as it zooms past. If a dragonfly's territory is invaded by another of its kind, it can spot the intruder from a long way off. Can you spot this dragonfly's two hair-like antennae? They are in front of its large eyes.

Golden-ringed dragonfly

Two ants communicate using their antennae. Perhaps one is talking about the queen or asking for food.

SMELL-O-GRAMS

An ant has an excellent sense of smell. Instead of having a nose, like you do, the tips of the ant's antennae are made up of scent organs. The ant uses these scent organs to 'sniff' its way to and from its nest and to recognise friends and enemies. It also follows smells to find food, but most importantly the ant uses its antennae to receive scent messages from other ants.

FELLAS' FEELERS

The male emperor moth has feather-shaped antennae. He uses them to track down a female moth's scent. This moth can smell a female up to 11km away! Some male mosquitoes and midges also have fancy feelers. They use them to track down females, by sound and not by scent.

Can you tell butterflies and moths apart? Male moths, like this silk moth, have feathery antennae. Butterflies have antennae that are shaped like cotton buds.

A CLOSER LOOK

An ant antenna is covered in tiny, sensitive hairs. This is what these hairs look like close-up.

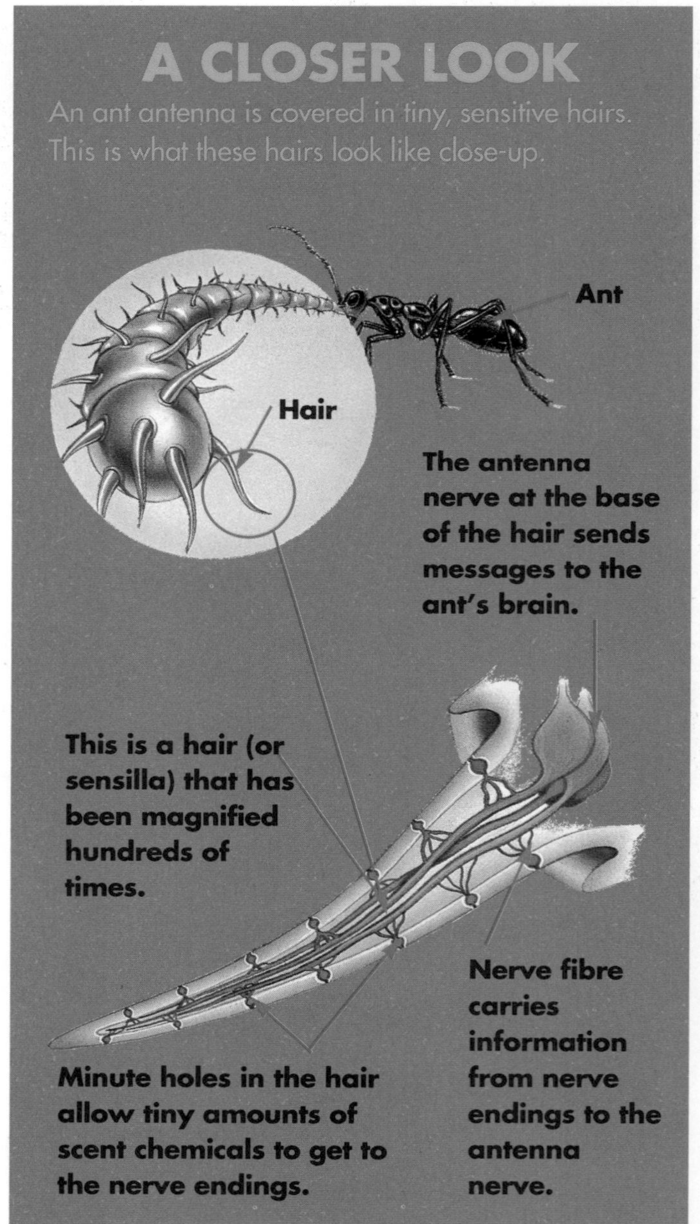
Ant
Hair
The antenna nerve at the base of the hair sends messages to the ant's brain.
This is a hair (or sensilla) that has been magnified hundreds of times.
Nerve fibre carries information from nerve endings to the antenna nerve.
Minute holes in the hair allow tiny amounts of scent chemicals to get to the nerve endings.

COMING OR GOING?

Some cunning butterflies have one set of real antennae on their heads, but they also pretend to have another pair sticking out behind them. The snail-headed butterfly, for example, has two long tail-pieces. A passing bird would be forgiven for thinking that these false antennae were on the butterfly's head. If the bird tries to grab them, though, the fragile tails break off very easily, giving the butterfly time to escape.

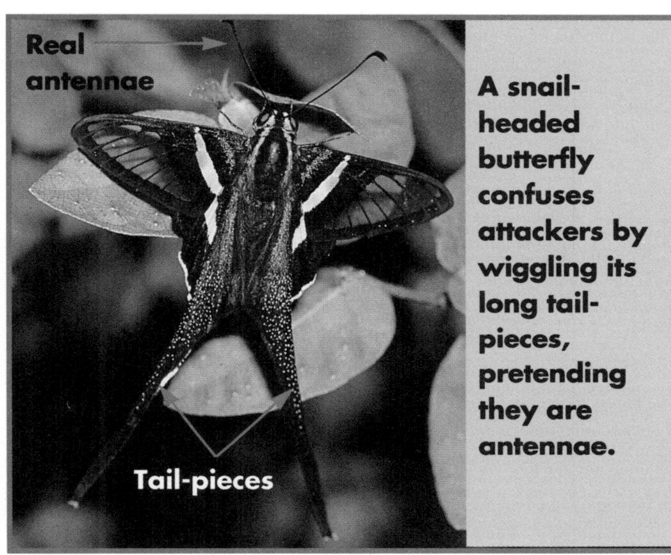

A snail-headed butterfly confuses attackers by wiggling its long tail-pieces, pretending they are antennae.

FEELING FINE

All crustaceans have two pairs of antennae. One pair is usually short and is used for tasting. The other pair is much longer and is used for defence. The blue spiny lobster (above) waves its long antennae around in the water to keep aggressive fish at bay. If a predator gets too close, it may get tangled up in the sharp spikes on the lobster's long antennae. The lobster also uses its antennae to give it a clear picture of all the goings-on in the murky sea water in which it lives.

ALL-ROUND ANTENNAE

Some crickets spend a lot of time in darkness. Cave crickets rarely leave the safety of their caves. Like other crickets, they grope around feeling for food and danger. But how do they know what is behind them? A cricket senses what is going on behind its back with its cerci (say 'ser-see'). These are a pair of sensitive prongs, which stick out from the cricket's abdomen.

The oak bush cricket has antennae that are nearly three times the length of its body. They are bendy so the cricket can pull them into its mouth to clean them.

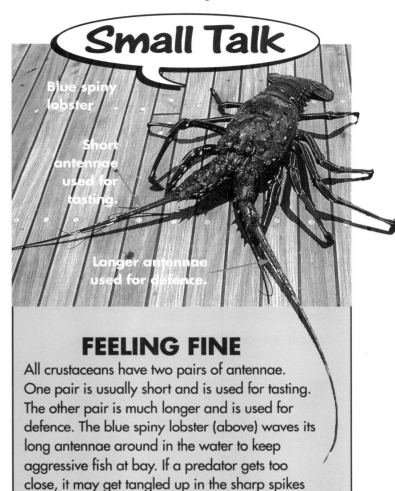

Doctor's orders

Imagine if, instead of giving you a bottle of pills, the doctor reached for a few beetles, a cricket or some maggots.

Your dentist may give you a painkiller for a toothache. If you had lived hundreds of years ago, you might have been given a beetle as a cure! In the last hundred years, science has taught us a lot about treating illness. In the past, people relied on strange cures, and sometimes they even turned to bugs. Some serious illnesses were treated in this way. Rabies, for example, was once thought to be cured by eating a few glow-worms!

WARTS

People would find you very odd if you got a bug to bite off your wart. Yet this is exactly what some people did right up until the beginning of this century. They let a wart-biter cricket nip off the wart with its powerful jaws. The cricket would then vomit liquid into the wound, which was believed to kill off the wart. This was how this cricket got its name.

Cricket

Maggots

Stag beetle

HOT HEADS

If you are feeling a bit under the weather, you try look after yourself. Perhaps you'd take some medicine, but you wouldn't deliberately take something that was going to give you a temperature. Yet that's what people did in the Middle Ages. They believed that fever was a good cure for many illnesses, including fits. The favourite treatment of the day was made of parts of a stag beetle.

WOUNDS

If you cut yourself, you'd probably put some disinfectant cream and a plaster on the wound. The last thing you'd dream of doing is letting maggots loose on it! The ancient aborigines in Australia and hill people in Burma would disagree. They knew that some maggots, such as blowfly maggots, attack only diseased or dead tissue. This means they can be used to clean out infected wounds.

BLOOD LETTING

Most doctors nowadays give patients a prescription. In the 16th and 17th centuries, they were more likely to reach for a leech. Leeches live off blood, and the doctors of the time thought that draining off some of a patient's blood let the badness out of their body and did them good. Luckily, the leech's jaws release a painkiller. This meant that its 'victim' felt nothing.

BLEEDING
If you have a cut that won't stop bleeding, you cover it with a plaster. The Japanese used to think beetles, such as oil beetles (right), could stop the flow of blood. They also believed that beetles were good for asthma, stomach upsets, cancer, warts and coughs. In some places, spiders' webs were used as bandages.

Oil beetle

FIDGETING
Hundreds of years ago, doctors in Europe had a special treatment for anyone who couldn't keep still. They fed them a nasty treat – ground-up tarantulas (above).

STITCHING WOUNDS
Imagine trying to stitch a wound using an ant! The South Americans used to do just this (main picture). They put the ant's jaws on either side of the wound and allowed it to bite on the skin. This pinched the two sides of the wound together. They then broke off the ant's body, leaving the jaws in place. The ant's body had become an instant bug stitch! When the wound had healed, they pulled out the jaws. Surprisingly, ants produce a special healing substance from a gland in their bodies. This gunge helped the South Americans to heal their wounds.

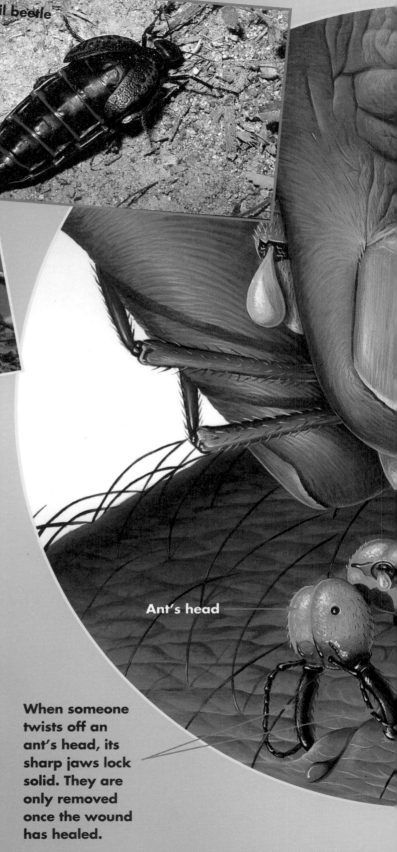

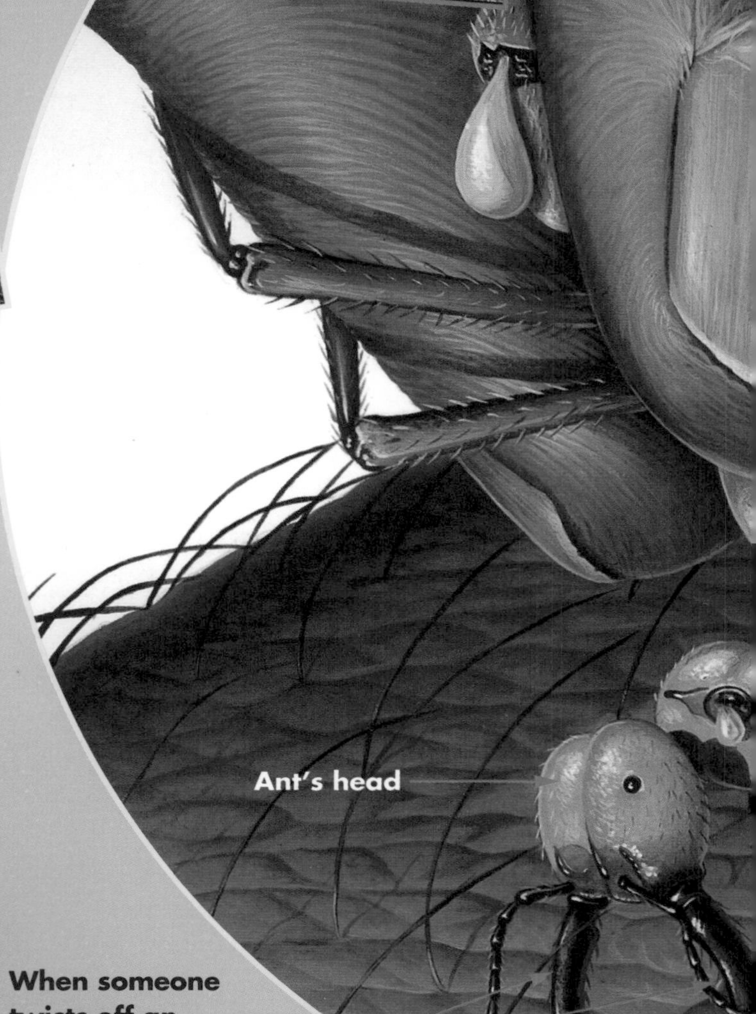

Ant's head

When someone twists off an ant's head, its sharp jaws lock solid. They are only removed once the wound has healed.

The ants produce a gunge that kills germs and helps the cut to heal quickly.

TOOTHACHE

Imagine going to the dentist and complaining about worms in your teeth. He or she would probably think you'd gone mad. But that's exactly what people long ago would have done. They believed that toothache was caused by worms boring inside the tooth. Beetles, such as blister beetles (below), kill worms. People thought that, if they swallowed them, the beetles would eat the worms that caused the pain. About 500 years ago, chemists sold ground-up ladybirds as a toothpaste.

Blister beetle

PLAYING SAFE

You have injections to protect you against serious diseases. Before people knew about injections, they tried to protect themselves in all sorts of strange ways. People in the Middle Ages believed that if you bit the head off the first cockchafer beetle of the year (left), you would be safe from fever for the rest of the year!

Cockchafer beetle

REMEMBER ...

Although, people in the past used bugs to try to cure themselves, don't try this yourself. Always get someone to take you to the doctor if you feel unwell.

Improve and test your knowledge with...

See if you can get to the bottom of this quiz, before 26 quarter-pounder hamburgers come crashing to the ground.

1 Which bug lays its eggs underneath a caterpillar's skin?
a) the blue-banded damselfly
b) the braconid wasp
c) the brown-tail moth

2 How many pairs of antennae do crustaceans have?
a) 2
b) 4
c) 6

3 What do land hermit crabs like to eat?
a) fish and chips
b) dried cat food
c) bread

4 What colour is the adult cat flea?
a) brown
b) black
c) white

Fat caterpillar

The larval stage of many bugs is the one when they eat most food. Some bugs, especially caterpillars, can eat an enormous amount of food during this part of their life. The caterpillars of the large silk moths eat so much that they grow from 4mm to 130mm in only 28 days. If a human baby were to grow at this rate it would be as long as a coach before its first month of life was over!

Singing thermometer

Some bugs can be used to find out what the air temperature is. The colder it gets, the slower most bugs become. This affects both their movement and the sounds they make. If you count the number of chirps a tree cricket makes in 15 seconds and add 40 you will have the temperature in degrees Fahrenheit. You can then convert this figure to degrees Celsius.

Beetle power

For their size, beetles are some of the strongest animals on Earth. Some species of scarab beetle can carry nearly 3kg – that's more than 26 quarter-pound hamburgers. This is over 200 times their own body weight, and would be the equivalent of a human carrying 15,254kg, the same weight as two adult elephants.

Joined for life

Some flatworms remain joined together for life after they meet a partner wandering about on the gills of fish. Once they start to mate, the cells of their bodies begin to mingle and soon the two flatworms are permanently joined together. In this way, they can fertilise eggs continuously. They will stay like this until they die.

5 How does the male cave cricket get the female's attention?
a) he sings
b) he knocks on the floor of the cave
c) he rubs his wings together

6 What does the cuttlefish do when it's being attacked?
a) grabs the attacker with its arms
b) swims away
c) squirts ink

7 What did the Japanese use instead of bandages in the past?
a) spiders' webs
b) silk worms' cocoons
c) cloths soaked in beetle juice

8 How many tentacles does the cuttlefish have?
a) 2
b) 10
c) 12

9 The tarantula-hawk wasp and the tarantula have a special relationship. Which is the parasite?
a) the tarantula
b) the tarantula-hawk wasp
c) neither

10 What were ground ladybirds used to make, many years ago?
a) toothpaste
b) wigs
c) face powder

Answers to the questions on the inside back cover

Matthew Robertson, who spent 12 years working with bugs at London Zoo, here answers all your creepy-crawly questions.

Why do moths fly towards lights?

Moths, which fly at night, use the light of the moon to help tell them where they're going. When a moth sees a bright light, such as a street lamp, it thinks it's the moon and flies towards it. However, the moth will not usually fly directly at the light, but flutters around it until it either falls exhausted to the ground or hits the light. Many insect collectors use special lights to attract and trap insects.

Does the female praying mantis always eat the male?

No. For a long time people thought that the female mantis always bit her mate's head off before, during or after mating. But most of the tests that 'proved' this were done in laboratories. These unnatural surroundings made the mantises nervous. In the wild, it is likely that only a few types of aggressive female mantis munch their mates on a regular basis. However, if the female does eat the male she is sure of getting a good meal before she lays her eggs.

Do bugs have noses?

No, bugs do not have noses. Unlike most backboned animals, bugs do not breathe through holes in their head. Insects, for example, breathe through openings in the sides of their bodies. Many worms breathe through their skin. Spiders have a number of slits underneath their abdomens and snails have a tube underneath their head. Sea cucumbers have a breathing organ that surrounds their mouths and looks a bit like a Christmas tree!

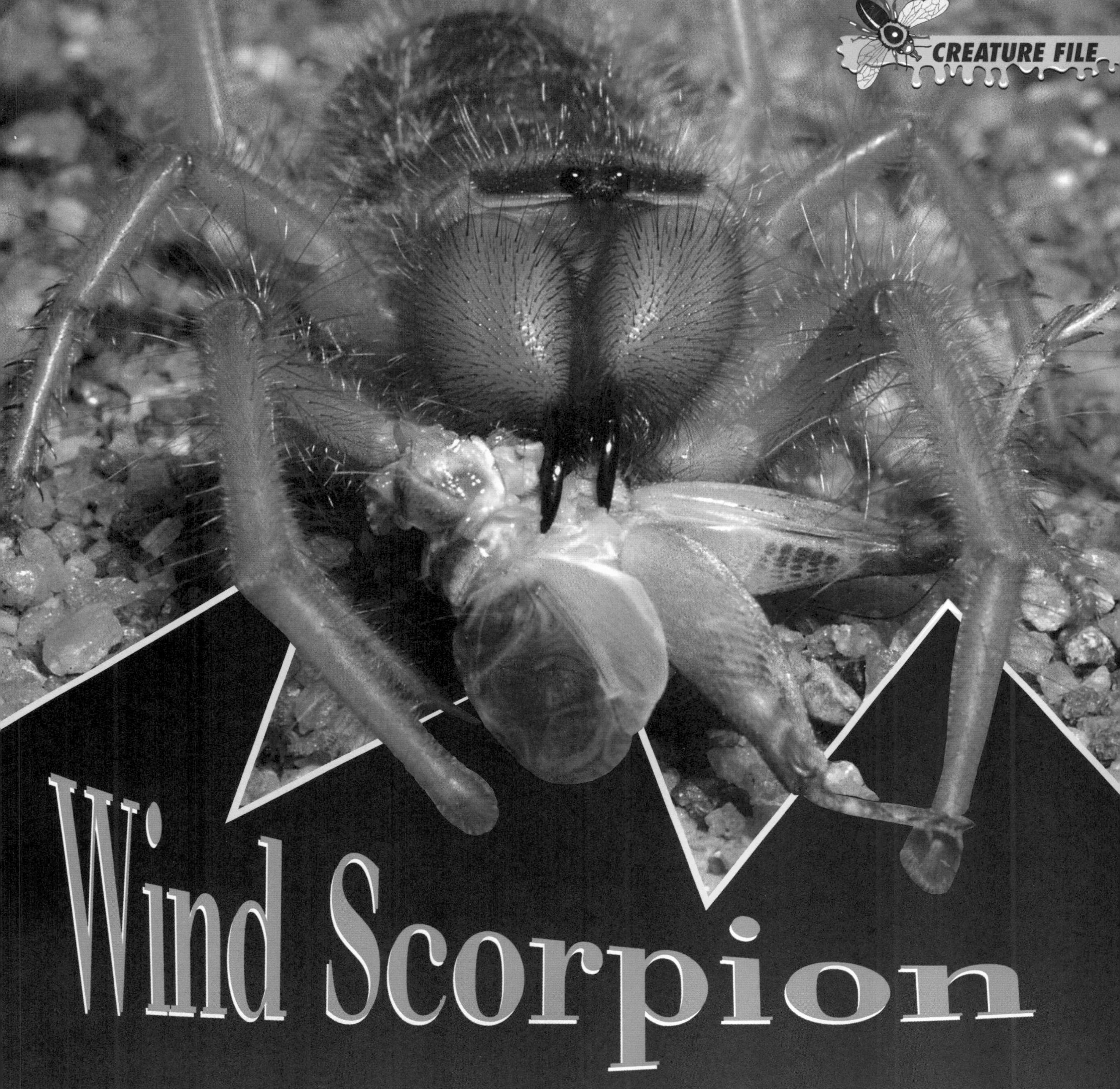

Wind Scorpion

When hunting prey, a wind scorpion runs at great speed, grabbing at anything that is in its way. It is a terrifying predator with huge, crushing jaws, excellent eyesight and an enormous appetite.

Most wind scorpions live in hot, dry deserts. By day, most of them hide away in burrows in the sand or soil, or in secret places under stones. At night, they come out to hunt. Some wind scorpions come out in the daytime when the sun is shining – these wind scorpions are called 'sun spiders'.

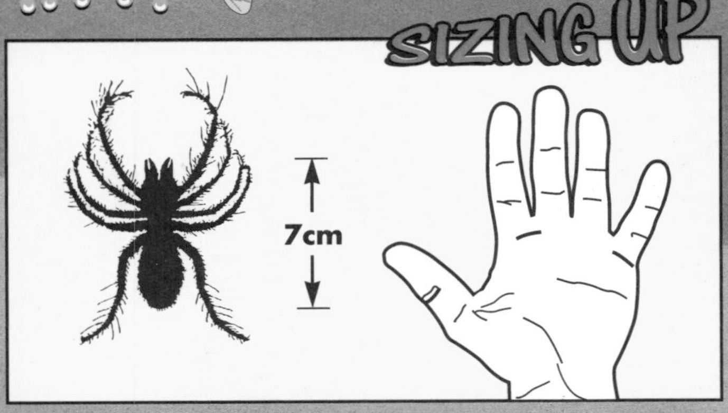

- **SCIENTIFIC NAME:** Solpugida
- **SIZE:** body up to 7cm long, legspan 15cm
- **LIVES:** usually in deserts of Africa, Asia and North and South America
- **EATS:** insects, spiders, worms, scorpions, lizards, birds and small mammals

LONG LEGS

The wind scorpion has quite a small body, but it has four pairs of very long, hairy legs. With its legs stretched out on either side, it would be almost as wide as a saucer!

HIGH SPEED

This bug gets its name because it can run so fast – 'as fast as the wind'. It can change direction quickly, too, and can even go backwards! Some wind scorpions can climb trees and walls, or even smooth, slippery surfaces like glass.

FINDING ITS PREY

The wind scorpion is a ferocious, meat-eating hunter. Using its six back legs for running, it races along with its pedipalps (feelers) and front pair of legs stretched out in front, 'feeling' for any possible victim. The long, yellow or brown bristles covering its body and legs also act as sensitive 'feelers'. It can see its prey, too, with the pair of powerful eyes on its head.

GIANT JAWS

Once it finds a victim, the wind scorpion grabs it in its strong jaws and sucks the goodness out of its body. Compared with the size of its body, the wind scorpion's jaws are probably the largest in the animal world. They are not venomous to humans, but they could give you a painful bite.

BIG APPETITE

The wind scorpion will eat all kinds of creatures – insects, spiders, worms, other scorpions, and even small lizards, birds and mice. It is very greedy and will go on eating until it is so full that it can hardly move.

TRICK OF NATURE

Mating can be a dangerous business for the male wind scorpion. The female is so fierce that she sometimes attacks a male that gets too close. When a male wants to mate with a female, he sidles up to her and starts stroking her. This sends her into a dreamy trance, but she does not stay in it for long. Once she is wide awake, the female might kill and eat her mate so he doesn't hang around for long.

MEGA MOTHER

After mating, the female wind scorpion eats as much as she can to give her strength for the hard work she has to do. Then she digs a burrow with her jaws, in which she lays 100 – 250 eggs.

Small Talk

FACING THE ENEMY

The wind scorpion can 'feel' an enemy approaching. Its pedipalps and two front legs are so sensitive that they can feel the ground moving as larger animals walk over it – in the same way that you would feel a wooden floor shaking if someone jumped on it. The wind scorpion does not run away from its enemies. Instead, it makes itself look as frightening as possible by rearing up and opening its gruesome jaws.

Pedipalp

Upper and lower jaws clamp together crushing the prey.

LIVING WITH MOTHER

Many female wind scorpions stay in their burrows to guard their eggs, driving away any other creatures that try to come in. When the eggs hatch, the mother goes out hunting to bring back food for her babies. She stays with them until they are big enough to leave their home and look after themselves.

BURROW BRAWL

A wind scorpion lunges at an African quelea bird. It wouldn't normally attack such large prey, but this bird is asking for trouble. It has strayed too near the wind scorpion's burrow and needs to be taught a lesson. Reaching out with its pedipalps and gnashing its jaws, the wind scorpion lunges at the bird, which takes off in fright.

Wind scorpions sense prey by reaching ahead with their front legs and pedipalps.

Powerful eyes help it to hunt its prey.

Six long back legs for running after prey.

Long bristles on legs and body act as feelers.

For most of its life this bug is an ugly, smelly caterpillar. But then it becomes the beautiful swallowtail butterfly.

Swallowtail Butterfly

The swallowtail butterfly begins life as an egg. After 8 – 10 days, a caterpillar hatches from the egg and begins munching the leaves of the wild carrot. The food gives the caterpillar the energy it needs to grow. As it grows, its skin peels off and is replaced by new skin underneath. If the caterpillar is growing really fast, it may shed its skin as often as once a week.

KEEPING SAFE

At first, predators don't notice the caterpillar because its back is black with a white patch. To a predator, it looks just like a bird dropping.

NATURAL DEFENCES

The caterpillar is green with black and orange bands. It has two orange horns, from which it squirts a smelly liquid to put off attackers. The caterpillar lives for a month, changes into a pupa for 2 – 20 weeks and then becomes a butterfly.

INVISIBLE COLOURS

The butterfly is attracted to flowers by their scent and colour. The swallowtail, which lives for only a month, can see colours that are invisible to humans.

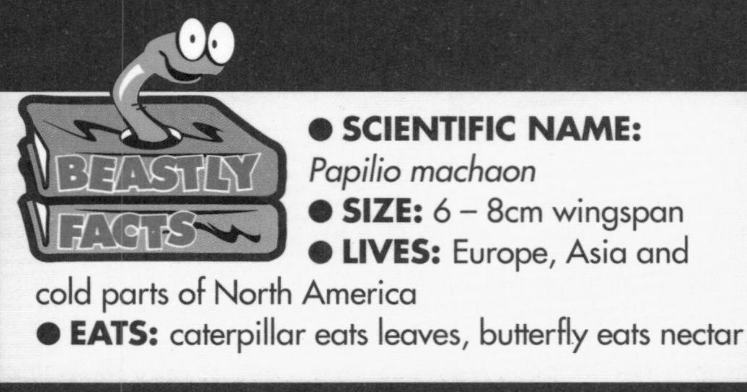

- **SCIENTIFIC NAME:** *Papilio machaon*
- **SIZE:** 6 – 8cm wingspan
- **LIVES:** Europe, Asia and cold parts of North America
- **EATS:** caterpillar eats leaves, butterfly eats nectar

SIZING UP

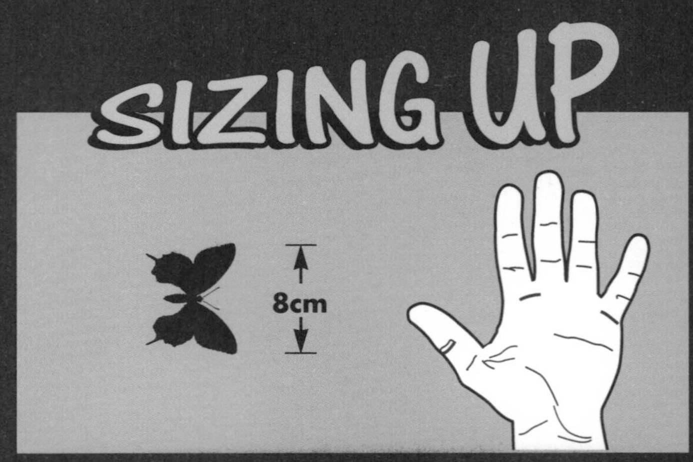

Giant Clam

A fully grown giant clam is too heavy to move!

Weighing just over a tonne, the giant clam is too heavy to move about. It stays in the same place all its life – often for as long as 100 years!

HANGING ON

When they are young, giant clams are covered in strong, silky hairs. These help them cling on to coral. Older clams just stay in place because of their great weight.

DANGEROUS SHADOWS

Inside the clam's shell is a fleshy lining called a mantle. All along the edge of its mantle are eyes that can detect light and shade. If the clam sees the shadow of a predator, it closes its shell to protect itself.

FILTERING OUT FOOD

The clam sucks water in through a tube in its mantle and passes it out through another tube. The sea water is full of microscopic sea creatures called plankton. The clam filters the plankton from the water and eats them. It also feeds on algae (tiny plants) that make their home on its mantle.

SAFE HOME

Pairs of small pea crabs sometimes live inside the clam's shell. They are useful to the clam because they eat any small parasites that try to invade their home.

SIZING UP

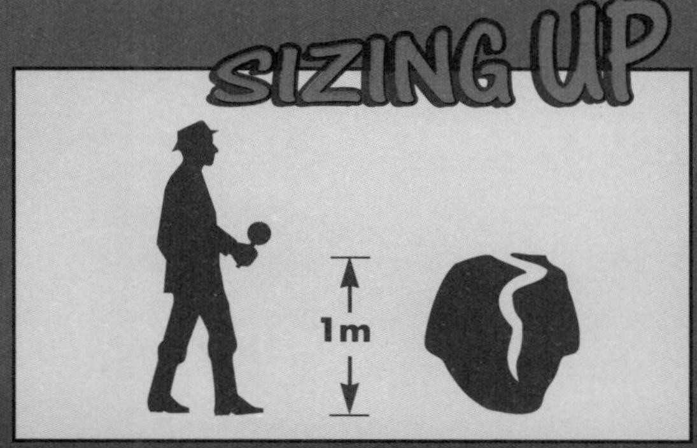

- **SCIENTIFIC NAME:** *Tridacna gigas*
- **SIZE:** about 1m long
- **LIVES:** coral reefs in the Indian and Pacific oceans
- **EATS:** plankton and algae

Paper houses

The common wasp likes company – it lives with hundreds of other members of its family in a purpose-built home. Here's how it makes its nest.

The queen starts the nest of the common wasp. She begins work on the home because she needs a safe place to raise her enormous family.

The side of this nest has been pulled away so that you can see inside.

A young wasp chews its way out of a cell.

Cells

SAFE HOUSE

First, the common wasp queen looks for a good spot to build her nest. She chooses a sheltered site such as up a tree, in the roof of a house or even in an up-turned saucepan!

1 A NEW HOME

Once she has found a good building site, the queen makes a shelter that looks rather like a mushroom. Next she builds a narrow stalk, from which she hangs a small cap. Inside there are either three or seven hexagonal cells, which are joined together. Eventually the whole nest will hang from this first stalk.

2 NEAT NURSERIES

Each cell is a tiny nursery and the queen lays an egg in each one. To protect her babies from cold winds and predators, the queen begins to build the walls of her house.

3 WRAP UP WARM

The queen makes her nest out of 'paper' which she makes by chewing up wood and then spitting it out again. She builds up layers of paper until only a small opening remains at the bottom of the nest. Air is trapped in between these layers and this helps to keep the nest warm, but stops it getting too hot. If you wore lots of thin jumpers, they would keep you warmer than one thick jersey, because of the air between each jumper.

First outer wall

This larva is the biggest. It probably contains a young queen wasp.
6
Every layer of wood pulp has been carried by wasps from a different place.
5
Paper walls
A tiny door keeps out drafts and stops the nest from getting too humid. It also protects the babies from large predators and other queens which might try to take over the nest.

5 STRIPY WALLPAPER

The workers fly off to different places to look for wood fibre to extend the nest. Because they all use a slightly different coloured wood, each layer of the nest has a different colour. This gives the outside of the nest a stripy effect.

6 MASTER BEDROOMS

When summer comes, the wasps build some special cells. The eggs laid in these cells develop into larvae, which are given VIP treatment. They get extra food and develop into males and queens. They fly from the nest and mate.

4 BORN TO BUILD

The queen's eggs hatch into larvae and she brings tiny insects and honey to the nest for them to eat. The young grow into workers, which are all female. They are born to build and immediately start to lend a helping hand. As the nest gets bigger, the workers eat the inner walls which were built by the queen. The space they leave makes room for new, larger groups of cells. As each cell becomes vacant, an egg is laid in it.

Is it true . . . that wasps use paper to build their nests?

Yes. Instead of bricks and mortar, wasps use chewed-up wood pulp to make their home. The same sort of pulp is used to make paper. If you have ever tried making anything with papier maché you will know how bendy soggy paper can be and how hard it dries. Wasps chew away at a piece of wood and fly back to the nest site with the wood pulp in their mouths. They spit it out and mould it to make the curved walls of their nests.

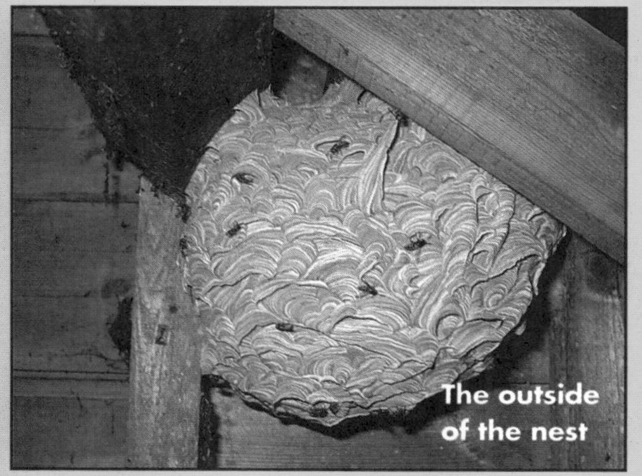
The outside of the nest

Different designs

Now you know how the common wasp builds its nest, take a look at the homes other wasps build.

Do you live in a flat, a house, a bungalow or a palace? We build many types of home, and so do wasps. Some are very hard to spot and others are quite bizarre!

BLOWN-UP RUBBER GLOVE

This nest in Costa Rica (above) looks a bit like a rubber washing-up glove that has been blown up! In fact, it's a clever water-collecting nest. During the night, dew settles on the rounded walls of the nest. As the day begins and the weather starts to warm up, the dew starts to run down the sides of the nest and on to the 'fingers' of the nest. It collects there for the wasps to have an early morning drink.

OLD SOCK

This may look like a old sock hung up in a tree to dry, but in fact it is the nest of a very wary wasp. The door to the nest is at the bottom of the long, thin tube (right). If predators, such as ants, try to get at the cells inside, they have to fight their way past the wasps that line the tube. The door is well away from the branch from which the nest hangs. This makes it even harder for hungry ants to get in the nest.

Door to the nest.

Small Talk

BIG BEACH BALL

The common wasp's nest can reach 35cm in diameter – that's about the same size as a big beach ball. The nest may contain up to 2,000 adults. In countries where the weather is always warm the wasps don't die in the winter – they just keep on building and the nests can be much larger.

STICK

This might look like a twig to you (right), but in fact it is a very thin wasps' nest. It was found in Peru, where the rainfall can be very heavy. Rain drops could easily run into the nest and drown the baby wasps, so it has been built with the doors facing towards the ground. Adult wasps put hungry ants off even more by rubbing an ant repellent from the back of their bodies on to the nest.

Doors

The doors of this nest point downwards.

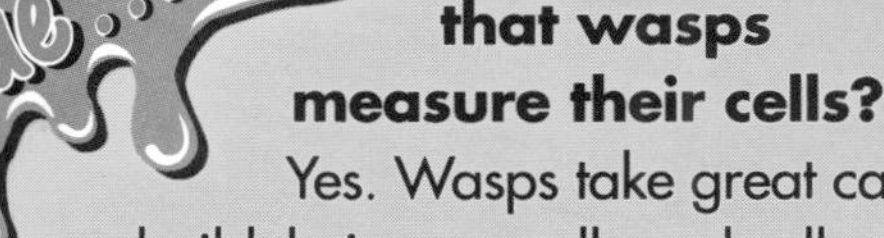

that wasps measure their cells?

Yes. Wasps take great care to build their nest walls and cells to just the right size. These clever builders don't have tape measures so they use their antennae to measure their cells and judge distances between the walls.

FRUITY FRAUD

The green wasps that have gathered on this hanging nest (right) on the island of Madagascar make it look like a half-eaten piece of fruit. This disguise fools most insect-eating birds and animals, which might try to eat the wasps. During the dry season, the wasps cluster quietly on the nest for several months while it is not being used.

Green wasps find safety in numbers.

SMALL AND COSY

This may be the smallest wasps' nest in the world (below). It has been built out of plant fibres and hangs under a leaf. This means that it can't be seen by predators. The wasps that live here eat tiny bugs, called springtails, which they drag back to their nests and munch at their leisure.

This tiny nest was discovered in Costa Rica.

ROCK POOLING

Peer into a rock pool and discover a whole world of watery minibeasts.

You will need:
- plastic jar
- water
- washing-up liquid
- notebook
- pencil

Next time you are by the seaside, take some time to look at the minibeasts that lurk in the rock pools beneath your feet. Whether you use a special rock pooling view tube, or you just sit and watch, you will see plenty of life which will keep you busy for hours.

1 First of all, make your rock pooling view tube. Ask in a sweet shop if they have a plastic sweet jar they do not need (or use any large, plastic jar). When you get it home, fill it with water, just to check that there are no leaks. Then soak the jar in warm, soapy water to remove any labels. You should also clean and rinse the inside of the jar, in case it has a sticky or sugary coating.

2 Now put your view tube in a rucksack with your notebook and pencil, tell someone where you are going and head for the beach. Once you are on the beach, select your rock pooling area. Remember that rocks can be sharp and slippery – particularly if they're covered in seaweed – so be careful. If you fall over, not only will you hurt yourself but you will also frighten away any minibeasts nearby.

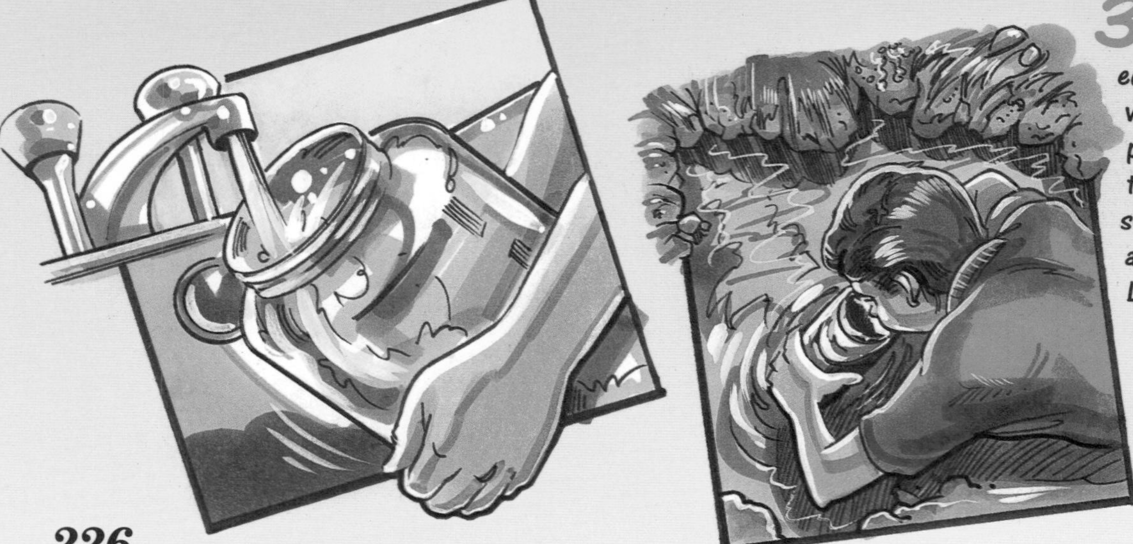

3 When you have chosen your rock pool, lie down near the edge of it. Gently lower your view tube into the water and peer through the hole where the lid was when it was a sweet jar. Hold it perfectly still and wait to see what emerges. Lying down might become uncomfortable so try just sitting and watching the pool. A pair of sunglasses will help reduce the glare from the water.

4 As you watch and wait, the minibeasts will reveal themselves. If you have brought sandwiches with you, drop a tiny bit of bread into the water – this should attract some animals. Look out for leggy creatures, such as crabs and shrimps. You may also see five-legged starfish moving on their rubbery legs and the many-tentacled anemone waving its arms as it waits to catch its prey.

CAUTION!

BEFORE YOU GO...

It is a good idea to check, before you start out, what time the tide goes out and comes in. The best – and safest – time to go rock pooling is just after the tide has gone out. The rock pools will be exposed and you will have plenty of time to explore your pool. Leave well before the tide is due to come in. Always let someone know where you are going – better still, go with a friend.

5 Not all the minibeasts you are likely to see will show any sign of movement unless you are very lucky. The soft-bodied shellfish, safe in its hard case, for example, may remain quite still. After a while, when you think you have seen everything in your pool, give a piece of seaweed a gentle nudge – this may encourage some more minibeasts to move. If you see anything you don't recognise, draw a quick picture of it. Remember to note down its colour, how many legs it has and where you found it. When you get home, look it up in a book, or in BUGS!.

Here comes the sun:
When you walk towards a rock pool, walk into the sun rather than away from it. This way your shadow will not fall across the water, which could frighten creatures and send them scuttling for cover.

6 Before you leave the beach, have a quick look in between the rocks. It is also worth looking under loose stones and rocks for bugs that like to hide there. Always remember to put the rocks and minibeasts back where you found them.

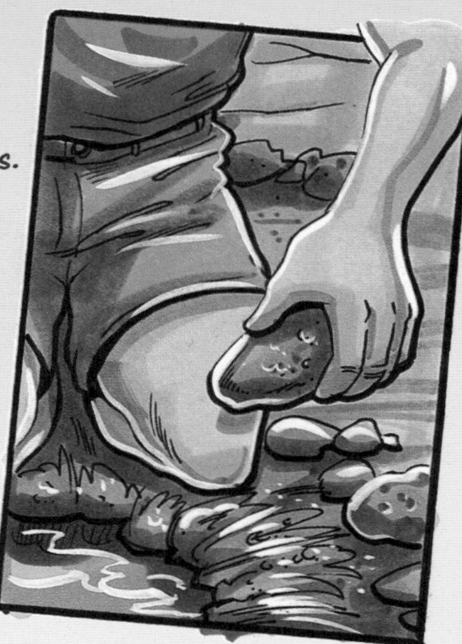

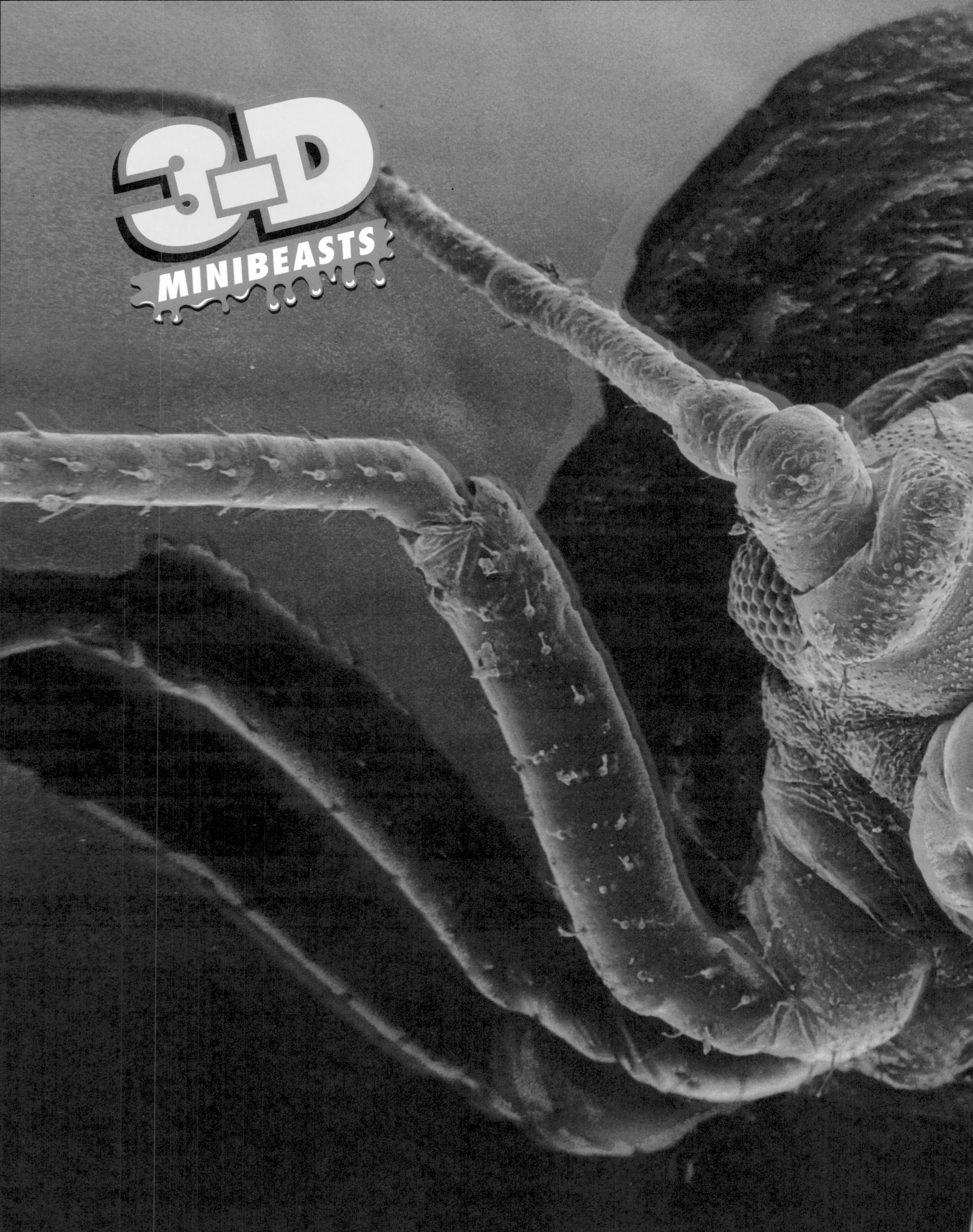
3-D
MINIBEASTS

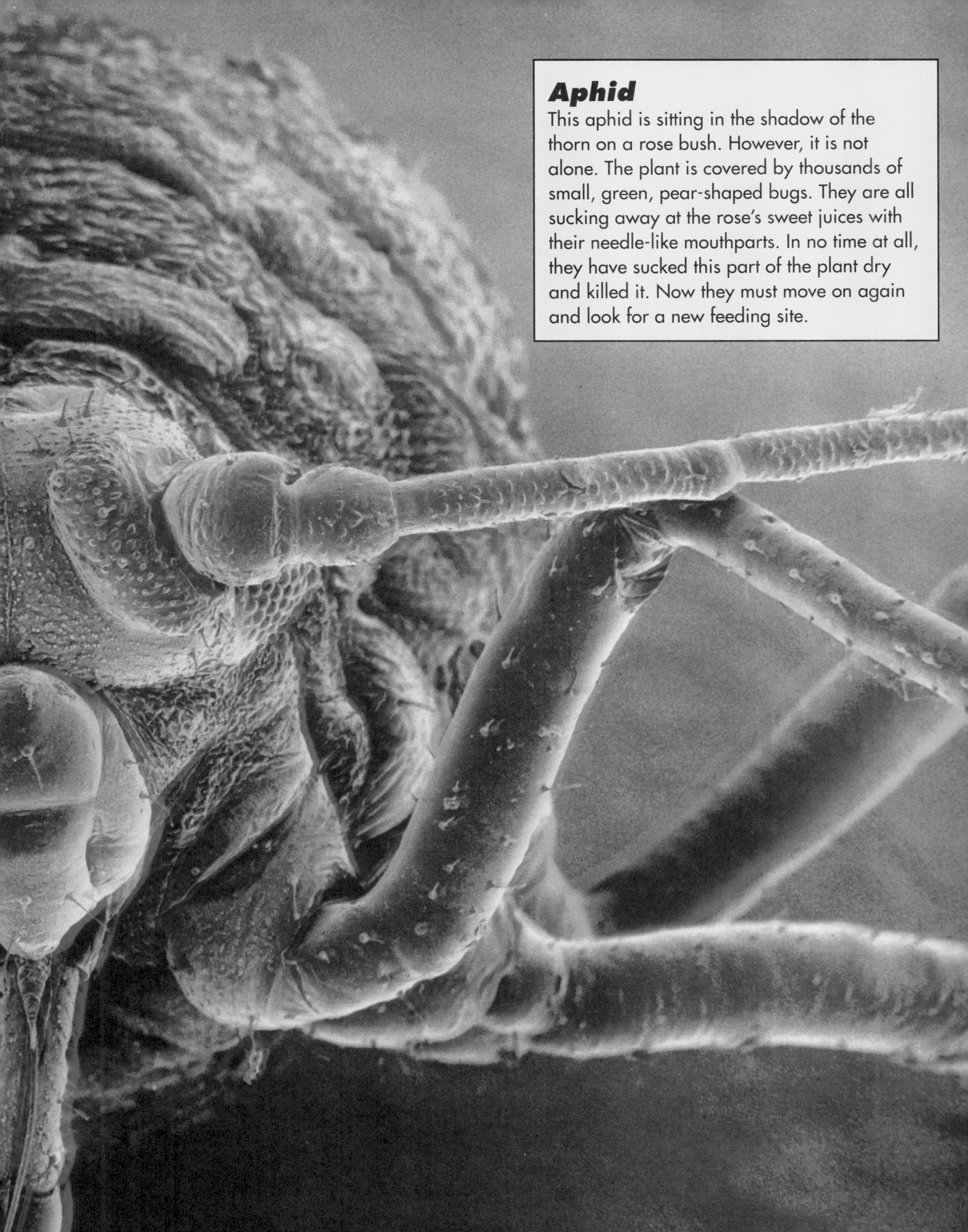

Aphid

This aphid is sitting in the shadow of the thorn on a rose bush. However, it is not alone. The plant is covered by thousands of small, green, pear-shaped bugs. They are all sucking away at the rose's sweet juices with their needle-like mouthparts. In no time at all, they have sucked this part of the plant dry and killed it. Now they must move on again and look for a new feeding site.

ALL CHANGE

Insects go through various stages as they grow. A Greek word, metamorphosis, which means 'change in shape', is used to describe these changes.

Metamorphosis (say 'meta-morf-o-sis') is something that happens to all living creatures – including you. A human being begins life as an egg inside its mother. For nine months, it grows and changes until it is ready to be born. You will keep on growing and changing until you are a fully grown adult. Like you, some insects develop steadily, while others go through huge changes in shape and colour – until they eventually become adults.

Female cabbage white butterfly laying eggs.

This is where the complete metamorphosis story starts. A female cabbage white butterfly (above) has found a sheltered spot, underneath a leaf, in which to start her family.

COMPLETE METAMORPHOSIS

Some bugs go through a four-stage process called complete metamorphosis. They start life as an egg (1). The egg hatches into a larva (2). This then changes into a pupa (3). And finally, the pupa changes into an adult (4). The young of insects that go through these four stages have certain things in common:

- They look totally different from their parents.
- They live apart from their parents.
- They usually eat different types of food from their parents.
- They show no signs of having wings.

Adult

4

4 The adult butterfly emerges from the case. At first, its wings are weak and floppy. After a while, they harden and the butterfly flies off to look for a mate to start the cycle again.

Eggs

1 The cabbage white butterfly lays her eggs on a plant that the caterpillars will be able to eat as soon as they hatch. In the case of the cabbage white, this is usually the cabbage, cauliflower or turnip. Look out for eggs on leaves in spring and summer.

2 The eggs of the butterfly hatch out into larvae, which are called caterpillars. The caterpillars are brightly coloured to warn birds of their unpleasant taste. The caterpillars spend all their time eating. They need all the goodness they can get before they turn into pupae.

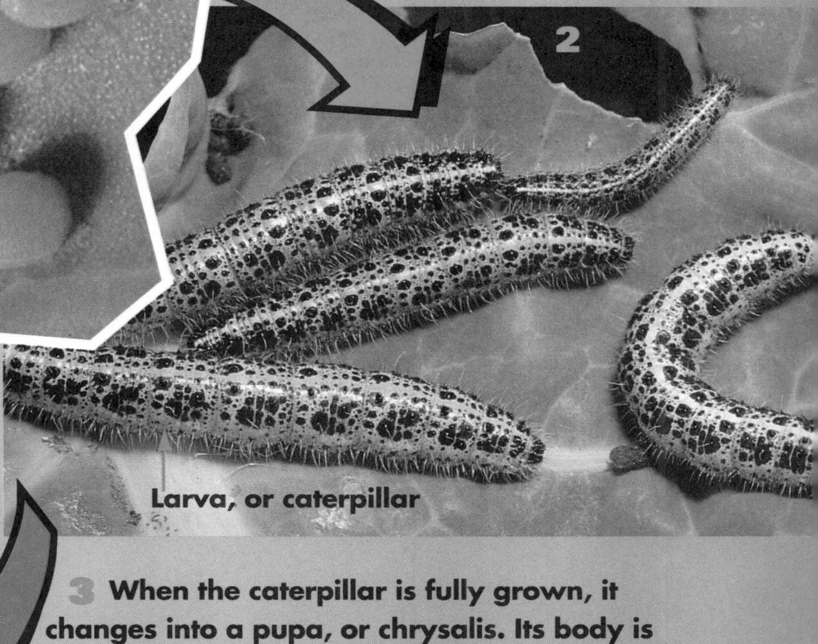

2

Larva, or caterpillar

3

3 When the caterpillar is fully grown, it changes into a pupa, or chrysalis. Its body is protected by a thin but hard case. Eventually, the caterpillar's body breaks down and rebuilds itself in the shape of the adult.

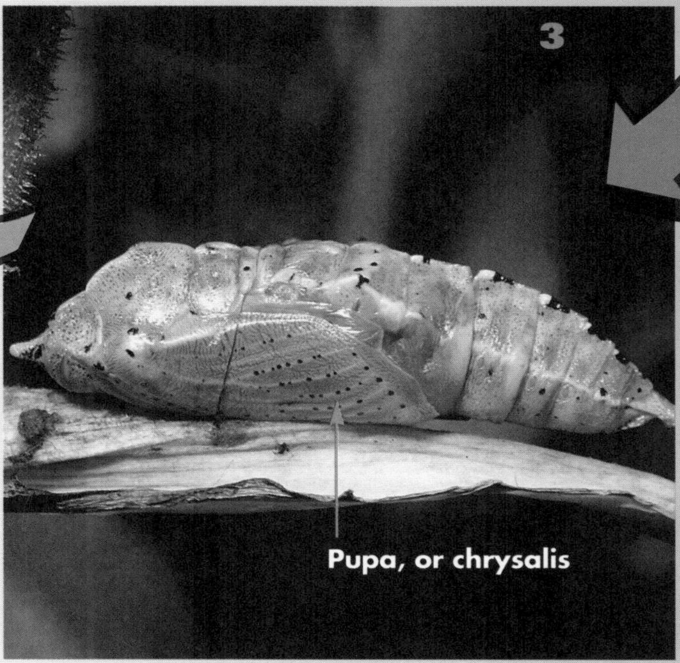

Pupa, or chrysalis

INSECTS THAT UNDERGO COMPLETE METAMORPHOSIS INCLUDE:

- ant
- bee
- beetle
- butterfly
- flea
- fly
- moth
- wasp

All change again

Some bugs gradually get bigger by shedding their skin.

Not all bugs go through complete metamorphosis. Some, such as the shield bug (right), miss out the pupa (or chrysalis) stage. Bugs that do this go through incomplete metamorphosis.

INCOMPLETE METAMORPHOSIS

As a shield bug grows, it looks more and more like an adult. It does this by moulting (shedding layers of skin). The growing bug changes size and shape very slowly with each moult. The young of bugs that undergo incomplete metamorphosis have the following things in common:

- They usually differ only slightly from their parents except in size.
- They usually live in the same place as their parents.
- They feed on the same type of food as their parents.
- Their wings appear gradually and tiny wing-buds can usually be seen before the insect is a full-grown adult.

INSECTS THAT UNDERGO INCOMPLETE METAMORPHOSIS INCLUDE:

- aphid
- cockroach
- cricket
- dragonfly
- earwig
- grasshopper
- locust
- mantis
- shield bug
- silverfish
- stick insect
- termite

1 **The mother shield bug starts off the process of incomplete metamorphosis when she lays her eggs. She leaves them on a plant that her babies will be able to eat as soon as they are born. She guards her eggs until they hatch.**

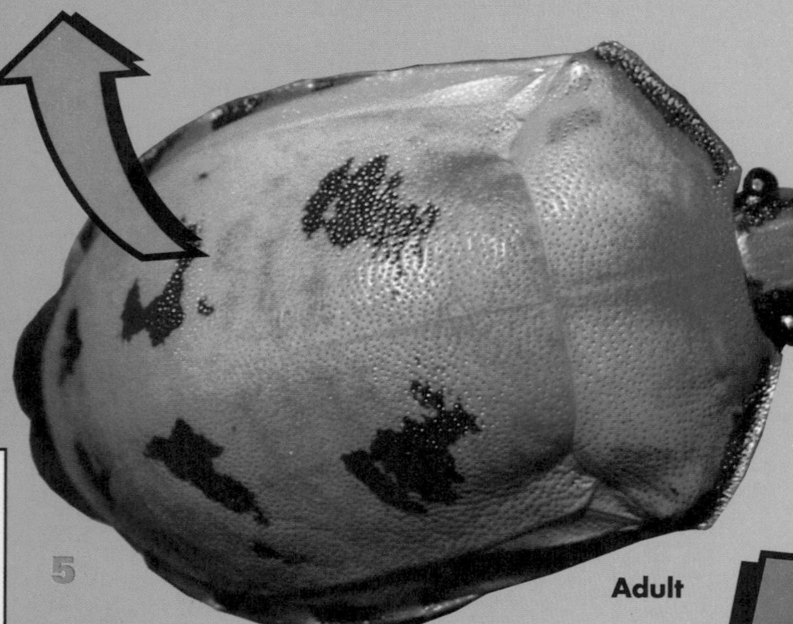

5 **The shield bug's wing-buds gradually get bigger with each moult. They are clearly visible before the bug is a fully grown adult. As the shield bug gets bigger, it looks more and more like the adult.**

2 The eggs of the shield bug hatch out into babies, which are called nymphs. They are much smaller than their parents, but they are basically the same shape.

3 The growing bugs gradually change in size. As they grow, they shed layers of skin – in a process known as moulting. This gradual change is the most important part of incomplete metamorphosis.

4 The fully grown adult bug is a large version of the much smaller nymph, with little difference in shape. The adult bug goes in search of a mate in order to start the lifecycle again.

Moulting shield bugs begin to look more like the adult (above left).

What is... moulting?

Young insects grow by shedding their tough skins. This is called moulting. Imagine if you had been born in a bendy suit of armour. You wouldn't have been able to grow without taking the armour off. Not all animals moult in order to grow – cats and dogs shed hairs in summer to stay cool.

Rain forest - a hothouse for bugs

Perching in the tree-tops or tunnelling under rotting leaves, millions of bugs make their homes in the lush, green rain forest.

If you lift up a leaf in a rain forest you are likely to find at least one bug, but they don't all live on the forest floor. Some like to live high up in the branches of massive trees. All of them love the moist, warm air and the thick greenery of the rain forest.

WHAT IS A RAIN FOREST?

Rain forests cover six per cent of the world's surface (that's about 10 million square kilometres – more than the area of the USA). They contain 50 – 70 per cent of all plant and animal species. The weather in rain forests is hot and moist. The temperature is usually about 24°C and as much as 3.8m of rain can fall each year.

ALL YEAR FOOD

There are no obvious seasons in the rain forest and so the plants that grow there are always in flower. This provides bugs with a year-round supply of sweet nectar.

Every minute of every day plants and trees are fighting for sunlight. The tallest trees stretch out their branches to soak up the sunlight, but shorter plants have to struggle just to get a few seconds of dappled light.

Small Talk

Rain forests are found on or near the equator in Central and South America, central Africa, South-East Asia and northern Australasia. The red areas on the world map (below) show where the rain forests are.

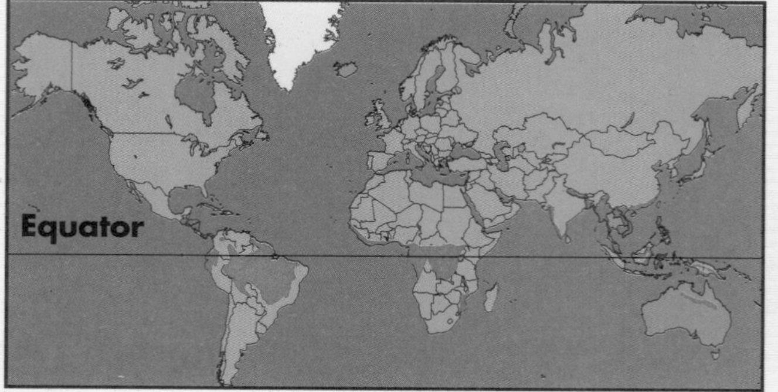

Leaf-cutter ants

LAYERS

If you were to stand in the middle of a rain forest and look up you would see a mass of leaves and branches. It may look like a jumble of trunks and greenery, but every rain forest has four separate layers.

1 CANOPY (up to 30 – 40m high)

The canopy or 'roof' of the forest is made up of broad tree-tops, which are tightly packed together. From the air, they look like one solid layer of vegetation. Like a huge, flat parachute, these tree-tops stretch for kilometres and are only interrupted by an occasional giant tree. These huge trees are called emergents because they 'emerge', or stick out, from the roof of the forest.

2 UNDER-STOREY (up to 6 – 12m high)

The under-storey is the densest layer in the forest. It includes palms and climbing plants. Many of the animals that live in the forest spend a lot of time foraging in the tree-tops. Some bugs hang out in the under-storey, looking for orchids and other brightly coloured flowers.

3 TRUNK

Below the under-storey, the branches thin out again and you can easily see the tree trunks. Wood-eating bugs live here. Some of the trunks are broad and tall, but the trees' roots are often very short. The trees are supported by buttress roots, which grow upwards from the ground and act like props, or scaffolding, for the trees.

4 GROUND

Only one per cent of the sunlight reaches the ground. The rest of the light is blocked off by thick vegetation. If a tree falls down, however, a small patch of sunlight reaches the forest floor and ground vegetation flourishes. In other places, though, it is dark and damp. Many bugs thrive on the dingy forest floor, eating fallen leaves and fruit.

Pack up your rucksack, put on your boots and grab your magnifying glass. You're going deep into the heart of the rain forest to look for bugs.

BUMP INTO A BUG

Lift up a rock, turn over a leaf. Bugs are easy to find in the rain forest – they're everywhere! It won't be long until you bump into a bug. Bugs live at four levels of the rain forest. Nectar-eating insects search out flowers that grow up in the canopy. Others clamber up and down the tree trunks or burrow through the thick undergrowth on the ground.

FOLLOW THAT SLIME

The flatworm may look like an orange rasher of bacon, but in fact it is a cunning hunter. It loves to eat snails so it follows the slimy trails that they leave behind. When it catches its prey, the flatworm sucks the fleshy part of the snail out of its shell through a mouth-like opening in its underside.

Its bright orange skin tells predators that the flatworm is poisonous. This snail didn't take the hint, or escape in time.

Land snail

Flatworm

HAIRY MENACE

Some of the largest spiders in the world live in the rain forest. Some live on the ground, while others spin thick webs in the trees. Bird-eating spiders can have a legspan as wide as this page. Most of the time they hunt large insects, but they also eat birds and may even attack small mammals, such as shrews and mice.

Behind you! A pink-toed bird-eating spider launches itself from one level of the rain forest to another and lands on a cicada.

Pink-toed bird-eatin spider

RAIN SONGS

The cicada is probably the noisiest bug in the forest. The male 'sings' to the female using bendy plates on either side of its abdomen. Like the curved surface of a drum, the plate is pulled in and out to make a clicking noise.

Imagine living under the ground until you are 17 years old! That's what a young cicada (right) has to do.

Cicada shedding its larval case.

CANOPY CAPERS

The male morpho butterfly (below right) flits high above the canopy. When the sun shines on his wings they shimmer. They are usually a beautiful, electric blue colour, but they can be red, yellow or brown. The female is less colourful and stays near the forest floor. The juice from rotting fruit and sap are the butterfly's favourite foods. The male only ventures down to the forest floor to drink from streams.

GOOD NEWS

In a rain forest, an area the size of a football pitch provides a home to over 20,000 different types of plants and animals. One in 10 of the drugs that modern doctors use to cure us comes from these plants and animals. About 1,650 of the rain forest plants can be eaten as vegetables. The trees also filter out some of the pollution that we pump into the air.

BAD NEWS

Humans have chopped down so many rain forest trees that thousands of animals and plants have become extinct. By destroying so much of the forests we are also upsetting the delicate balance of gases in the Earth's atmosphere. This may mean that in the future the world will get too warm for us.

A FOREST NO MORE

Humans have already destroyed half of the world's rain forests. If we carry on chopping down trees at this rate, there won't be a single tree left in the rain forests by the year 2035.

Morpho butterflies flock together for safety. This one has been caught by a cunning mantid. Collectors try to attract and trap them by waving bright blue scarves in the air.

Improve and test your knowledge with...

CREEPY~CRAWLY FACTS

Follow the ants' trail to the 'Egg-cellent' BUGS! quiz.

1 Where do wind scorpions live?
a) in cold, snowy mountains
b) in hot, dry deserts
c) in hot, wet forests

2 Why does an adult giant clam never move?
a) it's too heavy
b) it's too lazy
c) it cannot swim

3 What does the word metamorphosis mean?
a) change of clothes
b) lose the skin
c) change in shape

4 What is the best time to go rock pooling?
a) just after breakfast
b) just after the tide has gone out
c) when the sun has gone down

5 Where does the common wasp build its nest?
a) in a bright, sunny spot
b) in a sheltered site
c) in a damp, dark place

6 How does the tiger moth avoid being eaten?
a) it makes clicking noises
b) it changes colour
c) it sticks its tongue out

7 How does the common wasp get into its house?
a) through a large hole
b) it breaks its way in
c) through a small opening

Egg carriers

Biting house-flies have a strange habit. They hover above swarms of African driver ants and drop eggs in their path. Luckily for the biting house-flies, the African driver ants do not eat the flies' eggs. Instead they pick them up and carry them until they set up camp and build their bivouacs. Here the eggs hatch into maggots, which munch on the ants' rubbish.

Spider silk

Spider silk has been used for centuries. Over the years it has been used to make gloves, handkerchieves and parts for telescopes. Today, modern techniques mean that over 320m of silk can be removed from one female spider at a sitting. The spider is knocked out and the silk drawn out using a small motor. Luckily, the spider will recover after a short time. Spider silk is very tough, elastic and resistant to cold and heat. It is so stretchy and strong that it is also an excellent material for making parachutes and bulletproof vests!

Early warning

Tiger moths warn bats that they taste disgusting by making clicking noises. The banded woolly bear moth tastes much better to a bat, but it has learned to copy the tiger moth's clicking noises to avoid being eaten.

Slow grow

The clam is the slowest-growing animal on Earth. It took one clam 75 years to grow to its full size – 8mm long! Some clams grow only 10mm in 10 years.

8 What do rain forest trees use to support their trunks?
a) string
b) iron scaffolding
c) buttresses

9 How do collectors attract morpho butterflies?
a) they dress in black
b) they paint their faces blue
c) they wave bright blue scarves

10 What colour is the cinnabar moth?
a) green and blue
b) black and white
c) black and red

Answers to the questions on the inside back cover

Q and A

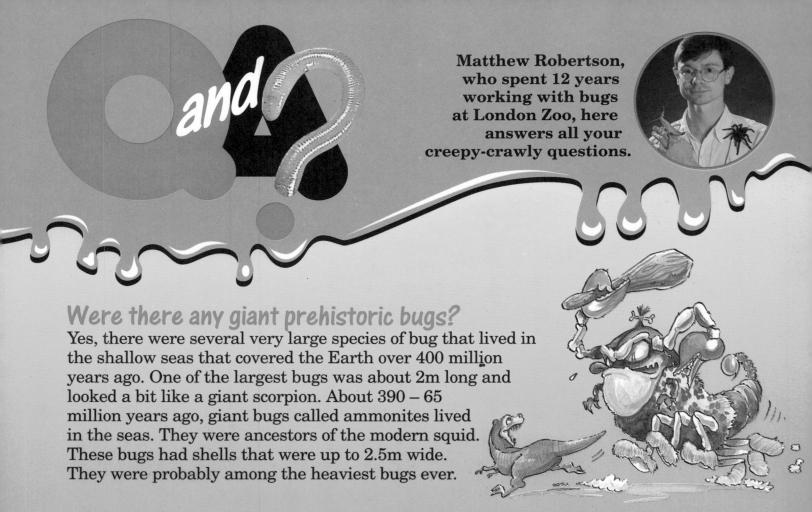

Matthew Robertson, who spent 12 years working with bugs at London Zoo, here answers all your creepy-crawly questions.

Were there any giant prehistoric bugs?

Yes, there were several very large species of bug that lived in the shallow seas that covered the Earth over 400 million years ago. One of the largest bugs was about 2m long and looked a bit like a giant scorpion. About 390 – 65 million years ago, giant bugs called ammonites lived in the seas. They were ancestors of the modern squid. These bugs had shells that were up to 2.5m wide. They were probably among the heaviest bugs ever.

Do bugs have brains?

Like you, most bugs have a brain in their heads (if they have heads, that is!). A brain is a control centre, which sends messages around the body through the nervous system (a network of nerves). Some animals, like the sponge, do not have a nervous system and therefore have no brain either. Simple-looking bugs have simple brains that are made up of a small clump of nerves. As bugs become more complex, so do their brains. However, we still do not really know how even the simplest bug brain works.

Can you get ill from a bug?

Like any animal, a bug can carry germs that can make you ill. In most cases, a bug germ will just make you feel sick. However, some germs can make you very ill and some can even kill. This is why you must always wash your hands after handling bugs. Bugs that have been kept in captivity for some time are unlikely to carry germs that would harm you. (Germs often need to live on other animals to survive.)

Emperor Dragonfly

With its incredible speed and amazing eyesight, the emperor dragonfly has no trouble capturing its prey.

There have been dragonflies on Earth for over 300 million years. In all that time, they have changed very little – even the first emperor dragonflies looked similar to the ones we can still see flying around today.

UNDERWATER LIFE

The adult dragonfly is a flying insect, but lives underwater when it is young. It begins life as an egg, tucked safely into the stem of a water plant, out of the reach of fish. When it hatches, the young dragonfly, or nymph (say 'nimf'), has no wings.

GROWING UP

A nymph takes about a year to grow up. As it gets bigger and fatter, its skin splits and comes off, to show a new skin underneath. This is called moulting. Each nymph may moult 10 – 15 times before it is old enough to crawl out of the water. As it sits in the warm sunshine, its skin dries and splits open – and out comes a new dragonfly.

SLOW FLAPPER

When its wings are dry, the dragonfly takes to the air. The adult dragonfly, which will only live for a few more weeks, has two pairs of wings. Unlike the wings of other insects, these beat up and down in turn – when one pair is up, the other pair is down. Although its wings beat only 20 – 30 times a second (about 10 times slower than a bee), the dragonfly is still one of the fastest flying insects.

The male's abdomen is bright blue with dark markings, while the female has a blue-green body with brown markings.

The nymph is a vicious hunter. It shoots out its flexible lower lip (called a mask), snatches its prey and draws it towards its mouth – all in just 25 milliseconds. A young nymph can easily catch and eat a tadpole that is half its size.

Two pairs of wings. When the dragonfly rests, it doesn't fold its wings back.

SEEING IS BELIEVING

The emperor dragonfly has incredible eyesight. Although its enormous eyes look round, they are in fact made up of thousands of tiny 'facets', or lenses, each facing in a slightly different direction. Each eye has about 30,000 facets, which means that the dragonfly can see all around. With its amazing sight, it can spot its prey up to 12m away.

KEEP OUT

The male spends almost all of his time in the air, flying about over his 'territory' – the patch of water that belongs to him. He guards his territory fiercely and will attack any other male that strays into it. When an unwelcome visitor arrives, the male flies underneath the intruder and forces it up and away from the water.

MID-AIR MOVES

No bug enters the male dragonfly's territory and gets away with it. Excellent wing control and brilliant eyesight helps the athletic flier to pounce on the trespassing greenbottle.

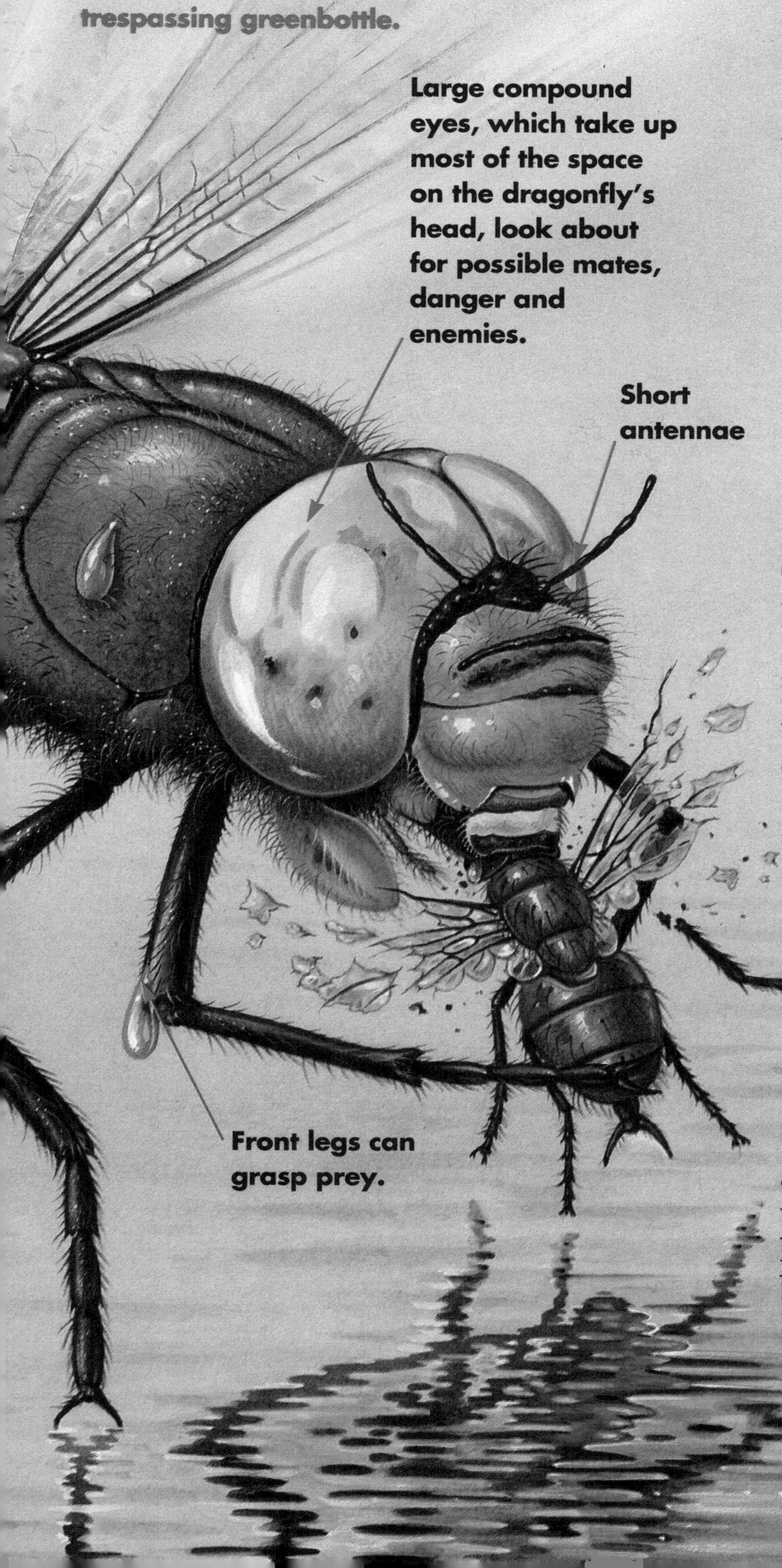

Large compound eyes, which take up most of the space on the dragonfly's head, look about for possible mates, danger and enemies.

Short antennae

Front legs can grasp prey.

BEASTLY FACTS

- **SCIENTIFIC NAME:** *Anax imperator*
- **SIZE:** wingspan 11cm
- **LIVES:** Europe, north Africa, the Middle East and parts of north-west India
- **EATS:** adults eat flying insects; nymphs eat tadpoles and other water creatures

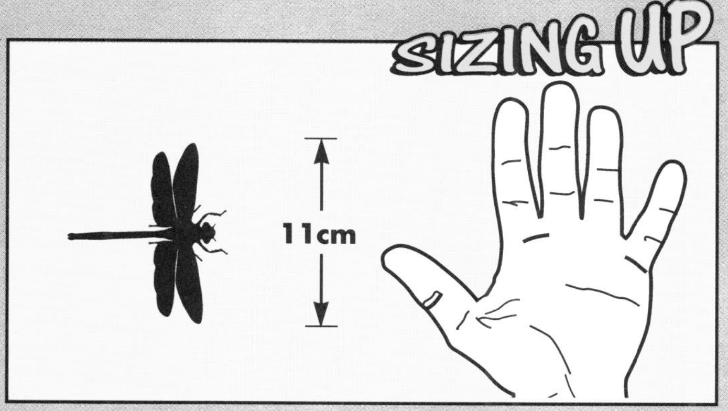

DIVE BOMBER

The emperor dragonfly is an excellent hunter. It swoops on its prey as it flies along, grabbing hold of victims with its legs. If its prey is small, the dragonfly won't even bother to land, but will just carry on with its meal in mid-air.

JAWS

The dragonfly nymph is just as ferocious as the adult. It can either move along by walking on its six legs or by pumping water out of the back of its body – like someone letting air out of a balloon. When it has caught up with its prey, the nymph shoots out its lower jaw at its victim and, in a millisecond, seizes it with the two hooks on the end. The nymph has been nicknamed 'the freshwater shark' because it is so fierce.

Money Spider

Like a trapeze artist swinging from a rope, the money spider floats gracefully through the air on a silky thread.

The money spider is hard to spot because it is so small. The best time to see this bug is in late summer and autumn, when millions of these little creatures take to the skies.

AIR TRAVEL

Before it can 'fly', the spider climbs up a blade of grass or a twig and releases a long thread of spider's silk. Warm air rising from the ground lifts the thread upwards until it catches on a solid object. When the spider feels the silk tighten, it lets go with its feet and is carried up into the sky!

SPINNING A WEB

As evening comes and the air gets cooler, the thread floats down again. Where the spider lands, it builds a fine, domed web. It sits underneath its trap and waits patiently for insects to drop on to the web.

COLOUR CHANGE

The money spider may be all black or black, white and brown. Some species can change their colour when they are disturbed, so that they blend in with their background and are harder to see.

LUCKY FIND

Finding a money spider on your clothes is supposed to be lucky – it means that you may become rich in the future.

SIZING UP

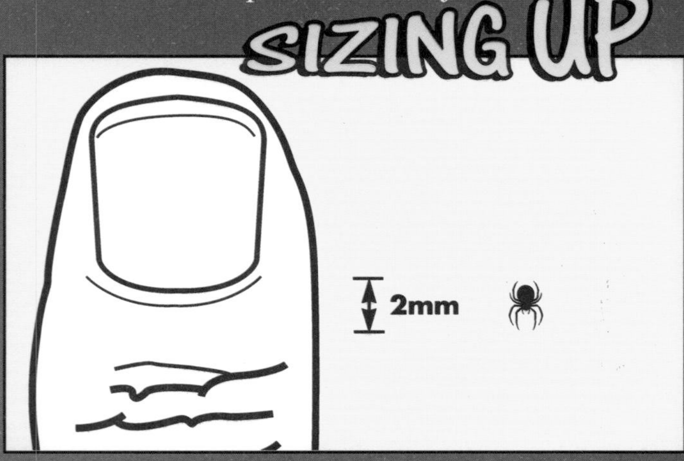

- **SCIENTIFIC NAME:** *Linyphia triangularis*
- **SIZE:** 2mm long
- **LIVES:** northern Europe
- **EATS:** insects

Fat-tailed Scorpion

The sting in the tail of this scorpion is so deadly that it could kill a human being.

BEASTLY FACTS

- **SCIENTIFIC NAME:** *Androctonus australis*
- **SIZE:** 8 – 12cm long
- **LIVES:** north Africa and the Middle East
- **EATS:** insects and other small animals

When the fat-tailed scorpion is threatened, it does not attack. It just rises up and lifts its tail over its head. It looks so terrifying that it frightens most enemies away.

SIZING UP

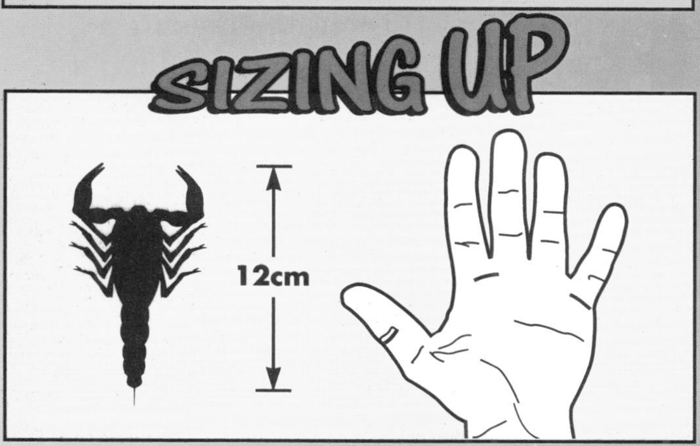

DEADLY STING

At the tip of the scorpion's tail is a sting that is so poisonous that, without treatment, it could kill a human in less than eight hours! The scorpion uses its sting for killing prey, but only if it cannot catch it with its claws, or if its victim fights back.

TAKE YOUR PARTNERS

Before mating, the male scorpion takes the female by her claws. He leads her backwards and forwards in a 'dance' that can last from 10 minutes up to an hour. After giving birth, the female carries her babies about on her back until they are big enough to look after themselves.

USEFUL HAIRS

The fat-tailed scorpion has four pairs of eyes, but it does not see very well. It finds its prey by smell and touch. Using the long, fine hairs on its feelers, it senses victims as they move about.

Letting off

Some bugs build up a head of steam before they attack. Their weapons include nasty liquids and horrible smells.

Bugs fight off their enemies in a variety of ways – some of them are quite nasty. Some give off foul smells or squirt yucky fluids, and some make threatening noises. Read on to find out what all the noise – and mess – is about.

MAKING A MESS

A species of bee from the West Indies, known as the tar baby, smears attackers with a sticky liquid, which it stores on its back legs. It makes the sticky substance in its abdomen and usually uses it to plug up holes in its nest. If a tar baby is upset, though, it will use the gunge to stop attackers in their tracks.

SPIT IT OUT

The American green lynx spider turns its head towards its target and then sprays a stream of venom from its fangs. It can hit a target as far away as 20cm. It seems to use this as a method of defence against predators, such as birds and lizards, rather than against other spiders.

A FLASH OF LIGHT

If it comes face to face with an enemy, the firework squid squirts a cloud of glow-in-the-dark ink. In the depths of the sea it is very dark and a spray of this ink will cause a sudden flash of light. For a moment, the attacker is blinded and the squid has time to escape.

steam

Startled by a nosy diver, a firework squid lights up the dark ocean with a spray of glow-in-the-dark ink. The sudden brightness stuns the diver and gives the squid time to swim away.

A serval (a type of African wild cat) gets an eye-full when it comes across a spitting assassin bug.

HOW IRRITATING!

The assassin bug (left) has long, needle-like mouthparts, which it can point in any direction. It uses them to squirt its attackers with a clear, irritating fluid. This nasty liquid can cause temporary blindness in any animal that decides to get in the assassin bug's way.

Not all bugs rely on liquids to defend themselves – some use sprays, smells or noises.

GOOD SHOT

A stick insect, known as the Florida walking stick, sprays a very smelly chemical from glands on the side of its thorax. Its aim is surprisingly good. If you were to get too close to the stick insect, it might spray you in the face. Not only is the smell disgusting, but the chemical also makes it very hard for the predator to breathe.

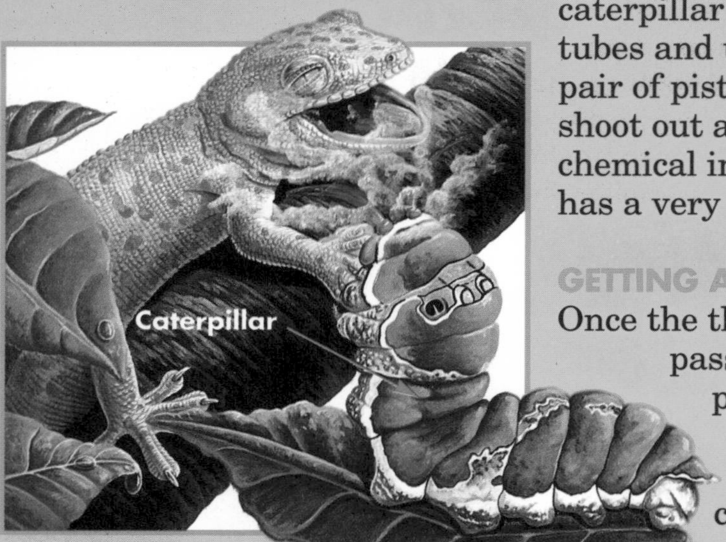

Caterpillar

A Trinidad orange dog swallowtail caterpillar gives a gecko a nasty surprise.

SHARP SHOOTER

The caterpillar of the Trinidad orange dog swallowtail butterfly has two brightly coloured tubes on its thorax, just behind its head. When it is threatened, the caterpillar sticks out the two tubes and uses them like a pair of pistols. The pistols shoot out a strong-smelling chemical in a fine spray. This has a very unpleasant stink.

GETTING AWAY WITH IT

Once the threat of danger has passed, the caterpillar pulls the two tubes back into its body. This smelly caterpillar doesn't always win, however, despite its efforts. Not all hungry predators are put off by a disgusting smell.

Soldier termites make a right rattling racket.

Purple-winged grasshopper

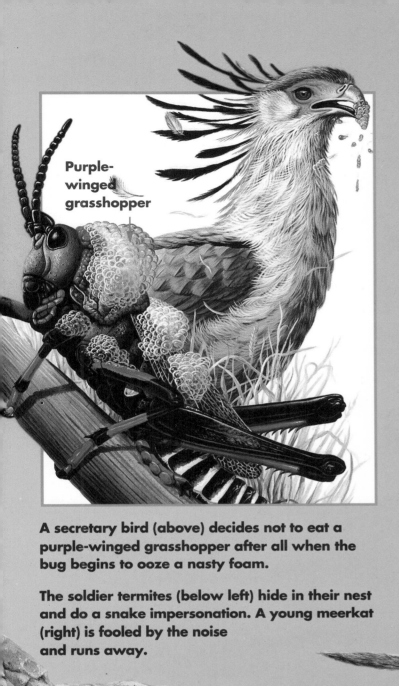

A secretary bird (above) decides not to eat a purple-winged grasshopper after all when the bug begins to ooze a nasty foam.

The soldier termites (below left) hide in their nest and do a snake impersonation. A young meerkat (right) is fooled by the noise and runs away.

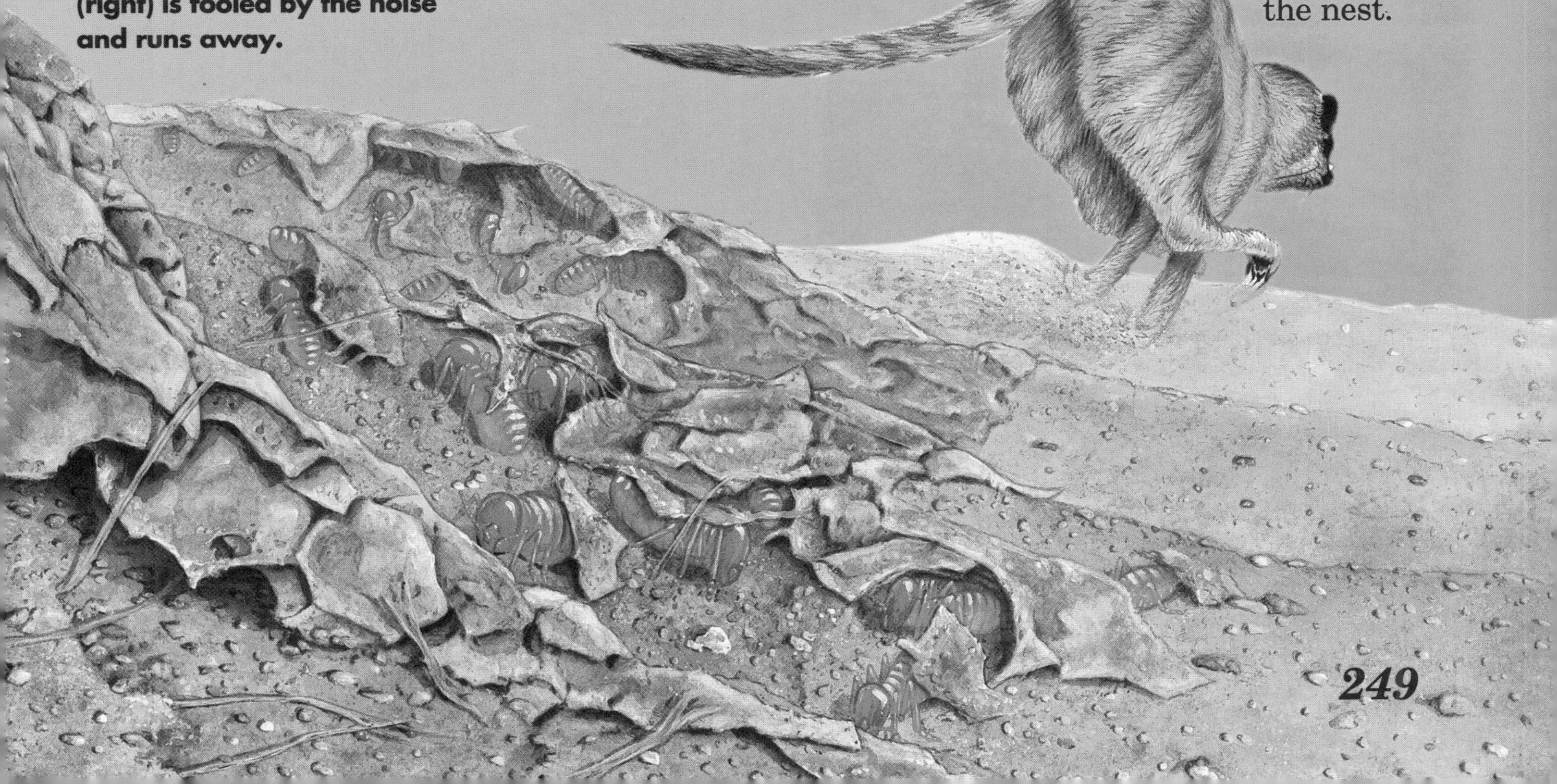

BUBBLING OVER

The African purple-winged grasshopper secretes a frothy foam from openings at the base of its back legs. Eventually, the grasshopper surrounds itself with a very off-putting chemical bubble. This not only tastes bad, but smells disgusting, too.

LEARNING A LESSON

Wart-biter crickets puke when they panic! In other words, they vomit a revolting brown liquid if attacked by predators. This liquid tastes foul and probably succeeds in putting off all but the most determined predators. The rest soon learn that these bugs have disgusting habits, taste horrid and are best left alone.

HEAD BANGER

The mound-building termite bangs its head against the inside of its nest. If lots of soldier termites do this at the same time, they make a loud hissing noise, which sounds just like a snake (main picture). They make such a racket that their hissing can be heard by predators outside the nest.

How good is

Do minibeasts flock to your garden or do they prefer next door's backyard? Take this test and find out how tempting your garden is to bugs.

Answer the following questions and award yourself points. The maximum number of marks you can score is eight. If that's what you get, give yourself a huge pat on the back for being such a minibeast fan.

SCORING

- If you answer YES to a question, tick the box and give yourself one point.
- If you answer NOT YET (but plan to do it soon), tick the box and give yourself half a mark.
- If you answer NO, tick the box and take a point away.

Make a note, too, of all the bugs you see on your tour round the garden. Write down the date and where you saw each one, together with the time and a brief description. If you don't know what it's called, make a rough drawing and you can look it up later in a book (or in BUGS!). Do all your survey on the same day, and make a count of all the insects you see. Obviously, the more you see, the better your wildlife safari park.

If you haven't got a garden, you may be able to form a club with a friend who has. Perhaps a few of you could club together. If none of you has a garden, perhaps you might be able make a survey of the local park – though you should, of course, get permission, both from a parent and from the park keeper.

YES NOT YET NO

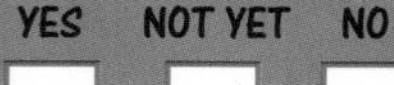

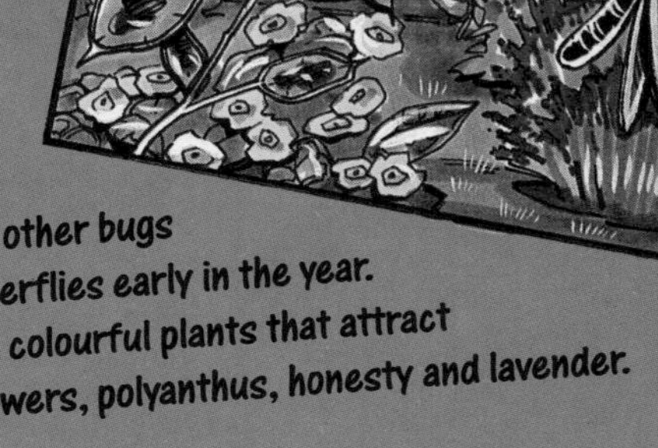

1 Have you created a butterfly border?

Butterflies and moths love plants to lay their eggs on, as well as plants they can eat. Plants such as aubretia provide cover for other bugs and a food source for butterflies early in the year. Other sweet-smelling and colourful plants that attract minibeasts include wallflowers, polyanthus, honesty and lavender.

YES NOT YET NO

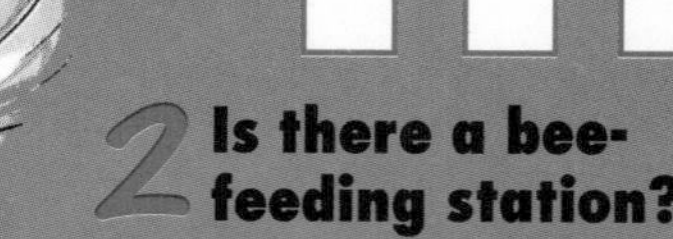

2 Is there a bee-feeding station?

Bees and their mimics, the hoverflies, are both useful in the garden. Bees pollinate flowers and hoverflies eat aphids. Great big yellow flowers such as sunflowers are good for attracting many insects, especially bees and hoverflies.

YES NOT YET NO

3 Do you have a pond?

Your pond could be nothing more than an old sink, or a hole only 60cm long and 1.2m wide. As long as there are plants in the pond that give off oxygen, such as water milfoil, you should start attracting all sorts of different insects.

your garden?

YES NOT YET NO

4 Is there a rockery or wall?

Old walls with holes in can play host to spiders. Stones and logs also provide hiding places for minibeasts that like to come out at night. You will also find woodlice under stones. There may even be a population of centipedes.

YES NOT YET NO

7 Do you have a compost heap?

A compost heap is an essential insect-attractor. You will also be able to spot and study worms there. When you spread compost over your garden soil, this provides a mulch for damp-loving minibeasts such as woodlice. A coating of leaf litter over your soil can encourage millipedes, centipedes and earwigs as well.

YES NOT YET NO

5 Do you have a grassy area?

A well-kept lawn may be a gardener's pride and joy, but worms also enjoy a large, grassy area. If a lawn is left to grow, it can also attract other bugs such as ground beetles and grasshoppers.

YES NOT YET NO

8 Is there a wood pile?

A wood pile provides food for wood-boring bugs. Other minibeasts can thrive in this habitat, too. Spiders can go on the prowl for their prey. A wood pile can provide cover and a handy meal of fungi for harvestmen. Loose bark can also provide cover for bugs to hide in and to escape the harsh winter months.

YES NOT YET NO

6 Is there a hedgerow or shrubbery?

Shrubs like pyracantha or forsythia are used by many spiders as hunting grounds. Small trees, roses and berberis all provide ladybirds and beetles with food and shelter. Don't forget to cover the ground with other plants like alyssum, aubretia and honeysuckle, all of which – brightly coloured, fragrant or both – should attract a lot of insects.

Small Talk

If you're pleased with your minibeast safari park, don't forget to tell people about it. Make a sign with the name of your bug safari park and offer your friends a creepy-crawly guided tour.

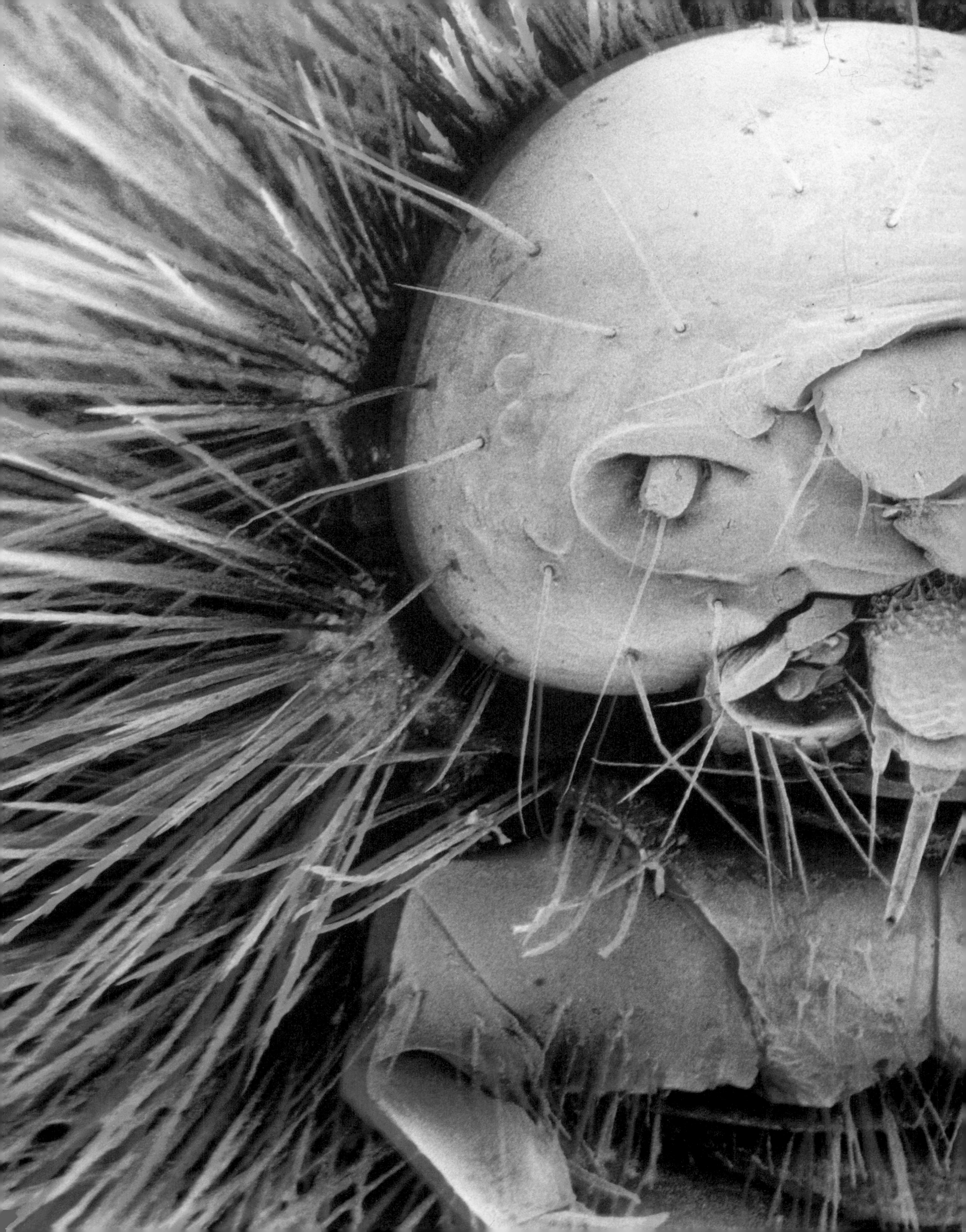

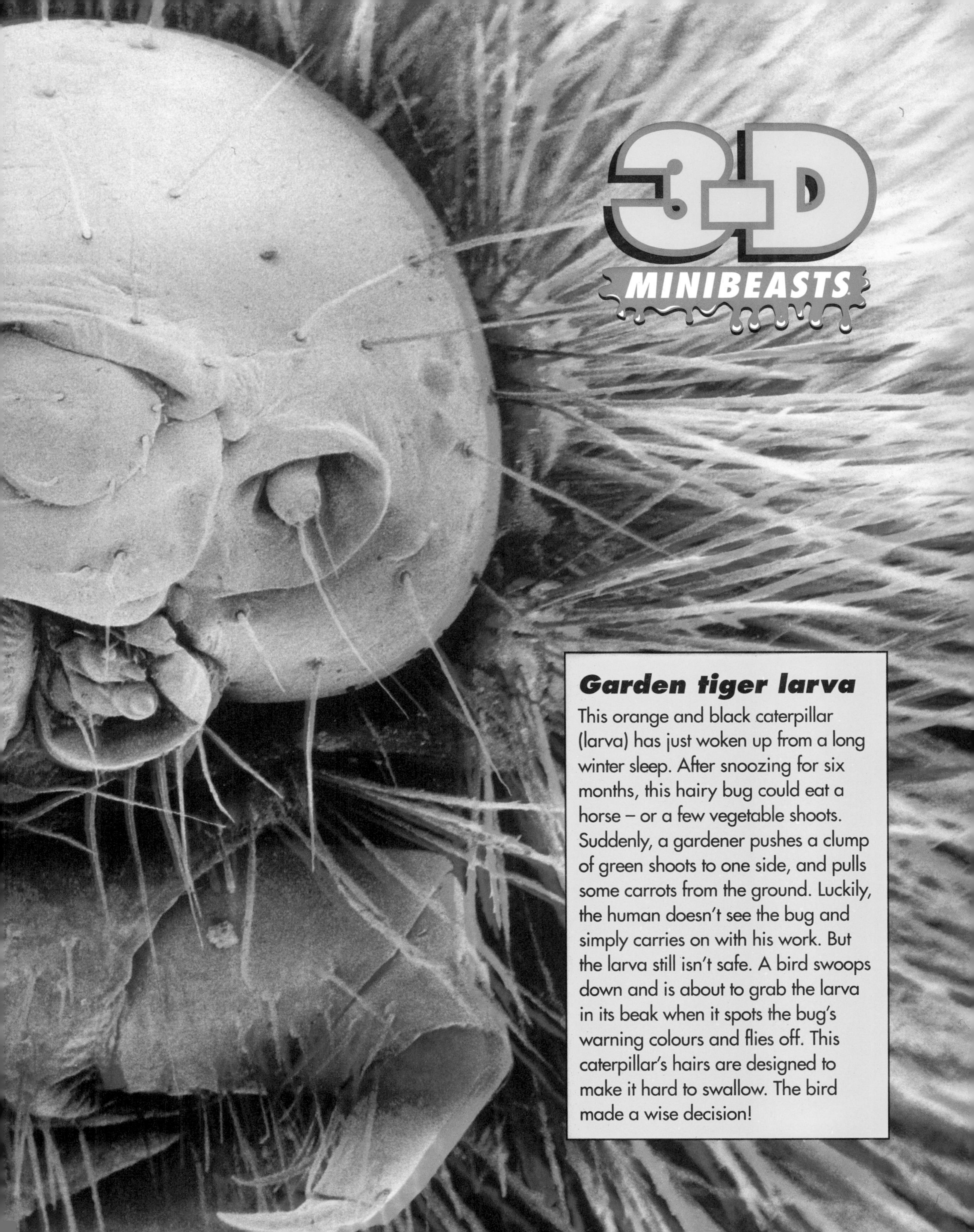

Garden tiger larva

This orange and black caterpillar (larva) has just woken up from a long winter sleep. After snoozing for six months, this hairy bug could eat a horse – or a few vegetable shoots. Suddenly, a gardener pushes a clump of green shoots to one side, and pulls some carrots from the ground. Luckily, the human doesn't see the bug and simply carries on with his work. But the larva still isn't safe. A bird swoops down and is about to grab the larva in its beak when it spots the bug's warning colours and flies off. This caterpillar's hairs are designed to make it hard to swallow. The bird made a wise decision!

Spot the difference

Males and females

Males and females from the same bug species often come in different shapes, shades and sizes.

Some female spiders eat their mates, but the male golden orb spider is quite safe. The female doesn't bother with him because he is so much smaller than the food she usually hunts. So the male can get close to the female and mate with her without having to worry about being eaten.

The female golden orb spider can be up to 100 times as heavy as the male.

Male and female bugs are designed for different things. While females spend most of their lives staying quite still, laying eggs and looking after their young, males move about a lot. Males may have to search long and hard to find a mate. When they do find a female, they often have to fight a rival to win her. Because of these different lifestyles, male and female bugs are often different sizes, shapes and colours.

BIGGER FEMALES

Most female spiders are bigger than the males of the same species. Look at the tiny male golden orb spider on this enormous female (main picture). Spiders lay hundreds of eggs at a time so the females need big bodies to house their ovaries (special organs where eggs are produced). Sometimes, it's hard to believe that a male and female spider belong to the same species because they look so different.

The small male golden orb spider clambers over his mate.

FIGHTING FIT

To help them fight off rivals many male bugs have ferocious jaws, or vicious pincers. The most terrifying looking beetle in the world is probably the male Hercules beetle (left, approaching the female). Including its huge, pincer-like horn, it measures an amazing 16cm. Male Hercules beetles are incredibly strong. They lock horns and fight until one manages to lift the other in the air and throw him to the ground. The females are less aggressive and not as strong.

The male Hercules beetle is larger and stronger than the female (above right). Like a deer stag, he also has impressive head gear.

LOOK, NO WINGS

Sometimes, male insects are much better at flying than the females. Often, the females can't fly at all. The female jungle nymph is a big, green stick insect that cannot fly. The male is much smaller and his wings are more developed. He can move about more easily and look for a suitable female to mate with.

Male jungle nymphs (left) are much lighter and better at flying than their bright-green mates (below).

BLOOD-SUCKING SISTERS

Males and females of the same species not only look and behave differently, they can also have quite different eating habits. The female mosquito, for example, eats blood, while the male never touches a drop. He prefers nectar, which he gets from flowers, and the juice of ripe fruit. The female needs a regular supply of blood, because it contains chemicals such as protein, without which she could not lay her eggs.

FIDDLING ABOUT

The fiddler crab got its name because of the male's enormous, brightly coloured claw. When he scuttles across the sand, it looks as though his giant claw is a fiddle and his ordinary claw is the bow. The male displays his special claw to the female, hoping it will make her want to mate with him, and shows it off to other males to warn them off his territory. He also occasionally uses it as a weapon in fights with other males.

The male fiddler crab stands at the entrance to his burrow and tries to attract the attention of passing females by waving his large claw (right). The larger claw can be either the right or the left one.

One of the circled stalk-eyed flies (above) is female, the other is male. See if you can work out which is which.

COLOUR MAD

The male jumping spider often has brightly coloured palps and body. The females are usually less colourful. Often, in the bug world, the male is very brightly coloured while females are a dull brown or grey. One of the reasons for the male's bright colours is that he needs to attract the female. She, however, is camouflaged. She spends a lot of her time in one place, laying eggs and looking after her young, so she doesn't want to be spotted.

EYE TO EYE

Not all male insects get into violent fights. Many don't fight at all. The stalk-eyed fly has another way of tackling rivals. It has a wide head with eyes set out on two long stalks. When two males meet they 'measure' each other up. The fly with the longer eye stalks wins the challenge. Female stalk-eyed flies have much shorter eye stalks than the males. But they always choose the male with the longest eye stalks.

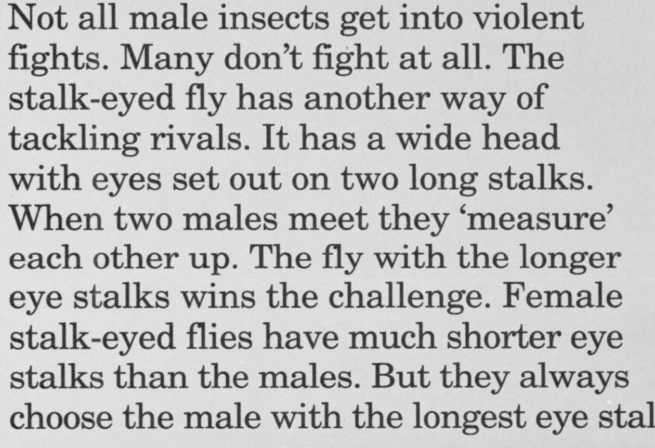

A female jumping spider (left) blends in with the background, while the male (below) shows off his bright colours.

BUGS ON YOU!

Some bugs go anywhere to grab a quick snack. Unfortunately, the human body is a fast-food paradise for many hungry bugs.

Bugs can live just about anywhere. They wander around the garden, crawl around the park and hang out at the beach, but some bugs prefer to live in your house and on your body! Many of them would love to live among the hairs on your head. So watch out, they may be closer than you think.

SNACKING ALL OVER THE WORLD

Parasites live all over the world and they're not at all fussy. They don't mind if their hosts are clean or dirty, rich or poor – just as long as they get a decent helping of their favourite dish – human blood.

DECLARE WAR

Some bugs make their homes inside humans' bodies, but many simply settle down on humans. Our bodies have few natural defences to fight off parasites, but we can easily get rid of stubborn bugs using special lotions.

CAN THEY MAKE YOU ILL?

Don't worry, most of the bugs that you may find living on you, and which are shown on these pages, probably won't make you ill. If you get bitten, the bite will itch. Try not to scratch it, this will make it sore, and it may become infected.

HOP OFF!

Some people's bodies react badly to certain bug bites, so these hungry minibeasts should be discouraged. Even if you really like bugs, don't let them live on you – get rid of them as soon as you can! Turn the page and take a closer look at human parasites.

If you were to shrink down to about 0.5mm tall and you took a walk across an infested human scalp, this is what you could see.

Is it true... that only people with dirty hair get head lice?

No. Anybody can have head lice. Like most parasites, head lice can survive for a while without blood, but they can't afford to be choosy. These blood-thirsty bugs are always on the look-out for food and will jump on to any head for their next meal.

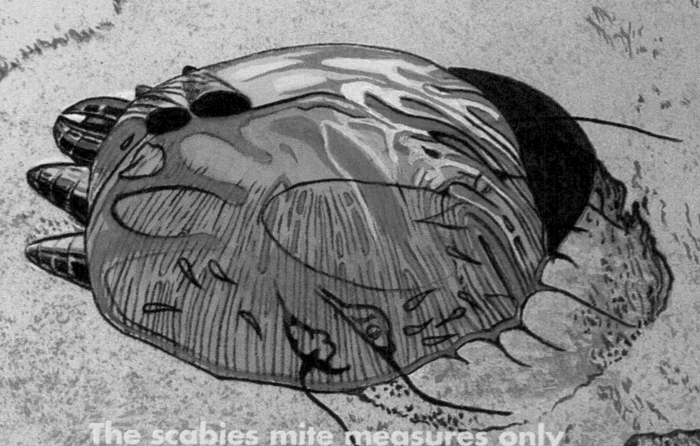

The scabies mite measures only 0.5mm. It burrows into the skin to lay its eggs and likes to live in eyebrows and on wrists.

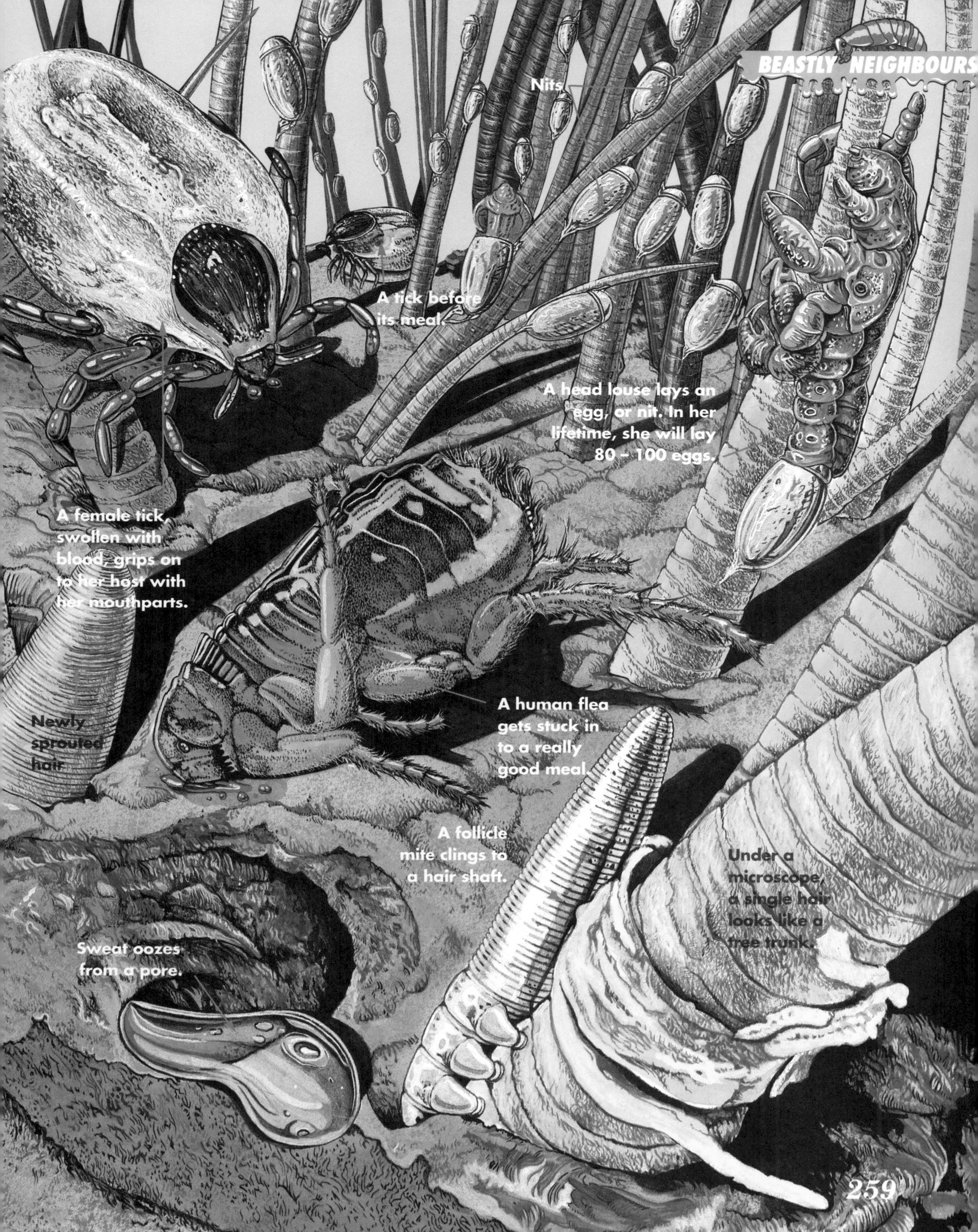
Nits
A tick before its meal.
A head louse lays an egg, or nit. In her lifetime, she will lay 80 – 100 eggs.
A female tick, swollen with blood, grips on to her host with her mouthparts.
A human flea gets stuck in to a really good meal.
Newly sprouted hair
A follicle mite clings to a hair shaft.
Under a microscope, a single hair looks like a tree trunk.
Sweat oozes from a pore.

This colourful selection of bugs looks like strange creatures from outer-space, but in fact they all live on humans.

HEAD LOUSE

You can probably guess from its name that the head louse lives on the human head. It likes to suck blood from the scalp. This bug, which is only 2 – 4mm long, leaves tiny red spots on the skin on the head, which can be very itchy. The females lay many tiny, pale-coloured eggs, known as 'nits', which she sticks to hairs for safe keeping. The nits hatch in about seven days and can live for several weeks. Head lice and nits are more common where there are crowds of people and a lot of heads, such as schools.

Head louse

The egg case (nit) has a lid. When the head louse is fully developed, it forces its way out.

Nit

The nit is attached to a strand of hair.

Head lice can spread rapidly in places where there are lots of heads, such as schools. A lot of schools do regular head checks for these minibeasts.

HUMAN FLEA

Another blood-sucking insect is the human flea. It is a champion among fleas, with an impressive jump, which it uses to escape danger or to jump on to a new host. Its strong hind legs enable it to jump as high as 20cm and as far as 33cm. That's the equivalent of a person doing a high jump of about 85m! It is found all over the world and likes cool, damp summers and mild, wet winters.

GET TOUGH

If you want to get rid of fleas for good, make their lives a misery. Treat the house with special cleaning products, wash the bites thoroughly, using soap and water, and calm the itching with a soothing ointment, such as calamine lotion.

Follicle mite

FOLLICLE MITE

The tiny human follicle mite (left) is about 0.5mm long. It is so small that the human host rarely even notices that it is there. It clings on to a hair and likes to live close to the skin. It is often found on people's eyebrows and up their noses! Sweat, which oozes out through pores (holes) in the skin, is the follicle mite's favourite food.

Hard tick

Body fills with blood as the tick feeds.

HARD TICK

Ticks are small, eight-legged creatures, which look a bit like little spiders and feed on blood. They are about 4mm long before feeding, but once they have eaten they can be up to 8mm long. Their bites are usually harmless, but very occasionally lead to diseases. Ticks attach themselves to the skin of their human hosts with their mouthparts. If the tick is still clinging to the skin, don't try to pull it off. Get an adult to cover it in petroleum jelly. The tick won't be able to breathe and will be forced to let go. Then wash the area thoroughly.

UNINVITED GUESTS

As well as all the bugs described here, another uninvited guest you might come across is the bed bug (below). This is a flat, wingless insect, which is only about 5 – 7mm long. It lives in furniture, especially beds and carpets, and comes out at night to track down human blood. Its bite can cause itchy sores, which may become infected, particularly if a person scratches them.

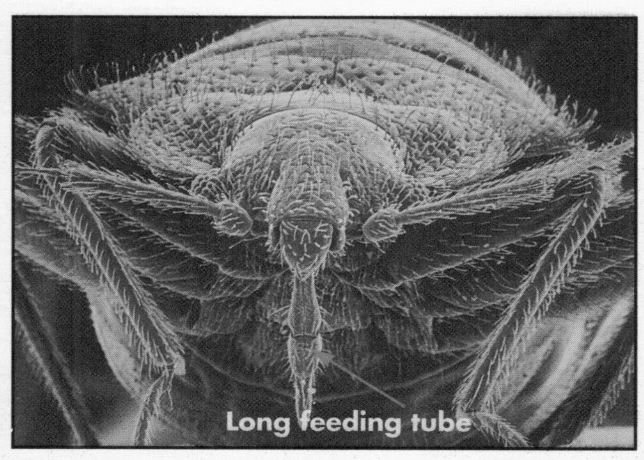

Long feeding tube

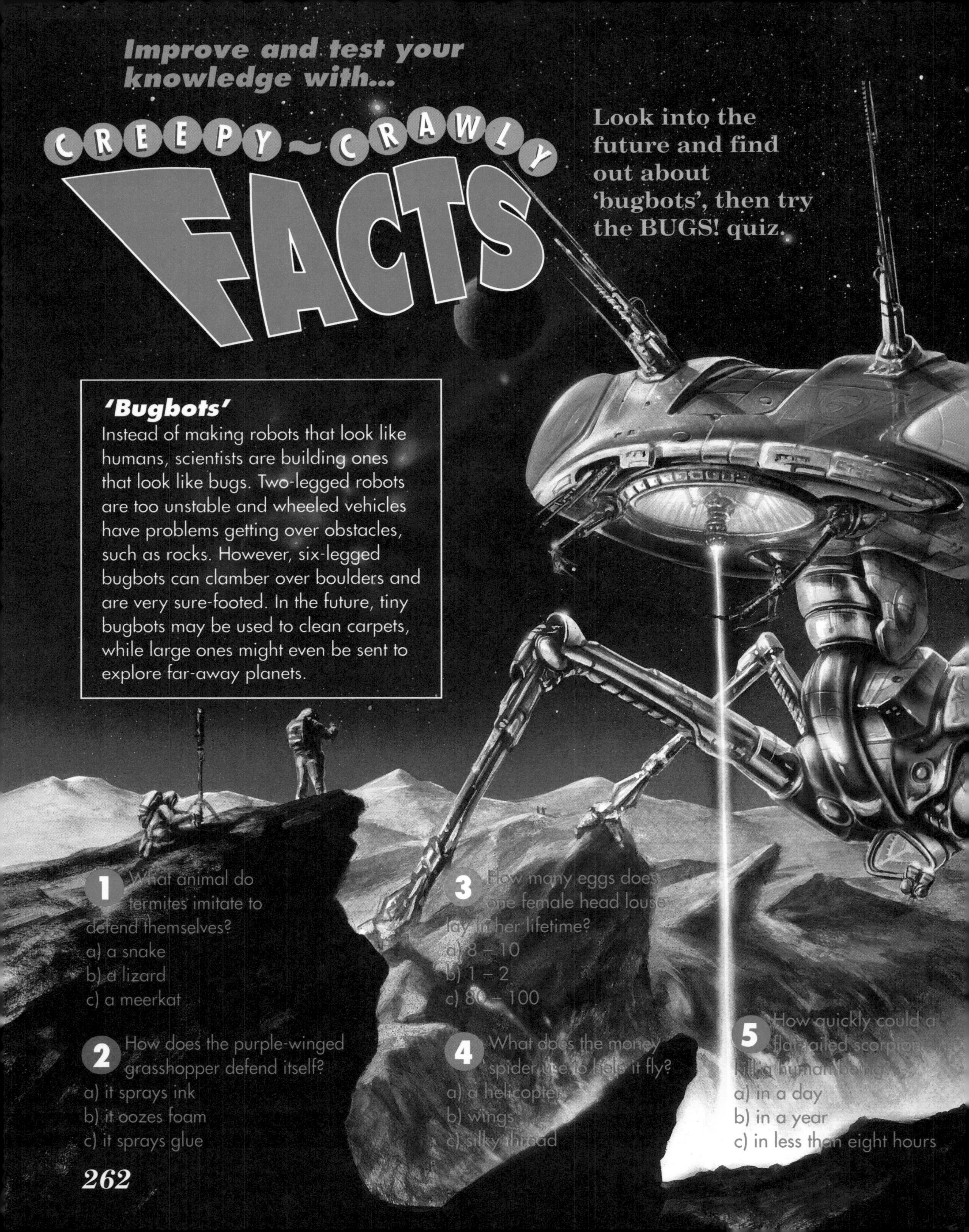

Improve and test your knowledge with...

CREEPY~CRAWLY FACTS

Look into the future and find out about 'bugbots', then try the BUGS! quiz.

'Bugbots'

Instead of making robots that look like humans, scientists are building ones that look like bugs. Two-legged robots are too unstable and wheeled vehicles have problems getting over obstacles, such as rocks. However, six-legged bugbots can clamber over boulders and are very sure-footed. In the future, tiny bugbots may be used to clean carpets, while large ones might even be sent to explore far-away planets.

1 What animal do termites imitate to defend themselves?

a) a snake
b) a lizard
c) a meerkat

2 How does the purple-winged grasshopper defend itself?

a) it sprays ink
b) it oozes foam
c) it sprays glue

3 How many eggs does one female head louse lay in her lifetime?

a) 8 – 10
b) 1 – 2
c) 80 – 100

4 What does the money spider use to help it fly?

a) a helicopter
b) wings
c) silky thread

5 How quickly could a flat-tailed scorpion kill a human being?

a) in a day
b) in a year
c) in less than eight hours

The 'cowardly' human bot fly has found a way of getting its eggs on to human skin. It spots a passing female mosquito and lays its eggs on her body. This blood-sucking bug acts as a flying taxi and she carries them to an unsuspecting human. As the mosquito drinks the human's blood, the warmth of the skin causes the bot fly eggs to hatch. The larvae then start to tunnel into the human's skin where they enjoy a meal themselves.

The slow-moving sloth, a tree-dwelling mammal, makes an unusual mobile home for eight species of moth. The small moths hide in the sloth's fur for safety. Once a week, when the sloth crawls down from the trees to go to the toilet, the moths fly off to lay their eggs on its droppings. Because the sloth is one of the slowest-moving animals on Earth, the moths have time to lay their eggs and fly back on to its coat before it moves too far.

6 Where is the Colorado beetle originally from?
a) central North America
b) Great Britain
c) Antarctica

Sticky situation

Aphids drink plant sap through their mouthparts. To get enough goodness from their food, they have to eat almost continuously. Aphids produce large amounts of waste called honey dew. In an area the size of a football pitch, there can be as many as 5 billion aphids and these will produce over two tonnes of this sweet-tasting liquid every day.

7 What's another name for a comb jelly?
a) sea walnut
b) water brazil nut
c) damp hazelnut

8 How many pairs of wings does a dragonfly have?
a) 12
b) 10
c) 2

9 What colour is a garden tiger caterpillar?
a) orange and black
b) pink and blue
c) green and white

10 Why does a male fiddler crab have an extra-large claw?
a) to play the fiddle with
b) to impress females and to fight
c) to cut up seaweed

Answers to the questions on the inside back cover

Q and A

Matthew Robertson, who spent 12 years working with bugs at London Zoo, here answers all your creepy-crawly questions.

Do earwigs crawl into your ears?

It is very unlikely that an earwig would set up home in an ear. Many bugs like to hide in places where they feel secure. Earwigs, especially, like to squeeze their bodies into narrow spaces. The human ear would make a warm, moist place for earwigs to live, but other factors make it an unsuitable home for bugs. They wouldn't like the hairs, wax and constant movement.

Which is the heaviest bug?

The heaviest bug in the world is the giant squid. It weighs over a tonne. It can cope with being this size because it lives in water, which supports its weight. On land, the heaviest bug is the robber crab. This has been known to weigh as much as 4kg, though it may actually grow even bigger than that.

Do bugs play?

No, bugs do not play. Scientists believe that mammals play in order to act out possible future roles in life – a sort of rehearsal for the real thing. Bugs do not need to do that. Play doesn't help young bugs to defend themselves or to reproduce in later life, so they don't bother to play when they are young. For a long time, experts thought that ants fought in play, but it was later discovered that they only fight in earnest – often to the death.

Orchid Mantis

It may look like a harmless flower – but the orchid mantis is really a deadly killer.

Compared with human beings, the mantis is very old – there have been mantises on Earth about 30 million years longer than people! The orchid mantis lives in forests where flowers called orchids grow.

FLOWER POWER

With wide, petal-like flaps on its legs and amazing colouring, the mantis looks just like one of the orchids in which it hides.

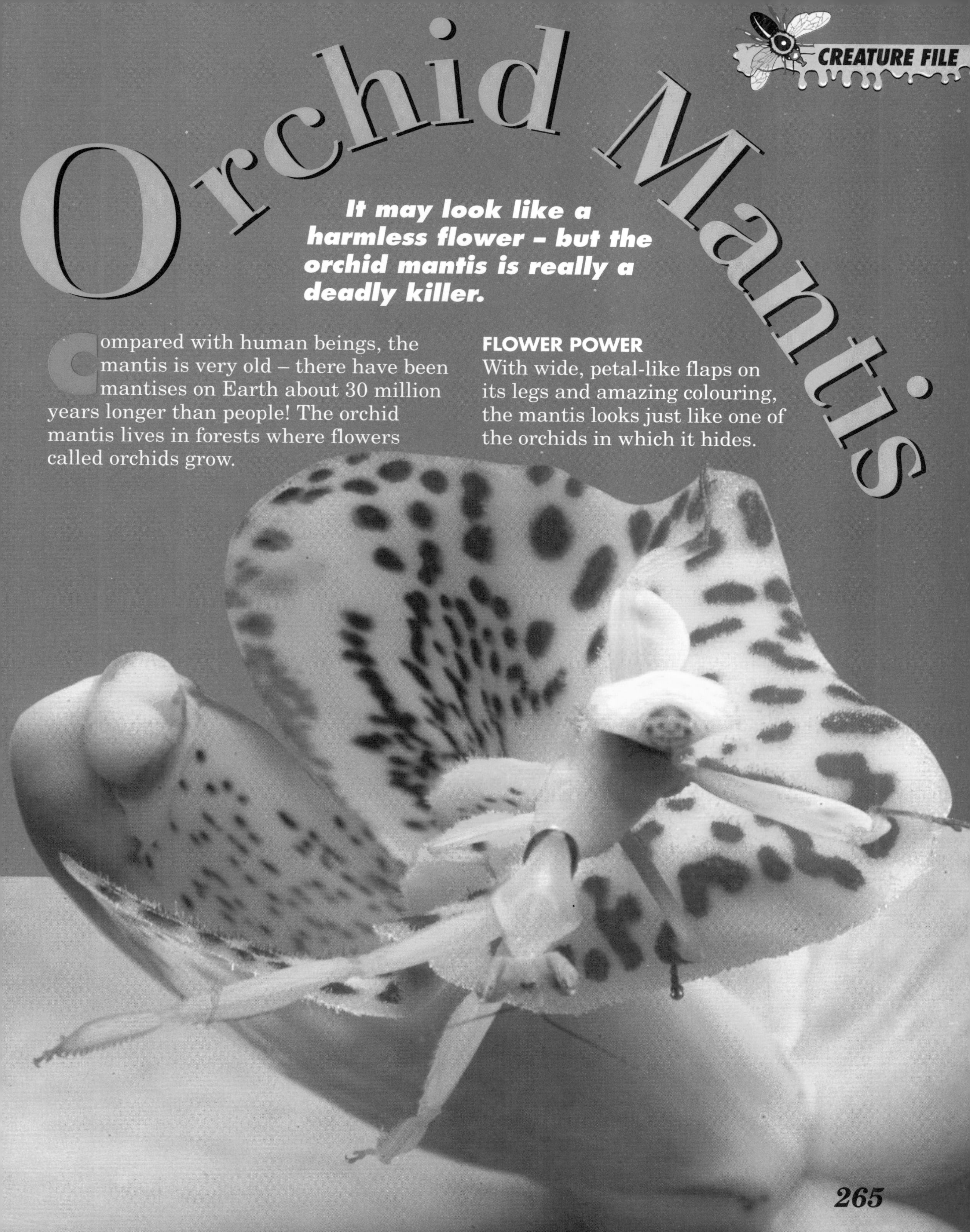

PERFECT DISGUISE
Looking like a flower gives the mantis the perfect disguise. Predators, such as birds and lizards, think it is just another orchid, and leave it alone. This cunning disguise also helps it to catch its prey.

DEADLY TRICK
Keeping very still, the mantis waits for a victim to come along. The only movement it makes is to rock gently backwards and forwards – just like a delicate flower swaying in the breeze. Unaware of this deadly trick, insects land on the orchids nearby to feed on the sweet nectar inside. When an insect is close enough, the mantis makes its move. It shoots out its front legs, grabs the victim, spiking it with its claws and the sharp spines on its legs so that the victim can't escape.

WATCH OUT!
Hoping to pick up some nectar, a bee buzzes towards an orchid. It aims for what it thinks is the centre of a flower – and flies straight into the arms of a deadly orchid mantis.

Antennae sense victims as they fly past.

Large eyes spot even the slightest movement.

Flexible neck means that the mantis can easily spin its head around.

Sharp spines help to trap struggling prey.

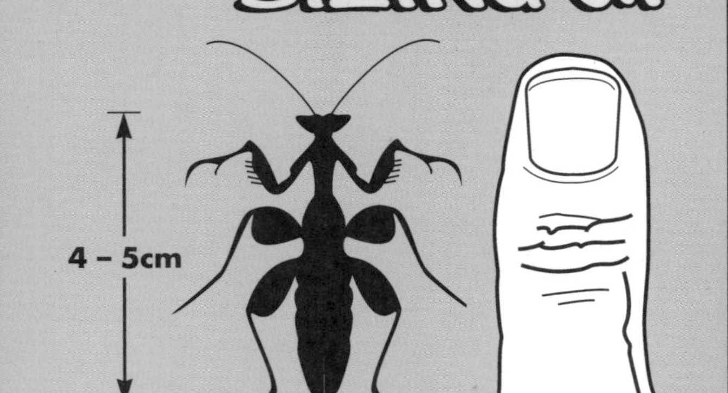

- **SCIENTIFIC NAME:** *Hymenopus coronatus*
- **SIZE:** 4 – 5cm long
- **LIVES:** Malaysia and other parts of South-East Asia
- **EATS:** other minibeasts such as grasshoppers, flies, moths, butterflies and bees

Small Talk

BENDY NECK

The orchid mantis does not chase after its prey, so it has had to develop other ways of picking out possible victims. With its huge, round eyes that stick out from the sides of its head, the mantis can see in every direction. It doesn't even need to turn around – this creature's neck is so bendy that it can spin its head right round to watch its victim approaching from behind!

LEFT OVERS

The mantis eats its prey alive. With its sharp jaws, it bites out pieces of flesh and chews them up until they are small enough to swallow. This meat-eater has a good appetite and eats up all the soft, juicy parts of its victim. It is, however, quite fussy and will leave behind all the tough bits, such as the legs and wings. When the orchid mantis has finished, it carefully cleans the spines on each leg to make them ready for the next victim.

MALE AND FEMALE

The male and female orchid mantis look slightly different. The female is twice as big as her mate. Her size means that she is a weak flier. Her wings are a pale colour, while the male, which is good at flying, has transparent wings.

MOTHERS AND BABIES

Orchid mantis eggs develop inside their mother's body. She lays her eggs in a kind of foam. Three to six months later, the young hatch. They are bright red and pretend to be stinging ants to put predators off. As they grow and change into adults, they moult (shed their old skins) several times.

AT PRAYER

The orchid mantis is also one of the 'praying' mantises. These minibeasts get their name because they sit very still and hold up their front legs in front of their faces – as if they are saying their prayers.

Great Diving Beetle

Pulling itself along with its oar-like legs, the great diving beetle is a champion swimmer.

The great diving beetle makes its home in shallow ponds or streams. Although it lives mostly underwater, it has to come up for air several times an hour.

FRANTIC FREESTYLE

This minibeast is perfectly made for swimming! Its body is flat and smooth so that it can slide easily through the water. The great diving beetle paddles through the water using its broad legs. Fringes of hairs on its legs spread out and help it go even faster. At top speed, the beetle manages two strokes per second – and covers an incredible 50cm!

GOING HUNTING

The beetle hunts tadpoles, water worms, insects and even small fish. It may also eat dead animals. When prey is scarce, the beetle can go without food for up to two months.

- **SCIENTIFIC NAME:** *Dytiscus marginalis*
- **SIZE:** 3.5cm long
- **LIVES:** ponds and streams throughout the northern hemisphere
- **EATS:** small water creatures

SIZING UP

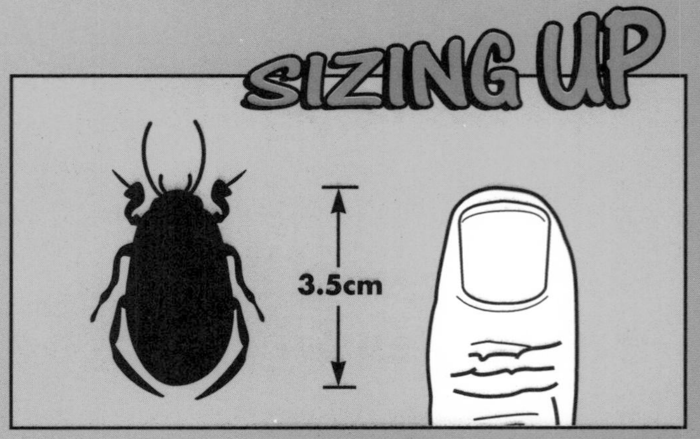

Giant African Land Snail

If you put this bug on the scales, it would weigh as much as a small bag of flour.

From head to tail, the giant African land snail can measure 30cm or more. Its stripy shell is 20cm long and its whole body weighs up to 500g. This monster is the biggest snail in the world.

GIGANTIC PEST

In East Africa, where it originally came from, this huge snail causes little trouble. It eats fallen fruit, dead animals and rotting leaves. In other places where it now lives, there are none of its natural predators to keep it under control. With nothing to stop it, the hungry snail greedily attacks valuable food crops.

FAST BREEDER

Like other snails, it is a hermaphrodite (say 'her-maf-ro-dite'). This means that it has both male and female sex organs and that it can mate with any other giant African land snail. After mating, it lays up to 300 eggs a month.

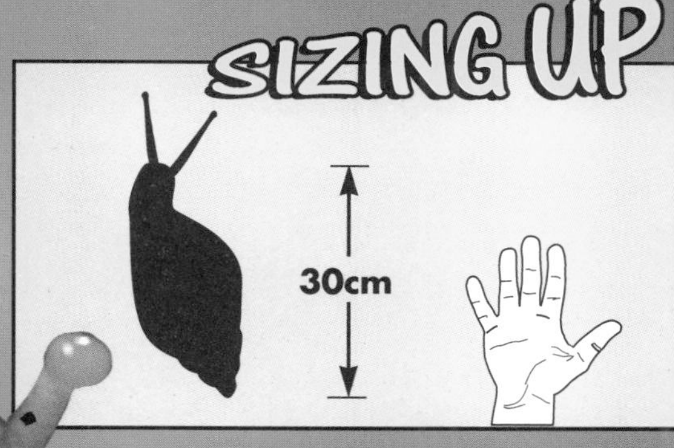

- **SCIENTIFIC NAME:** *Achinata fulica*
- **SIZE:** body 30cm long, shell 20cm long
- **EATS:** vegetation and dead animals
- **LIVES:** east Africa, India, China, South-East Asia, southern Europe, North America

The mysteries of migration

At certain times of the year, millions of bugs suddenly leave an area and travel, sometimes thousands of kilometres, to another place. This strange habit is known as migration.

But why do bugs do this, and how do these creatures manage to get so far? Bugs migrate for three main reasons. Some do it to avoid bad weather, others head off in search of food and some bugs migrate to mate and lay eggs.

INCREDIBLE JOURNEY

Every autumn, the monarch butterfly makes an incredible journey all the way from south eastern Canada to California, USA, and southern Mexico to avoid winter frosts. That's a distance of 4,000km! This butterfly has such powerful wings that in just one day it can fly an amazing 130km. A few months after they arrive in their new winter home, the monarch butterflies mate and then die. Their young make the return journey to Canada. But how do they know their way home? Scientists still don't know the answer to this question.

Monarch butterflies flock together in a eucalyptus tree.

Some bugs, including the monarch butterfly (background picture), migrate to avoid cold weather. This butterfly leaves the cool forests in autumn for sunny areas further south.

The monarch butterflies (above) have warning colours and release foul smells to put off predators. They stress these warning signals by flocking together, also finding safety in numbers

About 20 million driver ants, all walking in the same direction, form a well-trodden path.

QUICK MARCH

Colonies of African driver ants spend most of their lives migrating in search of food. There can be as many as 20 million ants in each colony. These large colonies are very well organised, with soldiers to guard the workers. There are so many of them, and they have such huge appetites, that the ants would soon run out of things to eat if they stayed in one place all the time. The ants simply never stop eating. They will munch through just about anything that gets in their path – even venomous snakes.

African driver ants (background picture) are completely blind! They manage to stay together in a line because each ant leaves a strong chemical trail, which all the others in the colony are able to recognise and follow.

Colonies of driver ants (above) are huge and, at the same time, highly organised. Here, some of the larger ants guard a column of workers as they cross a road.

Is it true ... that not all migrating bugs reach their destination?

Yes. Milkweed bugs migrate from the southern USA to the north in spring and summer. Sadly, none of the bugs that starts the journey will reach the final destination. The trip is too long and difficult. On the way, the milkweed bugs mate and so do their babies. It is the young of these babies that eventually reach northern USA – just in time to start the return journey!

The walls on either side of the ant trail are like the walls of a castle. The soldier ants stand on top of them and watch out for enemies.

CRAZY CRABS

Every spring on Christmas Island, off western Australia, about 120 million large red crabs scramble out of the forests and head for the rocky beaches, where they lay their eggs in the water. This migration is perfectly timed. The Christmas Island crabs know when to go to the beaches by the strength of light from the moon. The brightness of the moon tells them exactly what the tides are doing and when is the best time to lay their eggs.

On their way to the beach, Christmas Island crabs (below) don't let anything get in their way. They invade houses and litter roads and gardens. They can even clamber up steep cliffs (background picture).

FOLLOW MY LEADER

At the beginning of autumn in the Bahamas, hordes of spiny lobsters leave the shallow waters where they spend the summer months and head off in search of deeper, calmer seas. Like a squadron of marching soldiers, the lobsters line up one behind the other. No one knows exactly why they do this, but experts think they may be avoiding the pull of the water as they walk against the current. Try an experiment to find out how this works. Put your hand under a cold running tap with the palm of your hand pointing upwards. Then turn your hand until your thumb is pointing up towards the tap. You won't feel as much force from the flow of water when your hand is turned sideways.

Christmas Island crabs finally reach the sea to lay their eggs.

Ladybirds huddle together for warmth.

FLOATING BY

A ladybird doesn't get too attached to its home, and it won't think twice about moving to another country or flying across the sea to settle down in a completely new home. If you see huge swarms of ladybirds around coastlines or even bobbing about on the surface of the sea, you will know that these bugs are moving home. Should these hordes of ladybirds decide to land in your garden, it really would not be such a bad thing. Ladybirds are fierce predators and they would eat all those greedy aphids that love to munch their way through all your favourite plants.

Ladybirds (left and background) gather together in large numbers before hibernating (settling down in a safe, comfortable place for the winter). They gather together in this way for two reasons. Ladybirds know that there is safety in numbers and they like to huddle together to keep warm.

What is ... a swarm?

A swarm is a large, closely packed cluster of animals. Bugs swarm when they migrate. They get together in large groups and head off in search of food, a mate or a new home. Locusts swarm after a spell of good weather, the perfect conditions for breeding and laying eggs. The females lay so many eggs that when their offspring grow up, there is not enough food for all of them. So, the young locusts take to the air. Helped by gusts of wind, they travel for many kilometres until they spot some food. Farmers dread the arrival of a swarm of locusts – just one locust swarm can eat up to 20,000 tonnes of food in a single day!

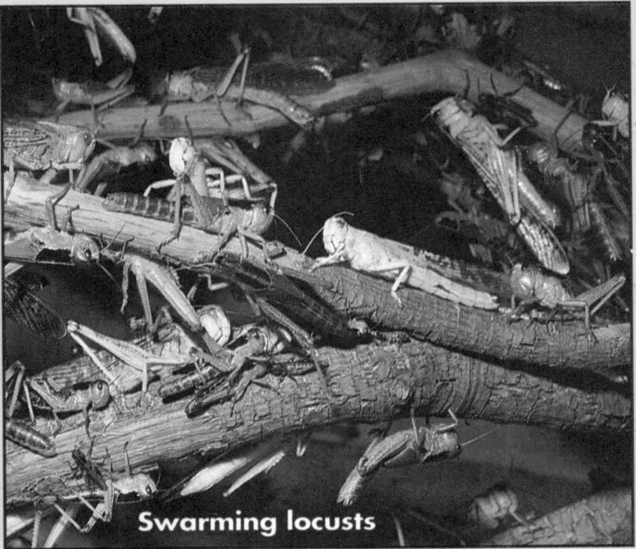
Swarming locusts

Metamorphosis

The aim of the metamorphosis game is to change from a caterpillar to an elegant moth. It's not as easy as it sounds.

There are three stages to this game. During the first (green) stage, you are a newly hatched caterpillar. When you reach the pale brown section, you become a pupa. Only when you reach the pale yellow section do you turn into a moth. The object of this game is to complete the metamorphosis process, lay an egg and start a new family.

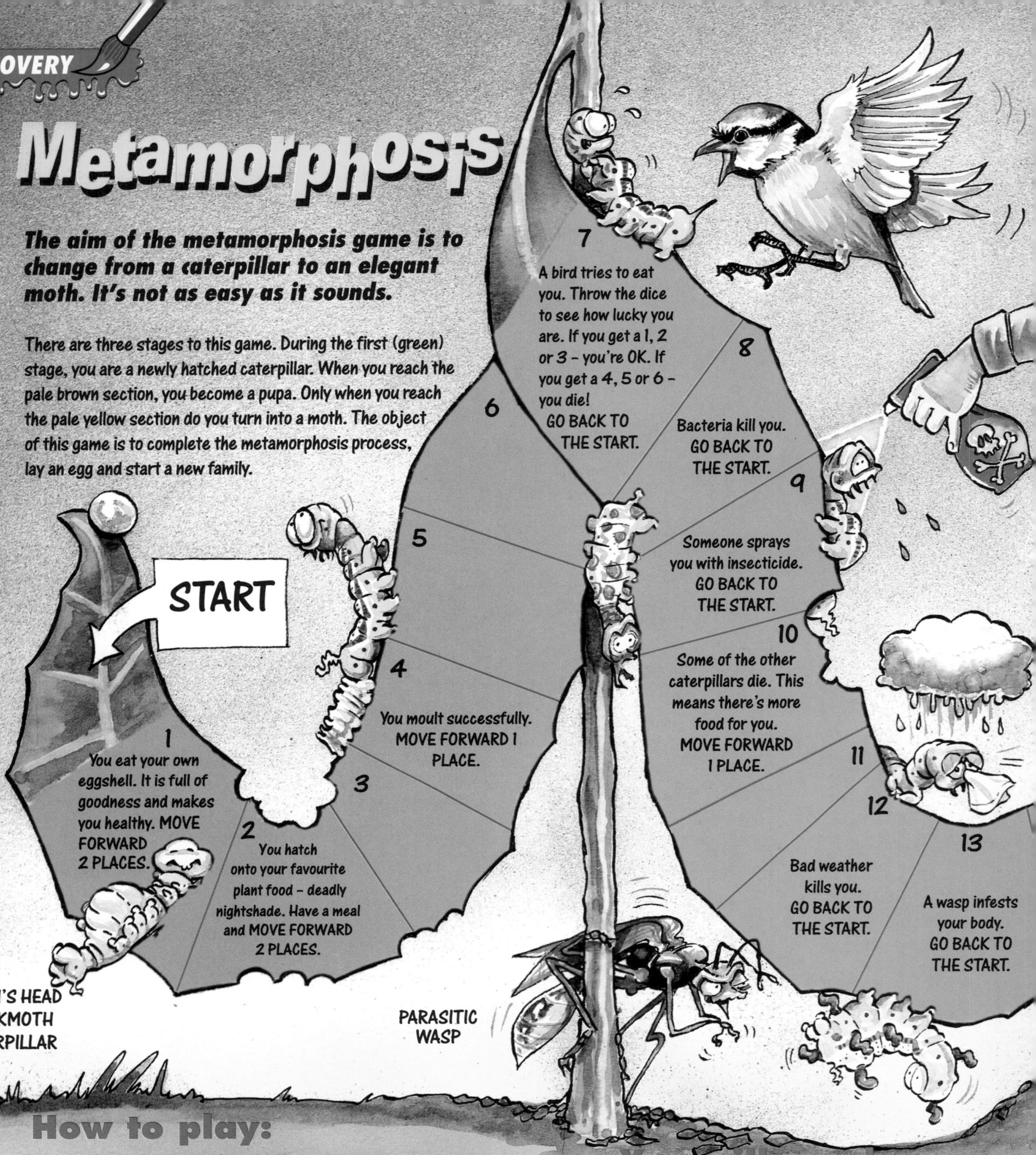

START

1 You eat your own eggshell. It is full of goodness and makes you healthy. MOVE FORWARD 2 PLACES.

2 You hatch onto your favourite plant food – deadly nightshade. Have a meal and MOVE FORWARD 2 PLACES.

3

4 You moult successfully. MOVE FORWARD 1 PLACE.

5

6

7 A bird tries to eat you. Throw the dice to see how lucky you are. If you get a 1, 2 or 3 – you're OK. If you get a 4, 5 or 6 – you die! GO BACK TO THE START.

8 Bacteria kill you. GO BACK TO THE START.

9 Someone sprays you with insecticide. GO BACK TO THE START.

10 Some of the other caterpillars die. This means there's more food for you. MOVE FORWARD 1 PLACE.

11

12 Bad weather kills you. GO BACK TO THE START.

13 A wasp infests your body. GO BACK TO THE START.

DEATH'S HEAD HAWKMOTH CATERPILLAR

PARASITIC WASP

How to play:

Put all the counters on START. Take it in turns to throw the dice and see where you land. Don't be surprised if you get sent back to the start – in real life most caterpillars don't live long enough to become moths or butterflies. Keep on taking turns until one player reaches the end and lays an egg.

You will need:

- one or more friends to play with

- a counter for each player (make caterpillar counters using strips of fabric or pieces of plasticine)

- a dice

37
You find a mate.
MOVE FORWARD 2 PLACES.
38
You fly into a candle flame.
GO BACK TO THE START.
36
39
35 You find some lovely flowers and eat their nectar.
MOVE FORWARD 3 PLACES.
40
FINISH
You've laid an egg and started a new family – WELL DONE.
26
A bug collector catches you, but puts you back carefully on the plant.
MOVE FORWARD 3 PLACES.
27
28
25
34
29
24
Your wings haven't dried out yet and you fall to the ground.
GO BACK 2 PLACES.
30
33
31
23
Your bright colours put off predators.
VE FORWARD 4 PLACES.
WELL DONE – you've taken off. GO FORWARD 2 PLACES.
32
22
DEATH'S HEAD HAWKMOTH
15
WELL DONE – you've turned into a pupa. MOVE FORWARD 3 PLACES.
21
WELL DONE – you've emerged as a moth.
MOVE FORWARD 1 PLACE.
18
16
17
Your caterpillar hasn't eaten enough to pupate.
GO BACK 6 PLACES.
PUPA (OR CHRYSALIS)
19
20
A mole eats your pupa.
GO BACK TO THE START.

Aphid – with parasite

This aphid is so fat that it can hardly move. It hasn't eaten too much – its body has been taken over by a parasite. Inside its swollen body is the larva of a wasp. The wasp's mother laid an egg in the aphid's body because she thought it would be a safe spot. She also knew that when her baby hatched it could grow big and strong by eating away at the aphid's body. Now the larva has outgrown its nursery and is about to escape from the aphid's body. The last thing that the aphid will feel is the fully grown wasp cutting a hole in its skin to make an escape hatch.

3-D
MINIBEASTS

What is an

Does the thought of a tarantula or a scorpion sends shivers down your spine? How do you feel about other spiders, and what about ticks and mites?

These bugs all belong to the group known as arachnids. All of its creepy crawly members have certain things in common.

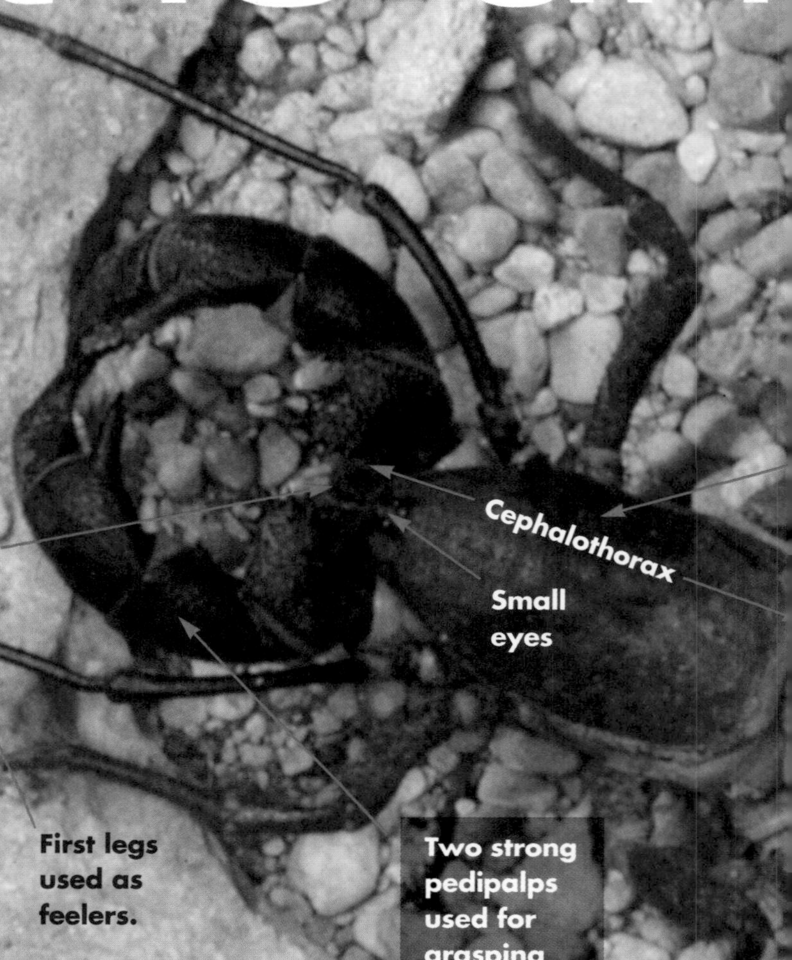

NO ANTENNAE

Arachnids have pedipalps at the front of their bodies. These sometimes look a bit like legs, but they aren't used for walking. Spiders use their pedipalps as feelers, while scorpions use them for seizing prey. Most insects have antennae, which can detect smells and tastes at an amazing distance. Arachnids don't need antennae to tell them what's going on a long way away because they don't have wings to get there.

SPECIAL JAWS

At the front of an arachnid's mouth is a pair of jaws, or chelicerae (say 'chell-iss-a-rye'). A spider's chelicerae end in sharp fangs, which the animal uses to pierce its prey, defend itself from enemies and burrow holes in the ground. Spiders, ticks and mites have hollow chelicerae to inject venom into their enemies. The animals suck their victims' blood through their chelicerae, just as you would suck a drink through a straw.

EYE EYE

Most arachnids have several small eyes, which are probably able to detect only blurs of light and dark. Unlike most insects and crustaceans, arachnids don't have large compound eyes, which are made up of hundreds of tiny lenses.

arachnid?

Like many arachnids, the whip scorpion is built to kill. But when it isn't hunting, this bug is quite shy – it likes to hide under rocks and stones.

Two main body parts.
Abdomen
All arachnids have four pairs of legs.
An arachnid has a book lung on either side of its body. They are underneath its abdomen.

LOOK, NO WINGS!

Can you imagine anything more terrifying than flying scorpions and spiders? Don't worry, you will never see a flying arachnid because they don't have wings.

LIQUID DIET

Most arachnids are carnivores. They usually eat insects. But they can only digest their food in liquid form. Once they have killed their prey, they start to produce saliva, which pours down their chelicerae into the body of their victim. The juices break the meat down until it is runny. The animals suck away at the soupy substance.

DIFFERENT BODIES

All arachnids' bodies are divided into two parts – the cephalothorax (say 'kef-alo-thaw-racks'), which is a word used to describe both the animal's head and chest, and the abdomen. Arachnids have more legs than insects – four pairs in total. (Remember, insects have three main body parts and only three pairs of legs.)

BOOK LUNGS

Arachnids have two pairs of lungs. These are called book lungs because they are made up of many fine layers, rather like the sheets of paper in a book. The layers are held apart by supports so that air can circulate freely between them. Arachnids take in air through the 'pages' in their book lungs. Without them, spiders and scorpions would not be able to breathe.

Spot the

Remember the arachnid rules

Most arachnids:
- have two main body parts (cephalothorax and abdomen).
- don't have wings.
- have four pairs of legs.
- have two pedipalps (grasping feelers) and chelicerae (jaws).
- don't have antennae or mandibles.
- are carnivores.
- have simple eyes, not compound eyes.

Use your new-found knowledge to try and work out which of the minibeasts on these pages are arachnids.

There are five bugs (A –E) pictured on these pages. Three of them are arachnids and two are insects. Take a look at the arachnid rules and try to work out which of these creatures are arachnids and which are not.

A
Yellow crane fly
Clue: takes to the air

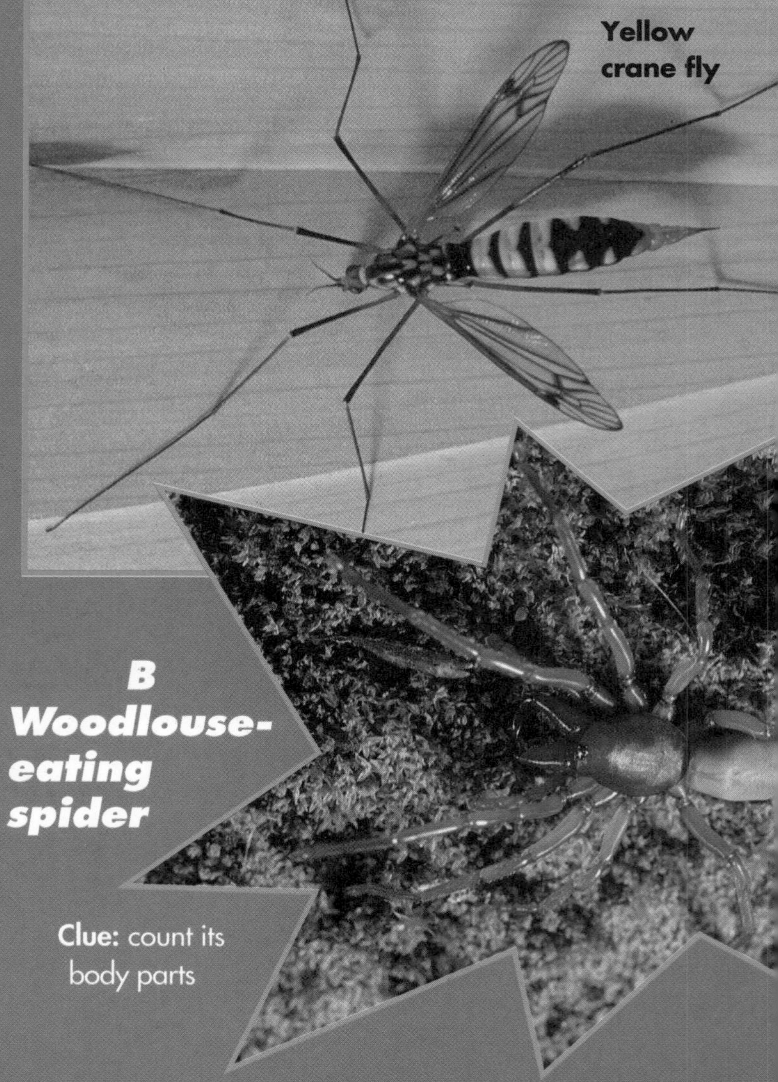

B
Woodlouse-eating spider
Clue: count its body parts

Is it true... that all arachnids are dangerous?

No. Not all arachnids are dangerous. Throughout the world, no more than 2 per cent of the 63,000 species of arachnid are harmful to humans. This means that 98 per cent are totally harmless. The daddy-long-legs, for example, is an innocent arachnid that lives in forests and grassland. (In Britain and North America, they are called harvestmen because they are usually seen around September, at harvest time.) Every year, more people are killed by bees and wasps, which are insects, than by arachnids, such as scorpions, spiders and ticks.

arachnids

Water scorpion

C Water scorpion

Clue: what big eyes you have!

D Harvestman

Clue: how many legs?

Harvestman

E Ant-mimic jumping spider

Clue: how does it feel?

Ant-mimic jumping spider

Woodlouse-eating spider

What is... arachnophobia?

People who are terrified of arachnids are said to have arachnophobia. But why are they so scared of these animals? Most spiders are harmless, and a scorpion's sting is rarely deadly. One of the reasons why these people are frightened of arachnids is because they never know where these bugs are – many arachnids are small, able to run fast and hide away in dark places.

ANSWERS

A YELLOW CRANE FLY

This bug has wings. Arachnids never have wings, but insects often do. The yellow crane fly is an insect.

B WOODLOUSE-EATING SPIDER

This bug has two separate body parts – a cephalothorax and abdomen – and four pairs of legs. It is an arachnid.

C WATER SCORPION

Despite its name, the water scorpion is not a real scorpion. It has compound eyes and only three pairs of legs. The water scorpion is actually an insect.

D HARVESTMAN

The harvestman is an arachnid. It has four pairs of legs and two separate body parts, but the latter are not easy to see.

E ANT-MIMIC JUMPING SPIDER

Don't be fooled – this bug is an arachnid. At a glance, it looks a bit like a well-known insect – the ant. Take a closer look. It doesn't have antennae because it is a spider. Like all spiders, it is an arachnid.

THE BLACK DEATH and how it happened

More than 600 years ago, millions of people died of a horrible disease. The cause of their deaths was a tiny bug that can only be seen under a microscope.

This dangerous bug was a germ, which lived inside fleas. The disease it caused was bubonic plague, which was commonly called the Black Death. Nobody in Europe was safe from this terrible illness.

BUGS ON BOARD

In the 14th century, many European people sailed to distant parts of the world – to trade, discover new lands and sometimes to fight in wars. They often brought back beautiful new things. But in 1348, some ships came back from Constantinople (now called Istanbul), in eastern Europe, with a deadly enemy on board. This was a tiny germ that infected fleas.

RAT TRIP

The infected fleas were carried back to western Europe by black rats, which lived on board trading ships. The rats chose to live on ships as there was lots of food on board for them to eat. The voyages were long and by the time the ships reached their destination, the rats had bred and increased in number. When they arrived in the new lands, the black rats jumped ashore and mixed with the local rats.

Carried inside the bodies of infected fleas (below), the plague germ spread across Europe.

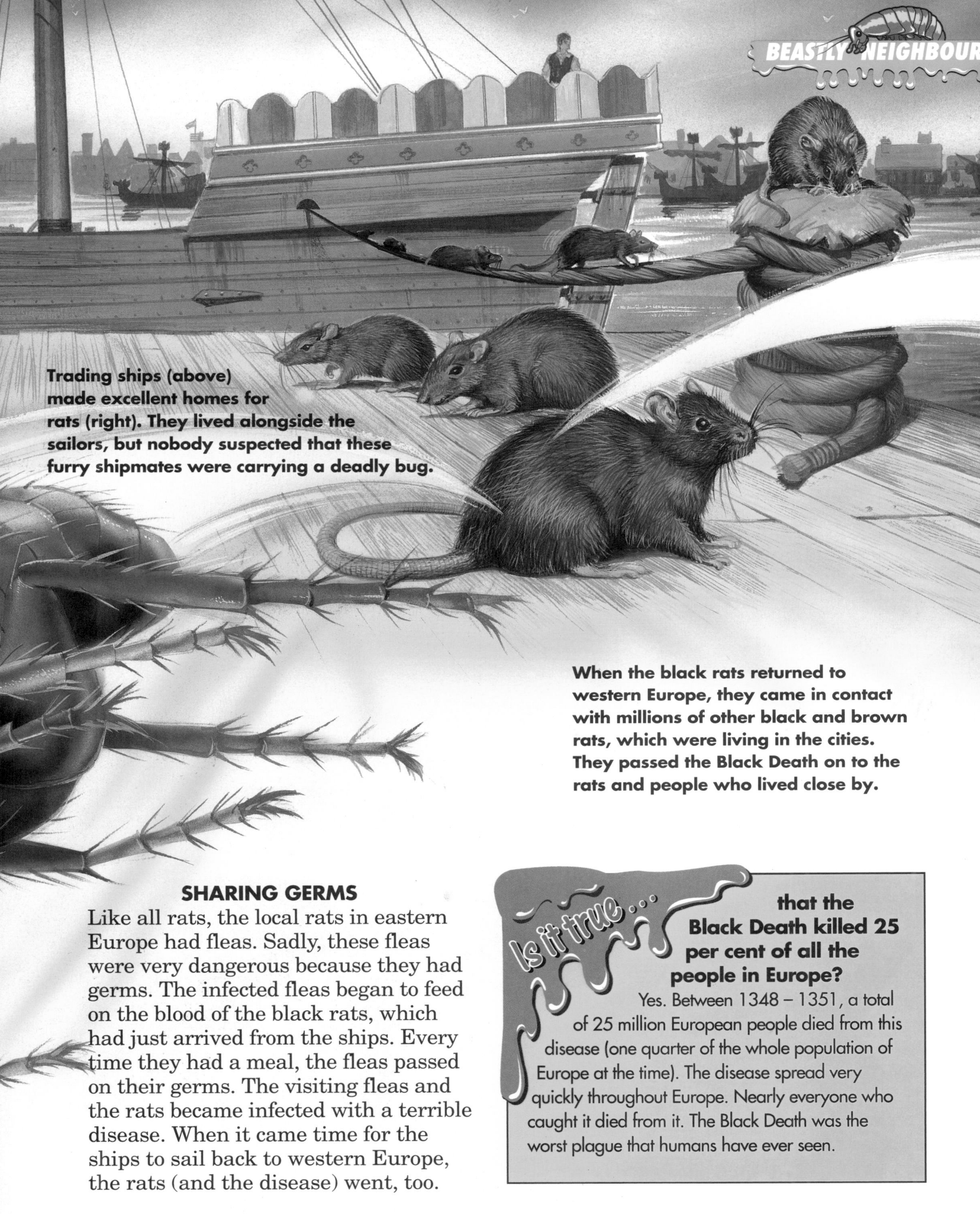

Trading ships (above) made excellent homes for rats (right). They lived alongside the sailors, but nobody suspected that these furry shipmates were carrying a deadly bug.

When the black rats returned to western Europe, they came in contact with millions of other black and brown rats, which were living in the cities. They passed the Black Death on to the rats and people who lived close by.

SHARING GERMS

Like all rats, the local rats in eastern Europe had fleas. Sadly, these fleas were very dangerous because they had germs. The infected fleas began to feed on the blood of the black rats, which had just arrived from the ships. Every time they had a meal, the fleas passed on their germs. The visiting fleas and the rats became infected with a terrible disease. When it came time for the ships to sail back to western Europe, the rats (and the disease) went, too.

Is it true... that the Black Death killed 25 per cent of all the people in Europe?

Yes. Between 1348 – 1351, a total of 25 million European people died from this disease (one quarter of the whole population of Europe at the time). The disease spread very quickly throughout Europe. Nearly everyone who caught it died from it. The Black Death was the worst plague that humans have ever seen.

In the 14th century, the streets in the big cities of Europe were very crowded and dirty. Lots of people lived in cramped conditions and their rubbish piled up in the streets.

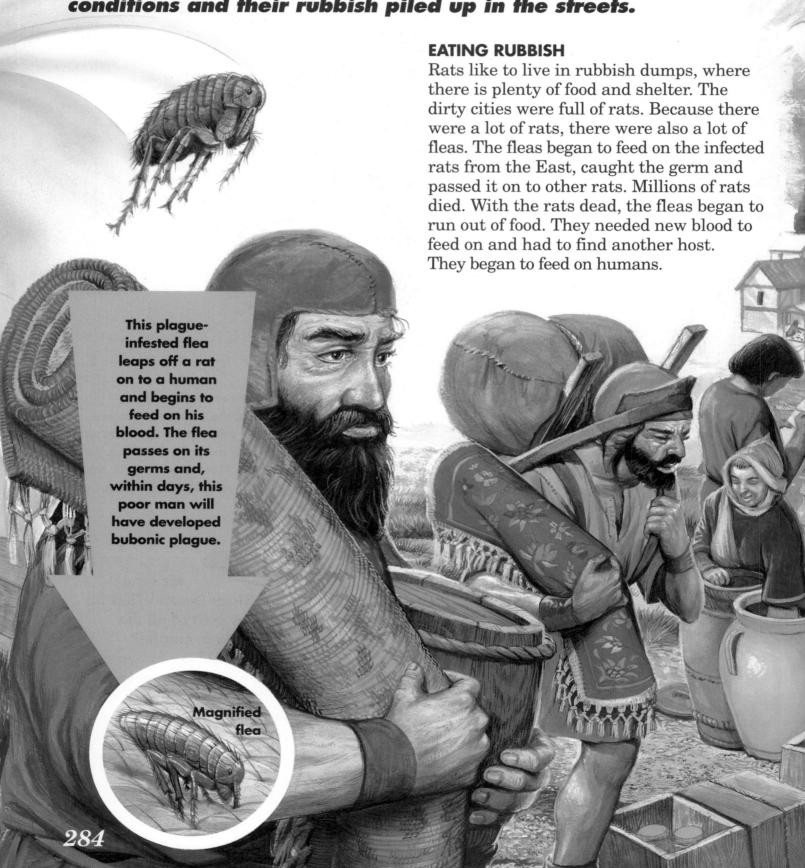

EATING RUBBISH

Rats like to live in rubbish dumps, where there is plenty of food and shelter. The dirty cities were full of rats. Because there were a lot of rats, there were also a lot of fleas. The fleas began to feed on the infected rats from the East, caught the germ and passed it on to other rats. Millions of rats died. With the rats dead, the fleas began to run out of food. They needed new blood to feed on and had to find another host. They began to feed on humans.

This plague-infested flea leaps off a rat on to a human and begins to feed on his blood. The flea passes on its germs and, within days, this poor man will have developed bubonic plague.

Magnified flea

SYMPTOMS OF THE PLAGUE

The plague was a horrible and painful disease. Victims suffered from terrible headaches, then they caught a fever. They sweated and shivered, had dizzy spells and began to imagine they were seeing things that were not there.

THE FINAL SIGN

The bubonic plague got its name from buboes, which are red, pus-filled swellings. These appeared under the victims' arms, on their necks or at the tops of their thighs. Eventually these buboes turned black and by this time there was little hope for the victims.

MILLIONS DIE

So many people died that there was soon no room to bury the bodies. Many were left in the street or in their houses. At the time, people were frightened because they didn't know what was causing the deaths. They blamed anything they could think of, including the dead rats. But no one gave a thought to the fleas.

RICH AND POOR

The plague was not just a disease for the poor. It killed rich and poor alike. Queen Eleanor of Aragon, Spain, died from it and the daughter of the English king, Edward III, was struck down by the plague on her way to her wedding in Spain.

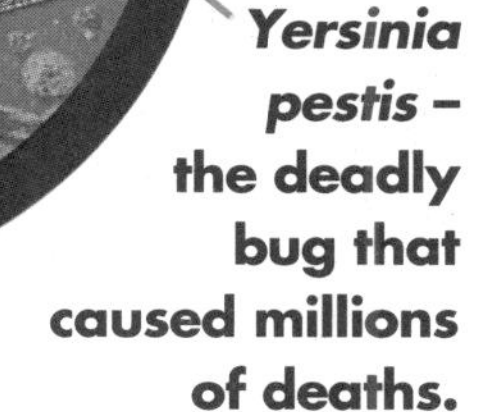

Yersinia pestis **– the deadly bug that caused millions of deaths.**

THE PLAGUE GERM

Experts have identified the germ that caused the plague. It is called *Yersinia pestis* (magnified 10,500 times above) and is very tiny. When several germs enter a flea's body, they form a lump in the flea's throat and block it up. This means that the flea is unable to swallow and it vomits the blood and the germ back into its host's bloodstream. If the host is a human, *Yersinia pestis* is carried around the body very quickly.

Small Talk

RECENT PLAGUES

There was another outbreak of bubonic plague in Britain in 1665 – 1666. This time, 70,000 people died. Then, in 1666, the Great Fire of London caught hold. Although it was a terrible disaster, it helped to wipe out the plague because it killed many of the rats and destroyed the dirty places where they bred. Today, it is still possible to catch the plague. Fleas that live on chipmunks in Colorado, USA, have been found to carry the plague germ.

Improve and test your knowledge with...

CREEPY-CRAWLY FACTS

Look up into the sky, learn some new minibeast facts and test yourself with the BUGS! quiz.

Creepy creche

The female lace bug is an excellent mother. She carefully guards her eggs and young against predators – she has even been seen head-butting ladybirds. Quite often, other female lace bugs will take advantage of a particularly good mum and place their eggs in her care. Several females may try this, leaving the original lace bug with a huge family.

Moth heatin'

Next time you see a silk scarf, spare a thought for the bugs that provided the raw material. Silk is made from the cocoons of domesticated silkmoth larvae. Once a larva has finished spinning its cocoon, the moisture is taken out of its body. This usually kills the bug. Then it is plunged into boiling water to loosen its cocoon. Over 60,000 tonnes of silk are produced each year, which means the death of about 3 billion bugs.

Out to lunch

Starfish like eating mussels. Mussels are not so happy about this, though, and hold their shells firmly shut. When mussel is on the menu, the starfish prises the shell open a few millimetres with its powerful legs. It then forces its stomach out through its mouth and into the mussel shell, where it can chomp away at its leisure.

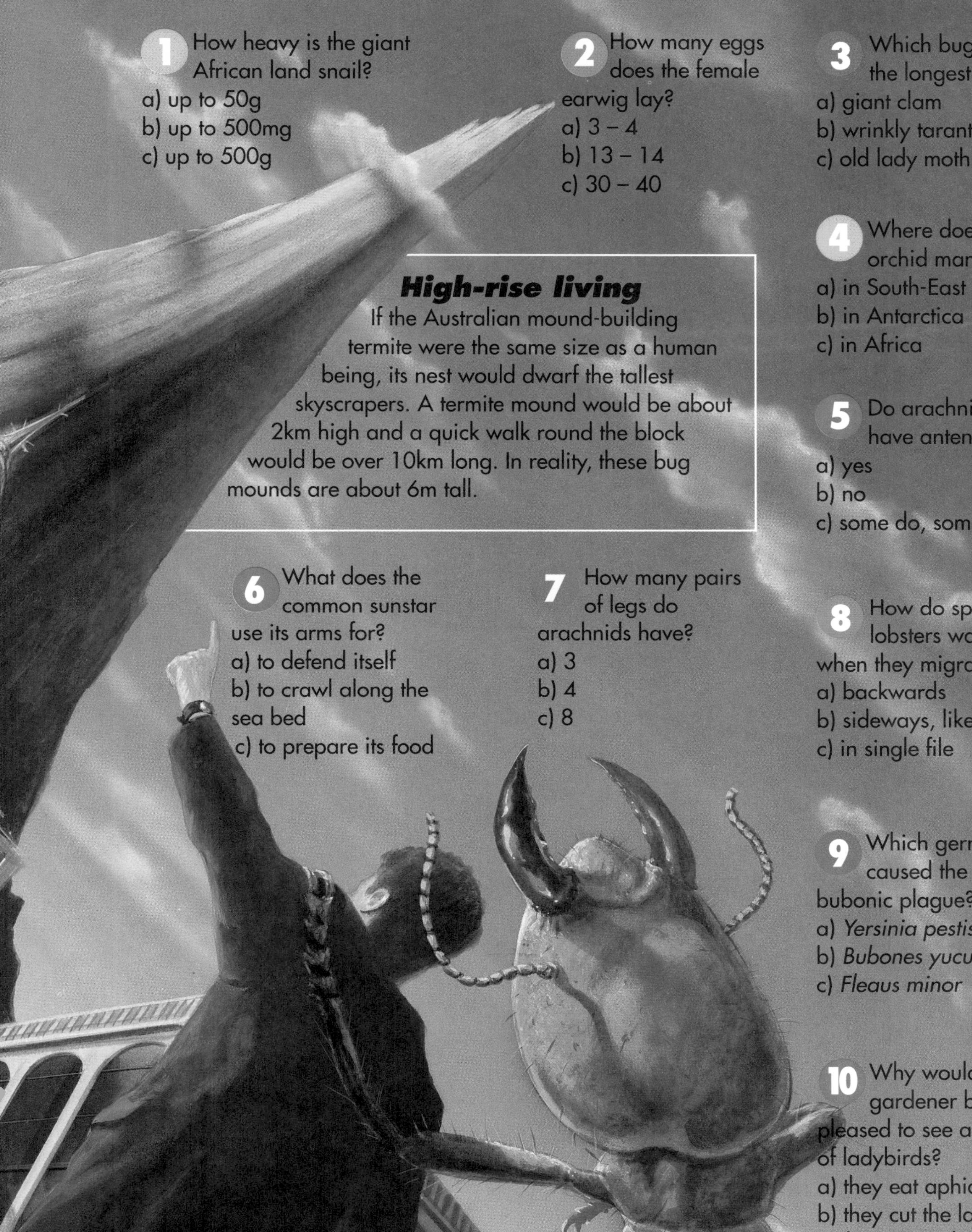

1 How heavy is the giant African land snail?
a) up to 50g
b) up to 500mg
c) up to 500g

2 How many eggs does the female earwig lay?
a) 3 – 4
b) 13 – 14
c) 30 – 40

3 Which bug lives the longest?
a) giant clam
b) wrinkly tarantula
c) old lady moth

4 Where does the orchid mantis live?
a) in South-East Asia
b) in Antarctica
c) in Africa

High-rise living

If the Australian mound-building termite were the same size as a human being, its nest would dwarf the tallest skyscrapers. A termite mound would be about 2km high and a quick walk round the block would be over 10km long. In reality, these bug mounds are about 6m tall.

5 Do arachnids have antennae?
a) yes
b) no
c) some do, some don't

6 What does the common sunstar use its arms for?
a) to defend itself
b) to crawl along the sea bed
c) to prepare its food

7 How many pairs of legs do arachnids have?
a) 3
b) 4
c) 8

8 How do spiny lobsters walk when they migrate?
a) backwards
b) sideways, like crabs
c) in single file

9 Which germ caused the bubonic plague?
a) *Yersinia pestis*
b) *Bubones yucus*
c) *Fleaus minor*

10 Why would a gardener be pleased to see a horde of ladybirds?
a) they eat aphids
b) they cut the lawn
c) they water the plants

Answers to the questions on the inside back cover

Matthew Robertson, who spent 12 years working with bugs at London Zoo, here answers all your creepy-crawly questions.

Do bugs have blood?

Yes, bugs do have blood. However, it is not always red like our own. Bugs may have blue, green or even colourless blood. Blood contains oxygen, which is carried in the blood by a special chemical. It is this chemical that affects the blood's colour. If the chemical is iron, the bug will have red blood, if it is copper, the bug's blood will be blue.

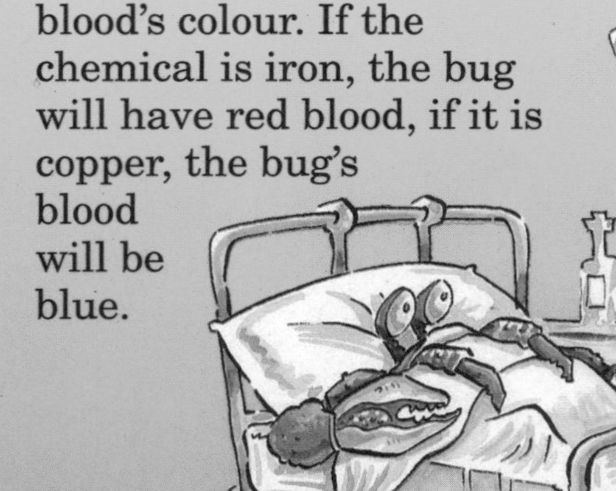

How high can bugs live?

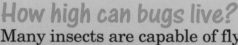

Many insects are capable of flying at a height of about 3,000 – 4,500m, although most never go that high. (Aeroplanes fly at an altitude of about 9,000m.) Creatures called aerial plankton are so tiny that they can live up in the clouds. Some spiders can live even higher – close to the top of Mount Everest. In the 1920s, a scientist called Major Hingston climbed this huge mountain and discovered jumping spiders at a height of 7,000m.

Which bug lives the longest?

Scientists think that certain molluscs live the longest. A type of clam, called a quahog, was found to have 215 growth rings. Each ring represents a year of growth, as it does on a tree. The rare giant clam, which is found in the South Pacific, usually lives for 150 years, but may live for as long as 200.

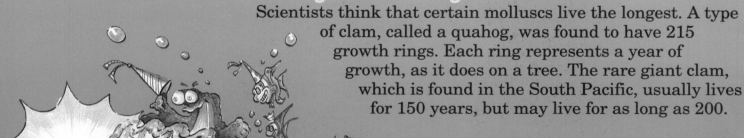

Portuguese man-of-war

A beautiful, pearly balloon floats on the water's surface. But don't touch. This 'balloon' is the Portuguese man-of-war – one of the ocean's deadliest killers.

The Portuguese man-of-war floats about in warm, tropical and sub-tropical oceans – often in huge crowds with thousands of others. When 18th-century sailors first saw one, they thought it was a Portuguese warship, known as a 'man-of-war' – which is how this strange-looking animal got its name.

SAILING THE OCEAN

The balloon-like 'float' – the part that you see above the water – is about 15cm high, and is filled with gas. Like the sail on a boat, it catches the wind, which then pushes the man-of-war across the water.

SINKING FOR SAFETY

If the weather is very stormy and the sea is rough, the man-of-war 'lets down' its gas-filled float, as if it were a rubber ring. It then sinks safely into the calmer waters below the waves.

JELLYFISH COLONY

Although it looks like a single jellyfish, the man-of-war is in fact a whole colony of polyps (say 'poll-ips') – tiny sea creatures – clustered together.

EACH TO THEIR OWN

Different groups of polyps have different jobs to do. Some form the float above the water, some have stinging tentacles that drift in the water and catch prey, and some digest the prey.

VENOMOUS DARTS

Like giant fishing lines, the man-of-war's tentacles trail a long way – they can be 50m long! (That's the same as the width of a football pitch.) If a fish brushes against the tentacles, tiny, hollow darts shoot out from inside the tentacles and inject a venom.

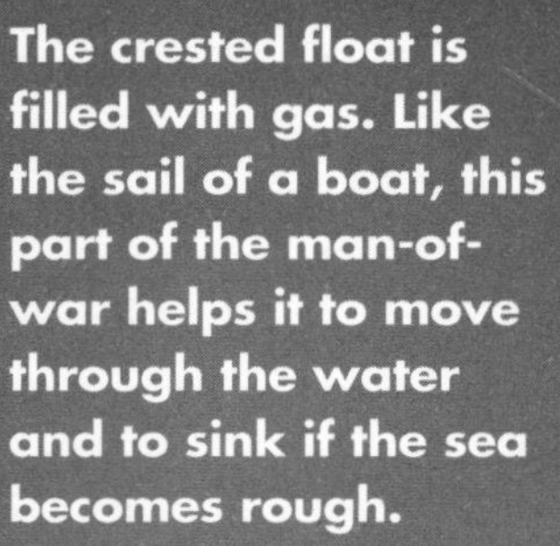

The crested float is filled with gas. Like the sail of a boat, this part of the man-of-war helps it to move through the water and to sink if the sea becomes rough.

REELING IN THE FISH

Then the tentacles lift the fish up to the polyps close to the float. These are covered in digesting juices, which dissolve the fish. Other polyps suck up the remains of the fish and share it around with other members of the colony.

- **SCIENTIFIC NAME:** *Physalia physalis*
- **SIZE:** body 9 – 35cm long, tentacles 15 – 50m long
- **LIVES:** tropical and sub-tropical oceans
- **EATS:** small fish

SIZING UP

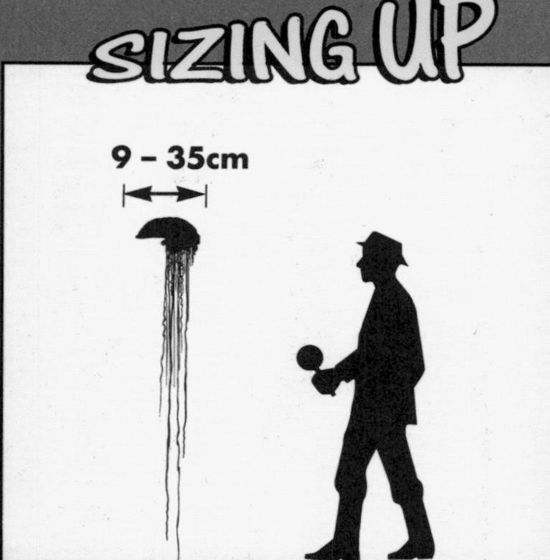

Muscular tentacles pull the fish up towards the jellyfish's polyps.

FEARSOME FINGERS

This Portuguese man-of-war is about to have tea. It has caught a passing fish in its long tentacles and injected it with deadly venom. The man-of-war will reel in its catch and slowly digest the fish.

DEADLY DANGER

The man-of-war is very dangerous to humans as well as fish. Swimmers who touch the tentacles may drown because the sting is so painful. Some people are allergic to the man-of-war's venom and die after they get stung. The tentacles are still venomous even if they are torn away from the body.

NEW COLONIES

The man-of-war has its own strange way of producing offspring – some of the polyps just break away to form a new cluster of jellyfish! Each man-of-war lives for only a few months. When it dies, scientists believe that it may also shed eggs and sperm into the sea, which then join together to produce baby jellyfish.

Shorter polyps, closer to the float, coat the fish with digestive juices.

Long tentacles are covered in stinging cells, which look pretty, but contain venomous barbs.

Tentacles can sting even if they break off from the body. They are sometimes found in fishing nets or washed up on the beach.

Atlas Moth

Once caught in thousands by bug collectors, the atlas moth is now quite rare.

Unlike many other moths whose wings are dull in colour, the atlas moth is as brightly coloured and beautifully patterned as a butterfly. It is also one of the biggest moths in the world. The female's wingspan, which is larger than the male's, can be 30cm wide. That's as wide as this page is long.

IN DANGER

In the past, people caught and killed thousands of atlas moths for their bug collections, so that there were very few left in the wild. Today, its natural habitats are threatened and so the atlas moth is in trouble once again.

FAT CATERPILLARS

The caterpillars of the atlas moth have speckled green and brown bodies, which may be 10cm long and 2cm thick – that's about as big as a grown-up's finger. Each caterpillar's body has several segments – rather like the folds in a concertina. Once the caterpillar becomes a moth, it will never feed again because the adult does not have a mouth! So the caterpillar can be excused for spending most of its time fattening itself up – it needs the food to grow and to survive as a moth. It feeds on the leaves of trees and shrubs.

- **SCIENTIFIC NAME:** *Attacus atlas*
- **SIZE:** 30cm wingspan
- **LIVES:** India and the Far East
- **EATS:** caterpillar eats leaves, adult doesn't eat

SIZING UP

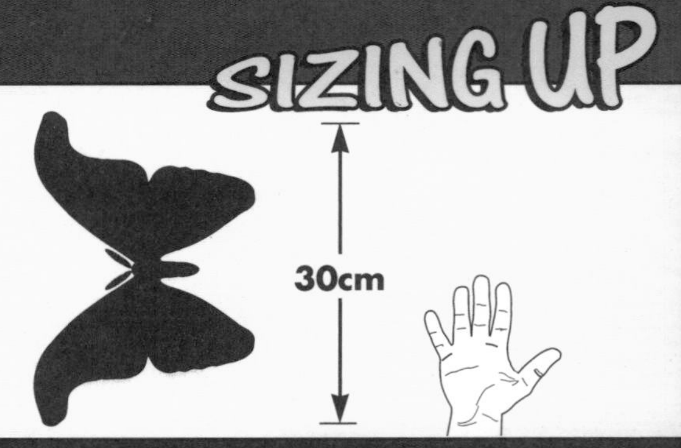

Giraffe-necked Weevil

When it meets a rival, the male giraffe-necked weevil shows who is boss by bending its long neck and nodding its head up and down.

The giraffe-necked weevil gets its name because of its extra-long neck. It lives in the rain forests of the island of Madagascar, off the east coast of Africa, where there is plenty of vegetation for it to eat.

LEAF ROLL

The leaves of the forest not only provide food for the weevil, but also a safe home for its young. When it is time for a female to lay her eggs, she chooses a leaf and then rolls it up into a tube. She squeezes the eggs out through her ovipositor (say 'oh-vi-poz-i-ter'), which is an egg-laying nozzle at the end of her abdomen. She squirts them into the leaf, rather like someone piping ice cream into a cone! Here, the eggs are out of sight of predators. When the young hatch, they eat their way out of their leafy home.

SHOWING OFF

If two male weevils meet in the forest, they don't attack each other. Instead, they stand face-to-face and nod the heads on the end of their long necks up and down at each other! The 'fight' is over when one of the males gives up and backs away.

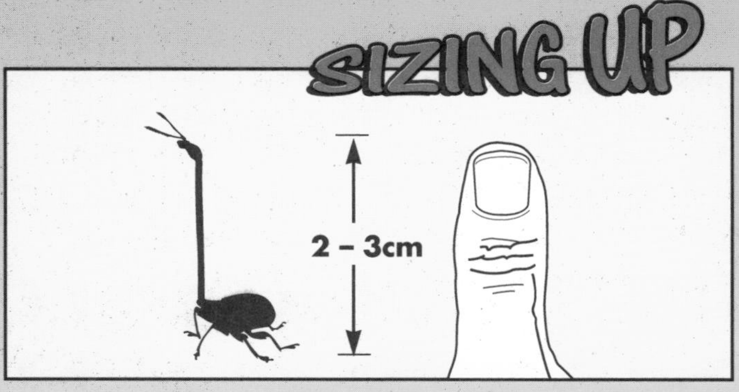

- **SCIENTIFIC NAME:** *Trachelophorus giraffa*
- **SIZE:** 2 – 3cm tall
- **LIVES:** Madagascar
- **EATS:** vegetation

Good parents

Many land bugs make excellent parents. As soon as their babies are born they provide them with food, shelter and protection.

Many bugs look after their eggs until they hatch and then carry on caring for their young larvae. Other bugs just find the best place to lay their eggs and leave their young to hatch and fend for themselves.

BEST START

The wild is a dangerous place for eggs and newborn bugs. Eggs can dry out, get too wet, go mouldy or be eaten. Female bugs go to a lot of trouble to find the best place to lay their eggs. Some make a protective covering for them or bury them underground. Others simply wait for their babies to hatch and take them wherever they go.

This mantis (above) has laid her eggs on the bark of a tree. She is covering them with foam that sets, like concrete, and keeps her babies safe.

This wolf spider's abdomen (above) is covered in tiny, red babies.

PIGGYBACK RIDE

Imagine a mother giving a piggyback ride to a hundred children. That is what the female wolf spider does (above). For several weeks before her babies are born the female wolf spider carries her eggs around in a large, specially made sac. When she senses that her young are rea to hatch, she tears open the bag and releases them. The babies climb on to he back and hitch a ride until they are old enough to look after themselves.

MANTIS MOTHER LOVE

The female mantis doesn't hang arounc watch her babies hatch. She simply lay her eggs then dashes off to lay some m elsewhere. Before she leaves, she cover her eggs in a foam case (left). This har into a tough shell that you would find to pull apart with your fingers. The eg need this protection against disease a stop them from drying out. They stay in their hard coating for 3 – 6 months

SECURITY BLANKET

The brown-tail moth recycles its sticky hairs and uses them as a protective rug. When it is a caterpillar, the brown-tail moth is covered in hairs. These crumble away when the bug turns into a pupa. When it emerges as a moth, it picks up the hairs and sticks them back on its tail by wiggling its abdomen. When the female lays her eggs, she arranges the hairs over them, like a rug (right). If predators have any sense they will stay away from this irritating blanket.

Tiny, pearl-like eggs (above) nestle in irritating brown-tail moth hairs.

WORKER NURSES

Sometimes, young bugs are not looked after by their parents at all. Instead, the have nurses to do the work. Ants live in huge colonies. All the ants in a colony ha the same mother (queen). She doesn't have time to look after all her young, so the worker ants take control. They clea the nests, go out in search of food and f the larvae (below).

OUT OF HARM'S WAY

The female lacewing lays her eggs in such a way that her babies can't get into trouble. She hangs her eggs by thin lines from leaves (above). The eggs look like tiny lightbulbs hanging from a ceiling. Each egg line is placed a little way from the others so that the babies that hatch first, which might be very hungry, can't eat their 'brothers' and 'sisters'! The lines also make it hard for prowling bugs to get at the eggs.

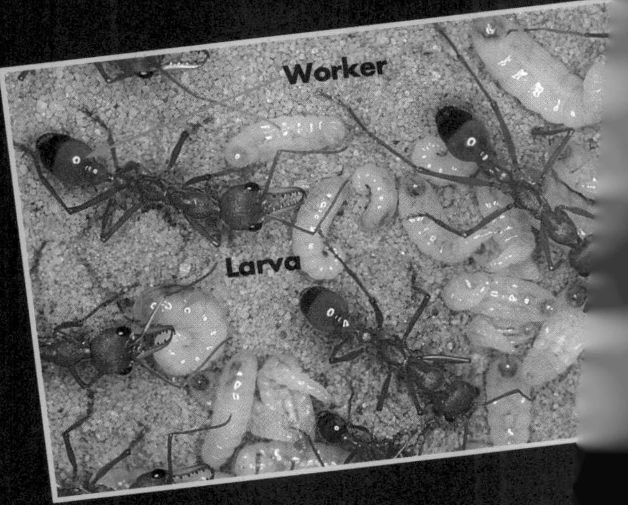

Bullant workers (above) have an importa They keep an eye on the larvae, feed the make sure that the next generation of an grows up to be big and strong.

NURSERY TENT

The nursery web spider carries her eggs around in a huge sac until they are ready to hatch. When they are about to emerge, she attaches the egg sac to a piece of grass or a leaf and builds a nursery around them (main picture right). Using her spinnerets (silk-producing organs), she weaves a large web, which is shaped like a circus tent. The babies stay inside the tent with their mother until they are old enough to scurry off and look after themselves.

The female nursery web spider watches over her babies as they grow up in the nest (right). She will stay with them until they have moulted (shed their skins) twice.

LIVE BABIES

Not all bugs lay eggs. Some give birth to live young. The female cockroach (below) keeps her eggs inside her body until they are ready to hatch. When they are born, their mother carries them around under her abdomen.

These young cockroaches (right) have just hatched – their bodies are still white. If they didn't have their mother to look after them, they would be seen and eaten by predators.

Is it true...

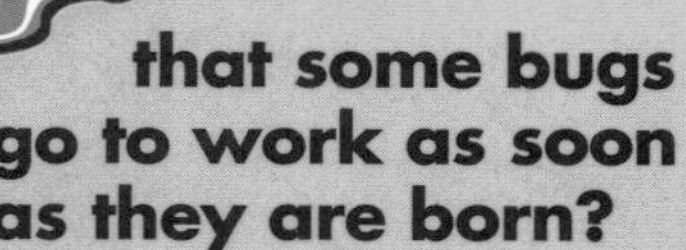

that some bugs go to work as soon as they are born?

Yes. The adult weaver ant (right) from South-East Asia, uses its newly hatched young to build a shelter. The larva produces a silky thread, which the adult uses to 'knit' herself a home. The female ant holds the larva in her mouth and moves her head from side to side, passing the larva across a leaf or between two stalks of grass.

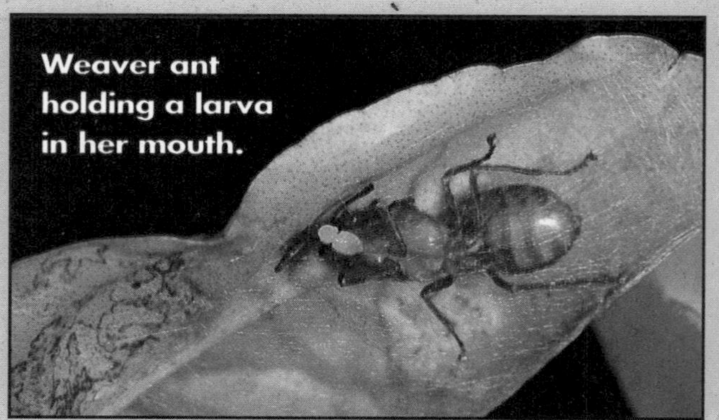

Weaver ant holding a larva in her mouth.

Predators will simply step over these eggs (above), which belong to several species of stick insects. They are designed to look like pebbles or seeds.

TAKE-AWAY EGGS

Some bugs don't need to look after their eggs. The female stick insect, for example, scatters her eggs on the forest floor (left). Each egg stays just where it lands for up to two years. It is protected from the rain by a hard shell. Because it looks just like a seed, insect-eating predators don't usually notice it. Eventually, a young insect emerges and climbs the nearest tree to enjoy its first meal.

Small Talk

TOUGH MUM

Earwigs take great care of their eggs and their young. After mating, the female earwig digs a burrow in the soil in which she lays 20 – 50 eggs. For the next two or three weeks she stays in the burrow, guarding her eggs from predators. Every so often she cleans and turns the eggs. This is to stop them getting infected by fungus. Once the babies hatch, the mother looks after them for a week or so. After this, she becomes less interested in being a mother and pushes them out of the burrow. If her young don't hurry up and leave, the mother knows that there is something wrong with them. She eats the weaklings that stay around. Any slowcoaches had better get a move on!

Wasp deposits an egg using its egg-laying tube.

This wasp (above) plans for the future when it lays its eggs inside the host's body.

FIRST FOOD

When human babies are born, one of the first things they do is have a meal. Some animals, like the braconid wasp (above), have a meal ready for their baby when it hatches. This wasp lays one egg inside an aphid's body, which the wasp larva can eat as soon as it hatches.

Keep a tarantula

The tarantula has a fearsome reputation, but it doesn't deserve this. It makes an excellent pet and is surprisingly simple to keep.

A tarantula has advantages over many other pets. You'll only need to feed it once a week and you won't need to take it for walks. Tarantulas aren't smelly, messy or noisy and they don't carry any diseases that can be caught by humans. In short, they make perfect pets! A tarantula that you buy in a pet shop may live for 5 – 20 years, depending on its species and sex. Get as much information about your spider from the pet shop as you can. (Don't buy from a shop that doesn't give information!)

- a large tank with close-fitting lid
- heat pad with thermostat
- strip thermometer
- sand or gravel
- one or two rocks
- one or two tree branches
- shallow dish
- tarantula food, such as crickets or mealworms

Small Talk

- Remember that tarantulas are cannibalistic (in other words, they will eat each other!), so do not attempt to keep more than one in the same tank.
- The Mexican red-kneed tarantula has been almost wiped out by the pet trade. So if you buy a tarantula, make sure that it was not taken from the wild, but bred in captivity.
- Many people are sensitive to their pets' hairs. Some humans are allergic to the hairs that cover a tarantula's body, which occasionally cause rashes.

1 You can use a fish tank for your spider, or buy a special tank for land animals – known as a terrarium. Tarantulas are experts at escaping so make sure that the lid of the tank is tight-fitting and secure.

2 Place the heat pad under your tank. Move it to one end and check the temperature inside the tank with a strip thermometer. It should be about 22 – 24°C.

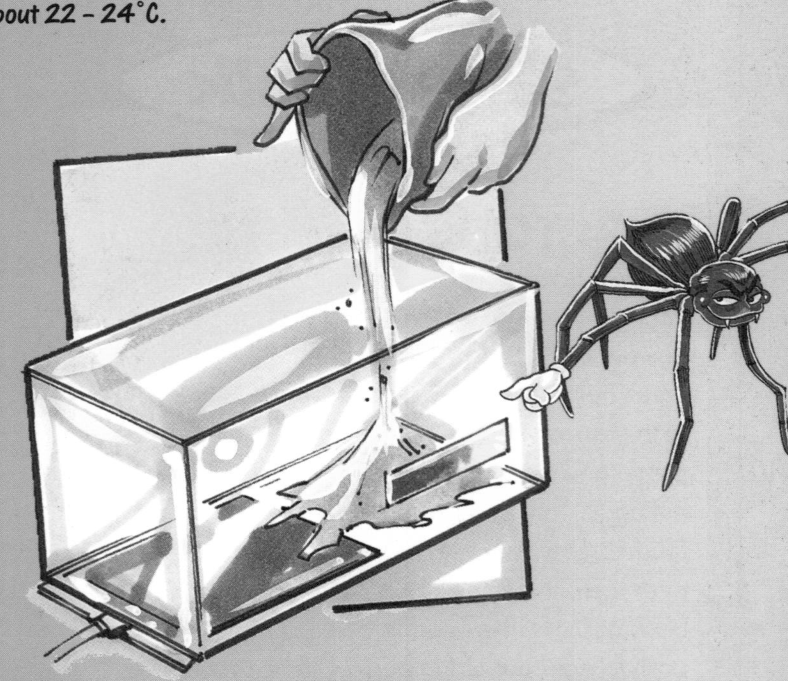

3 Pour a layer of sand or gravel into the tank. If you use sand, buy silver sand from a garden centre. If you choose gravel, use an odourless, parasite-free type of gravel suitable for fish and available from a pet shop. It should be about 6cm deep, allowing the tarantula to burrow into it.

Is it true... that a tarantula bite can kill a human?

No. The bite of nearly all species of tarantula is about as harmful as a bee sting. The venom that a tarantula produces is designed for overpowering prey smaller than itself – not humans. A tarantula bite will, however, hurt! If you get bitten, you must go to the doctor, who will make sure that your bite doesn't get infected.

6 If, at any time, you find your tarantula lying on its back on the floor of its tank, do not touch it. Leave it for a day or two and you will probably find that it is shedding its skin. When it has moulted, wait a week, by which time its new skin should have hardened.

Tarantulas are very sensitive when they have just moulted and should not be handled for several days after the moult.

4 Now furnish your tarantula's new home. Put a rock or two in it, along with one or two branches, especially if you have chosen a tree-climbing species of tarantula. You can buy a dead tree branch, complete with base, from a pet shop, which will reduce the risk of introducing parasites. Place a shallow dish of water in the tank. Always make sure that the dish is kept clean and change the water daily to stop it going stale. Put your tarantula in its new home and make sure the lid fits tightly.

Small Talk

HANDLING A TARANTULA

On the whole, it is better not to handle your tarantula. Being handled is not something that it needs or even particularly enjoys. It is not possible to under handle a tarantula, but it is possible to over handle it. If you must handle it, remember that tarantulas can bite, so you must hold them correctly. Very gently scoop the spider up in your hands with your palms facing upwards (right). Once you are more confident, grip your tarantula firmly with your thumb and forefinger between its second and third pairs of legs. Be careful not to drop your tarantula as a fall can easily kill it.

5 Tarantulas need to feed on live prey. They will kill and eat all sorts of large insects, such as crickets, grasshoppers, beetles and cockroaches. It is probably simplest to find out what your pet shop has to offer, and stick to this. Tarantulas will also eat a dead insect or even minced meat or pieces of fish, but only if they think the food is alive. Attach the food to a piece of string and jiggle it about in front of your spider. Most tarantulas need only one or two crickets (depending on the size of the crickets) a week.

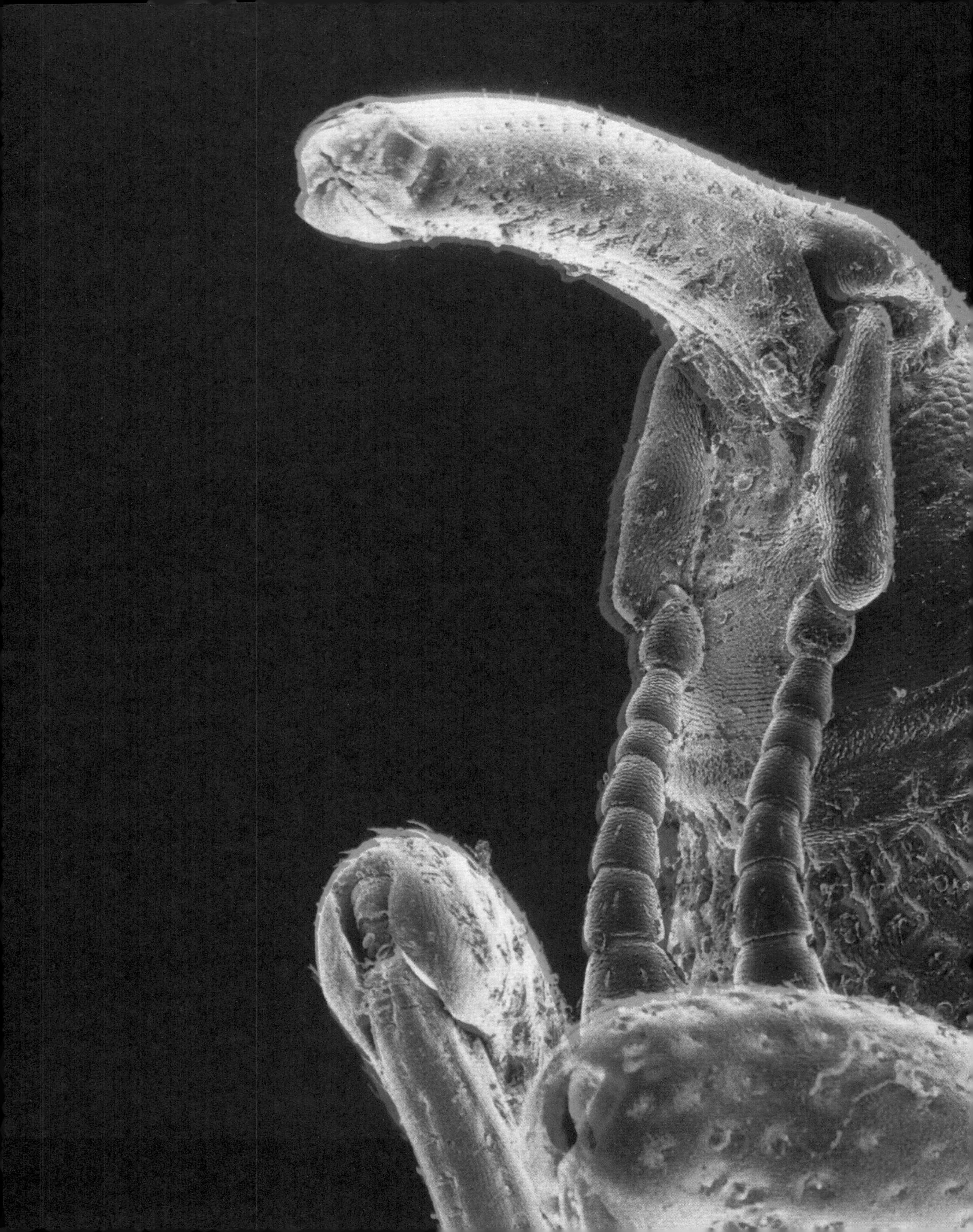

Grain weevil

After crawling through a bag of flour all morning, this female grain weevil is exhausted. To her, it feels a bit like walking across a sandy beach. She stops to take a breather, gives her long nose a wipe and chews away at a tiny grain of flour. The weevil's strong shell stops the moisture in her body from evaporating. This means that she can live in very dry places like cereal, grain and flour stores. Just as she's thinking of laying her eggs, a human opens the bag of flour. Sunlight pours in and the weevil runs for cover.

Walking without legs

Some of the bugs that live on the land do not have any legs. So how do they get from A to B? Read on and find out.

There are many ways for legless bugs to get around on land. Earthworms, leeches and slugs are just three slippery bugs that have developed clever ways of getting about without feet or legs.

WRIGGLING WORMS

An earthworm does not have legs. Its body is thin and is divided into segments (tiny sections). Each segment has four hairs on it, which it uses to grip the soil. Worms wriggle through the soil using two sets of muscles. Some of the muscles are long and run from the earthworm's head to its tail. The others are circular and surround each segment.

THICK AND THIN

When an earthworm is at rest, its body segments are all the same size (below, A). To move forward, a worm stretches the front part of its body as far forward as it can. This makes the front body segments longer and thinner (B). When the worm stops stretching these front segments, they get thicker. The front segment hairs stretch into the soil and hold the worm in place (C). Then the earthworm stretches and thickens all its body segments, in turn, right down to its tail (D). By the time the worm has stretched the last segments of its body, the front end is already stretching again (E).

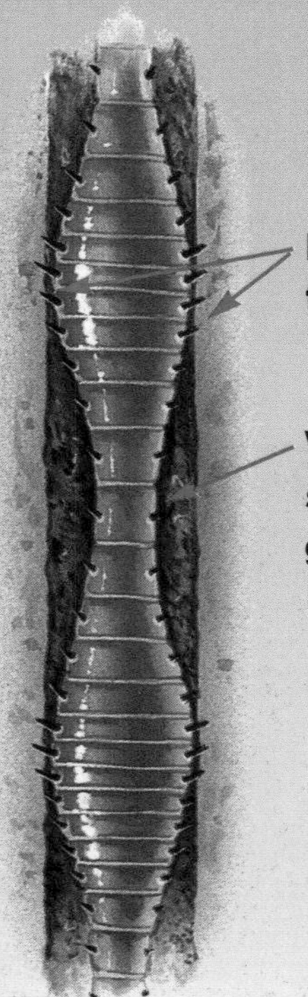

Extended hairs hold the worm in place.

When the worm stretches, the hairs go back in.

Direction of movement

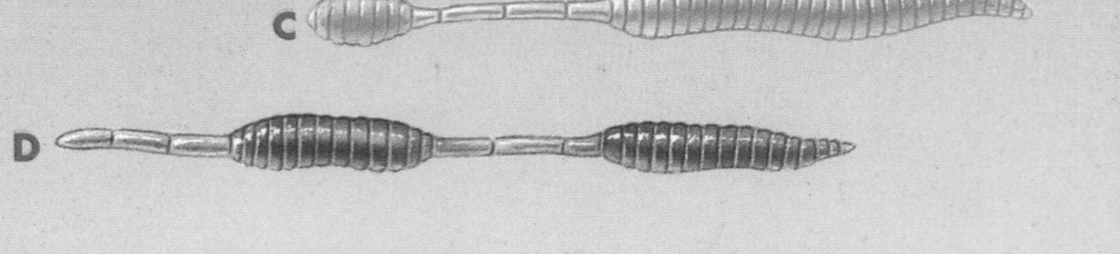

Direction of wave

A When an earthworm is at rest, all of its body segments are the same size.
B To move forward, the earthworm stretches the front segments of its body.
C The front segments thicken and hairs anchor the worm in the soil.
D The wave continues along the body as the head stretches forward.
E As the wave reaches the end of the body, the front is ready to stretch forward again.

A MEXICAN WAVE

As it wriggles along, the earthworm moves its body segments one-by-one. If you look at a worm very closely, you will be able to see a wave-like movement travelling down its body. (This movement is like a 'Mexican wave', which spectators sometimes do at big sporting events, jumping out of their seats in a certain order with their arms in the air.) In worms, this type of wave-like movement is called peristalsis (say 'perry-stal-sis'). A wave passes down an earthworm's body 7 – 10 times a minute.

The smooth earthworm (left) spends most of its time in narrow tunnels underground. Without any limbs, it moves along quite easily.

This jackdaw is trying to pull a worm out of the ground (right). The worm has anchored itself firmly in the soil, using its muscles and the hairs on each body segment.

Is it true ... that earthworms swallow soil to help them move forwards?

Yes. When an earthworm is tunnelling through tightly packed soil, the only way it can move the soil in front of it is to swallow it. In the soil are tiny food particles, such as the eggs and larvae of small animals, which the worm eats. When the worm reaches the surface, it excretes (expels) the rest of the soil, leaving small piles of droppings by its burrow. These little mounds of soil are called casts. If you see one on the grass, you'll know that this is the entrance to a worm's tunnel. A worm also pulls leaves into its burrow to eat (right). It only digests some of the leaves and, on its next trip to the surface, the remains become mixed up with the soil in the casts.

Now you've seen how worms wriggle, find out how leeches loop and slugs slither.

LOOPING LEECHES

A leech has a segmented body, like an earthworm, but it gets about in a completely different way – it loops its body. Instead of legs, a leech has two suckers – a small one at the front of its body and a larger one at the back.

SUCTION POWER

When it moves, a leech attaches its back sucker to the surface it is on and stretches its body as far forward as it can. It then attaches the front sucker, releases the back one, and brings its body together in a large loop. Then it starts all over again. A leech can move forward or backwards.

Most leeches live in water, but a few, like this Malaysian painted leech (right), can be found on land. They prefer places where it is damp and hide under leaves on the ground, or in trees.

SENSING PREY

Land-living leeches lurk underneath leaves, waiting for larger animals, such as humans to pass by. When a leech senses something or someone approaching, it moves the front of its body around in circles to sense where the movement or smell is coming from. When the host comes near enough, the leech attaches itself painlessly to the skin and begins to drink the blood.

This leech is 'looping' across sheet of glass (below). You can see its two suckers clearly. The small sucker at the front has three rows of sharp, saw-shaped teeth, which it uses to bite through the skin of its host and suck its blood.

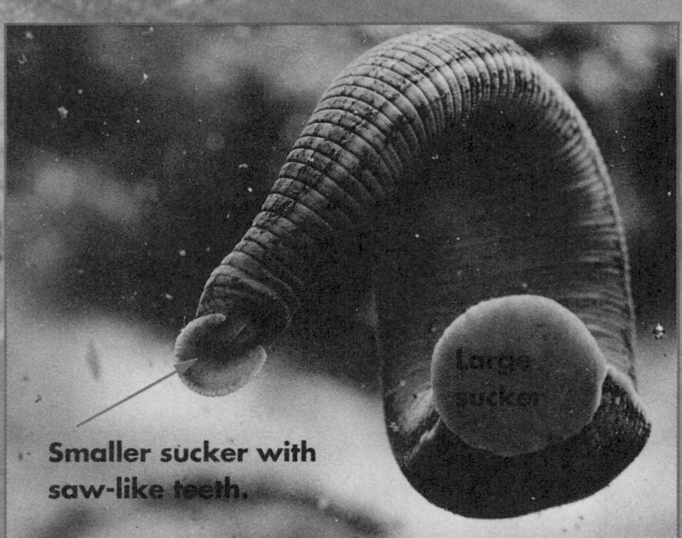

A Leech attaches back sucker to surface and releases front sucker.

B It stretches as far forward as it can and attaches front sucker.

C Releases back sucker and brings body forward in large loop.

D Starts the whole movement again.

Direction of movement

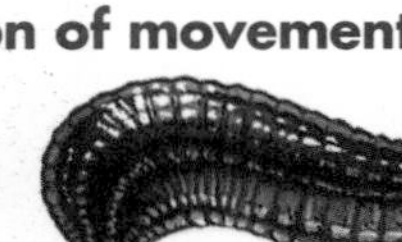

Malaysian painted leech stretches its body across a leaf.

SLITHERING SLUG

The whole of the underneath of a slug's body is a long, muscular foot, which is covered with a slimy substance called mucus. The mucus is very thick and sticky and helps the slug grip on smooth surfaces. A slug leaves a tell-tale trail of mucus wherever it goes.

MOVING IN WAVES

When a slug moves, it looks like it is skating along on a smooth surface, but it is really moving its foot in a series of wave-like movements. It lifts one part of its foot and moves it a little way forward. It then moves the next part and so on. The movements ripple from the back to the front of the slug's foot.

Although slugs only have one big foot, they can get about very well. This one (above) is slithering over a toadstool.

The mucus that a slug leaves behind is very thick. This slime protects the slug's foot and allows it to move safely over rough objects.

Small Talk

LAZY MAGGOTS

The larva of a fly, such as a bluebottle, is called a maggot. It has a very simple body, with two holes at one end for breathing, and two hooks at the other end for eating. A maggot does not have any legs, but unlike a worm, slug or leech, a maggot can't move. Because it can't go and look for food, its mother lays her eggs in a place where there is plenty of food for the maggot when it hatches. A bluebottle often lays her eggs in rotting meat. A maggot can eat and eat until it is ready to pupate, without having to go anywhere.

When the slug is still, its muscular foot does not move.
The slug lifts a small part of its foot and moves it forward.
By lifting each part separately, a wave moves up the foot.
The wave reaches the front of the foot and the slug begins again.
Direction of movement and wave

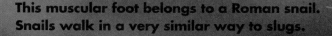

This muscular foot belongs to a Roman snail. Snails walk in a very similar way to slugs.

Freshwater bugs

Whenever you come across an area of fresh water, whether it's a pond, a river or lake, stop and peer into the water. Here are some of the bugs that you might see.

Bugs that live on the water's surface or fly among the reeds and plants around a pond are easy to spot. But beneath the surface there is a totally different world and the bugs that live there are much more difficult to see.

IT TAKES ALL SORTS

A freshwater pond, lake or river is home to many bugs. Some, such as caddisfly larvae, live at the bottom. They hide from predators in protective cases made from pebbles. Others, such as dobson fly larvae, are much braver. They swim around looking for other animals to eat.

After swimming to the surface for a breath of air, this great silver beetle (right) dives back down to the bottom, scaring off a tadpole. Lives: Europe.

The common mayfly nymph (right) has sensitive eyes and antennae. This bugs is a peaceful plant-eater. Lives: Europe.

Tadpole

Three long, thin tails used for breathing.

The freshwater crab (below) comes out at night to hunt small animals, such as fish and newts. It spends its days hiding under stones. Lives: North America.

Large, sharp claws for grabbing prey.

Newt

The ramshorn snail (right) lives in slow-moving water with lots of vegetation. It eats algae and other small plant remains. It often slithers to the surface to breathe, but it also has a gill, so it can breathe underwater. Lives: worldwide.

SUBAQUA BUGS

Some freshwater bugs, such as the larvae of dragonflies and caddisflies, never come to the water's surface. They can stay underwater and breathe through gills (slits in the sides of their bodies). The water scorpion and the great silver beetle, however, swim to the surface to breathe.

MOVING ON

The water scorpion and freshwater crab spend their whole lives underwater. But dragonfly and mayfly larvae only start their lives in the water. For the first 2 – 3 years, they live underwater and eat all the time. They shed their skin as they grow. When they are ready to turn into adults, they crawl out of the water, moult once again and take to the air.

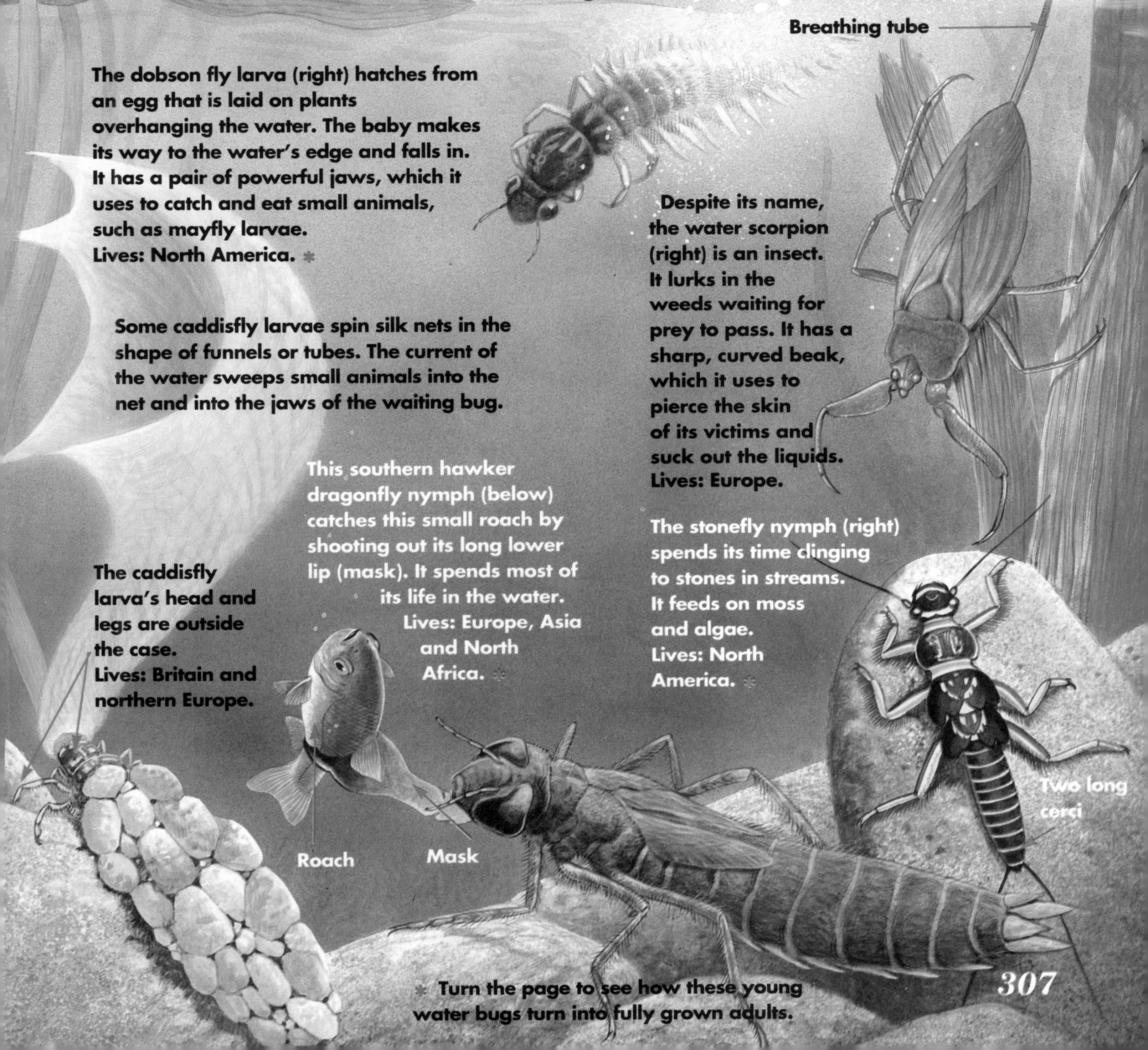

Breathing tube

The dobson fly larva (right) hatches from an egg that is laid on plants overhanging the water. The baby makes its way to the water's edge and falls in. It has a pair of powerful jaws, which it uses to catch and eat small animals, such as mayfly larvae. Lives: North America. *

Despite its name, the water scorpion (right) is an insect. It lurks in the weeds waiting for prey to pass. It has a sharp, curved beak, which it uses to pierce the skin of its victims and suck out the liquids. Lives: Europe.

Some caddisfly larvae spin silk nets in the shape of funnels or tubes. The current of the water sweeps small animals into the net and into the jaws of the waiting bug.

This southern hawker dragonfly nymph (below) catches this small roach by shooting out its long lower lip (mask). It spends most of its life in the water. Lives: Europe, Asia and North Africa. *

The caddisfly larva's head and legs are outside the case. Lives: Britain and northern Europe.

The stonefly nymph (right) spends its time clinging to stones in streams. It feeds on moss and algae. Lives: North America. *

Roach

Mask

Two long cerci

* **Turn the page to see how these young water bugs turn into fully grown adults.**

Some of the bugs that lived under the water as larvae have turned into adults. Now they live above the water, where they hunt, eat and mate.

MAY BUGS

Every year, when the weather's right you may see bugs leaving the water and shedding their skins. Mayfly nymphs are unusual because they all leave the water on the same day. They usually only live for one day and spend that day looking for mates. You may even see a male mayfly putting on a spectacular flying show to impress a female.

TAKE TO THE AIR

You have already met the bugs that live under the water. Some of them stay in their watery homes all their lives, while others move above the water's surface. Other bugs are born and bred on land, but gather around the water's edge to find their dinner. Look carefully and you might see an athletic dragonfly or an elegant damselfly resting on the pond plants. If you're lucky, you may spot a pond skater darting across the water, leaving ripples as it goes.

The yellow and black southern-hawker dragonfly (left) uses its four strong wings to fly at speed.

Powerful legs snatch prey.

Pond skater

Moth

The pond skater (above) is one of the few bugs that can walk on water. It can do this because it doesn't weigh very much and it has four special walking legs. It holds its legs out in an X-shape, which helps spread the bug's weight evenly. Only the tips of its feet touch the water.
Lives: Europe, Middle East and North Africa.

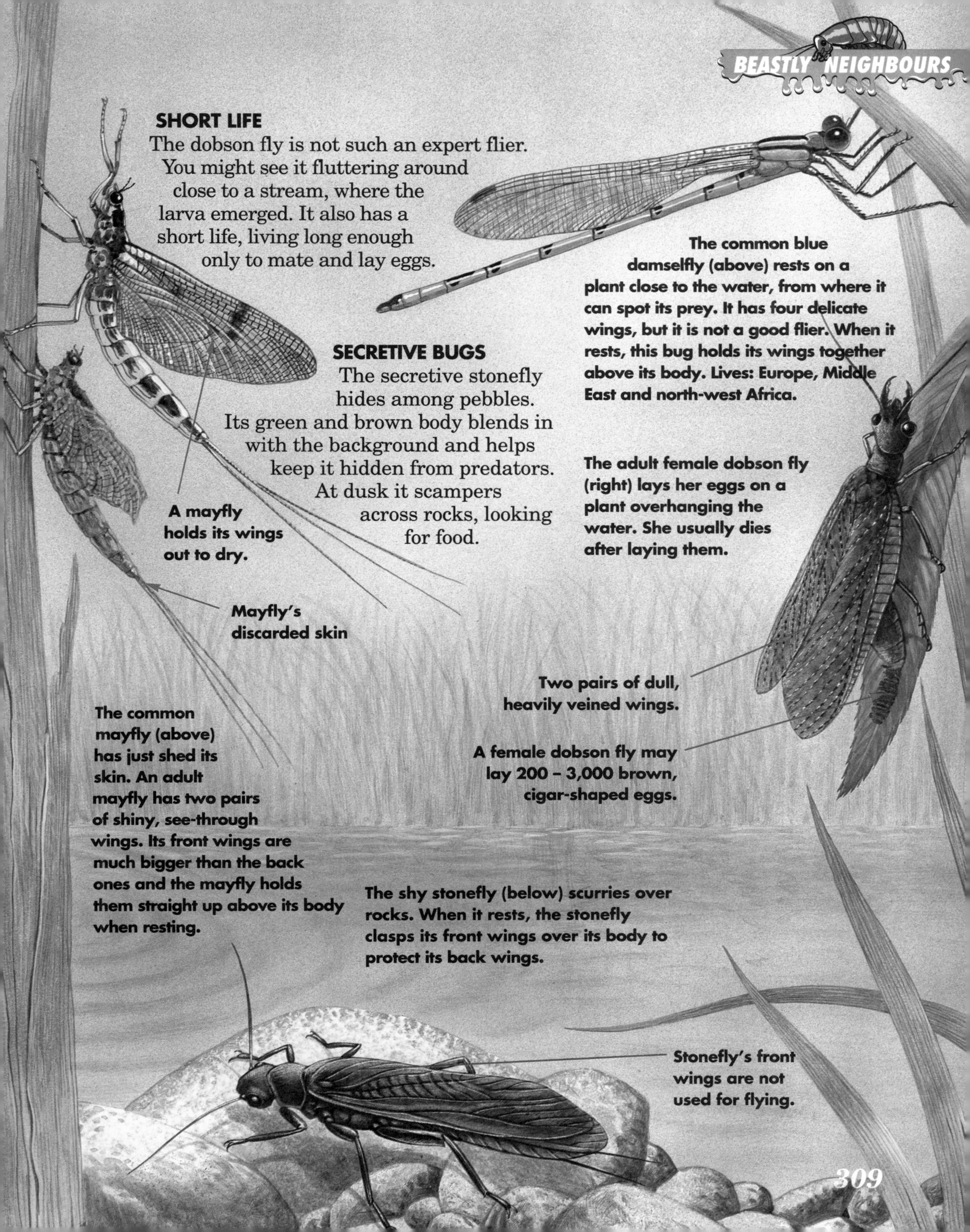

SHORT LIFE

The dobson fly is not such an expert flier. You might see it fluttering around close to a stream, where the larva emerged. It also has a short life, living long enough only to mate and lay eggs.

The common blue damselfly (above) rests on a plant close to the water, from where it can spot its prey. It has four delicate wings, but it is not a good flier. When it rests, this bug holds its wings together above its body. Lives: Europe, Middle East and north-west Africa.

SECRETIVE BUGS

The secretive stonefly hides among pebbles. Its green and brown body blends in with the background and helps keep it hidden from predators. At dusk it scampers across rocks, looking for food.

A mayfly holds its wings out to dry.

Mayfly's discarded skin

The adult female dobson fly (right) lays her eggs on a plant overhanging the water. She usually dies after laying them.

Two pairs of dull, heavily veined wings.

A female dobson fly may lay 200 – 3,000 brown, cigar-shaped eggs.

The common mayfly (above) has just shed its skin. An adult mayfly has two pairs of shiny, see-through wings. Its front wings are much bigger than the back ones and the mayfly holds them straight up above its body when resting.

The shy stonefly (below) scurries over rocks. When it rests, the stonefly clasps its front wings over its body to protect its back wings.

Stonefly's front wings are not used for flying.

Improve and test your knowledge with...

CREEPY~CRAWLY FACTS

Don't lose your cool – try the BUGS! red hot quiz. Then test your friends.

Bee blockers

During World War II, there was a series of plane crashes in South Africa. A man was arrested for deliberately making the planes unsafe to fly. Experts studied the wrecks and found that all the crashes had happened for the same reason. A small tube on the outside of each plane, which told the pilot how fast he was flying, was stuffed with leaves. An insect expert, called Dr Skaife, took a look and found the real culprits – leaf-cutter bees. They had used the tubes as nests and filled them with leaves for their young to eat.

Rampant rubbish

A village in Indonesia was once terrorised by a horde of huge centipedes. During the night, the village's rubbish tip caught fire. After a short time, thousands of centipedes, each one over 10cm long, scurried out of the burning rubbish dump, where they had made their home. The people were so scared of these giant bugs that they fled from their village.

Bushman's bug

In order to eat, the bushmen of the Kalahari desert, southern Africa, have to hunt animals. Without guns, these hunters need to make their own powerful weapons. They coat their arrowheads with poison from the larva of the leaf beetle. If a bushman hits his prey, the poison can kill an animal as large as a giraffe in just 30 minutes.

1 How long is the caterpillar of the atlas moth?
a) 1cm
b) 5cm
c) 10cm

2 How does the female mantis protect her eggs?
a) she covers them with a foam case
b) she lays her eggs underground
c) she covers them in thick mud

3 What happens when two rival male giraffe-necked weevils meet?
a) they fight
b) they nod their heads
c) they shake hands

4 How often does a pet tarantula need to be fed?
a) every day
b) once a week
c) once a month

5 Why do communal daddy-long-legs huddle together in groups?
a) for safety
b) they get lonely
c) to keep warm

6 Why does a male mayfly put on flying shows?
a) to find food
b) to impress the females
c) to make themselves tired

7 What disease can the cone-nosed bug cause?
a) cone-nose disease
b) malaria
c) Chagas' disease

8 What does a Portuguese man-of-war do when the sea is rough?
a) puts up its sails
b) lets down its float
c) swims to shore

9 Why can a dragonfly larva live underwater?
a) it has gills
b) it doesn't breathe
c) it can hold its breath for a long time

10 How does an earthworm move the soil that is in its way?
a) it pushes it into its burrow
b) it makes a spade with a leaf and shovels it out
c) it swallows it

Eggs-traordinary

Many insects lay their eggs in water, but sometimes they get confused. A shiny, black car, which was parked by a lake, was once mistaken for a pool of dark water. Its owner returned to the car to find that hundreds of dragonflies, damselflies and mayflies had all laid their eggs on it. The result was a huge bug omelette and a bill for the car to be re-sprayed.

Answers to the questions on the inside back cover

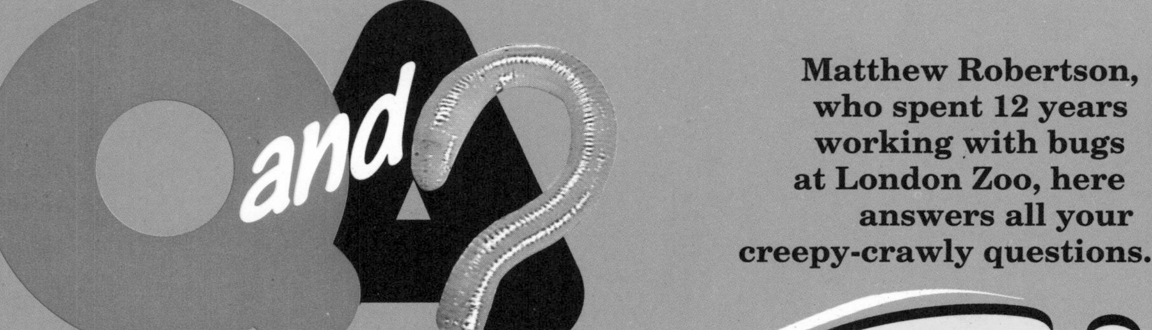

Matthew Robertson, who spent 12 years working with bugs at London Zoo, here answers all your creepy-crawly questions.

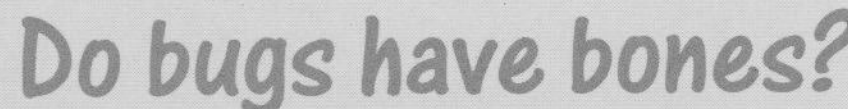

Do bugs have bones?

Unlike humans and other animals, most bugs do not have bones. Some, such as octopuses, don't have skeletons at all, while others, such as beetles, have hard shells on the outside of their bodies. Squids have bone-like plates inside their bodies, which help to support them.

Do any bugs use tools?

Bugs are so well adapted to the life they lead that they don't really need to use tools. However, some experts think that certain species of solitary wasp use little stones as 'hammers'. These bugs dig a hole, bury food for their young and cover it in pebbles. To secure their valuable supplies, they pick up a tiny stone in their jaws and knock the other stones into place.

Do bugs make good pets?

Yes and no. Because many bugs are quite small, it is possible to make homes for them that are very similar to those that they inhabit in the wild. However, as we learn more and more about bugs we find that many bugs have special needs, which are difficult to copy in captivity. Another problem with bug pets is that you can't cuddle them or take them for walks.

Bluebottle

The bluebottle is a common fly with some weird habits. It vomits on its food, walks on ceilings and loves sunbathing!

The bluebottle belongs to the fly group known as 'Diptera' (say 'dip-ter-a'). This name is a Latin word, which means 'two-winged'. Like the bluebottle, most of the flies in this group have only one pair of wings.

FAST AEROBATICS

The bluebottle has two well developed front wings, but no back wings. In their place are a pair of stick-like organs, called halteres (say 'hol-tears'). These work like stabilisers on a bicycle. They help the bluebottle to stay on course and stop it from rolling over in mid-flight. If the bluebottle loses one, or both, of its halteres, it can't fly. Even though a bluebottle only has two wings, it can fly quickly in just about any direction. It can also land anywhere – even upside-down on ceilings.

HOME LOVING

You have probably seen bluebottles in your home, particularly in the kitchen. If a bluebottle senses food, which has been left uncovered, it simply can't resist it.

- **SCIENTIFIC NAME:** *Calliphora vomitoria*
- **SIZE:** 11mm long
- **LIVES:** in and around houses throughout the world
- **EATS:** maggot eats rotting flesh and dung, adult eats animal flesh and sweet food

GOOD SENSES

Bluebottles have such a good sense of smell that they can sniff out food from a long way off, and will soon find their way to your home for a meal. When they land on some food, they 'taste' it with their feet, using special pads on the bottom of their feet that are sensitive to smell and taste.

ROTTING FLESH

These flying bugs love to eat flesh, particularly if it is slightly old and rotting. They don't eat solid food because they can't chew it up, like you can. Their stomachs can only cope with runny food.

Is it true... that bluebottles like to sunbathe?

Yes. They rest on leaves or twigs and soak up the warm sun. Like athletes, who warm up before a race to loosen their muscles, bluebottles need to keep their bodies and flight muscles warm. This means they can fly quickly to escape from predators, such as spiders and birds.

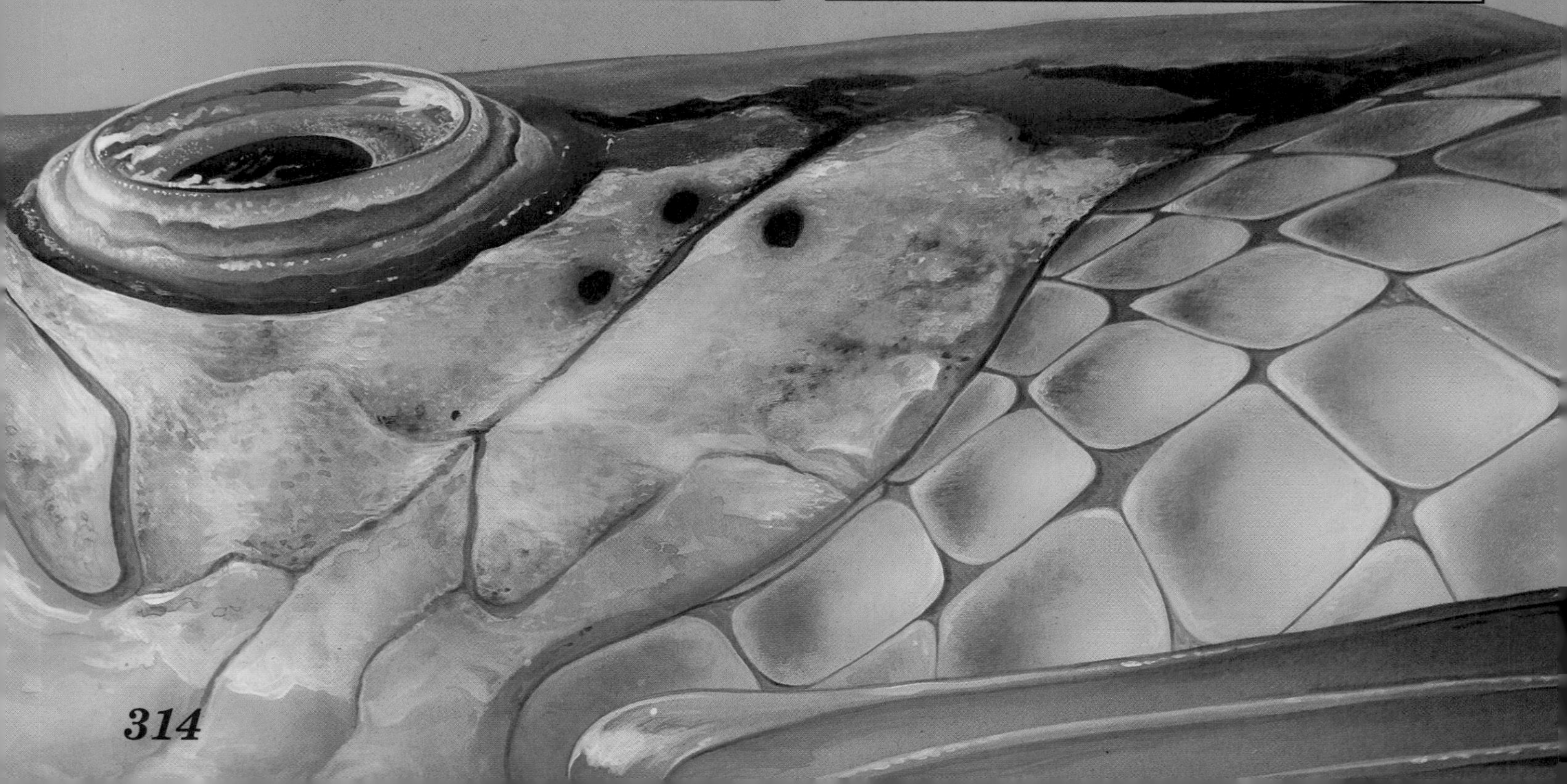

SUCKING UP

Before a bluebottle has its dinner, it vomits up some juices from its stomach and spits them on to the food. This helps to make it nice and runny and easy to suck up. Like many other insects, the bluebottle has mouthparts that work like a sponge and soak up the liquefied food.

MEAT PESTS

Bluebottles can spoil food and spread disease. Females lay their eggs in raw or cooked meat or fish. If you keep meat for any length of time, make sure that it is stored in the fridge, out of the reach of the bluebottle.

LIQUID FEEDER

An old piece of fish has been thrown out by a chef. A split in one of the fish's scales means that this bluebottle can get at the rotting flesh below.

A bluebottle's wings are see-through and can flap at great speed.

Compound eyes

Fish scales

Special juices to make the food runny.

A bluebottle can taste and smell food, using 'taste buds' on the bottom of its feet.

Mouthparts to soak up the food.

CREATURE FILE

Banana Slug

This bug looks as if it has slithered straight out of a fruit bowl!

Although it is well known for its yellow skin, the banana slug isn't always brightly coloured. At certain stages in its life, its yellow flesh is covered in dark brown patches. It is these darker markings that make the banana slug look like an over-ripe banana.

LOOK LIKE A LEAF

The banana slug's yellow colouring may not seem to be a very efficient form of camouflage. However, it does help this slimy bug to blend in well with its natural surroundings. It lives among the yellow and brown leaves that fall from the maple trees in North America. Without this colouring, the slug would be easily spotted by predators.

MIGHTY MUNCHER

Apart from munching through leaves, the banana slug also loves to eat fruit and mushrooms. These eating habits make it very unpopular with gardeners.

LEAVING A MESS

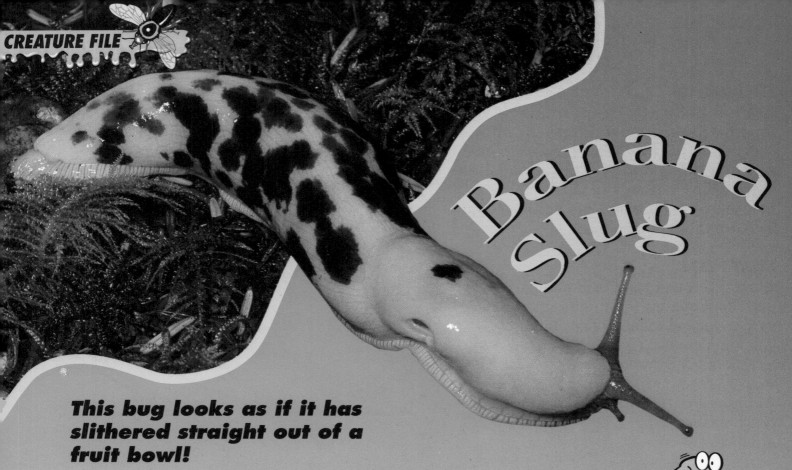

Although they leave behind a thick and sticky trail of slime, you would be very lucky if you actually saw a banana slug. They are nocturnal (they only come out at night).

- **SCIENTIFIC NAME:** *Ariolimax columbianus*
- **SIZE:** up to 20cm long
- **LIVES:** cool, wooded regions of North America
- **EATS:** leaves and fruit

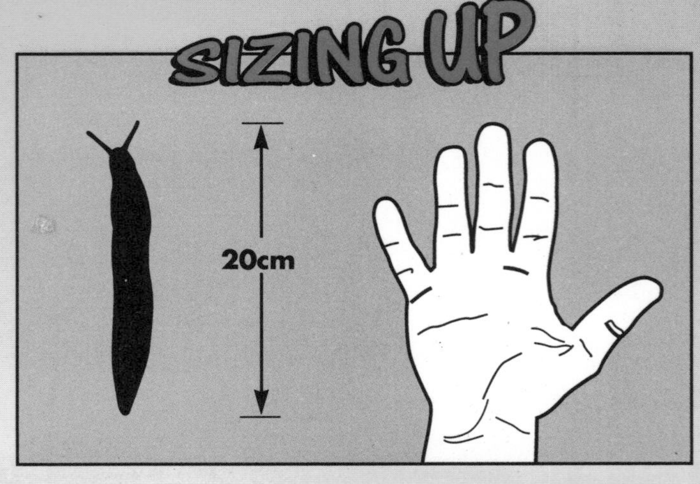

Red Velvet Mite

Despite its furry red coat, this velvet mite can live in hot and cold countries.

The red velvet mite belongs to the huge arachnid group of animals. Its relatives include spiders, scorpions and ticks. When it is young, the mite is a parasite, but as it gets older it eats all sorts of other bugs and eggs.

TINY FRIEND

The adult red velvet mite doesn't always live and feed off a host. If it needs to, it can also fend for itself. The adult red velvet mite is often considered to be a friend to humans. This fluffy bug is a natural insecticide – it likes to eat other creepy-crawlies that we think are pests, such as locusts and their eggs.

SLY SUCKERS

Like other arachnids, the adult red velvet mite has eight legs and two main body parts. It also has similar eating habits. It sucks up body fluids or solid food and turns them into liquids before swallowing them.

GETTING HUNGRY

Mites can go hungry for very long periods. Their young, called harvest mites, can survive for six months to a year without eating. When they find some tasty food, they gorge themselves. After a large meal, the female can lay several thousand eggs in one go.

- **SCIENTIFIC NAME:** Trombidiidae
- **SIZE:** 8 –12mm
- **LIVES:** worldwide
- **EATS:** other bugs and eggs

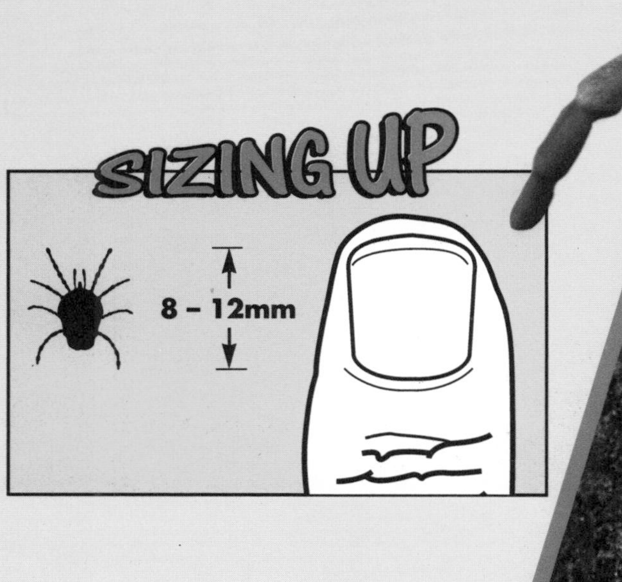

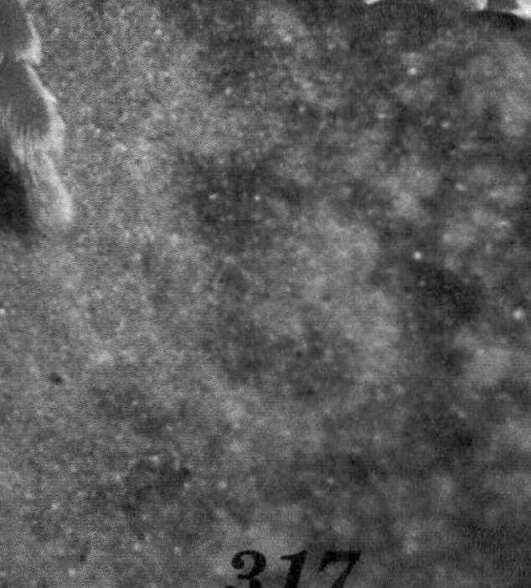

Glowing in the dark

Lurking at the bottom of the sea are many bugs that rarely – if ever – see the light of day. The oceans can be so dark and murky that the only way that these bugs can 'talk' to each other is by giving off light.

Imagine living in total darkness, in a world without light – no electricity, torches, or even matches. Now think what it would be like if you could make yourself glow in the dark. It sounds silly, but this is exactly what some sea animals do. These creatures are described as bioluminescent (say 'buy-oh-loom-in-ess-ent').

WHAT DOES IT?

Most glow-in-the-dark animals live in the sea. In the ocean depths, luminescence (say 'loom-in-ess-ence') is quite common, especially in jellyfish, shrimps and squids. They all have special light-producing glands. These may be on or near the head, or – as in the case of the squid – connected to the ink sac.

Jewel shrimps are covered in tiny, light-producing spots.

Small jewel shrimps (below left) swim towards microscopic sea creatures (plankton), which are attracted to a light. This light is a glow-in-the-dark trap, which a cunning angler fish has set (right).

WHY DO THEY DO IT?

Creatures produce light for a variety of reasons. Some do it simply to spot other bugs of the same species, just as teachers identify their pupils by their school uniform. Other creatures glow to attract their next meal, or to confuse and put off predators. In some animals, light signals are an important part of their courting and mating rituals.

ANGLING FOR A MEAL

The deep-sea angler fish is not something that you would like to meet on a dark night. It catches supper in its ferocious teeth by dangling some glow-in-the-dark bait from the tip of its 'nose'. This bait looks just like a salt-water bug, floating by.

THE GREAT ESCAPE

The jewel shrimp has light-producing spots all over its body and creates showers of luminesence. The lights confuse most predators and create a diversion, which allows the shrimp, meanwhile, to make its escape. The jewel shrimp isn't the only glowing shrimp. Its relative, the flashing prawn, is usually bright red, but when it is frightened it throws out a strange bright-green light. This is guaranteed to shock all but the toughest predator.

Angler fish

What is... luminescence?

Luminescence is the ability to give off a special type of glowing light. Something is described as luminescent if it gives off this light without getting hot. The glow-in-the-dark face of an alarm clock, for example, is luminescent. Living creatures that glow in the dark are said to be bioluminescent. The beginning of this word ('bio') means 'life'.

In the depths of the oceans, fantastic sea bugs are putting on a light show.

A colony of pyrosomes can be as long as a tennis court. One was once mistaken for a torpedo!

SPOTS BEFORE YOUR EYES

The odd-eyed squid (below) is so called because it has one large eye and one small eye. Its 7cm-long pink body is covered in lots of dark spots, each of which is a light organ.

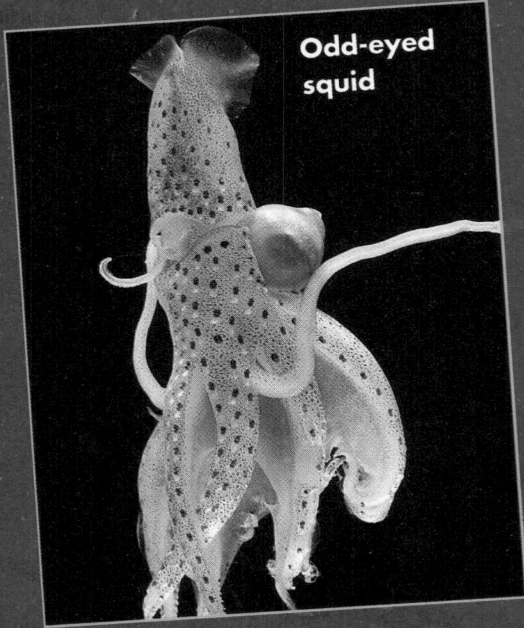

This odd-eyed squid (above) was photographed using a camera with a flash. This has spoiled the effect of the luminescence. Drawing A (below) shows what the same squid would look like if you met it in a dark sea. During the day, it uses its lights to hide from predators. If an enemy swims beneath the squid, it probably won't see it. The lights on the squid's body blend in with the sunlight shining through the water's surface. This makes it hard to see the animal's silhouette (drawing B).

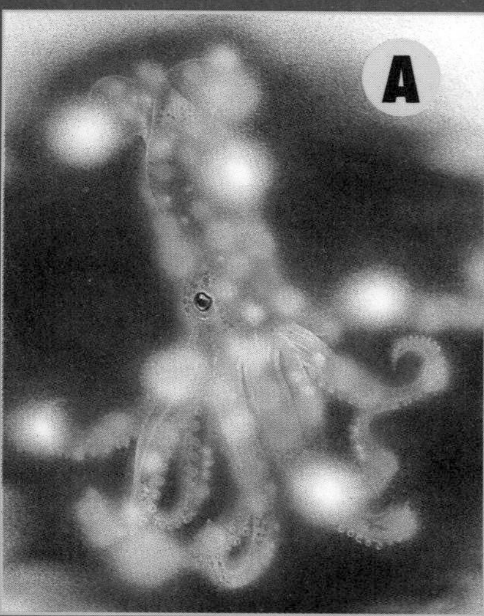

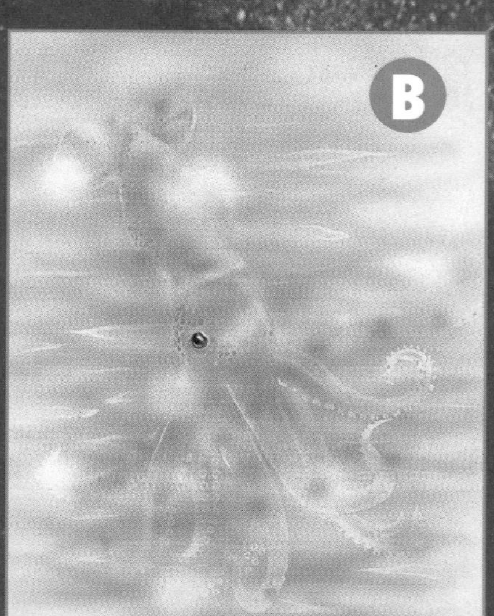

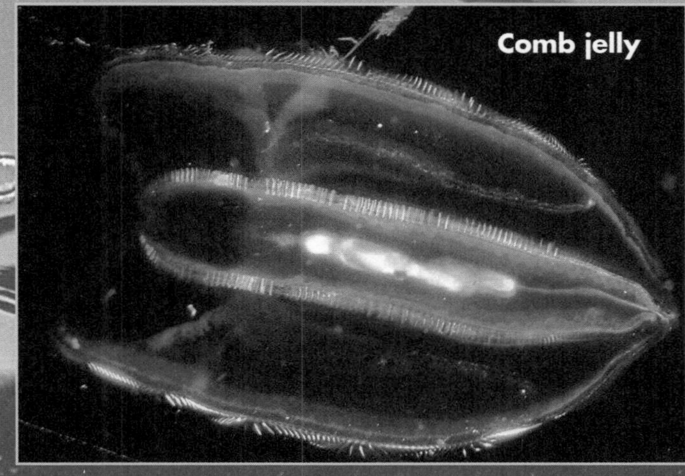

Comb jelly

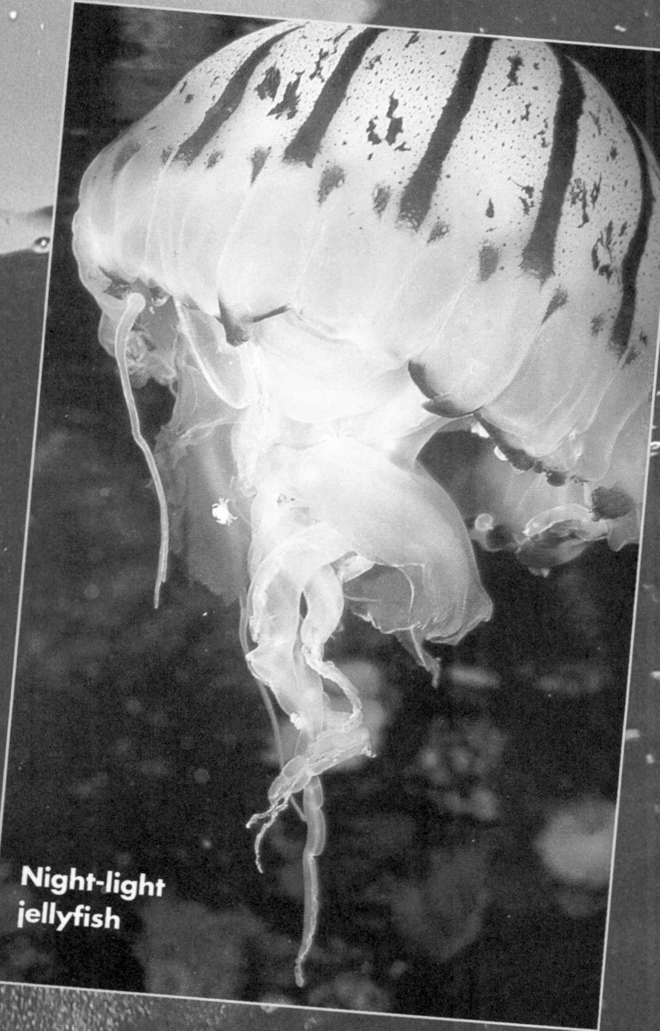

Night-light jellyfish

STRANGE, BUT TRUE

The see-through comb jelly (above) is one of the strangest creatures in the sea. A ghostly bag of transparent jelly, it glows in the dark – a bit like a bright-green electric light floating in the water. The light comes from tiny bugs that live in the creature's digestive system.

LET THIS BE A WARNING

A colony of pyrosomes (background picture) can measure 15m in length and is made up of masses of tiny bugs. Each animal is about 17mm long and lies with its mouth facing the outside of the colony. If it is disturbed, this crowd of bugs responds by glowing brightly. Its lights are a warning to others that something is up. The word pyrosome is taken from a Latin phrase, meaning 'fire body'.

Tiny sea gooseberry

FISHERMAN'S FRIENDS

The night-light jellyfish (above) is common in the Mediterranean sea. It is often seen from ships at night. Large groups of these creatures, with their 6cm-wide bells, float along and light up the sea with green lights.

NO FOOL

The tiny sea gooseberry (left), only 1cm in diameter, is a delicate little comb jelly. It is so transparent that it is almost invisible in the water. If it is disturbed as it glides through the waves, this luminescent bug flashes bright green.

Potty about

No garden and pushed for space? Don't worry – you can still create a mini bug farm.

You don't need a lot of space to attract bugs. Simply plant a window-box or place a large pot of flowers in the yard. These will provide a mass of colour, which you'll enjoy, but – most importantly – so will the bugs! Follow these easy instructions and you will soon have a bonanza of bees, butterflies, hoverflies and anything else that likes nectar. And don't forget those underground creepy-crawlies, like woodlice and beetles, that will collect in the soil.

Choosing your container

There are many different types of container that you can use. You can buy window-boxes or big pots from the garden centre, but you can also use old sinks or cooking pots, barrels, even old dustbins.

You will need:

- container
- stones or pebbles
- compost, preferably from a compost heap (ask a friend if you don't have one)
- soil-based (not peat-based) compost
- a selection of plants
- watering can

Optional:

- thick gloves
- nettles
- bucket of water

Choosing your plants

Here are some plants that attract flying bugs.

- aubretia
- alyssum
- catmint
- cornflowers
- ice plants
- lobelia
- nasturtiums
- ox-eye daisies
- poppies
- stocks

WHAT TO DO

1 Once you have decided on your container, start preparing it for your bug-attracting plants. First of all, make sure it has drainage holes so that excess water can flow away. (Don't water your plants when it rains, as this will drown them.) If it hasn't got drainage holes, ask an adult to put some in for you.

2 Now put a layer of stones or pebbles in the container. This will help with drainage. The layer should be thick enough to cover the bottom completely.

3 Next, fill the container with bulky compost from a compost heap until it is about half full. Finally, put a layer of soil-based compost from the garden centre on top. The compost should come up to about 3cm below the top of the container.

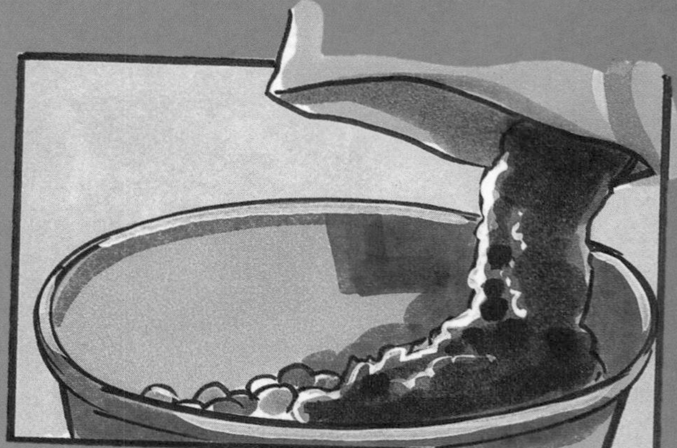

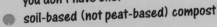

bugs

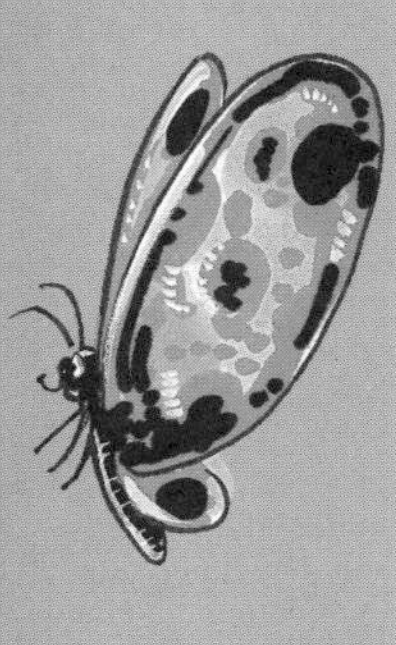

6 Feed your plants regularly – once a week in summer – with organic seaweed feeds. You can make your own plant food. Put on a pair of thick gloves, collect some nettles and put them in a bucket of water. Put a lid on the bucket and leave it outside for a couple of weeks. Eventually, a dark liquid will form. Put a little of this in your watering can and feed plants when you water them.

4 You are now ready to plant your bright, bug-attracting flowers. Find out how tall your plants will be when they are fully grown. Put the taller plants, such as cornflowers, red field poppies or ox-eye daisies, towards the back of the container if it is against a wall, or in the centre of a free-standing tub. Put low-growing plants, such as aubretia, near the front, or around the edge. Remember that your flowers will spread out as they grow, so give them space.

5 It is always important to keep the compost in containers damp. Container-grown plants dry out much more quickly than those that grow in open ground. Water your plants whenever the top of the compost feels dry. Watch how quickly the water is absorbed – if it disappears quickly, you are probably doing it right; if the plants are wilting, you need to give them more water.

Small Talk

BOX CLEVER

Be careful with your window-boxes, or with any other containers on window-ledges. Never lean out of the window. Don't put containers high up on a window-ledge without getting an adult to fix a guard to stop them falling off. Otherwise, they could fly off in a gust of wind and land on someone's head!

Mites on a bee's leg

Dozens of tiny mites have climbed aboard this bumble bee's leg. On their own, these mites find it hard to move about, so they catch a ride on a more mobile bug. These ones managed to clamber on board when the bee stopped to gather nectar from a bright sunflower. Measuring just 0.8mm long, the mites can afford to travel in huge numbers, there's plenty of room for quite a few. They all hang on tightly with their needle-like chelicerae (pincers). These hijackers don't really mind where they are going, just as long as refreshments are provided on the flight. Today, there is bee juice on the menu!

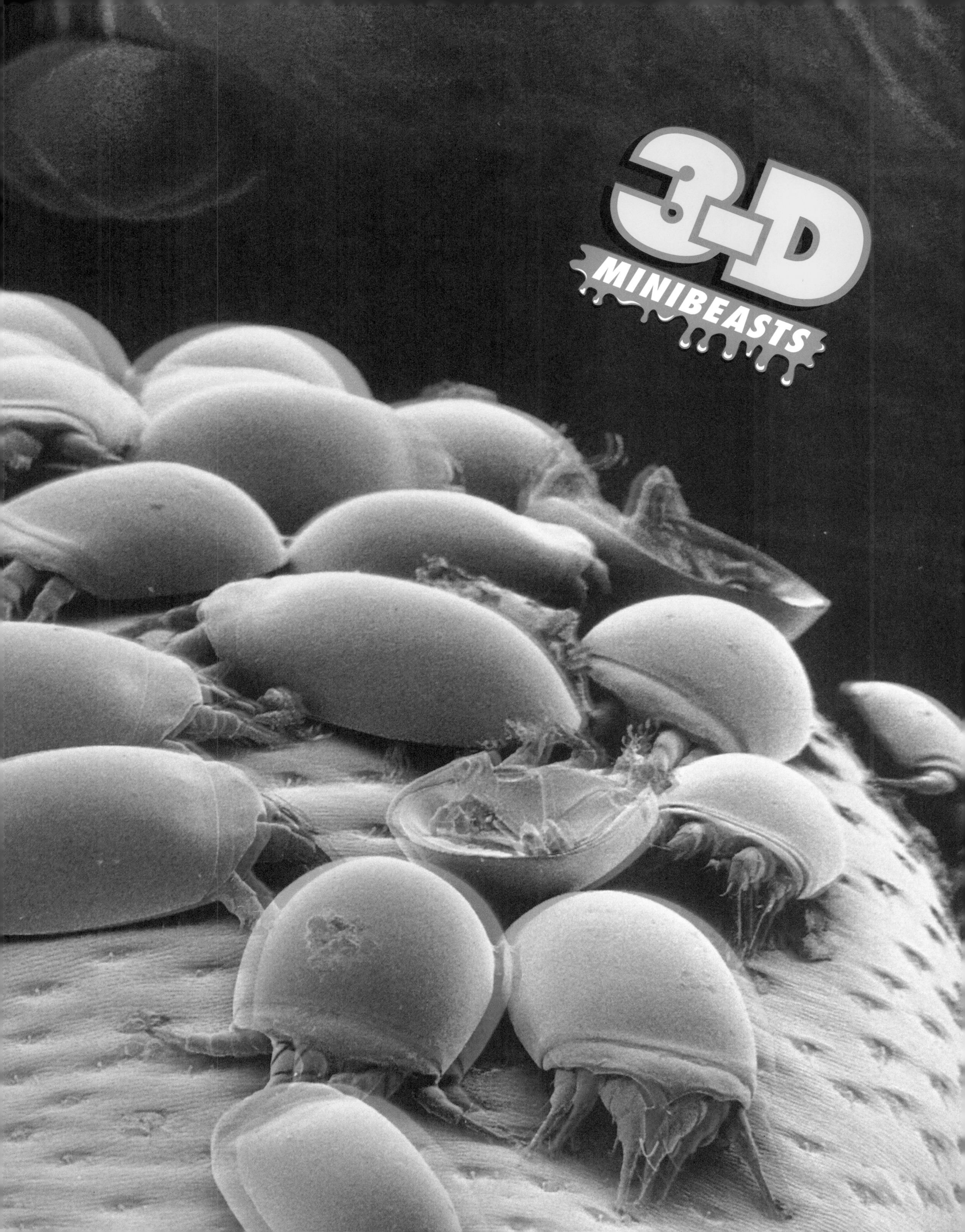
3-D
MINIBEASTS

Breathing without

All adult insects breathe air. Like humans they need oxygen to live. But unlike humans, they do not have a nose.

Insects don't have a nose to breathe through, and they don't have lungs either.

They breathe through special holes in the sides of their bodies. These holes are called spiracles (say 'spy-ric-als'). Each breathing hole leads into an air pipe called a trachea (say 'track-ee-a').

SWING DOORS

All spiracles have valves at the point where they open to the air. Valves are like tiny swing doors. They work by using muscles to control the flow of air into the insect's body. If a bug is flying or running about a lot, the valves open to let air in through the spiracles. If it is resting, the bug's spiracles close.

BRANCHING OUT

Tracheae (the plural of trachea) branch out through the insect's body, carrying air to its muscles and other organs. These air pipes branch into smaller tubes, called tracheoles (say 'track-ee-oles'), that go straight to cells around the bug's body. In this way, air is taken directly from outside the animal's body, through the spiracles, to the muscles that need it.

The locust's spiracles come in pairs, one on each side of the body. Insects have about 10 pairs of spiracles along their abdomens. Some have a single pair on their thoraxes, too.

UNDER THE MICROSCOPE

a nose

After entering through the spiracle, air travels to all parts of the insect's body. The blue lines on this diagram (below) show the routes that the air takes around the body.

A close-up picture of a spiracle on the side of a fruit fly's body.

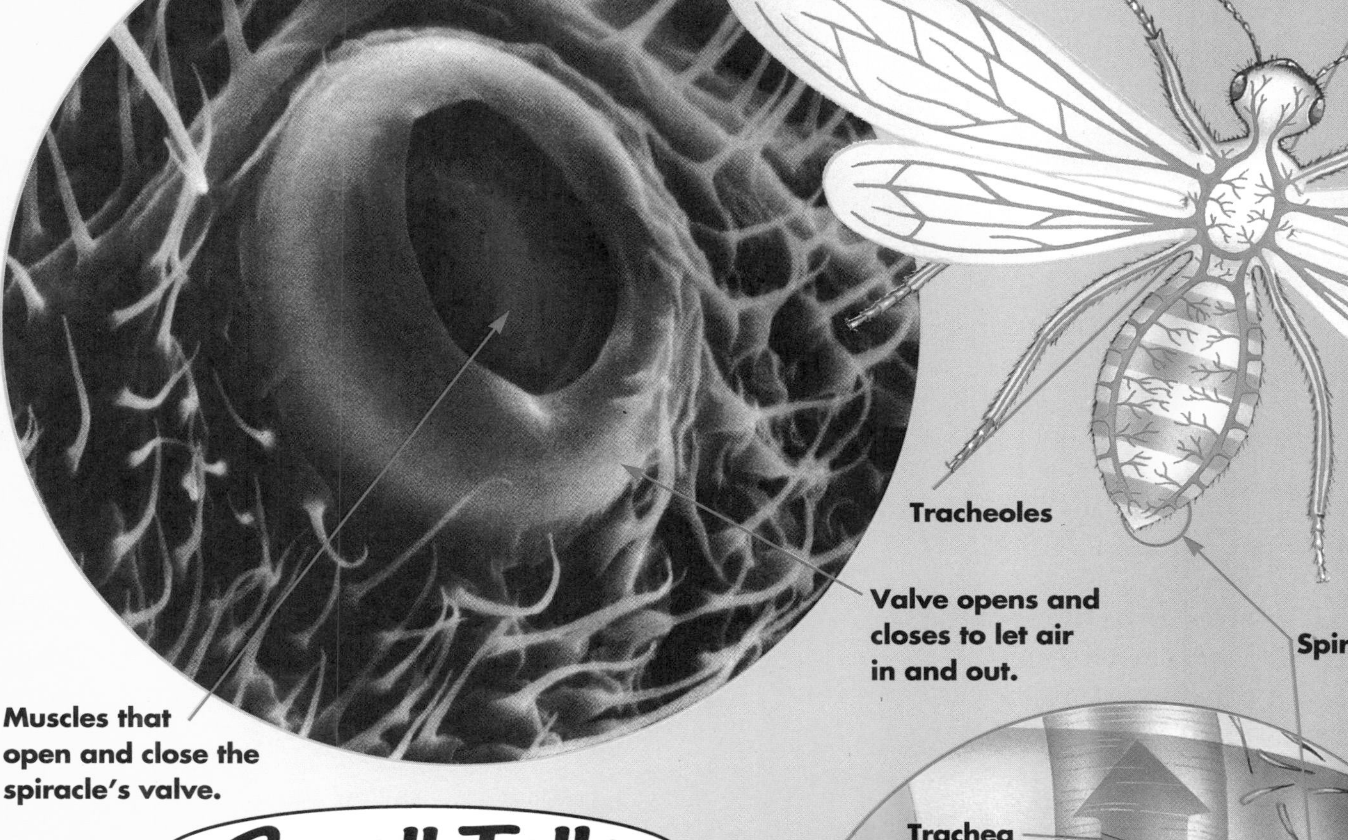
Trachea
Tracheoles
Valve opens and closes to let air in and out.
Spiracle
Muscles that open and close the spiracle's valve.

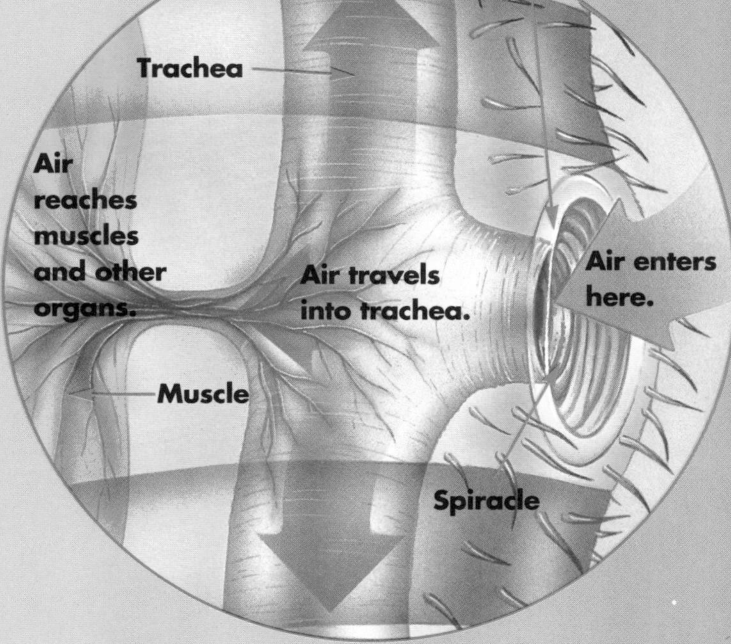
Trachea
Air reaches muscles and other organs.
Air travels into trachea.
Air enters here.
Muscle
Spiracle

Small Talk

LIVING ON AIR

Why does an insect need to breathe? Like most animals, it breathes to get oxygen from the air. Oxygen reacts with food in its body, giving it energy to live and move. As the food is broken down, a gas called carbon dioxide is also produced. This gas is not needed, and goes back out of the body the same way the air came in. When you breathe, you take in oxygen from the air and breathe carbon dioxide back out, just like an insect!

PUMPING UP THE POWER

If you run about a lot and then stop, you will find yourself breathing much harder. This is because you are taking more air into your lungs. Insects that do a lot of flying, such as bees and dragonflies, need to take in extra air, too. They use muscles to push the walls of their abdomens in and out. This pumping action helps them suck more oxygen into their bodies. Insects need this extra oxygen to power their flying muscles – without it they wouldn't be able to fly.

ONE-SIDED LUNG

Land slugs and snails breathe in air using a lung. In slugs, it is easy to see the opening to the lung. It is a hole called a pneumostome (say 'new-mo-stome'). When the slug (below) breathes, you can see the hole opening and closing. However, in some slugs, the breathing hole stays open all the time.

GASPING FOR AIR

When a dragonfly rests after it has been flying around, you can easily see the sides of its body pumping in and out. The next time you see a dragonfly (below) resting by a pond, take a close look and see if you can see it 'panting'.

After buzzing around all day, a dragonfly takes a well earned rest.

The breathing hole is on the right hand side of the slug's body.

What is... an air sac?

An air sac is an inflatable pouch connected to an insect's air pipe, or trachea. Bees have large air sacs in their abdomen. These fill with air and supply the flight muscles in the bee's thorax with oxygen. The air sacs also store oxygen during a bee's long winter rest.

BOOK LUNGS

Many spiders breathe air through a lung. This is a chamber made up of overlapping folds, which look like the pages of a book. It is called a book lung. Air gets into the lung through tiny slits in the spider's abdomen. The book lung helps take oxygen from the air into the spider's blood. The outside of a book lung is a hairless patch on the underside of the spider's abdomen. The diagram (below) shows what a book lung looks like and where it is situated in a spider's body. Most spiders have one on each side of their bodies. More active spiders also have a system of spiracles and tracheae, just like insects.

UNDERWATER SURVIVAL

An earthworm doesn't have a special organ for breathing. Instead it breathes through its moist body surface, called a cuticle. Tiny blood vessels lie just below the cuticle. The blood that circulates in the worm's body takes in oxygen and gives off a gas, called carbon dioxide, through the moist body surface. If its cuticle dries out, the worm will not be able to breathe, and dies.

As rain filters down into a worm's burrow, air spaces in the hole fill up with water. This means that the earthworm (left) has to come to the surface to breathe.

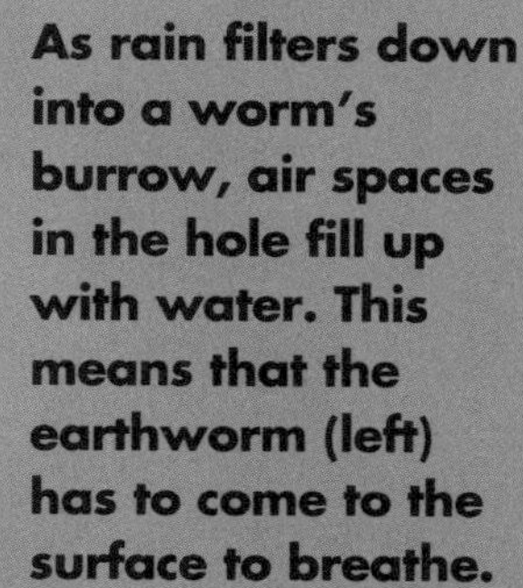

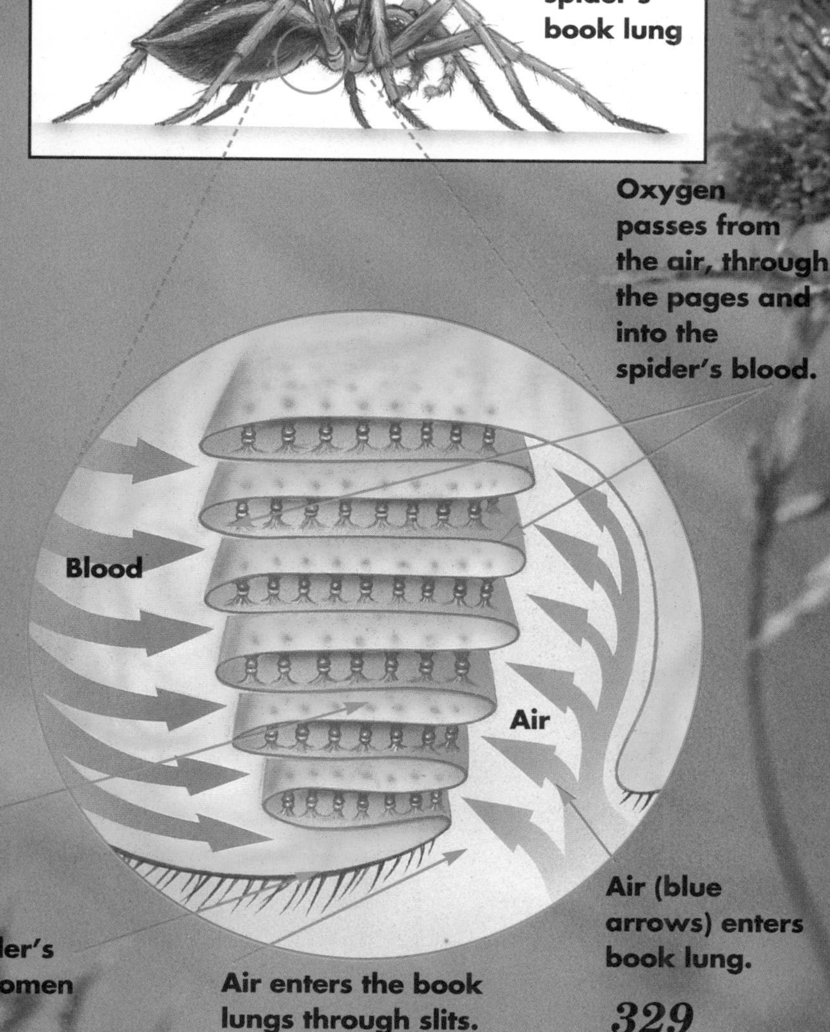

Position of spider's book lung
Oxygen passes from the air, through the pages and into the spider's blood.
Blood
Air
Air (blue arrows) enters book lung.
Spider's abdomen
Air enters the book lungs through slits.

Blood (red arrows) fills the spaces between the 'pages' of the book lung and takes oxygen from the air.

Busy, busy

You've probably been eating honey for most of your life. People have been keeping bees for their honey for 4,000 years.

A honeybee approaches a flower, covered in pollen. The bee's body is dusted with pollen and its pollen baskets (yellow bulges) on its hind 'knees' are full.

honeybees

Bees make honey to feed the young bees. They make it from nectar, which is the sweet-smelling, watery sugar solution produced by flowers.

FORAGING

The foraging worker bee collects nectar from flowers with its long tongue, or proboscis (say 'pro-boss-kiss'). It stores it in a special honey sac in its abdomen. A bee visits 500 – 1,000 flowers before its honey sac is full. When it gets back to its nest, the worker bee passes the nectar on to one of the younger worker bees before setting out again.

A honeybee (left) sucks nectar from a flower, using its long, reddish-brown proboscis.

FIRST OF ALL SPIT

The young worker bee mixes the nectar with its saliva (spit). This contains chemicals that change the sugars in the nectar from one type, known as sucrose, to other types known as glucose and fructose. The baby bees find these easier to digest. The nectar is then placed in cells where it thickens. The liquid becomes more concentrated and the worker bee chews it up again. It is now true honey, which we all know – and love.

Honeybees feed from a new comb (above left). Honey gives bees the energy they need to fly about and helps their young to grow big and strong.

THEN SPIT AGAIN

The worker bee spits out the honey into a special storage cell, which is then sealed over with a cap of wax. All the bees in the colony can break through the wax covers and help themselves to honey from the storage cells. A collection of cells form a comb. The comb is built vertically.

IN THE WILD

Most of the honey we eat comes from hives. In the wild, honeybees don't live in hives. They set up home in any empty space they can find, such as dead, hollow trees. Unfortunately, these are quite scarce because humans chop them down. But humans are not the honeybees' only enemies. Bee-eater birds, hornets and wasps can all spell trouble for a honeybee.

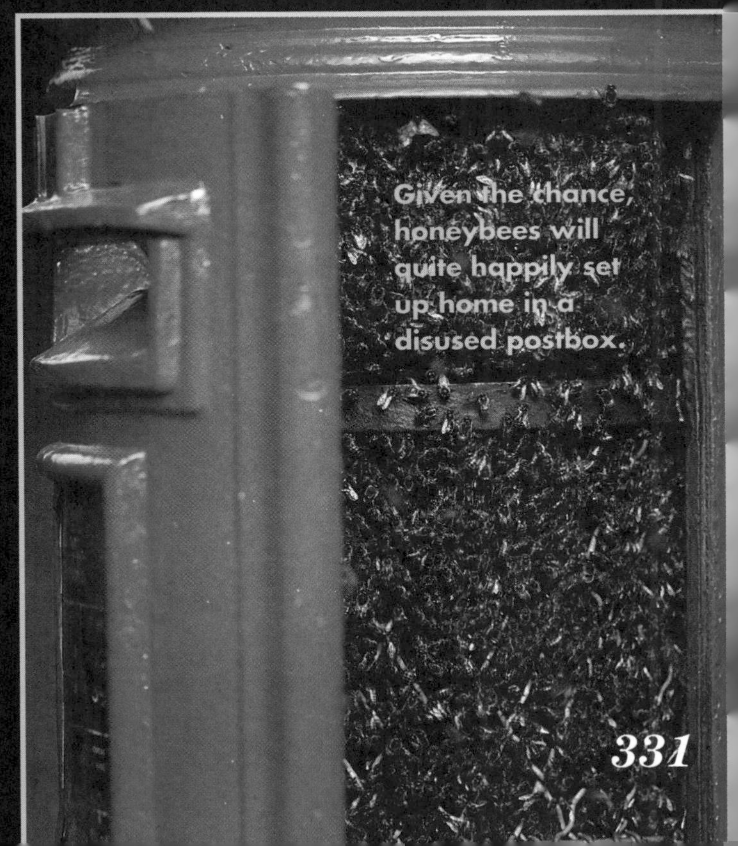

Given the chance, honeybees will quite happily set up home in a disused postbox.

After all their hard work, the bees' job is finally done and the honey is made. But how does it get from the comb to the honey pot?

EASY ACCESS

Getting honey from a comb is easy if you're a bee. You just stick your head in the honeycomb and suck. If you're a human, though, the process is a very different one.

INTO GEAR

The correct kit is important for both bees and beekeeper. Bees need to be kept happy if they are to produce honey. So beekeepers house them in specially designed hives. Beekeepers need to wear the right protective clothing – full body suit and face visor or veil – to stop the bees from stinging them.

It is important for beekeepers to equip themselves correctly for the task – both for the bees' comfort and for their own safety.

FOOD FOR THE WORKERS

Bees make honey to feed the young bees and to see them through the cold winter months. The queen bee would not be able to survive if she did not have her workers to feed and clean her. They also care for her eggs and the larvae, so it's very important that several hundred workers survive the winter. Honey provides their winter food store. Honey is important throughout the year, too, as a source of food for the developing larvae. There are many bees that busily work and never leave the hive. They rely on the honey for their food, too.

Both in the wild and in hives, the honeybees' combs stand upright.

COLLECTING COMBS

First of all, the beekeeper has to carefully remove the honeycombs, which are full of fresh honey, from the hive. The combs are then loaded into a special extractor, which spins the combs round and round so that the honey flows out. This whirling motion is known as centrifugal (say 'sen-tree-few-gal') force.

STRAIN AND SETTLE

During this process, bits of wax and other rubbish get mixed in with the honey. All the rubbish has to be removed by straining. Air bubbles will also have formed as a result of the motion of the extractor. These air bubbles will rise to the surface when the honey is allowed to stand in a special settling tank. The honey can then be put into jars.

Is it true ... that bees help flowers?

Yes, bees don't just help us by making honey. They help flowers, too, by transferring pollen from the male part of a flower to the female part – either of the same flower, or of other flowers of the same species. This process, known as pollination, is necessary for a plant to produce seeds or fruit. Although it doesn't realise it at the time, a bee transfers pollen when it collects nectar and pollen from a flower. While visiting a flower, the bee gets covered in pollen dust, but some of it drops off and pollinates the flower. It then combs its body free of pollen, moistens it with saliva and packs it into pollen baskets. The pollen is then taken to the hive and fed to both adults and young.

Hive bees have to visit 45 – 65 million flowers to make just 1kg of honey (left).

KEEP OUT

By the way, if you've ever wondered why you never find baby bees and eggs in your honey, this is because a special queen 'excluder' is always put in the hive. This prevents the queen laying eggs in those parts of the honeycomb that the beekeeper wants to use for honey.

Frames full of combs are placed in an extractor. When the beekeeper turns the handle (below), the honey flows out under centrifugal force.

Improve and test your knowledge with...

CREEPY~CRAWLY FACTS

Blast into space with these high-flying spiders, and expand your mind with this tricky BUGS! quiz.

Maggot and chips?

Some Chinese scientists suggest we stop breeding cows, which take up lots of room and need a lot of care, and farm housefly maggots instead. They breed quickly, don't need much care, and take up little space. They are low in fat and high in protein, and some experts claim they are a great substitute for other meats. Other people aren't quite so sure!

Fly lie

Millions of years ago, bugs got stuck in the sticky resin that oozes out of tree trunks. The resin hardened to form amber and the bugs were fossilised. Scientists have learned a lot about prehistoric bugs from these creatures. But one fossil fly was not what it seemed. Instead of being millions of years old, it turned out to be only 100. It had been glued in place in the late 19th-century by a joker!

Small, but powerful

The ferocious tiger beetle larva – with its powerful, sabre-like jaws and armour-plated head – has very few enemies. However, a tiny, wingless wasp has found a way to beat the beast. After finding a tiger beetle larva, it allows itself to be grabbed in the beast's jaws. It then neatly slips its thin body through the jaws, twists round and stings the larva in the neck, paralysing it. The wasp then lays a single egg which will hatch and eat the helpless beetle larva.

Eight small steps...

In 1973, astronauts on an Apollo space mission carried out a series of experiments on spiders. They took two spiders up into space with them. The astronauts let one spider run about in a cage. The second spider was kept in a small tube and only let out after four weeks. The first spider had had time to adjust to the feeling of weightlessness and, with practise, could spin perfect webs and run along a strand of silk. The spider that had been confined in the tube hadn't practised and found it hard to spin a web.

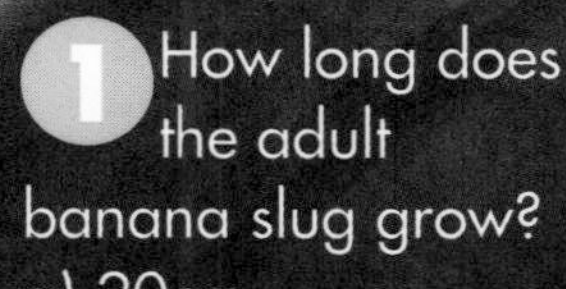

1 How long does the adult banana slug grow?
a) 20cm
b) 2cm
c) 20mm

2 What does the confused flour beetle eat?
a) other bugs
b) fresh leaves
c) grain

3 What do honeybees use to make honey?
a) pollen
b) nectar
c) wax

4 What does the bluebottle use to taste its food?
a) its feet
b) its wings
c) a fork

5 How many wings does a bluebottle have?
a) four
b) six
c) two

6 Which of these creatures have book lungs?
a) spiders
b) worms
c) librarians

7 Where was the Cooloola monster discovered?
a) in Australia
b) in South Africa
c) in Antarctica

8 What does the adult red velvet mite eat?
a) other bugs
b) velvet
c) leaves and fruit

9 Which is the largest damselfly in the world?
a) the Costa Rican giant damselfly
b) the blue-banded damselfly
c) the distressed damselfly

10 How did the cottonstainer bug get its name?
a) nobody knows
b) it spreads a fungus over the seed heads of the cotton plant
c) it never wipes its muddy feet

Answers to the questions on the inside back cover

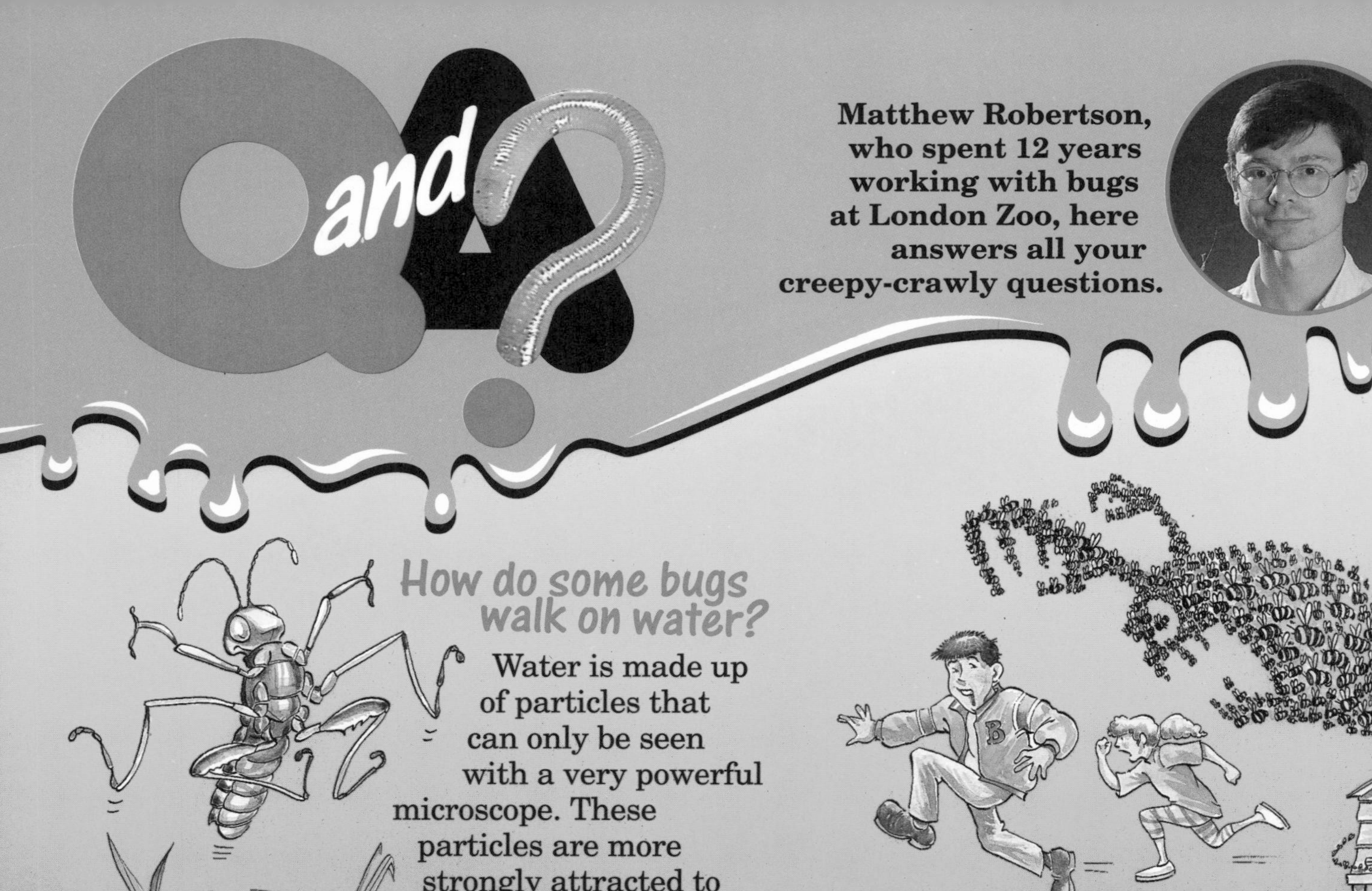

Matthew Robertson, who spent 12 years working with bugs at London Zoo, here answers all your creepy-crawly questions.

How do some bugs walk on water?

Water is made up of particles that can only be seen with a very powerful microscope. These particles are more strongly attracted to each other than to the air above them. This bonding forms a surface that very light bugs can walk on. Some bugs, such as the pond skater, have special hairs on their feet, which repel water and support the bug above the water. They also have long, widely spaced legs. They spread the pond skater's weight across the water's surface and stop it from sinking.

Why do crabs walk sideways?

The crab doesn't have a long body. This means that on either side of its body, its legs are very close together. There's not enough room for the crab's legs to move freely and it can't take big steps forward. Instead, the crab steps sideways.

Do bugs chase people?

Most bugs will ignore or avoid you because they think that you are a predator. Others may seem to be chasing you, but they are simply following you for a very good reason. In some hot countries, if you walk near a river, you might find yourself being shadowed by hordes of dragonflies. In Africa, a large red dragonfly deliberately follows humans and any other large animals. By walking through the grass, people disturb tiny insects, which fly into the dragonfly's waiting jaws. Sometimes, more than 50 hungry dragonflies will join in the pursuit.

Cone Shell

This colourful sea snail is related to the snails in your garden. But don't let this bug crawl across your hand – it's a killer.

The cone shell is a snail that lives in the sea – in the warm, shallow waters around coral reefs. Like a garden snail, it can tuck all of its body up inside its colourful, patterned shell. Once its body is safely inside, a flap comes down over the shell opening, and seals it up.

DAYTIME NAP

During the day, the cone shell rests. It hides in the sand, or in a crevice in the coral. It comes out at night, when it is time to go hunting! Like other snails, the cone shell crawls along on its foot. Squeezing and stretching its muscles, it sends ripples along its foot to push itself forward.

SENSE OF SMELL

The cone shell feeds on worms, molluscs and fish. Each of these creatures gives off a scent that is carried in the water, like a smell floating in the air. The cone shell picks up this scent by passing water through a special 'smelling' tube on its body – so it can tell when its prey is near.

SLOW MOVER

Because the cone shell is only a slow-moving snail, it would never be able to chase after fast-moving prey, such as fish. So, this lethal bug has developed a special way of catching its victims.

STICKING OUT ITS TONGUE

The cone shell has a long tongue, called a proboscis, which it uses as a weapon for catching its prey. On its tongue is a set of 20 – 30 hollow teeth filled with venom, and tipped with tiny darts, which are as sharp as needles. When its prey is close enough, the cone shell shoots out its tongue and stabs its victim with one of these darts.

QUICK-WORKING VENOM

The venom flows out into the body of the prey. Immediately, the prey becomes totally powerless. Then, with its victim still pinned to the dart – like a fish on a hook – the cone shell draws it up to its mouth and slowly swallows it whole! The cone shell can even use its tongue to pull worms out of the sand, like a bird pulling a grub out of the earth.

HANDS OFF!

The cone shell's venom is so powerful that it can even kill a human being, by causing a heart attack or stopping a person's breathing. No one should handle a live cone shell with bare hands!

SEAFOOD

For certain brave sea creatures, the deadly cone shell is a tasty snack! Some fish have such strong jaws that they can crack open its shell, and pull out and eat the snail inside. They are very careful, though, not to touch the venomous parts.

CAMOUFLAGE

Other creatures help the cone shell. Minute animals and plants help to disguise this deadly snail from its enemies. They grow on the snail's shell, like seaweed on a rock.

SNAIL'S PACE

Although snails are famous for their slow pace, this one has acted very quickly. In the blink of an eye, the cone shell has fired its deadly spike and harpooned its startled victim, [illegible] fish.

When the cone shell dies, small sea creatures, such as hermit crabs, move into its empty shell.

The snail slides along on its muscular foot.

As soon as the venom enters its side, this mandarin fish (below) will become stunned and defenceless.

A cone shell can only use each venomous tooth once. New teeth are always growing to replace the ones that have been used.

- **SCIENTIFIC NAME:** *Conus textile*
- **SIZE:** shell grows up to 13cm long
- **LIVES:** Indian and Pacific Oceans
- **EATS:** worms, molluscs and fish

Mouth can stretch to swallow a large fish whole.

Sensory tentacles work like an insect's antennae.

SIZING UP

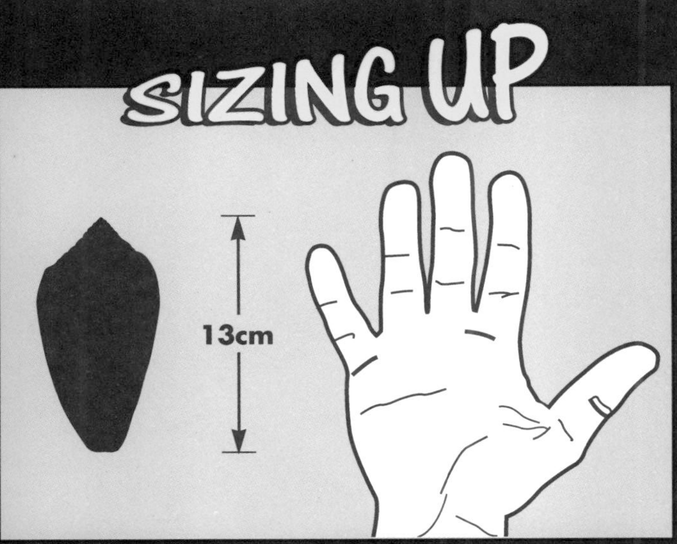

A close-up photo of a cone shell tooth.

Fine and sharp, like the point of a needle, the cone shell's dart can kill other animals, large and small.

Robber fly

Once it has spotted its target, the robber fly moves in for the kill, swooping down on its victim.

With its huge appetite, the robber fly isn't choosy about what it eats and even attacks insects that are bigger than itself, such as grasshoppers and dragonflies. Some types of robber fly will even steal baby bees from a nest. This is how this fly got its name.

SURPRISE ATTACK

The robber fly hunts by day, seizing its prey in mid-flight and quickly stabbing it with its proboscis, which is sharp enough to pierce the toughest skin. Then it carries its victim off to a quiet spot, where the robber fly sucks out the victim's insides, leaving only the hard, outer covering. Sometimes the robber fly is lazier, and sits on a log or the ground, waiting for unsuspecting prey to wander by. Thick bristles around its bulging eyes protect them against struggling victims.

PLAYING SAFE

Robber flies are so fierce that they may even eat each other! The only time it is safe for the male fly to mate with the female is when she is busy eating. If not, she may turn on him.

- **SCIENTIFIC NAME:** *Asilus crabroniformis*
- **SIZE:** 2 – 4cm long
- **LIVES:** Europe, Asia and north Africa
- **EATS:** adult eats insects, larva eats dead bugs

SIZING UP

4cm

The woodlouse could easily die if it gets too much sunlight, so it hides in cracks and crevices.

Woodlouse

This bug belongs to the same group of animals as crabs and lobsters, but over millions of years the woodlouse has learned to live on dry land. Like a tiny, armour-plated tank, this bug's body is protected by a hard shell, which is divided into overlapping layers.

SIZING UP

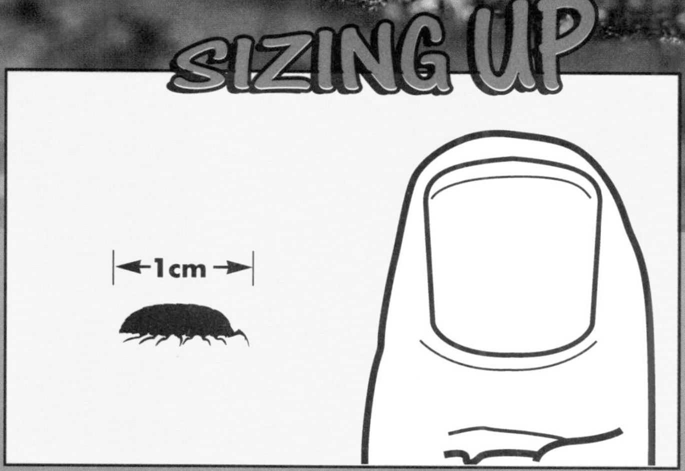

1cm

DEADLY SUNSHINE

Its shell does not have a waterproof coating to keep moisture in, like the shell of a beetle, so if it gets too dry it will die. To survive, the woodlouse shelters from the sun and open air, in dark, damp places, such as under stones, logs or rotting leaves. It comes out at night to eat, when the air is damper and cooler.

IN THE BAG

To keep her eggs moist and healthy, the female woodlouse carries them around in a wet pouch underneath her body – rather like a kangaroo! The babies do all their growing inside the eggs, until they hatch as tiny copies of the adults.

HALF AND HALF

As the woodlouse grows, it sheds its old shell – but not all in one go! First, it sheds the back half. The woodlouse waits for three days, while the new shell underneath hardens. Then the bug pushes off the front half and eats this part of its shell.

- **SCIENTIFIC NAME:** *Oniscus asellus*
- **SIZE:** up to 1cm long
- **LIVES:** Europe
- **EATS:** decaying plants and dead animals, sometimes living plants

Tough bugs

Bugs can live in places where conditions are so unbearable that no other animals could survive. Some are so hardy that they could probably even survive a nuclear war.

Some people believe that certain bugs with hard outer shells, such as crabs, cockroaches and scorpions, could survive a nuclear explosion. Tests have shown that atomic radiation, which is made up of harmful waves of energy, can be very dangerous for humans. But it does not have the same effect on bugs. They can stand up to 300 times more radiation than a human.

NUCLEAR FAMILY

Most of the toughest bugs, such as cockroaches and scorpions, have large families. This means that if a bomb was dropped, at least a couple of creatures would survive. With a bit of luck, the family would not die out. However, nobody really knows if these bugs could survive after a nuclear bomb, in a world full of deadly radiation.

EATING ANYTHING

Cockroaches have hard shells, but they have tough stomachs, too. They will eat just about anything, including other cockroaches, paper, leather, plastic, ink and the bindings of books. Some can even eat wood. Because they are not fussy eaters, these unbeatable bugs can survive when there is little food around and other bugs starve and die.

DEADLY AND DURABLE

Ever since people realised that mosquitoes carry the bug that causes malaria, humans have tried to wipe them out. But these tough blood suckers won't give up. They have been sprayed time and time again with lots of different chemicals. But all attempts to wipe them out have failed. The mosquitoes are so hardy that they have become immune to these chemicals and are still getting tougher.

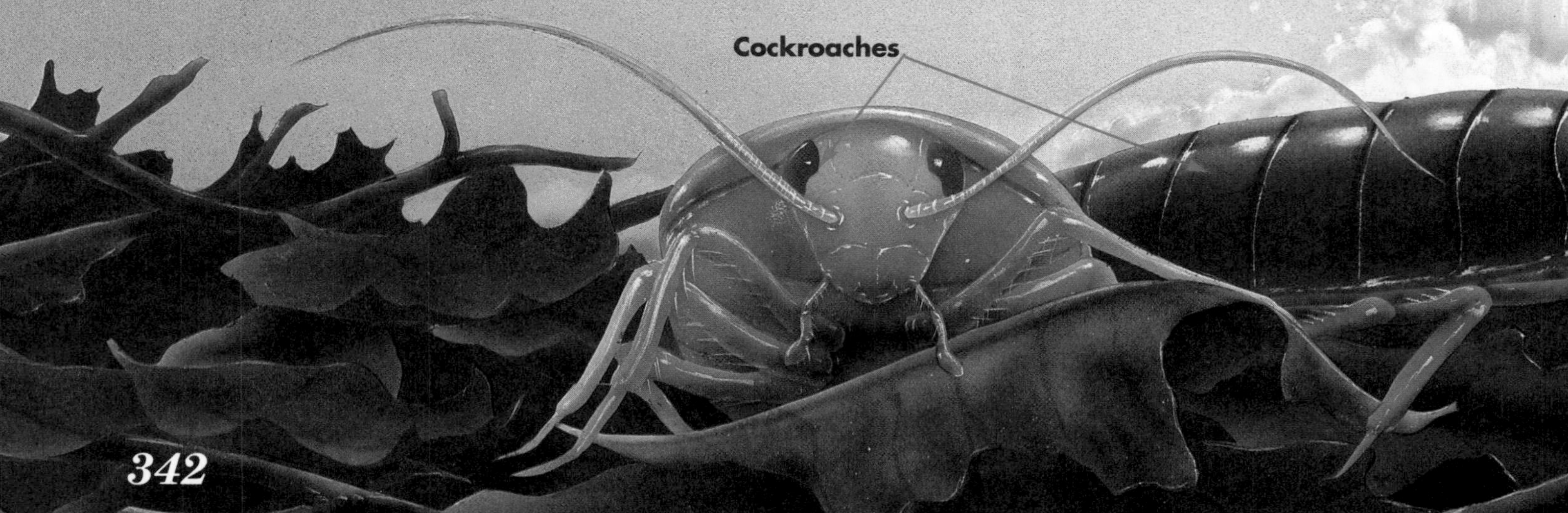

STICKY BUSINESS

When a tanker spills thousands of barrels of oil into the sea, the thick, sticky substance poisons fish, mammals and sea birds. The oil also ruins birds' feathers and stops them flying away. But some hardy bugs take it all in their stride.

PETROLEUM FLIES

Certain tough bugs can live quite happily in oil. In California, USA, the larvae of petroleum flies live in pools of thick crude oil, eating insects that get trapped on the surface of the sticky liquid. The larvae swim about under the oil, holding the ends of their breathing tubes above the surface, like snorkels. Adult petroleum flies walk on tiptoe across the surface of the oil, but they will get stuck if their wings or body touch the oil.

If a nuclear bomb were to fall, most animals and plants would die. Cockroaches would cope by eating rubbish. Scorpions, though, only eat live food. Perhaps they would live off the hardy cockroaches!

Small Talk

HARD TO KILL

The delicate-looking sponge, which lives under the sea, is a very tough bug. Its body is made up of lots of separate cells. Each cell has its own life and reproduces by splitting in half. If a sponge is damaged or trampled on, the hardy sponge doesn't die. Instead, it simply rebuilds itself. When the cells of a sponge become separated from each other, they crawl around in the water until they come across other sponge cells. The cells stick together and slowly grow into new sponges. This is a slow process, and a sponge may take years to re-grow.

A scorpion could kill a cockroach with its deadly sting (above).

Scorpion

When it is very hot or cold, you can choose to stay in or go out. Bugs don't have this choice – many have to face extreme temperatures.

Small Talk

- When food is short, a ribbon worm can eat 95 per cent of its own body to survive – that's tough!
- Bugs are so tough that they have been on Earth for about 3,500 million years. Insects first appeared 405 million years ago – that's 185 million years before dinosaurs. Humans have only been around for about 35,000 years.
- Sea anemones and sea cucumbers survive at great depths. They can live almost 11km beneath the sea under pressures that would crush humans.
- If necessary, a sheep tick can survive without food for over seven years.

SUN BAKED

Life in the desert is hard. It is always hot and dry – often there is no rain for years on end. Yet many bugs manage to live there. In the desert, the sand can reach unbearable temperatures, especially on the surface. (If you have ever walked barefoot across a sandy beach on a very hot day, you'll know how hot sand can get.)

SAND RUNNERS

The long-legged darkling beetle (below), which lives in the Namib desert, Africa, can run quickly across scorching sand on long, thin legs. Only the tips of its feet touch the sand, and because it has such long legs, the beetle's body is held away from the blistering heat of the sand.

SAND SWIMMERS

Other types of darkling beetle (below) burrow into the sand and swim through it as if it were water. They usually spend the day buried under the sand, where it is cooler. At night, when the temperature drops, burrow darkling beetles come out in search of food.

Burrowing darkling beetles have flattened bodies, so they can dive to find cooler sand.

Compared to its body length, the long-legged darkling beetle (left) has the longest legs of any insect.

A BUG FOR ALL SEASONS

Humans have heating and air-conditioning to keep the temperature of their homes at a comfortable level. Springtails manage without either. Measuring about 2mm long, springtails are small but tough.

ANTI-FREEZE

Some springtails live in the Arctic and can survive in temperatures of -30°C (more than three times colder than your freezer). They can do this because they have special fluids in their bodies, called glycerols (say 'gliss-er-olls'). These fluids act like anti-freeze, which is a liquid that prevents car engines from freezing up. Glycerols stop the springtails' bodies from getting so cold that the bugs die.

When the weather is freezing, a springtail (above) does not move around. Instead, it sleeps until the weather warms up.

Some springtails (left) also live in the desert, where it is very hot and dry.

This water bear (right) can live for about eight hours, in temperatures as low as -272°C. This is about as cold as it is possible to get.

HOMELESS BUGS

Water bears, or tardigrades, are microscopic aquatic bugs, which live in the thin layer of water that surrounds freshwater plants. When the weather warms up, a water bear is in danger of losing its home. If conditions suddenly become hot and dry, the water bear's watery home dries up.

A SWELL BUG

To survive this threat, the water bear pulls in its legs, loses nearly all the water in its body and shrivels up into a small ball, called a tun. All its body functions slow down until it is barely alive. While it is in this sleepy state, a water bear cannot eat, but can survive for up to 10 years. As soon as it rains again, the water bear swells and becomes active in just a few hours.

FREEZING UP

Some water bears live in the Antarctic. As the winter approaches and the temperature falls below freezing, these tiny bugs turn themselves into tuns and wait out the winter. In this state, they can survive the lowest winter temperatures.

Springtails have a special jumping organ on their abdomens called a furca (say 'fur-ka'). When a springtail releases this 'spring', it jumps high into the air, which is how the bug got its name.

Using a microscope

A microscope gives you the power to enter the world of minute minibeasts. Here's what it can do and how to use it.

As the word *suggests*, minibeasts are small. They hide away and it's often difficult to see them clearly with the naked eye. *Some are so small* that the keen bug watcher really needs a microscope, which magnifies things, or makes them look bigger than they really are.

Magnifying glass

The simplest microscope is a magnifying glass. It has only one lens and can magnify an object 10 – 20 times (x10 – 20). This means that if you look at a bug that is 1cm long through a lens, it will appear to be 10cm long. A magnifying glass is fine for studying the details on a large bug, but less useful for seeing smaller minibeasts clearly.

How a microscope works

If you want to see minute details, you need to use a compound microscope, which has two sets of lenses. In many microscopes, the lenses work by bending rays of light so that, when you look through the lenses, the object looks bigger. The first set of lenses, known as the objective lenses, form an enlarged image of the object. The second set of lenses are the eyepiece lenses. They enlarge the image even more. Small microscopes, like the ones used in schools, magnify about 100 times. Big microscopes that are used by scientists magnify up to 2,000 times. The most powerful microscopes are electron microscopes. Instead of bending light rays, these microscopes bend beams of electrons (tiny particles with a negative electrical charge, found in atoms). They can magnify up to 2 million times!

Amoebas (say 'am-ee-baaz'), common in pond water, are invisible to the naked eye (left). This one has been magnified about 300 times.

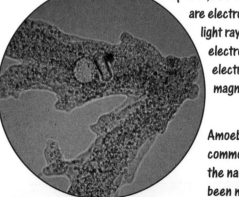

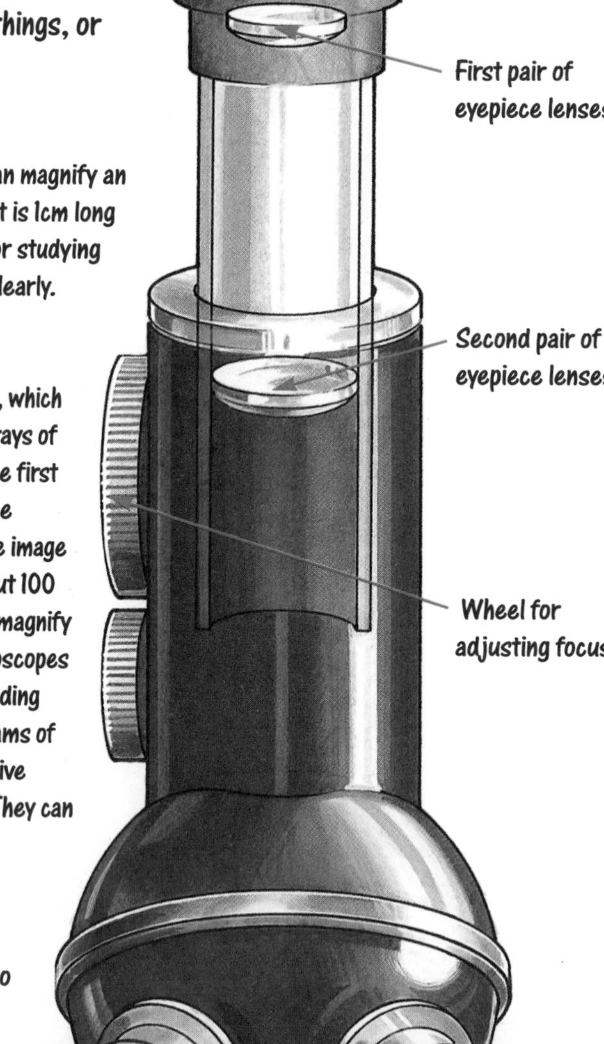

Using your microscope

A drop of pond water is bursting with animal life. Use your microscope and you'll discover a whole new world. If you have a microscope (or if you can borrow one from a friend or school), try this simple test.

1. Collect a little pond water in a clean jar.
2. Place a drop of pond water on a slide using a pipette. Put a slide cover over the top of it.
3. Place the slide, pond water and slide cover on the specimen table of your microscope.
4. Look into the eyepiece and down the tube. Turn the wheel to adjust the focus, until you can see the image clearly.
5. Sketch the bugs that you see.

You will need:

To get the most from you microscope, you will need a few simple tools.

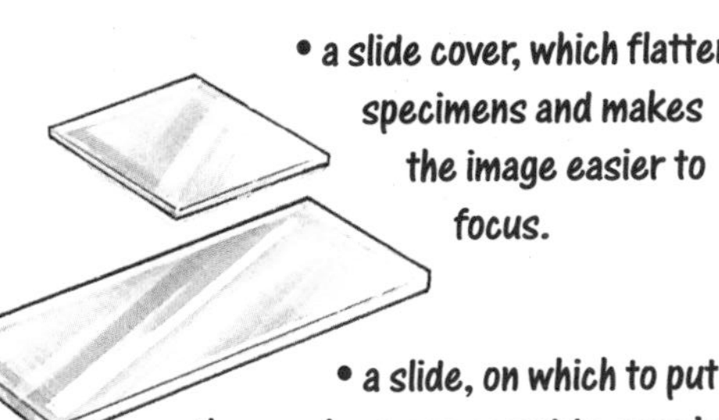

- a slide cover, which flattens specimens and makes the image easier to focus.
- a slide, on which to put the specimens you want to examine.

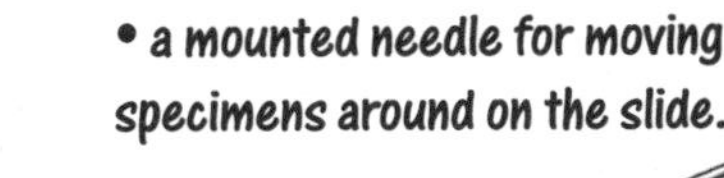

- a mounted needle for moving specimens around on the slide.

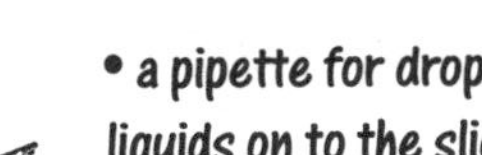

- a pipette for dropping liquids on to the slide.

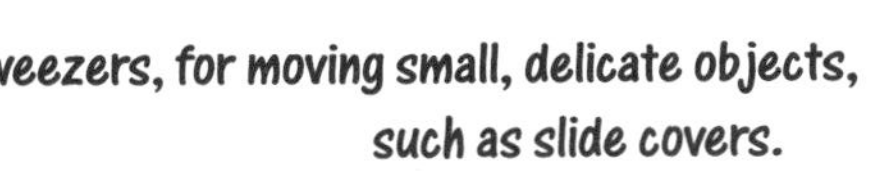

- tweezers, for moving small, delicate objects, such as slide covers.

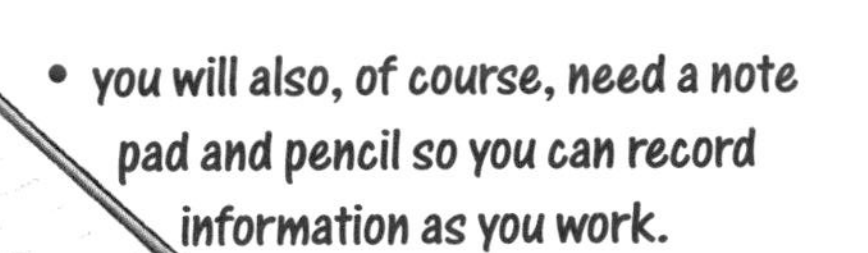

- you will also, of course, need a note pad and pencil so you can record information as you work.

First pair of objective lenses

Second pair of objective lenses

Table

Legs keep microscope stable

Mirror reflects light so that the lenses can magnify the object

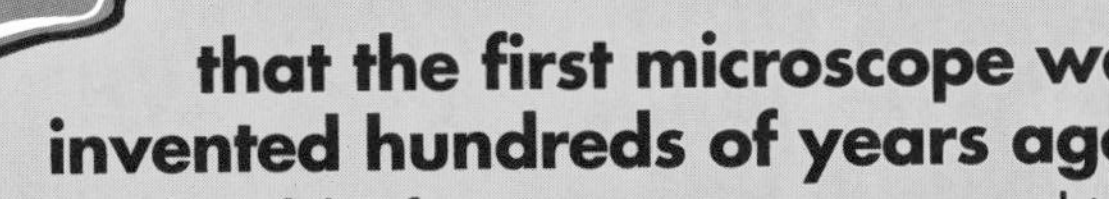

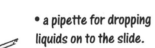

Chlorophytes (say 'clor-oh-fights') (right) are common in pond water.

Is it true... that the first microscope was invented hundreds of years ago?

Yes. One of the first microscopes was used in the 1600s by a Dutchman called Anton van Leeuwenhoek. His microscope had a magnifying power of 275 times (x275). Among other things, he used his microscope to see baby fleas hatching. Before this, no one had ever seen the eggs and people thought that fleas somehow came from mud or sand.

3-D MINIBEASTS

Pea beetle

This lucky adult pea beetle had a good start in life. Soon after it hatched, it found a field full of peas, its favourite food, and ate and ate. On its own, a pea beetle larva doesn't cause much damage. In large numbers, however, it can munch through whole fields of peas. Sometimes, these half-eaten vegetables are picked, dried and packaged before the larvae have had time to escape. This one was lucky. It moved house in the nick of time and lived to tell the tale.

Spot the difference

MOTH

Long, plain antennae

Hairy body

Hawkmoth

Dull colours allow the moth to hide during the day.

Wings folded flat at rest

Can you tell the difference between a butterfly and a moth? Read on and it will all become clear.

Together, butterflies and moths make up one of the largest groups of insects. This group is called Lepidoptera (say 'lep-i-dop-tera'), which means 'scaly winged'. It contains over 170,000 different species. There are many more moths than butterflies, but can you tell the difference between them? There is no single feature that makes all butterflies different from all moths, but there are certain clues you can look out for.

BUTTERFLY

This peacock butterfly, which flies around during the day, is sunning its wings (above). When it rests, the butterfly holds its wings upright.

THE DIFFERENCES

In general, butterflies are much more brightly coloured than moths and usually fly during the day. Most moths fly around at night when it is cooler. They generally have thicker, hairier bodies. Most butterflies' antennae are clubbed at the tips, but moths' antennae are either plain or feathery. Both moths and butterflies use their antennae to find food and mates.

The large blue butterfly's antennae (above) have clubbed tips.

The Emperor moth (above) has sensitive, feather-like antennae.

Butterflies and moths

TAKING A REST

You can also tell the difference between a butterfly and a moth by the way they hold their wings. If a butterfly sits perfectly still and rests, it will usually fold its wings together and hold them upright. A moth will lay its wings flat. The clouded yellow butterfly (below right) rests with its wings folded together and held upright. With its wings lying flat, the white ermine moth (below) looks like it is wearing a soft fur cloak.

Clouded yellow butterfly

White ermine moth

ON THE LATCH

Butterflies and moths have four wings. Many moths have a bristle on the hind wing that is held by a tiny hook on each fore wing. These work like a tiny latch to link the wings together. When the moth flies, its four wings work like two. Butterflies don't have this mechanism – their wings just overlap.

Hook on fore wing

Bristle on hind wing

Close-up of elephant hawkmoth's wing

COLOUR VISION

Butterflies' eyes are very sensitive to colours, and they particularly like red flowers. Moths are more attracted to light-coloured flowers. They are also attracted by lights at night, which is why you often see moths flying around an electric light bulb, or bumping into windows at night.

Blood red skipper butterfly from Peru

Both of these bugs are butterflies. The one above left is brightly coloured, but holds its wings out sideways at rest. The one below left has the colouring of a moth, but holds its wings up above its body, like a butterfly.

Hooked antenna

European small skipper butterfly

Moths and butterflies are cunning bugs. Not only can they fool insect spotters – they also try to fox their enemies.

FOLLOW THE CLUES

Now you know all about the differences between moths and butterflies. Here are a selection of butterflies and moths that make spotting the differences very difficult. Read on and meet the bugs that break all the rules!

HALFWAY HOUSE

Skippers are real rule-breakers. Their fast wing-beat and darting flight give these bugs their name. Although many of them look like moths, they are all butterflies. In many ways, a skipper is halfway between a butterfly and a moth! Some skippers close their wings like moths, and others rest with their wings open. One skipper butterfly, called the Australian regent skipper, even has a latch on its under wings, just like a moth. All skipper butterflies have hooked antennae.

Is it true... that there are more moths than butterflies?

Yes. There are 10 times more species of moths than there are butterflies. When moths first appeared on Earth, they flew at night because there were fewer predators about. Today, there are many more night-time predators, but moths still manage to outnumber their colourful relatives.

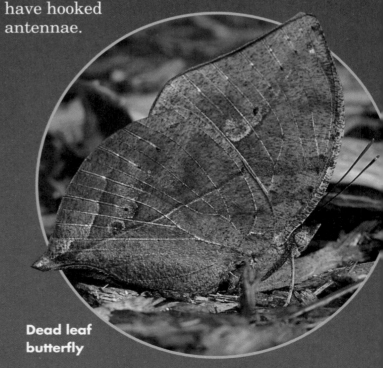

Dead leaf butterfly

Small Talk

LONG STRAWS

Butterflies feed through a proboscis – long, straw-like mouthparts that are perfect for sucking up liquid. When not in use, the proboscis is coiled neatly under the insect's head. Some moths have different eating habits because they feed at night. They often drink the sap of trees. Some moths do not have mouthparts and so they do not eat at all. Others have biting jaws and feed on pollen.

bee hawkmoth

Eyed hawkmoth

BEE CAREFUL

The narrow-bordered bee hawkmoth (above) looks just like a bumble bee, so its enemies treat it with respect. You can tell it's a moth by the way its back wings are attached to its fore wings and because it has feathered antennae.

GET MOTHED!

Like a butterfly, the brightly coloured burnet moth flies during the day. If attacked, it gives out a yellow, poisonous liquid. The moth's bright colours act as a warning. Once a bird has tasted a burnet moth, it won't attack one again.

Six-spot burnet moth

BEAT THE ENEMY

Some butterflies and moths have developed defences against enemies, such as birds and bats. The dead leaf butterfly (left), which lives in Asia, is superbly camouflaged. During the day, the eyed hawkmoth (above) hides by staying completely still on a tree trunk, with its wings closed. If a bird flies past, the hawkmoth opens its fore wings and flashes a pair of bright 'eyes' that stare at the enemy and frighten it away.

Woodland trail

Imagine you are walking through a wood. It has recently been visited by several different bugs. Take a look around and try to spot the clues that the bugs have left behind.

As a creepy-crawly detective, you'll need a good knowledge of bugs, a sharp eye and a magnifying glass. Unlike humans, bugs don't leave hefty footprints – their tracks are harder to spot.

THIS IS WHAT YOU DO

Gather the evidence, piece together the clues and guess which eight bugs have made their marks on these pages. Then turn over and see if you were right!

CLUMSY CLUES

What gives these minibeasts away? A few leave tiny footprints in mud or sand. Others leave trails with their bodies as they slither along the ground, or squirm through the vegetation. Sometimes, bugs give the game away when they eat, build their nests or lay eggs.

1 ◀ What has left a bit of its body behind – and why?

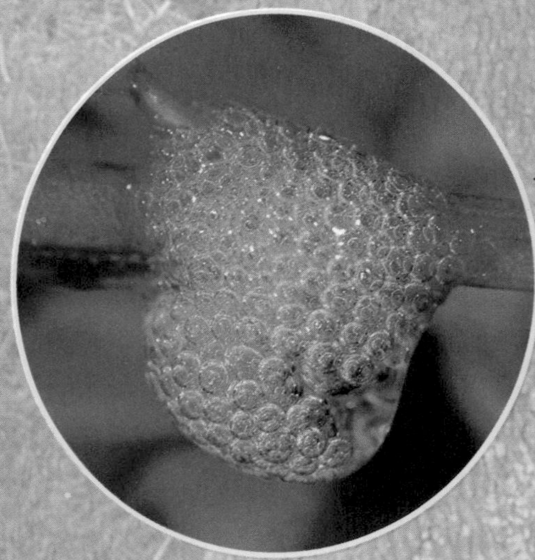

2 ◀ What made this bubbly gunge? You often find it on leaves, tree bark or stalks of grass.

3 ◀ This is a bug's front door. Can you name the earthy character?

4 ◀ This pattern shows the corridors in the home of a tiny bug. What used to live here?

VANDALS WERE HERE

Some bugs leave a trail of destruction. Like a messy crowd of humans on a picnic, they don't bother to clear up after they have eaten. These careless creatures eat other insects and simply throw away their half-eaten bodies. Others munch their way through leaves, plants and trees leaving bite marks and other damage.

HOUSES FOR SALE

Certain insects abandon their homes. They don't clear them out and thoughtfully board them up – they just leave them to rot. Occasionally, bug dwellings are 'vandalised' by insects. Ants and wasps won't think twice about raiding a nest for twigs, dirt or bits of leaf litter to use to build their own homes.

SQUATTERS

'Lazy' bugs move into ready-made homes. They live in disused nests or use them as warehouses to store their eggs. Some creepy-crawly home-owners fix up the place with a spot of DIY or extend the original nest to make room for their family. Species of bees and spiders that don't mind squatting will move into a sheltered spot, such as an old snail's shell, to build their nest.

Bugs have been about. But which ones? Follow the woodland trail and pick up the bug clues. Then turn the page and see if you were right.

5

These leaves weren't damaged by frost. An animal made these marks. Can you name the vandal? ▶

6

Something has taken very neat chunks out of these leaves. It must be a very tidy bug!

7

An animal with only one foot left this trail. Was it a hopping bug? ▶

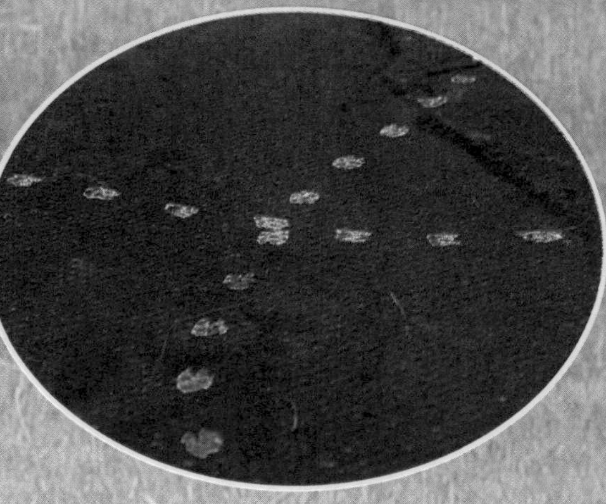

8

Is this a flower bud or a safe place to keep valuable property? ▶

What did you spot?

1 CAST-OFFS ▼

A lime hawkmoth has outgrown its coat and left it on the ground! The green larva, which feeds on lime and other trees, has shed its pupa and turned into an orange-brown adult moth.

Lime hawkmoth

2 MIND YOUR MANNERS ▼

A spittle bug nymph oozes a protective froth, called cuckoo spit. The froth stops the young bug from drying up and puts off hungry enemies. The soft-bodied nymphs grow into spindly adults.

Spittle bug nymph

3 DUMPING GROUND ◄

Mounds of earth, called casts, are clues that an earthworm has recently passed this way. Worms dig tunnels under the soil by swallowing earth and then dumping it above ground.

Earthworm

Elm bark beetle

4 WOODWORK ◄

Beetles that breed in bark and wood tunnel into tree trunks and lay 20 – 100 eggs at a time. When the larvae emerge, they burrow out through the wood, leaving a network of tiny tunnels.

Leaf-mining moth larva

5 MERRY MINERS ▲

The tiny leaf-mining moth larva makes tunnels, called 'mines', through leaves as it eats. These show up on the surface of the leaf as brown grooves. Other caterpillars roll the leaves while they eat, neatly tying the ends together with silk. So also look out for rolled and silken leaves on trees and shrubs.

6 MADE TO MEASURE ▼

The culprit responsible for the tidy hole in the rose leaf is the European leaf-cutter bee. The female collects building materials for her new home, but she isn't satisfied with any old piece of leaf. She knows exactly which shapes she needs. She cuts pieces out of leaves with her jaws so that they fit perfectly into her partly built nest.

European leaf-cutter bee

7 SLIPPERY CUSTOMER ◄

These sticky, silvery trails are the footprint of a snail making its getaway. The sticky slime helps it to move forward and climb up walls and trees without falling off.

Garden snail

8 WHAT A GALL! ►

This may look like a strange flower, but it's actually a robin's pincushion gall. It is made by a gall wasp, a 3mm-long wasp that lays its eggs in the twigs of plants and trees. When their young hatch, they produce a chemical, which causes this abnormal growth. Galls can be up to 10cm wide and provide the young gall wasps with a safe place to live. Some galls look like smooth, shiny apples – but don't eat them, they're poisonous!

Gall

Gall wasp

Improve and test your knowledge with...

CREEPY~CRAWLY FACTS

Put your feet up in front of the TV and get a 'pizza' the action! Find out some more amazing facts and try the BUGS! quiz.

1 Compared with its body length, which insect has the longest legs?
a) daddy-long-legs
b) long-legged darkling beetle
c) millipede

2 What does a leaf-cutter bee use to cut leaves?
a) sharp claws
b) scissors
c) its jaws

3 How many eggs does the crown-of-thorns starfish lay each year?
a) 20 million
b) 2 million
c) 200,000

4 How does a petroleum fly move across oil?
a) it tiptoes across
b) it jumps on the backs of other insects
c) it swims

5 What does the robber fly larva eat?
a) live insects
b) nectar
c) dead bugs

6 Who discovered the microscopic world of minibeasts?
a) van Leeuwenhoek
b) von Lindenberg
c) van Leadenhook

7 Why does the cone shell stick out its tongue?
a) it's very bad mannered
b) to catch its prey
c) to have a drink

8 What does the woodlouse do with its shell once it has shed it?
a) it buries it
b) it sets fire to it
c) it eats it

9 What is the water bear's real name?
a) water bug
b) tardigrade
c) tardis

10 Which of these statements is true?
a) butterflies are always brightly coloured
b) moths always lay their wings flat when they rest
c) moths are never brightly coloured

Silk fish nets

Spiders' webs are very effective traps. Flies and other insects stand no chance once they've been caught. Some big webs can even hold small birds. In Papua New Guinea, the local people use spiders' webs to catch fish! The silk of the golden orb spider is so thick that expert anglers can land fish weighing up to 500g.

Eye don't believe it!

Even though bugs have amazing eyes, they are nowhere near as refined as ours. With our single lens eyes, we can see objects far more clearly than any bug. If you were to swap your eyes for multi-lens, compound eyes, but you wanted to see as clearly as ever, your bug eyes would have to measure at least 1m across!

Star-struck fleas

In the 18th and 19th centuries, fleas became very popular as pets. They were also used in comic performances, made to wear fancy dress and trained to do tricks. In flea circuses, scenes were created in which fleas danced around a pretend ballroom, while others played cards. On one occasion, a flea's strength was demonstrated by making it pull a toy battleship, which was nearly 400 times its own weight.

Flying spiders

Does the thought of a flying spider turn your knees to jelly? If so – picture this! There is an Australian spider that comes as near to flying as any spider ever will. Although it has no wings, its legs are specially flattened and these act like the wings of a glider – allowing the spider to make long, gliding leaps.

Matthew Robertson, who spent 12 years working with bugs at London Zoo, here answers all your creepy-crawly questions.

How can you tell the sex of a bug?

It is not always easy to tell whether a bug is male or female. In some species of bug, males do not exist at all. In others, you can only tell the difference by looking through a microscope. But there are also many bugs in which the differences are obvious. Many male beetles have long horns, while male stick insects are usually much smaller than the females and may have bigger wings.

How do you get spiders out of the bath?

The steep, smooth sides of your bath are almost impossible for a spider to climb up. Without your help, its only way out is down the plug hole. This escape route can result in a watery death. If you don't want to pick the bug up (especially if it's a big, hairy spider), all you have to do is give it a ladder. A length of toilet roll will do the trick – simply hang it over the edge of the bath. Once it has climbed to safety, the spider will usually head for cover.

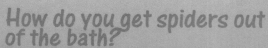

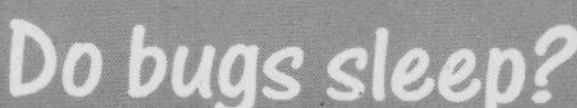

Do bugs sleep?

It is impossible to say whether bugs sleep or not. Some ants curl up and stop moving when they are not working. When they are gently shaken, they uncurl slowly and, for a few seconds, they appear to be dazed – rather like someone who has just been woken up from a deep sleep. Some sea bugs also become inactive at certain times of the day. It is difficult to understand how bugs can sleep at all when most of them cannot shut their eyes.

Ichneumon Wasp

The female ichneumon wasp injects her eggs into a host which she can't even see!

The ichneumon (say 'ik-new-man') wasp lives in the pine forests of Europe, North America and New Zealand. Unlike other wasps that live together in colonies, the ichneumon spends most of its time alone.

EGG-LAYING TUBE

With their long, slender, black bodies and two antennae, the male and female wasp look very similar – except that the female has an ovipositor (say 'o-vi-pozi-tor') at the end of her abdomen. This looks like a long, fine needle and the female uses it to lay her eggs – 'ovipositor' means 'egg-placer'.

DETECTIVE WORK

When it is time to lay her eggs, the female ichneumon flies around the forest, looking for a suitable spot in one of the pine trees. Settling on one of the trunks, she tiptoes over it and gently taps it with the ends of her antennae to listen for a tell-tale hollow sound. This means that deep inside the wood, tasty wood wasp larvae are tunnelling through the tree.

DEEP DRILLING

When she has found what she is looking for, the female ichneumon points her ovipositor straight down towards the trunk. With the sharp tip, she pierces through the bark – like a person giving an injection. She drills all the way through to a wood wasp larva and lays a single egg in its body. So that she can reach her victims, her ovipositor is especially long – it may be one and a half times longer than her body.

QUICK WORK

Although drilling is hard work, it takes the ichneumon only a few minutes to finish the job. It can be a dangerous time, though. While she is drilling, she is pinned to the tree and cannot move, so she could easily be attacked by any predator.

TUNNELLING OUT

In a few days' time, the tiny ichneumon young hatch and live inside the wood wasps' bodies. Eating away at their hosts' soft flesh, they slowly grow inside them until they are big enough to munch their way out. Then they tunnel out of the tree and take to the air.

FLOWER-LOVERS

Unlike its young, which eats the larva it hatches in, the adult ichneumon likes to drink nectar from flowers. It is attracted by their bright colours. Like a moth, it is also attracted by light.

This wasp has two veined, transparent wings. However, some ichneumons do not have wings.

Female ichneumon wasp

Body bends to allow wasp to drill at the right angle.

Sheaths protect the ovipositor and guide it in the right direction.

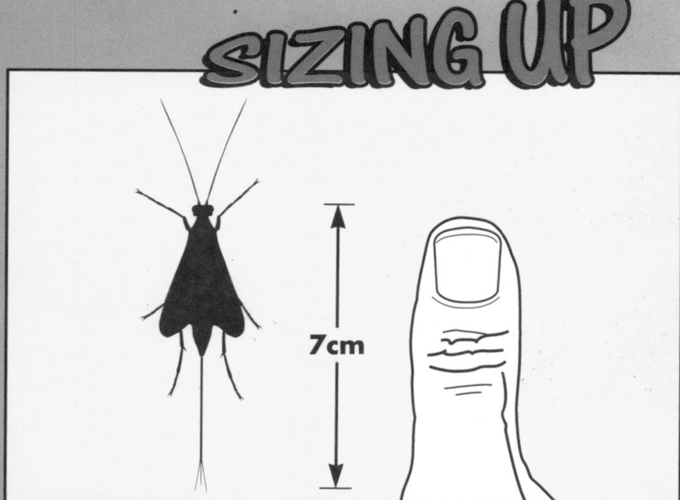

- **SCIENTIFIC NAME:** *Rhyssa persuasoria*
- **SIZE:** body 2 – 3.5cm long, ovipositor 3 – 3.5cm
- **LIVES:** Europe, North America, New Zealand
- **EATS:** young eats the insides of wood wasp larvae, adult drinks nectar

KILLER DRILLER

A female ichneumon crawls slowly up the branch of a tree. Tapping gently with her antennae, she tries to sense if a wood wasp larva is living inside the branch. A hollow noise tells her that a fat grub is lurking below.

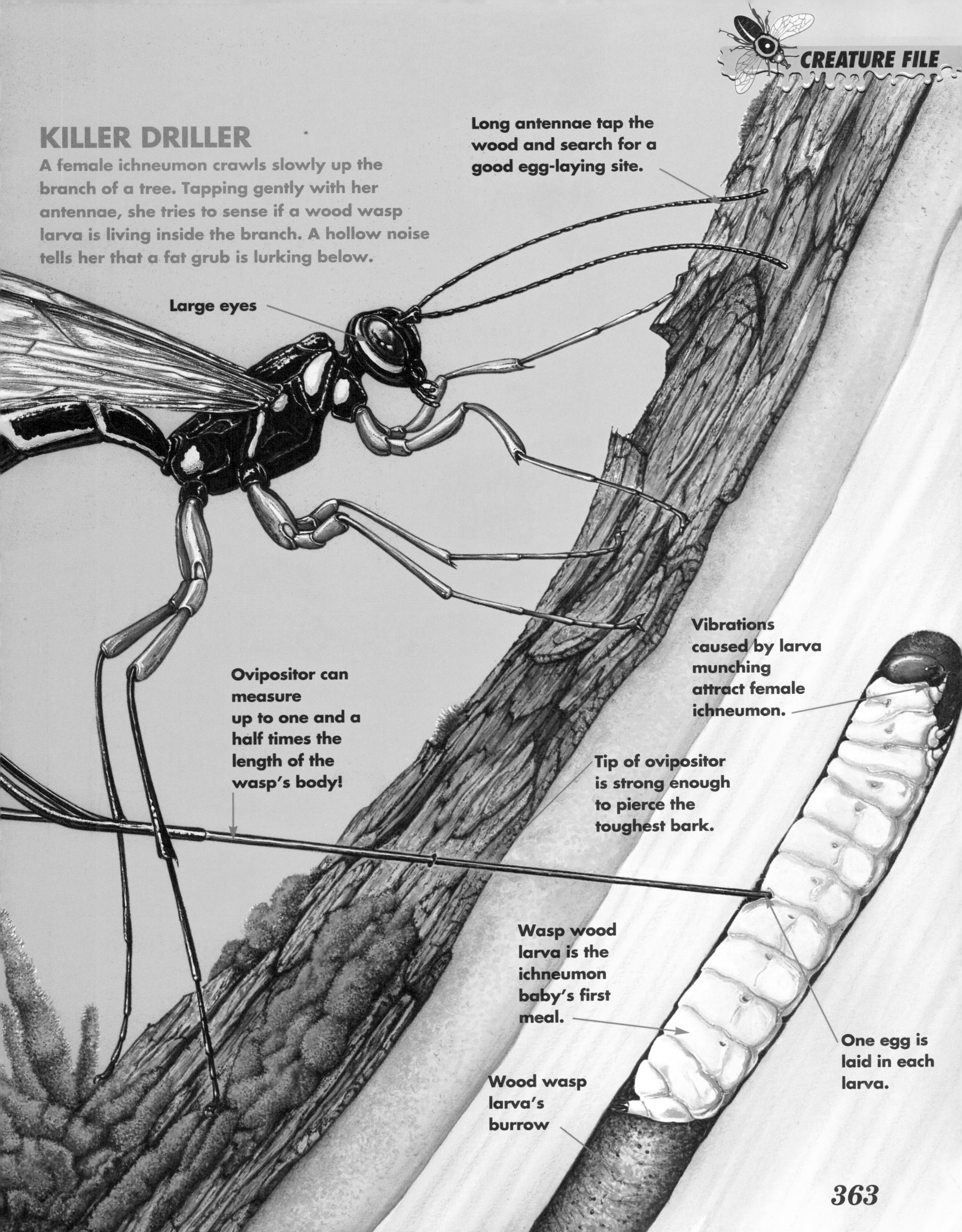
Long antennae tap the wood and search for a good egg-laying site.
Large eyes
Vibrations caused by larva munching attract female ichneumon.
Ovipositor can measure up to one and a half times the length of the wasp's body!
Tip of ovipositor is strong enough to pierce the toughest bark.
Wasp wood larva is the ichneumon baby's first meal.
One egg is laid in each larva.
Wood wasp larva's burrow

Daddy-long-legs

Its long, trailing legs have earned the crane fly the nickname daddy-long-legs.

Although it looks a bit like a big mosquito, the daddy-long-legs does not feed on human blood. In fact, it hardly bothers to eat at all, except to suck up water or nectar from flowers. A daddy-long-legs only lives for one day. During this time, it has to mate and produce its young. This means that there is no time for food.

BIG APPETITES

The female lays about 300 eggs. Using the pointed tip of her abdomen, she pushes her eggs deep into damp soil. Two weeks later, the young burrow through the soil. They eat the roots and stems of plants and can ruin lawns by nibbling through grass roots. The young have tough skins and are sometimes called 'leather-jackets'.

FLIGHT CONTROL

Two halteres, which stick out from either side of the bug's thorax, help it to keep its balance and to fly straight. A daddy-long-legs can only fly if the weather is calm.

SIZING UP

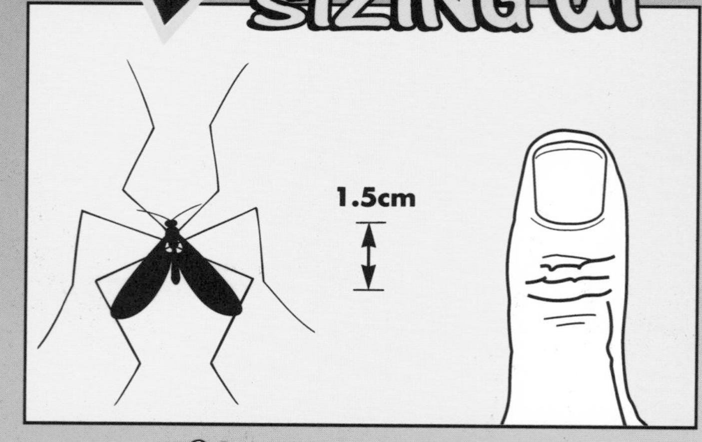

- **SCIENTIFIC NAME:** *Tipula maxima*
- **SIZE:** female body 2.5cm long, male body 1.5cm long
- **LIVES:** all over the world, especially in areas where there is damp vegetation
- **EATS:** young eats nectar, adult lives on roots, stems of plants and rotting vegetation

Box Jellyfish

Swimmers may not notice the see-through box jellyfish, until they feel its venomous sting.

The box jellyfish gets its name because of its square, box-like body – or 'bell'. From each corner of its bell hang groups of venomous tentacles. These trail through the water, stinging and killing any prey that accidentally touches them. Then the tentacles lift the victim up to the jellyfish's mouth, which is hidden under its bell.

INTO THE OCEAN

The jellyfish starts its life in a river, near to where it joins the sea. Heavy rains flush it out of the river and into the shallow waters along the seashore, where it grows to its full size.

HARD TO SEE

Its colourless, transparent bell makes the jellyfish almost invisible in the water – and especially dangerous to swimmers. If a person bumps into a box jellyfish, some of its tentacles stick to the victim's skin, injecting them with venom. Pouring vinegar on to the tentacles kills them and allows them to be removed. The sting of a box jellyfish is always very painful and is capable of killing a human in less than three minutes!

- **SCIENTIFIC NAME:** *Chironex fleckeri*
- **SIZE:** bell up to 25cm wide, tentacles 15m long
- **LIVES:** ocean shore off north-eastern Australia
- **EATS:** fish and small sea bugs

SIZING UP

Take your

In the bug world, finding a mate can be easy. But once a couple of bugs have met each other, the difficulties start. They have to go through all sorts of fancy routines called courting rituals.

Courting is when one animal goes out of its way to impress another and to find a mate. The animal kingdom is full of courting rituals. Bugs dance, fight and generally show off to impress members of the opposite sex. These posing sessions give a bug a chance to see if another bug is a suitable mate.

BUNGEY-JUMPING SLUGS

Slugs perform a courting ritual which can last for up to two and a half hours. They meet on a leaf, then trail each other in a circle. Then they 'embrace' and tumble off the leaf. Luckily, the slugs are attached to the leaf by a thread of mucus as they fall towards the ground – just like bungey-jumpers.

'Dancing' scorpions

LET'S DANCE

Before two scorpions mate, they 'dance' together. While 'dancing', the male looks about for a good spot to place his spermatophore (say 'sperm-at-oh-four'). This is a tube containing his sperm (seed), which he sticks into the ground. Then he leads the female round until he has positioned her over the spermatophore. The female picks up the sperm with special organs underneath her body.

partner

'Will you be my mate?' (main picture). Two slugs court on a leaf in the rain forest.

LOVE AT FIRST FLIGHT

Some bugs get together in huge numbers before they mate. Male mayflies gather in large groups and hover over a suitable spot, such as a pond, a lake or even a rubbish tip. Females are attracted to the site chosen by the males. They join the swarm and fly above the males. The males have to fly upwards to mate.

Mayflies hover over a lake and prepare to mate.

THEY'RE PLAYING OUR TUNE

Have you ever heard a cricket sing? If you have, it will have been a male, serenading its partner. Some singing attracts both male and female admirers. (The other males come to join in the chorus.) The male knows how to spot a female because they are the quiet ones. She settles down beside him and he sings to her alone! Female North American grasshoppers often sing as well as the male. The two of them sing a duet before mating.

A male cricket (left) uses his burrow as a loud-speaker. The hole that he sits in amplifies his singing (makes it louder).

HOT WORK

Some female Namib desert beetles let their suitors chase them up and down sand dunes in the heat of the mid-day sun. Sometimes the female gathers a whole crowd of followers. The one that manages to keep up with her is chosen as her mate. She only wants a partner that is fit enough to father their offspring.

Female beetle

Two Namib desert beetles chase a female in the desert (above). Only the toughest male will catch her.

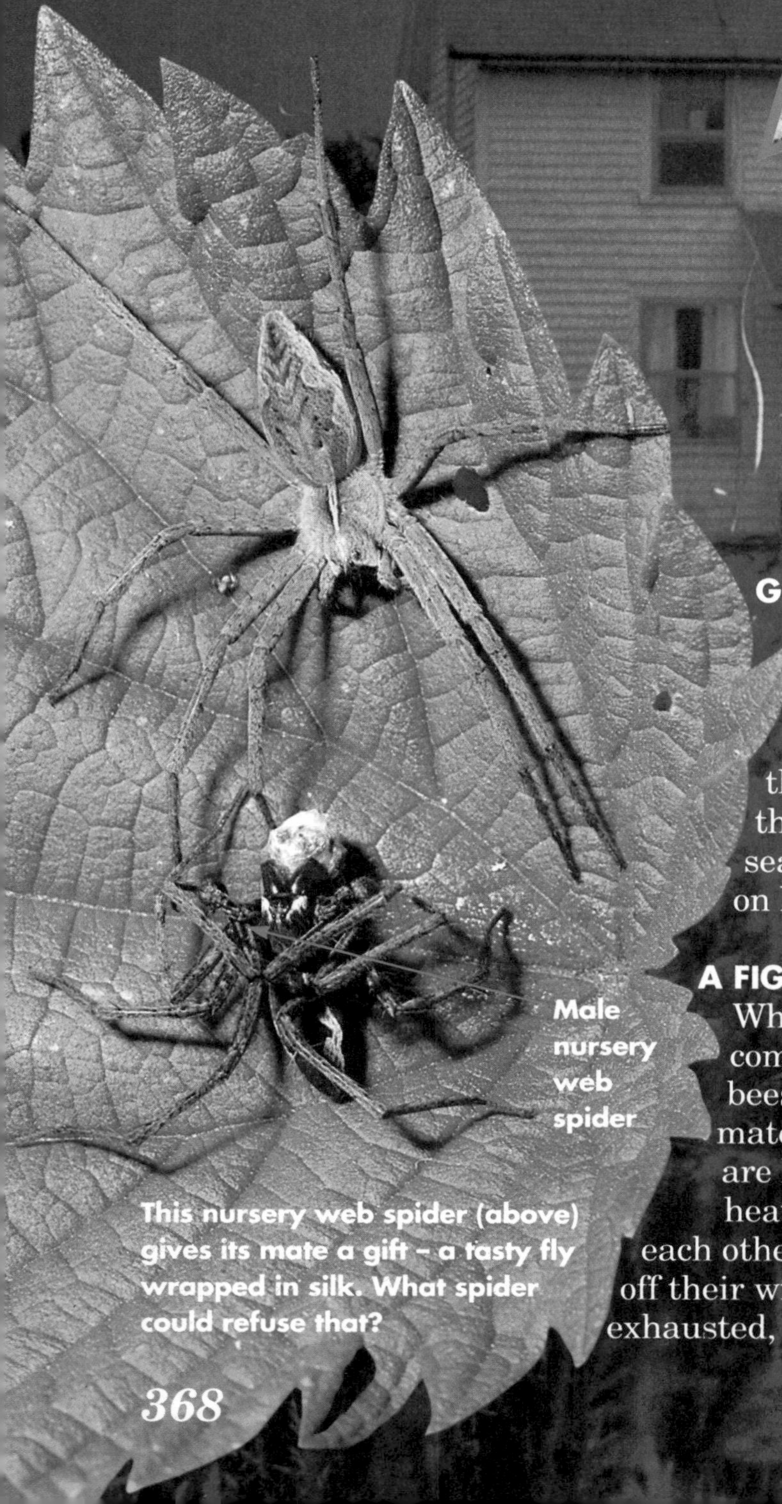

GIVING PRESENTS

Some insects impress their mate with a gift before they mate. Hangingflies and dance flies give their partners tasty snacks, such as little flies and moths. The bigger the gift, the longer the female will take to eat it. While she's eating, the male mates with her. During the mating season, females often stop looking for food and rely on handouts from interested males.

Male nursery web spider

This nursery web spider (above) gives its mate a gift – a tasty fly wrapped in silk. What spider could refuse that?

A FIGHTING CHANCE

When a female bee, which hasn't mated before, comes out of the nest she'll usually find 5 – 20 male bees waiting for her. These males are so eager to mate with her that they fight over her. These tiffs are known as 'mating balls', and can get a bit heated. The male bees jostle and occasionally fly at each other, pushing rivals out of the way or trying to tear off their wings. They fight until the weaker bees give up, exhausted, and make way for the stronger male bees.

LIGHT OF MY LIFE

A male firefly knows how to attract a female. He produces a chemical in his abdomen which gives off light that can be seen clearly at night. Once the sun has gone down, the male fireflies flit around, switching their lights on and off. Each firefly creates its own spectacular light show and draws the females closer.

It's lighting up time as a swarm of fireflies (background picture) search for mates near a farm at dusk.

What is... courtship?

Just as male lions fight each other for the attention of a lioness in the wild, so male bugs compete for the best partner by showing off, fighting or simply grabbing a female. This is called courtship. A male bug needs to impress a female bug or she will go and find another partner. Because bugs need to mate to produce young, competition for suitable females is fierce. This often means that only the strongest bugs get to mate. With a bit of luck, the babies they produce will also be strong enough to survive in the tough world.

SHOWING OFF

The male jumping spider goes to great lengths – and heights – to woo his partner. This bug has good eyesight and the male is especially attractive. When he is performing his mating rituals, he shows off the brightly coloured hair and scales on his legs, face and abdomen.

GIVE US A TWIRL

First, the male spider flashes his front legs. If that doesn't work, he does a twirl, then stands on tiptoe in front of the female and shows off his colourful abdomen! Other spiders are less charming. The Columbian nursery web spider simply ties his partner's legs up with silken thread – a 'bridal veil' – and leaves her to struggle free after he's gone.

The male jumping spider (right) waves one of his legs in the air. If this doesn't attract a mate, he'll simply flash another part of his body.

How to trap bugs

It may sound obvious, but the very first thing you have to do if you're going to be a bug watcher is catch your bugs. Follow these instructions and try your luck with a pitfall trap.

If you want to trap bugs that crawl on the ground, try a pitfall trap. This is an efficient way of catching bugs without harming them. Most bugs have enough problems in their short lives – avoiding predators, finding food, getting squashed by careless feet – without you adding to them. It is therefore important that you behave responsibly if you are going to be a bug watcher. When you catch a bug, remember to let it go later on.

You will need:

- a clean, empty ice-cream tub
- a darning or knitting needle
- a few small leaves
- a small plank of wood
- at least four small rocks
- a jam jar lid
- cotton wool
- water

WHAT TO DO

1 Punch about 20 holes in the bottom of the ice-cream tub with a fat needle. (Ask an adult to do this with a darning or knitting needle). This will prevent water collecting in the trap and drowning the bugs.

2 Dig a hole in the ground and fit the ice-cream tub into the hole so that the soil is level with the top of the tub.

3 Scatter a few small leaves in the tub, but make sure that they don't come anywhere near the top of it or the bugs will be able to crawl out again. Put a small, flat dish in the ice-cream tub, such as the lid of a jam jar. Place a little cotton wool in the dish and sprinkle it with water. Bugs can drink this water without drowning.

Small Talk

EXPERIMENTING

When you've made your pitfall trap, there are a number of experiments you may like to do. You can, for example, compare the bugs you catch during the night with those that you catch during the day. You can also compare the bugs you catch in different parts of the garden, the park or wherever you can use your trap. You can try attracting bugs with different sorts of food and noting which bugs are attracted to which food. Try using various different fruits – a very ripe banana will be popular – and small pieces of meat.

4 Give your bugs protection from the rain. Put a rock at each corner of the ice-cream tub and balance a small plank of wood on them so that it rests about 2cm above the tub. Use more rocks if you need them.

5 Weigh the plank down by placing a brick on top of it. The plank will provide cover for the bugs. It will allow them to get in, but will keep the rain out. Otherwise, if it rained the bugs would drown.

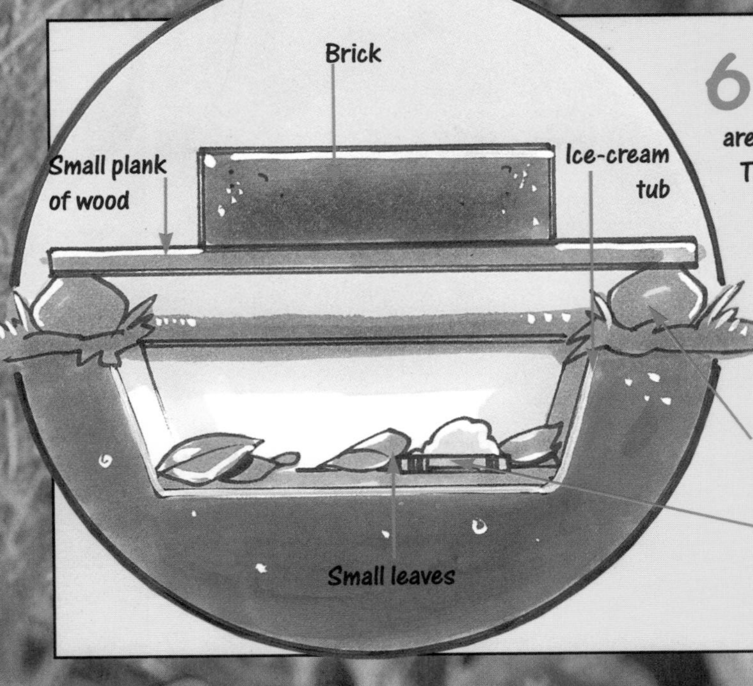

6 Now leave your trap overnight – many bugs are more active at night. Then, in the morning, check to see what bugs you have caught. Do not leave them in the trap for longer than this, as they will eat each other.

7 Once you have set up your pitfall trap, remember to keep an eye on it. Release the bugs when you have finished studying them. Do this simply by letting them crawl out. In the next issue of BUGS! we shall tell you how to identify the most common types of creepy-crawlies. Why not wait until you have the next issue of BUGS! before you set up your trap?

3-D
MINIBEASTS

Biting midge

The blood-sucking female midge may be tiny, but when she gets together with her friends they can be very irritating to humans. These bugs swarm in large numbers during the summer months, buzzing around rivers, lakes and boggy areas. It is at this time that they can make life unbearable for people trying to enjoy the warm weather. Biting midges fly around humans in search of blood. They sink their mouthparts into their flesh and then buzz off to find another victim. Some cheeky midges will even attack mosquitoes that are already full of juicy blood.

Excellent eggs

Some bugs lay millions of eggs at a time, others just lay one. Certain bugs lovingly look after their eggs, while others simply dump them and run.

Just like the bugs that lay them, eggs come in many shapes and sizes. Some are coated in jelly, foam or hard cases and most are protected in some way. This ensures that the babies hatch safely and prevents the species from dying out.

A window-winged moth (above) coats a blade of grass with hundreds of pearly eggs.

Tiny, 4mm-long octopuses (right) emerge from their egg cases. The white lumps inside the egg cases are food stores, which keep the unborn babies alive before they hatch.

GOING WITHOUT

Before she lays her eggs, the female octopus looks for a suitable shelter to house them in. She might choose an empty cockle shell, the ceiling of her home (a hole in a rock), or even an empty bottle! She guards and cleans them for several months and never lets them out of her sight. During this time, she goes without food. Sadly, she never sees her young grow up – the female octopus dies soon after her babies are born.

EGG WHITE

For some wasps, laying an egg can be a complicated and exhausting business. First, the female tarantula-hawk wasp has to find a tarantula. The wasp injects it with paralysing venom and takes the spider prisoner. Then she searches for a good nesting site and drags the dozy tarantula back to her burrow. The wasp lays a single, 1cm-long egg on its body (right). Once the egg has hatched, the wasp larva eats the soft parts of the tarantula's body.

Small Talk

MEETING THE NEIGHBOURS

Butterflies are very fussy about where they lay their eggs. Firstly, the mother carefully picks a leaf, looking it over and flicking it with her antennae. Then she checks to see if a lot of other females have laid their eggs nearby. If it looks like a crowded neighbourhood, she will move on to find a quieter spot. A caring mother, she wants to keep her babies safe from overcrowding, starvation and disease.

THE QUEEN MUM

The bug record for egg-laying goes to the queen termite. The common queen termite can lay around 30,000 eggs a day. She lives for up to 16 years, during which time she can produce over 150 million babies. Other termite species have queens that can lay up to 86,400 eggs in a day.

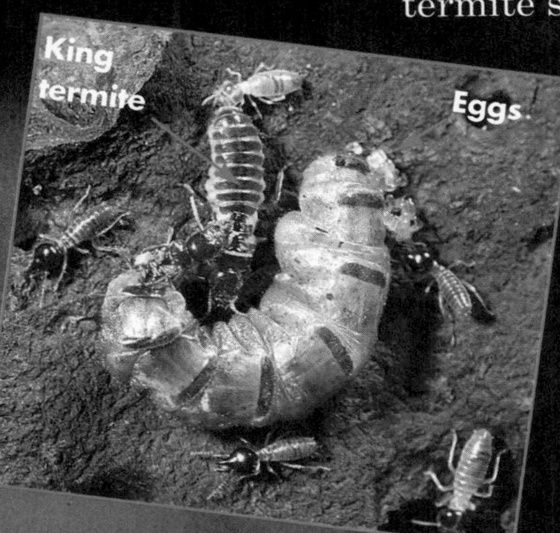

This queen termite's body is full of eggs (above).

TURNING OVER A NEW LEAF

Imagine starting life under a pile of damp leaves, or a stone. That's where baby slugs usually begin their short lives. The eggs hatch in early autumn, about 30 days after they've been laid. Many baby slugs don't survive the harsh winter months.

A baby leopard slug takes its first look around.

Each egg is 4mm wide.

Eggs bound together with silk.

The rafter spider (left) carries her eggs around until the spiderlings (baby spiders) hatch.

WRAPPED IN SWADDLING CLOTHES

Female spiders make the most of their spinning skills to tuck up their eggs safely until hatched. They carefully sew a cocoon of silk around the eggs and hang them from their web. The wolf spider and rafter spider hold their egg sacs in their jaws and carry them around with them (above left). Some species – like jumping and sack spiders – build a shelter, which protects the mother as well as her eggs.

ALL YOUR EGGS IN ONE BASKET

Just as women go to hospital to have their babies, many bugs choose one special spot to lay their eggs. Alderflies get together in huge numbers and lay their eggs on leaves by rivers. Tiny female thrips also gather together to lay their eggs. These bugs, which are also called thunder flies, are guarded by males, which hang around the egg-laying site. Each male hopes to mate with a female just before she lays her eggs, ensuring that the young will be his offspring.

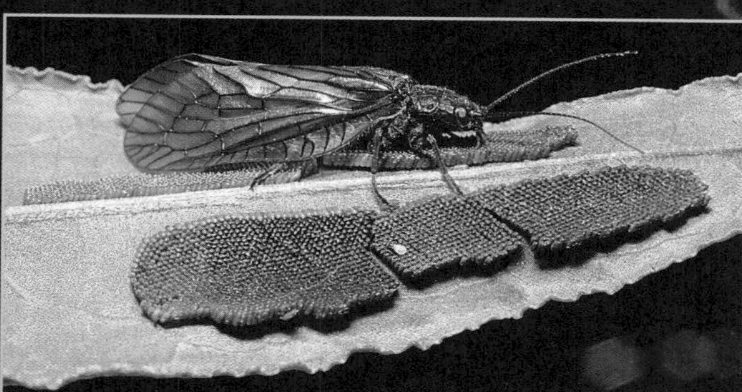

An alderfly (above) lays her tiny eggs next to a batch that belongs to another female.

Each lacewing egg, which is the size of a pinhead, is attached to the underside of a leaf by a stalk.

Small Talk

- When it comes to laying eggs, spiders differ enormously. Raft spiders, for example, can lay as many as 2,000 eggs in four egg sacs. Cave spiders, on the other hand, lay just one egg at a time! Spiders that stay with their eggs until they hatch usually have medium-sized families and lay up to about 20 eggs.
- The pork tapeworm can carry 102 million eggs in her body at the same time – that's 102 million babies. It's just as well she lays so many, because, unlike the queen termite, few of her babies survive.
- Some species of stick insects have to wait six months before they hatch out of their eggs. But the patient brine shrimp takes the prize. It can survive for 3 – 4 years before hatching!

A nursery full of baby squid

EGG PLANT

Look under a few leaves and you may spot the eggs of the pretty lacewing fly. The female lays each egg on a 'stalk' so that it looks like a tiny balloon on a stick (above). She glues the stalks in place with a special sticky liquid and leaves them dangling in the breeze. If she simply left the eggs lying side-by-side, the greedy little baby insects would try to eat each other.

EGGS EVERYWHERE!

Squids search around for a good spot to lay their eggs and make this area their nursery. Hundreds of squids use the same area and attach their jelly-covered egg capsules to stones, shells or clusters of other females' eggs. Together, their white eggs can cover several kilometres of the sea bed! When the baby squids hatch out (above), they are in good company – it's just like being born into an underwater kindergarten!

Tasty sea bugs

Have you ever thought of eating bugs? Many sea bugs are bred especially for humans to eat.

You can find sea bugs on menus all over the world. Which of these bugs would you fancy eating for your tea?

SNACK ATTACK

If you're really hungry, why not get to grips with a big squid or octopus? The octopus (far right) has a large brain and is probably the most intelligent bug humans eat. Chefs use the mantle, which is the fleshy part around the body, and the tentacles – suckers and all!

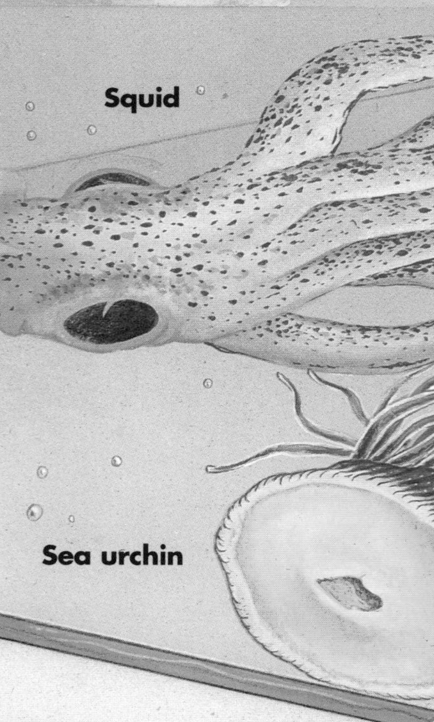

BLUSHING LOBSTERS

Despite their tough shells, crustaceans, such as prawns, crayfish and crabs (top right), have soft, chewy flesh. Lobsters are also tough, but tasty. In the wild, they can be dark-brown, green, blue, white or red, depending on their species and diet. When they finally end up on your plate, they will always be red. As soon as they are put into boiling water, the chemicals in their bodies, which determine their colour, are destroyed.

SEARCHING FOR AN URCHIN

Islanders who live in the Pacific Ocean hunt for sea bugs and eat them raw. Sea urchins, which are served with a sprinkling of lemon juice, are particularly popular.

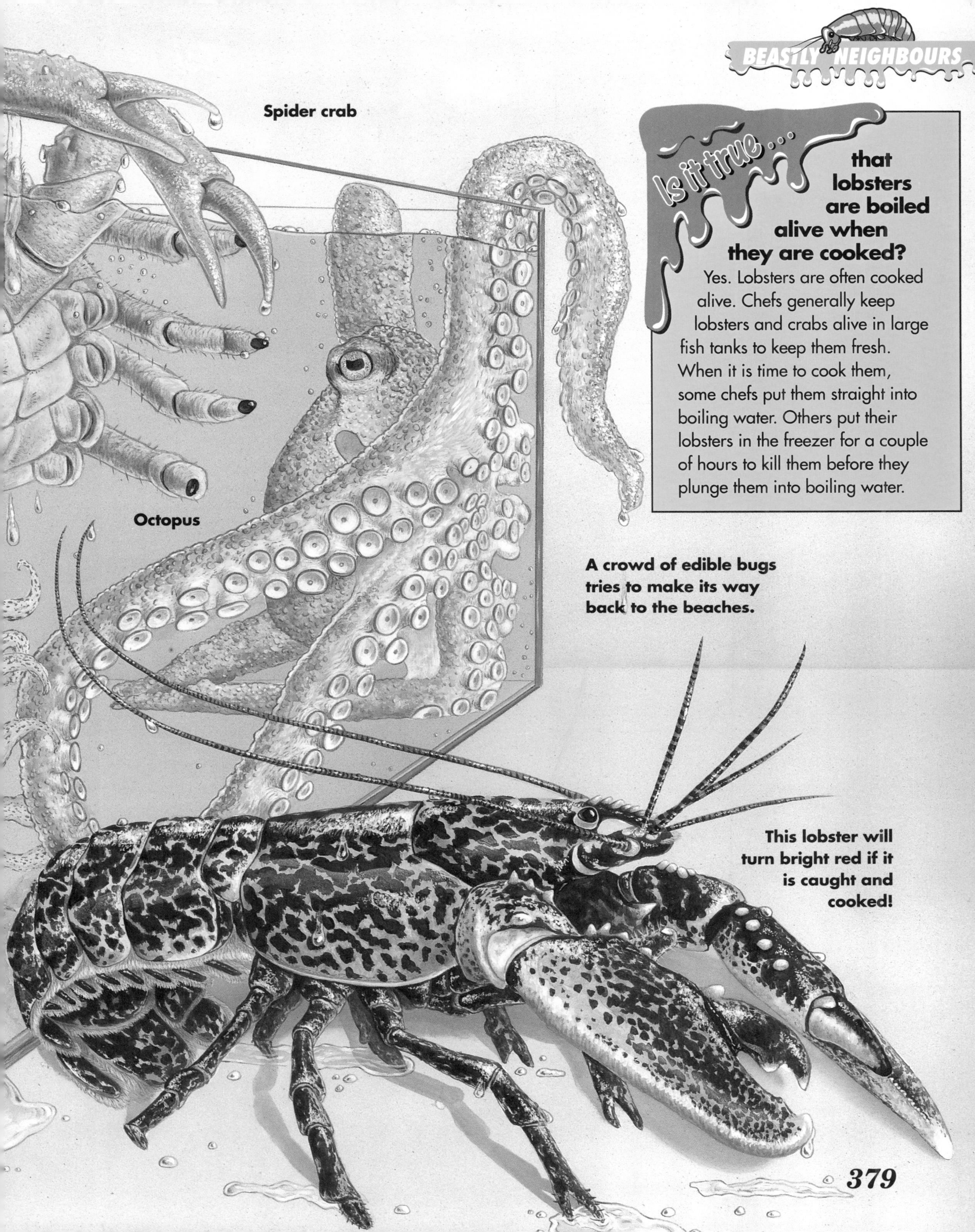
Spider crab
Octopus
A crowd of edible bugs tries to make its way back to the beaches.
This lobster will turn bright red if it is caught and cooked!

Is it true... that lobsters are boiled alive when they are cooked?

Yes. Lobsters are often cooked alive. Chefs generally keep lobsters and crabs alive in large fish tanks to keep them fresh. When it is time to cook them, some chefs put them straight into boiling water. Others put their lobsters in the freezer for a couple of hours to kill them before they plunge them into boiling water.

SMELLY SPAGHETTI

Palolo worms (below) look like green spaghetti! The people of Samoa and Fiji in the Pacific Ocean eat them by the plateful, either lightly fried or raw. But they have to stay up all night to catch them. These wriggling worms, which are each about as long as these two pages, live in the cracks in dead coral reefs and venture out at night to feed.

A NIGHT TO REMEMBER

One night, every year, the palolo worms swarm in their millions. However, it is only half the worm that swarms. The front half stays hidden among the rocks, while the rear half swims to the surface to mate. Meanwhile, hungry Samoans use nets to gather up what remains of the worms and take them home to eat.

Is it true… that oysters and mussels should only be eaten in a month with an 'r' in its name?

This is an old-fashioned guide to tell how fresh shellfish are. In the past, people who lived in the northern hemisphere didn't eat shellfish in the summer months (May, June, July and August). None of these months has an 'r' in its name. During this summer period, harmful plankton breed and fill the seas. The shellfish eat the plankton and become poisonous. This danger is a problem throughout the world. The Pacific razor clam, which buries itself in sandy beaches, is also poisonous in the summer. Today, shellfish are often farmed, so it is perfectly safe to eat them all year round.

Mussels

The day when the palolo worms surfaced used to mark the beginning of the Samoan New Year.

Palolo worms

GUZZLING GASTROPODS

Whelks are shellfish with curly homes on their backs. They are gastropods, which literally means 'belly-footed'. Along with cockles, they are a traditional British seaside snack. People in the West Indies eat a gastropod with a more glamorous image – the beautiful pink conch. They use it to make a thick soup, called chowder.

Stalls that sell sea bugs (left) are a familiar sight at British seaside resorts.

Sea cucumbers (above) can grow up to 2m long.

COOL CUCUMBERS

Only some of the 600 species of sea cucumber are edible. Chinese people, in particular, love the slippery, shiny texture of the sea cucumber. They boil these long, bendy bugs and then pickle them in jars.

THEY DIE TO DYE

Young cuttlefish, measuring just 3 – 6cm long, are cleaned, fried and eaten whole. Nothing is wasted in the careful preparation. The dark ink they squirt when attacked in the wild is often used to dye noodles, which are served, with the cuttlefish, as a side order. In Thailand, cuttlefish are laid out to dry and sold by the roadside. Toasted or raw, they are a popular and healthy snack.

Small Talk

RICH MAN'S FEAST!

Oysters were once called 'poor man's beef' because they were so cheap that even the poorest people could afford them. They were so popular that if you were to dig up an ancient rubbish pit, you would probably find lots of ancient oyster shells. Today, in most places, they are one of the most expensive foods you can buy.

A rich catch of oysters

A cuttlefish makes a healthier snack than sweets!

Improve and test your knowledge with...

CREEPY-CRAWLY FACTS

Take a refreshing look at water bugs and then try to tackle the brain-tingling minibeast quiz!

Cheers!

Modern water supplies are a lot cleaner than they used to be. Today, our water is treated and filtered so that when we turn on a tap we expect to get clean, clear water. However, water that hasn't been treated can contain more animals than an average zoo! They range from minute single-cell creatures to relatives of the crab and shrimp. Luckily, most water bugs are harmless and invisible to the naked eye – the ones in this picture have been magnified many times!

Seeing the lice

In the past, it was common for humans to be infested with parasites. Like many people of his day, Thomas à Becket (who was Archbishop of Canterbury, England, in the 12th century) was overrun with parasites. Official records in Canterbury Cathedral describe how his clothing was removed (in preparation for burial) to reveal thousands of fleas and mites.

1 Which bug holds the record for laying the most eggs?
a) superbug
b) termite
c) spider

2 What colour is the darter dragonfly?
a) bright red
b) red and black striped
c) bright green

3 Where does the ichneumon wasp lay her eggs?
a) in a curled-up leaf
b) in the body of the wood wasp larva
c) in an egg box

4 What is the cyclops named after?
a) a mythical giant
b) a bicycle
c) a cyclone

5 What does the adult daddy-long-legs eat?
a) blood
b) nectar
c) other bugs

6 Which sea bugs used to be called 'poor man's beef'?
a) sea urchins
b) sea cows
c) oysters

7 How did Darwin's beetle get its name?
a) it was first found in Darwin, Australia
b) its parents named it
c) it bit Charles Darwin

8 How does the male cricket attract the attention of a female?
a) he shares his dinner with her
b) he gives her presents
c) he sings to her

9 How big is a slug's egg?
a) 4m wide
b) 4mm wide
c) 12cm wide

10 How did the box jellyfish get its name?
a) because of its shape
b) because it lives in a box
c) because it boxes with its victims before eating them

Fanger lickin' good!

Everyone knows that spiders love to eat flies. Some, however, enjoy a much larger meal. The Australian barking spider, with its legspan of about 15cm, likes to eat chicken! After following a 15m trail, a farmer finally tracked down his missing chicken lying on the ground. When he tried to pick it up, he discovered that a determined barking spider was trying to pull the chicken down into its burrow.

Stinging the bees

Wasps and bees have been enemies for millions of years, but few wasps strike as much terror into the hearts of bees as the dreaded pirate wasp. This menacing wasp loiters around bee hives, waiting for bees to return. When the pirate wasp spots a victim, it pounces on it, forces it to the ground and stings it. Before the bee dies, the wasp sucks all the nectar, which the bee has collected, out of its body. Bees are so scared of these wasps that they will cower in the hive until the evil pirates have gone away.

Answers to the questions on the inside back cover

Matthew Robertson, who spent 12 years working with bugs at London Zoo, here answers all your creepy-crawly questions.

Can bugs tell the time?

Bugs do not have watches, but they are able to tell what time of day it is. Like all animals, bugs have special nerve cells near their eyes that act like internal clocks. Just as a clock constantly ticks away, so these cells send regular signals to the bug's brain reminding it that time is passing. Even if the bug cannot see any natural light, it can still keep a rough track of the time.

Do bugs get fat?

Because many bugs have hard, outer skeletons on their bodies, it is difficult for them to get fat. However, some bugs have bodies that are specially built to allow them to swell. Female bugs, such as the queen termite, often get very fat when they are producing eggs. Bugs that live in harsh places, like deserts, have to eat whenever they can. When these bugs are brought into captivity, they often overeat and become dangerously fat.

Do bugs lose their temper?

It is unlikely that bugs lose their temper in the same way as we do. However, if a bug feels threatened it may well fight to protect itself and its home. Social insects, such as bees, will gang up. When a bee stings, it releases a smell, which warns other bees of danger. Those that aren't being attacked will rush to help the others fight off an intruder. Ants, termites and wasps will also help to defend their nests.

Flambeau Butterfly

Bright colours, bold patterns and a very nasty taste keep predators away from the flambeau butterfly.

The flambeau (say 'flamm-bow') is one of the longest-lived of all butterflies. Some females can reach the ripe old age of six months, which is ancient in the butterfly world.

A HEALTHY DIET

One reason why the flambeau is able to live to this great age is because of its diet. It eats food that contains special extras that other butterflies do not get. Like you, the flambeau eats food that is rich in proteins and minerals. These ingredients help you, and it, to grow big and strong.

DIFFERENT MOUTHPARTS

The flambeau's mouthparts are different from those of most other butterflies, which means it can feed on the pollen of flowers. It is this pollen that provides it with protein. The flambeau gets minerals from a very strange source – it drinks the tears and urine of a type of alligator called a cayman!

An alligator's tears are not like yours. It doesn't shed tears when it is sad or hurt, but it does cry for an important reason. An alligator's body contains too many minerals and it has to get rid of some of them. The alligator gets rid of the excess minerals by passing them out in its urine and by 'crying' these salty tears. These tears also help to clean the alligator's eyes.

KEEP OUT!

Flambeau butterflies live in forests, where each male has his own territory – or space – just as you have your own home with a fence or wall around it. He fiercely guards his territory. If another male dares to enter, he bears down on it, flapping his wings and forcing it nearer the ground. The intruder usually gives up and flies away.

After mating, the female flambeau lays her eggs on the passionflower plant. If, after hatching, there are too many caterpillars in one place, they have a simple way of making more space for themselves – they eat each other! To stop this from happening, the female tries to lay her eggs in many different places on the plant.

POISONOUS FOOD

The passionflower plant not only provides the caterpillars with food, but it also helps to protect them from predators. The plant is poisonous and the caterpillars are able to store this poison in their bodies without becoming ill – but it does make them taste very nasty to any predator which tries to take a bite! The adult butterflies still contain enough of this poison in their bodies to make them an unpleasant snack.

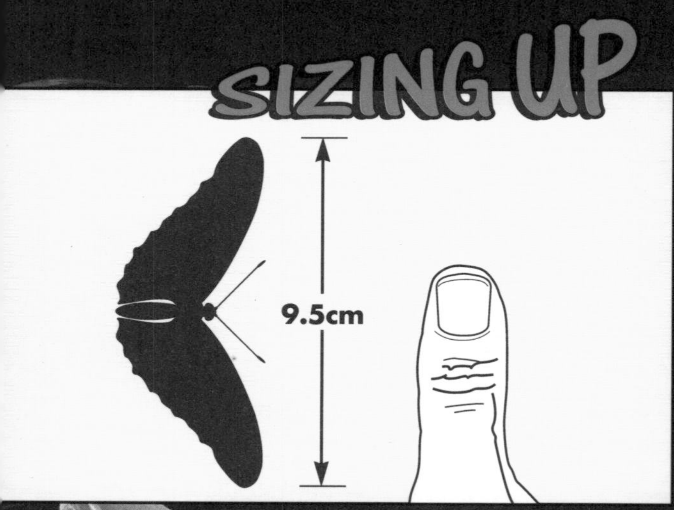

SHARE A TEAR

A flambeau spots a baby cayman (a type of alligator) and flutters down for a salty drink of its tears. The fierce animal will even allow several butterflies to feed at once.

- **SCIENTIFIC NAME:** *Dryas julia*
- **SIZE:** wingspan up to 9.5cm, caterpillar 4cm long
- **LIVES:** North, Central and South America
- **EATS:** caterpillar eats passionflower leaves; adult butterfly drinks cayman tears and eats pollen

The long spines of the caterpillar and the bright colours and bold patterns of the butterfly warn predators that the flambeau is not good to eat. Other butterflies and moths imitate these colours and markings to trick predators into thinking that they, too, taste nasty.

ALL CHANGE

When the caterpillar is ready to change into a butterfly, it spins a sticky, silk cocoon. The cocoon hardens, and its rough, dark brown surface fools predators into thinking that it is just a piece of wood. Safe and snug inside the cocoon, the pupa makes its incredible change from caterpillar to butterfly.

Small Talk

PLANT PROTECTION

To protect itself from being eaten up by hundreds of hungry caterpillars, the passionflower plant has a clever trick. At the base of its leaves – where the female butterfly prefers to lay her eggs – it produces small, pale green lumps, which look like flambeau eggs. When the female arrives, she thinks she has already laid eggs there, and goes somewhere else.

Clubbed antennae
With its wi[ngs] outstretche[d] flambeau butterfly measures 9
The butterfly sucks up liquid through its straw-like proboscis.
Basks in the sun with wings open.
Bright colours on the tops of its wings warn predators that this bug is poisonous.

Ogre-faced Spider

Like a fisherman throwing his net to catch fish, the ogre-faced spider spreads its web over its prey.

During the day, the ogre-faced spider rests among the leaves and fallen branches of the forest. With its eight legs neatly folded underneath its body, it looks like a twig from a tree and is difficult to see. But after sunset, this large, big-eyed spider wakes up and prepares to hunt for its supper.

SETTING A TRAP

The ogre-faced spider doesn't wait patiently and quietly, like other spiders, for insects to stumble into its web. It has another plan. Each night, it builds a thick, very sticky and stretchy web. Then, hanging upside down, it holds the web up in its four front legs – and waits!

LOOK OUT BELOW

When an insect comes near, the ogre-faced spider stretches the web out wide, drops it down over its victim and scoops it up. The spider usually eats its web when it has finished hunting at the end of each night. But sometimes it tucks it away among the twigs and branches for use the next night.

SIZING UP

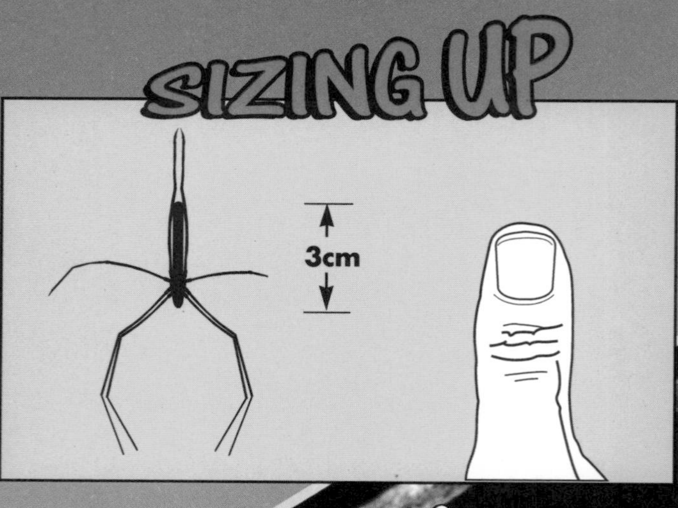

- **SCIENTIFIC NAME:** *Dinopis guatamalensis*
- **SIZE:** 12– 30mm
- **LIVES:** tropical forests of Central and South America
- **EATS:** insects

Horseshoe Crab

- **SCIENTIFIC NAME:** *Limulus polyphemus*
- **SIZE:** up to 60cm long, including tail
- **LIVES:** eastern shores of North America, also parts of the Far East
- **EATS:** algae, seaweed, worms, small fish and shellfish

SIZING UP

The huge, round shell of the horseshoe crab hides a creature that looks almost like a spider.

Horseshoe crabs, and their ancestors, have lived on Earth for over 300 million years and they have changed little since then. Under its horseshoe-shaped shell, the crab looks rather like its relation, the spider, except that it has five pairs of legs – not four.

USEFUL LEGS

The front four pairs have pincers for tearing food, such as worms or small fish, into bite-sized pieces. The back pair is used to crack open the shells of smaller shellfish, like clams.

RIGHT SIDE UP

Like a boatman with a long pole, the crab uses its tail to push itself along over the sand, and also to help flip itself over if it is turned on to its back. With nothing to protect its soft body, an upturned crab is helpless, and easy prey for predators.

ON TOW!

When it is time to breed, each female crab tows a male to the shore. Once the eggs are laid, fertilised and covered with sand, the pair go their separate ways.

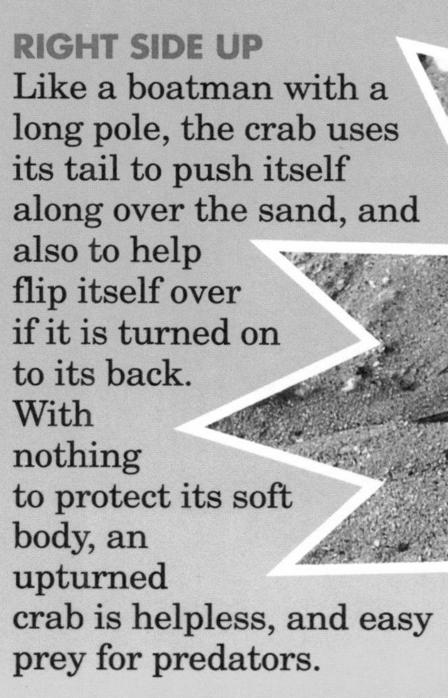

Veggie bugs

While many bugs love to sink their fangs into flesh, what some bugs long for is a juicy green leaf!

Not all bugs eat other small creatures. Some don't like meat, they prefer to eat plants. Animals that only eat plants are called herbivores – that's the same as being a vegetarian.

THE MUNCH BUNCH

The codlin moth larva (right), for example, thinks that there is nothing tastier than a crunchy apple. This is the young of a small, brown moth. Among humans, it has a bad reputation because of its fruit-eating ways. It has powerful jaws for cutting and boring its way through the toughest apples.

If you spot a caterpillar in your apple, look on the bright side – at least the fruit hasn't been filled with harmful pesticide!

CATERPILLAR ON THE COB

In the USA, humans check their corn on the cob carefully before they sink their teeth into it. Occasionally, they find that a wiggly corn ear worm (a type of caterpillar) has been munching its way through the corn and is still there! When it can't find corn, this worm eats cotton plants and tomatoes.

POTATO MANIA

Potatoes, tomatoes and other plants make a filling tea for the hungry hawkmoth caterpillar. Like other caterpillars, this one needs to eat a lot of food in order to build up its strength and survive its pupal stage. Some species eat trees.

STRAWBERRIES AND GREENS

Young weevils have more refined tastes. These larvae love plant stems, leaves and fruit. Among their favourites are cherries, plums, strawberries, pears, peaches and apples. Though tiny, these animals eat their food at an alarming rate, and a crowd of them could chomp their way through several plants in a few days! Some weevils prefer stodge – they choose grains, breakfast cereal or flour.

DINNER CUCUMBER

No prizes for guessing what the spotted cucumber beetle likes to munch. Cucumbers – though not necessarily spotted ones! It is partial to any member of the cucumber family, such as marrows, courgettes and juicy melons.

MINI MILLERS!

Harvester ants are little herbivorous millers. When they find seeds, they bite off their tips to stop them sprouting, before carrying them back to store in tiny granaries inside their nest.

A codlin moth larva pops up, juice dripping from its jaws, to find out who has taken a bite out of its apple.

ACCIDENTAL MEAT-EATER

Stick and leaf insects are such slow-movers and bad fighters that they can never catch live food! The leaf insect usually eats only leaves, but when it is living in very overcrowded places, it occasionally takes a bite out of another leaf insect by mistake.These bugs are so well camouflaged that they easily mistake each other for real leaves!

A cicada uses its sharp mouthparts to suck sap.

In spring, the larva of the lackey moth (right) hatches from its egg and spends its 'childhood' in the treetops munching through leaves.

MUNCH OR SUCK?

One tree can provide a whole crowd of bugs with food. Whether a creepy-crawly prefers bark, nectar, pollen, fungus or leaves – there's something for every kind of bug in a tree. Most vegetarian bugs don't need big jaws to catch, kill and chew up their prey. Let's face it, leaves and flowers can't escape and don't fight back! Instead, bugs either have long feeding tubes, munching mouthparts or sap-sucking beaks, depending on what they eat.

SUGAR PLEASE

Bees have a very sweet tooth. They live on sugary nectar and pollen from plants. Some have developed especially long tongues to reach into the centre of flowers. They also look for pollen, which they collect in baskets on their back legs and carry back to their nests to feed their young.

BIG AND BEAUTIFUL

The violet bee (left) is one of the biggest bees in the world. Its proboscis is sometimes longer than its body. This 2.5cm-long bug uses its proboscis like a bendy straw to reach the nectar inside narrow flower heads. The females have hairy back legs, which they use to collect pollen from the flowers.

The long-tongued violet bee makes a bee-line for the blossom.

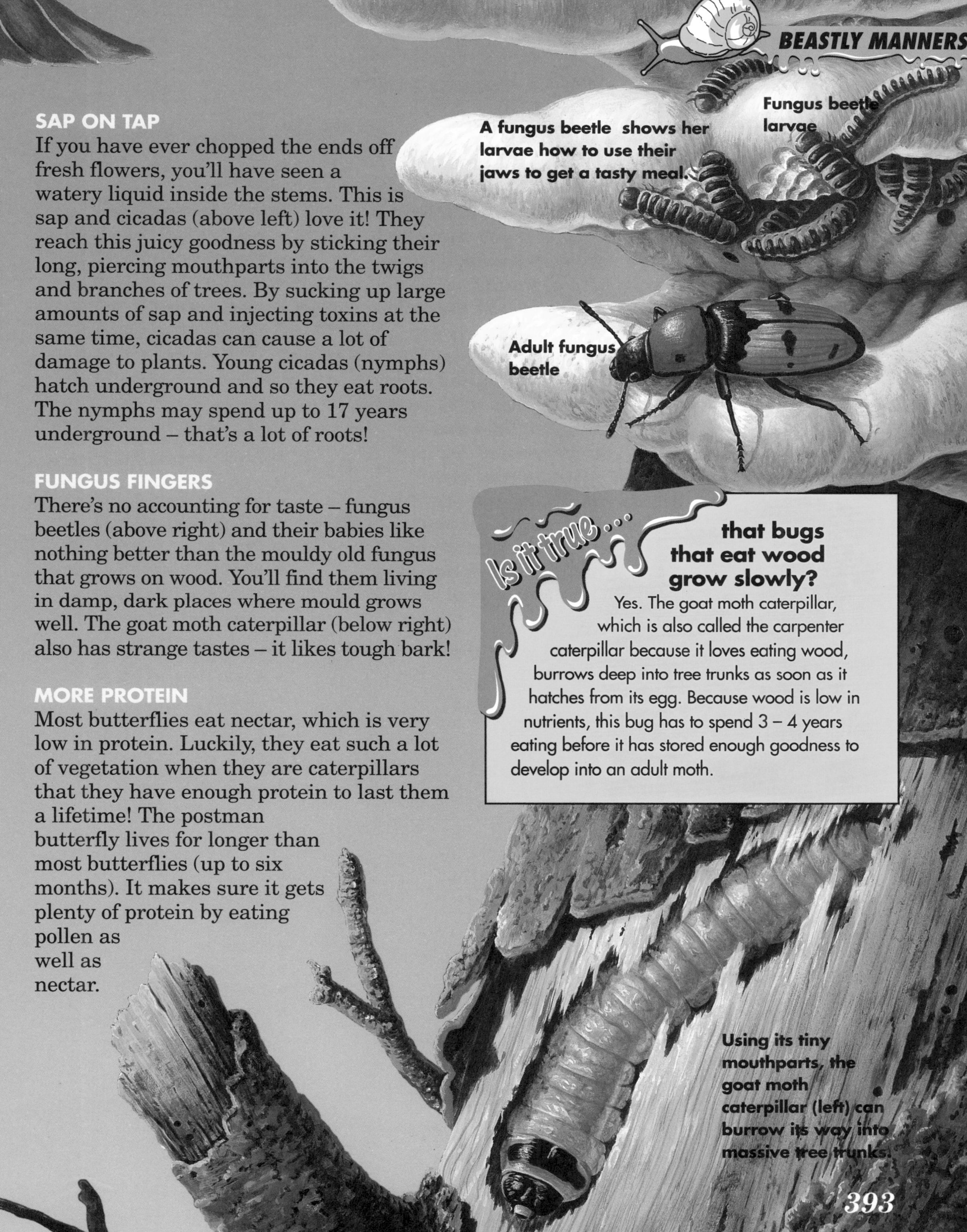

A fungus beetle shows her larvae how to use their jaws to get a tasty meal.
Fungus beetle larvae
Adult fungus beetle
Using its tiny mouthparts, the goat moth caterpillar (left) can burrow its way into massive tree trunks.

SAP ON TAP

If you have ever chopped the ends off fresh flowers, you'll have seen a watery liquid inside the stems. This is sap and cicadas (above left) love it! They reach this juicy goodness by sticking their long, piercing mouthparts into the twigs and branches of trees. By sucking up large amounts of sap and injecting toxins at the same time, cicadas can cause a lot of damage to plants. Young cicadas (nymphs) hatch underground and so they eat roots. The nymphs may spend up to 17 years underground – that's a lot of roots!

FUNGUS FINGERS

There's no accounting for taste – fungus beetles (above right) and their babies like nothing better than the mouldy old fungus that grows on wood. You'll find them living in damp, dark places where mould grows well. The goat moth caterpillar (below right) also has strange tastes – it likes tough bark!

MORE PROTEIN

Most butterflies eat nectar, which is very low in protein. Luckily, they eat such a lot of vegetation when they are caterpillars that they have enough protein to last them a lifetime! The postman butterfly lives for longer than most butterflies (up to six months). It makes sure it gets plenty of protein by eating pollen as well as nectar.

Is it true... that bugs that eat wood grow slowly?

Yes. The goat moth caterpillar, which is also called the carpenter caterpillar because it loves eating wood, burrows deep into tree trunks as soon as it hatches from its egg. Because wood is low in nutrients, this bug has to spend 3 – 4 years eating before it has stored enough goodness to develop into an adult moth.

Bug identikits

In the last issue, we showed you how to make a pitfall trap. Now you can catch some bugs in your trap and identify them with the help of these bug identikits. These are some of the most common bugs you may catch. As you find each bug, write in the spaces provided where you found it and what the date was. You may also catch bugs that are not on this list. Once you've got the idea, you can use our A-Z and CREATURE FILES to make your own, longer list. Another thing you might like to do is to draw bugs that you find, or trace the identikit picture on this page and then colour it in according to the colours of the bug in your trap.

Name: Earthworm

- Size: 7 – 15cm
- Legs: 0
- Wings: 0
- Body parts: from 30 upwards
- Date ________________
- Where you found it ________________

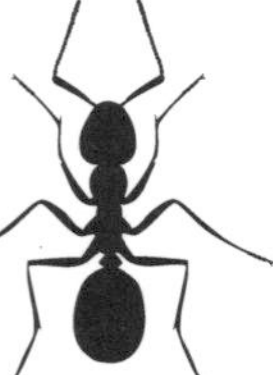

Name: Ant

- Size: 2 – 14mm
- Legs: 6
- Wings: 0 – 4
- Body parts: 3
- Date ________________
- Where you found it ________________

Name: Harvestman

- Size: 7mm (body length)
- Legs: 8
- Wings: 0
- Body parts: 2
- Date ________________
- Where you found it ________________

Name: Springtail

- Size: 1 – 9mm
- Legs: 6
- Wings: 0
- Body parts: 3
- Date ________________
- Where you found it ________________

Name: Rove beetle

- Size: 2 – 32mm
- Legs: 6
- Wings: 0 – 2
- Body parts: 3
- Date ________________
- Where you found it ________________

Name: Ground beetle

- Size: 9 – 14mm
- Legs: 6
- Wings: 0
- Body parts: 3
- Date ________________
- Where you found it ________________

Name: Ladybird

- Size: 2 - 9mm
- Legs: 6
- Wings: 2
- Body parts: 3
- Date ______________________
- Where you found it ____________

____

Name: House spider

- Size: 5cm
- Legs: 8
- Wings: 0
- Body parts: 2
- Date ______________________
- Where you found it ____________

____

Name: Earwig

- Size: 5 - 30mm
- Legs: 6
- Wings: 0 - 2
- Body parts: 3
- Date ______________________
- Where you found it ____________

____

Name: Woodlouse

- Size: 7 - 15mm
- Legs: 14
- Wings: 0
- Body parts: 12
- Date ______________________
- Where you found it ____________

____

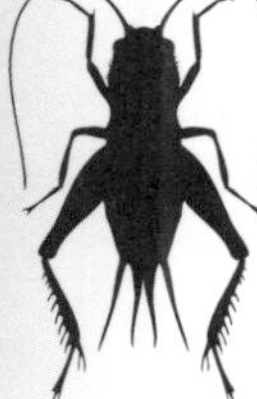

Name: Cricket

- Size: 2 - 50mm
- Legs: 6
- Wings: 0 - 4
- Body parts: 3
- Date ______________________
- Where you found it ____________

____

Name: True bug

- Size: 3 - 40mm
- Legs: 6
- Wings: 0 - 4
- Body parts: 3
- Date ______________________
- Where you found it ____________

____

Name: Centipede

- Size: 4cm
- Legs: 30
- Wings: 0
- Body parts: 18
- Date ______________________
- Where you found it ____________

____

Small Talk

FREEDOM FOR BUGS

Once you have studied your bugs, you must release them. By keeping them prisoner, you will cause them harm. Simply let the bugs crawl out of the pitfall trap and they will return to their natural home.

3-D
MINIBEASTS

Garden spider

This might be the first time you've come face to face with a garden spider! Despite being difficult to spot, the common garden spider lives up to its name and really is the most common spider in Europe! This female is thinking how lucky she was to be born a girl. She's much bigger and hardier than a male, and what's more she can spin herself a mean-looking web to catch flies and rest her eight legs. Baby spiders of both sexes can build webs, but when you see that huge, beautiful orb (round) web stretched between two branches, you can bet it was an adult female that built it!

What is an annelid?

Think of a worm and you probably imagine a slippery earthworm. In fact, that's just one of 8,700 types of worm!

The proper scientific name for worms is annelids (say 'anna-lids'). They are shy bugs, which hide under the ground, in sand or deep in the sea.

MUSCLEY TUBES

The name annelid means 'ringed body'. All annelids have certain things in common. Their bodies are all divided into similar-sized segments (parts). They all have very strong muscles, which run across and down their bodies and they do not have legs or bones. They do have a gut, which runs from their head to their tail end.

OUT OF SIGHT

Annelids are defenceless animals. They don't have sharp claws, big jaws or a sting. To keep themselves out of danger, they lurk in safe places.

TAKE THREE

Like all bugs, each type of worm has a fancy scientific name, which is almost as long as the worm itself! There are three classes of worms. These are:

- Oligochaeta (say 'oli-go-key-ta')
- Hirudinea (say 'here-ru-din-ee-a')
- Polychaeta (say 'pol-ee-key-ta')

EAT DIRT

Oligochaeta, which means 'few bristles' includes the familiar earthworm (below) and its cousins, which live in fresh water. Most of the members of this group eat dirt. When it is tunnelling through the ground, the earthworm swallows the earth in its path. Most of the soil that is swallowed is dumped above ground as waste. The worm squeezes it out of its body through its anus (the opening at the end of the gut) and leaves it at the entrance to its burrow. This little pile is called a cast. While the soil was travelling through the worm's body, the bug absorbed all the goodness from the earth, including vegetation, seeds and eggs.

An earthworm is a long, muscular bug that usually only ventures out of its underground burrow at night.

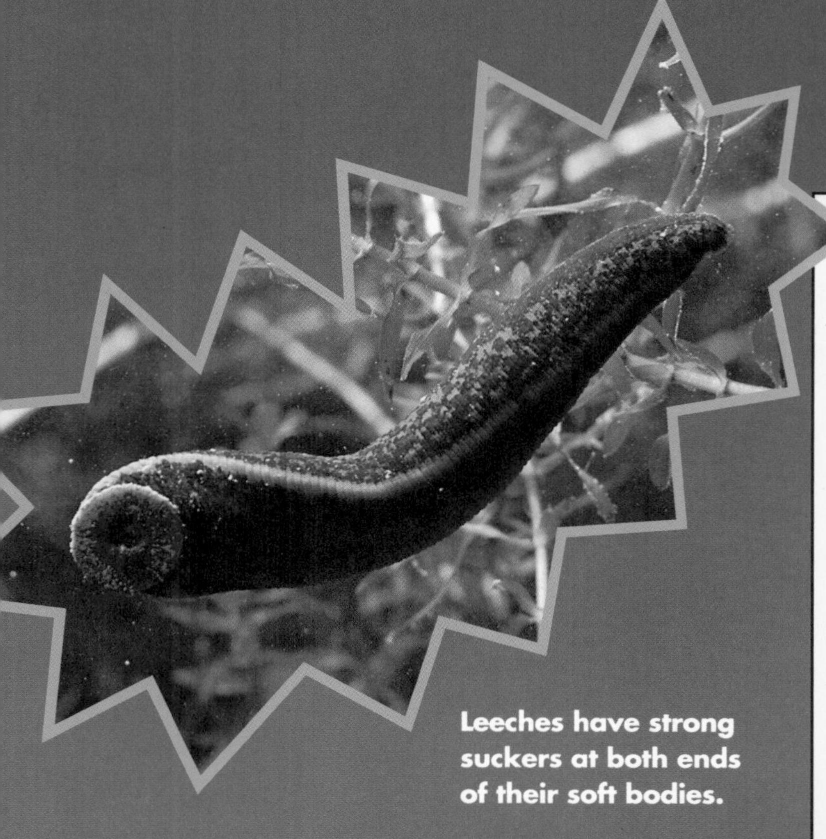

Leeches have strong suckers at both ends of their soft bodies.

Small Talk

A LONG STORY

Earthworms and sea worms are some of the longest annelids. Certain species, which live in the Mediterranean sea, grow up to 80cm long. In warmer places, such as Australia, giant land worms can grow up to 3m! That's almost as long as a small car! Imagine that wriggling up your leg! The record for the longest ever worm found is held by a South African giant worm which measured over 6.5m. 'Head' to 'tail', two of these massive annelids could easily span a tennis court. The smallest worm is a parasitic worm, which is just 0.5mm long!

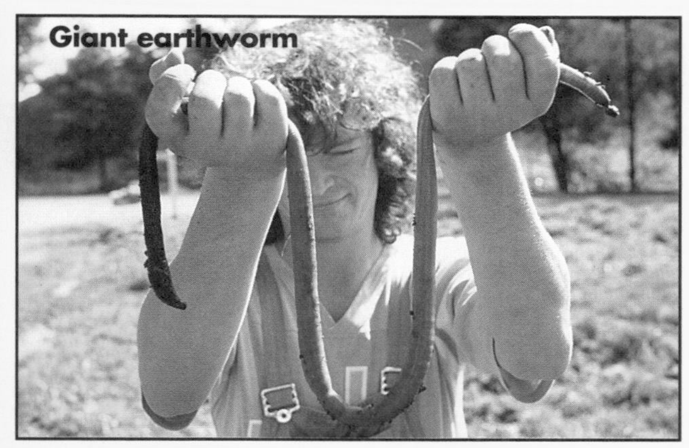

Giant earthworm

HEY SUCKER

Hirudinea is the scientific word for leeches (above), which usually live in shallow, fresh water or humid forests. Leeches, the vampires of the worm world, live on the blood of animals. They stick to their unsuspecting host and inject it with a chemical to help the blood flow freely and to numb the area they are feeding on. As the host can't feel any pain, the leech can drink away at the blood un-noticed.

FANNING FOR FOOD

Polychaeta, which means 'many bristles', is the scientific name for bristleworms. They are almost always found in salty water. Famous members of the bristleworm group include lugworms and fan worms. While some swim and burrow to find food, others, like fan worms (right), attach themselves to rocks and stay there! They wave their tentacles to trap microscopic bugs as they float by.

Fan worms are lazy. They use their long tentacles as a fishing net, waving them in the water to catch tiny bugs that float by.

bugs dash around
ng for food. Annelids
move very far or fast.
w do they manage?

LAZY LUGWORMS

A lugworm is a wriggly, red creature, which is found at the seaside. Under the sea, it makes burrows, which can be up to 50cm deep. These slippery engineers build U-shaped tunnels with two entrances. The lugworm crawls up one side of the tunnel to catch its food and then reverses the other way to leave its cast on the surface of the sand. Their homes are easy to spot in damp sand, when the tide goes out.

Lugworm

BEFORE AND AFTER

Some of the prettiest worms are the bristleworms that live in the oceans. The peacock worm (left), builds itself a protective funnel from sand, mud or chalk. It mixes its building material with mucus (slime) to make it easier to mould. It sits inside the tube and shows off its bright fan of feathery tentacles, which can be red, pink or green. These are used to breathe and to filter the water for food, but any sudden movement or bright light will make it withdraw into its tube.

Mouth

vith
s

tective
nel

1 Like many sea worms, the peacock worm gets its food straight from the water. Tiny hairs on each stiff tentacle waft food particles towards the worm's mouth. Only the smallest pieces of food are selected, anything else is spat out. The tentacles also provide a surface through which oxygen can pass – without them, the peacock worm wouldn't be able to breathe.

Christmas tree worm

A Christmas tree worm isn't decorated with fairy lights and it isn't green. In fact, this marine bristleworm can be deep blue, red or white.

Light catches the long, iridescent bristles that surround a sea mouse's body. This one has been turned upside-down.

Sea mouse

UNDERWATER CHRISTMAS TREE

The Christmas tree worm (above) has feathery tentacles, which look just like the branches of a fir tree. It lives on areas of living coral, where it waves its 'branches' around and waits for tiny pieces of food to pass by. The worms come in all different colours, but this one looks like it is covered in snow!

GLOW-IN-THE-DARK MOUSE

With a furry coat and a ring of bristles, the sea mouse (above) looks more like a little rodent than a worm! When its fringe of long bristles catches the light, it gives off rainbow colours. Underneath its fur coat it has a scaly body, which is about 15cm long. The sea mouse crawls along the sea bed and eats other worms and bugs.

Peacock worm with tentacles closed

2 Bristleworms' tentacles are sensitive to movement and changes in light. A sudden burst of light will make the peacock worm close them together and go back into its tube.

Is it true... that if an earthworm gets cut in two, both ends can survive as separate animals?

No. If an earthworm is cut in two, the larger section will survive and the smaller one will die. If, for example, an earthworm loses its tail end, it will re-grow a new replacement tail and this larger section will survive. Similarly if an earthworm loses its head end, it will grow a new head. It will not become two new worms.

Grassland

Grasslands are areas where grass grows naturally. For some of the year, cattle keep the grass short, but for the rest of the time it grows long and lush. Many bugs make it their home.

Long grass provides a home to a wide range of bugs. Those living on the ground are well hidden from predators, such as birds. Crickets sing and spiders sunbathe or weave webs between blades of grass.

FIERCE HUNTER

When a tiger beetle larva (left) hatches from its egg, it digs a deep burrow – sometimes over 1m deep – in which to hide from its prey. It is a fierce predator itself and has huge upward-pointing jaws on its head and lots of eyes so that it can see all around. When hunting, the larva sits at the entrance of its tunnel, with its head blocking the opening. When the prey comes near, the larva makes a sudden grab for it with its large jaws and drags it into its burrow.

Meadow ant

Tiger beetle larva

This tiger beetle larva grabs a meadow ant in its large jaws. It will pull it into its tunnel and eat the struggling bug. Turn the page to see what this vicious predator looks like when it grows up.

bugs

Small Talk

GRASS, NOT ROADS!

Grasslands are among the fastest disappearing habitats in the world. Over the years, many of these areas have been turned into motorways or railway lines. Although many people want to save the grasslands and protest against the building of more roads, still the destruction goes on. It is important to protect the grasslands from further damage. Once they are destroyed completely, the bugs and other wildlife that usually live there will become homeless.

LITTLE AND LARGE

The male ladybird spider has a red body with black spots which are ringed with white hairs. At a glance, it looks like a ladybird, which is how it gets its name. The male doesn't eat and spends its short life wandering freely over the ground, looking for a mate. The female ladybird spider has a sinister black coat and is about three times bigger than the male. She lives in a shallow silk-lined burrow. A fierce hunter, she will eat most things that come her way.

The female ladybird spider (below) spins a web close to the burrow entrance to capture other bugs. She never has to leave the safety of her burrow to feed. The male spider (left) can come as close to his mate as he wants, without fear of being eaten.

RARE SINGER

The field cricket loves to live in warm, grassy habitats, which have soft soil. This dark, bulky bug isn't very good at flying. Instead, it walks or makes short hops as it searches for food, such as leaves, seeds, roots and sometimes small animals. The male spends its life sitting close to its burrow, singing. If another male ventures too close, they will threaten each other and may even fight to the death.

The male field cricket (left) sings by rubbing veins on one forewing against veins on the other forewing. He sings to attract females and warn off rivals. In good weather, he may sing all night, stopping for a short period just before dawn.

Clinging to the blades of grass, or flying high above the flowers, some bugs prefer to live in the open air above the grasslands.

SUNBATHING MOTHER

The nursery web spider likes dry, grassy areas, where it can lie out in the sun. The female seeks an open spot on a leaf, where she sits in a strange position. Drawing her legs into her sides, she pushes the front part of her body forward and exposes her egg sac to the warm sunshine. This stops her bag of eggs from getting mouldy in damp weather and speeds up the development of the young spiders inside it.

VICIOUS HUNTER

A heavy-bodied, dark-green insect with black spots, the wart-biter cricket is a fierce hunter. It has powerful jaws and sharp mandibles for capturing prey and will kill and eat an adult grasshopper whenever it can find one. It will also eat plants, seeds and roots. The wart-biter is a great singer. Its song is made up of long bursts of clicking sounds. Starting slowly, the clicking gets faster and faster and the song lasts for several minutes at a time. In some parts of Europe, wart-biters are becoming very rare.

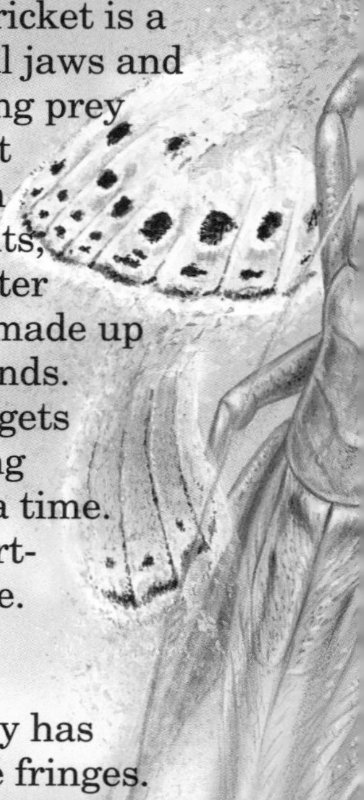

RARE BEAUTY

The adult large blue butterfly has bright blue wings with white fringes. It may measure 28 – 38mm from wingtip to wingtip. The large blue butterfly flutters between flowers, sipping nectar. Like most butterflies, it has a short life. Sadly, this beautiful bug is quite rare in parts of Europe, but it can still be seen in some countries from May to August. It is extinct in Britain.

When the young spiders are ready to hatch, the female nursery web spider (above) attaches the egg sac to a bunch of leaves and spins a silken tent over it. She stands guard until the youngsters are ready to scurry off on their own.

In grasslands, the large blue butterfly has many enemies, such as this wart-biter cricket (above left). But by destroying the grasslands and making this beautiful bug homeless, it is humans who are its greatest enemy.

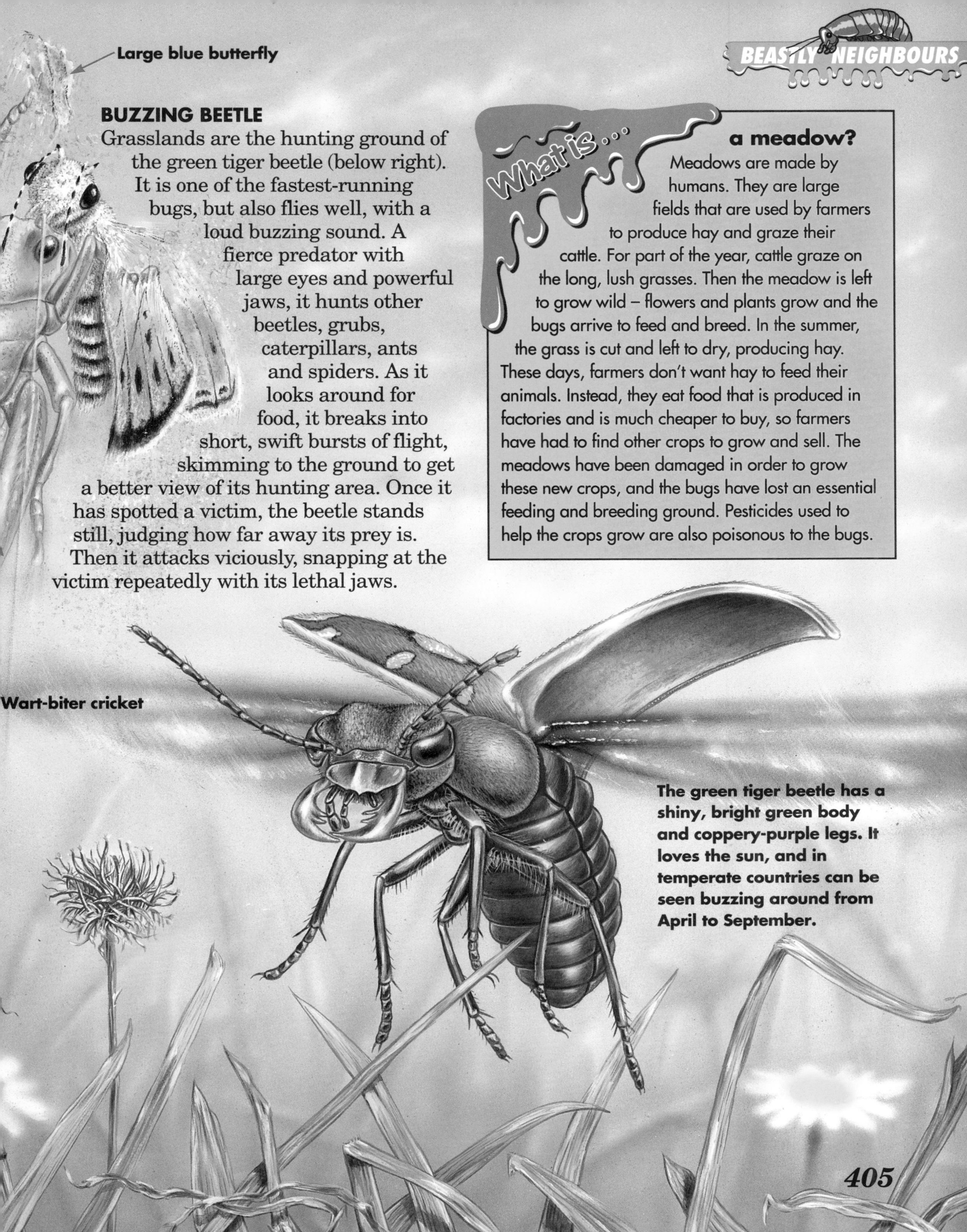

BUZZING BEETLE

Grasslands are the hunting ground of the green tiger beetle (below right). It is one of the fastest-running bugs, but also flies well, with a loud buzzing sound. A fierce predator with large eyes and powerful jaws, it hunts other beetles, grubs, caterpillars, ants and spiders. As it looks around for food, it breaks into short, swift bursts of flight, skimming to the ground to get a better view of its hunting area. Once it has spotted a victim, the beetle stands still, judging how far away its prey is. Then it attacks viciously, snapping at the victim repeatedly with its lethal jaws.

What is... a meadow?

Meadows are made by humans. They are large fields that are used by farmers to produce hay and graze their cattle. For part of the year, cattle graze on the long, lush grasses. Then the meadow is left to grow wild – flowers and plants grow and the bugs arrive to feed and breed. In the summer, the grass is cut and left to dry, producing hay. These days, farmers don't want hay to feed their animals. Instead, they eat food that is produced in factories and is much cheaper to buy, so farmers have had to find other crops to grow and sell. The meadows have been damaged in order to grow these new crops, and the bugs have lost an essential feeding and breeding ground. Pesticides used to help the crops grow are also poisonous to the bugs.

The green tiger beetle has a shiny, bright green body and coppery-purple legs. It loves the sun, and in temperate countries can be seen buzzing around from April to September.

Improve and test your knowledge with...

Don't get caught out in a shower of crabs – instead, try the mega minibeast quiz!

Artistic bugs

Artists have used many different methods to create paintings. Some use brushes, while others use cloths, wheels and even their feet. One artist has chosen to use an earwig. First, he coats some glass with soot and then lets the earwig walk across it. Its footprints leave a pattern. If you want to own one of these works of art, you should either make your own or start saving up – at more than £1,000 a picture, they're not cheap!

Flower power

Bees are famous for being tireless workers. A worker bee will visit up to 10,000 flowers a day collecting pollen and nectar. On average, the bees from a single nest will visit more than 27,600 million flowers a year. This is why bees are one of the most important pollinators of plants.

Can you sing?

A male cricket 'sings' to attract a female. It needs to mate with as many females as it can to make sure that plenty of babies are born. This means that it has to 'sing' loudly so that females a long way off can hear. Most crickets use their burrows as amplifiers. This means that the holes that they live in make their 'song' louder and travel further, just like a loud speaker. However, one clever field cricket made its home by an empty soft drink can. He nested just outside the can opening, so that when he 'sang', it made his mating song louder than ever!

It's raining crabs

Occasionally, people report that they have seen strange things falling from the skies. Showers of nuts, frogs, fish and even prawns have been recorded. Once, in May 1930, a small town in northern Australia was caught in a downpour of bright-red crabs! It is thought that they were sucked up into the sky by a small tornado out at sea, called a waterspout, only to be dumped 80km away, several hours later.

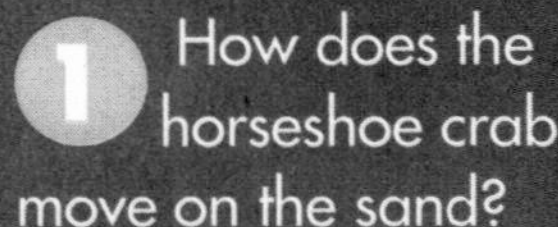

1 How does the horseshoe crab move on the sand?
a) it hops
b) it walks
c) it pushes itself along with its tail

2 How long can the average flambeau butterfly live?
a) 6 months
b) 6 weeks
c) 16 weeks

3 How does the ogre-faced spider catch its prey?
a) it waits for insects to fly into its web
b) it drops its web over its victim
c) it paralyses its victim

4 Which is the most common spider found in Europe?
a) the house spider
b) the garden spider
c) the funnel web spider

5 Why does the tiger beetle dig a burrow?
a) to have a sleep
b) to lay its eggs
c) to ambush its prey

6 What does the adult deer fly like to eat?
a) shrimps
b) blood
c) it never eats

7 What does 'annelid' mean?
a) ringed body
b) slimy body
c) wriggly body

8 Why does the nursery web spider put its eggs in the sun?
a) to cook them
b) to show them off
c) to help its babies develop and to stop the eggs from going mouldy

9 Why are goat moth caterpillars known as carpenters?
a) because their heads look like little hammers
b) because their teeth look like nails
c) because they eat wood

10 What does a death's-head hawkmoth's proboscis look like?
a) a long straw
b) a dagger
c) a spoon

Answers to the questions on the inside back cover

Q and A?

Matthew Robertson, who spent 12 years working with bugs at London Zoo, here answers all your creepy-crawly questions.

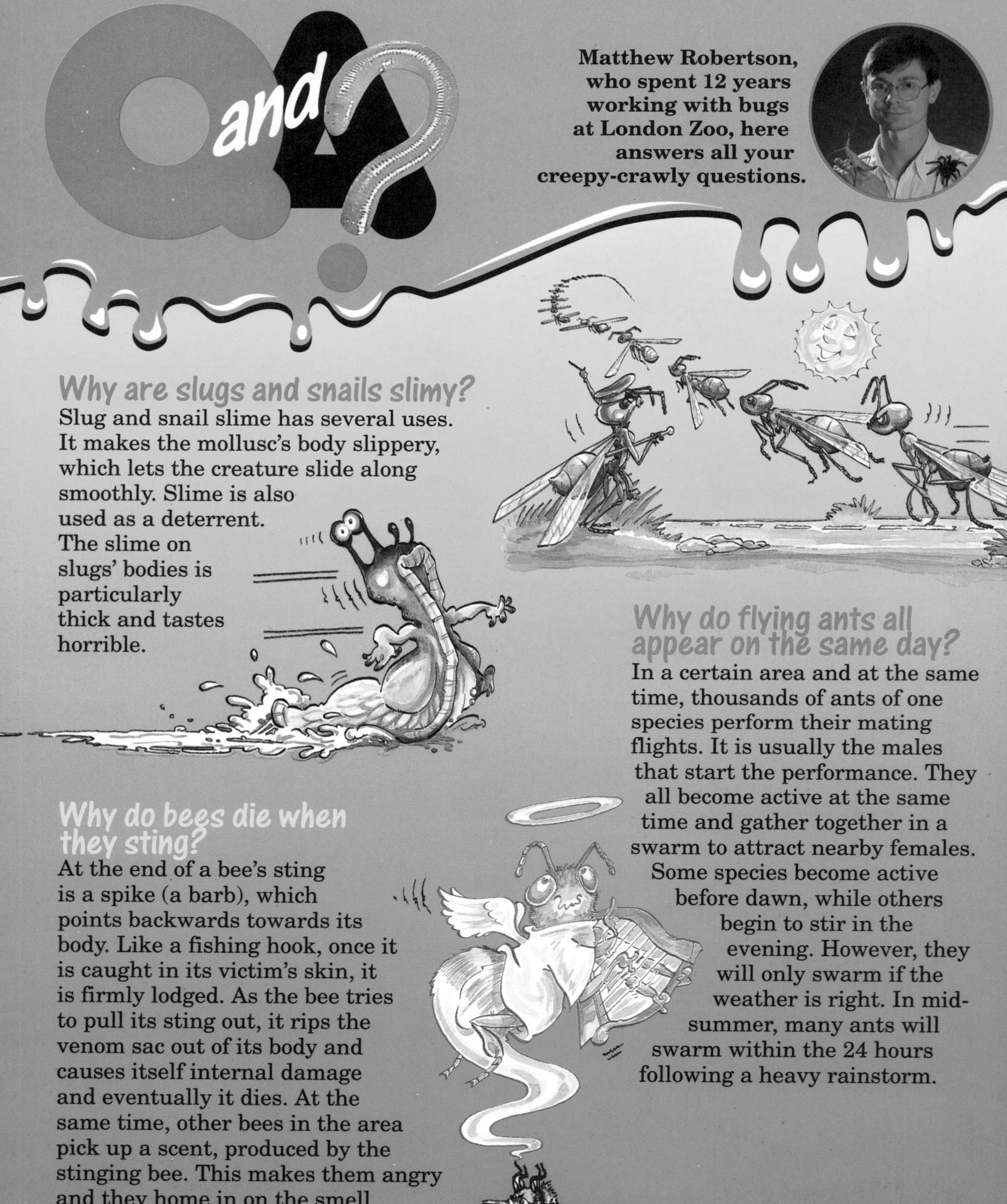

Why are slugs and snails slimy?

Slug and snail slime has several uses. It makes the mollusc's body slippery, which lets the creature slide along smoothly. Slime is also used as a deterrent. The slime on slugs' bodies is particularly thick and tastes horrible.

Why do bees die when they sting?

At the end of a bee's sting is a spike (a barb), which points backwards towards its body. Like a fishing hook, once it is caught in its victim's skin, it is firmly lodged. As the bee tries to pull its sting out, it rips the venom sac out of its body and causes itself internal damage and eventually it dies. At the same time, other bees in the area pick up a scent, produced by the stinging bee. This makes them angry and they home in on the smell from the dying bee.

Why do flying ants all appear on the same day?

In a certain area and at the same time, thousands of ants of one species perform their mating flights. It is usually the males that start the performance. They all become active at the same time and gather together in a swarm to attract nearby females. Some species become active before dawn, while others begin to stir in the evening. However, they will only swarm if the weather is right. In mid-summer, many ants will swarm within the 24 hours following a heavy rainstorm.

Pseudoscorpion

Pseudoscorpions first appeared on Earth over 65 million years ago. In all that time, this eight-legged bug has hardly changed.

The tiny pseudoscorpion (say 'syoo-doe-score-pion') is not easy to find. It never grows to more than about 1cm long and lives in small, secret places. It crawls under stones or piles of leaves, into bark, or even into the nests of ants or bees. To keep itself warm in the winter time, or when it needs a safe place to shed its skin or lay its eggs, it makes itself a nest out of silk. This silk is like that used by spiders for their webs.

FALSE SCORPION

The pseudoscorpion gets it name because it looks like a real scorpion, except that it doesn't have a long, stinging tail. The first part of the word ('pseudo') means 'false'.

DEAD STILL

Like a real scorpion, the pseudoscorpion walks with its huge claws held out in front. If it is threatened, it pulls its claws in over its body and lies perfectly still until the danger has passed.

Flat body can squeeze under rocks.
Pseudoscorpions never have stings.
Tiny armoured plates protect the bug.
Silk is made in the bug's mouthparts.
Sensitive bristles cover its claws.
Eight legs
The tips of its claws contain venom.
An ant gives the lazy pseudoscorpion a lift. It will not be harmed by its passenger.

TAKEN FOR A RIDE

Why walk – when you can get a lift? This pseudoscorpion has leaped off a blade of grass and landed safely on a passing ant. It picked up the sound of the ant with the hairs on its sensitive claws.

Small Talk

LONG-DISTANCE TRAVEL

Although it cannot travel very far on its own, this does not stop the pseudoscorpion getting about. It just hitches a ride to faraway places and new supplies of food – by holding on to insects, or to birds and mammals!

SAY HELLO

When two pseudoscorpions of the same species meet, they shake their claws at each other as a kind of greeting – or to warn each other away.

SENSITIVE TOUCH

Because it has such small, weak eyes – or even no eyes at all – the pseudoscorpion finds its prey by touch, feeling for it with the long, sensitive bristles on its claws. The tips of these claws are venomous and it uses them to stab its victim.

ON THE RIGHT TRAIL

Different species of pseudoscorpion have various ways of producing their young. To start with, the male places some sperm in a little case on the ground. The female has to find this sperm and take it into her body to fertilise her eggs. Some males just leave the female to find the sperm by herself. Some spin two long threads of silk leading to the sperm – all the female has to do is follow the pathway between the threads.

LET'S DANCE

Other males attract the female by doing a 'dance', waving their claws, tapping their legs and shaking their abdomens! If the female decides to join in, the male takes her claws and dances backwards and forwards, guiding her to the sperm.

BUILDING A NEST

Before laying her eggs, the female collects tiny scraps of wood and other bits and pieces and arranges them in a circle around herself. She then sticks them together with silk to make a nest.

BABY CARE

Inside her nest, she lays between 2 – 50 eggs in a pouch under her body. The eggs hatch and the babies grow inside this pouch, where they live on fluid from their mother's body.

- **SCIENTIFIC NAME:** Pseudoscorpionida
- **SIZE:** up to 1cm long
- **LIVES:** all over the world
- **EATS:** small insects and spiders as well as other small land creatures

Spanish Fly

The adult Spanish fly is a vegetarian, but its young prefer a more meaty diet.

The Spanish fly isn't a true fly at all, but a beetle. It comes out into the open in mid-summer.

NESTING PLACE

The female lays her eggs near the nests of solitary bees (bees which live on their own). When the young hatch, they make their way into the bee's nest. Here, their bodies go through a dramatic change – they shed their skins and emerge as tiny, maggot-like creatures. These live in the nest and feed on the young of the bee.

POISONOUS BODY

Although a Spanish fly has a strong smell, there is another reason not to get too close to this bug. It belongs to a group of insects called 'blister beetles'. When they are frightened, they ooze a burning poison that would make your skin blister. The Spanish fly is one of the most poisonous of all blister beetles. Long ago, people made poison from the bodies of blister beetles, or used them for medicine.

- **SCIENTIFIC NAME:** *Lytta vesicatoria*
- **SIZE:** 1 – 2cm long
- **LIVES:** central and southern Europe, Siberia, North America
- **EATS:** young eats bee larvae; adult eats the leaves of trees and branches where it lives

SIZING UP

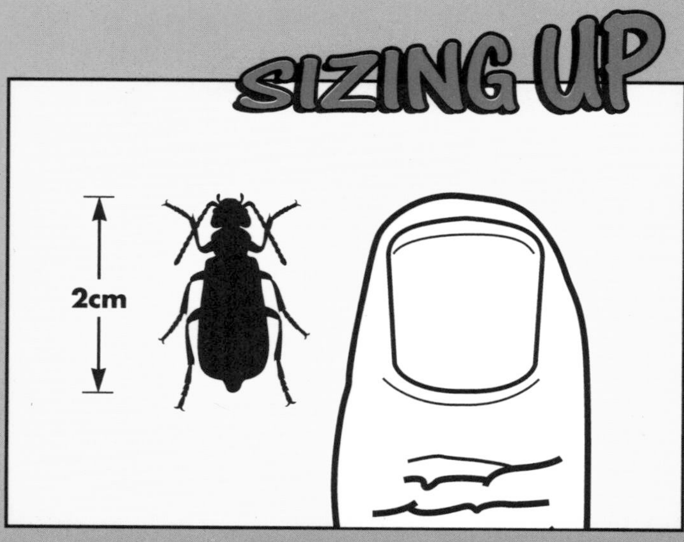

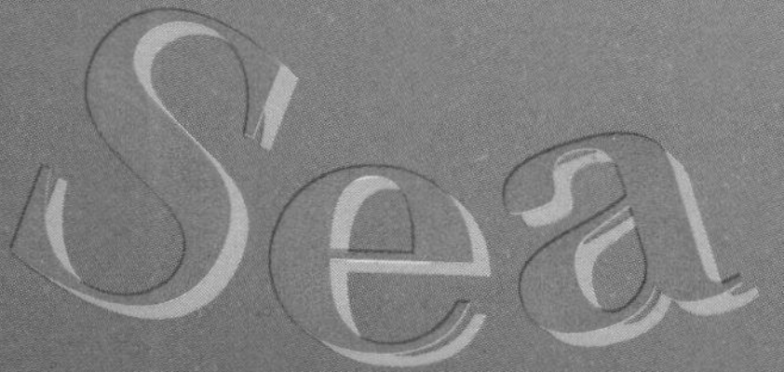

Sea Anemone

Although it looks like a beautiful flower, the sea anemone is really a flesh-eating animal.

Waving gently in the water, the 'petals' of the sea anemone are really its tentacles. These sting any small sea creature that brushes against them, paralysing it with their venom. Then they draw the victim down into the anemone's mouth, which is tucked away in the centre of the ring of tentacles.

FIRM HOLD

This bug clings to rocks or coral, using a sticky sucker at its base. It holds on so firmly that not even waves can budge it.

MAKING BABIES

Different sea anemones have different ways of reproducing themselves. Some produce eggs, and some grow a ring of baby anemones around their base. These break away when they are big enough and float off to find a new home. Others have an even simpler method – they just divide themselves in half to produce two anemones instead of one!

NO RELATION

If a new anemone settles too close to another from a different parent, the first anemone may attack it!

- **SCIENTIFIC NAME:** *Actinia equina*
- **SIZE:** 10cm wide with its tentacles spread out
- **LIVES:** seas all over the world
- **EATS:** small fish and other sea creatures

SIZING UP

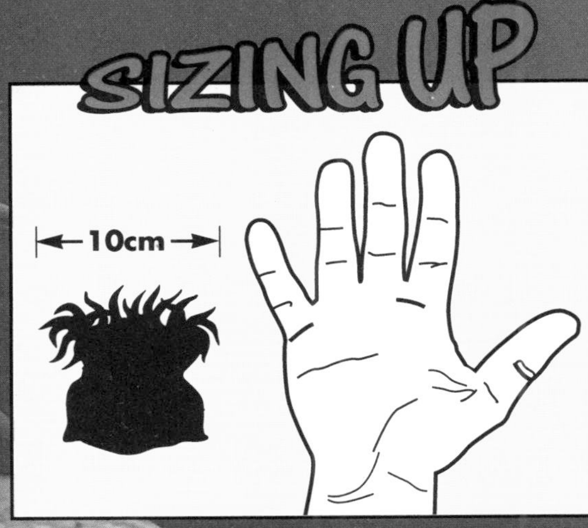

Mucking around!

The sight of a fresh pat of elephant dung causes great excitement to a group of scavengers – the dung beetles.

Dung beetles gather around a freshly laid pat as soon as they get their first whiff! To these bugs, it's a feast, the perfect place to stash their eggs and a valuable food source for their young.

CLEAN-UP JOB

As these bugs go about their daily duties, they are unaware that they are doing us a favour. By eating elephant dung, these beetles are providing a useful clean-up service!

LITTLE DIGGERS

In areas that are used to grow crops, dung beetles help farmers by fertilising the land. By rolling, digging and eating the dung, the beetles break it down and turn it into compost, which is full of goodness. Burrowing dung beetles also help to circulate air through the soil.

TAKE AWAY

Dung beetles don't just eat dung, they lay their eggs in it, too. Droppings are such valuable property that dung beetles don't dare eat them out in the open. Instead, they roll the dung into balls and drag it into tunnels. Burying the dung keeps it for longer – just like putting food in the fridge. They can then tuck in to their food later without having to share it with rival beetles.

Is it true... that dung is a nutritious feast for bugs?

Yes. Dung may not be your cup of tea, but it's rich in carbohydrates, vitamins, minerals and undigested food – all the good things that a growing dung beetle needs. It's not too fattening, either. In a 1kg pile of dung, there are about 460 – 500 calories. That's slightly more than an 85g bar of chocolate, which has about 420 calories.

STEAMING IN!

There are often fights between beetles, which are all longing to take home a piece of dung. As many as 15,000 beetles can battle for a share of one pat. One type of beetle, called an elephant dung beetle, is so large (10cm long) that it can take away a whole pat before any other bug can get a look in! Competition for dung is especially fierce in the rainy season when valuable droppings can be washed away by a single downpour.

Dung beetles will fly for several kilometres to visit a fresh dung pat.

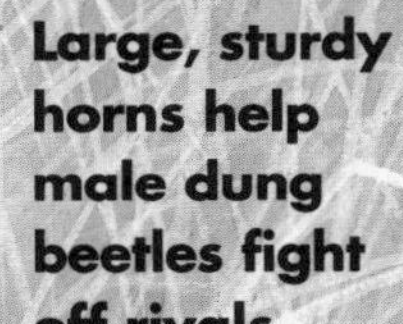

Large, sturdy horns help male dung beetles fight off rivals.

MEALS ON WHEELS

An adult pill rolling beetle makes sure that it has two dung balls in its underground burrow. One, which is called a brood ball, is for its larvae and the other is for the adult to eat. It takes them home in a very unusual way, walking backwards on its front legs, while holding the ball with the claws on its back legs.

UNINVITED GUEST

A dung ball is so precious that if its owner meets another beetle that doesn't have one, it will fight to hang on to its dung. Sometimes it loses and the newcomer makes off with the feast. Often a pushy male will roll a ball of dung for a female and then, when it has safely reached her home, invite himself to dinner!

PREPARE FOR TAKE-OFF

Dung beetles have wings, but when they're busy on the ground they keep them tucked away under protective wing cases. To fly, the beetles shake out their wings and get ready for take-off. Unlike flies, dung beetles don't make quick getaways. They have to puff themselves up with air by taking lots of deep breaths and quickly flapping their wings.

A female dung beetle cuts herself a piece of dung using her spiked forelegs and the jagged edge on the front of her head. Then she shapes it into a ball with her front legs.

In a few hours, there will be nothing left of this pile of elephant's dung. It will have been broken down, rolled into balls and buried underground.

Dung beetles are only interested in fresh, steaming dung.

1 AN UPHILL STRUGGLE

Rolling a huge lump of dung home is hard work and a beetle won't give up without a fight. A beetle pushing a precious ball of droppings is the equivalent of a man pushing a small car up a hill at about 65km/h!

2 GOING UNDERGROUND

Beetles build a huge network of tunnels in which to set up home and hide their dung. Beetles flatten the walls of their burrows with their tiny feet. Then the bugs work in pairs to build underground nests for their young. In many species, it is usually the female that decides where the burrow will be. She brings the first dung ball back to the new 'home'. Once the female has made the main structure, the male takes over, carrying away soil and bringing back balls of dung for the larvae's brood chamber (nursery).

Walking backwards, with its back feet in the air, a beetle may well use its head to defend its dung (below). Sometimes it will head-butt an opponent and send it flying.

Dung beetles are great builders, they can dig the deepest burrows of any insect – some set up home 3.5m below ground. A male pushes a ball of dung down an underground chamber (left) to the female, which is ready to roll it into a brood ball.

Some lazy beetles don't do the dirty work themselves. Rather than collecting and rolling dung, they lay their eggs in egg balls made by other, larger, dung beetles.

3 BORN IN DUNG

The female beetle kneads the brood balls as if they were lumps of dough. Then she lays an egg on each one and covers it with a cap of dung. This forms a pear-shaped lump of dung (below left). When it is born, the larva is surrounded by a ready-made supply of food (bottom).

WHAT A MUM!

Some female dung beetles are so caring that they build the tunnels, make the balls, lay the eggs and then stay with them until the larvae hatch. During this period, which lasts for about four months, the mother has no time for eating and often dies.

Egg covered over with a cap of dung.

FLY PATROL

Dung flies also lay their eggs in dung. In some places, there are so many flies that they can cause disease. Dung beetles are often brought in to help. These busy beetles remove the dung before the flies get a chance to lay their eggs.

Small Talk

NO MEAT PLEASE!

Are you fussy about your food? Dung beetles are. They prefer the dung of herbivores (vegetarian animals). One British local council decided to bring dung beetles to London to get rid of dogs' droppings on the streets. But the idea was a failure. Beetles would never make good pooper-scoopers because dogs eat meat!

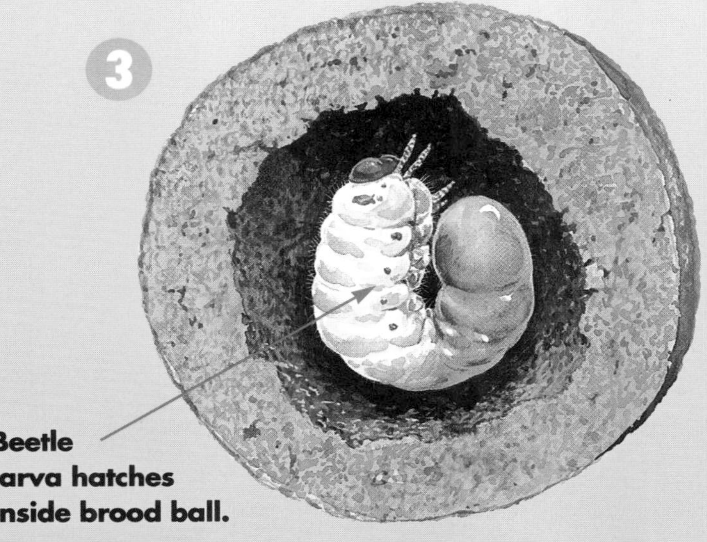

Beetle larva hatches inside brood ball.

Keeping a woodlouse

The woodlouse is not a fussy bug and its needs are simple – food (and it doesn't really care what!) and a damp atmosphere. There are few things you need to do to keep your woodlouse well and happy.

A woodlouse is easily pleased. It is one of the simplest bugs to keep.

Woodlice are easy to find and they're also easy to keep. You'll find them lurking under stones, rocks, planks of wood or flowerpots in the garden. If you've already invested in a tank – perhaps to keep another of the creepy-crawlies that you've read about in BUGS! – you'll be able to keep your woodlouse in that. If you haven't got a tank, the easiest thing is to keep it in an ice-cream tub – the flat, shallow kind is best. Don't worry if the tub isn't see-through – this won't worry the woodlouse and will only make it feel more secure. After all, in the wild it lives in dark, secret places.

You will need:

- an empty ice-cream tub with a lid
- soil or compost
- a small lump of wood
- a few bits of raw fruit or vegetable, such as apple, banana and mushroom
- a variety of dead leaves
- a water spray
- a thick needle, such as a darning or knitting needle

WHAT TO DO

1 Wash the ice-cream tub in soapy water and rinse. You needn't dry it on the inside as they like a damp atmosphere.

2 Put some soil or compost in the bottom of the ice-cream tub so that it is about 1.5cm deep.

Small Talk

THE HAPPY COUPLE

You may like to put two woodlice in your tub. If you are lucky, you will have a male and a female, in which case they will soon produce babies and you can have a whole family living in the tub. The female keeps her young in pouches underneath her body until they can fend for themselves.

3 Then place a lump of wood (or two) on top of the soil. This will give the woodlouse something to hide under.

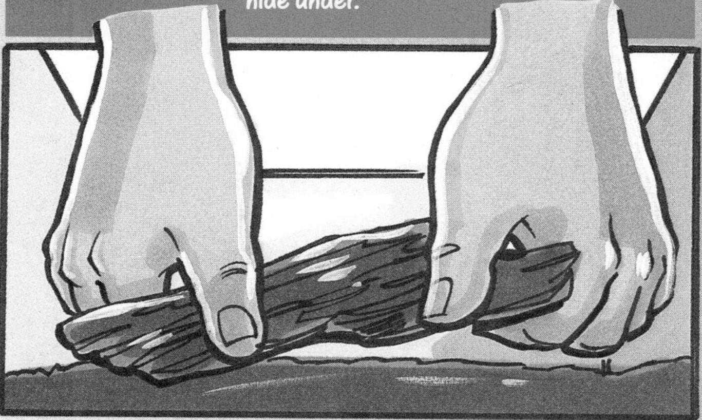

4 Put a few pieces of fruit or vegetable, such as apple or mushroom, in the ice-cream tub for your woodlouse to eat. The woodlouse does not have a big appetite, though, so don't be surprised if it doesn't eat much. Change the food every other day.

5 The woodlouse lives largely on rotting plant material, so make sure that you provide it with a variety of dead leaves to eat.

6 Now put your woodlouse in the tub. To stop it from escaping, put a lid on your ice-cream tub. Pierce a few holes in the lid with a thick needle, such as a darning needle, and place the lid on top of the tub.

7 Using a water mister, such as the kind you use to spray plants, water the contents of the ice-cream tub. Spray gently every day, but do not over-water your woodlouse's home. The woodlouse likes to be neither too wet nor too dry.

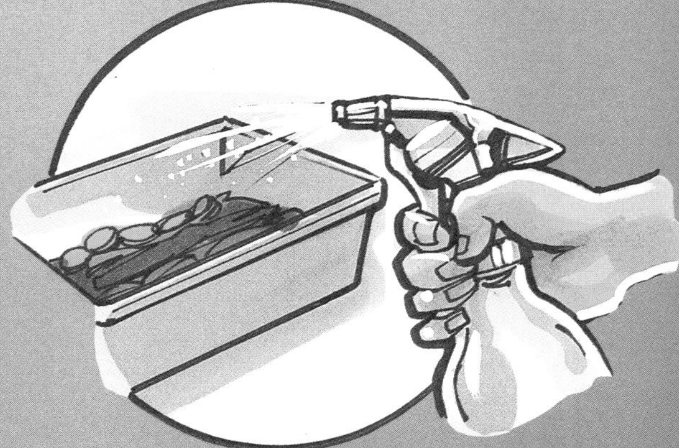

What is... a woodlouse?

A woodlouse is a land-living crustacean. This tiny bug is a relative of crabs and prawns. It is the only crustacean, in fact, that doesn't have to go back to water to lay its eggs. Woodlouse is not its only name. It is also known as the sow or pill bug.

3-D
MINIBEASTS

Centipede

This is the centipede that you may find in your house – especially in moist places such as basements and bathrooms. It has large compound eyes as well as useful feelers. Eyes and feelers play an important role in helping the centipede to find its food. Yummy treats for a centipede include silverfish, flies, cockroaches and other small insects. It's a welcome visitor in any household because it keeps down the numbers of these less welcome visitors. So, come in centipede, take the weight off your legs (all of them!), and make yourself at home.

Legging it!

Sometimes it's hard enough getting just two feet to work together. Imagine running with eight, or even 100, legs!

Bugs with legs can escape from attackers and chase after prey. Like you, they don't think about how they move – they just do it. But each bug has its own special way of getting about.

Centipedes always have an odd number of pairs of legs. This one has 15 pairs, but they can have up to 177.

BEST FOOT FORWARD

The pictures below show a centipede running and then slowing down. Each one shows a split second of time. The green areas mark which legs are touching the ground at that time, all the rest are lifted up in the air.

A This centipede is running. When it is moving fast, only a few legs are in contact with the ground.

B Like the oars of a boat, the legs of a centipede push the bug forward but also slightly sideways. This is why its body wriggles as it moves.

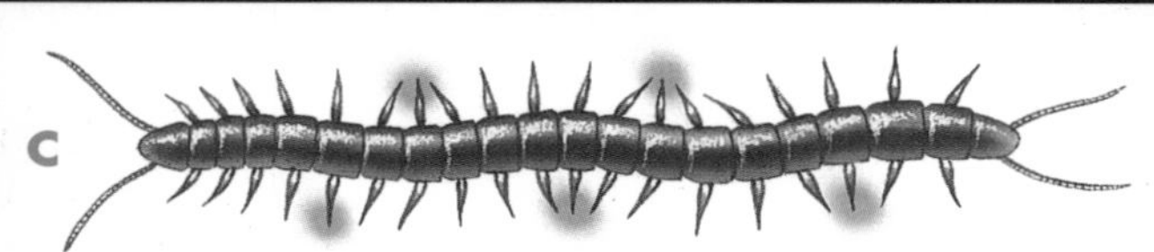

C Here the bug has slowed down a bit, so its body has become straighter. By bending its body from side to side slightly, the centipede can take longer steps without treading on its own 'toes'.

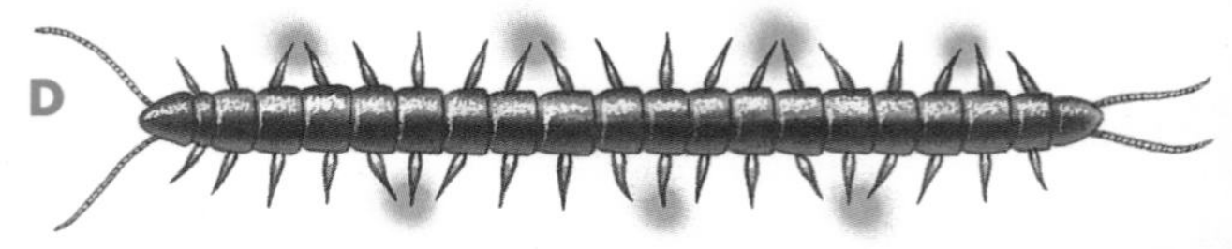

D When it walks slowly, the centipede's body becomes much straighter and the bug keeps more legs on the ground at one time. When it stops moving, all of its legs rest on the ground.

Is it true... that the fastest running bugs tend to be meat-eaters?

Yes. You need to be fast to hunt and catch another creature for your dinner! Herbivorous bugs, on the other hand, tend to be slow movers. You don't have to be able to run fast to catch a leaf or a vegetable!

A 'looping' caterpillar grips with its four leg-like back limbs and pushes its body forward.

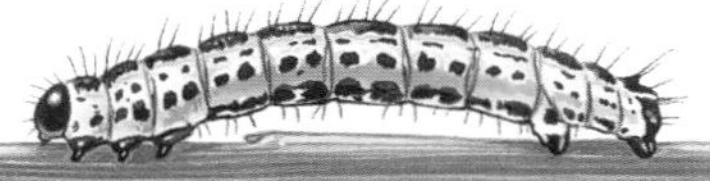

It has six 'true' legs at the front of its body, which clasp the ground where it lands.

Now it lifts up its back limbs and pulls its under-belly forwards.

Finally, it places its back limbs near its front legs, ready for its next 'loop'.

ALL TOGETHER NOW

Bugs that have many legs are called myriapods. They walk in many different ways. Both centipedes and millipedes have loads of legs, but only centipedes are able to move quickly. Despite all their limbs, millipedes move quite slowly. You lift up one leg at a time, but these bugs have to lift up several limbs at once. The fastest centipedes have shorter bodies and fewer, longer legs.

MORE THAN ENOUGH

Millipedes can have anything between 9 – 200 pairs of legs. They have learned to live with all these limbs and co-ordinate them quite well. They lift up about 22 pairs of legs at a time, in small groups.

LIKE LEAPFROG

With all those legs being lifted and placed in front of each other, why don't bugs trip over or stand on at least some of their feet? Some have longer rear legs and shorter front legs so they can step over the short ones. Others place their back legs outside the ones in front, a bit like leap-frogging.

A millipede lifts up groups of legs.

WALL WALKING

Isn't it strange how some insects can walk upside down? Flies and other bugs can walk across ceilings or straight up walls without sliding off. This is because they have cushioned pads on their feet. These pads are covered with hairs, which help these insects to stick to the smoothest surfaces.

Long legs help desert beetles to run fast and to raise their bodies away from the scorching sand.

WALKING IN A STRAIGHT LINE

Beetles and cockroaches are among some of the fastest bugs. Just as many Olympic runners have very long legs, so the quickest bugs, such as the American cockroach, have very long limbs. Although they are so speedy, beetles and cockroaches don't run in a completely straight line. Instead, they move their legs in such a way that their bodies zig-zag across the ground. Like many insects, they always have three legs on the ground and three legs in the air when they are walking.

HOW IT'S DONE

The diagrams below show how a beetle walks. Each arrow shows how a leg is lifted up and moved forward. The legs without arrows are still on the ground.

BUGS ON SKIS!

Just as we have special footwear for every type of weather, so bugs have adapted to cope with different conditions. To a tiny bug, clambering over a large sand dune is like trying to scale Mount Everest. Many desert bugs have hairs on the bottom of their legs, which stop them from sinking through the sand.

Leaving a trail of tiny footprints, this desert beetle skims easily over the sand. It uses the hairs on its legs like old-fashioned snow shoes.

The beetle moves its two outer left legs and its middle right leg forward. The insect's body moves to the right.

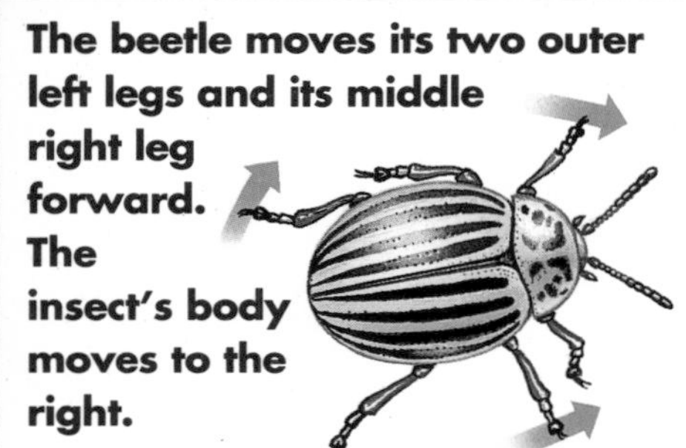

Using its other three legs, it pushes itself back in the opposite direction.

Keeping three legs on the ground, the beetle holds its body steady while the other three legs move.

Is it true . . . that wind scorpions are the fastest land bugs?

Yes. No other bug can out-run the wind scorpion, or sun spider as it is sometimes called. It is called the wind scorpion because it can 'run like the wind'. Found in hot countries and desert areas, it is a hunter and can chase and catch lizards and other creatures that it likes to eat. Wind scorpions use only six of their eight long legs for running. The first two limbs are used as feelers. The wind scorpion can run about 330 times its body length in 10 seconds. The fastest humans can only run 50 times their body length in that time!

Wind scorpion

FISHY BUSINESS

Some bugs swim on land! The silverfish, which is a six-legged creature, gets its name from the way it moves its body from side to side like a fish wriggling through the water. It likes moist places, but desert bugs also 'swim'. They use their legs to paddle through the sand.

LOVELY LEGS

Spiders have four pairs of walking legs. They don't pick up all four left legs and then all four right legs. If they did they would topple over! Generally they lift up two on one side and then two on the other side. (The second and fourth on the left and the first and third on the right.)

STICKY TRAIL

Spiders coat the surfaces they walk on with a fine film of water, which helps them stick to smooth and slippery surfaces. Many also have a clump of thousands of thick hairs in between the tiny claws on their feet. These hairs give the spider extra staying power on slippery surfaces, such as baths.

Although it is the biggest spider in the world, the goliath spider (right) can still climb up vertical surfaces. This is because it has thousands of tiny hairs on each foot.

Goliath spider

The silk makers

A talented insect, the oriental silkmoth is responsible for making one of the world's most beautiful natural products – silk. Next time you see a silk dress, spare a thought for the silkmoth.

The cute-looking silkmoth (main picture) is a feeble bug. It doesn't eat or fly and usually lives for less than 72 hours.

The oriental silkmoth originally came from Asia, but is now extinct in the wild. It can only survive on farms, where millions of them are bred for the silk thread that they produce to build their cocoons.

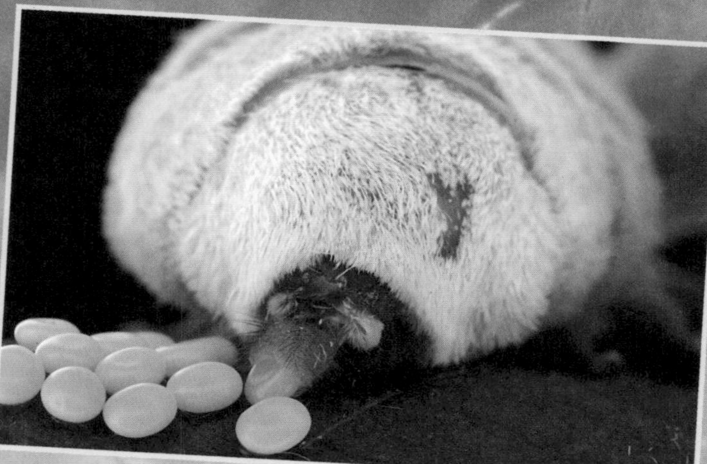

SOWING THE SEED

During its short life (2 – 3 days), a silkmoth is only interested in mating and laying eggs. A female silkmoth lays up to 500 yellow eggs (left). In natural conditions, she would lay her eggs in the middle of March, on the leaves of the mulberry tree. But in captivity, the female produces eggs at any time of year. She lays them on pieces of card, which can be stored throughout the winter in warm conditions which will encourage the eggs to develop.

Silkmoth farmers call the moths' yellow eggs 'seeds'. They sell them to other farmers by weight. They are so light that 40,000 eggs weigh just 28g.

Silkmoth caterpillars (left) eat the leaves of the mulberry tree. Tests have shown that if they eat other types of vegetation, they produce silk of a poorer quality.

EATING AND GROWING

After about six weeks, the caterpillars hatch from the eggs. They are pale grey and have wrinkled, hairless skin and a small horn at the end of their bodies. The caterpillars eat all the time and grow quickly, shedding their skin four times. They are fully grown after about three weeks and are ready to spin their large, silk cocoons, inside which they will turn into adult moths.

LIQUID SILK

A caterpillar produces silk using special glands inside its body. The silk comes out through an organ called a spinneret, which is near the caterpillar's mouthparts. When it first emerges, the silk is a liquid, but it hardens as soon as it reaches the air.

A silkmoth caterpillar, which is also called a silkworm, takes about two days to spin its cocoon of silk threads (above).

THE FINEST SILK

For thousands of years, people have known that caterpillars produce silk. The first silk was produced from wild silkmoths. But about 3,500 years ago, the Chinese set up the first farms. They chose the oriental silkmoth because it was the biggest and produced the finest silk. The Chinese were the first people to produce silk on a large scale.

Small Talk

SECRETS OF SILK

Large-scale silk production began in China about 3,500 years ago. As the centuries passed, the industry spread through India and other parts of Asia. However, the method was a closely guarded secret. Anyone caught trying to take silkmoths out of the country was put to death. About 1,400 years ago, some eggs of the oriental silkmoth were smuggled out of China and reached Europe.

Feeding silkworms (China 1834)

On a silkmoth farm, the caterpillars are treated like VIPs. They eat until they are big and fat, but as soon as they have spun their beautiful silk cocoons, they are killed.

SPECIAL QUALITIES

The oriental silkmoth makes an ideal farm animal! It is easy to look after and it can't escape. These moths used to be able to fly, but since they have been bred in captivity they have become too fat to take to the air. The farmer never has to worry about his livestock flying – or creeping – away. The caterpillar, too, has lost its ability to crawl. These bugs would not be able to survive in the wild today because they can't search for food to eat.

CLEAN CATERPILLARS

While they are alive, the pale grey caterpillars are kept in excellent condition. They are housed in sterile (clean, germ-free) plastic trays and fed their favourite food – fresh mulberry leaves. Farmers have to be very careful that the caterpillars don't become ill. By over-feeding the caterpillars, farmers can make them grow quickly.

SAVING THE BEST

Once the caterpillars have spun their cocoons on specially prepared trays, some of them are allowed to develop and emerge as silkmoths. These lucky moths are usually the largest and strongest and will be used for breeding. The other caterpillars are less fortunate.

A silkmoth's cocoon is rough on the outside because it is covered with a sticky, glue-like substance that holds the threads together. Inside, the silk is soft and smooth.

When the caterpillars are ready to pupate (right), the farmers provide them with a wooden frame, where they can spin their cocoons (top).

When a silkmoth emerges from its cocoon, it damages the valuable silk threads. This coocon will not be used to make silk.

KILLING THE CATERPILLARS

Farmers cannot allow the rest of the fully grown moths to emerge from their cocoons because they damage the silk. The caterpillars spin their cocoons with a single thread of silk and the farmers do not want the threads to get broken. Most of the cocoons are taken away and placed in a hot, dry room. Sadly, this kills the pupating caterpillars.

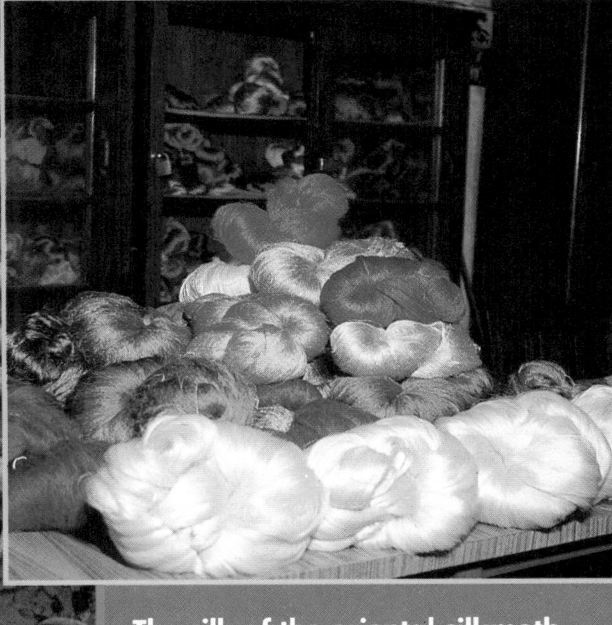

The silk of the oriental silkmoth (above) is often dyed beautiful colours before it is woven into cloth.

Is it true... that silkmoth caterpillars can spin different coloured silks?

Yes. The oriental silkmoth produces white or yellow silk, but other moths produce different coloured silks. The Indian emperor moth produces a beige coloured silk, called Eri silk. Another Indian silkmoth produces Tussor silk, which is much darker. Muga silk, made by a Chinese silkmoth, is a dull bronze colour. The Japanese oak moth (below) produces a pale green silk. Thousands of years ago, only members of the Japanese Emperor's household were allowed to use this beautiful silk.

UNRAVELLING AND REELING

Once the caterpillars are dead, the cocoons are put into boiling hot water. This dissolves the glue that holds the cocoon together. The soft silk, which is on the inside of the cocoon, can now be unravelled and wound on to a reel. The silk is very fine and often several strands are wound up together. The threads can be strengthened even more by twisting them round each other, like a rope.

MILLIONS KILLED

Each caterpillar produces a single thread of silk, which is more than 900m long (you could wrap this thread around a football 1,111 times). Despite this incredible length, it still takes many thousands of cocoons to produce just 500g of silk. Each year, over 60,000 tonnes of silk are produced around the world. This means more than 3 billion silkworms have to die.

Improve and test your knowledge with...

CREEPY-CRAWLY FACTS

Do these facts grab you? If not – try the creepy-crawly quiz!

What's lurking down there?

When humans first began to explore the seas, sailors came back with tales of mysterious monsters. In 1787, a large sailing ship floated on a still sea off the west coast of Africa. Some crew took advantage of the peace to chisel barnacles off the bottom of the boat. Suddenly, enormous tentacles rose out of the sea and tried to grab the sailors. Only after they had stabbed its tentacles did the giant 'beast' slip silently away. It may well have been a giant octopus. The world's seas are still largely unexplored and it is quite possible that there are more huge bugs living in the depths of the oceans.

1 What is another name for the wind scorpion?
a) breeze bug
b) fat-tailed scorpion
c) sun spider

2 What do sea anemones eat?
a) small sea animals
b) sharks
c) coral

3 Why is the Spanish fly dangerous to predators?
a) it has vicious jaws
b) it can give a venomous sting
c) it oozes a nasty, burning poison

4 What does the oriental silkmoth like to eat?
a) small berries
b) tiny insect larvae
c) the leaves of the mulberry tree

5 How does the dung beetle protect its wings?
a) it covers them in grease
b) it keeps them under wing cases
c) it lifts them in the air

6 Which one of these bugs is closely related to the woodlouse?
a) dragonfly
b) prawn
c) headlouse

7 How does the centipede find its food?
a) it oozes a sticky liquid to trap bugs that pass by
b) it never eats
c) it uses its eyes and feelers to find food

8 When did pseudoscorpions first appear on Earth?
a) 65,000 years ago
b) more than 65 million years ago
c) 65 years ago

9 How big is a digger wasp?
a) 24mm long
b) 24cm
c) 4mm

10 Which bugs tend to run the fastest?
a) meat-eaters
b) vegetarian bugs
c) slugs

All-round defence

Young insects have a lot of predators – staying alive is not always easy. Although the larvae of the Asian owlfly have large jaws, they are slow-moving and so are always in danger of attack. To avoid this, they huddle together as soon as they hatch, each with its mouthparts facing outwards. Few predators are brave enough to attack this crowd of gnashing jaws.

Supermoth

The death's-head hawk moth has excellent defences. Its wings look just like the bark of a tree, while the markings on its thorax look like two large eyes. The hawk moth has yellow and brown stripes on its abdomen so that if a determined predator comes any closer, it suddenly finds itself face-to-face with what looks like a huge wasp. If all else fails, the moth hisses loudly and raises its front legs. Finally, if an attacker tries to grab the moth, scales on its body rub off, so it can slip through the firmest grasp!

Waste not, want not

The larva of the tortoise beetle has a cunning disguise. From the day it hatches, it collects all its droppings and the skins that it sheds and sticks them to the end of its abdomen. This forms a disgusting-looking umbrella. To flying predators, a crowd of tortoise beetle larvae looks like a rubbish dump. At ground level, the smell puts even hungry ants off their tea!

Answers to the questions on the inside back cover

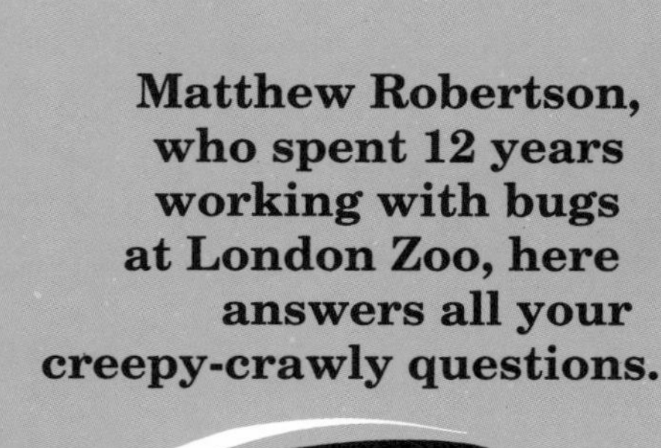

Matthew Robertson, who spent 12 years working with bugs at London Zoo, here answers all your creepy-crawly questions.

Can bugs see in the dark?

Many types of bug can see in the dark. Those that hunt at night probably have the best night vision of all bugs. Spiders, such as the ogre-faced spider, have such sensitive eyes that they can see almost as clearly at night as we can see in broad daylight. However, many bugs that see well at night find it difficult to see different colours.

Why do beetles walk when they have wings?

Some beetles do spend a lot of their time flying about. These bugs are usually lightly built. However, many beetles are heavy creatures and they have to use up a lot of their valuable food reserves just to get their muscles warm enough for take-off. Large beetles save their energy by walking from place to place. They only use their flying skills on important occasions, such as finding a mate or a suitable site to lay their eggs.

How do bugs crawl through narrow gaps?

If humans try to crawl through a narrow gap that is smaller than their body, they simply won't be able to get through. But many bugs have a flexible external skeleton, which allows them to squeeze through very narrow cracks. However, they still have to be careful not to damage their valuable internal organs, without which they would die.

Wart-biter cricket

The wart-biter cricket will try eating anything – even the warts on people's skin!

Like many other grasshoppers and crickets, the wart-biter lives in grassland – in open meadows, mountain pastures, or in damp, marshy places. It isn't very choosy about its food and will eat whatever it can find, but is particularly fond of insects and plants.

CAMOUFLAGE

The wart-biter may be green or brown, with patchy, spotty markings. Its colouring and patterns make it hard to see among the grass, and this protects it from predators.

TOO HEAVY

The wart-biter has a pair of wings that it keeps folded neatly under wing covers. Its ancestors would have used these wings for flying. Now, with its heavy body, the wart-biter would need much more powerful wings than these to allow it to fly well.

BOUNCING ALONG

Instead of flying, the wart-biter usually gets around by jumping. It has three pairs of legs, but its back legs are much longer and stronger than the front ones. It keeps them bent backwards, ready to spring.

IN A FLAP

When it wants to jump, the wart-biter shoots out its back legs to push itself forwards and upwards, like an athlete doing a high jump. Males and young females occasionally put their wings to good use. If they need to escape from a predator or travel just a little bit faster, they can open up their wings as they leap, to give them extra lift.

SINGING IN THE SUN

Like crickets and grasshoppers, the wart-biter 'sings'. But, unlike some of its relations that chirp away at night, the wart-biter sings in the daytime, especially if the weather is sunny. It produces its 'song' by rubbing the tops of its wings together. Only the male wart-biter sings, but he doesn't do this because he's happy! He sings to attract a mate, or to tell other males that he is there and to warn them to keep their distance.

A hobby (a bird of prey) gets ready to pounce.

EAT UP!

The wart-biter gets its strange name because people once used it to get rid of warts. Always on the look-out for food, it will try taking a mouthful of anything edible it finds. So, if it found a wart on a person's skin, it would take a bite out of that, too, and eat it up! (Don't try this – it hurts). Part of its scientific name – 'verrucivorus' (say 'ver-roo-kee-vor-rus') – means 'wart-eater'.

Ovipositor sticks out behind the bug's body when it isn't being used to lay eggs.

Powerful back legs

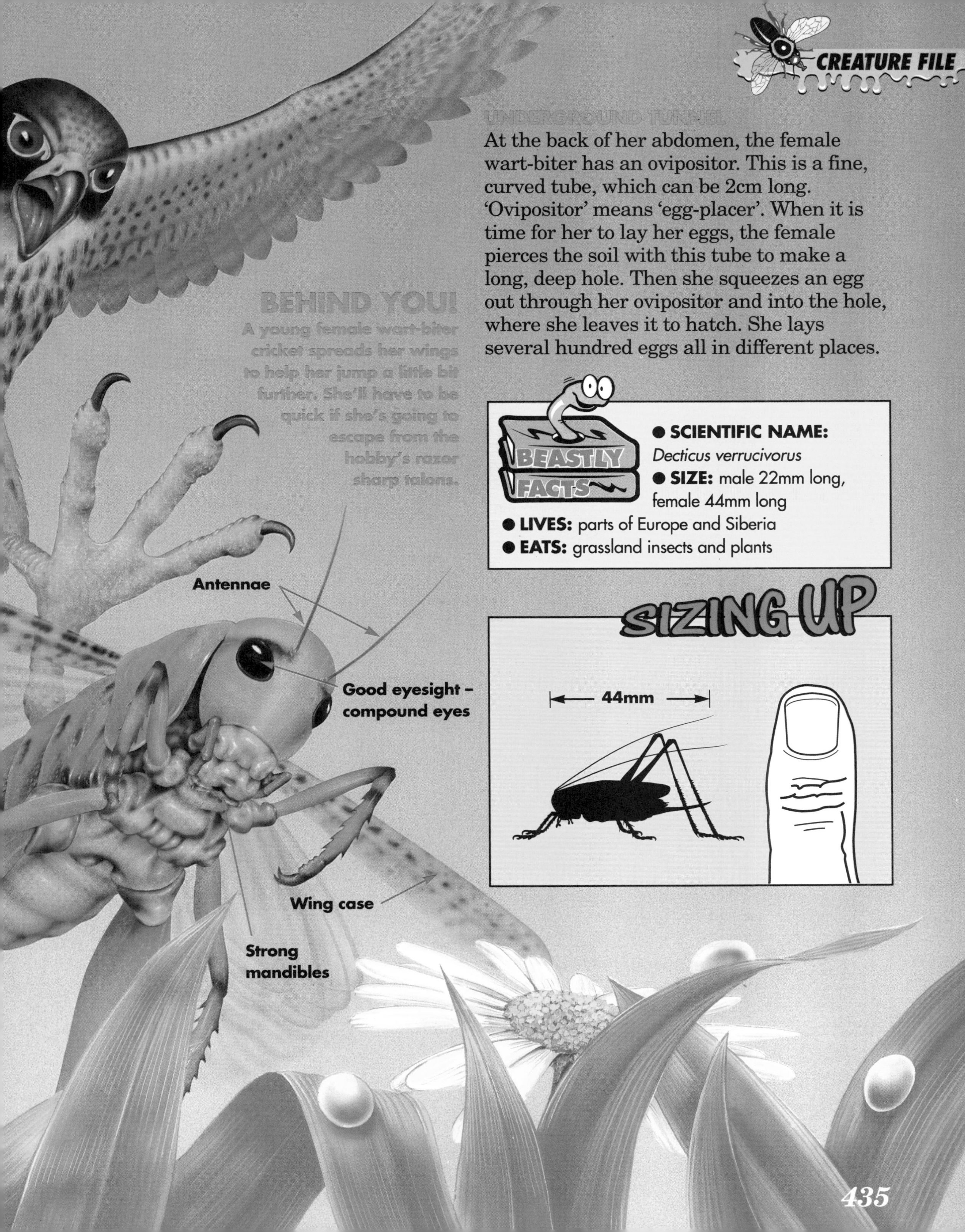

UNDERGROUND TUNNEL

At the back of her abdomen, the female wart-biter has an ovipositor. This is a fine, curved tube, which can be 2cm long. 'Ovipositor' means 'egg-placer'. When it is time for her to lay her eggs, the female pierces the soil with this tube to make a long, deep hole. Then she squeezes an egg out through her ovipositor and into the hole, where she leaves it to hatch. She lays several hundred eggs all in different places.

BEHIND YOU!

A young female wart-biter cricket spreads her wings to help her jump a little bit further. She'll have to be quick if she's going to escape from the hobby's razor sharp talons.

- **SCIENTIFIC NAME:** *Decticus verrucivorus*
- **SIZE:** male 22mm long, female 44mm long
- **LIVES:** parts of Europe and Siberia
- **EATS:** grassland insects and plants

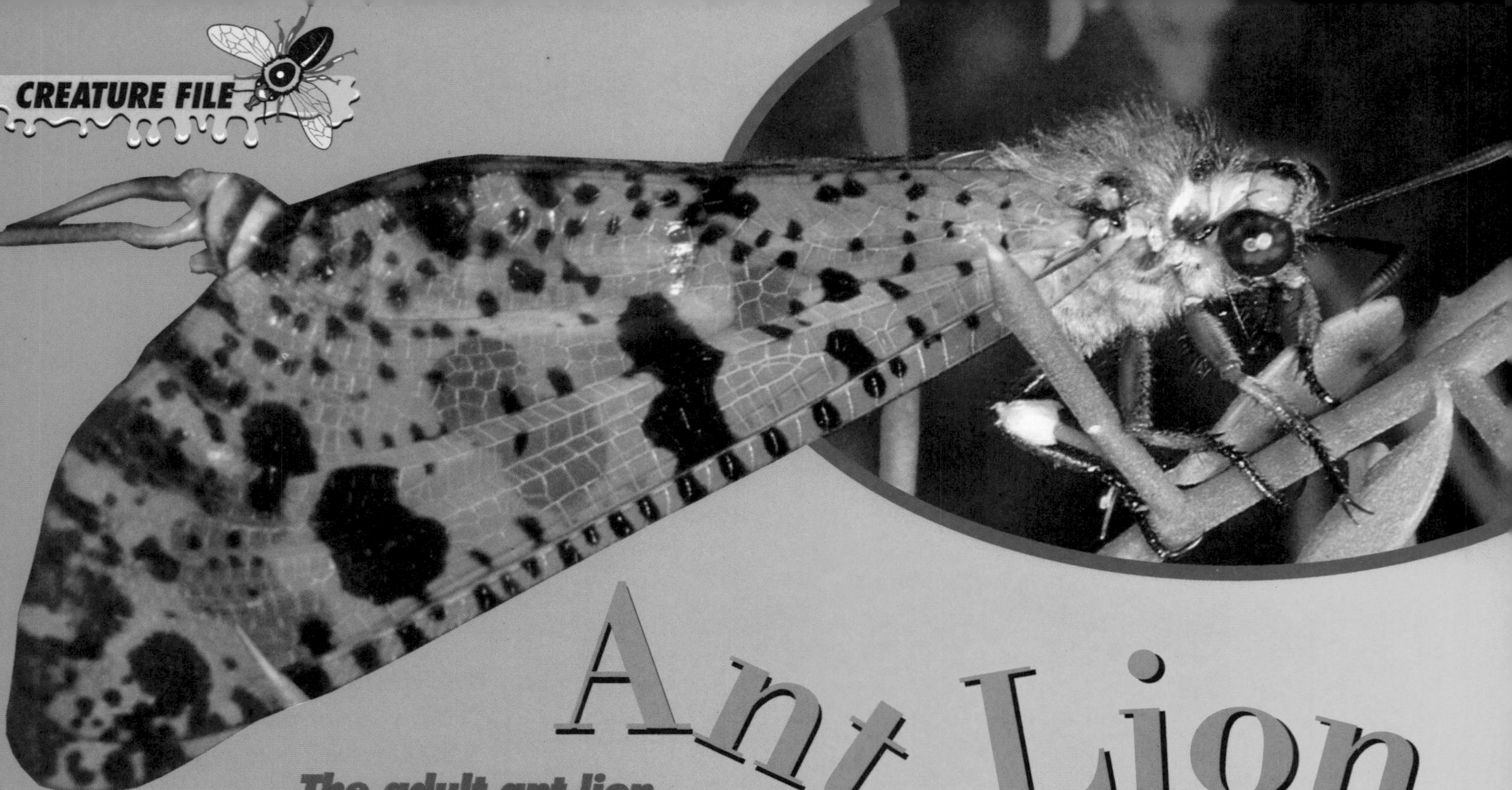

Ant Lion

The adult ant lion looks frail and delicate, but its larva is a skilled and ruthless hunter.

With its large wings and long body, the ant lion looks similar to a dragonfly. You can easily tell the difference between them by looking at their antennae – an ant lion has thick ones with a wide, blunt end, but a dragonfly's are tiny.

LACY WINGS

Although the ant lion has large wings, it is not a strong flier and never travels far. It flies about during the day, often in dense swarms. When it rests, the ant lion folds its wings back to cover its body, like a lid.

SNATCH AND GRAB

The short, fat young of the ant lion have large, spiny jaws, and are fierce. They burrow down into sand or loose soil and here – with only their heads sticking out – they quietly wait. When a suitable victim comes along, they dart out of their hiding place and grab their prey in their jaws. They catch mostly spiders and small insects, especially ants, which is why they are called 'ant lions'.

- **SCIENTIFIC NAME:** *Palpares libelluloides*
- **SIZE:** 10cm wingspan
- **LIVES:** countries around the Mediterranean sea
- **EATS:** adult eats fruit, small flies and the juice of aphids; young eats spiders and small insects

SIZING UP

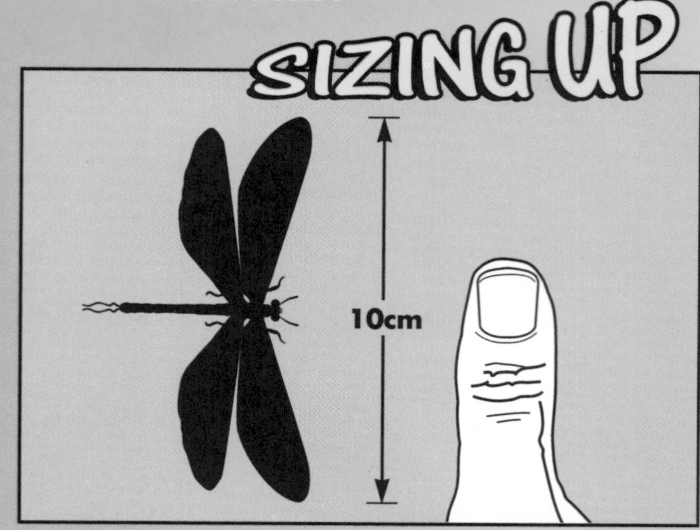

Caprellid Shrimp

The caprellid shrimp is hard to spot among the waving seaweed of its home.

The tiny caprellid (say 'cap-rel-lid') shrimp is only 2cm long. With its skinny body and dangly legs, it is sometimes also called the skeleton shrimp.

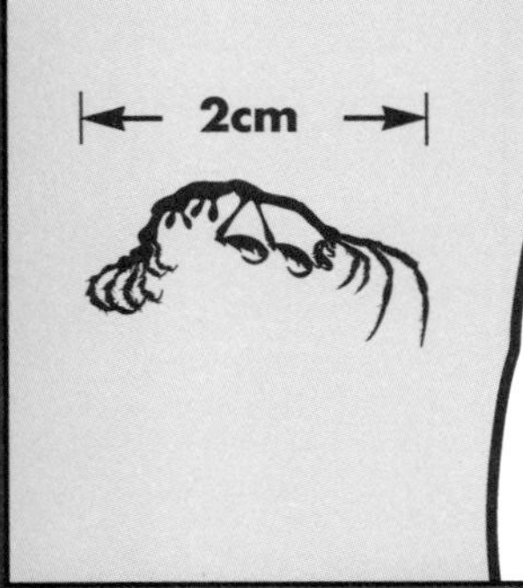

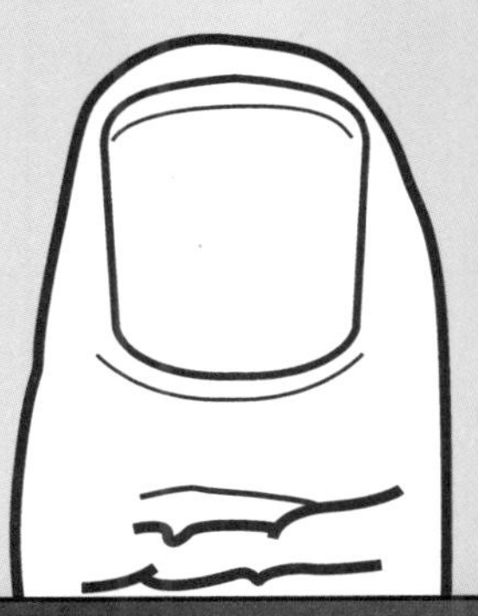

SEAWEED HOME

The caprellid lives in the warm Mediterranean Sea, in places where seaweed grows. It clings to one of these underwater plants with its back legs, leaving the rest of its body free to float. As it sways gently in the moving currents, it looks just like another piece of harmless seaweed.

FEELING FOR PREY

The caprellid can 'feel' its prey approaching. The feelers on its head are so sensitive that they can detect the tiny ripples made by plankton – minute sea creatures – as they swim through the water. It has good eyesight, too, and looks to see where its prey is. Then, when the victim is close enough, it shoots out its long arms and grabs it. Strong jaws tear the victim's body up into pieces. An adult caprellid may even grab the young of other caprellids as they drift about in the sea currents.

- **SCIENTIFIC NAME:** *Caprella linearis*
- **SIZE:** 2cm long
- **LIVES:** in the Mediterranean Sea
- **EATS:** plankton

Beware of the

Poison doesn't always come in bottles – it also comes in bugs. If they are eaten, many of these creatures can cause sickness or even death.

A poisonous bug has a toxin (poison) in its body. When a hungry predator tries to eat it, it gets a nasty shock. The poison, which is released into the enemy's body, can taste horrid, or have far more deadly results.

POISON OR VENOM?

Poisonous animals don't inject toxins into their victims. Instead, they keep the poison inside their bodies. It is only released when the bugs are sucked, bitten or eaten. Bugs that inject their toxins, such as bees, spiders and scorpions, are called venomous. They use claws, a sting or fangs to inject their victims and they can use the venom as a defence or to attack.

Is it true... that bugs can poison humans?

Yes. If you were silly enough to eat a poisonous bug you would probably suffer the same unpleasant symptoms as other predators. However, humans are usually bigger than the predators that attack bugs in the wild. This means that there is not usually enough poison in a bug to kill a human. However, it may make the person very sick.

Milkweed bugs (above) make a meal out of the plant's poisonous seed pods. Their orange coats are fair warning to attackers.

ONCE BITTEN, TWICE SHY

To warn their enemies that they are poisonous, some bugs are brightly coloured or marked with eye-catching patterns. Poison is a brilliant defence. Often the toxin inside a bug's body won't kill a predator, but it will taste disgusting and may make the attacker very ill. Once a predator has tried a poisonous species, it will learn its lesson and avoid the foul-tasting bug in the future.

BLISTERING BEETLES

If they are upset, blister beetles (right) give off a nasty, acid-like liquid. If this poison touches a human, he or she will get a nasty blister. If swallowed by an animal, this poisonous acid could burn away the predator's insides. Usually, hungry hunters are put off by the beetle's brightly coloured orange and black coat before they ever take a bite.

bugs!

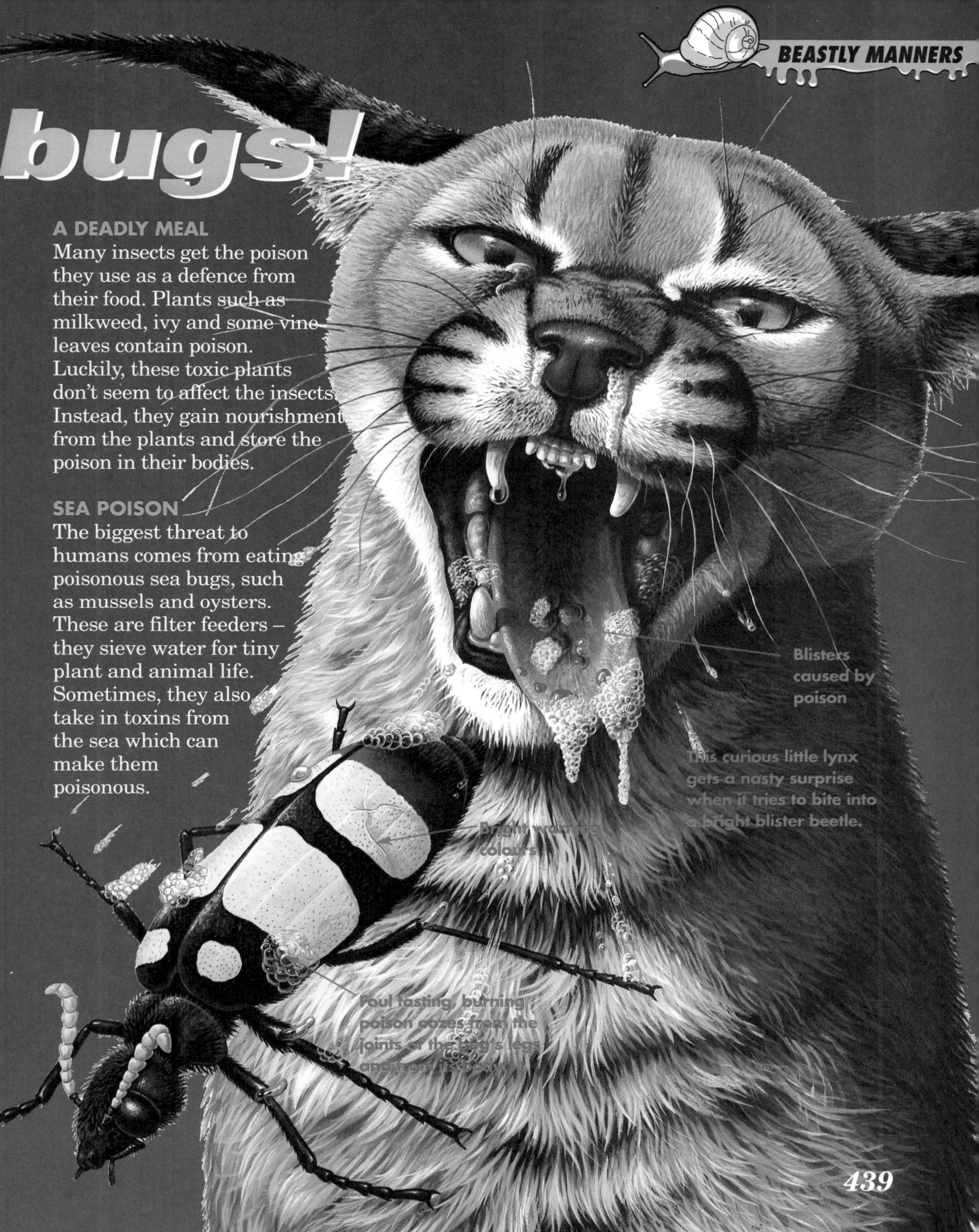
Blisters
caused by
poison
This curious little lynx
gets a nasty surprise
when it tries to bite into
a bright blister beetle.
Bright warning
colours
Foul tasting, burning
poison oozes from the
joints of the bug's legs
and from its body.

A DEADLY MEAL

Many insects get the poison they use as a defence from their food. Plants such as milkweed, ivy and some vine leaves contain poison. Luckily, these toxic plants don't seem to affect the insects. Instead, they gain nourishment from the plants and store the poison in their bodies.

SEA POISON

The biggest threat to humans comes from eating poisonous sea bugs, such as mussels and oysters. These are filter feeders – they sieve water for tiny plant and animal life. Sometimes, they also take in toxins from the sea which can make them poisonous.

Back off!

Animals have to learn to avoid poisonous bugs by looking out for the warning signs. These signs are often colourful or noisy.

BEAUTY AND THE BEAST

Moths and butterflies are among the most poisonous of insects. Both as adults and caterpillars, their bodies can contain lethal doses. It's not surprising that butterflies are so bright and eye-catching. Their vivid colours are a constant warning to hungry hunters that may be tempted to try them.

BAD BABY FOOD

Monarch, or milkweed, butterflies are poisonous to birds and other animals. The caterpillars eat the leaves of the milkweed plant, which are poisonous. Both the caterpillars and the fully grown adults store up lots of the toxins from the plant in their bodies and both are very colourful. If eaten, the poisons their bodies contain make a predator's heart beat wildly and it also finds it hard to breathe.

LISTEN OUT

Many moths fly at night. Bright warning colours would go unnoticed by night-time predators, such as bats, which are very short-sighted. Instead, some moths give off high-pitched noises to warn bats that they taste unpleasant.

TIGER'S BITE

Just to be on the safe side, tiger moths have eye-catching patterns and make warning noises, too. They fly about at dawn and dusk when both nocturnal and daylight animals can be about. They can either put off a night-time attacker by making a high-pitched noise, or give day-time predators a warning flash of their brightly patterned wings. Sensible predators give up and leave the moth alone.

DEADLY DART

Some poisonous insects are hunted by humans, who use the toxins in the bugs' bodies to defend themselves. Kalahari bushmen from Africa, for example, hunt for the larvae of the bushman arrow beetle and squeeze out its poisonous juices on to an arrowhead. One of these poisonous darts can kill a massive elephant in just 30 minutes!

Is it true... that poisonous bugs are always the same colours?

No. They come in many different shades. However, quite a few poisonous bugs are black and orange or black and yellow. The monarch butterfly, milkweed and Colorado beetles, and the African lycid beetle are all poisonous and all orange and black. The Peruvian hawk moth caterpillar also stands out from the crowd, but its body is covered in yellow and purple stripes.

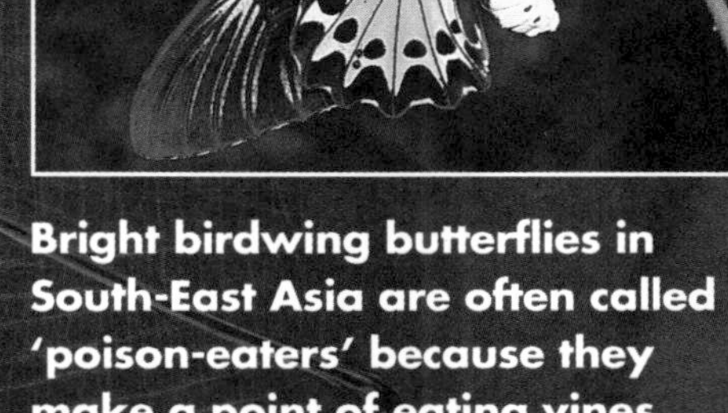

Bright birdwing butterflies in South-East Asia are often called 'poison-eaters' because they make a point of eating vines that are toxic.

Eye-catching yellow and black bands on the body of the monarch butterfly larva warn predators of its dangerous eating habits. Like some other bugs, this one eats milkweed.

A bat narrowly escapes food poisoning (main picture). The bat was alerted in the nick of time by a warning noise made by the moth. The furry predator realises that it is a poisonous tiger moth, not a tasty treat.

Is your house

From cellar to attic, your home is also home to bugs. Track them down by doing a survey of your house.

How many people do you live with? That's easy – you just need to count them. But do you know how many bugs you share your home with? Start by drawing a picture of your house, showing each room. Then sketch each bug that you find and, if you can, give it a name. Here are some hints to where you might find bugs.

ATTIC

It's warm, it's dry, and it's out of harm's way.

Wasp
Attics are the favourite nesting site of the common wasp. Females build their nest in spring and the colony breaks up in autumn.

Wood-boring beetle
Watch out! There's a beetle about. It munches its way through rafters and any bits of wood it can find.

BEDROOM

While the rest of the house sleeps, bugs run riot!

Mosquito
While its victims sleep, the female mosquito zooms in to suck their blood.

Clothes moth
Quietly munching in your drawers, the clothes moth is found all year round. It will eat any kind of fabric so watch our for your woollies!

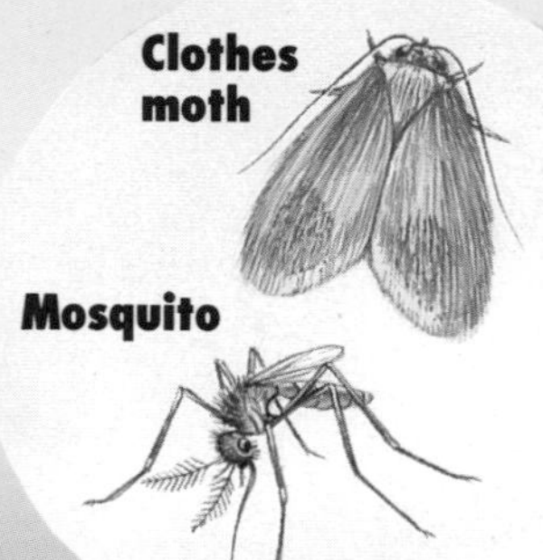

LIVING ROOM

There are lots of attractions for bugs in the living room. These include pets, houseplants, carpets and furniture.

Garden spider
Look on the windowsill for a garden spider coming in from the cold. The window is a favourite place for spiders to lurk because it gives them the chance to catch other insects that are attracted to the light.

Mealy bug
If you find white bugs under the leaves of your houseplant, they may well be mealy bugs. They lay hundreds of white eggs at a time under leaves.

Firebrat
The firebrat, with its three tails, looks for warm places, such as near radiators and fires.

Furniture beetle
The furniture beetle is dark brown. A table leg or a coffee table will easily get its mouth watering. Its larva, called woodworm, tunnels inside wood, leaving small, but obvious exit holes. It can cause serious damage.

Carpet beetle
The larva of the carpet beetle is a hairy little bug and its nickname is the woolly bear. It lives, alongside the adult, in carpets, rugs and furniture.

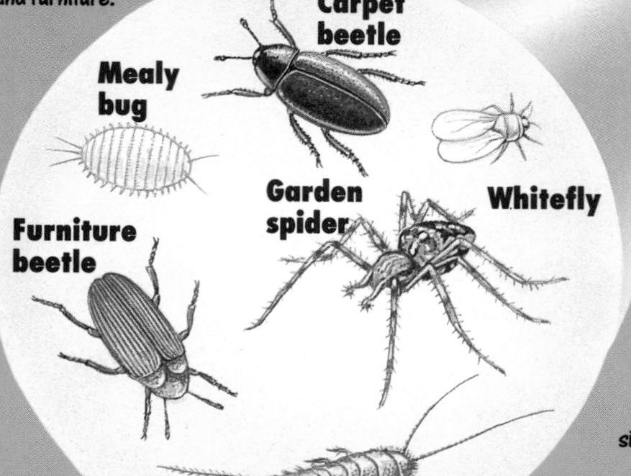

Whitefly
Houseplants encourage whitefly, which look like tiny moths with waxy, white wings. Look for them on the under sides of leaves.

bugged?

BATHROOM

Usually warm and damp, the bathroom offers just the right conditions for many bugs.

House spider
The large house spider is often seen running around the bathroom, especially in autumn when males are looking for females.

House spider

Silverfish
The three-tailed silverfish is pale grey in colour, likes damp surroundings and often lives in the bathroom or toilet. It comes out at night, so you will probably only see it in the morning if it got stuck in the bath the night before.

KITCHEN

Food is the big attraction here, for humans and creepy-crawlies alike!

Bluebottle
The bluebottle buzzes about looking for uncovered food. If it's rotting – so much the better.

Larder beetle
Look behind your fridge or cooker and you may well find a larder, or bacon, beetle. Their larvae are hairy bugs, which also love food, particularly meat.

Weevil
The grain weevil lives and breeds in stored grain products, such as cereal and flour.

Black garden ant
Ants track down food using their antennae. They will happily tramp across your kitchen floor in search of titbits that you have dropped. If they can, they'll also crawl into cupboards, especially those with jam in them!

Caterpillar
Next time you unpack the shopping keep your eyes peeled for a caterpillar as it crawls out of the vegetables.

Cricket
If you live in a hot country, or if your neighbour has a lizard or tarantula that feeds on crickets, keep your ears peeled for these singing bugs. They love to lurk noisily behind the fridge.

Cockroach
If you creep down to the kitchen at night, keep a look out for foraging cockroaches. Under cover of darkness, they search for food. They will eat dead bugs, paper or even wine bottle corks.

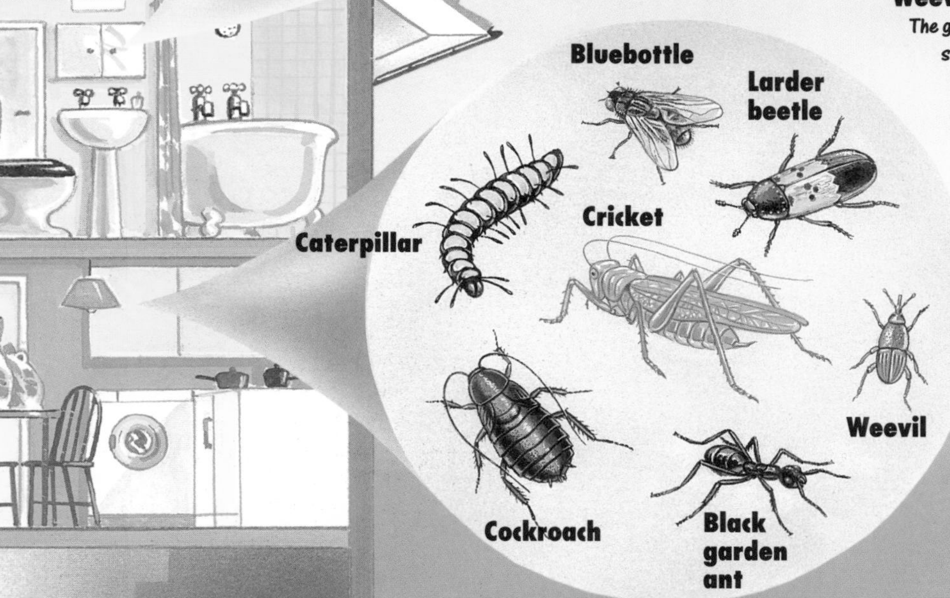

CELLAR

Quiet and out of the way, the cellar is a marvellous base from which to make expeditions to the kitchen.

House centipede
This long-legged centipede doesn't have 100 legs, but a maximum of 30. It lives mostly on walls where it hunts other bugs.

Cellar spider
This long-legged spider, also known as the daddy-long-legs spider, hangs upside-down from ceilings in a tangled web, which catches flies, little moths, mosquitoes, ants and other spiders.

Old lady moth
Hiding in cellars during the day, this elegantly patterned brown moth is so called because it looks like it is wearing a shawl.

Slug
Dark, cool and damp, the cellar is the slug's idea of heaven. The cellar may also have convenient access to and from the garden.

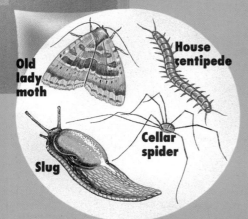

Old lady moth
House centipede
Cellar spider
Slug

3-D
MINIBEASTS

Springtail

Sitting in a bed of cosy leaf litter, the tiny springtail senses a tasty bit of fungus. It doesn't walk towards this tempting treat, but literally leaps after the food. Underneath the springtail's body is a tiny mechanism, which is like a two-pronged fork or spring. When the bug is resting, this 'fork' sits close to the underside of the body. When the springtail is frightened or it fancies a snack, the prongs spring apart and the bug shoots through the air like a rocket!

Imperial scorpion

The biggest scorpion in the world, the imperial scorpion lurks under a rock in a rain forest in central Africa. Using hairs on its legs and tail, it senses a tiny mouse nearby and prepares its deadly sting. Once it has grasped its prey in its huge pincers, there is no way out. One sting is not usually enough. The imperial scorpion injects its prey with venom over and over again until it stops struggling. The defenceless mouse will be dragged back to the scorpion's lair and torn apart.

3-D
MINIBEASTS

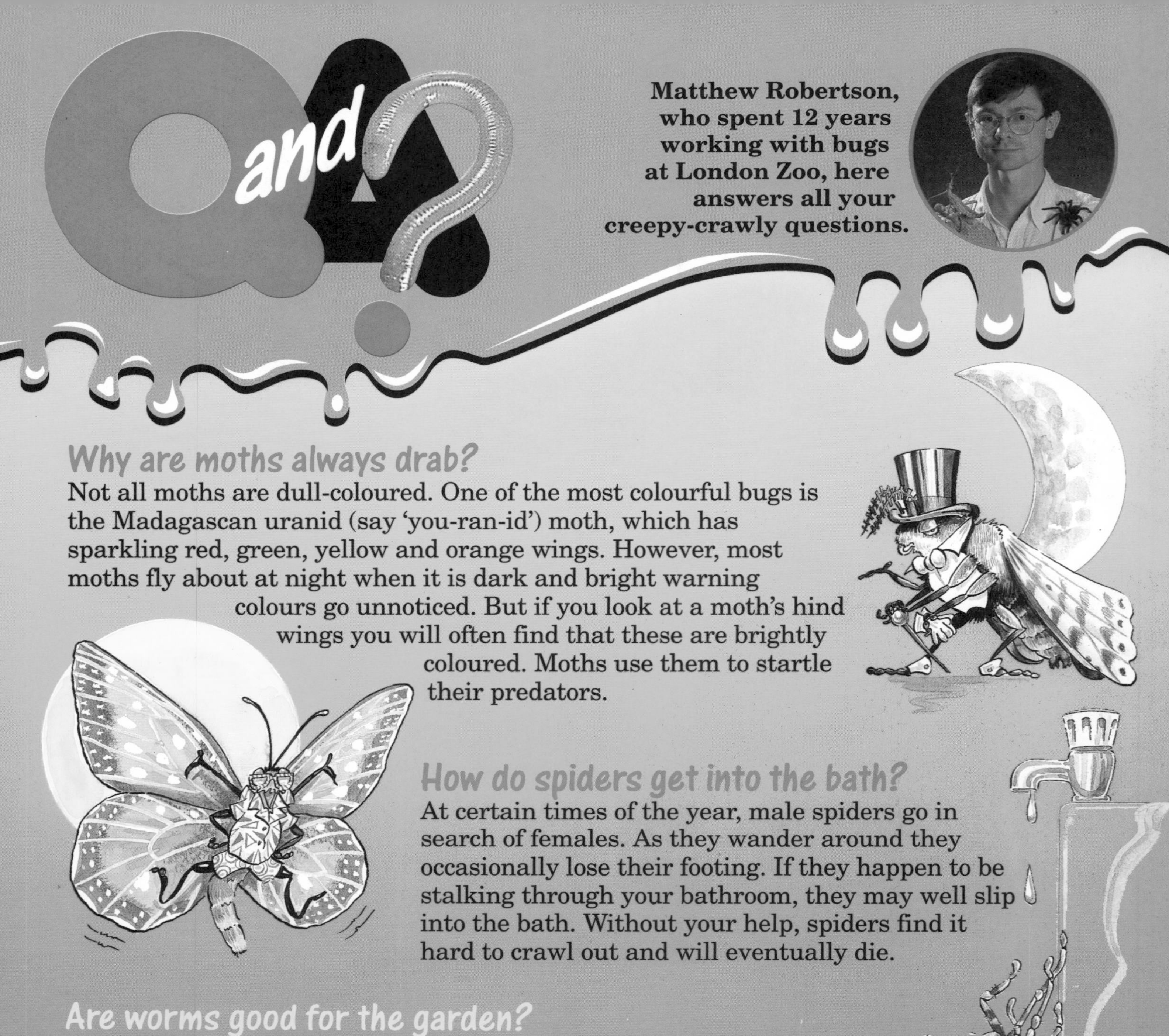

Matthew Robertson, who spent 12 years working with bugs at London Zoo, here answers all your creepy-crawly questions.

Why are moths always drab?

Not all moths are dull-coloured. One of the most colourful bugs is the Madagascan uranid (say 'you-ran-id') moth, which has sparkling red, green, yellow and orange wings. However, most moths fly about at night when it is dark and bright warning colours go unnoticed. But if you look at a moth's hind wings you will often find that these are brightly coloured. Moths use them to startle their predators.

How do spiders get into the bath?

At certain times of the year, male spiders go in search of females. As they wander around they occasionally lose their footing. If they happen to be stalking through your bathroom, they may well slip into the bath. Without your help, spiders find it hard to crawl out and will eventually die.

Are worms good for the garden?

Yes. Worms help the soil by making drainage holes in it. They also take plant material, which is full of goodness, from the surface of the soil to their burrows. Recently, a flatworm from New Zealand was accidentally introduced into Britain. Unfortunately, it eats earthworms. If the flatworm preys on all the worms in one area, the quality of the soil will certainly decline. Only then will we really appreciate the common earthworm.

Creepy Crawly Facts Answers

Page:	Answers:
22, 23	1b, 2b, 3a, 4b, 5c, 6b, 7b, 8b, 9a, 10b
46, 47	1c, 2b, 3c, 4a, 5b, 6b, 7a, 8c, 9a, 10b
70, 71	1b, 2a, 3c, 4b, 5b, 6c, 7a, 8a, 9c, 10b
94, 95	1c, 2b, 3b, 4a, 5a, 6a, 7c, 8c, 9b, 10c
118, 119	1b, 2c, 3a, 4b, 5c, 6a, 7c, 8a, 9a, 10c
142, 143	1a, 2c, 3a, 4b, 5a, 6a, 7c, 8a, 9b, 10c
166, 167	1b, 2b, 3c, 4a, 5a, 6a, 7a, 8b, 9b, 10c
190, 191	1c, 2a, 3c, 4a, 5b, 6c, 7a, 8a, 9b, 10b
214, 215	1b, 2a, 3b, 4a, 5c, 6c, 7a, 8b, 9b, 10a
238, 239	1b, 2a, 3c, 4b, 5b, 6a, 7c, 8c, 9c, 10c
262, 263	1a, 2b, 3c, 4c, 5c, 6a, 7a, 8c, 9a, 10b
286, 287	1c, 2c, 3a, 4a, 5b, 6b, 7b, 8c, 9a, 10a
310, 311	1c, 2a, 3b, 4b, 5a, 6b, 7c, 8b, 9a, 10c
334, 335	1a, 2c, 3b, 4a, 5c, 6a, 7a, 8a, 9a, 10b
358, 359	1b, 2c, 3a, 4a, 5c, 6a, 7b, 8c, 9b, 10b
382, 383	1b, 2a, 3b, 4a, 5b, 6c, 7c, 8c, 9b, 10a
406, 407	1c, 2a, 3b, 4b, 5c, 6b, 7a, 8c, 9c, 10b
430, 431	1c, 2a, 3c, 4c, 5b, 6b, 7c, 8b, 9a, 10a

Picture Acknowledgements

Front Cover: Andy Teare/Trevor Smith's Animal World; Planet Earth Pictures (tr); Heather Angel/Biofotos (spine).

Heather Angel/Biofotos 398, 400, 401, 413; David Burder/3-D Images 10-11, 36-7, 60-1, 84-5, 108-9, 132-3, 156-7, 180-1, 204-5, 228-9, 252-3, 226-7, 300-1, 324-5, 348-9, 372-3, 396-7, 420-1, 444-5; Natural History Museum 182(t), 183(c), 185(tl,tr,c); NHPA 1, 15(b), 7(t), 9(b), 27, 32-3, 39, 40(cr,br), 41, 49, 52, 53, 56(bl), 64-5(bkgd), 64(tl), 65(tc,tr), 86-7(b), 89(br), 97, 111(bl), 115(3), 117(2,3,4), 134, 135(b,tr), 136, 137, 148, 149, 151(cl), 160(bl,c), 161(l), 172, 174-5(bkgd), 176-7(bkgd), 176(tl), 185(tr), 199(cl), 206-7, 207(tr), 208(t), 209(br), 212(l), 268, 269, 272(bkgd), 281(l), 328-9, 337, 339(bl), 344(bkgd,br), 350(tr,r), 351(c), 352(br), 353(tr), 354-5, 354(bl), 355(r,br), 356-7, 364, 365, 399 (tl,r,br), 400(r), 412, 423 (b,br), 424(tr), 425(l,br), 427(bl,br), 428(c), 428-9, 433, 441(cr), 446; Oxford Scientific Films 29, 40(tr), 40-1, 44-5, 88(tl,cl,bl), 101, 111(tl,br), 115(l), 116, 117(l), 223(br), 242(l), 254-5(bl), 256-7(t), 289, Kathie Atkinson/OSF 151(br), 256-7, 303(br), 375(br), David Baag/OSF 344, Fred Bavendam/OSF 160(tl), Terry Button/OSF 340, 436, G.I.Bernard/OSF 305, 317, 332-3, 426(br), 426-7, 429(tl), Scott Camazine/OSF 12-13(bkgd), 24(tl), 48(tl), 72(tl), 96(tl), 120(tl), 144(tl), 168(tl), 192(tl), 216(tl), 222-3, 240(tl), 264(tl), 258, 288(tl), 312(tl), 336(tl), 360(tl), 384(tl), 408(tl), 432(tl), 448(tl), Waina Cheng/OSF 151(tr), J.A.L. Cooke/OSF 54-5(t), 122, 173, 244, 278-9, 294(bl), 369(b), 375(t), Jack Dermid/OSF 381(bl), David B.Fleetham/OSF 320-1, Michael Fogden/OSF 174(b), 199(tr,br), 212(t), 213(r), 217(t), 273(tl), 316, 366(bl), H.L. Fox/OSF 280(br), Bob Frederick/OSF 354(l), Dan Guravich/OSF 270(bkgd), Paul Kay/OSF 380(r), Richard Kirby/OSF 201(br), Rudie Kuiter/OSF 381(c), London Scientific Films/OSF 245, 354(r), Alastair Macewan/OSF 225(tr), Raymond Mendez/OSF 121, 273(bkgd), 375(bl), OSF endpapers, Godfrey Merlen/OSF 209(tr), Muzz Muray/OSF 328(br), Patti Murray/OSF 151(cr), 439, Ben Osbourne/OSF 332(tr), Peter Parks/OSF 321(br), 346(br), 347(t), James Robinson /OSF 367(r), Alastair Shay/OSF 135(c), 220(t), 292, 441(tr), Tim Shepherd/OSF 355(bl), David Specker/OSF 295(tr), Sinclair Stammers/OSF 4, 124, 437, Harold Taylor/OSF 304, 381(br), David Thompson/OSF 15(br), 329(br), Barrie Watts/OSF 305(tr), Babs and Bert Wells/OSF 294(tr), Nick Woods/OSF 64(tc), Norbert Wu/OSF 377(r); Ken King/Phasmida 41(br); Planet Earth Pictures 14(A,C), 28, 34-5, 40(tl,cl), 44(bl), 65(cr), 77(t), 88(bc), 89(tr), 111(tr), 115(2,4), 125(tr), 158-9(bkgd), 158(br), 161(br), 177(br), 187(t), 188(tr,bl), 193(b), 207(br), 208(bl), 209(cl), 213(bl), 221(br), 222(cl,b), 234(tr), 241, 256(l,t), 270(r), 273(br), 281(c), 295(br,l), 296(br), 297(r), 302(tr), 302-3, 303(r), 305(l), 320(tl), 321(tl,br), 330-1, 331(br), 332(br), 374(b), 376-7, 385, 388, 389, 409, 427(t); Premaphotos Wildlife 196(tl), 222(t), 224(cl,cr), 225(tl,bl,br), 230(br, tr), 231(bl,cr,tl), 232(tr,br), 233(tl,tr,bl), 257(r,c), 271(bkgd,r), 293, 352(tl,t), 353(br), 354(br), 355(l), 361, 366-7, 367(br), 368(l,tr), 374-5, 376(b), 424-5, 447; Robert Harding Picture Library 429(bl); Science Photo Library 3, 5, 62, 75(l), 76(b), 88(bkgd), 100, 145(l), 175(tr), 260(fp,br), 261(bl,r,t), 280(r), 281(tl), 285(tr), 285(tr), 296(c), 296-7, 297, 304(r), 313, 326, 327(tl), 330(fp,r), 343(tr), 345(bkgd,tr,l), 368-9, 376(t), 422-3, 429(r), 447(tl,bl,b), SPL/Martin Dohm 45(r); Andy Teare/Trevor Smith's Animal World 1, 25, 73(br), 169, 265; Windrush Photos 350(bl,br), 351(l), 353(l); ZEFA 33(r), 164-5(bkgd), 370-1(bkgd), 381(tl).

Artwork: Mike Atkinson/Garden Studio 2, 6, 7(b), 20(tl,tr,br); Andy Bezear 63; Robin Bouttell/Wildlife Art Agency (WLAA) 234-5, 236-7, 310-1, 382-3; Robin Carter/WLAA 74(bl), 110-1, 112-3, 154-5, 208(r), 266-7, 302, 304, 305, 320, 327, 329, 351, 356-7, 422, 423, 424, 434-5(b), 442-3; Jim Channell/Bernard Thornton Artists (BTA) 98-9; Tom Connell 162-3, 246-7, 290-1, 338-9, 440-1; Joanne Cowne 258-9(bkgd); Barry Croucher/WLAA 410-1; Richard Duckett 318-9; Dale Edna Evans 362-3; John Francis/BTA 140-1; George Fryer/BTA 282-3, 284-5; Lee Gibbons /WLAA 22-3, 42-3, 46-7, 70-1, 94-5, 110-1, 118-9, 142-3, 166-7, 190-1, 238-9, 262-3, 286-7, 334-5, 358-9, 406-7, 430-1; Angela Hargreaves/WLAA 8, 9(t); Tim Hayward/BTA 104, 105, 122-3, 414-5, 416-7; David Holmes/Garden Studio 50-1; Andrew Hutchinson/Garden Studio 38-9; Roger Kent/Garden Studio 55(r), 56(tr), 57; Adrian Lascom/Garden Studio 18-19, 20(bl), 30, 32, 66-7, 68-9, 78-9, 126-7, 152-3, 210-1, 248-9, 314-5, 378-9, 380, 402-3, 404-5; Paul Mitchell/Black Hat 12-13, 34, 35, 58-9, 82-3, 106-7, 130-1, 178-9, 202-3, 226-7, 250-1, 298-9, 322-3, 370-1, 418-9; Ray Mumford/WLAA 434-5; Colin Newman/BTA 26, 90-1, 102-3, 164-5, 184-5, 186-7, 242-3; Richard Orr/BTA 92-3, 146-7, 170-1, 200-1; Terry Pastor/WLAA 114-5, 116-7, 194-5(bkgd), 342-3, 344-5; Maurice Pledger/BTA 150-1, 218-9, 306-7, 308-9; Steve Roberts/WLAA 16, 17, 264, 360; Stephen Seymour/BTA 138-9, 188-9; Patrick Simon 182-3(b); Ray Straw/WLAA 24, 48, 72, 96, 120, 144, 168, 192, 216, 240, 264, 274-5, 288, 312, 336, 360, 384, 408, 432, 448; Studio B 21(b), 80-1(insets); Myke Taylor/Garden Studio 31, 68-9(insets), 80-1, 128-9, 153, 212-3, 247(inset), 248-9, 248(inset), 386-7, 390-1, 392-3, 438; Chris West/Black Hat 346-7.

Measurement Conversion Chart

Approximate conversions from customary to metric units and vice versa.

When you know:	You can find:	If you multiply by:
LENGTH:		
millimeters	inches	0.04
centimeters	inches	0.4
meters	yards	1.1
kilometers	miles	0.62
inches	millimeters	25.4
feet	centimeters	30
yards	meters	0.9
miles	kilometers	1.6
AREA:		
square centimeters	square inches	0.16
square meters	square yards	1.2
square kilometers	square miles	0.4
square hectometers (hectares)	acres	2.5
square inches	square centimeters	6.5
square feet	square meters	0.09
square yards	square meters	0.8
square miles	square kilometers	2.6
acres	square hectometers (hectares)	0.4
MASS AND WEIGHT:		
grams	fluid ounces	0.035
kilograms	pounds	2.2
megagrams (metric tons)	short tons	1.1
fluid ounces	grams	28
pounds	kilograms	0.45
short tons	megagrams (metric tons)	0.9
LIQUID VOLUME:		
milliliters	ounces	0.034
liters	pints	2.1
liters	quarts	1.06
liters	gallons	0.26
ounces	milliliters	30
pints	liters	0.47
quarts	liters	0.95
gallons	liters	3.8